MW00815476

Guide to United States Customs and Trade Laws

After the Customs Modernization Act

Third Edition

Kluwer Law International

Guide to United States Customs and Trade Laws

After the Customs Modernization Act

Leslie Alan Glick, Esq.

Third Edition

AUSTIN BOSTON CHICAGO NEW YORK THE NETHERLANDS

Published by:
Kluwer Law International
P.O. Box 316
2400 AH Alphen aan den Rijn
The Netherlands
E-mail: sales@kluwerlaw.com
Website: http://www.kluwerlaw.com

Sold and distributed in North, Central and South America by:
Aspen Publishers, Inc.
7201 Mc Kinney Circle
Frederick, MD 21704
United States of America

Sold and distributed in all other countries by:
Turpin Distribution Services Ltd.
Stratton Business Park
Pegasus Drive, Biggleswade
Bedfordshire SG18 8TQ
United Kingdom

ISBN 978-90-411-2704-4

About the Author

Leslie Alan Glick specializes in international trade and business and customs law in Washington, D.C. In addition, he handles a significant amount of work in the areas of intellectual property, food and drug law and legislative representation.

Mr. Glick is a 1967 graduate of Cornell University and a 1970 graduate of Cornell Law School. After serving a clerkship with an appellate court in the state of New York, Mr. Glick began active practice in Washington, D.C. in 1971. In addition to private law practice, Mr. Glick has served as counsel to the Subcommittee on International Trade of the Select Committee on Small Business of the US House of Representatives and as a Special Assistant Attorney General of the State of Maryland. He is a former member of the Maryland Democratic State Central Committee.

Mr. Glick has written several books in the international trade area including books entitled, *Trading with Saudi Arabia*; *Multilateral Trade Negotiations* and *Understanding the North American Free Trade Agreement*, 2nd ed. (Kluwer Law International). Mr. Glick has also written Chapter 34 entitled 'Legal Aspects of US–Mexico Trade' in the two-volume Matthew Bender Treatise entitled *Doing Business in Mexico*. He has also contributed to several other books including the West Publications law school text on *International Business Transactions*. His articles have appeared in the *Harvard International Law Journal, The Cornell Law Review, The Fordham Law Review, The Trademark Reporter, The Federal Bar News and Journal,* the *Business Lawyer* and the *International Lawyer*. Mr. Glick is co-editor and a contributor to the Kluwer Law International treatise entitled *Manual for the Practice of US International Trade Law 2001*.

Mr. Glick is Chairman of the American Bar Association, International Trade and Customs Law Committee of the Section on Administrative and Regulatory Practice. Mr. Glick has served as Chairman of the International Law Section of the Federal Bar Association and previously as Chairman of the International Trade and Customs Law Committee of the Federal Bar Association. He has served as Chairman of the Legal Education and Communications Committee of the Inter-American Bar Foundation. He has served as adjunct professor of law at George Mason University Law School (State University of Virginia).

Acknowledgements

The author would like to acknowledge the following persons who assisted with revising, editing and typing this third edition: Interns David Chen, Jon Brodergad, Ashley Brott and Evan Tarkington, and Secretaries Carolyn Kay, Angela Benson, and Karen Johnson.

Table of Contents

Chapter 1

Introduction and Overview of the Customs Modernization Act

The US customs laws have certain similarities to the US tax laws. Both were intended as revenue raising measures in the past; both are complex and not easily understood; and both were administered by branches of the Treasury Department, although this is no longer the case since the transfer of customs functions to the Department of Homeland Security. While there are numerous books and articles explaining and commenting on the US tax laws, the body of literature on the customs laws is much smaller. The few works that exist tend to be multi-volume scholarly tomes intended for experienced practitioners, and are both lengthy and expensive. It was with this in mind that I first discussed with Kluwer Law International the need for a one volume 'handbook,' or 'guidebook,' for the layman. I use the term layman somewhat cautiously, since many of the people that will use this book will be customs brokers, freight forwarders, export managers, in-house counsel, and others who are deeply involved in day-to-day import/export practice. However, it is anticipated that most of the readers will not be customs lawyers who deal with the arcane complexities of customs statutes and regulations on a day-to-day basis.

It has been our goal, therefore, to keep this book as nontechnical as possible, while addressing the laws, regulations and rulings that those involved in international trade activities need to know. This is a hard line to walk, since there is always the danger of leaving out an important concept that may be too technical for the needs of most of the readers. Our goal is to enable in-house counsel at a multinational company or an export manager to pick up this book and find enough information to alert him/her to a potential customs problem, so that he/she may seek proper guidance. This *caveat* is particularly valid since customs rulings are issued daily; and no book of this nature can remain completely up-to-date. This book, therefore, is not intended to be a substitute for consultations with experienced customs attorneys.

While the primary purpose of this book is to cover US customs laws, we have also included a discussion of US international trade laws administered by other agencies as well. The distinction between these two types of laws is somewhat hazy. All US international trade laws are, to some degree, enforced by US customs officials because customs is charged with collecting duties, enforcing marking requirements, enforcing quotas or exclusion orders and interdicting contraband goods at the border. What we categorize in this book as customs laws and regulations are those laws which customs both administers and enforces. International trade laws, such as the antidumping and countervailing duty laws, are generally enforced by customs, but administered by other agencies such as the US International Trade Commission or the US Department of Commerce. Customs plays a smaller role in regard to such international trade laws, generally becoming involved only in the enforcement stages of the proceedings. It was our feeling that a book of this nature would be most useful, given its purposes as a one volume deskbook or handbook, if it covered these international trade statutes as well. However, these laws are diverse and complex. In order to keep within the scope of this book, our treatment must be limited in length and depth. Again, it is our intention to enable the user to know enough about each particular area to be aware of a potential problem, and to seek necessary guidance, not necessarily to pose or answer every question.

We look forward to comments from the readers concerning our approach so we may make adaptations in future editions and revisions to further suit the needs of the exporting community. These comments can be sent to me at Porter Wright Morris & Arthur, 1919 Pennsylvania Ave. NW, Suite 500, Washington, D.C. 2006, or at lglick@porterwright.com.

The second edition was the first update of the book since it was originally written. Various chapters were updated and revised to reflect changes in laws, regulations, and in some cases rulings. Most importantly, the second edition reflected the significant changes in customs law and procedure made in the Customs Modernization Act, often referred to simply as the (Mod Act). Because of the importance of this new law, and 'overview' section was prepared and appears below as part of this introduction. This third edition is a departure from the first two editions insofar as it is intended to be updated. The appendix has also been expanded significantly and new chapters have been added.

I. OVERVIEW OF THE CUSTOMS MODERNIZATION ACT

The Customs Modernization Act (Mod Act) was passed by Congress as Title VI of H.R. 3450: The same legislation that contained the North American Free Trade Agreement (NAFTA). *See* Chapter 21, IIB. While many people are familiar with NAFTA, few people other than customs officials, customs brokers and customs attorneys are equally aware of all the changes brought about by the Mod Act and their significance. It is fair to say that the Mod Act is the most important revision of US Customs laws in recent history. Not only did it make many substantive changes in the Customs laws, but it also changes the philosophy and approach of these laws – shifting more of the legal burden to the importing community under the concepts of 'informal compliance' and 'reasonable care.'

The primary purpose of the Mod Act, and Title VI, of which it was part was to streamline and automate the commercial operations of the US Customs Service, and to improve compliance with the Customs laws and provide safeguards uniformity and due process rights to importers.

The Act is divided into four sections, briefly summarized below:

Subtitle A – contains improvements in Customs enforcement and changes required by Customs increasing transition to electronic processing. For example, new provisions were required to deal with electronic transmission to Customs of false and altered documents. New procedures concerning the accreditation of private Customs laboratories were established that for the first time established the right of the importer to conduct his own tests at an officially accredited private laboratory whose testing must be given the same weight by Customs as its own laboratories.

Subtitle B – authorizes the Secretary of Treasury (now the Secretary of Homeland Security) to establish a National Customs Automation Program for processing commercial imports and permit filings of entries from remote locations. This means that a customs broker or a company with an in-house customs department no longer has to have an office at each port of entry but can make computer entries from one office for entries at each port. It indicates that eventually the need for local offices and local entries may be replaced with one centralized computer entry system. Also, claims for duty drawback and certain other documentation can be filed electronically. Provisions are made for admissibility of such electronically transmitted information in judicial and administrative proceedings. This highlights the need for the importer to retain, 'hard copies' and save them in a safe place in case needed for filing protests, responses to penalty notices, and appeals in judicial cases to the Court of International Trade. Moreover, unless hard copies are made, it can be difficult for legal counsel to give effective advice or assistance to the importer. Alternatively, back-up copies can be kept on disks for printouts when needed, and copies of the disks can be made to give to legal counsel for safekeeping.

Subtitle C – deals with various miscellaneous Amendments to the Tariff Act of 1930, dealing with collection of duties and disposal by Customs of seized or unclaimed merchandise. Customs is also authorized for the first time to use private collection agencies to collect debts owed to the US Customs Service.

Subtitle D – deals mostly with internal changes required by Customs to support the transition to automation. It discusses the Customs Compliance Measurement Program which is the basis for Customs audits to determine the level of compliance by importers.

Many of the provisions in the Mod Act are technical and concern mostly Customs own administrative procedures for streamlining and modernizing recordkeeping and filing. The concept is to eliminate the need for as much paperwork at the time of entry as possible. At the same time, an increased burden is placed on the importer to keep adequate records so that if and when they are needed they will be available. In this regard, Customs has moved from a system that required exhaustive documentation to one more similar to the system used by the IRS that does not require the filing of supporting documents, but requires that they be available when requested. Customs is using a 'carrot and stick' approach to encourage good recordkeeping. A recordkeeping compliance program is being established that will assist importers in developing good recordkeeping systems with the assistance of Customs and reward them with the use of warnings, rather then penalties in certain situations where a recordkeeping program is in place. Moreover, the use of more electronic filings and less paperwork presented at the time of entry only increases the need for aggressive auditing of compliance by Customs.

II. RECORDKEEPING

Records must generally be kept for a five year period from the date of entry. Drawback claims need only be retained for three years. The parties subject to recordkeeping requirements have been expanded to include parties whose activities require the filing of an entry or declaration, parties transporting or storing merchandise carried or held under bond, parities who file drawback claims and parties who cause an importation or the transportation or storage of merchandise held under bond. New provisions are added specifically providing for penalties for the nonproduction of records when requested. The amount of penalty will depend on whether the failure to produce the records is due to willful conduct or negligence. In addition to the penalty, if the record that is not produced relates to the eligibility for special reduced duty rates under Column 3 (e.g., NAFTA, Generalized System of Preferences), customs may also liquidate the entry at the higher Column 1 tariff rate. However, companies that are 'certified' by Customs as participating in a recordkeeping compliance program and are in 'general compliance' with such programs shall, 'in the absence of willfulness or repeated violations' be issued a written warning notice in lieu of a penalty, if they fail to comply with a demand for production of records.

Since the Mod Act, Customs has been moving ahead with automation, first the Automated Commercial System (ACS) and, more recently, the Automatic Commercial Environment (ACE).

> *PRACTICE NOTE:* The trend toward electronic filing has both streamlined record keeping but created new challenges. Companies should consult both their attorneys as to record retention requirements and their information technology departments as to the mechanics of electronic records retention and preservation.

Chapter 2

Overview of US Customs and Trade Laws

It has been said that the oldest institutions known to mankind are taxes and prostitution. Perhaps almost as old is the imposition of customs duties. The first line of a government published booklet entitled 'This is Customs'[1] reads 'The collection of revenue and the control of trade are almost as old as man himself.' The booklet then proceeds to provide a short history of customs laws in the US starting with the Tariff Act of July 4, 1789. In the early years, customs laws were essentially revenue collecting measures. The new democracy found itself without many funds or lines of credit, and not much income to tax. Imports have provided a good source of revenue since generally goods that are imported are ones that are either scarce locally or otherwise highly in demand because of their price and quality. Customs points out in its 'This is Customs' booklet that due to customs revenues, the US actually reduced its national debt to zero by 1835.

Now, over 173 years later, this country's national debt is in the billions. Yet Customs revenues are no longer a major or even significant source of total US revenues. This is due to several reasons. Other revenue sources such as personal and corporate income tax have become a major source of government revenue and Customs duties have been reduced over the years through various multilateral trade negotiations to the point that their significance as a revenue producing medium has been diminished. What then are the functions of US customs laws in the 2000s and beyond? Are they still important?

US Customs duties will still serve a significant, albeit diminished, role as a revenue raising measure.

---

1. US Customs Service, 1976.

> *PRACTICE NOTE:* For example, miscellaneous tariff bills that reduce or remove duties can only be passed if there are offsetting revenue-raising measures.

However, more importantly, they serve as either a portal or a barrier to access to the world's largest and richest consumer market. A great deal of the personnel and efforts of customs today are not devoted solely to collecting duties, but also to the regulation of trade, excluding products that are not permitted or requiring conformity to US laws before the goods can enter the US. For exporters in foreign countries, their US importers, brokers, bankers and customers, and their lawyers, understanding the role of US customs and the laws it enforces is the *quid pro quo* of success in the US market. While the revenue aspects of customs duties may be declining, each year the non-revenue aspects are becoming more significant. The laws that customs enforces have become more complex. No one needs to tell this to the importer who has 40,000.00 USD (US dollars) in goods languishing in a customs warehouse, with customers threatening cancellations and lawsuits, all because the country of origin marking was put in the wrong place. No one needs to tell this to the importer of canned foods whose goods are embargoed because Customs has decided that the label does not meet the requirements of the US Food and Drug Administration.

The battleground in today's trade wars is not exclusively tariffs, but what is sometimes referred to as 'non-tariff barriers.' These are regulatory procedures that restrict the flow of goods in international markets. Sometimes these barriers are necessary and justified. Every country has the right to regulate access to its market to protect its citizens' health, safety and welfare. It is only when these laws are administered in an arbitrary or capricious manner, or in a manner designed to protect local markets rather than to enforce valid health and safety concerns, that they become a barrier to international trade.

Moreover, even monetary aspects of customs tariffs are still important in many instances. Some product areas have become so competitive that even a few cents price difference may make or break a sale. Whether an importer can qualify for duty free treatment under the Generalized System of Preferences, or pay a 6.2 per cent duty, may make the difference between success and failure. Duties become extremely important when penalty duties under the antidumping and countervailing duty laws are tacked on to the normal duties. While most statutory duties today are under 10 per cent (although some are 32 per cent and higher), antidumping duties have been imposed in the range of 70 per cent to 80 per cent *ad valorem,* and even in three figures. This can obviously put a company out of the market very quickly.

The author has practiced for over 30 years in international trade and customs law and handled just about every type of trade or customs case and has generally found that customs is a fair agency in its practices, though, one under considerable pressure to be enforcement oriented. The traditionally heavy emphasis on drug interdiction and smuggling, and now since September 11, on anti-terrorist activities, has given Customs some of the trappings of a paramilitary organization. Many Customs personnel carry guns. Their mandate is to enforce the US customs law and to collect the revenues of the United States. It is not the mandate of Customs to help you as an exporter or importer to reduce your duties or find more creative ways to import into the US at lower costs. This is not to say that many individual Customs officials are not helpful and friendly. They are. However, the responsibility for minimizing your duties, and avoiding problems with various laws enforced by Customs relating to quotas, marking, etc., is on the exporter and the importer and their legal advisors. There is a famous Supreme Court case which held that every person has the right to arrange his affairs to pay the lowest tax legally possible. While we have an obligation to pay taxes we do not have an obligation to pay one cent more than we legally owe. This is equally true for customs duties. While we must comply with the law, we may, through understanding the laws, find ways to minimize Customs duties and barriers.

Unfortunately, US trade and customs laws have become so complex that very few people, other than lawyers and officials directly involved in their enforcement, really understand them all. In 1988, Congress passed the Omnibus Trade and Competitiveness Act of 1988. In 1994, there was a major overhaul of the Customs laws in the Customs Modernization Act. This law was over 1000 pages long and made changes to many customs and trade laws. As pointed out in the book, we have at least four government agencies involved in the day-to-day administration and enforcement of trade and Customs laws and several others that become involved at different times. Information on these new laws and regulations does not filter down very quickly to the exporter, customs broker or import manager. Local Customs offices do not always receive copies of these new laws or regulations for some time. Lawyers have sometimes been asked by Customs officials to send them copies of new decisions or laws. The average Customs office may have a few loose-leaf books with bulletins and information on recorded trademarks, but these are often out of date and difficult to use for the layman. Import specialists are available to answer questions, but they are very busy people and have limited time. Their verbal answers, like those of tax advisors on the Internal Revenue Service information lines, are non-binding. Moreover, under the new Customs Mod Act, the importer now has a burden of 'reasonable care' and 'informed compliance.' These concepts mean that it is now *required* that the importer learn what the current laws and regulations are and if he does not know he must consult experts who do. Customs encourages companies to develop compliance programs and have compliance manuals. It is our hope that this book will be a helpful start to such programs and can even be integrated into them.

Information is power, and power is the tool to success in international trade as in other areas. While this book cannot answer every question, we hope it will provide enough information to educate the laymen in how to navigate through the maze of US customs and trade laws so their business can be more competitive. Understanding trade and customs laws is more than just understanding statutes and regulations. It also involves understanding trade policy. Trade is a very political area. It involves international and diplomatic relations as well as dollars. Trade issues are now linked to such diverse matters as drug enforcement, policy on oil exports, protection of patents and trademarks and international labor rights standards. Unions and even environmental groups have now become major players in the trade policy field. They are responsible for much of the 'protectionist' legislation. They were a moving force behind the Textile and Apparel Trade Act of 1988 that passed both houses of Congress, but was vetoed by the President. This bill would have imposed quotas on most textiles entering the US. Unions and environmental groups played an important role in the debates and regulation implementing the North American Free Trade Agreement, and more recently the Central American Free Trade Agreement (CAFTA) as well as other 'free trade agreements.' Some trade decisions are motivated more by military or defense concerns than by trade issues. Note the recent growth in Free Trade Agreements with moderate Middle Eastern countries such as Kuwait and Bahrain. Others are linked to domestic considerations such as unemployment. All of this is made more difficult by the lack of a single uniform US trade policy. Congress, the State Department, the US Trade Representative, the Department of Agriculture, the President and his national security staff, the Commerce Secretary and many others espouse trade policy on an *ad hoc* basis. There, unfortunately, are inconsistencies in the approach taken by various government officials, and between our trade policies and our socioeconomic-military policies towards some countries. On the same day that the President removes 25 million dollars in trade preference benefits for a country, under the Generalized System of Preferences, we might give them 50 million dollars in economic and military aid. There have been repeated talks about reorganizing international trade functions into one super agency and in the Commerce Department without results.

All of this tends to make the customs and international trade area an interesting and stimulating one. In the 30 years I have practiced in this area, it has never been boring.

Chapter 3
Administration of Customs and Trade Laws

I. US CUSTOMS SERVICE OPERATIONS AND PRACTICES

A. History under the Department of the Treasury

The US Customs Service operated under the auspices of the US Treasury Department for most of its history. It was a principal branch of the Treasury Department, with 42 district offices across the country,[1] approximately 300 ports of entry throughout the US,[2] Puerto Rico and the Virgin Islands, and at one time seven regional Commissioners. The Headquarters of the Customs Service was located at 1301 Constitution Avenue, N.W., Washington, D.C. 20229. The Secretary of the Department of the Treasury originally appointed the Commissioner of Customs. The top leadership of the Customs Service includes a Deputy Commissioner, a Comptroller, five Assistant Commissioners (one for each of the major offices), and seven Regional Commissioners. The organizational structure of Customs is divided into six major departments: Enforcement, Inspection and Control, Commercial Operations, International Affairs, Management and Internal Affairs. Each office is headed by an Assistant Commissioner, except that general administration is overseen by the Comptroller of Customs. Oversight of the Customs Service was originally vested in the Assistant Secretary of the Treasury for Enforcement. The Assistant Secretary coordinated Customs policy and reviewed policy issues. The Office of Tariff and Trade Affairs in the Treasury Department was under the auspices of the Assistant Secretary for Enforcement and was in charge of the

---

1. *See* Part IX-Forms and Reference Appendix, listing all 45 Districts.
2. *See* 19 C.F.R. 101 (1987) Customs facilities that operate as points of entry into the US are referred to as 'port' even if not actually a water-borne entry point. The 'ports' that do not involve waterways are often referred to by the oxymoron 'land ports'.

day-to-day review of Customs operations relating to trade and tariff issues. Importers with legal problems involving policy issues often sought to involve the Office of Tariff and Trade Affairs in the Treasury Department.

B. Transfer to the Department of Homeland Security

1. US Customs Service Reorganization – The Homeland Security Act of 2002

As a response to the September 11, 2001 terrorist attacks, President George W. Bush and Congress passed the Homeland Security Act of 2002 which established the Executive Department of Homeland Security on March 1, 2003. The creation of the Department of Homeland Security was the largest reorganization of the Federal Government in over 50 years. The Department of Homeland Security is charged with the vital mission of protecting America by deterring and responding to terrorist attacks, threats and other hazards to the nation, securing and ensuring safe and secure borders, welcoming lawful immigrants and visitors, and promoting the free-flow of commerce. The reorganization brought the former US Customs Service that had operated under the auspices of the US Treasury Department, under the Department of Homeland Security. Together with the US Customs Service, the former US Border Patrol and the Immigration and Naturalization Service (INS) of the US Department of Justice as well as the import/export inspection duties of the Animal Plant Health Inspection Service (APHIS) of the US Department of Agriculture (USDA) were consolidated to form the new US Customs and Border Protection. However, certain Customs revenue functions of the US Customs Service remains with the Department of Treasury. The mission of the Customs and Border Protection is to guard America's borders as America's frontline defense to safeguard the American homeland at and beyond its borders, protect against terrorism and the instruments of terror, enforce the laws of the United States while fostering America's economic security through lawful international trade and travel, and to serve the American public with vigilance, integrity, and professionalism.

II. US CUSTOMS AND BORDER PROTECTION OPERATIONS AND PRACTICES

A. Headquarters and the Customs and Border Protection

The US Customs and Border Protection operate under the auspices of the US Department of Homeland Security. It is a principal branch of the Department of Homeland Security with 20 Field Operations offices across the country that provide centralized management oversight and operational assistance to 317 official ports of entry throughout the US, Puerto Rico, and the Virgin Islands and an additional 14 pre-clearance offices in Canada, Ireland, and the Caribbean. The Headquarters of the Customs and Border Protection is currently located at 1300 Pennsylvania Ave., N.W., Washington, D.C. 20229. The Commissioner of the Customs and Border Protection is appointed by the President and confirmed by the Senate. The top leadership of the Customs and Border Protection includes a Deputy Commissioner, a Chief of Staff, five Staff Members, and twelve Assistant Commissioners (one for each of the major functional departments). The Commissioner's Staff is divided into five Staff Offices: Office of Chief Counsel, Office of Anti-Terrorism, Office of Equal Employment Opportunity, Office of Intelligence and Office of Policy and Planning. The organization is further divided into twelve major functional departments: Office of Customs and Border Protection Air and Marine, Office of Border Patrol, Office of International Trade, Office of Congressional Affairs, Office of Field Operations, Office of Finance and CFO, Office of Human Resources Management, Office of Information and Technology, Office of Internal Affairs, Office of International Affairs and Trade Relations, Office of Public Affairs, and Office of Training and Development. Each office is headed and administered by an Assistant Commissioner. Oversight of day-to-day operations is vested in the Deputy Commissioner. Importers with legal problems involving policy issues often seek to involve the Office of Trade Relations and the Office of International Trade. The Customs and Border Protection as reorganized, is significantly larger than the former US Customs Service, comprising of a workforce of over 40,000 employees, including inspectors, canine enforcement officers, Border Patrol agents, aircraft pilots, trade specialists, and mission support staff. The reorganization consolidated all customs and border protection duties into a single uniform agency, a notable change from the prior fragmented multi-agency structure.

PRACTICE NOTE: Notably, the functions of the Food and Drug Administration in relation to imports are still separate. However a memorandum of understanding (MOU) between the two agencies exists to increase coordination and cooperation.

B. Customs-related Staff Offices

1. Office of Intelligence

The Office of Intelligence is tasked with producing timely intelligence data in support of the Customs and Border Protection mission to secure the nation's borders. The Office serves as the primary information gathering unit of Customs and Border Protection and serves as the primary liaison to the Department of Homeland Security Headquarters, the intelligence community, and other Federal law enforcement agencies. The Office supports a variety of Customs and Border Protection programs, including the National Targeting Center, the Customs Trade Partnership against Terrorism (C-TPAT), and the Container Security Initiative (CSI). The

Office maintains partnerships with various intelligence agencies to increase Customs and Border Protection's ability to obtain and deliver timely intelligence data to decision makers at all levels.

2. Office of Chief Counsel

The Chief Counsel is the chief legal officer of the US Customs and Border Protection and reports to the General Counsel of the Department of Homeland Security. The Chief Counsel advises the Commissioner on the legal aspects of Customs and Border Protection practices and operations. The Office of Chief Counsel has both a Headquarters structure and a field structure. The Headquarters operations are divided into three functional areas: Administration, Enforcement, and Trade and Tariffs. Each division is headed by Associate Chief Counsels. Associate and Assistant Chief Counsels at field offices located in major cities across the United States advise Customs and Border Protection field managers in their geographic areas.

C. Customs-related Functional Offices

1. Office of Border Patrol

The Office of Border Patrol is the primary federal law enforcement organization responsible for preventing the entry of terrorists and terrorist weapons from entering the United States between official US Customs and Border Protection ports of entry. The Office of Border Patrol takes over traditional missions of the former Immigration and Naturalization Service (INS) in enforcing immigration laws and detecting, interdicting, and apprehending those who attempt to illegally enter or smuggle people or contraband across US borders between official ports of entry.

2. Office of Field Operations

Every person and product entering US territory must pass through Customs and Border Protection upon his or her arrival. Thus, another major function of the Customs and Border Protection is to process persons, baggage, cargo, and mail as they enter the US. This is accomplished through the Field Operations branch of the Customs and Border Protection, which controls carriers, persons and cargo entering and departing the US. During this process, the Office of Field Operations collects accurate import/export data with the use of technologies like Automated Commercial Environment (ACE) for compilation of international statistics. The Office of Field Operations oversees over 25,000 employees with more than 19,000 inspectors. The personnel of the Office of Field Operations are the persons that most of the public initially come into contact with at border crossings and ports of entry. They are generally uniformed and are stationed directly at the border crossings and airports. They have initial discretion to seize goods considered to be contraband, to be improperly marked with the country of origin or to be otherwise out of compliance with US Customs laws. The actual paperwork accompanying imports is generally forwarded to the import specialist who makes determinations as to duties owed, classification, etc.

The Office of Field Operations is responsible for a great variety of tasks from the assessment and collection of duties, excise taxes, fees and penalties on imported merchandise, to the seizure of contraband, narcotics and illegal drugs. The Office of Field Operations also enforces statutes administered by other agencies – e.g., Antidumping and Countervailing Duty Program, copyright, patent, and trademark provisions, (*See*, e.g., discussion of § 337 of the Tariff Act, 1930, *infra.*), quotas, marking of imported merchandise and other trade laws. In addition, the Office enforces import and export restrictions as well as certain navigation laws.

The Office plays an important role in the detection and apprehension of persons engaged in fraudulent trade practices, defined by Customs and Border Protection as fraudulent activity designed to circumvent import laws. Finally, Customs and Border Protection also operates in conjunction with over 40 other governmental agencies to enforce various provisions on their behalf. This includes the Federal Trade Commission (enforcement of textiles label and content laws), Food and Drug Administration (enforcement of labeling requirements), and the Environmental Protection Agency.

3. Office of International Affairs and Trade Relations

The Office of International Affairs and the Office of Trade Relations operate as co-equal offices under the Assistant Commissioner, International Affairs and Trade Relations.

The Office of International Affairs is responsible for all foreign initiatives, activities and programs within the CBP. It promotes and establishes collaborative relationships with foreign governments to foster and legitimate international trade, increase compliance, build alliances to combat transnational crime, reduce corruption, strengthen border controls, promote the rule of law and enhance economic stability throughout the world. It represents the CBP position in international forums, offers technical assistance and training, and negotiates or supports the negotiation of international agreements.

The Office of Trade Relations is tasked with fostering positive relationships with the trade community by serving as a liaison between industry and Customs officials. The office reviews concerns voiced by individuals or trade groups and furnishes recommendations to resolve justified complaints. The Director of the office is designated as the regulatory fairness representative for Customs and Border Protection, with responsibility for promoting compliance with the Small Business Regulatory Enforcement Fairness Act, which is administered by the Small Business Administration.

4. Office of International Trade

The Office of International Trade is responsible for CBP trade policy, program development, and compliance measurement. Consolidating these functions into one Office allows for strategic uniformity and clarity in trade enforcement. This Office not only develops regulations and issues legally binding rulings, but also directs enforcement responses and punitive actions against companies participating in predatory trade practices. Because the Office of International Trade includes the former Office of Regulations and Rulings, it may, upon request issue advance rulings on the proper classification, value, or country of origin marking of imported merchandise. The request must describe the relevant facts (the parties involved, country of origin, anticipated port of entry, and the nature of the transaction) and must also provide a sample or detailed description of the merchandise. Advance rulings are not available, however, if another division or field office is currently considering the same transaction or if it is being litigated before the Court of International Trade. The CBP is not bound by the advance ruling if the actual transaction varies from the facts originally relied upon. The advance ruling procedure for tariff classification is set out in Title 19, Sections 177.00–.10 in the *Code of Federal Regulations.* Advance rulings from Customs Headquarters on questions of valuation, country of origin, and other issues are covered by 19 C.F.R. §§ 177.21–.31. For goods which have already entered the US, an importer may prepare a request for internal advice to submit to the district director. District directors may then request internal advice from Customs Headquarters and the National Import Specialist (NIS) in order to assist them in their processing of importers' merchandise. A procedure for judicial review of advance ruling determinations is also available.

5. Office of Information and Technology

The Office of Information and Technology is responsible for managing all components of CBP technology. This includes software development, infrastructure services, tactical communications, the laboratory system, and research and development. This office directs the CBP Modernization Program, which is intended to build and efficient, user-friendly product that helps protect the nation's borders while facilitating commercial trade needs. One of the outgrowths of this program is the Automated Commercial Environment (ACE), a customized web-based system that connects CBP, the trade community and participating government agencies in one centralized, on-line access point.

D. Ports of Entry

Customs governs over 317 ports of entry through which merchandise may enter the US. A list of these ports along with the regions in which they are located appears in the appendix to the book. Title 19, Section 101 of the *Code of Federal Regulations* sets forth the guidelines by which these ports are established and administered. The terms 'port' and 'port of entry' are defined as 'any place designated by the Executive Order of the President, by order of the Secretary of the Treasury (now, the Secretary of Homeland Security), or by Act of Congress, at which a Customs official is authorized to accept entries of merchandise, to collect duties, and to enforce the various provisions of the Customs and navigation laws.'

E. Customs Attachés in US Embassies

Customs maintains offices located in US Embassies or Consulates in many countries. Included among these are Bangkok, Bonn, Dublin, Hong Kong, London, Mexico City, Ottawa, Paris, Rome, Tokyo, Seoul, Panama City, Vienna and The Hague. In addition, an attaché represents Customs in the US Mission to the European Communities in Brussels. These offices act as a liaison between American businessmen and foreign countries, as well as between foreign businessmen and the US. In conjunction with entities like the Office of East-West Trade and the Foreign Commercial Service under the Department of Commerce, the Customs attachés in US Embassies obtain information concerning foreign business enterprises and conduct investigations relating to the enforcement of US Customs laws. More recently, they play an important role in anti-terrorist activities.

III. ROLE OF OTHER AGENCIES

Customs and Border Protection cooperates with and enforces regulations of other government agencies, including the Department of Commerce, the International Trade Commission, the Office of the US Trade Representative and the Department of Agriculture. Customs is responsible for the enforcement of over 400 provisions of law on behalf of forty other government agencies.

A. United States International Trade Commission

The United States International Trade Commission (ITC) is a six member independent bi-partisan agency involved in the administration of international trade laws. It has concurrent jurisdiction with the US Department of Commerce in the administration of antidumping and countervailing duties statutes. It also can regulate agricultural imports under Section 22 of the Agricultural Adjustment Act. The ITC also conducts fact-finding investigations of numerous practices under Section 332 of the Trade Act of 1974, and makes determinations of market disruption caused by increased imports under Section 201 of the Tariff Act of 1974. The Commission also conducts investigations under Section 337 of the Tariff Act of 1930 relating to unfair practices that violate intellectual property rights.

No more than three commissioners may belong to the same political party. The Chairman of the Commission serves for two years. The Commission's responsibilities lie mostly in its investigative functions. It advises the President on various aspects of international trade. These include the effect of duties and other barriers on domestic industries, and preferential treatment of specific products. The Commission also conducts investigations into unfair trade practices and disruption of the domestic market when a petition is filed by industries or representatives of workers. Determinations of injury or threat of injury are made by the ITC in countervailing duty and antidumping cases. The ITC is also responsible for the preparation and publication of the harmonized tariff schedules of the US. *See* Chapters 12 *et seq*. for a complete discussion of the laws administered by the US International Trade Commission.

B. Office of the US Trade Representative

The Office of the United States Trade Representative (USTR) is a part of the Executive Office of the President which coordinates with other departments and agencies in the Executive Branch to advise the President on international trade policy matters. The US Trade Representative operates at the Cabinet level and holds the rank of ambassador, as do the two Deputy Trade Representatives. The USTR is primarily responsible for developing, implementing, and coordinating US international trade policy. The US Trade Representative, at least theoretically, is the chief negotiator for the US on bi-lateral and multilateral tariff and non-tariff barriers and on issues relating to the General Agreement on Tariffs and Trade (GATT) and the North American Free Trade Agreement (NAFTA).

> *PRACTICE NOTE:* In certain administrations, the Secretary of State and the Secretary of Commerce have shared and even dominated this role.

He or she also administers the Generalized System of Preferences (GSP) program that provides duty free benefits for designated products from beneficiary countries. (*See* Chapter 19). In the past, the President has sometimes allowed other officials, such as the National Security Advisor, to take the lead in these negotiations.

1. The Trade Policy Staff Committee

The Trade Policy Staff Committee (TPSC) is an interagency organization composed of members from various departments. A Senior Assistant Trade Representative chairs the TPSC. The Committee issues position papers on pertinent international trade issues and these are then forwarded to the Trade Policy Review Group (TPRG). The TPSC provides initial recommendations to the President on whether or not to impose quotas or to increase tariffs based on recommendations by the International Trade Commission in cases under Section 201 of the Trade Act of 1974, and on matters relating to GSP.

2. The Trade Policy Review Group

After receiving the TPSC's position papers, the TPRG reviews the policy position on that particular trade issue. The Committee is composed of assistant secretaries from all the relevant Executive departments.

3. The Trade Policy Committee

The highest level committee under the auspices of USTR, which affects national trade policy, is the Trade Policy Committee (TPC), chaired by the US Trade Representative. This Committee provides broad international trade policy guidance to the President at the Cabinet level. The Trade Negotiating Committee, which operates under the auspices of the TPC, coordinates the operational aspects of policy decisions and manages bilateral negotiations between the US and foreign countries.

4. Private Sector Committees

The USTR has established various private sector committees which aid the federal government in policy decisions. The Advisory Committee for Trade Negotiations (ACTN) is a presidentially-appointed committee of 45 representatives from various trades and industries in the US economy. The committee elects a private sector member to chair the meetings although the USTR convenes them. The ACTN offers broad policy guidance on trade issues. More specific policy recommendations, as they affect certain sectors of the economy, are offered by the policy advisory committees from various economic sectors, namely agriculture, commodities, defense, industry, investment, labor, services, and steel. Finally, private sector advice may also be proffered by the technical and sectorial policy advisory committees that are comprised of experts from the technical fields.

C. Department of Commerce

The Department of Commerce (Commerce) regulates non-agricultural trade activities, including implementation of the Multinational Trade Negotiations (MTN) and the administration of import regulating statutes. Commerce administers, in conjunction with the US International Trade Commission, specific import remedies such as the countervailing duty and antidumping statutes. It also administers national security regulations relating to trade matters. In addition, Commerce also engages in export promotion and control, trade adjustment assistance, and enforcement of anti-boycott laws.

A key unit within the Department of Commerce is the International Trade Administration (ITA). The ITA is headed by an Under Secretary and Deputy Under Secretary for International Trade. Three additional Assistant Secretaries also preside over three specific areas. The International Economic Policy division researches, analyzes and develops programs on trade investment and services. It coordinates the economic policy within the Department of Commerce and holds primary responsibility for the implementation of the MTN. The second division, which deals with the Trade Administration, regulates import/export administration issues such as licensing and enforcement of export control of critical goods or items in short supply. Antidumping and countervailing duty regulations are also administered by the International Trade Administration. Finally, the areas covered by the Assistant Secretary for Trade Development are trade expansion, direct assistance to US firms, trade promotion projects, and trade missions abroad.

Trade Development offices also provide support for local industries and businesses through the US Commercial Service, which assists US businessmen in foreign countries. This branch of Commerce has offices resident in most US Embassies tasked with assisting US businesses in promoting exports. In addition, the Office of East-West Trade, which initiates bilateral contacts with embassies and consulates, functions as a center for information regarding the economic conditions and market opportunities in communist countries. There has been legislation introduced to abolish the Department of Commerce. However, many of the existing trade functions will simply be transferred to other agencies.

D. Department of Agriculture

The Secretary of Agriculture plays an important role in the implementation of most major agricultural legislation and regulations. The most significant of these includes Section 22 actions under the Agricultural Adjustment Act which is jointly administered with the ITC. Under Section 22, the President is authorized to restrict the importation of agricultural products through the imposition of fees and quotas. The Secretary of Agriculture advises the President when an agricultural commodity may be endangered by excessive importations. If the President agrees, the ITC must conduct a further investigation. If the President accepts the Commission's finding, he may impose a fee or quota, set at no less than 50 per cent of the quantity imported during a prior representative period, although he may not impose both a fee *and* a quota. In cases of emergency, as determined by the Secretary of Agriculture, the President may act without a finding by the Commission. The action remains in effect until the Commission submits a report to the President.

The Secretary of Agriculture also plays a key role in the establishment of statutory quotas for specific products such as sugar, cotton, and meat (under the Meat Import Act of 1979). In addition, the Department of Agriculture participates in the establishment of international commodity agreements.

Chapter 4
Classification of Merchandise

I. TARIFF SCHEDULES OF THE US

Classification of merchandise is the method by which the tariff status of imported goods is determined. The Tariff Schedules of the United States (TSUS)[1] provided the basic framework by which the system operated prior to January 1, 1989 when it was replaced by the Harmonized Tariff Schedule (HTS or HTSUS). However, because of its historical significance and the fact that many court decisions and customs rulings are based on the TSUS, it warrants discussion here. The Tariff Schedules of the US provided statistical reporting guides and annotations. In addition, the General Headnotes and Rules of Interpretation aided in the proper classification of merchandise. The TSUS was organized into eight schedules and an appendix. The individual schedules applied to specific products were as follows:

Schedule (1) Animal and Vegetable Products
(2) Wood and Paper; Printed Matter
(3) Textile Fibers and Products
(4) Chemicals and Related Products
(5) Non-metallic Materials & Products
(6) Metals and Metal Products
(7) Specified Products, Miscellaneous and Non-enumerated Products
(8) Provisions for Total or Partial Duty Exemption under Certain Circumstances

Appendix: (9) Temporary Provisions Based on Legislation, Executive or Administrative Actions by Which Changes to Schedules 1–8 are Made.

1. 19 U.S.C. § 1202.

The first six schedules were organized as general categories according to the degree of processing performed on the basic raw material. Schedule 7 covered all products not encompassed in the first six, either specifically by name or as a 'basket' category. Every product which entered the US was included under one of the first seven schedules, although some products fell under a second, dual classification under either Schedule 8 or the appendix.

Schedule 8 classification took into account factors other than the product's intrinsic characteristics or commercial significance. For instance, some provisions implemented national policies not specifically related to international trade, and others included duty free or preferential treatment with certain conditions, or covered household products brought into the US by returning American residents. The Appendix included special tariffs and quotas of limited duration. Presidential 'escape clause'[2] actions and temporary duty suspensions on specific products were included under the provisions in the appendix.

The schedules were divided into parts and subparts, with each subpart more narrowly describing the imported merchandise. There were over 6,700 separate product categories under which products were classified. Each subpart provided a superior heading and an inferior heading for product description and assigned a five-digit item number. Column I duty rates applied to merchandise from most countries. These were the most favored nation (MFN) rates established under the General Agreement on Tariffs and Trade (GATT) and reflected the status of agreements reached over the last 50 years. Column I rates were the rates applied to most trading partners unless a special agreement existed or the country from which the product originated had been denied MFN status.

Higher tariff rates were provided under Column II. These were the rates established by the Tariff Act of 1930 before the emergence of the liberalizing trend in the tariff statutes. Countries not granted MFN status were subject to this rate. A list of these countries was found in General Headnote 3(d) of the Tariff Schedules. They included most communist countries. The special column rates granted preferential treatment to certain developing countries through various programs designed to enhance economic development. Since these programs still apply under the new Harmonized Tariff Schedules of the United States, they are discussed below.

A. The Generalized System of Preferences

The Generalized System of Preferences (GSP) originated as part of the Trade Act of 1974. Initially, 137 developing countries were eligible for duty free treatment, as authorized by the President, for a 10-year period. The GSP provisions were extended by the Trade and Tariff Act of 1984 for an additional eight years with a number of changes in the program. *See* more detailed discussion, *infra* at Chapter 19. In order to identify a product as eligible for the duty free rate, the country of origin must be listed in Headnote 3(e)(v) and designated by the letter 'A' next to the tariff number. However, the symbol 'A*' after the rate indicates that the product is not eligible if imported from certain countries otherwise eligible for GSP treatment

2. § 201 of The Trade Act of 1974. *See* Chapter 14. *infra.*

because of certain disqualifications. Headnote 3(e)(v)(C) aids in determining whether a country with A* is so disqualified. Products can be added and removed each year in an annual review. Products can also be removed if they exceed certain quantitative limits known as the 'Competitive Need Limits'. For a more detailed discussion of GSP *See* Ince and Glick, Manual of Practice of US. Import Law, Chapter 8, L. Glick, *The Generalized System of Preference* (Kluwer, 1990). The Generalized System of Preferences officially expired on July 1, 1995. Legislation to renew it retroactively passed on August 2, 1996, and it was signed into law by the President in September 1996. The GSP was renewed again for two years with certain modifications in a 'lame duck' session of Congress in December 2006. The changes place certain restrictions on competitive need limit waivers. *See* Chapter 19 *infra.*

B. The Caribbean Basin Economic Recovery Act

Most articles imported into the US from the Caribbean countries are entitled to duty-free treatment under the Caribbean Basin Economic Recovery Act if they satisfy certain requirements. Amendments to the law are currently being considered. Those Caribbean countries which qualify for this preferential status are designated by the letter 'E' after the 'Free' rate under the 'Special' column. If the designation 'E' appears after the rate, the product is not eligible for duty free treatment if imported from certain Caribbean countries even though other products originating from that country may be eligible.

C. Accelerated Reductions for Least Developed Developing Countries

Least Developed Developing Countries (LDDCs) were eligible for tariff cuts on an accelerated basis, under the TSUS. These reductions were negotiated during the Tokyo Round of GATT negotiations. A special column with accelerated tariff reductions for LDDCs appeared in the TSUS. They also receive special more favorable treatment under the GSP and are designated with an 'A+'.

D. US–Israel Free Trade Agreements

Preferential tariff treatment under the United States and Israel Free Trade Area Implementation Act of 1985 is extended to products from Israel in the form of 'free' or reduced rates under a schedule of reductions which should result in preferential treatment for all products imported from Israel until January 1, 1995.

E. The North American Free Trade Agreement (NAFTA)

The North American Free Trade Agreement commonly known as 'NAFTA,' was passed as part of the same legislation that included the Customs Modernization Act (H.R. 3450). It is the successor to the US–Canadian Free Trade Agreement discussed in Chapter 21, IIB although some provisions in that agreement continue in force. NAFTA was the most important trade agreement the US has entered into on other than on a multilateral basis. It covered a large amount of trade with our neighbors to both the North and South. For tariff purposes it provided for the elimination or phase out of all duties between the US, Canada and Mexico over a 15 year period for many products (such as those already duty free from Mexico under the Generalized System of Preference, discussed in Section 1 above). Others were subject to phase outs over 5, 10 and in a few cases for more sensitive products, 15 years. The phase in timetables for the three countries was not necessarily identical, recognizing the different levels of development between the countries. A provision was made for accelerated phase out and many petitions have been filed to expedite the duty phase out on certain products. Provisions, however, also exist for the reimposition of duties already removed or reduced and the non-reduction of future duties. This can occur under the so called NAFTA 'safeguard' provisions where a US industry producing a like a competitive product can file a petition with the US International Trade Commission to seek imposition of a duty if imports have increased and caused or threatened to cause material injury. The US tomato growing industry has made two attempts to implement this section – both unsuccessful (Note: the author represented certain Mexican tomato-growers in one of the cases).

NAFTA also made many important changes in areas not directly related to Customs duties. In fact, many commentators believe its most important accomplishment was in the area of so called 'Trade' in services – such as insurance, investments, banking, and professional (architects, engineers) that opened up these areas to 'national treatment'. A complete discussion of NAFTA can be found in L. Glick *Understanding the North American Free Trade Agreement* 2nd ed. (Kluwer Law International, 1995).

F. Other Free Trade Agreements

For a discussion of the US–Jordan Free Trade Agreement, US–Morocco Free Trade Agreement, US–Bahrain Free Trade Agreement, US–South African Free Trade Agreement, US–Australia Free Trade Agreement, US–Singapore Free Trade Agreement, Central American Free Trade Agreement (CAFTA), US–Columbian Free Trade Agreement, US–Peru Free Trade Agreement, US–Panama Trade Promotion Agreement, US–Korea Free Trade Agreement, US–Singapore Free Trade Agreement and the US–Morocco Free Trade Agreement, *see* Chapter 21.

II. THE HARMONIZED TARIFF SYSTEM OF THE US

The goal behind implementation of the Harmonized Tariff System (HTS) was to promote international uniformity in tariff systems. The organization of the HTS is similar to that of the Tariff Schedules of the US but the tariff headings are based on the Brussels Tariff Nomenclature, a system already used by most other countries in the world. The HTS replaced the TSUS upon passage of the Omnibus Trade and Competitiveness Act of 1988 and it took effect on January 1, 1989.

The Harmonized System is organized into 99 chapters. The first 97 chapters consist of the Rules of Interpretation, section and chapter notes, and tariff headings and subheadings with individual duty rates. Chapters 98 and 99 are analogous to the classifications found under TSUS Schedule 8 in their coverage of special, temporary classification provisions. They also provide classification categories resulting from special legislation, proclamations, and administrative actions.

Six General Rules of Interpretation (GRI) aid in the implementation of the Harmonized System. GRI 1 establishes that in the classification of goods, the primary consideration is the terms of the heading itself, which must be read in conjunction with the appropriate notes. This GRI is particularly important in the classification of parts and accessories because the Harmonized System does not contain a general rule on parts and accessories. It does, however, provide individual headings as well as chapter and section notes containing rules governing classification for parts and in some cases, accessories.

General Rule of Interpretation 2 fulfills two functions. First, it extends the provisions of the headings to include merchandise not yet completed or finished. It also extends the provisions of headings to include mixtures or combinations of materials under the heading dealing with the material itself. GRI 3 is designed to resolve classification questions when merchandise potentially falls under two or more headings. Conflicts are resolved in the following order:

(1) Specific description;
(2) Essential character; and
(3) The first heading under which the article may be classified.

The term 'essential character' as used in the General Rules has been interpreted to describe the attribute which most strongly distinguishes what the article is a characteristic which is indispensable to the structure, core, or condition of the merchandise.[3]

The first three General Rules of Interpretation are the most important in the application of the Harmonized System. The last three GRIs also provide important guidance; however, certain qualifications accompany their use. GRI 4 contains provisions for classification of goods by analogy to the merchandise which they most closely resemble; but it is only used as a last resort and applies only when no other rule can be effectively employed. Under GRI 5, containers and other packaging imported with merchandise are classified with the goods if the containers are of a kind normally sold with them. This rule does not apply, however, if the containers are suitable for repetitive use.[4] Finally, GRl6 states that classification of

---

3. *United China & Glass Co. v. United States,* 61 Cust. Ct. 386, 293 F. Supp. 734, 737 (C.A.F.C. 1968).
4. The US Customs Service originally interpreted this section as changing its long-standing interpretation that US-made packaging and containers were non-dutiable. In an initial ruling prior to implementation of the HTS, Customs indicated that only reusable packaging would be duty-

goods described in the subheadings is to be based on the terms of the subheading as well as any relevant notes and the other General Interpretive Rules.

Guidance in application of the Harmonized Code is also provided by additional rules of interpretation. For instance: the term 'parts' covers articles solely or principally used as parts; 'principal use' controls when classification is determined by a use other than actual use. Classification determined by actual use is subject to verification within three years.

III. COMPARISONS OF CLASSIFICATION OF MERCHANDISE UNDER THE TARIFF SCHEDULES OF THE US AND THE HARMONIZED SYSTEM

This Section is intended to supplement the discussions in Sections A and B of this chapter by further illustrating the differences of the Rules of Interpretation and Construction of the Tariff Schedules of the United States (TSUS) and the Harmonized Tariff System of the United States (HTS).

A. A Product Described by Reference to a Component Material

The most significant difference in the interpretation of the HTS and the TSUS is the method used to analyze a tariff category which refers to a material or substance. For example, many tariff headings under both the TSUS and the HTS refer to a product 'of' or 'wholly of' a named material. The TSUS and the HTS analyze such references differently.

B. The TSUS Approach

Under the TSUS, each term which appeared between the name of the product and a material or component had a specific definition and the importer determined whether a product was classifiable under that category by referring to that definition. For example, General Headnote 9(f)(i) of the TSUS defined the term 'of' when used between the description of an article and a material as meaning 'that the article is wholly of or in chief value of the named material.' The term 'in chief value' meant the cost of the named material exceeded the cost of every other component material in that article.[5,6] Thus, under the TSUS a product was 'of' a

---

free, if of US origin. In March 1998, a subsequent ruling extended this to all packaging of US origin which re-enters the United States without having been advanced in value or improved in condition.

5. General Headnote 10(f).
6. *See Request for Internal Advice* No. 15/80,061622 (March 25, 1980) (a braid at the intersection of the visor and crown of a cap running the width of the cap is a significant quantity of braid).

particular material when the cost or value of that material exceeded the cost or value of any other component material in that product.

General Headnote 9(f)(ii) of the TSUS defined the term 'wholly of' when used between the description of a product and a material as meaning 'that the article is, except for negligible or insignificant quantities of some other material or materials, composed completely of the named material.' This was different from a product being 'of' a given material as described above because it was a quantitative rather than a value analysis. A product was 'wholly of' the named material if, quantitatively, any other material was present only in insignificant amounts. The question of whether the named material is the material of chief value is less significant under the HTS.

General Headnote 9(f)(iii) of the TSUS defined the term 'almost wholly of.' when used between the description of a product and a material, as meaning 'the essential character of the article is imparted by the named material.' A component material imparted 'essential character' if that material served to distinguish what the article was. It had to be indispensable to the structure, core or condition of the article to impart the essential character to the product.

General Headnote 9(f)(iv) of the TSUS defined the terms 'in part of' or 'contains' when used between the description of a product and a material as meaning 'that the article contains a significant quantity of the named material.' For purposes of the TSUS, 'the word significant... implies a degree of usefulness, being meaningful or necessary, or denoting employment for a reason.[7] Thus, under the TSUS, a product was 'in part of' or 'contained' the named material if that material was necessary or useful to the product.

Under the TSUS, therefore, one would have resolved questions of whether a product could be classified under a heading which described the product by reference to a component material by referring to the term used between the product and the component material – 'of,' 'wholly of,' etc. – and analyzing whether the product satisfied the definition of that term.

C. The HTS Approach

The method of analyzing whether a product is classifiable under a heading which refers to a component material established by the HTS is somewhat different than the method outlined under the former TSUS. The general rule under the HTS is that whenever a heading describes a product by referring to a component material, any product which is made entirely of that material or is made of a mixture or combination of that material with other materials, may be classified under that heading; General Rule of Interpretation 2(b). This rule, however, is not a complete statement of the analytic process employed by the HTS.

---

7. The TSUS and the HTS both employ the *de minimus* rule in determining whether a product is 'wholly of,' 'in part of,' or 'containing' a certain material. Compare TSUS General Headnote 9(f), and HTS General Headnote 7(e).

General Headnote 7(e) of the HTS adopts the definitions of the terms 'wholly of,' 'in part of' and 'containing' used by the TSUS. Discussions with the international nomenclature staffs at both the US International Trade Commission and the US Customs Service indicate that, unless challenged through a court or administrative ruling, when these terms are used in an HTS category one should analyze them just as one would under the TSUS. Thus, to determine whether a product is classifiable under a category using one of these terms between a product and a component material, one must look to the definition of the term and determine whether the product satisfies that definition.

General Rule of Interpretation 2(b) of the HTS abandons the concept of chief value when analyzing whether a product is 'of' a named material. Rule 2(b) provides in relevant part: 'Any reference to goods of a given material or substance shall be taken to include a reference to goods consisting wholly or partly of such material or substance.' 'Of' is simply a general term referring to goods made entirely of, wholly of or partly of the named material; there is no reference to chief value.[8]

IV. WHERE A PRODUCT MAY BE CLASSIFIED IN TWO OR MORE CATEGORIES

Occasionally a product may be classified under two or more different headings. The TSUS and the HTS resolve this problem in different ways.

A. The TSUS Approach

Under the TSUS, when a product could be classified under two or more categories, it was classified under the category which most specifically described the product. The rules of 'relative specificity' described in this chapter controlled the determination of which category more specifically described the product.

If the problem could not have been resolved by reference to the specificity of the category, then the product would have been classified under the category which carried the highest duty rate.[9]

Finally, if the problem still was not resolved the product would have been classified under the category which appeared first in the schedules.[10]

B. The HTS Approach

Under the HTS, if a product may be classified under more than one category, the product is also to be classified under the one which most specifically describes it.[11]

8. General Headnote of the TSUS 10(c).
9. General Headnote of the TSUS 10(d).
10. *Id.*
11. General Rule of Interpretation of the HTS 3(a).

According to the International Trade Commission and the Customs Service, the same rules of relative specificity that existed under the TSUS apply to the HTS.

If a classification cannot be resolved by comparing the relative specificities of the headings, then the product will be classified as if it were made of the material which gives the product its 'essential character.'[12] The concept of 'essential character' is the same as it was under the TSUS.

If none of the preceding methods are applicable, the product is to be classified under the category which occurs last in the schedules.

This section briefly described the differences in the interpretation and construction of the TSUS and the HTS. The rules of interpretation not mentioned above (*i.e.*, classification by use, the classification of unfinished merchandise, or the classification of parts) do not appear to have been changed by the HTS. Also, until changed by the courts or by other means, the rules of construction such as the common meaning, commercial designation and relative specificity doctrines apply to the interpretation of the HTS.

V. RULES OF CONSTRUCTION

When the meaning of a particular tariff item is unclear or ambiguous, the legislative history of the particular provision in question may provide help in discerning the underlying intent. The Tariff Classification Study of November 15, 1960 provides useful legislative history and was recognized by the courts as a valuable source of guidance to the interpretation of the TSUS. It was published by the US Tariff Commission, now the International Trade Commission. In addition, the Brussels Tariff nomenclature has been a valuable source of interpretation when the tariff provisions are similar to those found in the TSUS. It is even more valuable as an interpretive aid now that the HTS is in force. The following rules of construction applied to the TSUS. As discussed above, some of these rules also apply to the HTS and others have been modified. However, since few court interpretations of the HTS originally existed, the many cases interpreting these rules under the TSUS are instructive.

A. Common Meaning

The *Simmon Omega*[13] decision provided valuable guidelines for the use of the common meaning doctrine. According to that decision, tariff terms are to be used in accordance with their common meaning. When no contrary legislative intent exists, the common and commercial meanings of a term are considered to be the same. Dictionary definitions, as well as the testimony of witnesses, are valuable sources for discerning the common meaning. Specialized dictionaries such as technical dictionaries are viewed as useful sources when technical terms are used.

---

12. General Rule of Interpretation of the HTS 3(b).
13. *Simmon Omega, Inc. v. United States,* 83 Cust. Ct. 14 (1979).

If the term is defined within the statute, however, the statutory meaning prevails over the common meaning.

The common meaning is a question of law to be determined by the court.[14] A presumption exists that the meaning of a term in a tariff statute is its commercial meaning. It is also presumed that this statutory meaning is the same as the common meaning.[15] The tariff schedules are intended to encompass even articles which have not yet been developed or those upon which basic design improvements have been made.[16] If the improved version basically resembles the article named in the statute, then that classification controls. If it bears little or no resemblance to the named article, a new classification may need to be determined.[17]

B. Commercial Designation

Terms which are well established in trade or commerce but differ from their common meaning are assigned their commercial meaning unless contrary legislative intent exists. The party asserting that a term's commercial meaning differs from its common meaning carries the burden of proof. Evidence establishing commercial designation includes definite, uniform and general use in trade.[18]

C. Relative Specificity

General Interpretive 'Headnote' of TSUS Rule 10(c) stated that when an article was described under more than one tariff provision it was to be classified under the provision which described it most specifically.[19] The following general rules applied:

(a) An *eo nomine* provision generally prevails over a term of general description; and
(b) A use provision generally prevails over an *eo nomine* provision.

Each case was determined on its own facts, including the merchandise and competing provisions involved. HTS 3(a) follows this rule.

---

14. *United States v. Brager-Larsen,* 36 C.C.P.A. I (1948) (principle that common meaning is a question of law and not of fact is well settled).
15. *Ameliotex, Inc. v. United States,* 65 C.C.P.A. 22, 565 F.2d 674 (1977).
16. *Kaysons Import Corp. v. United States,* 56 Cust. Ct. 146 (1966) (electric toothbrushes not in existence at time of Tariff Act of 1930 classified as toothbrushes due to their basic similarity).
17. *Texas Instruments, Inc. v. United States,* 82 Cust. Ct. 272, 475 F. Supp. 1183 (1979). *Aff'd,* 67 C.C.P.A. 57, 620 F.2d 269 (1980) (integrated circuit for use in digital watch not within scope of tariff term for 'watch movement').
18. *United States v. M.J. Brandenstein & Co.*, 17 C.C.P.A. 480 (1930).
19. *Novelty Import Co. v. United States,* 55 Cust. Ct. 169 (1965) (includes guidelines for determining which of two competing provisions is rnore specific).

D. Condition of Merchandise

The condition of the merchandise at the time of importation controls its classification. Processing or additions to the merchandise after importation are not considered in its classification.[20] The TSUS contained separate provisions for articles which were unfinished or unassembled. *See* Chapter 9 *infra* for discussion of processing of articles after they are imported into a foreign trade zone.

E. Finished and Unfinished Merchandise

TSUS General Interpretive Rule 10(h) stated that the tariff description of an article covered the article in any stage of assembly, finished or unfinished. If the material had been processed to the extent that it had been dedicated to making that article or was commercially fit only for use as that particular article, the merchandise would be classified as the article in unfinished form.[21] The *Daisy Heddon*[22] decision established that in order to qualify for classification as 'the article, unfinished or unassembled,' the articles had to be 'substantially complete.' In establishing whether an article was substantially complete and therefore ineligible for classification as the unfinished article, the following factors were taken into consideration:

(1) comparison of the number of omitted parts to the number of included parts;
(2) comparison of the time and effort required to complete the article with the time and effort required to place it in its imported condition;
(3) comparison of the cost of the included parts with the cost of the omitted parts;
(4) the significance of the omitted parts to the overall functioning of the article; and,
(5) trade customs.[23]

Another critical factor taken into consideration was the extent of work which remained to be done after importation.[24] This rule is similar under the HTS.

---

20. *Exxon Corp. v. United States,* 81 Cust. Ct. 87, 462 F. Supp. 378, *aff'd,* 66 C.C.P.A 129, 607 F. 2d 985 (1979) (product used in making motor fuel after importation not classified as motor fuel for tariff purposes).
21. *Pacific Fast Mail v. United States,* 68 Cust. Ct. 41, 338 F. Supp. 506 (1972) (locomotive models, finished except for wheels and boiler front assemblies, were classified under model locomotives as unfinished because they were so far processed that they were dedicated to the making of such models).
22. *Daisy-Heddon, Div. Victor Comptometer Corp. v. United States,* 81 Cust. Ct. 55, 460 F. Supp. 680 (1978), *aff'd,* 66 C.C.P.A. 97, 600 F.2d 799 (1979).
23. *Daisy-Heddon,* 600 F. 2d a1 803. *See also Toyota Motor Sales, U.S.A., Inc. v. United States,* 7 Ct. Int'l Trade 178, 585 F. Supp. 649, *aff'd,* 3 Ct. Int'l Trade 93, 753 F.2d 1061 (1985) (applying the *Daisy-Heddon* factors to hold that truck chassis without cargo box was substantially complete truck and thus classifiable under provision for trucks).
24. *Avins Indus. Prods. Co. v. United States,* 62 C.C.P.A. 83, 515 F.2d 782 (1975) (article must be so far processed toward its ultimate completed form as to be dedicated to the making of that

F. Parts of Merchandise

Under the TSUS, parts were classified under an *eo nomine* provision, which covered all forms of the article, unless specifically excluded.[25] These rules are unchanged in the HTS. Under the HTS, parts are governed by the GRI. The first consideration is to review the heading text to determine if the specifies part is named. The second consideration is to determine the heading which belongs to the article to which the part pertains. The HTS does not contain general rules for classification of parts and therefore provides no rules for the classification of a part as related to the classification of the original product.

In contrast, the TSUS General Interpretive Rules provided guidance for classification of parts. Rule 10(j) stated that a provision for parts would not prevail over a specified provision, the *eo nomine* provision, for that part.[26] A provision for parts, however, did prevail over a basket provision.[27] Thus Headnote 10(j) also stated that a provision for parts of a named class of articles only applied to merchandise chiefly used as parts of those articles. Accessories and optional equipment might also qualify as parts even though they might not be essential to the operation or functioning of the main article. However, the HTS 'Additional Rules of Interpretation' provide that, in the absence of special language or context, a provision for parts of an article covers products solely or principally used as a part of such articles. However, a provision for 'parts' or 'parts and accessories' should not prevail over a specific provision for such parts or accessories.

G. Entireties

The issue of whether two components shipped together with the intent that they be used together is classified separately or as an entirety under a single item number arises frequently, mostly in regard to imported clothing and apparel. The components will generally be considered an entirety if, when joined, they form a new article with a character or use different from the individual parts[28] or when one of the components predominates.[29] However, when the article is imported as a unit but the parts retain their individual character and are not subordinated to

article or that class of article in order to be classified under the *eo nomine* provision for that article, unfinished).

25. *Nomura (America) Corp. v. United States,* 58 C.C.P.A. 82, 435 F.2d 1319 (1971).
26. *Robert Bosch Corp. v. United States,* 63 Cust. Ct. 187, 305 F. Supp. 921 (1969) (automobile radio classified under provision for radiotelegraphic and radiotelephone apparatus rather than as parts of automobiles).
27. *Ideal Toy Corp. v. United States,* 58 C.C.P.A. 9, 433 F.2d 801 (1970) (miniature auto chassis and body were properly classified under parts of toys; TSUS number 737.90).
28. *James Betesh Import Co. v. United States,* 40 Cust. Ct. 186 (1958) (bowl and holder used together as ashtray are classifiable as smokers' articles, not specifically provided for).
29. *Artgift Corp. v. United States,* 30 Cust. Ct. 372 (1953) (base, dome and metal figure designed to be used together as statuette are classifiable as an entirety and different duties are not assessed against the individual parts).

the identity of the combination, duty is imposed on the individual parts as if they were imported separately.[30]

VI. METHODS FOR OBTAINING CUSTOMS RULINGS

Advance binding written Customs rulings can be an indispensable business aid to an importer. Upon request from a prospective importer, Customs personnel will generally provide an advisory opinion. Oral advisory opinions from local officials at the ports are considered non-binding rulings, are of limited value and are not generally recommended. Local port officials can no longer provide nonbinding written rulings. Certain types of binding written rulings can be obtained on the district level. This is generally limited to simple classification issues.

A. Procedure for Obtaining Advance Classification Rulings

Binding rulings on the classification of merchandise that has not yet been imported (prospective transactions) are generally obtained from the Commissioner of Customs, Office of Regulations and Rulings, US Customs Service that are located in Washington D.C. or the National Import Specialist in the New York Region.[31]

The request can be filed in the form of a letter and should include the following information relevant facts pertaining to the transaction; identification of the parties, country of origin, anticipated port of entry and the nature of the transaction. A sample of the merchandise or a detailed description of its anticipated condition on entry should also be supplied. In addition, research on past rulings on similar merchandise is highly recommended. Court decisions on such rulings are available in various court reporters in most libraries. Many, but not all, of the actual Customs private letter rulings that form the basis for most Customs decisions are not published in the Customs Bulletin. Others can be viewed on the Customs website. Unless research is undertaken on prior rulings relating to the same or similar merchandise the importer is limited in his ability to assert much influence over Customs decisions on classification. Generally, an experienced attorney should prepare these ruling requests.

> *PRACTICE NOTE:* Customs Brokers often obtain rulings for their clients at little or no cost but frequently do not research past rulings and case precedents as do attorneys.

30. *Donalds Ltd. v. United States,* 32 Cust. Ct. 310 (1954).
31. 19 C.F.R. 5 177.1–.10. A classification request can be addressed to a local district director but these are generally referred to the national import specialist in New York. More recently, field national import specialists have been designated in various cities. Also electronic or 'E' rulings or simple classification issues can be obtained from New York in as little as 14 days.

If the subject of the requested advance ruling is an issue currently being considered by the Customs Service or litigated or appealed before the Court of International Trade, an advance ruling may not be issued. If a ruling is issued, but the subsequent transaction materially varies from the facts submitted with the request, the ruling is not binding on the Customs Service.

B. Changes in Customs Practice

When Customs intends to make a change which diverges from 'established and uniform practice,'[32] it is required to publish a notice in the *Federal Register* and provide interested parties a chance to submit comments. A change in Customs practice is generally delayed for a 30-day period in order to provide importers with advance information regarding any adverse action which may affect their businesses.

C. Judicial Decisions on Classification

Customs applies the principles established by decisions of the Court of International Trade and the Court of Appeals for the Federal Circuit, according to the following guidelines, outlined in Title 19, Section 152.16, of the *Code of Federal Regulations:*

(a) If the principles espoused in the decision favor the government, all identical merchandise will then be classified according to those principles;
(b) If the principles are favorable to the government, they will be applied to all similar merchandise if its classification is affected by the principles and it has been entered or withdrawn from the warehouse after 30 days from the date of publication of the decision in the Customs Bulletin;
(c) If the court decision contains a 'definite statement that a higher rate' should be applied, that rate will be applied to all merchandise, identical or similar, which is affected by the principles in the court's decision. The 30-day delay rule will apply;
(d) If an American manufacturer's petition under Title 19, Section 1516, of the United States Code is upheld, the principles advanced in the decision apply to 'all merchandise of that character which is entered or withdrawn after the date of publication of the court's decision in the *Custom's Bulletin.*' The liquidation of entries covering the merchandise is suspended pending appellate review, pursuant to 19 C.F.R. § 159.57;
(e) If the court's decision is adverse to the government, the principles are applied in regard to non-liquidated entries involving the same issues.

---

32. *Biddle Sawyer Corp. v. United States,* 48 Cust. Ct. 30, 219 F. Supp. 239 (1962), *aff'd, 50* C.C.P.A. 85, 320 F.2d 416 (1963) (defining 'established practice' as the relative permanence or length of time a practice has been used). A ruling or practice is considered 'uniform' if it is published in the *Customs Bulletin and Decisions.* 19 C.F.R. 177.10(b).

They are also applied to any liquidated entry involving the same issue, if a timely protest was filed but not denied; however, Customs may apply a narrower interpretation than the court applied in its original decision; and

(f) Use of Private Laboratory Tests. The Customs Mod Act for the first time provided for certification of private testing laboratories. Customs must give equal weight to the results from these laboratories as they do to their own. Many classification issues, as well as those relating to proper visas, may rest on the technical nature of the composition of the goods. If Customs is in doubt, they may seek advice from their official laboratories, but the importer has little input into this process. Use of a private Customs laboratory provides the importer an opportunity to arrange its own testing and submit the results to Customs.

PRACTICE NOTE: The author has been involved in a case where the Customs Laboratory has made errors and in another case when private laboratories have been used. Under the old law, an importer could dispute findings of the Customs Laboratory but could not offer his own rebuttal laboratory data. The new law significantly strengthens the importer's ability to challenge the sanctity of Customs Laboratory findings which previously were given considerable weight in many court decisions.

Chapter 5

General Principles of Customs Valuation of Merchandise

I. INTRODUCTION

The purpose of this chapter is to discuss the general principles of customs valuation of merchandise. Valuation is a complex area. Since most tariffs are on an *ad valorem* basis (based on value), both valuation and classification together are required to determine the duties owed. This chapter will discuss basic principles of customs valuation. This is a complex subject and the treatment here is intended to be a general overview for the exporter and importer. Without a complete understanding of the facts and relationships between the parties, the costs of the merchandise, and the services performed in the US by any related importer, it is difficult to reach any conclusions about a specific transaction. The US adopted a new valuation system as part of The Trade Agreements Act of 1979. This new system took effect for most products on July 1, 1984. US customs duties are either specific rates (USD .10 per pound) or *ad valorem* (a percentage of the appraised value). Specific duties are less complex since they are based on weights or units and the real value of the merchandise need not be determined.

> *PRACTICE NOTE:* Duties can also be based on a combination of an *ad valorem* rate and a specific rate. (e.g., 5 per cent plus 10 cents per kilo).

II. DISCUSSION

A. Valuation of Merchandise

Title 19, Section 1401a of the United States Code governs the methods by which the CBP determines the dutiable value of imported merchandise. The statute derives its text from the Valuation Code of the General Agreement on Tariffs and Trade (GATT) to which the US is a signatory.[1] Based on the GATT Valuation Code, the value of imported Article III merchandise is to be appraised on a commercial basis. Thus, when importation results from a sale where the buyer and seller are unrelated parties, the dutiable value is determined by the selling price. This method, known as transaction value in the US, is the most frequently used and preferred method of customs valuation. Very few adjustments to price are permitted, and these must reflect the actual circumstances of the transaction in question. Commissions paid to the buyer's agent and selling expenses such as trademark royalties are not dutiable unless paid to the seller.

However, due in part to the growth of multinational corporations, frequently the buyer and seller are related parties and invoice sales prices do not always reflect the prices that would exist in an 'arms length transaction' between unrelated parties.

1. Methods of Valuation

As noted above, transaction value is the preferred method of valuation. It is the method most commonly and frequently used. Four alternative methods of valuation are employed where no price exists on which transaction value can be based. These alternative methods are to be applied in the following order:

(a) *Transaction value of identical merchandise,* established by the price in a direct sale to a US purchaser of merchandise produced in the same country at approximately the same time;
(b) *Transaction value of similar merchandise,* established by the price for nearly identical, commercially interchangeable merchandise from the same country;
(c) *Deductive value,* established by the price at which the article is ultimately sold in the US minus international freight, customs duties, clearance charges, federal sales tax, US inland freight, the commission earned or other usual general expenses and profits realized, and the cost of further manufacturing if any has been performed on the article; and
(d) *Computed value,* established by adding the manufacturer's actual costs for labor and materials and the usual general expenses and profit realized by the manufacturer. An importer may request computed value appraisement in preference to deductive value in a written request to Customs.

When none of the alternative methods apply, Customs determines a value through a method derived from one of the statutory methods. The derivations or adjustments must be based upon fact, must not be prohibited by law, and must reflect the actual experience of the manufacturer. For example, for some products such as perishable agricultural commodities,

1. For the text of the Code and a discussion of the GATT Customs Valuation Code, *see* L. Glick, *Multilateral Trade Negotiations: World Trade After the Tokyo Round*. Rowman & Allanheld. 1984, at 69.

Customs has based valuation on 'average' prices from a sample of sales of the commodity by groups of importers during a certain time-table period.

(e) The *transaction value* of the imported merchandise is the price actually paid or payable for the imported merchandise being appraised. The price paid or payable is subject to change where the contract-for-importation provides for a reduction on late delivery of the merchandise: Customs Ruling 543013 (February 15, 1983). However, where a price is renegotiated subsequent to importation for merchandise which is neither defective nor inferior, the new price is not considered as the price paid or payable; Customs Ruling 543609 (October 7,1985). Transaction value has been held to be the preferred method of appraisement; Customs Ruling 542658 (January 12, 1982).

The statute defines transaction value as:

> The total payment (whether direct or indirect, and exclusive of any costs, charges, or expenses incurred for transportation, insurance, and related services incident to the international shipment of the merchandise from the country of exportation to the place of importation in the United States) made, or to be made, for imported merchandise by the buyer to, or for the benefit of, the seller.[2]

a. Additions to Price

The actual quantity and level of trade is used in calculating the transaction value. The following items must also be added to the price to achieve the transaction value: packing costs incurred by the buyer, selling commission incurred by the buyer, the apportioned value of any assists, any royalty or license fee the buyer is required to pay as a condition of export sale of the merchandise, and the processes of any subsequent resale, use, or other disposition of the imported merchandise accrued to the seller. If sufficient information regarding these items is unavailable, this method of valuation cannot be used.

b. Exclusions from Price

The following items may be excluded from the price: cost of construction, assembly or maintenance of the merchandise after importation, the reasonable cost of transportation after importation, any US Customs duties, other import taxes and federal excise taxes on the imported merchandise. No exclusion is allowed for any rebate or reduction made after importation.

c. Restrictions on the Buyer

Certain restrictions on the buyer as to the disposition of the merchandise may eliminate transaction value as a possible method of valuation. These restrictions

---

2. 19 U.S.C. § 1401a (1980).

include limitations on the buyer's disposition of the merchandise; conditions attached to the sale or price of the merchandise and the accrual of any portion of the buyer's proceeds to the seller and related party transactions. Certain restrictions on the buyer, however, are acceptable and do not destroy transaction value. These include: restrictions imposed or required by law, restrictions limiting the geographical area in which the goods may be resold and other restrictions not substantially affecting the value of the goods. Some conditions relating to the sale or price which are not acceptable in a transaction value situation include a requirement that the buyer also buy other merchandise in specified quantities from the seller, requirements as to the price at which the buyer sells other goods to the seller and use of a form of payment extraneous to the imported merchandise. All of these situations can cause transaction value to be disregarded by Customs.

d. Use of Identical Merchandise

The transaction value of identical merchandise may be used when the use of transaction value of the imported article is not appropriate, for example, in related party transactions where transfer prices are involved. The additions to price specified under the primary value standard and any applicable adjustments must be added to this method of valuation. The transaction value of similar merchandise may also be used as an alternative method. The only difference between this method and transaction value of identical merchandise is the point of reference. Factors to be considered in determining whether merchandise is similar include the quality of merchandise, its reputation and whether or not it is trademarked. Thus, if Company A in the US purchases goods from its affiliated Company B in Mexico, and Customs questions the validity of the invoice prices due to the relationship, the importer may request that the value be based on the price of similar merchandise imported by unrelated parties.

e. Deductive Value

The deductive value is the price at which the imported merchandise or identical or similar merchandise is sold in the US with deductions for certain items. The price utilized is different than the invoice price between the exporter and importer. It is the price at which the importer resells the goods to an unrelated party minus certain expenses that are non-dutiable. The condition of the merchandise and the time of resale are also considered. In determining deductive value, Customs looks to the unit price at which the merchandise is sold to unrelated parties in the greatest aggregate quantity. If an assist is involved in the sale, that sale cannot be used in determining deductive value.[3]

Generally deductive value is calculated by beginning with a unit sales price. This price may depend upon the time of sale and condition of the merchandise. Additions are made for packing costs, unless already included in the price.

---

3. *See* discussion in Section 3, *infra.*

Packing costs are the cost of all containers and of packing, including both labor and materials. Certain deductions may then be made. These include deductions for commissions or profit and general expenses, transportation and insurance costs, customs duties and federal taxes and the value of further processing.

f. Computed Value

Computed value is the final method available to value merchandise when the other methods are considered inappropriate. Computed value is essentially a method of valuation based on cost of production. The following factors are used to arrive at the computed value: the cost of the materials and fabrication of the imported merchandise, the amount of profit and general expenses equal to those usually reflected in sales of merchandise of the same class or kind made by producers in the exporting country, any assist not otherwise included and packing costs. The figures for profit and expenses are based on the producer's actual figures unless they are inconsistent with what is usual in such sales.

Computed value may rely to a certain extent on information gathered from sources outside the US. If a foreign producer refuses to provide this information, or is in some fashion legally restrained from doing so, computed value cannot be determined. Computed value determinations are generally used in cases of sales, between related parties when other methods such as transaction value of similar merchandise cannot be used (for example, if there are no sales of similar merchandise by unrelated parties).

> *PRACTICE NOTE:* Importers generally prefer to avoid use of computed value because of the added cost required by detailed 'cost accounting' versus the simplicity of transaction value (using the invoice price).

2. Related-party Transactions

The principle behind different treatment of related-party transactions rests on the theory that commonality of ownership or control creates opportunities for non-market influences that can affect the legitimacy of price. In fact, transfer prices that do not reflect actual costs and profits are commonplace in intra-company transactions. An offshore production facility may be operated strictly as a cost center without regard to profitability. Customs will only accept a related-party sales price when the relationship between the parties does not affect the price and the transaction value determined under this method 'closely approximates' the value determined under other methods. Generally, related-party transfer prices are accepted as representative of transaction value if the parties can demonstrate that they dealt with each other at arms length. Thus if two related companies regularly conduct business as if they were unrelated, transaction value may be acceptable. Some criteria to determine this include: whether the seller or buyer, although related, also does business with unrelated parties, if their prices are different to their unrelated parties and if invoices are regularly sent and paid within commercially accepted time periods by check or other instruments. In addition, if the importer or manufacturer maintains its books and records in accordance with generally accepted accounting principles (GAAP), CBP will generally use this financial information.

The statute also provides that, if the transfer price approximates what the transaction value of identical or similar merchandise is for sale to unrelated US buyers or what the deductive or computed value of identical or similar merchandise would be, it must be accepted.

While it is the importer's responsibility to designate that a transaction is between related parties, Customs may not automatically disregard a sales price solely on the basis that the parties are related. Customs must have some basis on which to suspect that the relationship has affected the price. The determination whether the price paid or payable has been influenced by the relationship between the parties is made on a case-by-case basis.[4]

Transaction value has been held inapplicable in a related party transaction where there is no basis from which to ascertain whether the relationship influenced the price. In the absence of a transaction or deductive value, the computed valuation method is used in appraising the merchandise.[5]

3. Assists

Assists are items added into the dutiable value of merchandise for purpose of customs appraisement. Assists are certain production or selling inputs supplied to the foreign manufacturer or seller free of charge or at a reduced rate by the buyer or importer. The principle underlying this rule of adding the value of assists to the customs value of the product is that the foreign producer would have had to supply these inputs himself and bear the costs. These additional costs would normally have been reflected in the price to the importer and thus the value. The specified inputs include: the materials incorporated into the imported merchandise; tools, dies, molds or similar articles used in production; products consumed in the manufacturing process; and engineering, development, and designing costs performed outside the US. However, engineering, art and design work, and plans and sketches that are done in the US are not considered to be dutiable assists. Similarly, services, such as management, accounting, and legal advice, are not classified as dutiable assists.[6]

The value of any assists may be directly added to the price actually paid to determine transaction value. It may also be added as an element in constructing a value under the computed value method.

---

4. *See* Customs Ruling 543806 (March 12, 1987).
5. *See* Customs Ruling 542792 (March 25, 1983).
6. Customs Ruling 542122 (September 4, 1980).

Customs must determine the value of any assist and apportion it by prorating that value to the merchandise. This may be accomplished by using any method consistent with generally accepted accounting principles. The importer is required to supply appropriate documentation to support the method of apportionment. If the assist was acquired from an unrelated seller, the value of the assist is generally the cost of acquisition. In a related-party transaction, the value is normally the cost of production of the assist. Used, modified or repaired equipment can also be assists but are given different treatment in determining their value.

Assists frequently arise in related-party transactions, for example, where a US importer provides various machinery or equipment to an affiliated foreign manufacturer/exporter. However, sometimes the duty consequences of an assist can be avoided. For example, if the exporter leases the machinery at fair market value there would be no assist. Also, the value of any assist is the book value. If a machine is fully depreciated so that it has no book value, it may be an assist, but there is no dutiable consequence.

> *PRACTICE NOTE:* Assists are a frequently overlooked area and the source of advancement in value and often fines and penalties during Customs audits. If you do not understand assists, contact your customs advisor.

4. Difficulties in Appraisement and Valuation

Although the revision of the valuation statute resulting from the GATT Customs Valuation Code and the Trade Agreements Act of 1979 has simplified customs valuation to a great degree, many problems still exist. One problem area is the question of whether Customs has the authority to consider elements not specifically enumerated in the statute. One example is the payment of services which may be included in the 'price actually paid or payable for the merchandise,' but which are not payments for the merchandise itself. These may include payments for quota allocations, foreign inland freight, interest, or inspection costs.

The Customs Modernization Act, passed on December 8, 1993, has set forth standards for Shared Responsibility and Reasonable Care. Standards for Shared Responsibility and Reasonable Care were developed to foster mutual responsibility between the importer and Customs. 'Shared responsibility' requires that importers accurately evaluate and classify merchandise, and in turn, Customs must properly oversee entry and determine the duty amounts owed. In the event that an importer is uncertain of a classification or valuation issue, the importer must use 'reasonable care' in investigating any discrepancies.[7] A presumption of 'reasonable care' is found when the importer seeks expert advice from an attorney or an in-house employee with sufficient technical expertise in the particular

7. US Congress. Committee on Ways and Means. House Report (193–361).

merchandise in question, or when a valuation issue is involved, consults an attorney or public accountant, or any other appropriate personnel familiar with the importer's accounting system.[8] In addition, 'reasonable care' requires that the importer provide the expert with complete and full information sufficient for him/her to carry out entry or determine procedures for entry.[9]

III. CONCLUSION

The complexity of Customs valuation questions often requires an analysis of past rulings and cases. Only through such an analysis can a definite answer be given as to whether a particular transaction is consistent with the customs laws. Also, binding written rulings are issued on request by Customs headquarters. Such written ruling requests should include an analysis of prior Customs decisions on similar or related products, a discussion of the facts and legal issues and samples of the merchandise. Written Customs rulings are desirable to insure that a price used by an exporter will be accepted by Customs and that he will not be subjected to a later 'advancement' of value or to possible fraud or negligence penalties. Such rulings also insure uniformity of treatment between different ports and limit the discretion of local Customs officials. For example, in the antidumping case of Fresh Cut Flowers from Mexico imported into the US by some of the author's clients, different methods of valuation were being used by Customs at the ports of Miami, Houston and Laredo. The author had several meetings with Customs officials in the different ports in an attempt to achieve uniformity. Binding written rulings are issued by Customs in Washington.

If an exporter's present method of valuation is not in accordance with the law, fines and penalties and possible criminal action can be mitigated by making a voluntary disclosure before Customs begins an inquiry. *See* Chapter 10, *infra*.

---

8. *Id.*
9. *Id.*

Chapter 6
Country of Origin Marking

I. INTRODUCTION

This chapter provides an overview of the important topic of country of origin marking requirements. The chapter first summarizes the statutes and regulations dealing with country of origin marking requirements and then discusses the exceptions to the country of origin marking requirements. The concept of substantial transformation is also discussed, in light of the important role it plays in country of origin determinations. The chapter also analyzes Customs and court interpretations pertaining to the various concepts relating to country of origin marking requirements. In addition, the regulations regarding the terms 'Made in USA,' 'Made in America,' 'Assembled in the USA' and similar terms which are regulated by the Federal Trade Commission (FTC) are also discussed.

II. BACKGROUND

The US Customs laws require each imported article produced abroad to be marked as clearly and conspicuously as the nature of the article permits. The aim is to indicate to the ultimate purchaser[1] in the US the name of the country in which the article was manufactured or produced so as to enable the purchaser to choose between domestic and foreign-made products, or between the products of different foreign countries. In this sense, marking requirements could be considered a non-tariff barrier to trade since they tend to benefit domestic manufacturers *vis-à-vis* their foreign competition, on the theory that purchasers will prefer American-made

---

1. 'Ultimate purchaser,' in this context, is the last person in the US who will receive the article in the form in which it was imported. However, there are certain instances in which it is not always easy to state who will be the ultimate purchaser. *See* discussion, *infra*.

products when they know the difference.[2] There are, however, certain articles, which will be discussed below, which are specifically exempted from individual marking.[3]

A. Statutory Basis

The law regarding country of origin[4] marking is found in § 304 of the Tariff Act of 1930, as amended (19 U.S.C. § 1304), and in an implementing regulation contained in 19 C.F.R. § 134.

Pursuant to 19 C.F.R. § 134.11, every article of foreign origin (or its container) imported into the US must be marked in a conspicuous place as legibly, indelibly and permanently as the nature of the article (or container) will permit, in such, manner as to indicate to an ultimate purchaser in the US the English name of the country of origin of the articles.[5] Unless specifically exempted from marking, containers of articles must also be marked with the name of the country of origin.[6]

Articles of foreign origin imported into any possession of the US outside its customs territory and reshipped to the US are also subject to all marking requirements applicable to like articles of foreign origin imported directly from a foreign country to the US.[7] Special rules exist for an article of a kind which is usually combined with another article subsequent to importation, but before delivery to an ultimate purchaser. If the name indicating the country of origin of the original article appears in a place on the article so that the name will be visible after such combining, the marking shall include, in addition to the name of the country of origin, words or symbols which clearly show that the origin indicated is that of the imported article only and not that of any other article with which the imported article may be combined after importation (e.g., 'Handle made in Taiwan').

The general scope and purview of the rules regarding country of origin marking have been interpreted and extensively discussed in various customs and court decisions. Some of these decisions are discussed below.

---

2. *See* Note, *United States Country of Origin Marking Requirements: The Application of a Non-Tariff Trade Barrier,* 6 Law & Pol'y Int'l Bus. 485 (1974).
3. *See* discussion, *infra.*
4. 'Country of Origin' means the country of manufacture, production, or growth of any article of foreign origin entering the *US.* Further work or material added to an article in another country must effect a substantial transformation in order to render such other country the 'country of origin.' *See* 19 C.F.R. § 134.1(b) (1995).
5. However, generally understood variations from the English spelling, or abbreviations, are also permitted (e.g., 'Gt. Britain' for 'Great Britain'). In addition, variant spellings which clearly indicate the English name of the country of origin, such as 'Brasil' for 'Brazil,' and 'Italie' for 'Italy,' are acceptable; and the adjectival form of the name of a country shall be accepted as a proper indication of the name of the country of origin of imported merchandise provided the adjectival form of the name does not appear with other words so as to refer to a kind or species of produce. *See* 19 C.F.R. § 134.45(b) and (c) (1995).
6. *Id.*
7. 19 C.F.R. § 134.12 (1995).

B. Exceptions to Marking Requirements

Certain classes of articles are exempted from the country of origin marking requirements because they are not physically capable of being marked or can only be marked at the risk of damaging the article. Thus, the Secretary of the Treasury may, consistent with § 1304(a)(3) of the Tariff Act of 1930 that was amended, authorize the exception of any article from the requirements of marking if:

(a) Such an article is incapable of being marked;[8]
(b) Such an article cannot be marked prior to shipment to the US without injury;[9]
(c) Such an article cannot be marked prior to shipment to the US except at an expense economically prohibitive of its importation;
(d) The marking of a container of such article will reasonably indicate the origin of such article;
(e) Such an article is a crude substance;[10]
(f) Such an article is imported for use by the importer and not intended for sale in its imported or any other form.
(g) Such an article is to be processed in the US by the importer or for his account otherwise than for the purpose of concealing the origin of such article and in such manner that any mark contemplated by this section would necessarily be obliterated, destroyed or permanently concealed;
(h) An ultimate purchaser, by reason of the character of such article or by reason of the circumstances of its importation, must necessarily know the country of origin of such article even though it is not marked to indicate its origin;
(i) Such an article was produced more than 20 years prior to its importation into the US; or
(j) Such an article cannot be marked after importation except if there is an expense which is economically prohibitive, and the failure to mark the article before importation was not due to any purpose of the importer, producer, seller or shipper to avoid compliance with this section.[11]

'J – List' Exceptions – Under 19 U.S.C. § 1304(a)(3)(J), classes of articles named in certain notices published by the Secretary of the

8. E.g., gasoline or a pin.
9. Contact lenses and glass marbles, for example, cannot be individually marked without damaging them. Moreover, assuming *arguendo* that they could be marked without damaging them, such marking would, nevertheless, not achieve the desired result, because the letter size would be so small as to make the marking illegible.
10. Probably, even if crude substances were not excepted, they would qualify for exception as being incapable of marking, under category (a).
11. 19 U.S.C. § 1304(3) (1995). In addition, the regulations exempt the following articles from marking requirements: articles entered or withdrawn from warehouse for immediate exportation or for transportation and exportation; products of American fisheries which are free of duty; products of possessions of the United States; and products of the United States exported and returned. *See* 19 C.F.R. § 134.32(j)–(m) (1995).

Treasury in the late 1930s are not subject to the marking requirements. The articles named in such notices were those which had been imported in substantial quantities during the 5-year period ending December 31, 1936, and which had not been required to bear country of origin markings during that period. The 'J List' exceptions are all enumerated in the *Code of Federal Regulations* and attached as Appendix B11 to this book.[12]

C. Substantial Transformation

Substantial transformation is a legal principle used under US tariff laws in various contexts. In the case of country of origin marking, it deals with the concept of a product losing its identity as a product of one country because it undergoes a transformation in a second-country. Thus, when an article, material or component initially produced in one country is subsequently processed in a second country, that second country may be considered the country of origin of the product if the processing performed in the second country constitutes a substantial transformation of the article, material or component.

Substantial transformation occurs when, as a result of the manufacturing process, a new and different article emerges, having a distinctive name, character or use which is different from that originally possessed by the article or material before being subjected to the manufacturing process. The issue of substantial transformation arises in a variety of contexts relating to the administration of the US customs laws.[13] Although the fundamental principles underlying the concept of substantial transformation apply to the various areas of customs laws, tests applied by the US courts in determining whether a product has been substantially transformed are not necessarily identical within the various contexts.[14] For example, the rule applicable when determining the country of exportation in cases involving merchandise from communist countries is more stringent than the test utilized when determining the country of exportation generally.[15]

---

12. *See* 19 C.F.R. § 134.33 (1995).
13. In addition to country of origin marking requirements (*see,* e.g., *National Juice Prods. Ass'n v. United States,* 10 CIT 48, 628 F. Supp. 978 (1986)), other contexts in which substantial transformation issues arise are: country of production for GSP treatment (*see,* e.g., *Torrington Co. v. United States.* 764 F.2d 1563 (Fed. Cir. 1985)), country of exportation for purposes of Headnote *3(e),* TSUS (*see,* e.g., *Bellcrest Linens v. United Stares,* 741 F.2d 1368 (Fed. Cir. 1984)), duty applicable to products of communist countries (*see Belcrest Linens*), cases involving American goods returned (*see,* e.g., *Upjohn Co. v. United States,* 623 F. Supp. 1281 (CIT 1985)).
14. *See generally Coastal States Mktg. Inc. v. United States,* 646 F. Supp. 255 (CIT 1986), *aff'd,* 818 F.2d 860 (Fed. Cir. 1987), *Belcrest Linens,* 6 Ct. Int'l Trade 204, 573 F. Supp. 1149, 1152–54 (1983) *aff'd* 741 F.2d 1368 (Fed. Cir. 1984).
15. *Cf.* Foote, *The Caribbean Basin Initiative: Development, Implementation and Application of the Rules of Origin and Related Aspects of Duty-Free Treatment,* 19 Geo. Wash. J. Int'l 1. & Econ. 245. 320 (1985) (arguing that although each area of customs law requiring a country of origin determination may involve specific policy considerations that may or may not be

D. Country of Origin Marking under NAFTA

Country of origin marking under the North American Free Trade Agreement (NAFTA) is markedly different from the more subjective substantial transformation principle it replaced. Paragraph 1 of Annex 311 of NAFTA provides that NAFTA party countries shall establish 'NAFTA Marking Rules' to determine when a good is a good of a NAFTA country. The NAFTA Marking Rules established by the United States are set forth in 19 C.F.R. § 102 which are used to determine the country of origin for marking purposes. This is not the same as determining the country of origin for duty purposes. The NAFTA Marking Rules are distinct from the rules of origin under Article 401 of NAFTA that are used to determine whether a good is an originating good for duty purposes. The NAFTA Marking Rules are largely the same for all three of the current NAFTA countries, Canada, Mexico, and the United States. Our focus here is on the US NAFTA marking rules.

Instead of the more subjective substantial transformation principal used in the traditional country of origin analysis, the NAFTA Marking Rules are based on qualifying shifts in tariff classifications, based on the Harmonized Tariff System (HTS) of tariff classifications. Generally for individual goods, the country of origin of a good is the country in which 1) the good is wholly obtained or produced; 2) the good is produced exclusively from domestic materials; or 3) each foreign material incorporated in that good undergoes an applicable and qualifying change in tariff classification.[16] The rules are hierarchically applied. Like the substantial transformation principle, for goods made in one country with no foreign inputs, the country of origin determination is fairly easy under the first and second rules – it is the country of production. For goods processed in multiple countries using either exclusively domestic materials or both domestic and foreign materials, the country of origin determination is made according to the third rule. Under the third rule, the country of origin is the country where, through processes of manufacturing, a qualifying change or shift in tariff classification, as defined for specific tariff classification numbers in the tariff shift schedule found in 19 C.F.R. § 102.20, occurs. This change is also commonly referred to as a 'tariff shift.'

Determinations of the country of origin of a good under the third rule begin by examining the tariff classification of the finished good and then comparing the pre-processing tariff classifications of the non-originating components to determine whether an appropriate tariff shift has occurred. The tariff shift methodology can be viewed as a simplified, less subjective and more predictable means of ascertaining a substantial transformation. Manufacturing processes performed in the United States that cause non-NAFTA originating materials, that are inputs to acquire a different tariff classification when they become part of the finished good,

---

reflected in the controlling statute or implementing regulations. The fundamental principles underlying the concept of substantial transformation apply to all such laws).

16. *See* 19 C.F.R. § 102.11(b) (2005) (providing special country of origin marking rules for good described as a set good).

are deemed substantial enough to cause the finished good to become a product of that country. As a corollary, certain minor processing may not be substantial enough to cause a good's individual materials to acquire the tariff classification of the finished good. These include certain processes deemed mere 'finishing processes' which, depending on the circumstances, may include such processes as sorting, cutting, folding, and packaging.

However, not all of the non-NAFTA originating materials must necessarily undergo an appropriate tariff shift. The NAFTA Marking Rules require that the value of foreign materials that do not undergo an appropriate tariff shift to be no more than seven per cent of the value of the finished good. This is commonly called the *de minimis* requirement. However, the *de minimis* requirement does not apply to goods classified under certain chapters of the HTS.[17] When the requisite amount of foreign materials do not undergo an appropriate tariff shift and the good is a set, mixture, or composite good under the HTS, the country of origin is then determined by the materials or manufacturing processes that imparts the essential character of the finished good. Finally, when the materials or manufacturing processes that equally merit consideration for determining the 'essential character' of the good is inconclusive in determining the country of origin of the good, the country of origin of the good is the last country in which the good underwent production.[18]

The tariff shift methodology of the NAFTA Marking Rules attempts to provide a more objective and predictable country of origin marking determination than the substantial transformation principle by relying on the published tariff shift schedules in 19 C.F.R. § 102.20 based on Annex 401 to NAFTA.

E. Use of 'Made in USA'

The Federal Trade Commission (FTC) is charged with preventing deception and unfairness in the marketplace. The Federal Trade Commission Act grants the FTC the power to bring law enforcement actions against false or misleading claims including those that a product is of US origin.[19] In 1997, after an extensive review of its policies, the FTC reaffirmed its traditional requirement that a product advertised or marked as 'Made in USA' be 'all or virtually all' made in the United States. The FTC's Made in USA policy is commonly summarized as the 'all or virtually all' standard. Consumers who see Made in USA on a product expect the claim to be truthful and accurate.[20] The FTC suggests that the September 11, 2001

17. 19 C.F.R. § 102.13 (2005).
18. *See* definition of 'essential character' *supra* p. 25 and accompanying footnote.
19. 15 U.S.C. §§ 41–51 (2005).
20. Press Release, Federal Trade Commission, Selling 'American-Made Products? What Businesses Need to Know about Making Made in USA Claims' (October 2001), *available at* <www.ftc.gov/bcp/conline/pubs/alerts/usabalrt.htm>.

terrorist attacks have made consumers more sensitive to Made in USA claims and more interested in buying American-made goods.[21]

For most products sold in the US, automobiles and textile, wool, and fur products aside, there is no law that *requires* the products to be labeled 'Made in USA' or have any other disclosure about the amount of US content. Customs does not require such a marking. However, manufacturers who choose to make claims about the amount of US content in their products must conform to the FTC's Made in USA policy. The policy covers all claims appearing on products and labeling, advertising, and other promotional materials including all other forms of marketing such as digital or electronic claims made on the internet or through e-mail. The claims can be express or implied. In certain contexts, a symbol or geographical reference such as a picture of an American flag will be viewed as conveying a Made in USA claim. However, brand names and trademarks will not be considered, by themselves, as making a Made in USA claim, even when the brand name and trademark owners are well known US companies (e.g., US Steel). The FTC does not require that companies making Made in USA claims obtain pre-approval of their claims. Any manufacturer or marketer may make any Made in USA claim as long as the claim is truthful and substantiated. However, false claims risk enforcement action by the FTC. US Customs and Border Protection (CBP) works regularly with the FTC to enforce such claims.

Made in USA claims can be separated into qualified and unqualified claims. Unqualified Made in USA claims must satisfy the all or virtually all standards. Manufacturers choosing to make an unqualified Made in USA claim should, at the time the representation is made, possess and rely upon a reasonable basis that the product is in fact all or virtually all made in the United States. A product that is all or virtually all made in the US is one in which all significant parts and processing that go into the product are of US origin. In other words, the product should contain only a *de minimis*, or negligible, amount of foreign content. The *de minimis* standard under the FTC's Made in USA policy is not the same as the *de minimis* standard for country of origin marking under NAFTA. Under the FTC's *de minimis* standard and unlike NAFTA, there is no single 'bright-line' to establish when a product is or is not all or virtually all made in the United States. One must look at past cases or seek a ruling from the FTC.

However, there are a number of factors to which the FTC gives particular consideration. To begin with, the final assembly or processing of the product must take place in the United States. Under this requirement, it is a prerequisite that the product have been last 'substantially transformed' in the United States, as the term is used by the US Customs and Border Protection (CBP).[22] Beyond this initial threshold, the FTC will consider factors including but not limited to the portion of the product's total manufacturing costs that is of US origin, and how far removed from the finished product any foreign content is. There is no fixed point for all products at which a product becomes all or virtually all made in the

21. *Id.*
22. *See* discussion of 'substantial transformation' *supra* p. 48.

United States. A *de minimis* inquiry is made on a case-by-case basis, taking into account the proportion of US manufacturing costs and consumer expectations. How far removed incorporation of a foreign component is to a finished product is significant because foreign products incorporated early in the manufacturing process, especially in the case of complex products, are likely to be insignificant in terms of cost and also to consumers' purchasing considerations. For example, in the case of complex products such as computers, consumers are less likely to pay attention to the origin of the steel materials incorporated several steps back in the manufacturing process. In contrast, consumers will likely pay attention to the steel materials used to manufacture a steel pipe or wrench.

Qualified 'Made in USA' claims are warranted when a product is not all or virtually made in the United States. Qualified claims should adequately reflect the actual amount of US content and presence and amount of foreign content. Effective qualifications should be sufficiently clear, prominent, and understandable to prevent deception. Qualified claims, for example, can be general, such as 'Made in USA of US and imported parts' or specific, such as '60 per cent US content.' The appropriateness of qualified claims that denote a particular manufacturing process, such as 'Printed In' or 'Assembled In' are appropriate depending on the context. For example, consumers would likely understand that 'Printed In' used on printed goods is analogous in meaning to 'Made In' and thus, use of 'Printed In' on paper products should be used appropriately so as not to misrepresent. 'Assembled in' can denote a wide range of manufacturing processes. Thus, the FTC generally requires that 'Assembled in USA' may be properly used when the last substantial assembly is performed in the US.

The FTC routinely initiates formal law enforcement actions against violators of the Made in USA policy primarily to send a message to producers and marketers that Made in USA claims must be truthful and substantiated and that the FTC will actively enforce compliance. Many cases are settled informally or though the use of cease and desist orders and/or penalties.

PRACTICE NOTE: Although the FTC's current practice is to acknowledge receipt of complaints alleging 'Made in USA' violations, they will not provide any information on their investigations, which can take several years. In one case, the author was only able to learn that the FTC had contacted a company and sent a letter when informed by the target company itself as part of pre-litigation correspondence. Eventually, a private right of action under the Lanham Act was pursued.

III. CUSTOMS AND COURT INTERPRETATIONS

This section of the chapter discusses some of the important concepts in country of origin determinations that have been construed by the CBP and the courts.

A. 'Ultimate Purchaser'

The term 'ultimate purchaser' appears in § 1304(a)(H) of the Tariff Act of 1930, as amended. It is defined as 'the last person in the United States who will receive the article in the form in which it was imported.'[23] As the regulations make clear, it is not always certain who the ultimate purchaser is. Generally, if the imported article is distributed as a gift, the recipient is the ultimate purchaser unless the good is a good of a NAFTA country;[24] if the manufacturing process is merely a minor one which leaves the identity of the imported article intact, the consumer or user of the article, who obtains the article after processing, will be regarded as the ultimate purchaser.[25] If an imported article will be used in manufacturing, the manufacturer himself may be the ultimate purchaser,[26] and if an article is to be sold at retail in its imported form, the purchaser at retail is the ultimate purchaser. [27]

The concept of an ultimate purchaser was further clarified in the case of *Pabrini, Inc. v. United States*[28] In this case, an action was instituted by plaintiff after umbrellas imported from Taiwan were found in violation of the marking statute pursuant to § 304 of the Tariff Act of 1930, as amended (19 U.S.C. § 1304 (1982)).[29] Plaintiff contended, *inter alia*, that the umbrellas need not have been individually marked since they were distributed as gifts by a donor who was the ultimate purchaser and was aware of the country of origin.[30] However, the court held that racetrack patrons receiving the umbrellas upon payment of the regular price of admission were not donors of gifts but ultimate purchasers of the imported merchandise within § 304 of the Tariff Act.[31]

---

23. *See* 19 C.F.R. § 134.1(d) (1995).
24. 19 C.F.R. § 134.1(d)(4) (1995).
25. 19 C.F.R. § 134.1(d)(1) (1995).
26. 19 C.F.R. § 134.1(d)(2) (1995).
27. 19 C.F.R. § 134.1(d)(3) (1995).
28. 630 F. Supp. 360 (Cn 1986).
29. § 304 provides, in part: 'Except as hereinafter provided, every article of foreign origin (or its container ...) imported into the United States shall be marked in a conspicuous place as legibly, indelibly, and permanently as the nature of the article will permit in such manner as to indicate to an ultimate purchaser in the United States the English name of the country of origin of the article.'
30. Plaintiff argued that the donor, a racetrack, was aware of the umbrellas' country of origin, and that the umbrellas were therefore excepted from the marking requirement by 19 U.S.C. § 1304(a)(3)(H) (1995) and 19 C.F.R. § 134.32(h) (1995). The latter excepts from the marking requirements: 'Articles for which the ultimate purchaser must necessarily know the country of origin by reason of the circumstances of their importation or by reason of the character of the articles even though they are not marked to indicate their origin.'
31. *Cf. Uniroyal, Inc. v. United States,* 702 F.2d 1022 (Fed. Cir. 1983) (holding that US manufacturer, who bought imported footwear uppers and performed operations necessary to finish shoes, was not the 'ultimate purchaser' within meaning of Tariff Act since operations performed in the US did not substantially transform the identity of upper; thus, the footwear uppers had to be excluded from entry under the statute requiring that imported articles be marked so as to indicate country of origin to ultimate purchaser in the United States.)

B. 'Conspicuous Place'

Under the Tariff Act of 1930, as amended, the CBP may by regulations determine a conspicuous place on the article (or container) where the marking shall appear. [32] Consistent with this provision, 19 C.F.R. § 134.41 (b) states that 'the ultimate purchaser in the United States must be able to find the marking easily and without strain.' This means the ultimate purchaser must be able to detect the country of origin marking upon normal inspection prior to his purchasing decision. If the marking is hidden from sight when the merchandise is in its usual display or packaged condition, the marking may be unacceptable.

The Customs Court has held that whether the marking is conspicuous is a question of fact.[33] Thus, in *Pabrini, Inc. v. United States*,[34] it was held that a small label measuring 1 and 3/8 inches by 3/8 inches sewn to the inside seam of an umbrella, which could only be seen when the umbrella was opened, did not constitute 'conspicuous' marking within the meaning of 19 U.S.C. § 1304. A marking label on the tail of a dress shirt which was folded and placed in a transparent plastic bag so that only the shirt collar and front were visible to prospective purchasers also failed the test of conspicuousness.[35]

The general trend of the case law suggests that the question of whether a country of origin marking is conspicuous is a question of fact which is determined on a case-by-case basis.

C. 'Substantial Transformation'

The basic criteria applied by the courts in determining whether substantial transformation has occurred are those of name, character and use. These criteria were first enunciated by the US Supreme Court in *Anheuser-Busch Brewing Association v. United States*[36] as follows:

> Manufacture implies a change, but every change is not manufacture, and yet every change in an article is the result of treatment, labor and manipulation. But something more is necessary, as set forth and illustrated in *Hartranft v. Wiegmatin,* 121 US 609 [(1887)]. There must be transformation; a new and different article must emerge, 'having a distinctive name, character, or use.

---

32. *See* 19 U.S.C. § 1304(a)(t) (1995).
33. *See* e.g. *Midwood Indus. v. United States,* 64 Cust. Ct. 499, 503; 1 ITRD 1286 (1970); *if. Uniroyal, Inc. v. United States,* 542 F. Supp. 1026, 1029 3 CIT 220, 224, 3 ITRD 2193 (Court Int'l Trade 1982) (holding that substantial transformation for marking purposes is a question of fact), *aff'd,* 702 F.2d 1022 (Fed. Cir. 1983).
34. 630 F. Supp. 360 (CIT 1986).
35. *See Charles A. Redder, Inc. v. United States,* T.D. 44964, 59 Treas. December 1377 (Cust. Ct. 1931).
36. 207 U.S. 556, 562 (1908).

The Court of Customs and Patent Appeals in *United States v. Gibson-Thomsen Co.*[37] reiterated the rule. It is instructive to note, however, that whereas the court in *Anheuser-Busch* referred to the words 'name, character or use,' the court in *Gibson-Thomsen* used the conjunction 'and' in lieu of 'or.'[38] The regulations further confuse the situation by citing *Gibson-Thomsen,* but with the disjunctive 'or' which was used in *Anheuser-Busch.* The better view would seem to be that the words should be used in the disjunctive in determining whether substantial transformation has occurred. Thus, the test should be whether the article has a new name, character, or use.[39]

It must be noted, however, that the courts often look to whether the processing in question effects a change in the name, character and use of the merchandise. Thus, for example, although the court in *Data General Corp. v. United States*[40] noted that the regulation in question used the word 'or,' and thus technically required that there be a change in only one of the factors, the court went on to ascertain whether the merchandise in question satisfied all three criteria.[41]

Generally speaking, a change in *name* must be to a name having commercial (as opposed to merely proprietary) usage different from that of the pre-existing material or article. A change in *character* must be a change which materially affects the original article, such as by changing the physical or chemical identity of the article. And a change in *use* is a change which dedicates a multipurpose product to an exclusive use, or which changes a product's one specific and limited use to another).[42] A few other examples of the courts' holdings will further illustrate the concept of substantial transformation: *Uniroyal*[43] also held that if the

---

37. 27 C.C.P.A. 267 (1940).
38. *Gibson-Thomsen* referred to 'name, character and use.'
39. 19 C.F.R. § 134.35 provides: 'An article used in the United States in manufacture which results in an article having a name, character, or use differing from that of the imported article, will be within the principle of the decision in the case of *United States v. Gibson-Thomsen Co.,* 27 C.C.P.A. 267 (1940).' Under this principle, the manufacturer or processor in the United States who converts or combines the imported article into the different article will be considered the 'ultimate purchaser' of the imported article within the contemplation of section 304(a), Tariff Act of 1930 as amended (19 U.S.C. § 1304(a)), and the article shall be excepted from marking. The outermost containers of the imported articles shall be marked in accord with this part.
40. *See also* Foote, *supra,* note 15, at 321, fn. 453. In *Uniroyal, Inc. v. United States,* 542 F. Supp. 1026 (Court Int'1 Trade 1982), the court similarly held that the test to be applied was whether the imported article had undergone a 'substantial transformation' which results in an article having a name, character or use different from that of the imported article. *Id.* at 1029. The name, character or use test has been followed consistently by the courts. *See,* e.g. *Torrington Co. v. United States,* 764 F.2d 1563 (Fed. Cir. 1985); *Ferrostal Metals Corp. v. United States,* 664 F. Supp. 535 (Court Int'l Trade 1987); *Belcrest Linens v. United States,* 741 F.2d 1368 (Fed. Cir. 1984).
41. 4 Court Int'l Trade 182 (1982) (discussed in Foote, *supra* note 15, at 324–25).
42. 4 Ct. Int'l Trade at 186.
43. *Uniroyal* held, on its facts, that a manufacturing process in which the manufacturer added soles to footwear uppers which were manufactured in Indonesia from leather and other materials and then imported into the US did not effect substantial transformation of the uppers within the meaning of 19 C.F.R. §§ 134.11(d) and 134.35. Thus, the manufacturer was not the ultimate purchaser of imported uppers so as to exempt it from country of origin marking requirements.

manufacturing process is merely one which leaves the identity of the imported article intact, substantial transformation has not occurred, and an appropriate marking must appear on the imported article so that the consumer can know the country of origin.[44] In *National Juice Products Association v. United States,* the court specifically applied the criteria of name, character and use in determining that orange juice manufacturing concentrate is not substantially transformed in the process that converts the concentrate into frozen concentrated or reconstituted orange juice; and in *Carlson Furniture Industries v. United States,*[45] assembly of chair components was held to be substantial transformation for purposes of country of origin marking requirements. Except in the most routine cases, prospective exporters and importers are advised to seek binding written rulings on the acceptability of any marking. Samples should be submitted and research undertaken as to prior marking rulings and exceptions. Country of origin marking violations are one of the leading causes for seizures of imported merchandise and imposition of fines, penalties and forfeitures.

PRACTICE NOTE: It has been the author's experience that country of origin markings are more vigorously and consistently enforced at the 'land' parts along the US–Mexico border than at major seaports.

There have been a number of changes to the customs marking regulations. On September 5, 1995 customs issued regulations dealing with determinations of country of origin for textile materials. The new rules affect textile goods entered or withdrawn from warehouses for consumption on or after July 1, 1996. These rules, which are contained in the Appendix C, move to a system of determining origin based on the NAFTA method of looking at change in tariff classification for imported components rather than the 'substantial transformation test.' The NAFTA rules can be found in TD-9648, 61 Fed. Reg. 28932, June 6, 1996. Basically the textile rules of origin look first to the country in which the good was wholly obtained or produced. However, when the good is not wholly produced in one country then we would look to the country in which each foreign material incorporated in that good underwent an applicable change in tariff classification or tariff shift set out in 19 C.F.R. § 102.21 as amended. If there is no change in tariff category, customs will then look at the country in which the most important assembly or manufacturing process occurred or the last country in which an important assembly or manufacturing process occurred.

---

44. *See generally* Foote, *supra* note 15, at 324–25. A change in tariff classification may also be considered as a factor in the substantial transformation analysis. *See Ferrostal Metals Corp. v. United States,* 664 F. Supp. 535 (Court Int'l Trade 1987). *Cf. Torrington Co. v. United States,* 764 F.2d 1563 (Fed. Cir. 1985) (proper tariff classification is not dispositive of whether manufacturing process necessary to complete article constitutes 'substantial transformation' from original material to final product so as to qualify for duty-free entry under GSP statute Trade Act of 1974, §§ 501–505, 19 U.S.C. §§ 2461–2465).
45. *Supra,* note 24.

Chapter 7

Duty Drawbacks

I. INTRODUCTION

This chapter will discuss the concept of duty drawbacks in Customs laws. The discussion will first define the term drawback, then discuss the various types of drawbacks authorized by law and, finally, will briefly outline the procedures required to establish a drawback contract and liquidate a drawback claim.

II. DISCUSSION

A. Definition of a Drawback

A drawback is a refund upon re-exportation of the duties or taxes paid or assessed against certain imported merchandise.[1] A drawback makes certain imported materials duty-free,[2] encouraging manufacturing in the US by permitting manufacturers to exclude the duties on imported merchandise from the cost of manufacturing.[3]

1. Statutory Authority for Drawback

Title 19, Section 1313 of the United States Code, is the primary statutory authority for duty drawbacks. It provides for drawback on duty-paid merchandise which has

1. 19 C.F.R. § 191.2(a) (1995).
2. The refund granted under § 1313 is only 99 per cent of the duties paid. 1 per cent, is retained to cover costs. 19 U.S.C. § 1313(a) (1995).
3. *Campbell v. United States,* 107 U.S. 407 (1883); *Swan & Finch Co. v. United States,* 190 U.S. 143 (1903).

been used in the US and then re-exported. The basic requirements of Section 1313 are that the merchandise designated as the basis of a drawback claim has been imported, has had some duty levied against it and has been exported from the US. Under the terms of the statute, the exportation must occur within five years of the importation of the duty-paid merchandise.[4]

2. Duties Subject to a Drawback

There are a variety of duties and taxes subject to drawback. Under Section 1313, original customs duties, countervailing duties, antidumping duties and marking duties are all subject to drawback.[5]

Internal Revenue taxes may also be subject to drawback. Section 1313 provides for the drawback of Internal Revenue tax upon domestic alcohol used in 'flavoring extracts, medicinal or toilet preparations,' and upon 'bottled distilled spirits and wines manufactured in the United States.'[6] Taxes on imports of distilled spirits, beer and wine found to be unmerchantable, or nonconforming, are also subject to drawback.[7]

3. Substitution Drawback

It is important to note that, in certain cases, domestic or duty-free merchandise may qualify for drawback.[8] These substitution provisions allow a manufacturer or producer who maintains an inventory of duty-paid and duty-free material, to receive drawback of the duties paid without providing documentation that the articles being exported were the duty-paid items. The substitution provisions have certain particular requirements, time limitations and procedures which will be discussed below.

B. Types of Drawbacks

There are a variety of different types of drawbacks which will be discussed below.

1. Drawback Under 19 U.S.C. § 1313(a)

The most common drawback is the 'direct identification drawback' authorized in Title 19, Section 1313(a) of the United States Code.[9] Section 1313(a) provides

---

4. 19 U.S.C. § 1313(i) (1995).
5. 19 C.F.R. § 191.3 (1995).
6. 19 U.S.C. § 1313(d) (1995).
7. 26 U.S.C. § 5062(c); 19 C.F.R. § 191.151 (1995).
8. 19 U.S.C. § 1313(b), (j)(2) (1995).
9. 19 C.F.R. § 191.4(a)(I) (1995).

'[U]pon the exportation of articles manufactured or produced in the United States with the use of imported merchandise.... the duties paid upon the merchandise so used shall be refunded as drawback.'[10] Eligibility for drawback under this section depends on two factors: whether the article in question was 'manufactured or produced in the United States with the use of imported merchandise,' and whether the article has been 'exported'.[11]

The courts and the Customs Service have dealt many times with the issue of whether an article has been manufactured. In *Anheuser-Busch Brewing Ass'n. v. United States,*[12] the Supreme Court established the test for determining whether an article is manufactured. The court held that imported cork, used in beer bottle caps, was not an 'article manufactured in the United States,' within the meaning of the relevant drawback statute.[13] The cork had been stamped, cleaned, steamed and dried after importation in order to make it fit for use in the bottle caps. In holding this process did not constitute manufacturing the court stated: 'manufacturing implies a change, but every change is not a manufacture ... something more is necessary ... There must be transformation; a new and different article must emerge, "having a distinctive name, character or use."'[14]

The Customs Service emphasizes that the *Anheuser-Busch* test is a flexible one designed as a measure of the extent to which a particular operation 'requires a significant investment of American capital and labor ... promot[ing] domestic industry, employment, and capital investment.' For example, the Customs Service has held that formatting blank computer tapes, making the tape fit for 'use as other than blank computer tape,' is manufacturing.[15] Section 1313(a) also requires the articles to be 'exported' in order to be eligible for drawback. Courts have indicated that exportation requires some act of shipment coupled with the bona fide intent to have the product enter a foreign market.[16]

The intent to seek a foreign market must exist at the time the articles are shipped out of the US. If there is a shipment with the proper intent, then there has been 'exportation' for purposes of Section 1313. Once the articles have been exported they may be returned to the US without being disqualified for drawback.[15] For example, watches manufactured in the US and shipped to a Canadian sales and distribution center for shipment to other nations, including the US, were held to have been exported and were eligible for drawback.[16] The intended purpose of sending the watches to Canada was to seek a foreign market satisfying the exportation equivalent.[17]

On the other hand, a company which shipped trucks out of the US, disassembled the trucks outside the US, and then imported the parts did not satisfy the

10. 9 U.S.C. § 1313(a) (1995).
11. *Id.*
12. 207 U.S. 556 (1908). *See also* discussion in Chapter VI, *supra.*
13. *Id.* at 563–64.
14. *Id.* at 562.
15. Letter Ruling No. 209295 (1978).
16. C.S.D. 82-154, 16 Cust. B. & Dec. No. 46, p. 12 (1982).
17. *Id.*

exportation requirement.[18] The sole purpose of shipping the trucks out of the US was not to seek foreign markets and thus the *operation did not constitute* exportation for drawback purposes. The *bona fide* intention of the manufacturer controls the issue of exportation in the drawback context; if the purpose of shipping the materials from the US is to seek a foreign market, the goods are 'exported.'

2. Same Condition Drawback

Another often-used type of drawback is 'same condition' drawback. Where duty-paid imported merchandise is exported or returned to Customs' possession unused or destroyed in the same condition as when it was imported, a drawback will be paid.[19] The imported merchandise must be exported or destroyed by Customs within three years of the importation.

The primary issue in determining eligibility for this type of drawback is what constitutes use of the merchandise. The merchandise is not considered 'in the same condition' if it has been used in the US. Some incidental operations may be performed on the article without constituting a prohibited use of the article which would preclude drawback. Section 1313(j) provides: 'the performing of incidental operations (including, but not limited to, testing, cleaning, repackaging and inspecting)... shall not be treated as use of that merchandise.'[20]

Temporarily changing the condition of a substance for repackaging, or, e.g., having a captain living aboard an imported yacht before export, does not constitute a use of the article so as to disqualify it for same condition drawback.[21]

The incidental operations exception, however, is narrowly drawn, and many operations constitute use, rendering the same condition drawback inapplicable. An operation involving the dissolution and re-crystallization of a chemical rendered the chemical ineligible for same condition drawback.[22] Also, installation of imported components into another article rendered that merchandise ineligible for drawback.[23] Thus, the same condition drawback is available only in those instances where the merchandise was not used or subjected to more than incidental operations in the US. However, if the operations performed on the merchandise render the article ineligible for same condition drawback, it is important to determine whether the operations may satisfy the manufacturing test qualifying the merchandise for drawback under Section 1313(a).

18. C.S.D. 82-155, 16 Cust. B. & Dec. No. 46, p. 12 (1982).
19. 19 U.S.C. § 1313(j); 19 C.P.R. § 191.4(10) (1995).
20. 19 U.S.C. § 1313(j)(4) (1995).
21. C.S.D. 85-48, 19 Cust. B. & Dec. No. 49, p. 30 (1985); C.S.D. 83-17,17 Cust. B. & Dec. No. 751 p. 36 (1982).
22. C.S.D. 83-19, 17 Cust. B. & Dec. No. 15, p. 30 (1982).
23. C.S.D. 84-52, 18 Cust. B. & Dec. No. 23, p. 30 (1983).

3. Substitution Drawback

As was mentioned above, in certain circumstances domestic or duty-free merchandise may receive a drawback. The domestic or duty-free merchandise is substituted for duty-paid merchandise, allowing an importer to claim drawback on duties paid regardless of whether the merchandise for which the claim is being made is that merchandise upon which the duty was paid. Substitution drawbacks benefit manufacturers or producers who maintain inventories of duty-paid and duty-free material. For example, in Letter Ruling No. 209363 (August 16, 1987), a company which received a particular chemical from both domestic and foreign sources stored all the chemicals in one tank. Upon exportation of the chemical, there was no way to determine whether the chemical was from a lot upon which duties had been paid. Under the principle of substitution drawback, the company could claim drawback on the duties paid on the imported chemical regardless of whether the chemical it was subsequently exporting was in fact the identical chemical upon which duty had been paid.[24]

There are two substitution provisions in Section 1313 which are discussed separately below.

a. Substitution Drawback Under § 1313(b)

Section 1313(b) provides for a substitution drawback for manufacturers with duty-free merchandise which satisfies the Section 1313(a) manufacturing and exportation requirements.[25] The section in relevant part provides:

> If imported duty-paid merchandise and duty-free or domestic merchandise of the same kind and quality are used in the manufacture or production of articles within a period not to exceed three years from the receipt of such imported merchandise ... they shall be allowed ... not withstanding the fact that none of the imported merchandise may actually have been used in the manufacture ... an amount of drawback.[26]

It is important to recognize the different time limitations under this substitution drawback. Not only must the completed articles be exported within five years of the receipt of the imported duty-paid merchandise, but also that duty-paid merchandise must be used in the manufacture or production of articles within three years.[27]

There is another basic requirement to qualify for substitution drawback under Section 1313(b). Imported duty-paid merchandise and the duty-free merchandise must be of the same 'kind and quality.' 'Same kind and quality' merchandise is

---

24. Letter Ruling No. 209363.
25. 19 U.S.C. § 1313(b) (1995).
26. *Id.*
27. The Customs Service has approved first-in-first-out accounting as 'a practical method of identifying imported merchandise to account for its use within three years.' Letter Ruling No. 209243 (1979).

defined by the Customs Regulations as 'merchandise which may be substituted' under substitution drawback. Fungible merchandise is always 'same kind and quality' merchandise; however, same kind and quality merchandise is not always fungible.'[28] The determination of 'same kind and quality' questions is done on a case-by-case basis. For example, in holding that imported, duty-paid, reconstituted orange juice is not the 'same kind and quality' as orange juice extracted from domestic oranges, the Customs Service considered 'many sources such as the standards of grades for citrus products set forth in the regulations of the Department of Agriculture and the Food and Drug Administration, technical advice, and standards set by the industry.'[29] The Customs Service carefully analyzed the properties and uses of the orange juices to determine whether they were of the 'same kind and quality.'[30]

b. Substitution Drawback Under § 1313(j)(2)

Section 1313(j)(2) provides for substitution drawback. This program can be used by manufacturers or producers who have domestic or imported merchandise which is exported, or destroyed by Customs, and is 'fungible' with other imported merchandise which is exported or destroyed while in the same condition as when it was imported and was not used in the US Section 1313(j)(2) provides in relevant part:

> (2) If there is, with respect to imported merchandise on which was paid any duty, tax, or fee imposed under Federal law because of importation, any other merchandise (whether imported or domestic) that –
> (A) Is fungible with such imported merchandise;
> (B) Is, before the close of the three-year period beginning on the date of import of the imported merchandise, either exported or destroyed … ;
> (C) Before such exportation or destruction –
> (i) Is not used within the United States, and
> (ii) Is in the possession of the party claiming drawback…; and
> (D) Is in the same condition at the time of exportation or destruction as was the imported merchandise at the time of its importation; then upon the exportation or destruction of such other merchandise the amount of each such duty, tax, and fee paid regarding the imported merchandise shall be refunded as drawback …

First, it is important to note that in this type of substitution drawback the exporter must meet the basic requirements of the same condition drawback. The domestic or duty-free goods must be in the 'same condition' as the imported goods were upon importation. Also the domestic or duty-free goods may not have been 'used'

28. 19 C.F.R. § 191.2(1)(m) (1995).
29. 1980 Cust. Serv., C.S.D. 81–96.
30. *Id.*

in the US before exportation or destruction, and the domestic goods must be exported or destroyed within three years of the date of importation of the goods for which they are substituted.[31] However, to qualify for substitution same condition drawback the domestic goods must also be 'fungible' with duty-paid goods.[32]

'"Fungible merchandise" means merchandise which, for commercial purposes, is identical and interchangeable in all situations.'[33] Customs determines whether merchandise is fungible on a case-by-case basis. For example, in Letter Ruling No. 21854, (March 17, 1986), the Customs Service held that two batches of fruit were not fungible simply because both batches met the 'Good Delivery Standards'[34] of the Department of Agriculture. Such quality standards may be considered, along with other factors such as color, size and variety of the fruits, in determining whether two batches of fruit are fungible.

4. Manufacturing Substitution Drawback

Manufacturing substitution drawback is intended to alleviate some of the difficulties in accounting when the imported merchandise has been used in domestic manufacturing. *See* 10 C.F.R. Part 191–68, Fed. Reg. 50700 (August 22, 2003). New rules for calculating manufacturing substitution drawback involving chemical elements were adopted in August 2003. *Id.*

5. Other § 1313 Drawbacks

There are several types of drawbacks available under Section 1313 which are applicable only in particular cases. Drawback is allowed on duty-paid merchandise which is exported for 'not conforming to sample or specifications' or because it was 'shipped without the consent of the consignee.'[35]

Imported salt will be eligible for drawback if it is used for curing fish or meat under certain circumstances.[36] Fish cured with imported salt is not required to be exported, while the meat must be exported to qualify for drawback.[37] All of the duties paid on the salt used in curing fish are refunded while the duties on salt used to cure meat are refunded 'in amounts not less than USD 100.'[38]

Imported materials used in the US, for constructing and equipping 'vessels built for foreign account and ownership, or for the government of any foreign

31. 19 U.S.C. § 1313(c) (1995).
32. 19 U.S.C. § 1313(j)(2)(A) (1995).
33. 19 C.F.R. § 191.2(1) (1995).
34. 7 C.F.R. § 46.44 (1995).
35. 19 U.S.C. § 1313(c)(I) (1995).
36. *Id.*
37. *Id.*
38. *Id.*

country,' are eligible for drawback.[39] This section applies regardless 'that such vessels may not within the strict meaning of the term be articles exported.'[40]

Internal Revenue taxes paid on alcohol used to make flavoring extracts, medical or toilet preparations may also qualify for drawback.[41] These products must be made in part from domestic alcoho1.[42] Upon exportation of the products, a drawback on the tax will be paid. Unlike the drawback on duties paid, the entire tax paid is refunded.[40] The entire amount of tax paid on 'bottled distilled spirits and wine made in the US' will also be refunded upon exportation.[43]

Section 1313(h) provides a drawback on foreign-built jet engines which have been 'overhauled, repaired, rebuilt, or reconditioned in the U.S.' using imported duty-paid parts.

Finally, Section 1313 allows drawbacks on imported duty-paid packaging material used to package or repackage articles which qualify as a direct identification drawback under Section 1313(a).[44]

6. Miscellaneous Drawback Provisions

There are other provisions which provide drawback of duties paid. Title 19, Section 1309(b), of the United States Code provides a drawback on duties and taxes paid on supplies for vessels and aircraft. The articles may be withdrawn from 'any Customs bonded warehouse, from continuous Customs custody ... from a foreign trade'.[45] The merchandise must be supplies for vessels or aircraft described in the provision.[46]

Duty-paid merchandise which has been in Customs' custody since importation will be eligible for drawback when the merchandise is exported.[47] There is a five-year time limit on this drawback. There is a drawback for merchandise shipped to a foreign trade zone from Customs territory.[48] The refund of taxes paid on unmerchantable imported distilled spirits, wines, or beer has already been mentioned.[49]

C. Procedures for the Drawback Contract

To be eligible for and to receive payment of drawback claims, an applicant must follow the appropriate procedures. Compliance with the appropriate customs

39. *Id.*
40. 19 U.S.C. §§ 1313(e), (I) (1995).
41. *Id.*
42. *Id.*
43. 19 U.S.C. § 1313(g) (1995).
44. 19 U.S.C. § 1313(j)(4) (1995).
45. 19 U.S.C. § 1309(a) (1995).
46. *Id.*
47. 19 U.S.C. § 1557(a) (1995).
48. 19 U.S.C. § 81(c) (1995).
49. *Supra,* p. 54; 26 U.S.C. § 5062(c) (1995).

regulations is a condition precedent for allowing drawback. Once the drawback claim has been prepared and submitted in accordance with the laws and regulations, the drawback claim 'shall' be determined.[50] The process of establishing a drawback claim is begun with the preparation of the drawback contract.

1. Specific Drawback Contract

The Customs Regulations provide that a specific drawback contract consists of a drawback proposal, 'a written document ...which contains an offer to operate under the drawback law ...,' and the drawback acceptance as 'a letter from Customs ... accepting the proposal.'[51]

The drawback proposal must be submitted by a 'proper applicant ... each manufacturer or producer of articles intended for exportation.'[52] This includes all manufacturers or producers of the article: primary, intermediate, or final manufacturers, regardless of whether that manufacturer is the owner of the eligible merchandise.[53] A subcontractor engaged to do work which 'does not constitute a manufacture or production,' does not have to submit a drawback proposal.[54] The principal does, however, have to establish in its proposal how it will 'maintain the identity of the merchandise' while it is in the possession of the subcontractor.[55]

Each drawback proposal must contain certain information.[56] The proposal must describe the relevant manufacturing operations, outline how the drawback laws and regulations will be complied with, contain a statement that the necessary records will be maintained and include an agreement to follow required procedures and keep all records with regard to drawback procedures.[57] The specific requirements for submission of proposals are detailed in Section 191.21(f) of Title 19 of the *Code of Federal Regulations.* A drawback contract requires each manufacturer or producer to keep certain records for all relevant articles. Generally, these records must: (1) include the date of manufacture; (2) identify the quantity and identity of the duty-paid merchandise; (3) identify the quantity and description of the articles manufactured; (4) state the quantity of waste incurred; and (5) include a statement that the finished articles will be exported within the five-year limitation.[58] There are other requirements for the storage and identification of the records.[59]

---

50. 19 C.F.R. § 191.71(d) (1995).
51. 19 C.F.R. § 191.2(c), (d), (e) (1995).
52. 19 C.F.R. § 191.21(a) (1995).
53. 19 C.F.R. §191.21(a)(2) (1995).
54. *Id.*
55. *Id.*
56. 19 C.F.R. § 191.21(b) (1995).
57. *Id.*
58. 19 C.F.R. § 191.22 (1995).
59. *Id.*

Proposals which satisfy the requirements of the law and regulations 'shall' be approved by the regional commissioner or by Customs headquarters.[60] The contracts will run for 15 years and can be renewed upon request to the Commissioner or Customs headquarters.[61] A manufacturer may terminate the contract by writing to the appropriate Commissioner at Customs headquarters.

2. Procedures Used in Drawback Substitution

The procedures outlined above generally apply to drawback substitution.[62] However, because of the requirement that the duty-paid imported article be used within three years, the Customs Regulations establish certain extra procedures for record-keeping and other rules with regard to who must submit drawback proposals.[63]

3. General Drawback Contracts

There are certain 'common manufacturing operations' to which general drawback contracts have been granted.[64] A general drawback contract is a drawback proposal prepared by Customs in order to simplify drawback procedures. Customs Headquarters publishes the proposals in the 'Customs Bulletin' and the manufacturer need only notify a regional commissioner to accept the contract.[65] The manufacturer's acceptance must contain its name and address, the factories which operate under the contract, and the names of those authorized to sign the drawback documents.[66] Customs has granted general contracts to: (1) orange juice products, (2) steel products, (3) refined sugar, (4) general articles manufactured from component parts, (5) finished piece goods, and (6) by-products.

D. The Drawback Claim

1. Determining the Drawback Claim

Once a manufacturer or producer has gotten a drawback contract, there are a number of other procedures which must be followed. First, a manufacturer or producer claiming a drawback must establish that the articles have been exported. This is done by complying with one of five possible procedures.[67] The claimant

60. 9 C.F.R. § 191.23(a) (1995).
61. 19 C.F.R. § 191.26 (1995).
62. 19 C.F.R. § 191.31 (1995).
63. 19 C.F.R. § 191.32–.34 (1995).
64. 19 C.F.R. § 191.41 (1995).
65. 19 C.F.R. § 191.42 (1995).
66. *Id.*
67. 19 C.F.R. § 191.51 (1995).

may provide: (1) a notice of exportation,[68] (2) an exporter's summary,[69] (3) certified notice of exportation for mail shipments,[70] (4) notice of landing for supplies of certain vessels or aircraft,[71] or (5) notice of transfer for articles manufactured or produced in the United States which are transferred to a foreign trade zone.[72] Drawbacks under 19 U.S.C. § 1309 and 19 U.S.C. § 81c have different procedures for providing evidence of exportation.[73]

To complete drawback claims, a claimant must file a drawback entry and all other necessary documents within three years.[74] This involves, *inter alia,* filing a manufacturing drawback entry and certificate on Customs Form 331. There are additional uses for Form 331 established in the Customs Regulations.[75]

2. Liquidation of Drawback Claims

When the drawback claim has been completed, the documents have been filed as discussed above and the exportation of the articles in question has been properly established, the drawback claim can be liquidated.[76] The commissioner will determine the amount of the drawback due.[77]

The time at which the drawback claim is liquidated depends on the basis of the claim. First, drawback claims may be liquidated after 'final liquidations of the import entry.'[78] Second, if the drawback claim is based on the estimated duties of the imported merchandise, the claim is liquidated after the deposit of estimated duties and before liquidation of the import entry.[79] Finally, the commissioner certifies the amount of drawback to a person 'authorized to receive payment' under Section 191.73 of Title 19 of the Code of Federal Regulations.[80]

Drawback claimants claiming under 19 U.S.C. § 1313 (a), (b), or (j) may be eligible for an accelerated payment of the claim.[81] Upon approval of the claim, it will be certified for payment within three weeks of filing.[82] A claim for accelerated payment must contain the claimants' computation of the amount of drawback and 'a bond on Customs Form 301, containing the bond conditions set forth in 19 C.F.R. § 113.65.' [83]

---

68. 19 C.F.R. § 191.52 (1995).
69. 9 C.F.R. § 191.53 (1995).
70. 19 C.F.R. § 191.54 (1995).
71. 19 C.F.R. § 191.93 (1995).
72. 19 C.F.R. § 191.163 (1995).
73. 19 C.F.R. § 191.61 (1995).
74. 19 C.F.R. § 191.62 (1995).
75. 19 C.F.R. § 191.62(2) (1995).
76. 19 C.F.R. § 19.
77. *Id.*
78. 19 C.F.R.§ 191.71(a) (1995).
79. *Id.*
80. *Id.*
81. 19 C.F.R. § 191.72 (1995).
82. *Id.*
83. *Id.*

E. Special Duty Drawback Procedures under NAFTA

Article 303 of the North American Trade Agreement (NAFTA) provides special drawback provisions for goods exported to Canada on or after January 1, 1996, and for goods exported to Mexico on or after January 1, 2001. NAFTA provides that drawback calculations for these goods are subject to the 'lesser of the two' rule. The 'lesser of the two' rule allows the drawback to be based on the lower amount of (1) the total duties paid or owed in the US; or (2) the total duties paid on the good upon subsequent importation into Canada or Mexico. The 'lesser of the two' rule also applies to unused merchandise claimed under § 1313(j)(1) but not in the same condition.

The following rules apply in making a 'lesser of the two' comparison. For claims designating multiple imports and a single export, the duties paid on the imports have to be aggregated before a comparison is made with the Canadian or Mexican duty paid on the importation of the exported goods into Canada or Mexico. Once this comparison is made, no other claims should be made designating that exported good. The only exception to this is drawback claims that involve a combination of goods that are subject to the 'lesser of the two' calculation and goods subject to full drawback.[84] Also, goods covered by § 1313(j)(2). Unused Merchandise Substitution Drawback are not eligible for drawbacks if they involve exports to Canada or Mexico (as effective since January 1, 1994.)

For claims involving single import and multiple exports, a relative value calculation should be made, and the 'lesser of the two calculations' should be made separately for each individual exported good. Calculations for the relative value follow the same procedures as provided under Part 191.22 of the Regulations (prior to NAFTA). 'The value of the exported product designated on the drawback claim is divided by the total value of all products produced. This value is then multiplied by the duty which results in the allowable duty for the exported product. The relative value should be determined before the "lesser of the two" comparison is made.'

NAFTA drawback claims must be supported by 'satisfactory evidence' to be eligible for the 'lesser of the two' calculation. In particular, claimants must provide evidence of the duties paid on the designated exported goods upon importation into Canada or Mexico. In the case of Canada, for example, documents that may be used as 'satisfactory evidence' include the Canadian Customs Invoice or an affidavit from the drawback claimant which is based on information received from the importer of the goods into Canada. The documents must include the following information: the Canadian entry number, date of importation into Canada, Canadian Harmonized Tariff Schedule Number(s), Canadian rate of duty, and amount of duties paid to Canada. In submitting a NAFTA drawback claim, the

---

84. Goods eligible for full drawbacks are goods claimed under 1313(j)(1) that are in the same condition, goods claimed under 1313(c), goods which originate in Canada or Mexico and meet the NAFTA rules of origin, and goods included in Annex 303.6 of the NAFTA agreement. Goods eligible for full drawbacks are not considered NAFTA drawback claims.

drawback claims must be submitted separately from all other types of claims. A separate claim must be submitted for each exported product. Once an exported product is designated in a NAFTA drawback claim, it may not be designated again in a subsequent claim.

III. CONCLUSION

Drawback is a valuable tool allowing manufacturers in the US to compete in international markets by using imported components without being hampered by high import duties. Although the concept of drawback may seem complex, it is important to remember that a drawback is simply a refund of a Customs duty '… assessed… because of a particular use made of the merchandise.'[85] The exporter must always determine the merchandise on which duty has been paid and ascertain the use that has been made of that merchandise. This will determine the type of drawback which may be applicable.

85. 19 C.F.R. § 191.2(a).

Chapter 8

American Goods Returned and Other Special Exemptions

I. INTRODUCTION

This chapter will discuss the preferential treatment accorded to certain imported articles under the US Customs laws and the Harmonized Tariff Schedules of the United States (HTS).[1] Specifically, the discussion will address four principal classifications under Section 9802 of the HTS, foreign trade zones and bonded customs warehouses and their benefits to importers. In addition, the chapter will also provide a brief description of the *Maquiladora* (in-bond processing) program in Mexico, which is an example of utilization of these special tariff exemptions, and a program in which the author has been actively involved.

II. DISCUSSION

The provisions contained in Section 9802 of the HTS, as well as those relating to foreign trade zones and custom bonded warehouses all are designed to permit American businesses to reduce their costs, and reduce or eliminate certain duties while taking advantage of competitive benefits in undertaking certain types of operations overseas. HTS Section 9802 provides several special tariff classifications for certain articles that are exported from and returned to the US. This memorandum will discuss four such classifications: HTS items 9802.00.00, 9802.00.20, 9802.00.60 and 9802.00.80. These items are more commonly known by their prior designations under the Tariff Schedules of the US, which are TSUS items 800, 806.20, 806.30 and 807.

---

1. 19 U.S.C. § 1202 (1995).

A. HTS Item: Articles Assembled from U. S. Components Abroad – HIS 9202.00. 80

Item 9802.00.80 of the Harmonized Tariff Schedules of the US (HTS) provides beneficial duty treatment to articles imported into the US which are 'assembled' outside the US using components produced in the US.[2] Item 9802.00.80 applies to 'articles assembled abroad, in whole or in part of fabricated components, the product of the United States,' which were exported in a condition ready for assembly without further fabrication, which have not lost their physical identity in such articles by a change in form, or shape and have not been advanced in value except by operations incidental to the assembly process.[3] Such products can be re-imported into the US with duty paid only on the foreign value added. However, there are a number of strict requirements to obtain these benefits. These requirements are discussed below.

1. Fabricated Components, Products of the US

The question of whether the imported article is composed of fabricated components which are products of the US is the first issue that must be resolved. The term 'fabricated component' is defined as 'a manufactured article ready for assembly in the condition as exported.'[4] Thus, any article, not a raw material, which may be assembled into another article without undergoing any further manufacturing process, may qualify as a fabricated component.[5]

The fabricated component must also be a product of the US. 'A "product of the United States" is an article manufactured within the Customs territory of the United States.'[6] The fabricated component may be manufactured using imported materials or components and still qualify as a product of the US.[7] The Customs regulations provide:

Foreign-made articles or materials may become products of the United States if they undergo a process of manufacture in the United States which results in their substantial transformation. Substantial transformation occurs, when as a result of manufacturing processes, a new and different article emerges, having a distinctive name, character or use, which is different from that originally possessed by the article or material. 19 C.F.R. § 10.14(b).[8]

---

2. 19 U.S.C. § 1202 (1995).
3. 19 U.S.C. § 1202 (1995).
4. 19 C.F.R. § 10.12(d) (1995).
5. The US Supreme Court has defined manufacturing as a process creating a 'new and distinctive article.' *See Anheuser-Busch Brewing Ass'n v. United States.* 207 U.S. 556 (1908); *see also* Chapter 7, Duty Drawbacks.
6. 19 C.F.R. § 10.12(e)(1995).
7. *Id.*
8. *See also* discussion of substantial transformation in Chapter 6, *Country of Origin Marking.*

HTS 9802.00.80, therefore, applies to an imported 'component' which has been fabricated in the US and transformed into 'a new and different article' in the US Customs territory prior to re-exportation for assembly abroad.

2. 'Assembly' and 'Operations Incidental to Assembly'

In determining whether an article complies with the requirements of HTS item 9802.00.80, the initial question is whether the components were shipped in a condition 'ready for assembly without further fabrication.'[9] Specifically, the question is whether the foreign operations constitute 'further fabrication' or whether they are 'assembly.'[10] If the operations constitute further fabrication of the component, then it was not exported in a condition 'ready for assembly' and is not eligible for item HTS 9802.00.80 treatment.

Articles eligible for HTS item 9802.00.80 treatment must not only have been exported in a condition 'ready for assembly,' but also must not have been improved in condition or value while abroad except by assembly, or through operations incidental to assembly.[11] Operations 'incidental to assembly' are activities which, while not constituting assembly, are also not considered further fabrication and therefore, do not preclude articles from treatment under item 9802.00.80.[12]

The regulations give several examples of operations incidental to assembly including: cleaning, applying preservative coatings, trimming, filing, or cutting off excess material. Cutting to length from rolls or strips is generally considered to be incidental to assembly while cutting to width is not.[13] The courts have been more liberal than Customs in expanding the concept of incidental to assembly. For example, the courts found buttonholing on shirt cuffs and collars, buttonholing and pocket slitting on women's pants, and burning holes and slots into z-beams, all to be assembly or operations incidental to assembly.[14] Operations which are not incidental to assembly include 'any significant process... whose primary purpose is the fabrication, completion, physical or chemical improvement of a component... whether or not it effects a substantial transformation.' 19 C.F.R. § 10.16(c).[15] An important case that went to the US Supreme Court considered the question of whether perma-pressing via a heat treating process would disqualify

9. *Zwicker Knitting Mills v. United States,* 469 F. Supp. 727, 730 (Cust. Ct. 1979), *aff'd,* 67 C.C.P.A. 37, 613 F.2d 295 (1980).
10. Section 10.12(b) of Title 19 of the Code of Federal Regulations defines 'assembly' as the 'fitting or joining together of fabricated components.' The regulations also provide that 'assembly operations performed abroad may consist of any method used to join or fit together solid components.' 19 C.F.R. § 10.16(a)(1995).
11. 9 U.S.C. § 1202 (Schedule 8, Part I, Item 807) (1978).
12. 19 C.F.R.§ 10.16(b)(1995).
13. *Id.*
14. *See United States v. Oxford Indus.,* 668 F.2d 507 (C.C.P.A. 1981); *United States v. Mast Indus.,* 668 F.2d SOl (C.C.P.A. 1981). *Miles v. United States,* 567 F.2d 979 (C.C.P.A. 1978).
15. The Customs regulations give certain examples of operations considered not to be incidental to assembly. *See* 19 C.F.R. § 10.16(c)(l995).

a textile product from treatment under Section 9802 or if it were incidental to assembly. *See United States. v. Haggar Apparel Co.*, 1526 US 380 (1999).

3. Loss of Physical Identity

For fabricated components to be eligible for item HTS 9802.00.80 treatment they cannot have lost their physical identity through the assembly process.[16] 'The test specified in item HTS 9802.00.80 is whether the components have been changed in form, shape, or otherwise to such an extent that they have lost their physical identity in the assembled article.'[17] The component does not have to be divisible or detachable from the assembled article, but an importer may have to be able to verify that the component has not lost its physical identity through the testing of samples.[18] Articles which are eligible for classification under items HTS 9802.00.80 receive beneficial duty treatment. Item HTS 9802.00.80 articles are subject to duty upon the full value of the imported article reduced by the value of the components produced in the US.[19]

Thus, a manufacturer will pay duty only on the relatively small increase in value, from assembly and operations incidental to assembly, imparted to their products while they were outside the US.

B. HTS Item 9802.00.60: US Metal Products Exported for Further Processing

Another important tariff exemption classification is HTS 9802.00.60, formerly known as TSUS Item 806.30, which provides that 'any article of metal (except precious metal) manufactured in the United States . . . if exported for further processing' and returned to the US for further processing will be subject to 'a duty upon the value of such processing outside the United States' only.[20] In order to be eligible for item HTS 9802.00.60, a metal article (other than one of precious metal), which has been manufactured in the US, must have been sent to another country for processing and returned to the US for 'further processing.' Section HTS 9802.00.60 has a number of advantages over HTS 9802.00.80. The main one is that the operations performed overseas are not limited to strict assembly operations. In fact, under HTS 9802.00.60, any types of manufacturing or processing activities are permitted. However, there are other requirements under

16. 19 U.S.C. § 1202 (Schedule 8, Part I, Item 807(b)) (1978).
17. *Zwicker Knitting Mills v. United States,* 469 F. Supp. 727, 735–36 (Cust. Ct. 1979) (*quoting United States v. Baylis Brothers* Co., 451 F.2d 643, 646 (C.C.P.A. 1971)), *aff'd,* 67 C.C.P.A. 37, 613 F.2d 295 (1980).
18. *Special Classification Under the U.S. Tariff Schedules: U.S. Goods Returned.* 9 Law & Pol'y in Int'l Bus. 681, 690 (1977).
19. 19 U.S.C. § 1202 (1995).
20. 19 U.S.C. § 1202 (1995).

HTS 9802.00.60 that are unique. One is the requirement that after the product is returned to the US, it must undergo further processing.

1. Further Processing Within the US

In order to receive tariff preferences under HTS 9802.00.60, a metal article must undergo 'further processing' upon returning to the US. What constitutes 'further processing' under the customs laws has been the subject of many court interpretations. In *Intelex Systems v. United States*[21], the court held that removal of insulation and sheathing from communications equipment did not constitute 'further processing' for purposes of § 1615(g)(2)(B), Tariff Act of 1930, the predecessor statute to item 806.30 TSUS. The court held that the 'further processing' referred to in § 1615 (g)(2)(B) is a further 'manufacturing' process.[22] The article must undergo some operation which is part of the process of creating a 'new and different article.'[23] 'The article processed abroad and returned to the US is no more than an advanced material or article which will be subjected to further *manufacturing* processes in the US to get a completed article.'[24] Finishing operations are not 'further processing.'[25]

Generally, Customs has held that the further processing undertaken in the US must 'impact the metal.' Thus, drilling a hole would qualify while polishing might not.

2. Further Processing Outside the US

The metal items must undergo further processing both in the US and abroad. The Customs Court has also addressed the issue of when certain metal articles were subject to 'further processing outside the United States within the meaning of former item 806.30 TSUS.'[26] In finding the application of a coat of rubber to metal domes to be 'further processing' for purposes of former TSUS item 806.30, the court held that the construction of the term 'further processing' established in *Intelex* for operations within the US applied to 'further processing' outside the US.[27] It is required that the metal undergo some manufacturing process while outside the US.

The Customs Service also uses this definition of 'further processing.' The Customs Service stated that 'further processing' for purposes of item 806.30 referred to a further manufacturing process.[28] The process must be 'looking toward

---

21. *Intelex* 460 F.2d 1083 (C.C.P.A. 1972).
22. *Id.* at 1085.
23. *See supra* note 2.
24. 460 F.2d at 1085.
25. *Id.*
26. *Firestone Tire* & Rubber *Co. v. United States,* 364 F. Supp. 1394, 1395 (Cust. Ct. 1973), vacated on other grounds, 373 F. Supp. 564 (Cust. Ct. 1974).
27. 364 F. Supp. at 1397.
28. Letter Ruling No. 554160 (July 17, 1986).

the completion of an article, as distinguished from that [process] to which a substantially completed article may be subjected in order to adapt it for the purpose intended.'[29] Thus, where a metal article undergoes operations which 'will change [its] form or impart new and different characteristics,' both outside the US and upon its return to the US, that article may qualify for classification under item No. 806.30.[30]

C. THE *MAQUILADORA* INDUSTRY

Utilization of HTS No. 9802.00.60 and HTS No. 9802.00.80 prior to NAFTA was particularly great by the large Mexican in-bond industry known as *maquiladoras*. The term *maquiladora* refers to those firms which are involved in producing goods or rendering services in Mexico by importing materials and equipment into Mexico and assembling the materials into a product which is subsequently exported from Mexico. However, sections 9802.0060 and 9802.0080 apply to all eligible countries. Recently there has been a trend for these types of operations to be moved to China. Reference to Mexico in this chapter should be considered applicable to China and other countries. The materials, equipment and components which are imported into Mexico enter duty free, provided they are not to be sold in Mexico, but are re-exported for sale in foreign markets as part of assembled products. Mexico began the *maquiladora* program in the early 1960's as an attempt to reduce unemployment, generate foreign exchange and to bring modern technology into the country. Since its inception, the program has expanded tremendously.

There are many incentives for businesses to use *maquiladora* operations. Inexpensive Mexican labor allows manufacturers to significantly reduce their production costs. Mexico allows total foreign ownership of the *maquiladora* industries.[31] Finally, Mexico's proximity to the US allows for lower transportation costs, greater control of operations, and the possibility of personnel living in the US, all of which make Mexico a more attractive location in which to establish production facilities than Asia and elsewhere. The benefits of *maquiladora* production have made the *maquiladora* program a remarkable success attracting business from Asia and the US into the northern border region of Mexico.

The success of the *maquiladora* program has generated significant debate in the US Congress. The debate was originally with regard to items HTS 9802.00.60 and 9802.00.80, discussed above. Opponents of these programs, led by organized labor, have sought to eliminate the items from the tariff schedules, arguing that by levying a duty only on the 'value added' to an American product, these items

---

29. *Id.*
30. *Id.*
31. This was a notable advantage of the Mexican *Maquiladora* program, since foreign investment in Mexico was ordinarily limited to 49 per cent. However, on May 15, 1989, Mexico amended its foreign investment regulation to expand majority foreign ownership over non-*maquiladora* operations.

encourage manufacturers to transfer their operations to Mexico 'at the expense of US labor and the health of the entire US economy.'[32] Legislation has in fact been introduced to abolish former Section 807.[33]

Proponents of former tariff numbers 806/807 have historically argued that these items, along with the *maquiladora* program, actually save jobs in the US. Reduced production costs allow the manufacturers to maintain or increase their market share, protecting many highly skilled jobs in the US. The proponents also assert that it is better to have the foreign production facilities in Mexico rather than in Asia or elsewhere; the US has a vested interest in the economic health of its neighbors, the *maquiladora* program is a boon to the Mexican economy and much of the money spent in support of the Mexican facilities is returned to the US economy. A study on this system by the US International Trade Commission supports the theory that these programs create as many jobs in the US as they send abroad and have a neutral impact on employment.[34] Removal of duties under NAFTA has lessened the importance.

D. Other Special Classifications under Chapter 9

Section 9800, HTSUS, provides several other special classifications which will be noted in this discussion as items 9802.00.00, American Goods Returned; and 9802.00.20, Goods Repaired Abroad.

1. Item 9802.00.00: American Goods Returned

Item 9802.00.00 (former TSUS Item 800) allows 'products of the United States when returned after having been exported, without having been advanced in value or improved in condition by a process of manufacture or other means while abroad' to enter the US duty free.[35] The goods may undergo some operations or change while abroad, provided that the change does not constitute advancement in value or improvement of condition of the article.[36]

There are two significant issues under this item: the first is whether the articles imported are products of the US, and the second is whether the goods have been 'advanced in value or improved in condition' while abroad.[37] 'The first question to be determined is whether the imported merchandise is the merchandise that was exported.[38] If it was the same, advancement in value and improvement

32. Organized labor has traditionally been an opponent of the 807 program.
33. *See,* e.g., H.R. 3211, introduced by Congressman John La Faice in 1988.
34. *See 'The* Use and Economic Impact of TSUS items 806.30 and 807.00.' USITC publication No. 2053, January, 1988.
35. 19 U.S.C. § 1202 (1995).
36. *See United States v. John V. Carr & Son, Inc.*, 496 F.2d 1225 (C.C.P.A. 1974).
37. *Upjahn Co. v. United States*, 623 F. Supp. 1281, 1285 (Ct. Int'l Trade 1985).
38. To prevent factual questions as to origin, the exporter is advised to register the US article with Customs prior to exportation. This is done by filing Customs Form 4455 with the US Customs

in condition are of importance; if it was not the same, value and condition are inconsequential.'[39]

The Court of International Trade in *Upjohn Company v. United States*,[40] held that chemicals, crude BLD and pure MDl, extracted from an American-made chemical, crude 390 HOP, in the Netherlands, were not the same merchandise as that which was exported from the US and, therefore, were not eligible under former TSUS item 800. The court held that whether an imported article is the same as the article which was exported depends on whether that article was 'manufactured' while outside the US.[41] Thus, if an imported article has been manufactured, processed into a 'new and distinctive article,' while outside the US, it is no longer the article which was exported and is ineligible for item 800.[42]

The Court of International Trade addressed the second question, whether an article had been 'advanced in value or improved in condition,' in *Aviation Group, Inc. v. United States.*[43] In *Aviation,* the court denied summary judgment motions on the question of whether US-made airplanes equipped with convertible seating configurations and specialized avionics systems while in Canada were advanced in value or improved in condition.[44] The court stated 'the words "improved in condition" must be taken in a commercial sense and the actual nature of the commercial entity must be considered.'[45] Thus, an article which is a product of the US may be exported and re-imported duty-free if it has not been manufactured or if its commercial or economic value has not been otherwise increased while the article was outside the US.

2. Item 9800.00.20: Goods Repaired Abroad and Re-imported

HTS item 9802.00.20 (formerly TSUS item 806.20) provides that 'articles exported for repairs or alterations' may be re-imported to the US subject only to a duty on the value of the repairs or alterations.[46] The primary difference in item 9802.00.20 is that, unlike 9802.00.00, 9802.00.60 and 9802.00.80, the item need not be originally of US origin. The only issue is whether the operations performed outside the US constitute repair or alterations of the exported goods. The operations may change the 'name, appearance, size, shape and use of an article' and

---

Service and providing Customs with an opportunity to inspect the goods prior to exportation.

39. *Upjohn,* 623 F. Supp. at 1285 *(quoting Shell Oil Co. v. United States,* 27 C.C.P.A. 94, 98, C.A.D. 68 (1939)).
40. 623 F. Supp. at 1288.
41. *Id.* at 1285.
42. *Id.; see also Anheuser-Busch Brewing Ass'n v. United States,* 207 U.S. 556 (1908); Chapter VI, *Drawbacks.*
43. *Anheuser-Busch* 615 F. Supp. 597 (Ct. Int'l Trade 1985).
44. *Id.* at 602.
45. *Id.* (*quoting Amity Fabrics, Inc. v. United States,* 43 Cust. Ct. 64, 67 (1959)). ('[T]he economic value... is the key to classification' under item 800.).
46. 19 U.S.C. § 1202.

still qualify as 'repairs or alterations' under item 9802.00.20 and it is sometimes difficult to distinguish impermissible processes from repairs and alterations.

In distinguishing between 'repairs and alterations' and other processes which transform the article, the courts and the Customs Service focus on the purpose for which the process is carried out. If the operations are to obtain a finished product ready for sale it is unlikely to qualify under item HTS 9802.00.20, while operations which are carried out on already finished products will likely qualify as repairs under item 9802.00.20. For example, in *Doffiff & Co. v. United States*,[47] the court found that heat-setting, chemical scouring, dyeing, and treating with chemicals, did not qualify under former item TSUS 806.20. The court reasoned that the operations were steps 'necessarily undertaken to initially produce the finished fabric' and could not qualify as 'repairs or alterations.'[48] The Customs Service has found stonewashing denim,[49] and punching holes into leather belts,[50] so to be processes 'carried out to obtain a finished product,' and therefore, ineligible for treatment under former item 806.20. Thus, only where finished articles exported from the US are 'repaired or altered,' restored, inspected, tested, have components replaced, etc., without undergoing a finishing process, may they be re-imported into the US subject to duty only on the value of the operations performed outside the US.

---

47. 599 F.2d 1015, 1021 (C.C.P.A. 1979).
48. *Id.* at 1020.
49. Letter Ruling No. 554235 (September 15, 1986).
50. Letter Ruling No. 554345 (November 17, 1986).

Chapter 9

Foreign Trade Zones

The Foreign Trade Zones Act of 1934, as amended,[1] authorizes the Foreign Trade Zones Board to establish foreign trade zones in the US.

Foreign Trade Zones (FTZs) are 'isolated, enclosed and policed areas in or adjacent to a port of entry … subject equally with adjacent regions to all the laws relating to public health, vessel inspection, postal service, labor conditions, immigration, and indeed, everything except the customs laws.' FTZs are considered to be outside the Customs territory of the US and, therefore, not subject to US customs laws.[2] Foreign and domestic merchandise can be transferred into FTZs, subjected to certain operations and transferred out again (so long as it does not enter US Customs territory) without formal customs procedures, including payment of duties and quota restrictions.[3] When the merchandise is moved from the FTZ into the Customs territory, duty is paid on the product in the condition it is in at the time it enters the US Customs territory. This may be a lower duty than the one applicable to the product at the time it entered the FTZ. Quota categories may also be different or non-existent.[4]

---

1. 19 U.S.C. § 81a–u. (1978 Supp. 1995).
2. 19 U.S.C. § 81c. (Supp. 1995).
3. *Id. See also* 46th Annual Report of the Foreign Trade Zones Board to the Congress of the United States.
4. For example, US steel quotas cover products such as steel sheet and steel plate, but not most finished products made of steel. Thus, entering steel sheet into an FTZ and processing, may allow the resulting product to enter the US Customs territory free of quota restrictions despite the quota on the product that entered the zone.

A. General Information

FTZs are operated as public utilities by states, political subdivisions or corporations.[5] Grantees or operators of FTZs may enter into agreements with other 'persons, firms, corporations, or associations' to use the FTZ.[6] The users may establish such facilities in the zone as are necessary to meet their requirements.[7] Most zones are part of industrial parks with lots on which zone users can construct their facilities.

There are significant benefits for an importer or manufacturer using an FTZ: the importer may be able to reduce customs duty on imported merchandise; while in the FTZ, the goods are exempt from excise tax and are not subject to customs duty; goods can leave an FTZ without paying duty or tax if re-exported; and customs procedures are minimal.[8]

B. Status Designation of Merchandise in Foreign Trade Zones

The primary benefit of FTZs is that users can potentially reduce the customs duties paid on imported merchandise. The duty paid on an imported product depends on the tariff classification of the product and the value. The classification of merchandise in FTZs is affected by the status of the merchandise in the zone.[9] An importer may seek to establish the merchandise's status at the lowest tariff rate.

There are several status designations.[10] The first status designation is 'privileged foreign merchandise.'[11] For merchandise which qualities for privileged foreign status, (appraisement and classification is based on the condition and quantity of the merchandise when the status application is made).[12] Section 146.41 privileged foreign status (a.) foreign merchandise which has not been manipulated or manufactured so as to effect a change in tariff classification – or an application to district director. Although the duty is determined at the time application for the privileged status is made, it is not payable until the merchandise enters US Customs territory. To receive designation as 'privileged foreign merchandise,' an application must be properly filed 'before the merchandise has been manipulated or manufactured in the zone in a manner which has effected a change in tariff classification.'[13]

---

5. 19 U.S.C. § 81n (1978 and Supp. 1995).
6. 19 U.S.C. § 81m (1978 and Supp. 1995).
7. *Id.*
8. 'Foreign Trade Zones: US Customs Procedures and Requirements.' Customs Publication No. 537.
9. 19 U.S.C. § 81c, 19 C.F.R. §§ 146.41–.44 (1995).
10. 19 C.F.R. §§ 146.41–.44.
11. 19 C.F.R. § 146.41(e) (1995).
12. *Id.*
13. 19 C.F.R. § 146.41(b) (1995).

The second status designation is 'non-privileged foreign merchandise.'[14] Merchandise which qualifies for this status is appraised and classified according to its condition and quantity when it is transferred into US Customs territory.[15]

(a) Foreign merchandise – not privileged or zone restricted;
(b) Waste recovered from any manufacture of privilege foreign merchandise in a zone; and
(c) Any domestic merchandise which by reasons of noncompliance with regulations in this part has lost its identity as domestic merchandise.

These status designations give importers a great deal of flexibility in establishing the duty rates. If the importer is importing foreign merchandise which has a higher rate of duty than the finished and manufactured product, the importer can receive non-privileged designation, paying the lower duty rate for the completed manufactured goods. This is known as 'tariff inversion.' If, however, the imported merchandise has a lower rate of duty than the product manufactured using the merchandise, the importer can seek privileged status and pay the lower duty rate for the imported merchandise.

There are two other status designations: 'domestic merchandise' and 'zone restricted merchandise.'[16] Domestic merchandise is duty-free, duty-paid, or American-made merchandise transferred into an FTZ.[17] It may be returned to the US; Customs territory free of duty and quota.[18] Zone restricted merchandise is merchandise transferred into an FTZ 'for the sole purpose of exportation, destruction ... or storage.'[19] Once status granted cannot be abandoned and moved into US Customs territory.[20]

C. Activities Permitted in Foreign Trade Zones

Foreign or domestic merchandise can be moved into an FTZ for a variety of operations: storage, sale, exhibition, breaking up, repacking, distribution, sorting, grading, cleaning, mixing with other merchandise, assembly, and manufacture are all operations permitted within FTZs.[21] Before performing any operation in an FTZ, the importer must 'apply on Customs Form 216 for permission to manipulate, manufacture, exhibit, or destroy merchandise.'[22]

14. 19 C.F.R. § 146.42 (1995).
15. *Id.*
16. 19 C.F.R. § 146.44 (1995).
17. 19 C.F.R. § 146.43(a) (1995).
18. 19 C.F.R. § 146.43(c) (1995).
19. 19 C.F.R. § 146.44(a) (1995).
20. *Id.*
21. 19 U.S.C. § 81c; 15 C.F.R. § 400.803.
22. 19 C.F.R. § 146.52(a) (1995); 15 C.F.R. § 400.803(a) (1995).

Products which are subject to certain Internal Revenue taxes may not be produced in FTZ;[23] items such as cigars, cigarettes, products made with imported alcohol and guns may not be manufactured in FTZ'S.[24] Also, no retail trade in foreign goods is permitted from an FTZ.[25]

D. Administrative Process

In order to establish an FTZ, an applicant must file a written application with the Foreign Trade Zones Board. The application must be on letter-size paper, identify the applicant, be signed by an authorized corporate officer and contain the corporate sea1.[26] The application must be accompanied by 13 different exhibits which are detailed in the Customs regulations.[27] The Board reviews the application and will authorize the applicant to establish a zone if the application satisfies the standards set out in the Customs regulations.

The statute provides that each port of entry is entitled to at least one zone, but more than one zone may be authorized if a single zone will not 'adequately serve the convenience of commerce.'[28] The Customs regulations authorize the establishment of subzones as well as master zones.[29] Subzones are special-purpose facilities established by companies which cannot operate at a zone site.[30] A subzone may actually be established at a company's own plant if it is located in an area where there is a master zone.

Once a zone has been established, the zone operator or grantee must make an application to the Foreign Trade Zone Board to 'activate' the zone.[31] The application must contain 'a description of the zone sites…, any operations to be conducted therein and a statement of the general characteristics of the merchandise to be admitted.'[32] The application must also be accompanied by certain supporting documents including a blueprint of the zone area and a procedures manual outlining the inventory control and recordkeeping systems to be used in the zone.[33]

---

23. 19 U.S.C. § 81c.
24. *Id.*
25. *Id.*
26. 15 C.F.R. § 400.602 (1995),
27. 15 C.F.R. § 400.603(a)–(m) (1995). 19 U.S.C. § 816(a) (1995).
28. 19 U.S.C. § 816(b).
29. 15 C.F.R. § 400.304.
30. *Id.; see also* 'Foreign Trade Zones: US *Customs* Procedures and Requirements.' Customs Publication No. 537.
31. 19 C.F.R. § 146.6(a) (1995).
32. 19 C.F.R. § 146.6(a) (1995).
33. 19 C.F.R. § 146.6(b) (1995).

E. Guidelines for Adjacency Requirement

The FTZ Act and regulations require that zone sites be within or adjacent to a US Customs port of entry, as listed and defined in part 101 of the US Customs and Border Protection regulations (19 CFR §101.3). Each application must explain how the requested sites meet the adjacency requirement. The Customs Service is required to review this and the FTZ staff must certify to the Treasury Board member that the adjacency requirement is met.

The adjacency requirement can be satisfied if one of the following factors is met:

(1) The zone or subzone site is within the limits of a CBP port of entry (19 CFR §101.3);
(2) The zone or subzone site is within 60 statute miles of the outer limits of a Customs port of entry (19 CFR §101.3);
(3) The zone or subzone site is within 90 minutes' driving time from the outer limits of a CBP port of entry (19 CFR §101.3); or
(4) For subzones only: if a subzone site does not meet the adjacency requirement based on one of the above three factors, it may alternatively qualify to be considered adjacent if the CBP Port Director agrees that the three special Customs oversight factors are met. These factors are listed in the FTZ Board regulations (15 CFR § 400.21 (b)(2)(ii)):

Sec. 400.21 Number and location of zones and subzones.
The 'adjacency' requirement is satisfied if:

(1) A general-purpose zone is located within 60 statute miles or 90 minutes' driving time from the outer limits of a port of entry;
(2) A sub-zone meets the following requirements relating to Customs supervision:
   (a) Proper Customs oversight can be accomplished with physical and electronic means;
   (b) All electronically produced records are maintained in a format compatible with the requirements of the US Customs Service duration of the record period; and
   (c) The grantee/operator agrees to present merchandise for examination at a Customs site selected by Customs when requested, and further agrees to present all necessary documents directly to the Customs oversight office.[34]

34. <www.ia.ita. Doc.gov/ftzpage/ftznew/adjacency.html>.

F. BONDED WAREHOUSES

There are also other types of arrangements that allow various forms of activities similar to those permitted in a Foreign Trade Zone. Among these are bonded warehouses,[35] owned by importers and used exclusively by them, and public bonded warehouses, used by many parties. Some are used simply for storage of goods that are later exported. Others are used for actual manipulation of goods or manufacturing activities in bond for exportation.

Any party may make written application to the district director of Customs to establish a bonded warehouse. If a party wishes to manipulate goods in a bonded warehouse (e.g., cleaning, sorting, repacking), the goods may be entered with Customs Form 7501. A prior application to manipulate must have been filed with the district director using Customs Form 3499. If manufacturing is to be done in the warehouse, a list of articles intended to be manufactured in the warehouse must be filed with the district director indicating the names of the ingredients and materials that are dutiable or taxable. Imported merchandise to be used in a bonded manufacturing operation may be entered duty free, using Customs Form 7501. Withdrawal of the material from the warehouse must be under Customs supervision and only for direct exportation to a foreign country.

> *PRACTICE NOTE:* Alcohol, goods subject to antidumping orders and other classes of goods that might be considered contraband cannot be brought into a bonded warehouse.

35. *See* U.S.C. § 1955; 19 C.F.R. Part 19.

Chapter 10
Fraud Investigations

I. INTRODUCTION

This chapter will discuss the laws and procedures by which Customs investigates and imposes penalties on any importation involving negligence or false statements. Our discussion will focus on the administrative and judicial procedures involved in enforcing Title 19 § 1592 of the United States Code. The discussion will also address the penalties imposed for violation of § 1592 and the basis upon which these penalties may be assessed.

II. DISCUSSION

A. Section 1592

In Title I of the Customs Procedural Reform and Simplification Act of 1978, the US Congress significantly revised the provisions dealing with fraud and false statements contained in the Tariff Act of 1930, (Title 19 § 1592 of the United States Code).[1] The 1978 changes in the law include: establishing degrees of culpability for violations of the section; basing the penalties upon the degree of culpability; providing more procedural safeguards in the administrative proceedings; and establishing *de novo* judicial review of all issues.[2] Recently, the Customs Mod Act (Title VI of the NAFTA Implementation Act) has made some changes to Customs enforcement thereby creating the new version of Title 19 U.S.C. § 1592. The Mod Act changes § 1592 by specifically prohibiting electronic transmittal

---

1. *See* Peterson, *Civil Customs Penalties Under Section* 592 *of the Tariff Act: Current Practice and the Need for Further Reform,* 18 Vand. J. Transnat'l L. 679 (Fall 1985).
2. *Id.* at 688.

to Customs of false data; something that was not specifically considered under the old law.

Section 1592 is one of the primary provisions used by Customs to restrict unlawful import practices. The section provides that ('no person, by fraud, gross negligence, or negligence ... may enter, introduce, or attempt to enter or introduce any merchandise into the commerce of the United States by means of ... any document, or electronically transmitted data, written or oral statement, or act which is material and false, or any omission which is material, or false).'[3] The section is very broad, making it unlawful for any person to make, or to aid or abet another[4] in making 'any false and material statement or omission in connection with the importation of merchandise.'[5] (Mere clerical errors or mistakes of fact do not constitute violations of this section, but an importer may be liable for a simple negligent act or omission of material. The new version of § 1592 states however, that the mere unintentional repetition by an electronic system of an initial clerical error does not constitute a pattern of negligible conduct.[6, 7]) Also, a violation may occur regardless of whether there has been an actual loss of duties resulting from the practice.[8] Thus, § 1592 penalizes both fraudulent and negligent import practices which have a potential impact on the importation of an article, without regard to any actual loss of revenue to the United States. Furthermore, the new amendment to § 1592 emphasizes the standard of 'Reasonable Care.' *See* Chapter 5, Section 4 for discussion of the 'Reasonable Care' standard.

There are also other statutes which provide for criminal penalties for activities similar to those penalized in § 1592. For example, Title 18 § 542 of the United States Code penalizes the use of fraud or false statements to effect the entry of goods. Title 18 § 1001 is another more general statute sanctioning false statements.[9]

---

3. 19 U.S.C. § 1592(a) (1995).
4. Section 1592 prohibits any person from aiding or abetting another in violating the statute. 19 U.S.C. § 1592(a)(1)(B) (Supp. 1995). The importer will bear primary responsibility for any violation of Section 1592. But where collusion with the importer has been established, other parties have been held jointly liable with the importer. Apparently, bad faith is necessary for joint liability under Section 1592. In Letter Ruling No. 653382 (October 19, 1983), a customs broker's simple misunderstanding of the proper entry forms was held to be insufficient grounds upon which to impose liability for a penalty.
5. *United States v. R.I. T.A. Organics, Inc.*, 487 F. Supp. 75, 76 (N.D. III. 1980) (emphasis added). *See also* ('A document, statement, act, or admission is material if it has the *potential* to alter the classification, appraisement, or admissibility of merchandise ... ') *See also* (emphasis added). *United States v. Rockwell Int'l Corp.*, 628 F. Supp. 206, 209 (Cl. Int'l Trade 1986).
6. 19 U.S.C. § 1592 (a)(1)(A)(I).
7. 19 U.S.C. § 1592(a)(2) (1995); *see also United States v. Ven-Fuel, Inc.*, 758 F.2d 741, 759 (1st Cir. 1985).
8. 19 U.S.C. § 592(a)(2) (1995).
9. It is important to note that the Court of International Trade has held that the US is free to bring an action for civil penalties under § 1592 even after the persons have been subjected to criminal sanctions under Title 18 § 542 of the *United States Code*. *United States v. Loesche*, 688 F. Supp. 649, 651 (Ct. Int'l Trade 1988).

B. ADMINISTRATIVE PROCEDURES

1. Pre-penalty Notice

The penalty process begins when Customs discovers a possible violation of § 1592 through discrepancies or inconsistencies in the required documentation or through receiving information of possible violations from informers.[10] If a Customs officer determines that there is 'reasonable cause to believe that there has been a violation' and that there should be further proceedings, he must issue a written pre-penalty notice to the party concerned.[11] The pre-penalty notice is a written statement of the officer's intention to issue a claim for a penalty due to an alleged violation of Section 1592.[12] The notice must contain: a description of the merchandise; details concerning the alleged improper importation; the laws and regulations which may have been violated; all the facts establishing the violation; the degree of culpability; and the estimated loss of duties and the estimated penalty. Further, it must grant the person a 'reasonable opportunity' to explain why a penalty should not be imposed.[13] The pre-penalty notice is not required if the violation involves a non-commercial importation or if the claim is for less than USD 1.000.[14]

The person named in the pre-penalty notice will have 30 days in which to respond to the notice.[15]

> *PRACTICE NOTE:* The response may be either oral or in writing.[16] Extensions of time may be granted under certain circumstances.[17] The importer's written presentation need not be in any particular form, although it must contain certain required information.[18] The importer's response should contain information identifying it as a response to the pre-penalty notice, answering the allegations set out in the notice and providing reasons why a penalty should not be issued or should be issued for a lesser amount.[19]

---

10. 19 U.S.C. § 1619(a)(I)(B) (1995) provides for compensation to be given to persons who provide information 'concerning any fraud upon the Customs revenue ....'
11. 19 U.S.C. § 1592(b)(1)(A) (1995); 19 C.F.R. § 162.77(a)(1995).
12. 19 U.S.C. § 1592(b)(1)(A); (Supp. 1995) 19 C.F.R., § 162.77(a) (1995).
13. 19 U.S.C. § 1592(b)(1)(A); (Supp. 1995) 19 C.F.R., § 162.77(a) (1995).
14. 19 U.S.C. § 1592(b)(1)(B); 19 C.F.R. § 162.77(b) (1995).
15. 19 C.F.R. § 162.78(a) (1995).
16. The district director may shorten the time in which the named person must respond if there is less than one year until the statute of limitations runs on the Section 1592 cause of action. This shorter period of time cannot be less than seven days. *Id.*
17. 19 C.F.R. § 162.78(b) (1995).

> *PRACTICE NOTE:* At least one extension of time is routinely granted.

18. 19 C.F.R. § 162.78(c) (1995).
19. *Id.*

2. Determination as to Violation

Once the district director has received and considered the response to the pre-penalty notice, he/she must determine whether there was in fact a violation of Section 1592.[20] If the director determines there has been no violation, he/she 'shall promptly issue a written statement of the determination to the person to whom the notice was sent' stating that there will not be a claim for a penalty issued against that importer.[21]

If the director determines there was a violation, 'he shall issue a written penalty notice/claim to such person.'[22] The penalty claim is a written notice that a claim for a monetary penalty has been assessed against the person named. The notice must contain any changes from the pre-penalty notice and must inform the person named of the right to seek mitigation of the claim under Title 19 Section 1618 of the United States Code.[23] The petition for mitigation of the penalty will be discussed below.

If the person named chooses to seek mitigation of the penalty, the 'appropriate Customs officer shall provide to the person concerned a written statement which sets forth the final determination and the findings of fact and conclusions of law on which such determination is based.'[24] At this stage of the proceedings, the importer must decide whether to pay the penalty or to refuse to pay the penalty, forcing Customs to begin judicial proceedings to collect the penalty. The judicial process will be discussed below.

3. Prior Disclosure

Occasionally, an importer may recognize a violation of Section 1592 in his own operations before Customs has initiated an investigation. Section 1592 allows an importer to limit liability for the violation if the importer makes a 'prior disclosure' of the violation to Customs. 'A prior disclosure is made if the person concerned discloses the circumstances of a violation…, in writing to a district director before, or without knowledge of, the commencement of a formal investigation… and makes a tender of any actual loss of duties.'[25]

Although an importer may limit his liability through prior disclosure, there are certain risks involved in the process. Any prior disclosure is immediately referred for investigation, and any other undisclosed violation that is uncovered will not be subject to prior disclosure treatment.[26] Thus, by making a prior disclosure, an importer is calling attention to his operation and potentially opening himself to full liability for any undisclosed liability uncovered in the subsequent

20. 19 U.S.C. § 1592(b)(2) (1995).
21. 19 U.S.C. § 1592(b)(2); 19 C.F.R. § 162.79(a) (1995).
22. 19 U.S.C. § 1592(b)(2) (1995).
23. 19 U.S.C. § 1592(b)(2) (Supp. 1995); 19 C.F.R. § 162.79(b)(2) (1995).
24. 19 U.S.C. § 1592(b)(2) (1995).
25. 19 C.F.R. § 162.74(a) (1995).
26. 19 C.F.R. §§ 162.74(c), (i) (1995).

investigation. § 621 further expands 19 U.S.C. § 1592 by defining commencement of formal investigations, for prior disclosure purposes, as being the date recorded in writing by Customs when places and circumstances were discovered or when information received reveals a possibility that a violation of Section 1592 existed.

> *PRACTICE NOTE:* It is important to make certain to clearly fix the date and time of the disclosure if made orally and the date and time and Customs officer's name should be recorded and included in a formal letter which should be sent by service with proof of date and time of delivery.

4. Remission or Mitigation of Penalties

After receiving a penalty notice, the named party has 30 days in which to petition for mitigation of the penalty.[27] The petition may be either in writing, addressed to the Commissioner of Customs, or an oral presentation.[28] The petition should contain the facts surrounding the alleged violation and the reasons why the penalty should be mitigated.[29]

In determining whether to mitigate a penalty, Customs considers certain 'factors' set out in the Customs Regulations.

Customs will consider the following elements: (1) whether there was any error by Customs which contributed to the violation; (2) whether the importer cooperated with the investigation to an extent 'beyond that expected from a person under investigation'; and (3) whether the importer took immediate remedial action, including paying the duties actually lost 'prior to the issuance of a penalty notice'; (4) such other factors as the importer's inexperience, if it was relevant to the violation, and whether the violation was based upon fraud or gross negligence will also be considered; (5) customs will consider an importer's good record if it shows a consistent pattern of importations without a prior Section 1592 violation.[30]

Finally, there are also certain aggravating factors and extraordinary factors which Customs will consider.[31]

> *PRACTICE NOTE:* Mitigating factors are balanced against aggravating factors.

---

27. 19 U.S.C. § 1618 (1995); 19 C.F.R. § 17J.J2(d) (1995).
28. 19 C.F.R. §§ 171.11(c), 171.14(a) (1995).
29. 19 C.F.R. § 171.11(c) (1995).
30. 19 C.F.R. Part 171, App. B § (F) (1995). Importers' violations are regularly recorded in the Customs computer system. Companies with a record of violations are more likely to be subjected to intensive inspections and audits.
31. 19 C.F.R. Part 171, App. B, §§ (G), (H) (1995).

After the proceedings for remission or mitigation of the penalty have been completed, the 'Customs Service' will provide the importer with a written statement declaring the final determination as to the penalty.[32] The importer must either pay the penalty or refuse to pay and defend against the collection proceeding in the Court of International Trade.

C. Civil Penalties for Entry of Goods by False Statement

There are a variety of penalties available to Customs to deter improper importation practices. Section 1592 provides for monetary penalties as well as seizure and forfeiture of the goods in question. The monetary penalties vary according to the degree of culpability, the value of the merchandise in question and with the amount of any revenues lost. Also, Title 18 U.S.C. § 542, provides for criminal penalties including fines of not more than USD 50,000 or imprisonment for not more than two years for each offense.

> *PRACTICE NOTE:* Criminal prosecution for customs violations is rare. They are often pursued in intentional and egregious cases of mismarking of goods. The author had two clients where criminal penalties were pursued, both involving mismarking of country of origin. In one case, an informant alleged that foreign labels were removed and replaced with 'Made in USA' labels.

1. Maximum Penalty Amounts in Section 1592

If there was no prior disclosure or mitigation of the penalties, the maximum monetary penalty allowed under Section 1592 is determined by the degree of culpability of the importer. If the violations in question were fraudulent, then the maximum penalty authorized is the full domestic value of the merchandise.[33] An act or omission is considered to be fraudulent if 'the material false statement or act in connection with the transaction was committed (or omitted) knowingly, *i.e.*, was done voluntarily and intentionally, as established by clear and convincing evidence.'[34] If the violation was grossly negligent, the maximum penalty would be either; (1) 'the lesser of the domestic value of the merchandise, or four times the lawful duties of which the United States may be deprived'; or (2), 'if the violation did not affect the assessment of duties, 40 per cent of the dutiable value of the merchandise may be assessed.'[35] The violation is grossly negligent if it results from an act done with

---

32. 9 U.S.C. § 1592(b)(2) (1995).
33. 19 U.S.C. § 1592(c)(I) (1995).
34. 19 C.F.R. Part 171, App.B §(B)(3) (1995).
35. 19 U.S.C. § 1592(c)(2) (1995).

'actual knowledge of or wanton disregard for the relevant facts and with indifference or disregard for the offender's obligations under the statute.'[36]

If the violation was negligent, the maximum penalty would be either: (1) 'the lesser of the domestic value of the merchandise, or two times the lawful duties of which the United States may be deprived'; or (2), 'if the violation did not affect the assessment of duties, 20 per cent of the dutiable value of the merchandise.'[37] A violation is negligent if it was done 'through either the failure to exercise the degree of reasonable care and competence expected from a person in the same circumstances in ascertaining the facts or in drawing inferences there from in ascertaining the offender's obligations under the statute, or in communicating information so that it may be understood by the recipient.'[38]

2. Prior Disclosure

An importer may limit potential liability under Section 1592 by making a prior disclosure.[39] If the violator discloses a fraudulent violation the penalty will not exceed the value of the loss of duties.[40] A check for any duties owed should be tendered with the prior disclosure or the disclosure should indicate that the check will be tendered within 30 days.

> *PRACTICE NOTE:* There often is a psychological advantage in tendering your check with the prior disclosure. Customs, with the cash in hand may be more motivated to accept your offer. They must return the check if they reject it.

3. Mitigation of Penalties

Under Title 19 Section 1618 of the United States Code, a person may petition to have any penalty claims against him/her mitigated.[41] The Customs Regulations provide guidelines for the mitigation of monetary penalties assessed for violation of Section 1592.[42] These guidelines indicate that violations which result in revenue loss to the US will be mitigated differently from those violations which result in no revenue loss.

In the revenue loss cases, the penalty will be generally related to the lost revenues or the domestic value of the merchandise. If the violation is determined to be fraudulent, the penalty can be mitigated to 'an amount ranging from a minimum of five times the loss of revenue to a maximum of the lesser of the domestic value

---

36. 19 C.F.R. Part 171, App. B § (B)(3) (1995).
37. 19 U.S.C. § 1592(c)(3) (1995).
38. 19 C.F.R. Part 171, App. B. § (B)(I) (1995).
39. *See* text *supra* at B(3).
40. 19 U.S.C. § 1592(c)(4)(A) (1995) 41. *See* text *supra* at B(4).
41. *See* text *supra* at B(4).
42. 19 C.F.R. Part 171, App. B § (D)(2)–(6) (1995).

of the merchandise or eight times the loss of revenue.'[43] If the violation is grossly negligent, the penalty can be mitigated to 'an amount ranging from a minimum of two and one-half times the loss of revenue to a maximum of the lesser of the domestic value of the merchandise or four times the loss of revenue.'[44] Finally, if the violation was merely negligent, the penalty may be mitigated to 'an amount ranging from a minimum of one-half the loss of revenue to a maximum of the lesser of the domestic value of the merchandise or two times the loss of revenue.'[45]
In the cases where there is no revenue loss, the penalty is usually determined as a percentage of the dutiable value of the merchandise. In cases of fraud, the penalty may be mitigated to 50 to 80 per cent of the dutiable value of the merchandise.[46] In cases of gross negligence, the penalty may be mitigated to 25 to 40 per cent of the dutiable value of the merchandise.[47] In cases of mere negligence, the penalty may be mitigated to 20 per cent of the dutiable value of the merchandise.[48]

4. Seizure and Forfeiture

Section 1592 provides not only for monetary penalties but also for seizure and forfeiture of the merchandise at issue. However, the authority to seize goods under this section is limited.[49] To justify a seizure, the district director must first have 'reasonable cause' to believe that a violation of Section 1592 has occurred.[50] The district director must also have 'reasonable cause' to believe that the seizure is justified because the violator is insolvent, beyond the jurisdiction of the US, or the seizure is essential to protect the revenue of the US or to prevent the violator from introducing prohibited products into the US.[51] Seizure is not authorized in cases where a prior voluntary disclosure has been made.[52]

If the district director elects to seize the merchandise in question, he must provide written notice to all interested persons.[53] The notice must contain the facts supporting the alleged violations, a description of the merchandise involved, a statement of the laws alleged to have been violated, and an estimation of any duties lost due to the violation.[54] Any interested party may file a petition for relief from forfeiture according to the procedures established for seeking remission of a penalty.[55]

---

43. *Id.* at § (D)(2)(a) (1995).
44. *Id.* at § (D)(3)(a) (1995).
45. *Id.* at § (D)(4)(a) (1995).
46. *Id.* at § (D)(2)(b) (1995).
47. *Id.* at § (D)(3)(b) (1995).
48. *Id.* at § (D)(4)(b) (1995).
49. 19 U.S.C. § 1592(c)(6) (1995).
50. *Id.*
51. *Id.*
52. 19 U.S.C. § 1592(c)(4) (Supp. 1995); 19 C.F.R. § 162.75(b) (1995).
53. 19 C.F.R. § 162.75(c) (1995).
54. 19 C.F.R. §§ 162.759(c), 162.31(b) (1995).
55. 19 C.F.R. § 171.11(a), (d) (1995).

After the merchandise is seized, it may either be released under bond or remain to be subject to forfeiture. If there is a deposit of security adequate to cover the maximum penalty assessed against the violator, the district director 'shall return seized merchandise to the person from whom it was seized' or to any other interested party.[56]

If the merchandise is not released or the penalty mitigated, forfeiture proceedings will be carried out by the Department of Justice if the value of the merchandise seized is greater than USD 10,000.[57] This is generally handled by the US Attorney's Office in the applicable district. Otherwise, the forfeiture will be done as specified by the summary forfeiture procedures established in the Customs Regulations.[58]

Finally, it is important to note that Customs may consider merchandise seized under Section 1592 to be also subject to seizure and forfeiture under Section 1595a(c), which provides that any 'merchandise that is introduced or attempted to be introduced into the United States contrary to law *(other than in violation of Section* 1592) may be seized and forfeited.'[59] Customs construes this section to provide for seizure in all cases except those involving only a violation of Section 1592.

5. Deprivation of Lawful Duties

In addition to assessing monetary penalties and seizure, Section 1592 requires importers to pay any withheld or unpaid duties regardless of whether another penalty has been assessed.[60] Where an importer is liable for any actual loss of duties and there has been no penalty assessed or no notice of claim issued, the importer must receive written notice of the liability, identifying the merchandise, the transaction, the amount of liability and making a demand for payment within 30 days.[61]

D. Customs Brokers and Section 1641

Title 19 Section 1641(d) of the United States Code provides for disciplinary proceedings against customs brokers.[62] Section 1641 allows penalties to be assessed

---

56. 19 C.F.R. § 162.75(d)(1), (2) (1995).
57. 19 C.F.R. § 162.75(d)(3) (1995).
58. *Id.*
59. 19 U.S.C. § 1595a(c)(4) (emphasis added) (1995).
60. 19 U.S.C. § 1592(d) (1995).
61. 19 C.F.R. § 162.79(b) (1995).
62. Customs brokers are any persons, partnerships, associations, or corporations licensed under Section 1641 to transact business before the Customs Service on behalf of others. 19 U.S.C. § 1641(a)(1) (1995); 19 C.F.R. § 111.1(b) (1995).

against a broker for a variety of offenses[63] including having: 'counseled, commanded, induced, procured, or knowingly aided and abetted the violations by any other person of any provision of any law enforced by the Customs Service, or the rules or regulations issued under such provision.'[64]

Thus, customs brokers, like importers under Section 1592, may be subject to primary liability as well as liability for aiding and abetting the commission of an infraction. Section 1641 authorizes two types of sanctions for violations of the section: monetary penalties, or revocation or suspension of the broker's license or permit.[65]

Any complaint or charge against a broker which may indicate a violation of Section 1641 is investigated by a special agent.[66] The special agent makes a report to the director of the appropriate district, who in turn reports his findings to the Commissioner for a final determination as to whether charges will be brought against the broker.[67] If charges are to be preferred against the broker, the district director must issue a statement of charges 'which fairly informs the accused of the charges against him so that he is able to prepare his response.'[68] The statement of charges will also 'specify' the sanction being proposed.'[69] The proceedings for imposing the different sanctions vary.

1. Procedures for Monetary Penalties under Section 1641

The grounds for imposing monetary penalties on a broker are established in Section 1641 and the Customs Regulations.[70] The procedures established for imposing a monetary penalty are similar to those discussed above for Section 1592.

The statement of charges must advise the alleged violator of the charges against him and inform him of his right to respond to the charges.[71] The alleged violator then has 30 days in which to file a petition for relief under Section 1618.[72] After consideration of the application for relief, a written decision is issued containing the final determination with regard to the charges and the penalty.[73] If there is a penalty imposed, the broker has 60 days in which to pay the penalty or the matter will be referred to the Department of Justice.

---

63. There are guidelines established in the Customs Regulations regarding the imposition of penalties for violations of 19 U.S.C. § 1641, 19 C.F.R. Part 171, App. C (1995).
64. 19 U.S.C. § 1641(d)(1)(D) (1995).
65. 19 U.S.C. § 1641(d)(2) (1995).
66. 19 C.F.R. § 111.55 (1995).
67. 19 C.F.R. §§ 111.55–.57 (1995).
68. 19 C.F.R. § 111.58 (1995).
69. *Id.*
70. 19 U.S.C. § 1641(d)(2)(A). (The broker must show cause why he should not be subject to a monetary penalty, not to exceed USD 30,000), (1995).
71. *Id.*
72. 19 C.F.R. §§ 111.92–.93 (1995); 19 C.F.R. §§ 171.11–15 (1995).
73. 19 C.F.R. § 111.94.

a. *Procedures for Cancellation, Suspension or Revocation of a Broker's License*

The administrative procedures involved in revoking, suspending or canceling a broker's license for violation of Section 1641 are more complex than those discussed above.[74]

After the investigation and a statement of charges is issued by Customs, there is a preliminary proceeding. The broker has a right to participate in the preliminary proceedings and the district director must provide the broker with notice of the proceeding and an opportunity to participate.[75] The notice must be written and contain a copy of the statement of charges, a statement that formal proceedings are available to him, a statement of the broker's rights with regard to those proceedings, and an invitation 'to show cause why the formal proceedings should not be instituted.'[76] The district director reports to the Commissioner on the results of the preliminary proceeding along with his recommendations, who then determines whether to proceed on the charges against the broker.[77]

If the Commissioner decides to proceed against the broker, the district director prepares a notice of charges to be served on the broker.[78] The notice of charges must inform the broker of the relevant code section, and provide a statement of the broker's right to counsel and right to cross examine witnesses.[79] The broker will be notified within 10 days of receiving the notice of charges of the time and place of the hearing.[80]

The charges will then be heard before a hearing officer who 'shall be an administrative law judge.'[81] The hearing will be on the record with a copy of the transcript to be provided to the broker without charge.[82] After the hearing, the parties may submit proposed findings, conclusions and supporting reasons to the hearing officer for review.[83] The hearing officer then makes a recommended decision and certifies the entire record to the Secretary of Homeland Security.[84] The Commissioner then renders a decision and publishes a notice in the *Federal Register.*[85] Appeals from the decision must be made according to Section 1641(e).[86]

---

74. *See* 19 U.S.C. 1641(d)(2)(B) (1995).
75. 19 C.F.R. § 111.59(a), (b) (1995).
76. *Id.*
77. 19 C.F.R. § 111.61 (1995).
78. *Ibid.*
79. 19 C.F.R. § 111.62 (1995).
80. 19 C.F.R.§ 111.64(a) (1995).
81. 19 C.F.R. § 111.67 (1995).
82. 19 C.F.R. § 111.67 (1995).
83. 19 C.F.R. § 111.68 (1995).
84. 19 C.F.R. § 111.69 (1995).
85. 19 C.F.R. § 111.74 (1995).
86. 9 C.F.R. § 111.75 (1995); 19 U.S.C. § 1641(e) (1995).

E. Role of the US Attorney

The US Attorney may become involved in the enforcement of penalties under Sections 1592 and 1641. Title 19 § 1604 of the United States Code requires the 'appropriate customs officer to report promptly' any seizure or violation which may require legal proceedings, to the US Attorney for the district in which the violation or seizure occurred. Thus, if a violator refuses to pay the penalty assessed against him/her as a result of the administrative proceedings outlined above, or if there is to be a forfeiture of seized merchandise valued at more than USD 10,000, Customs must report the case to the US Attorney.[87]

Upon receiving reports of cases which may require legal proceedings from Customs, the US Attorney is obligated to investigate the facts of the case.[88] If, from the investigation, it appears probable that a violation occurred and formal legal proceedings are necessary for the recovery of any penalties or forfeiture; then the 'proper proceedings [are] to be commenced and prosecuted without delay.'[89] If the investigation reveals that formal legal proceedings should not be instituted, then the case will be referred for administrative action.[90] The US Attorney represents the US in proceedings in the Court of International Trade to enforce the penalties or forfeitures assessed under Sections 1592 and 1641.

> *PRACTICE NOTE:* US Attorneys are very busy, and do not consider smaller Customs forfeiture cases, not involving drugs, pornography or weapons high priority, and they are generally amenable to settling these cases without forfeiture.

F. Legal Proceedings

Exclusive jurisdiction over 'any civil action ... commenced by the United States to recover a civil penalty under Section 1592 is granted to the Court of International Trade in New York.'[91] This grant of exclusive jurisdiction has been upheld by the courts.[92] Thus legal proceedings to enforce Section 1592 will be brought by the US Attorney in the Court of International Trade.

1. The Statute of Limitations

Title 19 § 1621 of the United States Code establishes the time in which any action to 'recover any pecuniary penalty or forfeiture of property accruing under the

87. 19 U.S.C. §§ 1603, 1610 (1995); 19 C.F.R. § 162.49(a) (1995).
88. 19 U.S.C. § 1604 (1995).
89. *Id.*
90. *Id.*
91. 28 U.S.C. § 1582(1) (1995).
92. *See,* e.g., *United States v. Appendagez, Inc.,* 560 F. Supp. 50 (Ct. Int'l Trade 1983).

customs laws must be commenced.'[93] In Section 1592 cases which are based upon negligence or gross negligence of the importer, the action must be begin within five years of the date of the violation.[94] However, in all other cases, including Section 1641 and Section 1592 cases based on fraud, the action must be brought within five years of the date the violation was discovered.[95] The Court of International Trade has not ruled on the issue of what constitutes 'discovery' for purposes of Section 1621.[96]

2. Recovery of Monetary Penalties

Section 1592 provides that the Court of International Trade 'in any proceeding ... for the recovery of any monetary penalty claimed under this section' will try all issues *de novo*.[97] Trial *de novo* allows the alleged violator to freely litigate the basis and the amount of the penalty without being bound by previous administrative determinations.[98]

In these proceedings to recover monetary penalties, the US carries the burden of proof but the burden varies with the degree of culpability being alleged.[99] In an action based on fraud, the US must prove the violation by 'clear and convincing evidence.'[100] In an action based on gross negligence or negligence, the government must establish all the elements of the violation.[101] Once the US establishes the act or omission constituting the violation, the burden shifts to the importer to show that the act or omission constituting the violation did not result from negligence.[102]

3. Forfeiture

Forfeiture cases under Section 1592 are referred to the US Attorney or the Department of Justice.[103] Forfeiture proceedings may be instituted before all administrative procedures have been completed.[104] Title 19 §§ 1602–1619 of the United

---

93. 19 U.S.C. § 1621 (1995).
94. *Id. See also United States v. Joan & David Helpern Co.*, 611 F. Supp. 985, 988 (Ct. Int'l Trade 1986).
95. 19 U.S.C. § 1621 (1995).
96. One commentator has argued that the statute of limitations should begin to run when Customs comes into 'possession of information that, if investigated with due diligence,' would lead to actual discovery of the violation rather than when the investigator actually discovers a violation. Peterson, Civil Customs Penalties Under Section 592 of the Tariff Act: Current Practice and the Need for Further Reform, 18 Vand. J. Transnat'l L. 679 (Fall 1985).
97. 19 U.S.C. § 1592(e)(1) (1995).
98. *See United States v. Tabor*, 608 F. Supp. 658 (Ct. Int'l Trade 1985).
99. 19 U.S.C. § 1592(e)(2)–(4) (1995).
100. 19 U.S.C. § 1592(e)(2) (1995).
101. 19 U.S.C. § 1592(e)(3), (4) (1995).
102. 19 U.S.C. § 1592(e)(4) (1995).
103. 19 U.S.C. §§ 1603, 1610 (1995); 19 C.F.R. § 162.49(a) (1995).
104. 19 C.F.R. § 162.32(c) (1995).

States Code, generally control the procedures affecting the forfeiture of all property by the Customs Service.[105]

Upon receiving a report from Customs, the US Attorney will petition the court to order a sale of the property.[106] The court, in its discretion, may then order the sale.[107] Title 19 § 1613 of the United States Code and Title 19 § 162.52 of the Code of Federal Regulations controls the priority of the distribution of the proceeds from the sale of the property. The proceeds are to be distributed in the following order:

1. Internal Revenue Taxes;
2. Marshall's fees and court costs;
3. Expenses of advertising and sale;
4. Expense of cartage, storage, and labor;
5. Duties;
6. Any sum due to satisfy a lien for freight charges, or contributions in general average, provided notice of the lien has been given in the manner prescribed by law; and
7. The monetary penalty assessed under 19 U.S.C. § 1592.

Section 1613, as amended, allows any excess proceeds from the sale of the forfeited merchandise to be returned to the person against whom the penalty was assessed.

105. 19 U.S.C. § 1600 (1995).
106. 19 U.S.C. § 1612 (1995).
107. *Id.*

Chapter 11

Recordation of Trademarks and Copyrights with the US Customs

I. INTRODUCTION

This chapter provides an overview of the relevant laws and regulations relating to recordation of trademarks and copyrights with US Customs. It discusses the relevant statutes and administrative regulations pertaining to recordation of trademarks and copyrights, as well as some recent court interpretations of these statutes and regulations. This has been a particularly active and somewhat controversial area of Customs law due to the issues surrounding so called 'gray market' imports. 'Gray market' or parallel imports are imports of goods into the US that bear a valid trademark which a foreign company is legitimately entitled to use abroad. The issue arises when these goods are imported into the US and compete with US goods bearing the same trademark and where the exporter is not licensed to use the trademark in the US.

II. GENERAL OVERVIEW OF TRADEMARKS AND COPYRIGHT LAW

A. 'Trademark'

A trademark is a distinctive mark which a manufacturer affixes to the goods he produces so that they may be identified in the market and their origin may be identified. A trademark may be a word, symbol, design or combination of a word and design which distinguishes the goods or services of one party from those of another. A trademark is created chiefly by use. This use (which to obtain a federal registration must be in interstate commerce) must be general, continuous, and exclusive. The mark must be applied to the goods and used in trade under such circumstances as to indicate an intention to adopt the mark for specific goods.[1] Trademark rights can last indefinitely if the mark continues to be used. [2]

B. 'COPYRIGHT'

A copyright refers to an intangible property right granted by statute to the author or originator of certain literary or artistic works. It is a form of protection provided by the laws of the US to the authors of 'original works of authorship' including literary, dramatic, musical, artistic, and certain other intellectual works. The originator of such works is normally granted a specified time period within which he/she has the sole and exclusive right to reproduce copies of the work for publication or sale purposes. The protection is available to both published and unpublished works.

C. STATUTORY PROTECTION TO TRADEMARK AND COPYRIGHTS IN THE US

1. Background

Although a detailed discussion of the law of intellectual property is beyond the scope of this book, a brief overview of the subject is helpful to understand the application of international trade and customs laws to imported goods which infringe on patents, trademarks and copyrights.

The basic US trademark laws are contained in the Lanham Trademark Act of 1946, as amended,[3] and in the Tariff Act of 1930, 19 U.S.C. § 1526.

Section 1124 of 15 U.S.C. provides:

> Except as provided in subsection (d) of Section 1526 of Tide 19 [19 U.S.C. § 1526(d)], no article of imported merchandise which shall copy or simulate the name of… [any] domestic manufacture, or manufacturer, or trader, or of any manufacturer or trader located in any foreign country which, by treaty, convention or law affords similar privileges to citizens of the United States, or which shall copy or simulate a trademark registered in accordance with the provisions of this chapter or shall bear a name or mark calculated to induce the public to believe that the article is manufactured in the United

---

1. *Continental Corp. v. National Union Radio Corp.*, 67 F.2d 938, 942 (7th Cir. 1933).
2. This is in *contrast* to copyrights or patents, which have limited periods of validity. Trademark owners must file affidavits of continuing use or the mark may be deemed abandoned by the Patent and Trademark Office.
3. 15 U.S.C. § 1051 *et seq*. For updates, *see* the Trademark Classification Act of 1984, 15 U.S.C. §§ 1051–1127 (1988 and Supp. 1995).

> States, or that it is manufactured in any foreign country or locality other than the country or locality in which it is in fact manufactured, shall be admitted to entry at any customhouse of the United States;

Section 526(a) of the Tariff Act of 1930[4] also makes it

> unlawful to import into the United States any merchandise of foreign manufacture if such merchandise... bears a trademark owned by a citizen of, or by a corporation or association created or organized within, the United States, and registered in the Patent and Trademark Office by a person domiciled in the United States ... unless written consent of the owner of such trademark is produced at the time of making entry.

Section 526(b) subjects any such merchandise to seizure and forfeiture for violation of the customs laws, and 526(c) provides that any person dealing in such merchandise may be enjoined from doing so within the US or may be required to export or destroy the merchandise or remove or obliterate the trademark. It also subjects the dealer to the same liability for damages and profits for wrongful use of a trademark.

The copyright laws are contained in the Federal Copyright Act, 17 U.S.C. §§ 101–810. Section 601 (known as the manufacturing clause) requires that books in the English language be manufactured in the US or Canada as a condition of copyright.[5] When a book is authored by a citizen or domiciliary of the US and has been so manufactured and copyrighted, the importation of foreign manufactured reprints is prohibited.[6] Section 602 prohibits the importation of books, periodicals, newspapers, music, phonograph records, motion picture films, and similar articles bearing a false notice of copyright. Piratical copies[7] of works copyrighted and recorded with the Customs service are also prohibited from entry.[8]

---

4. 19 U.S.C. § 1526(a) (1994).
5. 17 U.S.C. § 601(a) (Supp. 1995).
6. The prohibition does not apply where: importation is sought under the authority or for the use, other than in schools, of the United States government of any State or political subdivision of a State (17 U.S.C. § 601(b)(3)(Supp. 1995)); importation, for use and not for sale, is sought by any person with respect to no more than one copy of any work at anyone time, or by any person arriving from outside the United States, or by an organization operated for scholarly, educational, or religious purposes and not for private gain (17 U.S.C. § 601(b)(4)(A)–(C)). The copies are reproduced in raised characters for the use of the blind (17 U.S.C. § 601(b)(5)).
7. 'Piratical' copies are those produced without the authorization of the copyright owner.
8. However, this prohibition does not apply to: (i) importation of copies or phonograph records under the authority or for the use of the Government of the United States or of any State or political subdivision of a State, but not including copies or phonograph records for use in schools, or copies of any audiovisual work imported for purposes other than archival use; (ii) importation for the private use of the importer and not for distribution, by any person with respect to no more than one copy or phonograph record of anyone work at anyone time, or by any person arriving from outside the United States with respect to copies or phonograph records forming part of such person's personal baggage; or (iii) importation by or for an organization operated for scholarly, educational or religious purposes and not for private gain, with respect to no more than one copy of an audiovisual work solely for its archival purposes, and no more

2. Trademarks

The federal registration of trademarks provides the registrant with certain distinct advantages over whatever trademark rights might exist under state laws or common law (non-statutory case law) including:

(i) The right to sue in federal court for trademark infringement;
(ii) Recovery of profits, damages and costs in a federal infringement action and the possibility of treble damages and attorney's fees;
(iii) Availability of criminal penalties in an action for counterfeiting a registered trademark; and
(iv) A basis for filing trademark applications in foreign countries.

3. Procedure for Registration of Trademarks

The US Patent and Trademark Office (PTO), which is a branch of the Commerce Department, processes applications for the federal registration of trademarks. The first part of the registration process is the filing of an application. An application consists of:

(i) a written application form;
(ii) a drawing of the mark;
(iii) five specimens showing actual use of the mark in connection with the goods or services; and
(iv) the required filing fee. A separate application must be filed for each mark for which registration is requested.

The application must be written in English, and be signed by the owner of the mark. Marks containing designs or logos require a separate application as do service marks of the owner of the mark. Samples of the mark as actually used on goods must be attached. In addition, the date of first use in interstate commerce must be indicated.

When an application is filed, it is assigned a serial number, and the applicant is sent a filing receipt. A trademark examiner will then determine whether the mark is suitable. Generally, the applicant or his attorney is sent an 'office action' in which certain additional information may be requested or in which the views of the examiner on the registrability of the trademark are set out.[9] The

---

than five copies or phonograph records of any other for its library lending or archival purposes (17 U.S.C. § 602(a)(1)–(3)) (1977 and Supp. 1995).

9. The Examining Attorney will refuse registration if the mark or term applied for does not function as a trademark to identify the goods or services as coming from a particular source; is immoral, deceptive or scandalous; may disparage or falsely suggest a connection with persons, institutions, beliefs or national symbols or bring them into contempt or disrepute; consists of or simulates the flag or coat of arms or other insignia of the United States, or a State or municipality, or any foreign nation; is the name, portrait or signature of a particular living individual, unless he has given written consent; or is the name, signature or portrait of a deceased President of the United States during the life of his widow, unless she has given her consent; so resembles a mark already registered in the PTO as to be likely, when applied to the goods of the applicant, to cause confusion, or to cause mistake, or to deceive; is merely descriptive or deceptively

applicant must respond to any objections raised within six months, or the application will be considered abandoned. If after reviewing the applicant's response the Examining Attorney makes a final refusal of registration, the applicant may appeal to the Trademark Trial and Appeal Board, an administrative tribunal within the PTO.

Once the Examining Attorney approves registration of the mark, whether on a first or subsequent review, the next stage is publication in the Trademark Official Gazette, a weekly publication of the PTO. Any other party then has 30 days to oppose the registration of the mark, or to request an extension of time to oppose.[10] If no opposition is filed, a registration is generally issued 12 weeks from the date the mark was published.[11] If an opposition is filed, an adversary 'interference' proceeding begins, culminating with a hearing by the Trademark Office.

4. Procedure for Customs Recordation of Trademarks

Once a Trademark is validly registered with the US Patent and Trademark Office, it can be recorded with US Customs. While registration with the Patent and Trademark office provides a right to sue infringers, this is often difficult when the infringers are located in foreign countries. The customs recordation procedures literally stop the infringing good at the border with US Customs acting to enforce the party's private trademark rights.

An application to record one or more trademarks must be made in writing addressed to the Intellectual Property Rights Branch of the US Customs Service in Washington, D.C., detailing the following information:

(i) The name, complete business address, and citizenship of the trademark owner or owners;[12]
(ii) The places of manufacture of goods bearing the recorded trademark;[13]
(iii) The name and principal business address of each foreign person or business entity authorized or licensed to use the trademark;[14] and
(iv) The identity of any parent or subsidiary company or other foreign company under common ownership or control which uses the trademark abroad.[15]

Pursuant to US Customs regulations on the recordation of trademarks, the application must be accompanied by a status copy (showing current ownership) of the certificate of registration certified by the US Patent and Trademark Office, and five

misdescriptive of the goods or services; is primarily geographically descriptive or deceptively misdescriptive of the goods or services of the applicant; or is primarily merely a surname.

10. An opposition is similar to a proceeding in the federal district courts, but is held before the Trademark Trial and Appeal Board.
11. On average, a mark will be registered within 13 months of the date the application for registration is filed.
12. 19 C.F.R. § 133.2(a) (1995).
13. 19 C.F.R. § 133.2(b) (1995).
14. 19 C.F.R. § 133.2(c) (1995).
15. 19 C.F.R. § 133.2(d) (1995).

copies of the trademark or copyright.[16] An application fee of USD 190 is required for each trademark to be recorded.[17]

The trademark recordation and protection becomes effective on the date an application for recordation is approved.[18] However, if there is a change in ownership of a recorded trademark, the new owner must re-apply by complying with the registration procedures outlined above, describing any time limit on the rights of ownership transferred,[19] submitting a status copy of the certificate of registration certified by the US Patent Office,[20] and paying a fee of USD 80.[21] If there is a change in the name of the owner of a recorded trademark, but no change in ownership, the owner is required to give written notice thereof to the Commissioner of Customs. This notice must be accompanied by a status copy of the certificate of registration certified by the US Patent and Trademark Office, showing title to be presently in the new name,[22] and a fee of USD 80.[23]

5. Copyrights

Only registered copyrights may be recorded with US Customs for protection against infringing imports. In general, copyright registration is a legal process which formalizes protection of a copyright. Registration, however, is not a requirement for protection. Under US law, publication of a work with a valid 'copyright notice' forms the basis of legal protection. This notice is generally the word 'copyright,' the author's name, and the date. However, the copyright law provides several inducements or advantages to encourage copyright owners to register their works. Among these advantages are the following:

(i) Registration establishes a public record of the copyright claim;
(ii) Registration is normally a prerequisite for filing of infringement suits;
(iii) If made before or within five years of publication, registration will establish *prima facie* evidence in court of the validity of the copyright and of the facts stated in the certificate; and
(iv) If registration is made within three months after publication of the work or prior to an infringement of the work, statutory damages and attorney's fees will be available to the copyright owner in court actions. Otherwise, only an award of actual damages and profits is available to the copyright owner.

---

16. 19 C.F.R. § 133.3(a) (1995).
17. 19 C.F.R. § 133.3(b) (1995). This was the fee in effect at the time this chapter was completed. All fees are subject to change and should be checked prior to filing.
18. 19 C.F.R. § 133.4(a) (1995).
19. *See* 19 C.F.R. § 133.5(b) (1995).
20. 19 C.F.R. § 133.5(c) (1995).
21. 19 C.F.R. § 133.5(d) (1995).
22. 19 C.P.R. § 133.5(d) (1995).
23. 19 C.P.R. § 133.6(a) (1995).

6. Procedure for Registration of Copyrights

To register a work, the following three items must be sent to the Register of Copyrights, in Washington, D.C.:

(i) A properly completed application form;
(ii) A nonrefundable filing fee for each application; and
(iii) A non-returnable deposit of the work being registered.[24]

Special deposit requirements exist for different types of work. In some instances, only one copy is required for published works, in other instances, only identifying material is required, and in still other instances, the deposit requirement may be unique.[25]

The following persons are legally entitled to submit an application form:

(i) The author;[26]
(ii) The copyright claimant;[27] and
(iii) The duly authorized agent of such author, other copyright claimant, or owner of exclusive right(s).[28]

> *PRACTICE NOTE:* Issues can arise as to who is the copyright owner if the creator of the work prepares the work as part of a job for which he is paid a salary.

7. Procedures for Recordation of Copyrights with the US Customs Service

The procedures for recordation of copyrights with US Customs are substantially the same as those for the recordation of trademarks discussed in Section C.4.

---

24. The deposit requirements vary in particular situations. If the work is unpublished, one complete copy or phonograph record is required. If the work was first published in the US on or after January 1, 1978, two complete copies or phonograph records of the best edition are required; if the work was first published in the US before January 1, 1978, two complete copies or phonograph records of the work as first published are required. 37 C.F.R. § 202.3 (1995).
25. For example, in the case of a published motion picture, only one copy of the work is required, but it must be accompanied by a separate written description of the work. In the case of works reproduced in three-dimensional copies, identifying material such as photographs or drawings is ordinarily required. Other examples of types of work having special deposit requirements include many works of the visual arts, such as greeting cards, toys, fabric, oversized material, video games and other machine-readable audiovisual works and contributions to collective works.
26. This is either the person who actually created the work or, if the work was made for hire, the employer or other person for whom the work was prepared. 37 C.F.R. § 202.3 (1995).
27. The copyright claimant is defined in Copyright Office Regulations as either the author of the work or a person or organization that has obtained ownership of all the rights under the copyright initially belonging to the author. 37 C.F.R. § 202.3 (1995).
28. Any person authorized to act on behalf of the author, other copyright claimant, or owner of exclusive right(s) may apply for registration. 37 C.F.R. § 202.3 (1995).

D. Gray Market and Parallel Goods

A gray market good is a foreign manufactured good bearing a valid US trademark that is imported for sale in the US without the authorization or consent of the US trademark holder.[29] Customs regulations permit importation of these gray market goods if the identical American and foreign trademarks are owned by the same or affiliated entities or if the American trademark owner has authorized the foreign entity's use of the trademark.[30] The regulations state that the general restrictions on importations bearing recorded trademarks do not apply when:

(i) Both the foreign and the US trademark or trade name are owned by the same person or business entity;[31]
(ii) The foreign and domestic trademark or trade name owners are parent and subsidiary companies or are otherwise subject to common ownership or control;[32] or
(iii) The articles of foreign manufacture bear a recorded trademark or trade name applied under authorization of the US owner.[33]

These gray market goods are said to be imported 'parallel' to goods imported by or with the permission of the trademark owner.[34]

These Customs regulations have given rise to protracted litigation in the US courts on the grounds that they go beyond the language of the statute they implement. The leading case is *Coalition to Preserve the Integrity of American Trademarks (COPIAT) v. United States.*[35] Plaintiffs, a trade association of US companies that own or are affiliated with the owners of American trademarks, and two of its members brought suit against the US in the US District Court for the District of Columbia seeking a declaration that Customs regulations permitting the importation of gray market goods into the US[36] were inconsistent with Section 42 of the Lanham Trademark Act of 1946,[37] as amended, and Section 526 of the Tariff Act of 1930.[38] Plaintiffs also sought an injunction prohibiting enforcement of the regulations and compelling enforcement of the express terms of the statutes.

The district court upheld the regulations as a reasonable interpretation of the governing statutes which was 'supported by the legislative history, judicial decisions, legislative acquiescence, and the long-standing consistent policy of the

29. *See K Mart Corp. v. Cartier, Inc.*, 486 U.S. 281 (1988).
30. *See* 19 C.F.R. § 133.21(c) (1995).
31. 19 C.F.R. § 133.21(c)(1) (1995).
32. 19 C.F.R. § 133.21(c)(2) (1995).
33. 19 C.F.R. § 133.21(c)(3) (1995).
34. *See Olympus Corp. v. United States*, 792 F.2d 315, 317 (2d Cir. 1986).
35. 598 F. Supp. 844 (D.D.C. (984)), *rev'd*, 790 F.2d 903 (D.C. Cir. 1986), *aff'd in part, rev'd in part, sub 110m. K Mart Corp. v. Cartier, Inc.*, 486 U.S. 281 (1988).
36. The regulation in question was 19 C.F.R. § 133.21(c) (1985).
37. *See* 15 U.S.C. § 1124 (1994).
38. *See* 19 U.S.C. § 1526 (1995).

Customs Service.'[39] However, the US Court of Appeals for the District of Columbia reversed and held that the Customs Service regulations violated Section 526 of the Tariff Act, which does not permit imports of any goods bearing registered US trademarks, except those trademarks which American owners have authorized to be used abroad.[40] Unlike the district court, the Court of Appeals found that deference to the interpretation by the agency of its governing statute was inappropriate where the language of the statute unambiguously expressed congressional intent on the matter at issue.[41] The Court of Appeals also held that Customs regulations were invalid because they did not constitute a reasonable interpretation of Section 526.[42] Reviewing the legislative history, the court concluded that Congress had intended Section 526 to confer 'an absolute, unqualified property right upon American companies that own registered trademarks.'[43]

The US Supreme Court reviewed the case and held the regulations valid in part as consistent with 19 U.S.C. § 1526 but invalid in part as violating the relevant statute.[44] A majority of the Court held that the 'same person' and 'common control' exceptions in Sections 133.21(c)(l) and 133.21(c)(2) were valid. They were held consistent with 19 U.S.C. § 1526 because Customs was enticed to interpret the statute as meaning that a foreign parent company 'owns' the US trademark of its domestic subsidiary, and that goods manufactured by a foreign subsidiary of a domestic company are not goods 'of foreign manufacture.'[45] A different majority of the Court, however, held that authorized use exception in 19 C.P.R. § 133.21(c)(3) was invalid because goods made in a foreign country by an independent foreign manufacturer could not reasonably be removed from the purview of 19 U.S.C. § 1526.[46]

The effect of the *COPIAT* decision is that 19 C.F.R. § 133.21(c)(3) is invalid. The rest of the regulations remain valid.

---

39. 598 F. Supp. at 852. The court reasoned that the construction of a statute by those charged with its execution should be followed unless there are compelling indications that it is wrong, especially when Congress has refused to alter the administrative construction. Under the circumstances, it concluded, Congress must be deemed to have approved the interpretation of and practice under Section 526 of the Tariff Act of 1930. *Id.* Shortly after the D.C. Circuit's decision in *COPIAT*, the US Court of Appeals for the Second Circuit decided that the Customs regulations, while unsound as a matter of policy, were not such a clear abuse of discretion that they should be considered unlawful. *See Olympus Corp. v. United States*, 792 F.2d 315 (2d Cir. 1986).
40. 790 F.2d 903 (D.C. Cir. 1986).
41. *Id.* at 914.
42. *Id.*
43. *Id.* at 910.
44. 486 U.S. 281 (1988).
45. 486 U.S. at 292–93.
46. *Id.* at 294.

Chapter 12
Antidumping

I. INTRODUCTION

The antidumping laws are international price discrimination measures 'designed to protect a domestic industry from sales of imported merchandise at less than fair value ('LTFV') which either causes or threatens to cause injury.'[1] Antidumping duties, designed to offset the LTFV sales, are imposed pursuant to Title 19, Section 1673 of the United States Code, and the relevant regulations.[2] This chapter will discuss the various legal issues which arise under the antidumping law, the roles played by the Commerce Department and the International Trade Commission in implementing the law, and the procedures for court review of antidumping orders.

II. DISCUSSION

A. Background Information

'Under the antidumping provisions ... if foreign merchandise is sold or is likely to be sold in the United States at less than its fair value, subjecting a US industry to material injury or a threat of material injury, an antidumping duty shall be imposed on such merchandise.'[3] There are two primary issues which arise in investigations under the antidumping law. The first issue is whether there has been a sale at less

---

1. *Badger-Powhatan, Div. of Figgie Int'l Inc. v. United States,* 608 F. Supp. 653, 656 (Ct. Int'l Trade 1985).
2. *See* 19 U.S.C. § 1673 (1995); 19 C.F.R. Part 353 (1995), as amended by 54 Fed. Reg. 12742, (1989).
3. *Consumer Prods. Div., SCM Corp. v. Silver Reed America, Inc.,* 753 F.2d 1033, 1035 (Fed. Cir. 1985).

than fair value. The second issue is whether there has been a material injury, or threat of material injury, to an industry in the US. If there is both an LTFV sale and a material injury (or a threat thereof) then 'there shall be imposed upon such merchandise an anti-dumping duty,' in an amount equal to the amount by which the foreign market value exceeds the United States price for the merchandise.[4] As will be discussed later, these two determinations are made by two separate US agencies. The International Trade Administration of the Commerce Department ('Commerce' or the ITA) determines whether there have been LTFV sales and the US International Trade Commission (the 'Commission' or the ITC) determines whether there is material injury, or threat thereof, caused by the LTFV sales.

B. Less than Fair Value

The concept of 'fair value' is not defined in the relevant statutes. However, Section 353.1 of Title 19 of the Code of Federal Regulations provides that 'fair value' is intended to be an estimate of foreign market value.[5] Therefore, one must look to the foreign market value to determine whether a sale in the US is at 'fair value.'

1. Foreign Market Value

Ordinarily, the foreign market value is determined by the price at which the merchandise in question is sold, or offered for sale,[6] in the principal markets of the country from which the merchandise is exported (home market sales).[7] If the merchandise is not sold in the exporting country or if it is sold in quantities which are too small to provide an adequate basis for comparison, such as when home market sales of a like or substantially similar product are less than 5 per cent of total sales, then the foreign market value may be determined in one of two alternative manners. First, the price may be determined by referring to the price at which similar merchandise is sold, or offered for sale, for exportation to countries other than the US (third market sales).[8] If no third market sales exist, the foreign market value

4. 19 U.S.C. § 1673 (1995).
5. 19 C.F.R. § 353.A2 (1995) *see also ICC Indus. v. United States,* 812 F.2d 694, 697 (Fed. Cir. 1987).
6. In determining foreign market value, offers generally will be considered only in the absence of sales. An offer, the acceptance of which is not reasonably expected, shall not be deemed an offer. 19 C.F.R. § 353.7, § 353.43 (1995).
7. 19 U.S.C. § 1677b(a) (1995). Section 1677b provides in pertinent part: 'The foreign market value of imported merchandise shall be the price at the time such merchandise is first sold in the United States at which *such* or similar *merchandise is sold or,* in the absence of sales, *offered for sale* in the principal markets of the country from which exported, in *usual commercial quantities* and in the *ordinary course of trade* for home consumption.' (emphasis added). The terms 'such or similar merchandise ... sold or, in the absence of sales, offered for sale,' 'usual commercial quantities,' and 'ordinary course of trade' all have specific definitions established by statute. *See* 19 U.S.C. § 1677 (1995).
8. 19 U.S.C. § 1677 (1995). *See also* 19 C.F.R. § 353.48 (1995).

will be determined by reference to the 'constructed value' of the product.[9] The concept of constructed value is somewhat akin to the concept of computed value used for Customs valuation purposes and discussed in the chapter on Customs valuation (Chapter 5).

In determining the foreign market value of merchandise, allowances can be made for price discounts in the US resulting from differences in quantities sold, differences in the circumstances of the sales, and differences in the physical characteristics of the merchandise.[10] If, after allowances for these variances in price, the prices of the sales of the merchandise vary, the determination of foreign market value normally will be based upon the weighted average of the sales prices of all merchandise used to determine foreign market value.[11] Also, in certain circumstances, the price at which merchandise is sold or offered for sale between related parties may be used to determine foreign market value.[12]

If there is no home market or third country market which can provide an adequate basis for comparison, then the foreign market value must be determined by referring to the constructed value of the merchandise. The constructed value is the sum of the costs of materials and fabrication of the merchandise, including costs of packing the goods ready for shipment, plus any expenses and profit 'usually reflected in sales of merchandise of the same general class of kind.'[13] Under Department of Commerce regulations, the constructed value can be increased by including certain predetermined amounts for profit and general administrative costs.[14] If the company records do not reflect at least these amounts, they will be applied by the ITA in its calculations. For example, if profits are less than 8 per cent, an 8 per cent profit will be assumed for purposes of the constructed value calculation.[15]

Non-market economies create certain difficulties in determining foreign market value. The price at which goods are sold is determined by the state rather than by the market. Section 1316 of the Omnibus Trade and Competitiveness Act of 1988 provides that the foreign market value of products exported from non-market countries will be determined under subsection (a) of Section 1677(b) as are the foreign market value of products from market countries when the 'administering authority finds that available information does not permit the foreign market value of the merchandise to be determined under subsection (a).'[16] If the foreign market value is not to be determined under subsection (a), then the 'administering authority' can determine the foreign market value in one of two ways: first, on the basis of the value of the various factors of production, plus general expenses, and

---

9. 19 C.F.R. 353.48 (1995).
10. 19 U.S.C. § 1677b(a)(1)(C), (B), (e) (1995); 19 C.F.R. §§ 353.55–.57.
11. 19 C.F.R. § 353.44(a).
12. 19 C.F.R. § 353.45(b).
13. 19 U.S.C. § 1677b(e) (1995); 19 C.F.R. § 53.50.
14. 19 C.F.R. §§ 353.50(a)(2).
15. *Id.*
16. The Omnibus Trade and Competitiveness Act of 1988, Pub. L. No. 100-A18, 102 Stat. 1186.

an amount representing profit[17] second, if the best information available is 'inadequate for determination of foreign market value,' the foreign market value may be determined on the basis of the price at which comparable merchandise is sold in one or more market economy countries.[18]

PRACTICE NOTE: This is referred to as use of surrogate country data.

All parties to the case are given an opportunity to comment on the most appropriate surrogate country and to submit surrogate country data. This amendment changed the prior practice by allowing the International Trade Administration (ITA) to determine the foreign market value pursuant to Section 1677b(a). Prior to the amendment, the ITA could not determine the foreign market value pursuant to this section, but instead was required 'to use either the prices or constructed value of such or similar merchandise in a nonstate-controlled-economy country.'[19]

2. The US Price

Once the 'fair value' of the merchandise in question is established by determining the foreign market value of the goods; the ITA must determine the US price of the merchandise in question. In general the term the 'US price' refers to the purchase price, or the exporter's sales price, of the merchandise, whichever is appropriate.[20] The 'purchase price' is the price 'at which the merchandise under investigation is purchased, or agreed to be purchased, prior to the date of importation from the manufacturer or producer of the merchandise for exportation to the United States.'[21] The purchase price is the proper basis of comparison where 'all shipments' of the product in question 'were sold to unrelated purchasers in the United States prior to the date of exportation.'[22] These would normally be direct sales to unrelated customers, not involving brokers. The 'exporter's sales price' is the price 'at which merchandise is sold or agreed to be sold in the United States, before or after the time of importation, by or for the account of the exporter.'[23] The exporter's sale price is used where the importer is related to the exporter and the transaction between the exporter and the importer is not an arm's length transaction. The exporter's sales price is the resale price from a related importer to the first unrelated purchaser or 'the price at which the goods are eventually transferred in an arm's length transaction, whether from the importer to an independent retailer

17. *Id.*
18. *Id.*
19. *In re Porcelain-on-Steel Cooking Ware from China,* 9 I.T.R.D. (BNA) 1244, 1247 (I.T.A. 1986).
20. 19 U.S.C. § 1677a(a) (1995); 19 C.F.R § 353.41(a) (1995).
21. 19 C.F.R. § 353.41(b).
22. *Certain Carbon Steel Plate From Poland,* 2 I.T.R.D. (BNA) 5318, 5319 (1979).
23. 19 U.S.C. § 16772(a).

or directly to the public.'[24] Exporter's sales price is also generally used in consignment sale situations.

In determining the US price, the purchase price or the exporter's sales price may be increased or decreased by certain factors.[25] The purchase price or the exporter's sales price may be increased by costs incidental to placing the merchandise in the US market, such as the cost of containers, or coverings and the amount of any duties or taxes imposed on the merchandise by reason of its exportation to the US.[26] The purchase price may be reduced by the costs described above, if included in the purchase price or the exporter's sales price, by any expenses, such as commissions, incurred by the exporter in selling substantially identical merchandise in the US, and by the value added by any manufacture or assembly operation performed in the US.[27] There are other adjustments, discussed below, which may be made when comparing the US price with the foreign market value.

3. Computation of the Dumping Margin

Once both the US price and the foreign market value of the merchandise have been determined, the two prices are compared to determine if a LTFV sale exists. The dumping margin is 'the amount by which the foreign market value of the merchandise exceeds the US price of the merchandise.'[28] In comparing the US price and the foreign market value of the merchandise, adjustments may be made to account for differences in quantities.[29]

Price adjustments will also be made for differences in circumstances of the sales if it is established to the satisfaction of the Secretary of Commerce that the amount of any price differential is wholly or partly due to such difference.[30] There are a multitude of cases dealing with adjustments due to differences in circumstances of the sales. Where commissions are paid in one market and not in the other market that is under consideration, then 'a reasonable allowance for selling expenses will be made.'[31] Advertising expenses may be the basis for adjustment where they 'are undertaken on behalf of the ultimate customer.'[32] Credit expenses directly related to sales made during the period under investigation may also be a basis for adjustment.[33] Technical services provided may be the basis of adjustment

---

24. *Smith Corona Group v. United States,* 4I.T.R.D. (BNA) 2297, 2300 *(Fed.* Cir. 1983).
25. 19 U.S.C. § 1677a(c)–(d) (1995); 19 C.F.R. 353.41(d)&(e).
26. *Id.*
27. *Id.*
28. 19 C.F.R. § 353.2(1)(1) (1995).
29. *Brass Sheet and Strip from Sweden,* 9 I.T.R.D. (BNA) 1879, 1883 (1987) (Quantity discounts are the basis for adjustments where specifically attributable to the production of the different quantities involved and the discounts are verified).
30. 19 C.F.R. § 353.56 (1995).
31. *Porcelain-on-Steel Cooking Ware from Taiwan,* 9 I.T.R.D. (BNA) 1303, 1313 (1987).
32. *Brass Sheet and Strip from Korea,* 9 I.T.R.D. (BNA) 1611, 1615, (1987).
33. *Carbon Steel Butt-Weld Pipe Fittings from Japan,* 9 I.T.R.D. (BNA) 1713, 1716 (1986) (Practice of borrowing dollars in order to earn additional yen during a period of currency adjustment is not directly related to sales of butt-weld pipe fittings).

where technical services are part of the terms of the sale and are not 'general sales promotion.'[34] Finally, after-the-sale warehousing costs which are directly related to particular sales are also a basis for adjustment. Simply maintaining inventory is not.[35] Other differences in sales which may be the basis of adjustment include guarantees, servicing, royalties, warranties and freight.

Price adjustments will be made for differences in the physical characteristics of the merchandise being compared, if it is established to the satisfaction of the Secretary of Commerce that the amount of any price differential is wholly or partly due to such differences.[36] This adjustment will take into account 'differences in material, differences in variable manufacturing costs, and differences in the weight' of the merchandise being compared.[37]

The comparisons of the US price and the foreign market value are to be made at the same levels of trade.[38] If there are differences in prices of the merchandise being compared resulting from the fact that they are sold in different markets at different levels of trade (e.g., wholesale in one market and retail in another), then the Commerce Department may make an adjustment.[39] To establish eligibility for this adjustment, the party must prove that the differences in the levels of trade affect the comparability of the US price and the foreign market value.[40] The purpose of all of these adjustments is to ensure that the price comparison will not be distorted.

If, upon comparing the US price and the foreign market value after any adjustments, Commerce determines that there have been LTFV sales, an antidumping duty will be imposed 'in an amount equal to' the dumping margin if the US International Trade Commission finds there has been injury to a domestic industry.[41]

C. Injury Requirement

In all antidumping cases, the US International Trade Commission must make a determination that an industry in the US has been materially injured, threatened with material injury, or that the establishment of this industry has been materially retarded 'by reason of imports' of the products in question before antidumping duties can be assessed. There is a causation element in the injury determination. 'Absent a finding of a causal link between injury and imports, the Commission

34. *Id.* at 1717.
35. *Malleable Cast Iron Pipe Fittings from Brazil,* 8 I.T.R.D. (BNA) 2101, 2105, (1986) (Maintaining an inventory is a general cost of doing business and, therefore is not considered directly related to particular sales).
36. 19 C.F.R. § 353.57 (1995).
37. *Certain Forged Steel Crankshafts from West Germany,* 9 I.T.R.D. (BNA) 2646, 2655 (1987).
38. 19 C.F.R. § 353.58 (1995).
39. *See Hercules, Inc. v. United States,* 9 I.T.R.D. (BNA) 1473 (Ct. Int'l Trade 1987).
40. *Certain Tapered Journal Roller Bearings from Italy,* 6 I.T.R.D. (BNA) 1092, 1096 (1984).
41. 19 U.S.C. § 1673 (1995).

is unable to provide the domestic industry with relief.'[42] The injury to the industry in the US must be 'by reason of imports or sales for importation of the merchandise with respect to which the administering authority has made an affirmative determination ... '[43] Thus, there must not only be a material injury, but also the product in question must have been a cause of that injury. Also, with the passing of the new GATT/WTO another factor has been added in determining injury. Now the size of the margin of dumping is considered when determining if dumping causes injury.

1. Material Injury

Material injury is 'harm which is not inconsequential, immaterial, or unimportant.'[44] Section 1677 also provides a list of factors which the Commission should consider when making an injury determination.[45]

One of the factors to be considered by the Commission in its injury determination is the volume and impact of the imported products. An amendment to this section in 1984 requires the Commission to 'cumulatively assess the volume and effect of imports from two or more countries ... if such imports compete with each other and with like products of the domestic industry in the United States market.'[46] This policy is referred to as 'cumulation' and means that even if imports from one country are so small that on their own they would not cause injury, they can be a source of material injury when combined or 'cumulated' with imports from other countries also alleged to be engaged in dumping. Prior to this amendment, the Commission frequently cumulated imports when it determined on a case-by-case basis that it was warranted, but it was not required to do so.[47] The amendment made cumulation mandatory where 'marketing of the goods in question into the United States is reasonably coincident, and there is a reasonable indication that the imports in question will have a contributing effect in causing, or threatening to cause, material injury to the domestic industry.'[48]

---

42. *Gilford-Hill Cement Co. v. United States,* 615 F. Supp. 577, 579 (Ct. Int'l Trade 1985).
43. 19 U.S.C. § 1673d(b)(1) (1995).
44. 19 U.S.C. § 1677(7)(A) (1995).
45. *See* 19 U.S.C. § 1677(7) (B)–(E) (1995). Section 1328 of the Omnibus Trade and Competitiveness Act of 1988 amends subparagraphs (B) and (C) of this section. Omnibus Trade and Competitiveness Act of 1988. Pub. L. No. 100-418, 102 Stat. 1204. This amendment is designed to clarify 'that the ITC is required, in every case to consider and explain its analysis of each of the three specified factors.' H.R. Conf. Rep. No. 100-576, 100th Cong., 2d Sess. 616, *reprinted in* 1988 U.S. Code Congo & Admin. News 1547, 1649 (1988). Also, the Commission 'may consider, on a case-by-case basis, such other economic factors as are relevant to an injury determination.' *Id.* (1995).
46. 19 U.S.C. § 1677(7)(G).
47. H.R. Rep. No. 98-725. 98th Cong., 2d Sess. 36, *reprinted in* 1984 U.S. Code Cong. & Admin. News 5127, 5163 (1984).
48. *Id.*

2. Threat of Material Injury

The injury requirement may also be satisfied by a threat of material injury.[49] Although there is no specific definition of threat of material injury, Section 1677(7)(F) establishes the relevant economic factors which are to be considered by the Commission.[50] A threat of material injury can be sufficient to satisfy the injury requirement if it is an immediate threat, but mere potential injury may not be sufficient. For example, in *Portland Hydraulic Cement from Colombia, France, Greece,*[51] the Commission found there was no threat of injury where the domestic industry was presently enjoying high levels of profitability and where any 'anticipated downturn in the business cycle' was not so 'imminent as to leave the industry vulnerable in the foreseeable future to a possible increase in imports.'[52] In another example, *Philipp Brothers, Inc. v. United States,* [53] the Court of International Trade upheld the Commission's finding of a threat of material injury where 'prices remained in decline for sponge delivered in the first half of 1984, future domestic sales to the stockpile were threatened, and ITI [Internor Trade, Inc.] was discouraged from making capital investment[s].'[54]

Section 1330 of the Omnibus Trade and Competitiveness Act of 1988, authorizes the Commission to cumulate where the imports 'compete with each other, and with like products of the domestic industry, in the United States market,' and are subject to any antidumping or countervailing duty investigation. [55] However, unlike material injury cases, cumulation in threat of material injury cases is discretionary. The Commission may cumulate if the above criteria are met but is not required to.[56] The WTO also authorizes the use of cumulative analysis (Article II of GATT 1994).

D. The Procedural Roles of the Department of Commerce and the International Trade Commission

Responsibility for the determinations under the antidumping law is shared between the Department of Commerce and the United States International Trade Commission. Section 1673 of Title 19 of the United States Code requires Commerce to determine whether 'a class or kind of foreign merchandise is being, or is likely

49. 19 U.S.C. § 1671(a)(2) (1995).
50. 19 U.S.C. § 1677(7)(F) (1995).
51. 9 I.T.R.D. (BNA) 1662, 1672 (1987).
52. *Id.*
53. 8 I.T.R.D. (BNA) 1022 (Ct. Int'l Trade 1986).
54. *Id.* at 1026.
55. Omnibus Trade and Competitiveness Act of 1988, Pub. L. No. 100-418, 102 Stat. 1207.
56. H.R. Conf. Rep. No. 100-576, 100th Cong., 2d Sess. 620, *reprinted in* 1988 U.S. Code Cong. & Admin. News 1547, 1653 (1988).

to be, sold in the US at less than its fair value,' and the Commission to determine whether there has been material injury.[57]

Investigations regarding antidumping duties are usually instituted through a petition filed by a producer in the US under the procedures established in the International Trade Administration, Department of Commerce Regulations.[58] A petition must be filed simultaneously with Commerce and the Commission.[59] Article 58 of the Antidumping Agreement 1994 establishes that National Authorities terminate an investigation if the authorities satisfy themselves that the margin of dumping is *de minimus.*

1. The Department of Commerce

Upon receiving the petition, Commerce must, within 20 days, determine the sufficiency of the petition.[60] The petition must contain sufficient information to support the allegations, and the petitioner must have standing to bring the claim.[61] The International Trade Administration regulations also contain more specific requirements for the contents of the petition.[62]

If the petition is sufficient Commerce must initiate an investigation, otherwise the proceeding is terminated.[63] Commerce must give notice of its sufficiency determination to the Commission and publish notice of the determination in the *Federal Register.*[64]

If the petition is sufficient, Commerce must then institute a formal investigation, in which Commerce will seek information necessary to make preliminary and final determinations.[65] Commerce obtains this information by issuing pricing questionnaires to foreign exporters. 'Ordinarily the Secretary will require a foreign manufacturer, producer, or exporter subject to the investigation to submit pricing information covering a period of at least 150 days prior to, and 30 days

57. 19 U.S.C. § 1673(1)–(2) (1995).
58. *See* 19 U.S.C. § 1673a(b) (1995); 19 C.F.R. § 353.12 (1995).
59. 19 U.S.C. § 1673a(b)(2) (1995); 19 C.F.R. § 3.12(c) (1995).
60. 19 C.F.R. § 353.13 (1995).
61. 19 U.S.C. § 1673a(b)(1); 19 C.F.R. § 353.12(a) (1995). To have standing, the petitioner must be an interested party filing the petition on behalf of an industry in the U.S. 19 U.S.C. § 1673a(b). In *Gilmore Steel Corp. v. United States,* 585 F. Supp. 670, 677 (Ct. Int'l Trade 1984), the court affirmed Commerce in dismissing a petition because it was not 'brought on behalf of the national steel plate industry.' The court interpreted section 1673a(b) as providing a two-step standing analysis. *Gilmore Steel,* 585 F. Supp at 676. First, the petitioner must be an interested party, 'a member of the affected industry.' *Id.* Second, the petition must be brought on behalf of an industry – a majority of the industry must back the claim. *Id.* Commerce has interpreted this standard loosely, rarely challenging standing. A petition is accepted on its face unless standing is challenged by other US producers. *See also* 54 Fed. Reg. 12,746 (1989), where the Commerce Department reaffirmed its position on this issue.
62. *See* 19 C.F.R. § 353.12.
63. 19 U.S.C. § 1673a(c)(3) (1995); 19 C.F.R. § 353.13(c) (1995).
64. 19 U.S.C. § 1673a(c)(2), (d) (1995); 19 C.F.R. § 353.13(d) (1995).
65. 19 C.F.R. § 353.15 (1995).

after, the first day of the month during which the petition was received.'[66] The information must be submitted in the form prescribed in the regulations.[67] Generally, the questionnaires cover a one-year period. These questionnaires are detailed and complex. Data on individual sales transactions must be submitted on computer tape. This adds to the complexity and cost of a response and is particularly difficult for the smaller companies.

Within 75 days of the institution of the investigation, the responses to the questionnaires are reviewed by Commerce.[68]

Within 140 days of the filing of the petition, Commerce must make a preliminary determination 'based upon the information available to it at the time of the determination, of whether there is a reasonable basis to believe or suspect that the merchandise is being sold, or is likely to be sold, at less than fair value.'[69] If Commerce determines that the case is 'extraordinarily complicated,' then the determination must be made within 210 days.[70] Notice of the determinations must be given to the parties, the Commission, and be published in the *Federal Register.*[71]

Within 75 days of an affirmative preliminary determination, Commerce must issue a final determination of the LTFV sale issue.[72] The information upon which Commerce will make its final determination generally must be verified.[73] The methods and procedures followed in verifications are set out in 19 C.F.R. § 353.36. Generally, the verification involves a visit by Commerce Department personnel to the exporter's office in the country of exportation to review records and documentation used to prepare the questionnaire response. If, after an opportunity to correct inadequate information, the information cannot be satisfactorily verified, Commerce will base its final determination on the 'best information available.'[74] 'Best information available,' however, may often be interpreted by Commerce as the information submitted by petitioner in the petition, or the highest rate reserved by another company that was verified.

All parties have an opportunity to present their views, both[75] orally and in writing, before the final determination. Any written submissions must be filed

---

66. 19 C.F.R. § 353.31 (1995).
67. *Id.*
68. (Supp. 1995).
69. 19 U.S.C. § 1673b(l)(A) (1995); 19 C.P.R. § 353.15 (1995).
70. 19 U.S.C. § 1673b(c); 19 C.F.R. § 353.15(b) (1995). If the preliminary determination is affirmative, then the liquidation of all entries of the merchandise in question is suspended by Customs (i.e., final duties are not assessed or paid). Estimated dumping duties must be posted to cover the antidumping margin and Commerce makes all relevant information available to the Commission. 19 U.S.C. § 1677b(d). If the preliminary determination is negative, there is no suspension of liquidation, but the case still proceeds.
71. 19 U.S.C. § 1673b(f) (1995).
72. 19 U.S.C § 1673d(a) (1995); 19 C.F.R. § 353.20(a) (1995).
73. 19 U.S.C. § 1677e(d) (Supp. 1995); 19 C.F.R. § 3.36(a) (1995).
74. 19 U.S.C. § 1677e(c) (Supp. 1995); 19 C.F.R. § 353.37(a) (1995), also known as 'Facts Available.'
75. 19 C.F.R. §§ 353.38 (1995).

in accordance with the regulations.[76] Upon request from any party, there may be a hearing before a designated official.[77] The hearing is not conducted according to the Administrative Procedures Act and does not provide for cross-examination of opposing witnesses.

If the final determination is negative, the antidumping case is terminated. If the final determination is affirmative, and if the Commission too makes an affirmative final determination, then an antidumping order is issued within seven days of receipt by Commerce of the Commission's decision.[78] Commerce transmits the information to US Customs which determines the duty and enforces collection.

2. The International Trade Commission

As noted above, an antidumping petition is filed simultaneously with the Commission and the Commerce Department. Upon receiving notice from Commerce that the petition is sufficient, the Commission begins its investigation with regard to the material injury requirement.

Within 45 days of receiving notice from Commerce, the Commission must make a preliminary determination of material injury.[79] Notice of the determination must be given to the parties, to Commerce, and be published in the *Federal Register*.[80]

In the preliminary injury determination, the Commission must determine 'whether there is a reasonable indication' of an injury to the US industry caused by the product in question. There has been some disagreement in the courts as to the appropriate standard to be applied by the Commission in making the preliminary determination. However, the Court of Appeals for the Federal Circuit has held that the 'reasonable indication' standard requires that the Commission issue a negative determination 'only when (1) the record as a whole contains clear and convincing evidence that there is no material injury or threat of such injury; and (2) no likelihood exists that contrary evidence will arise in a final investigation.'[81] Thus, the preliminary injury standard is not as high as is required for the final injury determination. If the preliminary determination is negative, the investigation is to be terminated.[82] If the preliminary injury determination is affirmative, the Commission must proceed with the final injury investigation, and Commerce proceeds with its parallel investigation of LTFV sales.

---

76. 19 C.F.R. § 353.38 (1995).
77. 19 C.F.R. § 353.38 (1995).
78. *See* 19 U.S.C § 1673d(c) (1995); 19 C.F.R. § 353.21 (1995).
79. 19 U.S.C § 1673b(a) (1995).
80. 19 U.S.C § 1673b(f) (1995).
81. *American Lamb Co. v. United States,* 785 F.2d 994.1001 (Fed. Cir. 1986).
82. 19 U.S.C. § 1673b(a) (Supp. 1995).

The Commission must also issue a final injury determination. Notice of the determinations must be given to the parties, to Commerce, and be published in the *Federal Register*.[83]

E. Annual Administrative Reviews of Antidumping Duty Orders

Section 1675(a) provides that Commerce may review an antidumping duty order at least once every 12 months after the first year of the order's publication.[84] Commerce will review 'the amount of any antidumping duty ... and review the current status of, and compliance with, any agreement by reason of which an investigation was suspended.'[85] The review is triggered by a request from any interested party and will normally cover 'entries, exports or sales of merchandise during the 12 months preceding the most recent anniversary month.'[86] The review actually determines the duty to be paid on liquidation of entries during the original period of investigation. An exporter may receive a refund, with interest, of the estimated duties paid, or may owe additional duties. Thus, even if an exporter receives a high antidumping duty in the original investigation, the amount he pays is actually only an estimated deposit that can be refunded with interest if the rate determined in the annual review is lower.

The procedures Commerce must follow in an administrative review parallel those followed in the investigation. Upon receiving a timely request, notice of the review must be issued,[87] questionnaires requesting information for the review are sent to all interested parties, and then a preliminary determination is made.[88] In administrative reviews, verification of the information is not always required. If Commerce does verify the information, it usually does so before the preliminary determination. The preliminary results must be published in the *Federal Register*.[89] Commerce is then authorized either to order Customs to assess any antidumping duties or to collect a cash deposit of any estimated duties for future importations.[90]

---

83. 19 U.S.C. § 1673d(d) (1988 Supp. 1995).
84. If there *is* no request for an administrative review, the Customs Service will assess antidumping duties on the merchandise ... at rates equal to the cash deposit of or bond for estimated antidumping duties required on that merchandise. 19 C.F.R. § 353.22(e) (1995).
85. 19 U.S.C. § 1675(a)(1)(B)–(C).
86. 19 C.F.R. § 353.22(b)(1).
87. 19 C.F.R. § 353.22(c)(1) (1995).
88. 19 C.F.R. § 353.22(c)(2) (1995).
89. 19 C.F.R. § 353.22(c)(5) (1995).
90. 19 U.S.C. § 1675(a) (Supp. 1995); 19 C.F.R. § 353.22(c)(10) (1995).

F. Sunset Review

The Antidumping Agreement of 1994 (Article VI of GATT 1994) added a new procedural rule to be applied by Commerce and the Commission in conducting five year reviews also known as Sunset Reviews.

This review of injury is required each five years after an anti-dumping order is issued.[91] If the review is not performed or if the review shows that injurious dumping would not persist if the order were lifted, the antidumping order will be terminated.[92]

G. Continued Dumping and Subsidy Offset Act

In October 28, 2000, Congress passed the Continued Dumping and Subsidy Offset Act ('CDSOA'), also called the Byrd Amendment named after its sponsor Senator Robert Byrd of West Virginia, which amended the Tariff Act of 1930 to provide for a system whereby US CBP will annually distribute after liquidation, duties assessed pursuant to an countervailing duty order, an antidumping order, or a finding under the US Antidumping Act of 1921 to (certified) domestic producers which supported the petition for the countervailing duty order, the antidumping order, or the finding under the US Antidumping Act of 1921. There is no statutory or regulatory requirement as to how to spend a disbursement. CDSOA disbursements to 'affected domestic producers' made as of December 2006 totaled over USD379 million.

The antidumping and countervailing duties eligible for disbursement are those assessed on or after October 1, 2000 pursuant to antidumping and countervailing duty orders in effect on or after January 1, 1999. The distribution is available to 'affected domestic producers for qualifying expenditures.' An 'affected domestic producer' is defined as a manufacturer, producer, farmer, rancher, or worker representative (including associations of such persons) that (1) was a petitioner or interested party in support of a petition and (2) remains in operation. Producers that have ceased production of the product covered by the order or that have acquired by a firm that opposed the petition will not be considered an affected domestic producer.

Under the CDSOA, the CBP is statutorily charged with the duty of the annual distribution of antidumping and countervailing duties assessed during the preceding fiscal year. The ITC's only role is to forward to CBP a list of potentially eligible 'affected domestic producers' that publicly indicated support for the petition through a response to an ITC questionnaire or by letter submitted to the ITC during the investigation. Potentially eligible affected domestic producers submit to CBP certifications of eligibility and desire to receive a portion of the disbursement. The disbursement-seeking producers must identify 'qualifying expenditures' incurred

---

91. Article 11.3 of Antidumping Agreement of 1994 (Article VI of GATT 1994).
92. *Id.*

since the issuance of the order. CBP distributes the disbursement according to the percentage of a party's qualifying expenditures to all such qualifying expenditures claimed by certifying parties.

On July 12, 2001, Australia, Brazil, Chile, India, Indonesia, Japan, Korea, Thailand and the European Communities requested that a WTO dispute settlement panel be established to examine the WTO-consistency of the CDSOA. A similar request was made by Canada and Mexico on August 10, 2001. The complaining parties argued that the CDSOA violated Article 18.1 of the GATT Antidumping Agreement (the 'AD Agreement') and 32.1 of the Agreement on Subsidies and Countervailing Measures (the 'SCM Agreement') by being a specific action against dumping or subsidies because there was an actual and unavoidable connection between the determinations of a duty and the offset payments and that the reimbursement program adversely affected the competitive relationship of dumped/subsidized goods with domestic producers. Furthermore, the complaining parties argued that the CDSOA violated Article 5.4 of the AD Agreement and 11.4 of the SCM Agreement by providing a financial incentive for domestic producers to file or support applications of antidumping or countervailing duty investigations because offset payments are made only to producers that file or support investigations. The WTO dispute settlement panel affirmed on appeal its decision in favor of the complaining parties and ordered the United States to bring the CDSOA in conformity with the Panel's interpretation of the AD and SCM Agreement provisions.

In 2006, Congress repealed the CDSOA, but permitted distribution of collected antidumping duties through October 1, 2007.[93] Because distribution continued through 2007, the complaining parties of 2001 at the WTO insisted that the repeal did not satisfy the WTO decision and requested status reports until full compliance was achieved.

93. Repeal of Continued Dumping and Subsidy Offset, Pub. L. No. 109-171, § 7601, 120 Stat. 154 (2006).

Chapter 13
Countervailing Duties

I. INTRODUCTION

A countervailing duty is an additional duty imposed on goods imported to the US, designed to offset any subsidy in the manufacture, production or export of the article. 'The fundamental purpose of the countervailing duty law is to provide a special duty to eliminate the advantage an imported product may obtain from forms of assistance termed "subsidies."'[1] The imposition of countervailing duties is controlled by Title 19 Section 1671, of the United States Code and the relevant Customs Regulations.[2] Proposed revisions to the regulations pertaining to continuous duties were issued on May 31, 1989.[3]

This chapter will discuss the various legal issues which arise under the countervailing duty laws, the roles played by the Commerce Department and the International Trade Commission in enforcing the laws and the procedures for review of countervailing duty orders.

II. DISCUSSION

A. Background Information

There are two basic types of countervailing duty cases: those in which an injury determination must be made before the countervailing duties can be assessed and those in which no injury determination must be made.

---

1. *Bethlehem Steel Corp. v. United States,* 590 F. Supp. 1237, 1241 (Ct. Int'l Trade 1984).
2. *See* 19 U.S.C. § 1671 (2004); 19 C.F.R. Part 351 (2006), as amended.
3. 54 Fed. Reg. 23, 366.

1. Cases in Which an Injury Determination Must be Made

Injury determinations must be made in all cases brought under Section 1671 unless the goods against which the duty is sought are imported 'from a country which is not a Subsidies Agreement country.'[4]

In these cases, the International Trade Commission ('Commission') is required to determine that 'an industry in the United States is materially injured, or is threatened with material injury, or the establishment of an industry in the United States is materially retarded, by reason of imports of that merchandise or by reason of sales (or the likelihood of sales) of that merchandise for importation' as a prerequisite to the imposition of countervailing duties.[5]

Section 1671 defines the term 'Subsidies Agreement Country.'[6] A Subsidies Agreement Country, for the purposes of this section, is a WTO member country, a country that has 'assumed obligations . . . which are substantially equivalent to the obligations under the Subsidies Agreement,' or a country which, under an agreement in force prior to December 8, 1994, requires most-favored-nation treatment with respect to articles imported into the United States. Thus, countries that are not WTO member countries but which have assumed obligations substantially similar to the code can also receive the benefits of an injury test.[7]

2. Cases in Which No Injury Determination is Required

As noted above, there are certain countervailing duty cases which do not require an injury determination. In the *Cementos Anahuac* case, Mexico had been recognized by the US Trade Representative (USTR) on April 30, 1985 as having 'assumed obligations . . . substantially equivalent to obligations under the Agreement,' bringing Mexico within the meaning of 'under the Agreement' for purposes of Section 1671.[8] Plaintiffs asserted that countervailing duties, therefore, could not be imposed upon imports of Portland hydraulic cement made in 1984 without an injury finding in the Section 751 review.[9] The court held that merchandise that had entered into the US before the agreement was not entitled to an injury determination before the assessment of countervailing duties.[10] However, as to entries after April 1985, the Commerce Department and USTR took the position that Mexico was entitled to an injury determination, and countervailing duties were revoked.

---

4. 19 U.S.C. § 1671(c) (2004).
5. 19 U.S.C. § 1671(a)(2) (2004).
6. 19 U.S.C. § 1671(b) (2004).
7. For example, in April 1985, Mexico entered into an 'Understanding' with the US on subsidies, and thus became eligible for an injury determination under Section 1671.
8. *Cementos Anahuac del Golfo, S.A. v. United States,* 10 I.T.R.D. (B.N.A.) 1586, 1598 (Ct. Int'l Trade 1988).
9. *Id.* at 1598.
10. *Id.* at 1603.

B. 'Subsidy' and 'Bounty or Grant'

Not every type of government grant or subsidy is countervailable. For example, generalized infrastructure benefits such as national defense, education, highways and utilities are not countervailable duties, even though they provide benefits that industries derive.[11] Therefore, a determination must be made as to what forms of government assistance are legally 'subsidies' and, therefore, countervailable. Section 1677 provides a list of benefits which are considered to be 'subsidies;' however, the list is merely illustrative and is not a comprehensive statement of all the benefits which may be countervailable.[12] This section has been amended by the Omnibus Trade and Competitiveness Act of 1988.

1. Determining What Types of Governmental Assistance Constitute a Subsidy

Direct payments to exporters in the form of grants or tax rebates and low interest loans or other types of assistance directly designed to stimulate exports are considered export subsidies and are almost always countervailable. Greater problems arise with so called 'domestic' subsidies that are not related to export promotion. Further definitions of export and domestic subsidies are contained in the proposed rules promulgated by the US Department of Commerce on May 31, 1989.[13]

The Department of Commerce, in the past, has applied a 'general availability test' to determine which forms of domestic subsidies are illegal for purposes of the countervailing duty laws. If the benefits are available to all companies and industries in a particular country then they are generally not countervailable.[14]

In *Cabot Corp.*, the Court of International Trade remanded the issue of whether certain loans by the Mexican government, and the sale of 'carbon black feedstock and natural gas at government set rates, constitute[s] a bounty or grant' for countervailing duty proposes.[15] The court held that the determination of whether a benefit constitutes a subsidy requires "focusing only on whether a benefit or "competitive advantage" has been actually conferred on "a specific enterprise or industry, or group of enterprises or industries." '[16] Thus, to determine whether a benefit is a subsidy, the Commerce Department should perform a two-part analysis: first it should determine whether there has been a benefit bestowed upon a specific class, and second, it should determine whether this benefit amounts to a competitive advantage.[17]

---

11. *Cabot Corp. v. United States,* 620 F. Supp. 722, 73 L (Ct. Int'l Trade 1985), *appeal dismissed,* 788 F.2d 1539 (Fed. Cir. 1986).
12. 19 U.S.C. § 1677(5) (2004).
13. 54 Fed. Reg. 23379.
14. *See Cabot Corp.,* 620 F. Supp. at 731.
15. *Id.* at 734.
16. *Id.* at 732.
17. *Id.* at 729.

In *Georgetown Steel Corp. v. United States,*[18] the Soviet Union and the German Democratic Republic had granted favorable exchange rates on sales of steel wire and potash that were below the official rate. The court analyzed the competitive effects of this benefit and determined that it was not a subsidy. The court determined that in non-market countries, the economic incentives offered by the state do not enable the exporters to make more sales in the US than they would have without the benefit because the state determines the cost and the quantity of the sales, not the market.[19] Therefore, the countervailing duty statutes do not apply to non-market economies because they do not provide a 'competitive advantage' to the recipients.[20]

Congress, in the Omnibus Trade and Competitiveness Act of 1988, amended Section 1677(5) directing Commerce to 'determine whether the bounty, grant, or subsidy in law or in fact is provided to a specific enterprise or industry, or group of enterprises or industries. Nominal general availability . . . is not a basis for determining that the bounty, grant or subsidy is not . . . provided to a specific enterprise or industry, or group thereof.'[21]

2. Upstream Subsidies

Another recent development with regard to the question of subsidies is the inclusion of 'upstream subsidies' as countervailable subsidies. The Trade and Tariff Act of 1984 amended Sections 1671 and 1677 to subject 'upstream subsidies' to countervailing duties. Upstream subsidies are subsidies granted to the manufacture or production of components or inputs used in making a product imported into the US.[22] The statute requires the Department of Commerce to find that upstream subsidies are a competitive benefit when 'the price of the input product . . . is lower than the price that the manufacturer or producer . . . would otherwise pay for the product in obtaining it from another seller in an arms-length transaction.'[23]

C. The Injury Requirement

In some cases, the Commission must make a determination that an industry in the US has been materially injured, threatened with material injury, or that the

18. 801 F.2d 1308 (Fed. Cir. 1986).
19. *Id.* at 1316.
20. *Id.* at 1318. In holding that the countervailing duty laws do not apply to non-market economies, the court also relied on its determination that the US Congress intended to deal with 'selling by non-market economies at unreasonably low prices' through the antidumping laws. *Id.* at 1316. Section 325 of the Omnibus Trade and Competitiveness Act of 1988, specifically includes non-market economies under the antidumping law.
21. Omnibus Trade and Competitiveness Act of 1988, at § 333. *See also* in *Roxxx Inc v. U.S.* – C.LT. 2y Cust. Bul. 23 (1990).
22. 19 U.S.C. § 1677-1 (1995).
23. Omnibus Trade and Competitiveness Act of 1988, at § 1677-1(b).

establishment of this industry has been materially retarded 'by reason of imports' of the products in question.

There is a causation element in the injury determination. The injury to the industry in the US must be 'by reason of imports of the merchandise' which is the subject of the investigation.[24] Also, Article 6, Paragraph 4 of the Agreement. On Interpretation and Application of Articles VI, XVI and XXIII of the General Agreement on Tariffs and Trade provides: '[I]t must be demonstrated that the subsidized imports are, through the effects of the subsidy, causing injury within the meaning of the Agreement.' Thus, there must be not only a material injury, but also the product in question must have been a cause of that injury.[25]

1. Material Injury

Material injury is defined as 'harm which is not inconsequential, immaterial, or unimportant.'[26] Section 1677 also provides a list of factors which the Commission should consider when making an injury determination.[27] One of the factors to be considered is the volume and impact of the imported products. This section authorizes the Commission to 'cumulatively assess the volume and effect of imports from two or more countries . . . if such imports compete with each other and with like products of the domestic industry in the United States.'[28] Section 621(a)(2) of Trade and Tariff Act of 1984 amended Section 1677(7)(C), essentially codifying the existing practice of the Commission. The Commission frequently cumulates the volume and effect of imports.[29] It can also 'cross-cumulate,' *i.e.*, cumulate the volume and effect of imports of like products which are subject to both antidumping and countervailing duty investigations.[30] '[P]rior to the 1984 Act, . . . cross-cumulation was not mandatory for all competing products.'[31]

---

24. 19 U.S.C. §§ 1671(a)(2) and 1671(b)(a) (2004).
25. The prior text of 19 U.S.C. § 1671 defined countries 'under the Agreement' as those countries to which the 'Agreement on Subsidies and Countervailing Measures of the General Agreement on Tariff and Trade ("GATT") applies.' *See* 19 U.S.C. § 1671(a) (1995). This referred to the Agreement on Interpretation and Application of Articles VI, XVI, XXIII, of the General Agreement on Tariffs and Trade of the Trade Agreements Act of 1979. 19 U.S.C. § 1677(8). *See* L. Glick, Multinational Trade Negotiations, – World Trade After the Tokyo Round (Rowman & Allanheld 1984) for discussion of the GATT subsidies. Code and complete text of the Code, at 52236.
26. 19 U.S.C. §§ 1671(a), 1671(a) (2004). 31. 19 U.S.C. § 1677(7)(A) (2004).
27. 19 U.S.C. § 1677(7)(B)–(E) (2004). Section 329 of the Omnibus Trade and Competitiveness Act of 1988 amends subparagraphs (B) and (C) of this section.
28. 19 U.S.C. § 1677(7)(G)(i) (2004). Cumulation is designed to protect US industries from the compounded effect of subsidized or dumped imports from more than one country. *Bingham & Taylor. Div. Va. Indus. v. United States,* 627 F. Supp. 793, 799 (Ct. Int'l Trade 1986).
29. *USX Corp. v. United States,* 655 F. Supp. 487, 494 (Ct. Int'l Trade 1987).
30. *Bingham & Taylor. Div., Va. Indus. v. United States,* 627 F. Supp. 793, 799 (Ct. Int'l Trade 1986).
31. *USX Corp. v. United States,* 655 F. Supp. at 497.

2. Threat of Material Injury

Countervailing duties may also be imposed when there is a threat of material injury.[32] Although there is no specific definition of threat of material injury, Section 1677(7)(F) establishes the relevant economic factors which are to be considered by the Commission.[33] The Court of International Trade has stated that the 'essence of a threat lies in the ability and incentive to act imminently.'[34] Therefore, a threat of material injury can be sufficient to satisfy the injury requirement if it is an immediate threat; mere potential injury may not be sufficient.

D. The Department of Commerce and the International Trade Commission

Investigations regarding countervailing duties are usually instituted through a petition filed by a producer in the US. The petition is filed with the Department of Commerce ('Commerce') which is the 'administering authority' of countervailing duty laws. A copy of the petition must be simultaneously filed with the International Trade Commission ('Commission').[35] Commerce will determine the question of whether there is a subsidy and the Commission will determine whether there is material injury.[36]

During the course of a countervailing duty investigation, both Commerce and the Commission are required to make certain preliminary and final determinations.[37] The Code of Federal Regulations requires the agencies to provide notice of the institution of an investigation and of the determinations to all parties to the proceedings, and to publish a notice in the *Federal Register*.[38]

1. The Department of Commerce

Upon receiving the petition, Commerce must, within 20 days, determine the sufficiency of the petition.[39] The petition must contain sufficient information to

---

32. 19 U.S.C. § 1671(a)(2) (2004).
33. 19 U.S.C. § 1677(7)(F) (2004).
34. *Republic Steel Corp. v. United States,* 591 F. Supp. 640, 650 (Ct. Int'l Trade 1984).
35. *See* 19 C.F.R. § 351.202(c) (2006).
36. The procedures for a countervailing duty investigation are prescribed in Sections 1671(a)–1671(h).
37. Section 1677e(b) provides in relevant part, 'In making their determinations . . . the administering authority and the Commission shall, whenever a party or any other person refuses or is unable to produce information requested in a timely manner and in the form required, or otherwise significantly impedes an investigation, use the best information otherwise available.' (This is now referred to as 'Facts Available').
38. *See,* e.g., 19 C.F.R. § 351(c)(1)–(2) (2006).
39. 19 C.F.R. § 351.203(b). Note that the 20-day period may be extended if support for the petition must be determined.

support the allegations and the petitioner must have standing to bring the claim.[40] If the petition is sufficient, Commerce must then make a preliminary determination 'based upon the information available at the time of the determination as to whether there is a reasonable basis to believe or suspect that a subsidy is being provided.'[41] This preliminary determination must be made within 65 days unless Commerce determines that the case is 'extraordinarily complicated' and should be postponed.[42] If the determination is affirmative Commerce must calculate the amount of the subsidy and require a deposit of estimated countervailing duties.[43]

Within 75 days of an affirmative preliminary determination, Commerce must issue a final determination on the issue of subsidies.[44] The information upon which Commerce bases its final determination must be verified.[45] A verification involves a visit to the foreign company's office to review its book and records along with the foreign government. If for some reason the information cannot be verified, Commerce will base the determination on the 'best information available'[46] (now known as 'facts available') which could be the information in the petition. Upon making the final determination, Commerce issues a final order which, if negative, terminates the investigation or, if affirmative, orders the assessment of countervailing duties.[47]

PRACTICE NOTE: The statute indicates that verification is mandatory, not discretionary. Commerce has frequently failed to verify companies on the grounds of lack of manpower and resources. In the author's opinion this is an undesirable policy that encourages non-compliance by exporters under investigation.

---

40. 19 C.F.R. § 351.203 (2006); 19 U.S.C. § 1671(a)(b)(1) (2004). To have standing the petitioner must be an interested party filing the petition on behalf of an industry in the United States. 19 U.S.C. § 1671(a).
41. 19 C.F.R. § 1671(b)(1) (2004).
42. 19 C.F.R. § 351.205(b) (2006); 19 U.S.C. § 1671b(c) (2004). If the subsidy is an upstream subsidy, then the period within *which* the preliminary determination *is* to be made *is* extended to 250 days. 19 U.S.C. § 1671(b)(g).
43. 19 C.F.R. § 351.205(d) (2006). A negative preliminary subsidy determination by Commerce does not terminate a case under § 1671. Thus, *if* the Commission makes a positive preliminary injury determination after Commerce's negative subsidy determination, Commerce will continue its investigation.
44. 19 C.F.R. § 351.210(b) (2006); 19 U.S.C. §1671(d)(1) (2004). All parties have an opportunity to present their views both orally and in written form before the final determination. 19 C.F.R. §§ 351.309–.310 (2006).
45. 19 U.S.C. § 1677e(a) (1995); 19 C.F.R. § 351.307(a) (2006).
46. 19 U.S.C. § 1617e(b) (1995); 19 C.F.R. § 351.308(a) (2006).
47. 19 U.S.C. §§ 1671(d)(e) (2004). In Section 1671 cases, however, the Commission is simultaneously conducting an injury investigation and a countervailing duty order may not be issued until both the Commission and Commerce have made positive final determinations.

Firms may be exempted from a Countervailing Duty Order if they can show that they receive no 'benefit from a subsidy alleged or found to have been granted to other firms producing or exporting the merchandise subject to the investigation.'[48] To be exempt from a Countervailing Duty Order, the firm must file an application requesting exclusion. The application must be made within 30 days of the publication of a 'Notice of Initiation of Countervailing Duty Investigation.' Thus, it is important to act quickly both in learning of the investigation and in obtaining legal counsel.[49]

2. The International Trade Commission

If the case is one which requires an injury determination, a petition is filed simultaneously with the Commission. Upon receiving notice from Commerce that the petition is sufficient, the Commission then begins its investigation with regard to the material injury requirement of Section 1671.

Within 45 days of receiving notice from Commerce, the Commission must make a preliminary determination of-material injury.[50] In the preliminary injury determination the Commission must determine 'whether there is a reasonable indication' of an injury to the US industry caused by the product in question. This is a very quick timetable and requires rapid action by foreign exporters and their legal counsel.

The Court of Appeals for the Federal Circuit has held that the 'reasonable indication' standard requires that the Commission issue a negative determination 'only when (1) the record as a whole contains clear and convincing evidence that there is no material injury or threat of such injury; and (2) no likelihood exists that contrary evidence will arise in a final investigation.'[51]

If the preliminary determination is negative, the investigation is terminated.[52] However, this is a relatively rare occurrence since the preliminary injury standard is much lower than required for the final determination. The Commission has, on a few occasions, made negative preliminary injury determinations. For example, the Commission made a negative preliminary determination in *Iron Bars from Brazil.*[53] To determine that there was no reasonable indication of material injury, the Commission relied on the fact that the imports of iron bars during the period under investigation were relatively low and the US industry supplied almost the entire domestic market.[54] The Commission has made other negative preliminary

48. 19 C.F.R. § 351.212 (2006).
49. *Id.*
50. 19 U.S.C. § 1671b(a) (1995).
51. *American Lamb Co. v. United States.,* 785 F.2d 994, 1001 (Fed. Cir. 1986); *but see Republic Steel Corp. v. United States,* 591 F. Supp. 640 (Ct. Int'l Trade 1984); *Jeannette Sheet Glass Corp. v. United States,* 607 F. Supp. 123 (Ct. Int'l Trade 1985), and *Armstrong Rubber Co. v. United States,* 614 F. Supp. 252 (Ct. Int'l Trade 1985).
52. 19 U.S.C. § 1671b (2004).
53. 5 I.T.R.D. (BNA) 1906 (I.T.C. 1983).
54. *Id.,* at 1908–09.

determinations. For example, the Commission made a negative preliminary determination in *Portland Hydraulic Cement from Columbia, France, Greece.*[55] In this case, the Commission determined that the domestic industry was 'enjoying high levels of profitability,' that the increased imports of the product reflected an increased demand in the US and that much of the importation of the product was 'attributable to domestic producers,' and that there was no indication that the foreign producers were likely to increase production. Therefore, there was no reasonable indication of material injury.[56] In another example, *Certain Steel Products from Spain,*[57] the Commission relied on the relative strength of the domestic industry and the consistently low level of penetration of imported products to find no reasonable indication of material injury with regard to three of the six steel products investigated.[58] Where there was no indication that the exporting nation intended to divert shipments of fresh cut roses from traditional markets and US supplies were inadequate to meet domestic demand, the Commission also found no reasonable indication of material injury.[59] Finally, where Canadian exports of frozen potato products were not a substantial share of the US market, there were no indications of price undercutting, depression or suppression, and there was an increase in US production capacity and exports of the products, the Commission found no reasonable indication of material injury.[60]

If the preliminary injury determination is affirmative, the Commission must proceed with the injury investigation. The Commission must issue a final injury determination. If Commerce has made an affirmative preliminary subsidy determination, then the final injury determination must be made before the later of (1) the 120th day after Commerce's preliminary subsidy determination or (2) the 45th day after Commerce makes its final subsidy determination.[61] If Commerce has made a negative preliminary subsidy determination and a positive final subsidy determination, the Commission must make a final injury determination within 75 days of the final subsidy determination.[62]

If the final injury determination and the final subsidy determination are positive, then Commerce issues a countervailing duty order.[63]

---

55. 9 I.T.R.D. (BNA) 1662 (I.T.C. 1986).
56. *Id.* at 1672.
57. 4 I.T.R.D. (BNA) 1200 (I.T.C. 1982).
58. *Id.* at 1206–14.
59. *Fresh Cut Roses – The Netherlands,* 1 I.T.R.D. (BNA) 5165, 5168 (I.T.C. 1980).
60. *Frozen Potato Products – Canada,* 1 I.T.R.D. (BNA) 5161, 5163 (I.T.C. 1980).
61. 19 U.S.C. § 1671(d)(b)(2) (2004).
62. 19 U.S.C. § 1671(d)(b)(3) (2004).
63. 19 U.S.C. § 1671(d) (2004).

E. Administrative Reviews of Countervailing Duty Orders

Section 1675(a) provides that Commerce may review a countervailing duty order at least once every 12 months after the first year of the order's publication. Commerce will review 'the amount of any countervailable net subsidy and review the current status of, and compliance with, any agreement by reason of which an investigation was suspended.'[64] The review is triggered by a request by any interested party and will normally 'cover exports of the subject merchandise during the most recent completed fiscal year of the government in question.'[65]

The procedures Commerce must follow in a review generally parallel those followed in the investigation. Upon receiving a timely request, notice of the review must be issued.[66] Questionnaires requesting information for the review are sent to all interested parties and a preliminary determination is made.[67] The preliminary results must be published in the *Federal* Register.[68]

Finally, '[n]ot later than 365 days after the month of the . . . initiation of the review' final results of the review must be published in the *Federal* Register.[69] Commerce is then authorized either to order Customs to assess any countervailing duties, order the deposit of any estimated duties for future importations or revoke the order after a review.[70]

The annual reviews are extremely important since they provide an opportunity for an exporter subjected to a high countervailing duty to seek a lower rate. If the exporter did not receive any subsidy during the review period it may apply for a zero rate. Even if it received a very small subsidy, if the amount is deemed to be *de minimus* (usually less than 0.50 per cent) a zero rate can also be granted. Also, the initial countervailing duty is really just a deposit; the actual amount paid is based on the results of the annual reviews.

---

64. 19 U.S.C. § 1675(a) (2004).
65. 19 C.F.R. § 351.213(d)(2) 2006).
66. 19 C.F.R. § 351.221(b)(1) (2006).
67. 19 C.F.R. § 351.221(b)(2) (2006).
68. 19 C.F.R. § 351.221(b)(4) (2006).
69. 19 C.F.R. § 351.221(b)(5).
70. 19 U.S.C. § 1675(a); § 3511.2212(b)(6) (2006).

Chapter 14

Section 201 of the Trade Act of 1974

I. INTRODUCTION

Section 201 of the Trade Act of 1974 is traditionally referred to as the 'escape clause.' This name developed since, for many years, the Congress has required that an escape clause be included in each trade agreement. It is aimed at providing *temporary*[1] relief for an industry suffering from serious injury, or the threat thereof, so that the industry will have sufficient time to adjust to the freer international competition.'[2] Article XIX. 1. (a) of the General Agreement on Tariffs and Trade (GATT) is a typical example of such an escape clause. Section 201 of the Trade Act of 1974[3] was enacted to improve the mechanism 'for providing relief to domestic industries injured by import competition.' However, in contrast to other trade laws discussed in this book, such as the countervailing duty and antidumping laws, Section 201 is not an 'unfair trade practices' statute; it may be invoked against a country that is trading fairly but causing market disruption in the US. This chapter will discuss the substantive and procedural requirements by which a US industry can utilize Section 201 and the roles the US International Trade Commission and the President of the US play in enforcing Section 201.

---

1. Under present law, 'the duration of the period in which action taken under this section may be in effect shall not exceed 8 years.' Omnibus Trade and Competitiveness Act of 1988, P.L. 100418 § 1401, 102 Stat. 1236, Section 203(e)(I)(A).
2. Senate Committee on Finance, S. Rep. No. 93-1298, 93rd Cong., 2d Sess. 195, *reprinted in* 1974 US Code Cong. & Admin. News 7186, 7263 (emphasis added).
3. 19 U.S.C. §§ 2251–2253 (1995).

> *PRACTICE NOTE:* Since no unfair trade practice is required for duties or quotas to be imposed, the US may be required to give other forms of compensation to the countries affected.

II. DISCUSSION

A Section 201 case has two stages. The first is an administrative process whereby the US International Trade Commission ('Commission' or ITC) determines certain factual issues which arise with regard to the increased imports and potential injury to US industries.[4] After making its recommendation, the Commission reports to the President who essentially makes a political decision that determines what action to take, if any, to remedy the injury.[5] This decision by the President is the second stage.

A. The Role of the Commission

As was stated earlier, the role of the Commission is to determine whether imports are increasing and causing serious injury or threat of serious injury to a domestic industry. Upon filing of a petition, the Commission is required to 'promptly make an investigation to determine whether an article is being imported into the US in such increased quantities as to be a substantial cause of serious injury, or the threat thereof, to the domestic industry producing an article like or directly competitive with the imported articles.'[6] Identical language in Section 201(b)(1) of the Trade Act of 1974, before the 1988 amendments, has been held to require the Commission to make four determinations: (1) the relevant domestic industry; (2) whether imports of like or directly competitive products have increased; (3) whether there is serious injury or threat of injury, and (4) whether imports are a substantial cause of any injury.[7]

---

4. Omnibus Trade and Competitiveness Act of 1988, P.L. 100-418 § 1401, 102 Stat. 1226, Section 202(b) *codified at* 19 U.S.C. § 2252(b) (1995).
5. Omnibus Trade and Competitiveness Act of 1988, P. L. 100-418 § 1401, 102 Stat. 1225, Section 201(a) *codified at* 19 U.S.C. § 2251(b) (1995).
6. P.L. 100-418 § 1401, 102 Stat. 1226, § 202(b)(I)(A) *codified as amended at* 19 U.S.C. § 2252(b)(1)(A) (1995). Before the amendments in 1988, the statute required that the Commission report to the President within six months of petition. Section 1401 of the Omnibus Trade and Competitiveness Act of 1988, however, requires that the Commission make its determination within 120 days of the petition. House Conf. Rep. No. 100-576 100th Cong. 2d Sess. 666, *reprinted in* 1988 U.S. Code Cong. & Admin. News 1547, 1966.
7. *See Carbon and Certain Alloy Steel Products,* 6 I.T.R.D. (BNA) 2232, 2240 (1984).

1. Determining the Domestic Industry

The first issue the Commission must address is to define 'the domestic industry producing an article like or directly competitive with the imported article.'[8] In making this determination the Commission generally follows a two step 'product-line' analysis.[9] The Commission first determines which 'articles are like or directly competitive with the imported articles.'[10] Second, the Commission determines which domestic facilities are producing the like or directly competitive articles.[11]

The Commission has performed this two-step analysis in many cases.[12] For example, in determining the domestic industry in *Wood Shakes and Shingles,*[13] the Commission examined 'both similarities and differences between the various shakes and shingles at issue' in the investigation to determine that both shakes and shingles constitute the relevant domestic product. Then the Commission considered 'the productive facilities, manufacturing processes, and the markets for the products at issue' to determine 'which producers constitute the domestic industry.'[14] Once the Commission determines the domestic industry, it turns to the question of whether there are increased imports of the article.

2. Increased Imports

In order to recommend relief, the Commission must find that imports of the articles in question have been increasing. The increase can be 'either actual or relative to domestic production.'[15] In *Unwrought Copper,*[16] for example, where in absolute terms '1983 imports of blister and refined copper exceed[ed] their 1979 levels by almost 24,000 and 282,000 short tons' there was an increase in imports. However, the Commission has also found there to be an increase in imports where total imports, in absolute terms, declined. In *Carbon and Certain Alloy Steel Products,*[17]

---

8. P.L. 100-418 § 1401, 102 Stat. 1227, Section 202(b)(I)(A) *codified at* 19 U.S.C. § 2252(b)(1)(A) (1995).
9. *Certain Canned Tuna Fish,* 6 I.T.R.D. (BNA) 2464, 2466 (1984).
10. *Id.* at 2465. 'Like' articles are defined . . . as 'those which are substantially identical in inherent or intrinsic characteristics (*i.e.,* materials from which made, appearance, quality, texture, etc.).' *(quoting* Senate Committee on Finance, S. Rep. No. 93-1298, 93rd Cong. 2d Sess. 122, *reprinted in* 1974 U.S. Code Cong. & Admin. News 7186.) 'Directly competitive' articles are those 'which, although not substantially *identical* in their inherent or intrinsic characteristics, are substantially equivalent for commercial purposes, that is, are adapted to the same uses and are essentially interchangeable.'
11. *See* note 10, *supra.*
12. *See,* e.g., *Apple Juice,* 9 I.T.R.D. (BNA) 1056, 1059 (1986) (appropriate domestic industry is the industry producing apple juice, including single-strength apple juice, three-strength frozen apple juice concentrate, juice concentrate, and various processed apple juice retail products).
13. *Wood Shakes and Shingles,* 8 I.T.R.D. (BNA) 2135, 2137 (1986).
14. *Id.* at 2138.
15. P.L. 100-418 § 1401, 102 Stat. 1228, Section 202(c)(1)–(C) *codified at* 19 U.S.C. § 2252(c)(1)(C) (1995).
16. *Unwrought Copper,* 6 I.T.R.D. (BNA) 1708, 1711 (1984).
17. *Steel Products,* 6 I.T.R.D. (BNA) 2236, 2246–51 (1984).

for example, the Commission found there to be an increase in imports where the decline in the imports was slower than the decline in domestic production. The imports were held to have increased relative to the domestic production.[18]

3. Serious Injury

The Commission must also find that there is serious injury or a threat of serious injury to the domestic industry. Although the statute does not explicitly define 'serious injury' or 'threat of serious injury' the Commission has stated that serious injury is 'an important crippling, or mortal injury, one having permanent or lasting consequences;' and threat of serious injury is 'real rather than speculative' and that serious injury is 'highly probable in the foreseeable future.'[19]

In determining serious injury or threat of serious injury, the Commission is to 'take into account all economic factors which it considers relevant.'[20] The Commission must examine 'the economic experience of the industry,' measuring overall trends within the industry.[21] For example, in *Electric Shavers*,[22] the Commission found no serious injury or threat of serious injury despite evidence that profits were down, growth was down and most indicators had declined for the first three quarters of 1985. The Commission relied on evidence that the domestic industry had shown marked improvement from 1979 to 1984 and that most indicators had stabilized by the fourth quarter of 1985, in determining there was no serious injury or threat or serious injury.[23]

4. Substantial Cause

Finally, the increase in imports must be a substantial cause of the serious injury or threat of serious injury to the domestic industry. '[T]he term "substantial cause" means a cause which is important and not less than any other cause.'[24] This

---

18. *Steel Products,* 6 I.T.R.D. (BNA) 2236, 2246–51 (1984).
19. *Electric Shavers and Parts Thereof,* 8 I.T.R.D. (BNA) 1827, 1830 (1986), *quoting Belts Nuts and Screws of Iron or Steel* Inv. No. TA-201-2, USITC Pub. No. 747, at 19 (1975).
20. Section 1401 of Omnibus Trade and Competitiveness Act of 1988 (P.L. 100-418 § 1401, 102 Stat. 1227-8, Section 202(c)(1)(A), (B) *codified at* 19 U.S.C. § 2252(c)(I)(A), (B) (1995)) includes certain economic factors which are to be considered by the Commission in determining serious injury or threat of serious injury.
21. *See Steel Fork Arms*, 9 I.T.R.D. (BNA) 1096, 1099 (1986) (By *most* indicators – production, shipments, and inventory, for example – the domestic industry's performance had not declined from 1981 *to* 1985, and in 1984 and 1985 the industry operated at a profit. Therefore, there was no serious injury or threat of serious injury).
22. *Electric Shavers*, 8 I.T.R.D. (BNA), at 1830 (1986).
23. *Id.*
24. Omnibus Trade and Competitiveness Act of 1988, P.L. 100-418 § 1401, 102 Stat. 1227, Section 202(b)(1)(B) *codified at* 19 U.S.C. § 2252(b)(i)(B) (1995).

definition 'requires that a dual test be met – increased imports must constitute an important cause and be no less important than any other single cause.'[25]

In determining whether increased imports are a substantial cause of injury, the Commission isolates 'each of the economic factors relevant to the question of serious injury and . . . compare[s] each of them with the factor of increased imports.' The other potential causes of injury are not to be aggregated and compared to the increased imports, and the increase in imports cannot be less of a cause than any other.[26] For example, in *Potassium Permanganate,*[27] the Commission held that increased imports were not a substantial cause of injury. The industry's loss of its major customer was a more important cause of injury than increased imports.[28]

Upon completing its investigation the Commission must submit a report to the President.[29] If the Commission determines that an article is being imported into the US in such increased quantities as to be a substantial cause of serious injury, or the threat thereof, to the domestic industry producing an article like or directly competitive with the imported article, the President shall take action.[30]

B. ROLE OF THE PRESIDENT

The granting of relief under Section 201 of the Trade Act of 1974 has historically been discretionary. While the statute establishes the basic issues and remedies which are to be considered by the President, the ultimate decision as to whether to provide a remedy was made by the President.[31] Prior to the Omnibus Trade and Competitiveness Act of 1988, once the Commission made an affirmative injury determination, the language of the statute granted the President discretion as to whether to provide import relief.[32] The amendments in the Omnibus Trade and

---

25. Senate Committee on Finance, S. Rep. No. 93-1298, 93rd Cong., 2d Sess. 195, *reprinted in* 1974 U.S. Code Cong. & Admin. News 7186, 7265.
26. The Omnibus Trade and Competitiveness Act of 1988 amends Section 201 of the Trade Act of 1974 to clarify that the Commission 'shall not aggregate causes of declining demand associated with a recession or economic downturn into a single cause of serious injury and requires the ITC to examine factors other than imports which may be a cause of serious injury.' House Conf. Rep. No. 100-576, 100th Cong. 2d Sess., 668, *reprinted* in 1988 U.S. Code Cong. & Admin. News 1547, 1701.
27. *Potassium Permanganate*, 7 I.T.R.D. (BNA) 1734, 1738 (1985).
28. *Id.* at 1738.
29. Omnibus Trade and Competitiveness Act of 1988, P.L. 100-418 § 1401, 102 Stat. 1234, Section 202(t) *codified at* 19 U.S.C. § 2252(t) (1995).
30. Omnibus Trade and Competitiveness Act of 1988, P.L. 100-418 § 1401, 102 Stat. 1234, Section 203(a) *codified at* 19 U.S.C. § 2253(a)(1)(A) (1995).
31. Because these import relief cases involve such a high degree of discretion by the President, courts have a very limited role in reviewing any action taken by the President. *Maple Leaf Fish Co. v. United States*, 596 F. Supp. 1076 (Ct. Int'l Trade 1984), *aff'd*, 6 I.T.R.D. (BNA) 2186 (Fed. Cir. 1985).
32. '[T]he President shall provide import relief for such industry . . . *unless he determines that provision of such relief is not in the national economic interest of the United States*.' § 202(a)(1)(A) of the Trade Act of 1974, 19 U.S.C. § 2252(a)(1)(A) (1980) (*emphasis added*). In recent years

Competitiveness Act of 1988 eliminate the discretionary language, instead stating that 'the President shall take all appropriate and feasible action within his power . . .'[33] The legislative history, however, indicates that 'the President should not be forced into taking action.'[34] Thus, in 'certain exceptional circumstances, when any action that would facilitate adjustment would result in greater economic and social costs than benefits,' the President may still decline to grant a remedy.[35]

The Omnibus Trade and Competitiveness Act of 1988 establishes those factors which the President must take into account in determining what action to take.[36] The President shall consider

(a) The recommendation and report of the ITC;
(b) The extent to which workers and firms are benefiting from adjustment assistance and other manpower programs and are engaged in worker retraining efforts;
(c) The efforts being made, or to be implemented, by the domestic industry to make a positive adjustment;
(d) The probable effectiveness of import relief and other actions within the authority of the President;
(e) The short and long-term economic and social costs of action that could be taken relative to the short and long-term economic aid social benefits of such actions and other considerations relative to the position of the domestic industry in the US economy;
(f) Other factors relating to the national economic interest of the US;
(g) The extent to which there is diversion of foreign exports to the US market by reason of foreign restraints;
(h) The national security interests of the US; and
(i) Other factors required to be considered by the ITC.[37]

The statute also provides a variety of remedies available to the President including: (a) tariff increases; (b) tariff rate quotas;[38] (c) quantitative restrictions;

prior to enactment of the Omnibus Trade and Competitiveness Act of 1988, the President had declined to impose import relief for various policy reasons despite the recommendation of the International Trade Commission. This angered protectionist elements in the US Congress who attempted to limit this discretion in the 1988 law.

33. Omnibus Trade and Competitiveness Act of 1988, P.L. 100-418 § 1401, 102 Stat. 1225, 1234, Sections 201(a), 203(a) *codified at* 19 U.S.C. § 2251(a), 2253(a) (1995).
34. House Conf. Rep. No. 100-576. 100th Cong. 2d Sess., 681, *reprinted in* 1988 U.S. Code Cong. & Admin. News 1547, 1714.
35. *Id.*
36. Omnibus Trade and Competitiveness Act of 1988, P.L. 100-418 § 1401, 102 Stat. 1234-5, § 203(a)(2) *codified at* 19 U.S.C. § 2253(a)(2) (1995).
37. *Id.*; *see also* House Conf. Rep. No. 100-576, 100th Cong. 2d Sess., 681, *reprinted in* 1988 *U.S.* Code Cong. & Admin. News 1547, 1716.
38. Tariff rate quotas allow entry at the existing tariff up to certain quantitative limits, and the increase the duty rate. This has elements of both a tariff increase and quota.

(d) auctioned quotas; (e) Orderly Marketing Agreements;[39] (f) international negotiations to address the underlying cause of the increase in imports or otherwise alleviate the injury; (g) adjustment measures, including trade adjustment assistance (other than entitlements); (h) legislative proposals; (i) any other action within his power; and (j) any combination of the above.[40]

C. Procedures

The Commission is authorized to initiate an investigation under this section upon petition by an entity on behalf of an affected domestic industry.[41] The petition must contain specific information including: a description of the product; names of the domestic producers of the product; data showing serious injury or threat thereof allegedly caused by increased imports; a statement on the efforts of the domestic industry to compete, and the relief sought by the petitioner.[42] After receiving a petition, the Commission is required to 'send copies of the petition to the Office of the United States Trade Representative and other Federal agencies directly concerned,' such as the Department of Commerce and the Department of Labor.[43]

1. Procedures at the Commission

Once the Commission has received a petition, it must make its injury determination within 120 days of the date on which the petition was filed.[44] The Commission is required to hold a public hearing in connection with an investigation, granting

---

39. Orderly Marketing Agreements are essentially voluntarily adopted quota agreements with foreign countries. One of the purposes of the Uruguay Round was to abolish 'gray areas' of safeguard measures. Article XI of the Agreement on Safeguards prohibits voluntary export restraints, Orderly Marketing Agreements or any other similar measures on the export or import side.
40. Omnibus Trade and Competitiveness Act of 1988, P.L. 100-418 § 1401, 102 Stat. 1235, § 203(a)(3) *codified at* 19 U.S.C. § 2253(a)(3) (1995); *see also* House Conf. Rep. No. 100-576, 100th Cong. 2d Sess., 684, *reprinted in* 1988 U.S Code Cong. & Admin. News 1547, 1717.
41. Omnibus Trade and Competitiveness Act of 1988 P.L. 100-418 § 1401, 102 Stat. 1224, § 202(a)(1) *codified at* 19 U.S.C. § 2252(a)(1) (1995); 19 C.F.R. § 206.8 (1995). Although a petition on behalf of a domestic industry is the usual method by which an investigation is initiated, the Commission is authorized to make an investigation 'upon . . . the request of the President or the Trade Representative, the resolution of either the Committee on Ways and Means of the House of Representatives or the Committee on Finance of the Senate, or on its own motion.' *Id.* at 102 Stat. 1226-7, § 202(b)(1)(A) *codified at* 19 U.S.C. § 2252(b)(1)(A) (1995).
42. 19 C.F.R. § 206.9(a)–(h) (1995).
43. Omnibus Trade and Competitiveness Act of 1988, P.L. 100-418 § 1401, 102 Stat. 1226, § 202(a)(3) *codified at* 19 U.S.C. § 2252(a)(3) (1995).
44. *Id.* at 102 Stat. 1227, § 202(b)(2)(A) *codified at* 19 U.S.C. § 2252(b)(2)(A) (1995). A 30-day extension on this deadline is authorized if within 100 days of the date on which the petition was filed, the Commission determines the case is extraordinarily complicated. Omnibus Trade and Competitiveness Act of 1988, P.L. 100-418 § 1401, 102 Stat. 1227, § 202(b)(2)(B) *codified at* 19 U.S.C. § 2252(b)(2)(B) (1995).

'[a]ll interested parties . . . an opportunity to be present, to present evidence, and to be heard at such hearings.'[45]

If the Commission makes an affirmative injury determination it must also make a recommendation of what relief 'would be most effective in facilitating the efforts of the domestic industry to make a positive adjustment to import competition.'[46] The statute requires that the Commission hold a public hearing with regard to its recommendation providing 'all interested parties . . . an opportunity to present testimony and evidence.'[47] Members of the Commission who did not agree with the injury determination are not eligible to vote on the recommendation of the remedy but may submit their separate views in the Commission's report to the President.[48]

No later than 180 days after the date on which the petition was filed, the Commission must submit a report of its determination and recommendation of remedy, if any, to the President.[49] That report must also be made available to the public, without any confidential information.[50] The report must include the Commission's findings that the criteria for relief have been met, the record upon which the Commission made its determinations, and a description of the economic effects that implementing and not implementing the Commission's recommended remedy will have 'on the petitioning domestic industry, its workers and communities where production facilities of such industry are located, and other domestic industries.'[51]

2. Action by the President

Upon receiving the report of an affirmative injury determination from the Commission, the President has 60 days in which to act to remedy the import injury.[52] The statute requires the President to consult with the Interagency Trade Policy Committee, established under § 242 of the Trade Expansion Act of 1962,[53] before any action is taken.[54] The President is authorized to enforce any action taken by providing regulations for the administration of any action taken.[55] No action taken by the President under this section may last longer than eight years.[56]

---

45. 19 C.F.R. § 206.5 (1995).
46. Omnibus Trade and Competitiveness Act of 1988, P.L. 100-418 § 1401, 102 Stat. 1231, § 202(e)(5) *codified at* 19 U.S.C. § 2252(e)(5) (1995).
47. *Id.* at 102 Stat. 1232, § 202(e)(5) *codified at* 19 U.S.C. § 2252(e)(5) (1995).
48. *Id.* at 102 Stat. 1232, § 202(e)(6) *codified at* 19 U.S.C. § 2252(e)(6) (1995).
49. *Id.* at 102 Stat. 1233, Section 202(1) *codified at* 19 U.S.C. § 2252(1) (1995).
50. *Id.*
51. *Id.* 19 C.F.R. § 206.6(a).
52. Omnibus Trade and Competitiveness Act of 1988. P.L 100-418 § 1401, 102 Stat. 1235, § 203(a)(4) *codified at* 19 U.S.C. § 2253(a)(4) (1995).
53. 19 U.S.C. § 2171 (1982).
54. *Id.* at 102 Stat. 1234, § 203(a)(1)(C) *codified at* 19 U.S.C. § 2253(a)(1)(C) (1995).
55. *Id.* at 102 Stat. 1237, § 203(g) *codified at* 19 U.S.C. § 2253(g) (1995).
56. *Id.* at 102 Stat. 1236, § 203(e) *codified at* 19 U.S.C. § 2253(e) (1995).

When the President decides whether to take action under this section, he must submit a report to the Congress which provides a description of the action to be taken, if any, and his reasons for the decision.[57] If the President reports to Congress that he will not take any action or will provide a remedy which is different from that recommended by the Commission, Congress may implement the remedy recommended by the Commission.[58] Congress must act by joint resolution within 60 days of receiving the President's report to override the President's action.[59] This is a new addition to § 201 that essentially provides for a congressional override of a decision by the President not to implement an ITC recommendation to impose import relief. It resulted from congressional concern over the President's failure to implement recommendations of the ITC in several past cases.

D. Monitoring and Modification of Relief

Although any relief under this section is temporary, the Commission is required to 'monitor developments with respect to the domestic industry' for the duration of the remedy.[60] These are commonly known as '203 reviews'. The Commission is to report biannually to the President and the Congress on the results of the monitoring. In preparing this report the Commission must hold a public hearing providing 'interested persons a reasonable opportunity to be present, to produce evidence, and to be heard.'[61]

After receiving the monitoring report from the Commission the President may reduce, modify or terminate the action.[62] The President can modify the action under two circumstances. The first is if certain 'changed circumstances warrant such reduction.'[63] The second is when 'a majority of the representatives of the domestic industry' requests the modification on the grounds that the industry has made a positive adjustment to import competition.[64] Under the Uruguay Round Agreement on Safeguards, the general rule under Article VII provides that safeguard measures should not last more than four years. An extension for up to an additional four years is allowed if, on the basis of additional investigation, it is established that serious injury, or threat of, is present and that the industry affected is adjusting. Section 203 is similar in accord with GATT provisions. It also provides for a four-year period of relief which may be extended to a total of eight years if the Commission determines it would be needed in order to prevent injury and that a positive adjustment is occurring. These changes in Section 201 will generally make the statute easier for US industries to use and may result in

57. *Id.* at 102 Stat. 1236, § 203(b) *codified at* 19 U.S.C. § 2253(b).
58. *Id.* at 102 Stat. 1236, § 203(c) *codified at* 19 U.S.C. § 2253(c).
59. *Id.*
60. *Id.* at 102 Stat. 1238, § 204(a) *codified at* 19 U.S.C. § 2254(a) (1995).
61. *Id.*
62. *Id.* at 102 Stat. 1238, § 204(b) *codified at* 19 U.S.C. § 2254(b) (1995).
63. *Id.*
64. *Id.*

increased use of this statute in the future as a trade relief measure against increased imports from abroad since no unfair trade practices are required to trigger Section 201 relief. It is difficult for foreign exporters to prevent exposure to actions under this statute. However, careful monitoring of their exports to the US to determine any pattern of increased imports can be useful. Special safeguard rules for NAFTA Signatories have been established as part of NAFTA.

E. Section 201 Safeguard Investigation of Steel Products (INV. NO. TA-201-73)

PRACTICE NOTE: This was one of the largest and most important Section 201 cases. It involved almost every type of steel and every steel-producing country. It also divided major US industries such as the steel industry and the automotive industry, which is a major consumer of steel and which has adversely affected its ability to obtain sufficient quantities of steel at reasonable costs. Because of the importance of this case it will be discussed in greater detail.

On June 22, 2001, at the request of the United States Trade Representative (USTR), the Commission instituted investigation No. TA-201-73 under Section 202 of the Act[65] to determine whether certain steel products are being imported into the United States in such increased quantities as to be a substantial cause of serous injury, or the threat thereof, to the domestic industry producing an article like or directly competitive with the imported article.[66] On July 26, 2001, the Commission received a resolution from the Committee on Finance of the United States Senate requesting that the Commission conduct an investigation of the same scope. On October 22, 2001, the Commission made its injury determinations. On December 7, 2001, the Commission announced its recommendations with respect to remedies and subsequently transmitted its report to the President on December 19, 2001.[67]

65. 19 U.S.C. § 2252.
66. 66 Fed. Reg. 35267, July 3, 2001.
67. *Id.* 67304, December 28, 2001.

Table I. Commission's Determinations in Investigation No. TA-201-73

Commission's Determinations	*Products*
Affirmative	Carbon and alloy flat-rolled products (slabs, plate, hot-rolled, cold-rolled, and coated), hot bar, cold bar, rebar, welded pipe and tube, fittings, stainless steel bar, and stainless steel rod.
Evenly divided	Tin, stainless steel wire, stainless fittings and flanges, and tool steel.[68]
Negative	Grain oriented silicon electrical steel (GOES), carbon and alloy steel ingots, billets, and blooms, carbon and alloy steel rails and railway products, carbon and alloy steel wire, carbon and alloy steel strand, rope, cable, and cordage, carbon and alloy steel nails, staples, and woven cloth, carbon and alloy steel heavy structural shapes and sheet piling, carbon and alloy steel fabricated structural units, carbon and alloy seamless steel pipe, seamless oil country tubular goods (OCTG), welded OCTG, stainless steel ingots, billets, and blooms, stainless steel cut-to-length plate, stainless steel woven cloth, carbon, alloy, and stainless steel rope, and stainless steel seamless and welded pipe.

Following receipt of the Commission's report,[69] the President, pursuant to his authority under Section 203 of the Act,[70] imposed import relief in the form of tariffs and tariff-rate quotas on imports of certain steel products for a three year and one day time period, effective March 20, 2002. *See* Table II.

68. The President took no action with respect to these products. Source: 66 Fed. Reg. 54285, October 26, 2003.
69. *See* Steel, Inv. No. TA-201-73, USITC Publication 3479, December 2001.
70. 19 U.S.C. § 2253.

Table II. Steel Safeguard Measures Imposed on March 20, 2002

Product Type	*Measure*	*First Year of Relief*	*Second Year of Relief*	*Third Year of Relief*
Certain carbon and alloy flat-rolled-steel:				
Slab	Tariff-rate quota (TRQ)	Increase in duties of 30% *ad valorem* for imports above 4.90 million metric tons	Increase in duties of 24% *ad valorem* for imports above 5.35 million metric tons	Increase in duties of 18% *ad valorem* for imports above 5.81 million metric tons
Plate	Increase in duties	30	24	18
Hot-rolled	Increase in duties	30	24	18
Cold-rolled	Increase in duties	30	24	18
Coated	Increase in duties	30	24	18
Tin	Increase in duties	30	24	18
Hot bar	Increase in duties	30	24	18
Cold bar	Increase in duties	30	24	18
Rebar	Increase in duties	15	12	9
Welded pipe and tube	Increase in duties	15	12	9
Fittings	Increase in duties	13	10	7

Table II. (continued)

Product Type	*Measure*	*First Year of Relief*	*Second Year of Relief*	*Third Year of Relief*
Certain carbon and alloy flat-rolled-steel:				
Stainless bar	Increase in duties	15	12	9
Stainless rod	Increase in duties	15	12	9
Stainless wire	Increase in duties	8	7	6

COUNTRIES EXEMPTED FROM IMPORT RELIEF

The Section 203 safeguard measures were applied to imports of the steel products investigated from all countries except Mexico, Canada, Israel, Jordan,[71] and developing countries that are members of the World Trade Organization (WTO) whose share of total imports of a particular product did not exceed 3 per cent (provided that imports that are the product of all such countries with less than 3 per cent import share collectively accounted for not more than 9 per cent of total imports of the product).

71. *See* Paragraph 11 of the President's Proclamation of March 5, 2002 (67 Fed. Reg. 10553, March 7, 2002). Mexico, Canada, Israel, and Jordan were exempted in accordance with the terms of four trade agreements the US has entered into with these countries.

Chapter 15

Section 301 of the Trade Act of 1974, as Amended

I. INTRODUCTION

Section 301 of the Trade Act of 1974,[1] as amended, establishes broad authority for the US to 'retaliate' against unfair foreign trade practices. In the legislative history of the Act, the Senate Finance Committee noted that, 'Foreign trading partners should know that we are willing to do business with them on a fair and free basis, but if they insist on maintaining unfair advantages, swift and certain retaliation against their commerce will occur.'[2] Retaliation is authorized against two different categories of foreign trade practices. First, retaliation is authorized where any rights or benefits of the US under any trade agreement are being denied. Second, retaliation is authorized where an act, policy or practice of a foreign nation burdens or restricts US commerce and is unjustifiable, unreasonable, or discriminatory. Thus, the US may retaliate against acts which are either inconsistent with trade agreements or burdensome to domestic commerce. This statute has received increased attention and utilization in recent years due to its broad scope. Unlike other trade laws that essentially cover trade in products or goods, Section 301 can be and has been applied to trade in services as well.

1. Omnibus Trade and Competitiveness Act of 1988, Pub. 1. No. 100-418, §§ 1301, 102 Stat. 1164.
2. S. Rep. No. 93-12911. 93rd Cong., 2d.Sess. (1974), *reprinted in* 1974 U.S. Code Cong. & Admin. News 7180, 7303.

PRACTICE NOTE: Under the old GATT System, Section 301 was an important weapon in the US arsenal of trade remedies. After the World Trade Organization (WTO) replaced the GATT as the administrative body, the WTO limitations against unilateral actions have limited the use of Section 301 in recent years.

II. DISCUSSION

The Omnibus Trade and Competitiveness Act of 1988 rewrote and significantly amended Section 301. Perhaps one of the most important changes is the transfer of authority under Section 301 of the Trade Act of 1974 from the President to the United States Trade Representative (USTR). Prior to these amendment, the President was authorized to determine whether action was appropriate and what action, if any, should be taken, and the USTR merely made recommendations to the President regarding whether action should be taken.[3] The President had broad discretion in determining whether to apply sanctions against offending countries with the only procedural requirements being that the President had to provide notice and an opportunity for comment. The Omnibus Trade and Competitiveness Act of 1988 transfers the authority to determine whether and what action may be appropriate from the President to the USTR.[4] Although the USTR has broad discretion in this area, the Omnibus Trade and Competitiveness Act does require the USTR to act in certain situations[5] and does establish somewhat more restrictive procedural guidelines. The rationale behind the transfer of authority was to insulate the President from political pressure from foreign governments that often resulted in his hesitance to retaliate. While the US Trade Representative is appointed by the President, it was thought that he or she was more likely to take retaliatory action. In practice, the change has not had this intended effect.

A. Determinations by the USTR

1. Preliminary Determinations

Upon petition or on its own motion, the USTR has broad discretion to determine whether to initiate an investigation under Section 301[6] If the USTR determines that retaliation under the section 'would be effective in addressing such act, policy, or practice,' then the USTR will initiate an investigation.

3. 19 U.S.C. § 2411(a).
4. *See* §§ 301 and 304, Pub. L. No. 100418, § 1301, 102 Stat. 1164, 1170.
5. § 301 of the Trade Act of 1974 as amended, provides that the USTR 'shall take action' under certain circumstances. *See* § 301 (a) of the Trade Act of 1974, as amended.
6. § 302(c) of the Trade Act of 1974, as amended.

2. Consultations

On the day that the USTR institutes an investigation under Section 301, the USTR 'shall request consultations with the foreign country concerned regarding the issues involved.'[7] The consultation requirement is designed to allow an opportunity for any dispute to be resolved without the US having to resort to any retaliatory action. If the investigation involves a trade agreement, the USTR is also required to request any formal dispute resolution procedures provided under the agreement if, after a period of time, there has been no resolution of the case.[8] Such consultations often enable the USTR to avoid unilateral retaliatory actions.

3. Statutory Standards

Once an investigation has been instituted, the USTR is required, by § 304(a)(1), to make a determination as to whether the criteria for action under Section 301 are met. The dual nature of § 301, discussed above, is reflected in the different standards for action.

a. Rights and Benefits under a Trade Agreement

Section 301 allows the USTR to retaliate to protect the rights or benefits of the US under any trade agreement. The USTR must determine whether:

> (A) The rights of the United States under any trade agreement are being denied; or
> (B) An act, policy, or practice of a foreign country
> > (i) violates, or is inconsistent with, the provisions of, or otherwise denies benefits to the United States under any trade agreement...[9]

Thus, to act on these grounds the USTR is required to determine whether there is a trade agreement involved to which the US is a party and whether the rights or benefits of the US under that agreement are being denied. An example of utilization of this provision was the petition of the American Meat Institute requesting an investigation under Section 301 and alleging that Korea's prohibition on all imports of beef for domestic consumption violated Article XI of the General Agreement on Tariffs and Trade (GATT).[10]

---

7. § 303(a)(1) of the Trade Act of 1974, as amended.
8. § 303(a)(2) of the Trade Act of 1974, as amended.
9. § 301(a)(1). As commentators have pointed out, there seems to be little difference between these provisions. It may be that the difference between these provisions would rest on a distribution between rights under a trade agreement, and benefits under a trade agreement. *See* Archibald, *Section 301 of the Trade Act of 1974*, contained in U.S. International Trade Laws Program Materials, Appendix V (Georgetown University Law Center, 1985).
10. 53 Fed. Reg. 10995 (1988).

b. Burden or Restrict United States Commerce

The USTR is also authorized to retaliate against acts, policies or practices of foreign nations which 'burden or restrict' the commerce of the US and are 'unjustifiable...unreasonable' or 'discriminatory.' This is a very broad section and, unlike other trade laws, it covers services as well as goods).[11] The USTR can retaliate against a foreign nation regardless of whether there are any trade agreements between that nation and the US provided there is a burden or restriction on US commerce. For example, on January 22, 1988, the US Cigarette Export Association filed a petition alleging that certain practices of the Republic of Korea burdened and restricted US commerce. There was no allegation of a violation of a trade agreement.[12] Although each of these standards can be separate grounds for action under § 301, petitioners frequently allege multiple grounds for relief under § 301. For example, in the *Indian Almond* case, the petitioners alleged that the actions of the Government of India 'deny rights of the United States under a trade agreement, are inconsistent with a trade agreement, and are unjustifiable and unreasonable and cause a burden on United States commerce.'[13]

c. Definitions

Although the USTR has a great deal of discretion in determining whether the criteria for retaliation under § 301 exist, § 301(d) does provide some guidance by defining the terms 'commerce,' 'burdens or restricts United States commerce,' 'unreasonable' 'unjustifiable,' and 'discriminatory.'

Section 301(d) indicates that the term 'commerce' is to be defined broadly. The term includes 'services associated with international trade, whether or not such services are related to specific goods and foreign direct investment by United States persons with implications for trade in goods or services.'[14] Thus, 'commerce' is not limited to those industries involved directly with products exported to the US. The industries may be service industries, 'associated' with international trade, such as insurance and banking, or with any direct investment which has foreign trade 'implications.'

Section 301(d) does not specifically define 'burden or restrict United States commerce.' The section does, however, state that such burdens or restrictions may include direct or indirect subsidies granted to the construction of 'vessels used in the commercial transportation by water of goods between foreign countries and the United States.'[15] Section 301(d)(2) of the Trade Act of 1974, as amended.

---

11. *See* Section 301(a)(1)(B)(ii), (b).
12. 53 Fed. Reg. 4926 (1988) (investigation terminated after dispute resolved by U.S./Korean agreement (53 Fed. Reg. 20406 (1988))).
13. 52 Fed. Reg. 6412 (1987) (investigation terminated (53 Fed. Reg. 21,757 (1988))).
14. Section 301(d)(1) of the Trade Act of 1974, as amended (*emphasis added*).
15. Section 301 is broad enough to cover most types of subsidies recognizable under the countervailing duty statute and can be used as an alternative to that statute. *See* Chapter 13.

The USTR interprets the burden or restriction requirement broadly. The USTR does not require allegations of injury in the traditional manner, such as is required in antidumping or countervailing duty cases (*see* Chapters 12 and 13), before instituting an investigation. For example, in the *Korean Cigarette Market Restrictions* case, the USTR instituted an investigation on a showing by the petitioner that Korea's practices 'deprive US tobacco companies of access to a cigarette market worth USD 2.1 billion at the retail level in 1986...[and] the US is losing USD 520 million of potential exports annually.'[16] While injury may be implicit in the allegation, technically there was no showing that the US industry was 'injured' by the denial of access to Korean markets.

In order to justify retaliation under Section 301, an act, policy, or practice of a foreign nation must not only burden or restrict US commerce, but also must be 'unreasonable,' 'unjustifiable,' or 'discriminatory.' Section 301(d)(3) indicates that the term 'unreasonable' is also to be interpreted broadly. 'An act, policy, or practice of a foreign country...is unreasonable if the act, policy, or practice...is otherwise unfair and inequitable.'[17] Section 301(d) also provides that such acts by a foreign country are not to be considered unreasonable if there is a showing that the actions are not 'inconsistent with the level of economic development of the foreign country.'[18] Thus, the USTR may retaliate where it is determined there is an unfair or inequitable burden or restriction on US commerce which is not justified by the level of economic development of the offending nation. The 'level of economic development' issue is an important defense for developing countries.

Unjustifiable acts, policies or practices are those which are 'in violation of, or inconsistent with, the international legal rights of the United States.'[19] This seems to refer to the rights and the benefits of the US arising under international obligations other than trade agreements covered in the other sections, including 'national or most favored nation treatment or the right of establishment or protection of intellectual property rights.'[20]

Discriminatory acts, policies or practices are those which discriminate between the foreign goods or services; for example, where 'national or most favored nation treatment [is denied] to United States goods, services or investment' and not to goods, services or investments from other nations.[21] An example might be where a country permitted certain foreign banks to have branches but not those of the US.

---

16. 53 Fed. Reg. 4926 (1987) (investigation terminated after dispute resolved by U.S./Korean agreement (53 Fed. Reg. 20, 406 (1988)).
17. Section 301(d)(3)(A) of the Trade Act of 1974, as amended.
18. Section 301(d)(3)(C)(i)(11) of the Trade Act of 1974, as amended.
19. Section 301(d)(4) of the Trade Act of 1974, as amended.
20. *Id.*
21. 15 C.F.R. 301(d)(5) of the Trade Act of 1974, as amended.

B. Time Limits and Procedures

This section of the chapter will discuss the regulations provided in the Code of Federal Regulations, 15 C.F.R. Part 2006, pertaining to Section 301. Note that these regulations may not all have been amended to reflect the changes established in the Omnibus Trade and Competitiveness Act of 1988.

1. Initiation of Investigations

Investigations may be initiated either by petition filed with the USTR by 'any interested person'[22] or by the action of the USTR.[23] The petition must contain: 1) the identity of the petitioner, and 2) facts to describe the relevant country, relevant product, and the trade practices being complained of.[24] Upon receiving the petition, the USTR has 45 days within which to determine whether to initiate an investigation. The USTR must publish the determination whether affirmative or negative, along with a summary of the reasons for the determination, in the *Federal Register.*[25]

2. The Investigation

Upon instituting an investigation, the USTR is required to provide 'any interested persons' with an opportunity to present their views. This may include a public hearing if an interested person so requests in writing. In order to present their views, either at a public hearing or otherwise, the interested persons should submit 20 copies of a written brief. Rebuttal briefs may also be submitted. The USTR will also obtain advice from the US International Trade Commission.[26]

The time period within which the USTR must make its determinations vary with the nature of the investigation. If the case involves a trade agreement, the USTR must make its determinations within 30 days after the dispute resolution procedures[27] have ended or 18 months after the initiation of the investigation. In most other types of cases, the USTR must make the determinations within 12 months of the initiation of the investigation.

---

22. '"Interested persons"... includes, but is not limited to domestic firms and workers, representatives of consumer interests, United States product exporters, and any industrial user of any goods or services that may be affected by actions taken.' *Id.* § 301(d)(9).
23. *Id.* § 302(a)–(b).
24. *Id.* § 2006.1 (1990).
25. 15 C.F.R. § 2006.3.
26. *Id.* § 304(b)(1)(B)–(C)
27. As discussed above, in cases involving a trade agreement, Section 303(a) requires the USTR to invoke any dispute resolution procedures provided under that trade agreement.

3. Implementation of Retaliation under Section 301

The USTR is required to implement any retaliatory action 30 days after the determination that such action is required. There are three primary actions the USTR is authorized to take in order to retaliate against the unfair foreign trade practices. The USTR may: 1) 'suspend, withdraw, or prevent the application of, benefits of trade agreement concessions;' 2) 'impose duties or other import restrictions on the goods... or restrictions on the services of, such foreign country;' or 3) 'enter into binding agreements with such foreign country that commit such foreign country to' eliminate or compensate for the unfair practices. 19 U.S.C. § 2411(c)(1)(A), (B) and (C).

These actions may be implemented 'on a nondiscriminatory basis... without regard to whether or not such goods or economic sector were involved in the act, policy or practice that is the subject of such action.' 19 U.S.C. § 2411(c)(3), (A) and (B). For example, on September 16, 1985, the USTR instituted an investigation under Section 302 of the Trade Act of 1974 regarding Brazilian trade restrictions on computer and computer related industries.[28] As a result of the investigation, the President announced plans to impose sanctions against certain Brazilian imports to the US. Included on this list were certain benzoid drugs and paper products produced in Brazil. Clearly, these products had no relation to the computer industry; but they were properly subject to retaliation under Section 301. Thus, exporters in a country targeted for Section 301 investigations should retain counsel and participate in any hearings relating to implementation of retaliation to avoid their products being the subject of retaliatory actions. The fact that the investigation itself involves a different product or industry is no guarantee of immunity from retaliatory tariffs or duties. For example, in the Brazilian investigation, the author represented certain Brazilian exporters of ceramic tiles and successfully had them removed from the list of articles subject to retaliation.

The USTR is under a duty to monitor the implementation of retaliatory actions and if the USTR 'considers that a foreign country is not satisfactorily implementing a measure or agreement,' the USTR will determine what other action may be necessary.[29] If the action taken is no longer appropriate or the conditions which occasioned the retaliation no longer exist, the USTR may terminate or modify the action after publishing notice in the *Federal Register* and providing written notice to the Congress.

Finally, any action taken under Section 301 terminates automatically after four years unless the petitioner or a 'representative of the domestic industry which benefits from such action' has made a timely request that the action be continued. Upon receiving such a request, the USTR is to review the efficacy of the action and its effects on the US economy, before determining whether to continue the action. It is important that exporters and importers understand the implications of

28. 50 Fed. Reg. 37.608 (1985).
29. 19 U.S.C. § 2416(b).

this law and take appropriate actions to defend their interests. The emphasis on trade in services increased interest in Section 301 in the past as a mechanism to retaliate against foreign countries that discriminate against US banks, insurance companies, accounting and law firms, and shipping companies. As in the case of Brazil, the law has been utilized against countries such as China that do not adequately protect intellectual property rights (patents, trademark and copyrights) of US companies.

> *PRACTICE NOTE:* Given the fact that the US Trade Representative is part of the Executive Office of the President, there have been concerns about the politicization of decisions under Section 301 and other statutes. Rejection twice by the George W. Bush Administration of a petition by the AFL-CIO involving interest rate practices in China raised concerns of this nature.

Chapter 16

Appellate Review of Customs Decisions

I. INTRODUCTION

Administrative decisions by the Customs Service and other agencies involved in enforcing the US trade laws are reviewable by the US Court of International Trade (CIT). Decisions by the CIT are then appealable to the Court of Appeals for the Federal Circuit (CAFC). Decisions of the United States International Trade Commission in Section 337 cases are appealed directly to the CAFC. This chapter will discuss the judicial review procedures, including the jurisdiction of the two courts involved, standing and the scope and standards of review in different cases.

II. THE COURT OF INTERNATIONAL TRADE

The CIT, formerly named the Customs Court, was established by the Customs Court Act of 1980,[1] which provides that the court is established under Article III of the Constitution of the United States.[2] The Customs Court Act of 1980 sought to resolve the confusion as to the proper relationship between the Customs Court and the US District Courts.[3] The CIT was upgraded to a full Article III constitutional court and was granted all judicial powers in law and equity, jurisdiction over counterclaims, cross-claims and third-party actions in 'any civil action' in the CIT,[4] and

---

1. Pub. L. No. 96.417, 94 Stat. 1727 (codified in various Sections of Titles 19 and 28 of the United States Code).
2. 28 U.S.C. § 251(a) (1993).
3. *See International Trade: United States Court of International Trade – Customs Court Act of 1980,* 22 Harv. Int'l L.J. 480 (1981).
4. 28 U.S.C. § 1583 (1994).

the authority to hear jury trials, in order to make the CIT the exclusive forum for resolving disputes arising out of tariff and international trade laws.[5] Title II of the Customs Court Act of 1980 establishes the jurisdiction of the CIT.

A. JURISDICTION

The CIT is granted exclusive jurisdiction over any civil action arising from the denial of an importer's protest or a domestic interested party's petition, discussed in the previous chapter, under Sections 515 and 516 of the Tariff Act of 1930.[6] In order to bring a case under one of these arms of jurisdiction, the protest or petition must have been properly filed and then denied.[7]

The CIT is also granted exclusive jurisdiction for any case arising from countervailing or antidumping duties proceedings.[8] Section 516A of the Tariff Act of 1930 controls judicial review of countervailing and antidumping duty proceedings and will be discussed later.

Section 1581(d) of Title 28 of the United States Code provides the CIT with exclusive jurisdiction to review 'any final determination of the Secretary of Labor' regarding the eligibility of workers for adjustment assistance.[9] Also, the CIT has exclusive review of 'any final determination of the Secretary of Commerce' regarding the eligibility of firms or communities for adjustment assistance.[10]

Review in the CIT is also granted over 'any final determination of the Secretary of Treasury' regarding nondiscriminatory US Government procurement under Section 305(b)(1) of the Trade Agreements Act of 1979[11] or the denial, revocation or suspension of a customs broker's license or permit.[12]

The final two arms of jurisdiction are perhaps the most interesting.

Section 1581(h) allows the CIT to review a case prior to the import transaction or determination which is the subject of the review. However, the court may only grant review 'if the party commencing the civil action demonstrates to the court that he would be irreparably harmed unless given an opportunity to obtain judicial review prior to such importation.'[13] This grant of jurisdiction is interpreted narrowly to apply only to 'specific contemplated import transactions which contain identifiable merchandise and which will feel the impact of the ruling with virtual

---

5. H.R. Rep. No. 1356, 96th Cong., 2d Sess. 28, reprinted in 1980 U.S. Code Cong. & Admin. News 3721, 3739.
6. 19 U.S.C. §§ 1515–1516 (Supp. 1995); 28 U.S.C. § 1581(a)(b) (1994).
7. *See*, e.g., *Detroit Zoological Soc'y v. United States*, 630 F. Supp. 1350, 1354 (Ct. Int'l Trade 1986).
8. 28 U.S.C. § 1581(c) (1994).
9. *Id.* § 1581(d)(1) (1994).
10. *Id.* § 1581(d)(2)–(3) (1994).
11. *Id.* § 1581(e) (1994).
12. *Id.* § 1581(g)(1)–(2) (1994).
13. *Id.* § 1581(h) (1994).

certainty.'[14] There is a four-part test to determine whether the court has jurisdiction under this section: (1) judicial review must be sought prior to importation of goods; (2) review must be sought of a ruling of the Customs Service, a refusal to issue a ruling or a refusal to change such ruling; (3) the ruling must relate to certain subject matter; and (4) irreparable harm must be shown unless judicial review is obtained prior to importation.[15]

The other interesting feature of the jurisdiction of the CIT is its so called 'residual jurisdiction' established in Section 1581(i). Under this section, the CIT has exclusive jurisdiction over any case that 'arises out of' laws, or the administration of laws, relating to revenue, tariffs, duties, fees, taxes from, or restrictions on, imported merchandise.[16] This arm of jurisdiction is a secondary type of jurisdiction to be invoked only 'when other available avenues of jurisdiction are "manifestly inadequate or necessary because of special circumstances to avoid extraordinary and unjustified delays caused by the exhaustion of administrative remedies."'[17]

The CIT also has exclusive jurisdiction in civil actions brought by the US and involving certain import transactions.[18]

B. Remedial Powers

As was stated earlier, the CIT is granted 'all the powers in law and equity of, or as conferred by statute upon, a district court of the United States.'[19] These powers include the authority to enter money judgments, to 'order a retrial or rehearing for all purposes,' to 'order . . . further administrative or adjudicative procedures,' and to 'order any other form of relief that is appropriate in a civil action.'[20]

C. Procedures

Title III of the Customs Court Act of 1980 defines the CIT requirements for standing, commencing an action, and the scope and standards of review.

1. Standing

The standing provisions of Section 2631 largely restate existing law as to what persons may commence an action. The section does, however, expand the definition

---

14. *Pagoda Trading Co. v. United States*, 577 F. Supp. 22, 24 (Ct. Int'l Trade 1983).
15. *American Air Parcel Forwarding Co. v. United States*, 718 F.2d 1546, 1551 (Fed. Cir. 1983).
16. *28 U.S.C.* § 1581(i) (1994).
17. *Detroit Zoological* Soc'y, 630 F. Supp. at 1353, n. 6 (*quoting Manufacture de Machines du Haut-Rhin v. van Raab*, 569 F. Supp. 877, 882–3 (Ct. Int'l Trade 1983)).
18. *28 U.S.C.* § 1582 (1994).
19. *28 U.S.C.* § 1585 (1994).
20. *28 U.S.C.* § 2643(b)–(c) (1994).

of 'party-at-interest' to include US workers, communities and manufacturers.[21] This section also grants standing to that class of persons who would have standing to sue under the Administrative Procedures Act.[22] 'This subsection is intended to correlate with and complement the broad grant of residual jurisdiction found in section 1581(i).'[23]

2. Commencement of an Action

Generally, a civil action in the CIT is begun by filing a summons and complaint with the clerk of the court.[24] In cases brought under Section 1581(a) or (b), however, the petitioner need only file a summons. A complaint is not necessary.[25] Similarly, under Section 1581(c), the action may be begun either by filing a summons or by filing a summons and compliant. At the time of filing a fee must be paid to the clerk of the court.[26]

The plaintiff must have the summons and/or complaint served upon the defendant according to the rules established by the court.

The time within which a case before the CIT must be filed depends on the grounds on which the case is being brought before the court. Cases brought under Section 1581(a) must be brought within 180 days of the mailing of a notice of denial of a protest. Cases brought under Section 1581(b) must be brought within 30 days of the mailing of the notice of denial of the petition.[27] In countervailing and antidumping duty cases, the interested party must file a complaint and summons within 30 days of the publication of the final determination in the Federal Register.[28] Any action brought under Section 1581(d) must be filed within 60 days of the notice of the determination by the Secretary of Labor or the Secretary of Commerce.[29] Actions brought under Section 1581(e) must be begun within 30 days of the publication of the determination in the *Federal Register.*[30] Section 1581(f) cases must be begun within 10 days after the denial of the request for confidential material.[31] An action contesting the denial, suspension, or revocation of a private laboratory accreditation must be brought within 60 days of the order

---

21. 28 U.S.C. § 2631(k) (1994).
22. 5 U.S.C. § 702; 28 U.S.C. § 263(1) (1994).
23. H.R. Rep. No. 1356. 96th Cong., 2d Sess. 52. reprinted *in* 1980 U.S. Code Cong. & Admin. News 3721, 3764.
24. 28 U.S.C. § 2632(a) (1994).
25. *Id.* § 2632(b) (1994).
26. This was USD 120 at the time this chapter was prepared. Ct. Int'l Trade R.3.
27. *Id.* at § 2636(b) (1994).
28. *Id.* § 2636(c) (1994); 19 U.S.C. § 1516a(a) (Supp. 1995).
29. *Id.* § 2636(d) (1994).
30. *Id.* § 2636(e) (1994).
31. *Id.* § 2636(f) (1994).

by the Customs service.[32] All other actions brought under Section 1581 must be brought within two years after the cause of action arises.[33]

Exhaustion of administrative remedies is only *required* in civil actions contesting the denial of a protest or a petition under Sections 515 and 516 of the Tariff Act of 1930. Actions which are instituted prior to the import transaction under Section 1581(h) do not require exhaustion of administrative remedies.[34] Otherwise the CIT 'shall, where appropriate, require the exhaustion of administrative remedies.'[35]

3. Amendments to Rule 22

The following amendment was added to the CIT Rules on September 30, 2003, effective January 1, 2004.

a. Rule 22 Interpleader

(1) Persons having claims against the plaintiff may be joined as defendants and required to interplead when their claims are such that the plaintiff is or may be exposed to double or multiple liability. It is not ground for objection to the joinder that the claims of the several claimants of the titles on which their claims depend do not have a common origin or are not identical but are adverse to the independent of one another, or that the plaintiff avers that the plaintiff is not liable in whole or in part to any or all claimants. A defendant exposed to similar liability may obtain such interpleader by way of a cross-claim or counterclaim. The provisions of this rule supplement and do not in any way limit the joinder of parties permitted in Rule 20.

(2) The remedy herein provided is in addition to and in no way supersedes or limits the remedy provided by Title 28 U.S.C. §§ 1335, 1397, and 2361. Actions under those provisions shall be conducted in accordance with these rules.

D. Scope and Standard of Review

The Customs Court Act of 1980 established the scope and standard of review that the CIT will exercise in the cases brought before it.

---

32. *Id.* § 2636(g) (1994). The Customs Mod Act provided for the first time the accreditation of private laboratories to do testing that can be used to challenge the results of Customs own laboratories.
33. 28 U.S.C. § 2636(i) (1994).
34. 28 U.S.C. § 2637(c) (1994).
35. *Id.* § 2637(d) (1994).

1. De Novo Review

In cases brought under Sections 1581(a), (b), (e), (f), (g)[36] and 1582, the CIT 'shall make its determinations upon the basis of the record made before the Court.'[37] This is a *de novo* review and the court, which is not bound by the findings of the agency from which the appeal is taken, will establish the record following the Federal Rules of Evidence, the Federal Rules of Civil Procedure and the Rules of the CIT.

The CIT rules provide that a trial may be either before a jury or before the Court.[38] Upon timely demand by a party the court will try all the issues triable by a jury before the jury.[39]

The *de novo* nature of CIT review does not mean that it may interpret statutes without giving deference to an agency's interpreting regulations.[40] Where an agency is charged with using its discretion to implement Congressional policy, or where a statute is ambiguous, the CIT should defer to the agency's expertise unless the court concludes that 'the regulation is inconsistent with statutory language.'[41] When a regulation is challenged, the CIT is charged with determining if the regulation is reasonable, not if it is the best interpretation.[42] This essentially applies the Chevron *doctrine to the CIT.*[43]

2. Review in Countervailing Duty and Antidumping Cases

As was stated above, review by the CIT of countervailing duty and antidumping cases are controlled by Section 516A of the Tariff Act of 1930.[44]

a. Review of Certain Determinations

Section 1516a of Title 19 of the United States Code provides for review of 1) a determination not to initiate an antidumping or countervailing duty investigation; 2) a determination by the International Trade Commission not to review a decision because of changed circumstances; or 3) a negative determination by the International Trade Commission as to whether there is a reasonable indication of material injury, threat of material injury, or material retardation. The CIT will

36. If the Secretary acted under Section 641(d)(2)(B) of the Tariff Act of 1930, the court will review the case as provided in Section 706 of the Administrative Procedures Act.
37. 28 U.S.C. § 2640(a) (1994).
38. Ct. Int'l Trade R. 38, 39.
39. Ct. Int'l Trade R. 39.
40. *United States v. Haggar Apparel Co.*, 526 U.S. 380, 391 (1999).
41. *Id.* at 392–93.
42. *Id.* at 394.
43. *Id.* at 487; *see also Chevron USA Inc. v. Natural Resources Defense Council, Inc.*, 467 U.S. 837 (1984).
44. 19 U.S.C. § 1516a (Supp. 1995). 28 U.S.C. § 2640(b) (1994).

'hold unlawful any determination, finding, or conclusion found . . . to be arbitrary, capricious, an abuse of discretion, or otherwise not in accordance with law.'[45] For example, in *Budd Company Railway Division v. United States*,[46] the Court upheld the International Trade Commission's finding of no material injury or threat of material injury. The court stated that a finding otherwise would be contrary to the evidence and 'arbitrary, capricious, an abuse of discretion or otherwise not in accordance with law.'[47]

b. Review of Determination on the Record

Section 1516a(a)(2) also provides for judicial review of any final determinations 'on the record.' The determinations which may be reviewed under this section are:

(1) Final affirmative determinations by the ITA and the ITC under Section 705 or 735 of the Tariff Act of 1930;
(2) Final negative determinations by the ITA and the ITC under Section 705 or 535 of the Tariff Act of 1930;
(3) Any final determination by the ITC or the ITA after a review under Section 751 of the Tariff Act of 1930;
(4) A determination by the ITA under Sections 704 or 734 of the Tariff Act of 1930;
(5) A determination of injurious effect under Section 704(h) of the Tariff Act of 1930; and
(6) A determination by the ITA regarding the class or kind of merchandise described in an order.[48]

The CIT will review the record to determine whether the determination in question is supported by 'substantial evidence on the record.'[49] For example, in *Kyowa Gas Chemical*,[50] the CIT remanded the case to the ITA because the ITA had erred by applying the wrong standard. The record contained no precedent or authority justifying the standard used by the ITA.

3. Review in Other Cases

Section 2640 provides that for any action not specifically provided for by Section 2640, the CIT is to apply the standard of review established in the Section 706 of the Administrative Procedures Act. Section 706 establishes either an 'arbitrary and

---

45. 19 U.S.C. § 1516a(b)(1) (Supp. 1995).
46. 507 F. Supp. 997, 1002 (Ct. Int'l Trade 1980).
47. *Id.* at 1002.
48. 19 U.S.C. § 1516a(a)(2)(B).
49. 19 U.S.C. at § 1516a(b)(1)(B) (Supp. 1995).
50. *Kyowa Gas Chern. Indus. Co. v. United States*, 5 I.T.R.D. (BNA) 2131, 2133 (1984).

capricious' standard or a 'substantial evidence' standard depending on the action in question.[51]

Review of determinations made under Section 22 of the Agricultural Adjustment Act of 1933, and Sections 201, 301 and 501 of the Trade Act of 1974, is severely restricted since in enacting the legislation Congress delegated a great deal of discretion to the President. In such cases, the court will review the action only to determine: (1) whether proper statutory procedures were followed; (2) whether the statutory language was properly construed; and (3) whether the action taken was within the scope of the delegated authority.[52]

The CIT has followed this test in numerous cases. For example, the CIT applied the test in upholding actions by the President and the ITC in a Section 201 case involving importations of frozen and breaded mushrooms.[53] In *United States Cane Sugar Refiners' Association v. Block*,[54] the court stated that, in a case under Section 22 of the Agricultural Adjustment Act, if the President's action was authorized and within the authority of the section cited then 'his motives, his reasoning, his finding of facts requiring the action, and his judgment, are immune from judicial scrutiny.'[55] The CIT has also followed this test in reviewing cases under Section 301 of the Trade Act of 1974. For example, in *Sunburst Farms, Inc. v. United States*,[56] the court stated that under Section 301, the President is authorized to exercise discretion and therefore the court is 'permitted only to determine whether the statutory language has been properly construed and whether the President's action conforms with the relevant procedural requirements.'[57] Section 301 of the Trade Act of 1974 was amended in the Omnibus Trade and Competitiveness Act of 1988 transferring the 'retaliation authority' from the President to the US Trade Representative. These have been no cases construing the scope and standard of review for actions by the Trade Representative under Section 301. However, since the Trade Representative is an executive officer, and is authorized to exercise broad discretion under Section 301, it is likely that the CIT will apply the standard of review discussed above.

III. COURT OF APPEALS FOR THE FEDERAL CIRCUIT

Pursuant to the Federal Courts Improvement Act of 1982,[58] Congress created the Court of Appeals for the Federal Circuit (CAFC) by combining the Court of Customs

51. 5 U.S.C. § 706 (1977).
52. *United States v. George S. Bush & Co.*, 310 U.S. 371 (1940).
53. *Maple Leaf Fish Co. v. United States.* 596 F. Supp. 1076, 1079 (Ct. Int'l Trade 1984) *aff'd*, 6 I.R.T.D. (BNA) 2186 (Fed. Cir. 1985).
54. 683 F.2d 399 (C.C.P.A. 1982).
55. *Id.* at 404.
56. 620 F. Supp. 735 (Ct. Int'l Trade 1985).
57. *Id.* at 737. *See also Luggage & Leather Goods Mfrs. of Am. v. United States*, 588 F. Supp. 1413, 1426 (Ct. Int'l Trade 1984).
58. Pub. L. No. 97-164, 96 Stat. 25 (1982).

and Patent Appeals and the Court of Claims. The CAFC now has the appellate jurisdiction which was shared between the two courts.

A. JURISDICTION

Unlike the other federal courts of appeals, the jurisdiction of the CAFC is defined by subject matter, not geography.[59] The CAFC is empowered to hear appeals from cases brought throughout the US, provided the cases are within the subject matter jurisdiction of the court.

1. Exclusive Jurisdiction

The court has exclusive jurisdiction to hear appeals from final decisions of district courts in patent cases.[60] However, in cases 'arising under any Act of Congress relating to copyrights, exclusive rights in mask works, or trademarks' which have no other claims under Section 1338(a), the CAFC does not have exclusive jurisdiction.[61] These cases are to be appealed to the appropriate circuit under Sections 1291, 1292 and 1294 of Title 28.[62]

The CAFC has exclusive jurisdiction over appeals from the US Claims Court and the Court of International Trade.[63] Appeals from the Board of Patent Appeals and Interferences of the Patent and Trademark Office, the Commissioner of Patents and Trademarks or the Trademark Trial and Appeal Board are also within the exclusive jurisdiction of the CAFC.[64]

Final determinations by the International Trade Commission under Section 337 of the Tariff Act of 1930 are appealed directly to the CAFC and are within the exclusive jurisdiction of the court. In these cases the CAFC reviews only final determinations of the Commission to determine whether the determination was 'arbitrary, capricious or otherwise not in accordance with law.'[65]

The CAFC also has exclusive appellate jurisdiction over determinations of the Secretary of Commerce '[u]nder US note 6 to subchapter X of Chapter 98 of the Harmonized Tariff Schedule of the United States' and over appeals brought under Section 71 of the Plant Variety Protection Act.[66]

---

59. *See* Note, *An Appraisal of the Court of Appeals for the Federal Circuit*, 57 S. Cat. 1. Rev. 301 (1984).
60. 28 U.S.C. § 1295(a)(1) (1994).
61. *Id.*
62. *Id.*
63. 28 U.S.C. § 1295(a)(3), (5) (1994).
64. 28 U.S.C. § 1295(a)(4) (1994).
65. *Fischer & Porter Co. Inc. v. United States Int'l Trade Comm'n*, 831 F.2d 1574, 1576 (Fed. Cir. 1987).
66. 7 U.S.C. § 2461 (1988); 28 U.S.C. § 1295(a)(7) (1994).

2. Interlocutory Appeals

Section 1291 controls the jurisdiction of the CAFC review of interlocutory (*i.e.*, non-final) decisions. The CAFC has jurisdiction to review interlocutory orders or decrees in any case in which it would have jurisdiction to hear a final determination.[67]

Section 1292 also grants the CAFC jurisdiction to hear certain interlocutory appeals by permission. If the chief judge of the CIT authorizes a judge to conduct an evidentiary hearing in a foreign country pursuant to Section 256(b) of Title 28, the CAFC has discretion to hear an interlocutory appeal from that order.[68] If any judge of a district court, the CIT or the US Claims Court issues an interlocutory order which includes a statement that a controlling question of law is involved with respect to which there is a substantial ground for difference of opinion and that an immediate appeal from that order may materially advance the ultimate termination of the litigation, the CAFC may elect to review that order.[69] An appeal under this section will not stay the proceedings in the court below unless a stay is specifically ordered.[70]

B. PROCEDURE

1. Appeals by Right

In order to take an appeal as of right, or an appeal under Section 1295 or 1292(a), the appellant must file notice of appeal with the clerk of the district court within 30 days (60 if the US is a party) of the date of the filing of the order or judgment appealed.[71] The notice of appeal must identify the parties taking the appeal, the judgment or order being appealed and the court to which the appeal is being taken.[72] The clerk of the court will serve the notice on all parties except the appellant.

After the notice of appeal has been filed, the appellant must also file the record on appeal, docket the appeal, and file a brief and appendix.[73] The CAFC may dismiss the appeal for the appellant's failure to take these further steps.[74]

67. 28 U.S.C. § 1292(c) (1994).
68. 28 U.S.C. § 1292(d)(i) (1994).
69. 28 U.S.C. § 1292(b)(d)(1), (2) (1994).
70. 28 U.S.C. § 1292(d)(3) (1994).
71. Fed. R. App. P. 3(a), 4(a).
72. Fed. R. App. P. 3(b).
73. Fed. R. App. P. 10–12, 28, 31–32.
74. Fed. R. App. P. 5(a).

2. Appeals by Permission

To seek an appeal by permission under Section 1292(b), (c), or (d), the appellant must file a petition for permission with the clerk of the CAFC within 10 days of the order being entered by the CIT. The petition must contain sufficient facts to describe the controlling question of law, a statement of the question itself, the reasons for a substantial basis of a difference of opinion, how an immediate appeal may materially advance the termination of the litigation, and a copy of the order in question.[75] The petition will be served on adverse parties who then have seven days in which to file an answer opposing the appeal.

3. Review of Agency Orders

The rules for appeals from agency orders to the CAFC differ slightly from those described above. To seek review of an agency order, the appellant must file a petition for review with the clerk of the CAFC.[76] The petition must identify the parties seeking review, name the agency which is to be the respondent, and identify the order in question.[77] The time in which the petition must be filed varies depending on the agency from which the appeal is being sought. A petition for review of an order of: 1) the International Trade Commission must be filed within 60 days; 2) the Secretary of Commerce must be filed within 20 days; and 3) the Secretary of Agriculture must be filed within 60 days.[78]

In appeals from agency actions, the record shall consist of 'the order sought to be reviewed, the findings or report on which it is based, and the pleadings, evidence and proceedings before the agency.'[79] Unlike appeals from district courts, the appellant is not responsible for assisting the clerk in assembling the record for review. The agency retains the record and submits a certified list to the court.[80] The court may order the agency to provide copies of the record, or any physical exhibits.[81]

C. Court Decisions

For a summary and discussion of some more significant decisions of the CIT and CAFC, *See* L. Glick, Chapter 18, at 353 *et seq. 'International Trade and Customs Law' in Developments in International Law and Regulatory Practice* (American University, Washington College of Law, 2004).

---

75. Fed. R. App. P. 5(h).
76. Fed. R. App. P. 15(3).
77. *Id.*
78. *See* Note of Advisory Committee on Appellate Rules to Fed. R. App. P. 15.
79. Fed. R. App. 16.
80. Fed. R. App. P. 17(a).
81. *Id.*

Chapter 17

Section 22 of the Agricultural Adjustment Act of 1933: A Remedy to Protect US Agricultural Programs

I. INTRODUCTION

Section 22 of the Agricultural Adjustment Act[1] is designed to

> insulate the US farm economy from the effects of international trade in agricultural commodities... [T]he Agricultural Adjustment Act of 1933 established a system of production and marketing controls and parity prices designed to raise the price farmers received for their crops. However... imports (at the lower world price) would prevent farmers from obtaining the price which the programs were designed to achieve[2].

Therefore, Section 22 authorizes the President to impose quotas or duties on imports of agricultural commodities. This chapter will discuss Section 22, the roles played by the Secretary of Agriculture, the President and the United States International Trade Commission (The 'Commission') in enforcing the law, the relevant statutory standards and the procedural requirements for action under Section 22.

PRACTICE NOTES: This section has not been utilized very much in recent years.

1. 7 U.S.C. § 624 (1982, as amended).
2. *Certain Tobacco*, USITC Inv. No. 22-47, Pub. No. 1644 (1985), F. 7.R.T.D. (B.N.A.) 1643, 1645 (1985).

II. DISCUSSION

Unlike many of the laws discussed earlier, domestic industries or individuals do not play a large role in Section 22 actions. Section 22 is designed to protect public programs as well as domestic industries or individuals. Thus, the various government agencies tend to play a more significant role in Section 22 actions than in actions brought under other laws. In a Section 22 case, the Secretary of Agriculture notifies the President when he/she 'has reason to believe that any article or articles are being or are practically certain to be imported into the United States under such condition and in such quantities as to render or tend to render ineffective, or materially interfere with' programs of the US Department of Agriculture (USDA).[3] After such notice, the President may choose to direct the Commission to investigate the complaint and develop a report for his consideration. Upon receiving the report from the Commission, the President may impose quotas or duties on the imports in question.

A. US Department of Agriculture

In the preliminary stages of a Section 22 investigation, both the USDA and the President have a great deal of discretion as to whether the investigation will continue. The roles of the various agencies are discussed below.

1. The Foreign Agricultural Service of the US Department of Agriculture

All Section 22 investigations are instituted in the USDA. A request for action is submitted to the Foreign Agricultural Service (FAS) which has administrative responsibility, within the USDA, for Section 22 investigations.[4] The administrator of the FAS reviews the application and if 'there is reasonable ground to believe' some action is warranted, he/she will order an investigation to be made.[5] A hearing may be held if the administrator determines that one is necessary.

Upon the completion of the investigation the FAS submits a report to the Secretary of Agriculture summarizing the information discovered by the FAS investigation and containing the recommendations of the FAS. The report must also contain a recommendation as to whether the President should take emergency action with regard to the imports.[6] If emergency action is recommended, the report should state the conditions which establish the need for such action.

---

3. 7 U.S.C. § 624(a).
4. 7 C.F.R. § 6.3(a).
5. 7 C.F.R. § 6.4 (a).
6. 7 U.S.C. § 624(b).

2. The Secretary of Agriculture

The Secretary of Agriculture reviews the recommendation submitted by the FAS and if he/she finds 'reason to believe' the imports in question warrant action under Section 22, either emergency or otherwise, the Secretary will recommend the appropriate action to the President.

3. Representation at Commission Hearings

The USDA is not only responsible for the preliminary investigation of Section 22 cases, but it is also present at the Commission hearing.[7] The FAS designates a person to present the recommendations of the USDA and the information and data supporting that recommendation to the Commission. Because of the expertise of the USDA with regard to the agricultural programs and the fact that the USDA has already gathered facts relevant to the Commission's determination, the Commission gives significant weight to testimony of the representative from the USDA.[8]

B. The US International Trade Commission

The Commission undertakes an investigation in a Section 22 case only if the President directs the Commission to do so.[9] The USDA and the President must determine only whether there was a 'reasonable ground' for belief that 'any article or articles[10] are being or are *practically* certain to be imported into the United States under such conditions and in such quantities as *to render* or *tend to render ineffective*, or *materially interfere* with[11] an agricultural support program.' The Commission must then determine if sufficient facts exist to warrant action. Essentially, the Commission acts as a fact finding body, analyzing the USDA program in question, its methods of operation and its goals, actual or potential increases in imports and any impact on USDA programs.[12] The Commission's investigation must be made pursuant to Sections 201 and 204 of the Code of Federal Regulations.

---

7. *Id.*
8. *See Certain Tobacco*, USITC Inv. No. 22-43, Pub. No. 1174 (1981), 3 I.R.T.D. (B.N.A.) 1266, 1277 (1981).
9. 19 C.F.R. § 204.2 (1988).
10. Unlike sections discussed earlier, the imported articles subject to investigation under Section 22 do not have to be the same as the domestic articles in question. The imported articles need only have the necessary impact on a USDA program.
11. 7 U.S.C. § 624(a) (emphasis added).
12. The Commission's 'role in these investigations is a limited one. [They] are not called upon to judge the wisdom of a particular commodity program or to propose changes to it' *Certain Tobacco*, USITC Inv. No. 22-47, Pub. No. 1644 (1985), I.R.T.D. (B.N.A.) 1643, 1645 (1985).

1. Substantive Issues before the Commission

a. The Import Test

The Commission must first determine whether any articles of the type in question are being or are practically certain to be imported into the US. The term 'being' indicates that the articles in question are presently being imported.[13] The test for 'practically certain,' however, is more complex.

In *Certain Articles Containing Sugar*,[14] the Commission found that the imported articles were practically certain to materially interfere. In analyzing the levels of imports, the Commission indicated that the phrase 'practically certain' raises two issues.[15] 'First, there must be a demonstration that there are sufficient *incentives* and *the capability* to *increase imports*..., Second, these imports must be *expected* to reach a level which will materially interfere with the price support program. The '"practically certain" standard means the probability of imports reaching a level so as to cause material interference must be highly likely.'[16] In finding that imports of the articles containing sugar were practically certain to materially interfere, the Commission analyzed the economic incentive to import the articles, the capacity of foreign producers to produce the articles for export to the US and the 'recent increase in newly created blends containing high levels of sugar.'[17] The Commission followed a similar analysis in *Certain Tobacco*[18] (flue-, fire- and dark air-cured tobacco and burley tobacco are not being imported and are not practically certain to be imported in such quantities as to tend to render ineffective or materially interfere with USDA programs for tobacco).

b. Harm to a USDA Program

If the import test is met, the Commission must also determine whether the USDA program in question is being harmed or is threatened with harm by the imports. The imports must be found to 'render or tend to render ineffective, or materially interfere with the program in question.'[19] There is no statutory definition of 'render ineffective' or of 'materially interfere.' However, the Commission has interpreted the statutory language in several cases.

In *Certain Tobacco*,[20] the Commission discussed the question of harm in a Section 22 investigation of fire-, flue- and dark air-cured and burley tobacco. The Commission seemed to indicate that the difference between 'rendering ineffective'

---

13. *Id.*
14. USITC Inv. No. 22-48, Pub. No. 2626 (1983), T.D. (B.N.A.) 2410, 2422 n. 11 (1983).
15. *Id.*
16. USITC Inv. No. 22-43, Pub. No. 1174 (1981), 3 I.R.T.D. (B.N.A.) 1266.
17. *Id.*
18. *Certain Tobacco*, USITC Inv. No. 22-47, Pub. No. 1644 (1985), I.R.T.D. (B.N.A.) 1643 (1985).
19. 7 U.S.C. § 624(a).
20. *Certain Tobacco*, (1981).

and 'materially interfering' with is a matter of degree. 'Renders ineffective' is the most severe harm and 'material interference' is the less stringent of the standards.[21] 'A program which has been rendered ineffective has also suffered material interference, although the reverse may not be true.' In this case, the Commission found the USDA programs to be presently healthy and found no indication of prospective harm. It therefore held that the increased imports of the articles in question did not have a sufficient impact on the programs to justify action under Section 22.

The Commission addressed the issue of material interference again in another investigation of tobacco imports.[22] In analyzing whether the imports materially interfered with USDA tobacco programs, the Commission stated that such 'interference can be defined in terms of the goals of the tobacco program rather than solely in terms of the mechanisms by which those goals are achieved.'[23] Thus, the Commission is to not only look at changes in the mechanics of the programs, levels of stock, production and acreage allotments, price support levels and costs of the program; it must also look at whether these changes interfere with or help to accomplish the overall goals for which the programs were established. In this case, the Commission concluded that the increased imports of tobacco in the categories in question did not have a sufficient effect on the USDA programs.

2. Procedures before the Commission

It is important to note that Section 22 authorizes two types of investigations: an investigation under Section 22(a) (7 U.S.C.S. § 624(a)) and a supplemental investigation under Section 22(d) (7 U.S.C.S. § 624(d)). Except for the way the investigations are instituted, the procedures for these investigations are the same.[24]

The Commission performs three functions in each Section 22 investigation: 1) it obtains the information needed to make its determination; 2) it holds a public hearing on the issue; and 3) it issues a report of its findings to the President.

The Commission has a variety of tools available to obtain the information necessary to make its determinations.[25] Normally, the Commission prepares questionnaires which are sent to growers, importers and other interested persons to obtain information relevant to its inquiry.[26]

---

21. *Id.*
22. *Certain Tobacco*, (1985).
23. *Id.*
24. The supplemental investigation allows the President to modify any provision of a proclamation made under Section 22(a). An investigation for the purpose of modifying the proclamation may be instituted either 'upon request of the President or upon the Commission's own motion' when in its judgment there is good and sufficient reason therefore. 19 C.F.R. § 204.4. Note that preliminary determinations by the USDA and the President are not required in supplemental investigations.
25. 19 C.F.R. § 201.9 (1988).
26. However, the Commission is also authorized to obtain 'pertinent information from its own files, from other agencies of the Government, through...correspondence and through field work by members of the Commission's staff.'

The Commission is also required to conduct a public hearing on the issues: The hearing is to be conducted by one or more of the Commissioners who are granted the broad authority to conduct a 'fair and impartial hearing.'[27] Any party, importer, or domestic grower, may participate in the hearing.[28] A representative from the FAS with an attorney from the Office of the General Counsel will also be present at the hearing.

Finally, upon completing the investigation, the Commission must submit a report to the President.[29] Neither the statute nor the regulations provide a deadline for the submission of the report. The report must contain the Commission's findings, a recommendation as to the appropriate remedy, a description of the Commission's investigation, and a transcript of the evidence presented at the hearing.

C. The Role of the President

The President plays two roles in enforcing Section 22. First, the President makes the preliminary determination, based upon the recommendation of the Secretary of Agriculture, as to whether to direct the Commission to instigate an investigation. Second, the President makes the final determination, based upon the report from the Commission, as to whether to provide a remedy under Section 22 and what that remedy will be.

1. **Preliminary Determinations**

Upon reviewing the report submitted by the Secretary of Agriculture, if 'the President agrees that there is reason' for the Secretary's belief that certain importations warrant action under Section 22, the President directs the Commission to institute an investigation. The President is also authorized to establish regulations regarding the conduct of the investigation.

If, as discussed above, the Secretary of Agriculture recommends that the President take emergency action with regard to the imports, the President has the discretion to impose quotas or duties on the imports before the Commission makes its determination. These remedies remain in effect until the Commission completes its investigation, reports to the President, and the President acts on the report.

2. **Action by the President**

After receiving the findings and recommendations of the Commission, the President may choose to provide a remedy against the imports in question.[30] If the

27. 19 C.F.R. § 201.13(b)(1), (2).
28. 19 C.F.R. § 201.13(c).
29. 19 C.F.R. § 204.5.
30. Although the President has broad discretionary powers under Section 22 (7 U.S.C. § 624(a), (b), (e)), the Court of International Trade will review the President's action to determine if the

President chooses to provide a remedy, the presidential proclamation must contain specific findings that the criteria established in Section 22 are satisfied.[31]

3. Available Remedies

The President is authorized under Section 22 to impose either a quota or additional duties on the imported article in question. The President may not impose both duties and a quota on the same article.[32] The duties or fees are limited to no more than 50% *ad valorem* and the quota may not reduce the total quantity of the article allowed to enter the US to less than 50 per cent of the normal quantity of the articles imported.

III. CONCLUSION

Section 22 is not a trade remedy that has been used frequently in the past. However, due to the increased importance of agricultural trade, it is likely that it will be implemented more often in the future.

President's authority 'has been exercised in conformity with the procedural requirements of statutory authority and whether such action of the President has been performed according to law.' *Farr Man & Co. v. United States*, 544 F. Supp. 908, 910 (Ct. Int'l Trade 1982).

31. *Best Foods, Inc. v. United States*, 218 F. Supp. 576 (Cust. Ct. 1963) (finding that domestic peanut processors needed relief from short supply in a presidential proclamation modifying an earlier proclamation did not constitute the funding required to be in a presidential proclamation).
32. 544 F. Supp. at 891–92.

Chapter 18

Enforcement of Health and Agricultural Laws

I. INTRODUCTION

US Customs enforces or assists in enforcing various agricultural policies and laws when they relate to the importation of products into the US. For example, Customs is involved in enforcing various health and safety restrictions as they pertain to the importation of food, plants, seeds, milk and cream. Except where Customs and the other regulatory agency issue regulations jointly, all of the relevant Customs Regulations are found in Part 12 of Title 19 of the Code of Federal Regulations.

This chapter will discuss the role the Customs Service plays in enforcing these laws and the interaction between the Customs Service and the various agencies such as the Animal and Plant Health Inspection Service (APHIS), the Agricultural Marketing Service (AMS) of the United States Department of Agriculture (USDA) and the Food and Drug Administration (FDA) of the Department of Health and Human Services (HHS).

II. DISCUSSION

A. THE FOOD AND DRUG ADMINISTRATION

In cooperation with the FDA, the Customs Service enforces certain import restrictions on adulterated foods, milk and cream.

1. Adulterated Foods

Customs cooperates with the FDA in enforcing Section 801 of the Federal Food, Drug and Cosmetic Act.[1] Under this section, any food which was not manufactured

1. 21 U.S.C. § 381(1995).

or processed in accordance with the requirements of the Act, is restricted in sale in the exporting country, is adulterated, manufactured, processed or packaged under unsanitary conditions, may not enter the Customs territory of the United States.[2]

Upon request of the district director of the FDA in the relevant port of entry, the customs officer must deliver samples of any food which is being offered for importation into the US.[3] The customs officer is then required to provide notice of the delivery of the sample to the owner or consignee of the article.[4] The sample is then inspected by the FDA to determine whether it will be refused admission under Section 801.[5]

While the FDA is determining whether to deny the article admission, the customs officer may authorize delivery of the articles in question if the owner or consignee posts a 'customs single-entry or term bond, containing a condition for the redelivery of the merchandise upon demand from the customs officer.'[6] The bond must be posted under the conditions established in Section 113.62 of the Customs Regulations on Customs Form 301.

If the FDA denies the articles' admission into the US, the articles must be destroyed under Customs supervision unless they are exported under Sections 18.25 and 18.26 of the Customs Regulations[7] within 90 days of notice of the denial of admission.[8]

2. Milk and Cream

Customs also assists the FDA in enforcing the Federal Import Milk Act.[9] Primary responsibility for enforcing this act lies with the FDA. However, under the Federal Import Milk Act, no Customs Officer may permit milk or cream to be imported into the customs territory of the US without a permit issued by the FDA.[10] Applications for a permit to import milk or cereal into the US must be filed with the Commissioner of Food and Drugs.[11] In order to obtain the permit, the farms, cows, plants and equipment from which milk or cream is to be imported into the US must be inspected before the importation.[12] Failure to allow the necessary

2. 21 U.S.C. § 381(a) (1995).
3. 21 C.F.R. § 1.90 (1995).
4. *Id.*
5. The FDA is required to provide the owner or consignee of the articles in question an opportunity to introduce oral or written testimony on the issues if it 'appears that the article may be subject to refusal of admission.' 21 C.F.R. § 1.94 (1995).
6. 21 U.S.C. § 381(b) (1995); 21 C.F.R. § 1.97 (1995).
7. To export the excluded articles, four copies of Customs Form 7412 must be filed. 19 C.F.R. § 18.25 (1995).
8. 21 U.S.C. § 381(a) (1995).
9. 21 U.S.C. § 141–9 (1995).
10. 19 C.F.R. § 12.7 (1995); *see* 21 U.S.C. § 141 (1995).
11. 21 C.F.R. § 1210. 20 (1995).
12. 21 C.F.R. §§ 1210.10–.17 (1995).

inspections or failure to meet the standards established by the FDA can result in denial, suspension, or revocation of a permit.[13]

The Federal Import Milk Act also provides for criminal sanctions against 'any person who knowingly violates any provision of this Act.'[14] The Department of Justice is responsible for the prosecution of any case under this section. Before the Justice Department will proceed in a case, however, a hearing will be held at the FDA providing the 'party against whom prosecution is under consideration' an opportunity 'to show cause why he should not be prosecuted.'[15] If, after the hearing, 'it appears that the law has been violated,' the facts will be referred to the Justice Department.[16]

B. Agricultural Marketing Service (AMS)

The AMS and Customs have issued joint regulations governing the enforcement of Section 402(b) of 'the Federal Seed Act of 1939.[17] This section prohibits the importation of 'any agricultural or vegetable seed' or 'screenings of any seed' which do not meet the statutory standards.

Upon importation of any seed or any screenings, a Customs officer must draw samples of the seeds and forward them to the Livestock, Meat, Grain, and Seed Division, of the AMS.[18] The AMS then inspects the seed to determine if it meets the statutory criteria. If the seed or screenings do not meet the criteria, then the AMS notifies Customs and the seed is refused entry into the US.

Customs must provide notice to the owner of the seeds or screenings that a sample has been drawn and the rest of the shipment is being held until the AMS determines whether the shipment may enter the US.[19] Pending decision of the matter by the AMS, Customs may deliver the shipment to the owner under 'a customs single-entry bond or a customs term bond' containing a redelivery condition.[20] In order to qualify for this delivery under bond, 'each container of such seed or screenings [must be] stenciled or labeled to show the name of the kind, or the kind and variety, and a lot number or other designation identifying the lot of seed.'[21] If the AMS denies entry to the seed or screenings, they must be

---

13. The PDA regulations also provide for administrative hearings to be held before the PDA if any person 'contests the denial, suspension. or revocation of a permit.' 21 C.F.R. §§ 1210.10, 1210.30 (1995); 21 U.S.C. § 143 (1972).
14. 21 U.S.C. § 145 (1972).
15. 21 C.F.R. § 1210.31 (1995).
16. *Id.*
17. 7 U.S.C. § 1581 (1995) *et. seq.*
18. 19 C.F.R. § 12.16 (1995); 7 C.F.R. §§ 210.208, 210.209 (1995). To ensure that the sample is representative of the quantity of seed the regulations establish the methods by which the customs officer is to obtain the sample. *See* 7 C.F.R. §§ 201.210–.216 (1995).
19. 7 C.F.R. § 201.217 (1995).
20. 7 C.F.R. § 201.218 (1995).
21. *Id.*

destroyed under Customs' supervision unless they are re-exported within one year of notice of denial of admission.[22]

C. Animal And Plant Health Inspection Service

With regard to the importation of plants, plant products, domestic animals and animal products, '[c]ustoms officers and employees shall perform such functions as are necessary or proper on their part to carry out such regulations and orders of the Department of Agriculture and the provisions of law under which they are made.'[23] APHIS, an agency of the USDA, operates the inspection and quarantine programs for all plants and animals which are imported into the US. Thus, Customs works in cooperation with APHIS to enforce the Plant Quarantine Act[24] and the laws regulating the importation of animals and animal products, including Section 306 of the Tariff Act of 1930.[25] The Customs officer at the point of entry for the plants, plant products, animals and animal products may not release the shipments until such release is authorized by the appropriate service.[26] The shipments may be released under a temporary bond, as discussed above.

1. Federal Plant Pest Act

Customs will not allow a plant pest to enter the customs territory of the US unless that importation complies with the requirements of the Federal Plant Pest Act. This act prohibits the movement of plant pests without a permit issued by the APHIS or a certificate of inspection issued by the appropriate officials of the country or state from which the plant pest is to be moved.[27]

Applications for such a permit must be made to the Plant Protection and Quarantine Program of APHIS prior to the importation by residents of the US.[28] The application for each pest must contain: 1) the scientific name of the pest; 2) stage; 3) quantity; 4) origin; 5) destination; 6) a statement as to whether that pest is established at the destination of the shipment; and 7) information regarding the shipment method, safety measures and final disposition of the pest.[29] The Deputy Administrator for the Plant Protection and Quarantine Program is responsible for considering the application.[30] The Deputy Administrator is authorized to consult any state or federal officials and to inspect the destination site for the shipment of

---

22. 7 U.S.C. § 1582 (1995).
23. 19 C.F.R. §§ 12.10, 12.24 (1995).
24. 7 U.S.C. § 150aa (1995) *et seq.*
25. 19 U.S.C. § 1306 (1995).
26. 19 C.F.R. §§ 12.10, 12.11, 12.8 (1995).
27. 7 U.S.C § 150bb(a)–(b) (1995).
28. 7 C.F.R. § 330.201 (1995) APHIS is now part of the Department of Homeland Security along with Customs.
29. *Id.*
30. 7 C.F.R. § 330.202 (1995).

pests in order to determine whether to issue the permit.[31] If the Deputy Administrator determines that there is a danger of dissemination of the pest, he/she will deny the application.[32] The Customs officer must hold 'all plant pests; means of conveyance; and their stores which the inspector may consider to be infested or infected by a plant pest until they have been inspected.'[33] Once the inspector notifies the customs officer that the plant pests may be released, the customs officer may release the plant pests for 'entry or onward movement.'[34]

2. Plant Quarantine Act

The importation of plants into the US is restricted by the Plant Quarantine Act and Parts 319, 320, and 321 of the APHIS Regulations. Under this act, Customs may allow plants to enter the US only if accompanied by a permit issued by the APHIS and a certificate of inspection.[35]

There are two kinds of permits: a general permit and a specific permit.

The general permit, established in the regulations, is a general authorization to move plants.[36] A person is not required to apply for a general permit. If the plants being imported do not satisfy the criteria to be entered under a general permit, then the importer must apply for a specific permit.[37] The application must be made prior to the arrival of the shipment in the US, and should be made to the Permit Unit, Plant Protection and Quarantine Programs, APHIS.[38] Permits are denied if 'it is not possible to prescribe conditions adequate to prevent danger of plant pest dissemination by the plants.'[39]

Upon the arrival of the shipment, the importer must notify Customs, in duplicate on form PQ-368.[40] Once notified of the arrival, Customs must hold the plants until authorized to release them by an inspector for APHIS.[41]

3. Animals and Animal Products

The Department of Agriculture is authorized to restrict the importation of animals and animal products in order to prevent the 'introduction or dissemination of the contagion of any contagious, infectious, or communicable disease of animals and/or live poultry.'[42] Generally, all animals and animal products may enter the Customs

---

31. *Id.*
32. 7 C.F.R. § 330.204 (1995).
33. 7 C.F.R. § 330.105 (1995).
34. *Id.*
35. 7 U.S.C. § 154(b)(1)–(2) (1995).
36. 7 C.F.R. § 352.5 (1995).
37. 7 C.F.R. § 352.6 (1995).
38. *Id.*
39. *Id.*
40. 7 C.F.R. § 352.7 (1995).
41. 7 C.F.R. §§ 352.10 (1995), 330.105 (1995).
42. 21 U.S.C. § 111 (1995).

territory of the US with a permit if they have been inspected and quarantined. However, Section 306 of the Tariff Act of 1930 prohibits the importation of cattle, sheep, swine and meats in certain cases.

a. *Restrictions on Entry into the US*

Customs may not permit the entry of animals or animal products if they are not accompanied by an import permit issued by a salaried veterinary officer of the national government of the country of Origin.[43] The applications must be made prior to the arrival of the shipment and must contain detailed information about the animals, their country of origin, the importer, their transportation and their destination.[44] At the time the application is made, the importer must pay a fee to reserve a quarantine facility.[45]

Upon arriving in the US, the animals are quarantined for a period of time.[46] The amount of time in quarantine depends on the type of animal. While in quarantine, an inspector from the Veterinary Services inspects the animals to determine whether they are free of communicable disease and have not been exposed to such.[47] The inspection may include certain diagnostic tests. If the inspector makes an affirmative determination that the animals are free from contagious disease, then at the end of the quarantine period, Customs may release the animals into the US.[48]

b. *Prohibitions on Entry into the United States*

Section 306 of the Tariff Act of 1930 prohibits the importation of cattle, sheep, swine, and meats from countries in which rinderpest or foot-and-mouth disease exists.[49] The Secretary of Agriculture has given the Secretary of Treasury notice that rinderpest or foot-and-mouth exists in all countries, except those listed in the regulations.[50]

There are a few narrow exceptions in which customs may allow these products to enter the US. Some cattle, sheep and swine may enter the US from one of the listed countries if those animals have passed through quarantine at the Harry S. Truman Animal Import Center. This quarantine area is specifically designed to quarantine animals which may have been exposed to rinderpest or foot-and-mouth disease.

---

43. Ruminants, swine, poultry, pet birds., commercial birds, zoological birds, and research birds may also require a certificate from a veterinary officer of the country from which they are transported. 9 C.F.R. §§ 92.104(a), 92.205(a), 92.405(a)–(c), 92.505(a)–(c) (1995).
44. 9 C.F.R. §§ 92.103(a), 92.204(a), 92.304(a), 92.404(a), 92.505(a) (1995).
45. *Id.*
46. 9 C.F.R. §§ 92.106(a), 92.209(a)(I), 92.308(a), 92.411(a), 92.510 (1995).
47. 9 C.F.R. §§ 92.105, 92.207, 92.306, 92.408, 92.507 (1995).
48. 9 C.F.R. §§ 92.106, 92.207, 92.306, 92.408, 92.507 (1995).
49. 19 U.S.C. § 1306 (1995).
50. 9 C.F.R. § 94.1 (1995).

Authorization to use the center is issued only to a limited number of importers and is granted on a lottery basis.[51]

An importer must apply for the lottery and pay a fee of USD 1,000 per head to be eligible for the lottery.[52]

Fresh, chilled, or frozen meat of cattle, sheep, and swine raised and slaughtered from a country that is listed disease free, but during shipment to the US, enters a port of a country where rinderpest or foot-and-mouth disease exists, may enter the US if certain conditions are met.[53] The meat must be inspected by and carry a foreign meat inspection certificate from an inspector of the Food Safety and Inspection Service.[54] An agent of the APHIS must have sealed the meat into the transport carrier in the country of origin of the meat so as to prevent contact of the meat with any other cargo. If, upon arrival in the US, the meat is as represented in the certificates as correctly certified and sealed, the Customs Service may allow the meat to enter.[55] Cured or cooked meat which has been imported under the strict guidelines established in the regulations may also enter the US.[56]

The Uruguay Round Agreement provides a number of requirements and procedures that member countries may take in establishing regulations to protect their country from animals, plants, or pests that may be diseased. In particular, the Sanitary and Phytosanitary (S&P) Agreement of the Uruguay Round Agreements are designed to preserve the ability of governments to regulate this area while guarding against the use of unjustified S&P measures to protect domestic industries.

The Agreement calls for governments to take necessary measures to protect human, animal or plant life and health form the risk of disease from animal, plant, pest or product introduced into the US from another country. The S&P measures are to be based on scientific principles. The term, 'scientific' is not defined in the Agreement and therefore the term is expected to be interpreted in good faith.

Article 3 of the Agreement calls for harmonization of the different government standards into a uniform international standard as a basis for establishing its S&P measures. However, the Agreement explicitly affirms the right of each government to maintain or adopt measures more stringent than the relevant international standard, so long as there is sufficient justification for doing so.

A transparency requirement is also introduced, in which each government must promptly publish its S&P measures and allow interested members access to such information.

The basic concept of the S&P Agreement is to recognize governments' rights to regulate this area, but not to use the S&P measures as a protectionist measure. While it allows for discrimination against other countries, it may not be arbitrary or unjustifiable.

---

51. 9 C.F.R. §§ 92.430, 92.522 (1995).
52. *Id.*
53. 9 C.F.R. § 94.1 (1995).
54. *Id.*
55. *Id.*
56. *Id.*

4. The Public Health Security and the Bioterrorism Preparedness and Response Act of 2002 (Bioterrorism Act)

In response to new concerns raised as a result of the events of September 11, 2001 on June 12, 2002, President Bush signed the Bioterrorism Act into law. The law required registration of certain foreign products and exporters of food products and prior notice of shipments of these products to give US Customs and FDA inspectors more time to be alerted to potentially hazardous shipments. Importers of these products were required to have registered agents in the United States available for contact at all times. For a discussion of the Bioterrorism Act, *See* L. Glick, *A Coordinated Response to Stop Bioterrorism at the Border*; *'Update' Issue 3, at 18* (Food and Drug Law Institute, 2004).

Chapter 19

The Generalized System of Preferences

I. INTRODUCTION

Among the duty exemption provisions enforced by US Customs, the most important is probably the Generalized System of Preferences (GSP). The Generalized System of Preferences is a program designed to help developing countries increase their export trade. It provides for duty-free importation into the US of a wide range of products from beneficiary developing countries (BDCs). The purpose of the program is to assist the economic growth of developing countries and to encourage diversification and expansion of their production and exports. For many developing countries, export earnings constitute the primary source of fimas needed for development, as well as foreign exchange for financing importations of basic commodities and machinery, and for repaying debts. Thus, through the GSP, developing countries are able to increase exports and diversify their economies, thereby decreasing their dependence on foreign aid. Twenty-seven developed nations have GSP programs, including the United States, the European Community, Canada, Australia, the Nordic Countries, Japan and the East European countries. The US program of the GSP has been instrumental in promoting economic development in developing countries. During the period since the GSP was initiated, developing countries have offered the fastest growing markets for US products.[1] The GSP also has contributed to this growth by enabling developing countries to earn increased foreign exchange, which they have partly used to purchase more US goods and services.[2]

---

1. *See* Annual Report of the President of the United States on the Trade Agreements Program, 1984–85, at 155 (1986).
2. *Id.*

II. STATUTES AND REGULATIONS

The GSP was enacted by the US as part of the Trade Act of 1974,[3] was implemented on January 1, 1976, and has been extended either prior to expiration or retroactively on each occasion of its possible expiration.[4]

The provisions of the GSP are implemented by Part 2007 of Title 15 of the Code of Federal Regulations.

Under Section 501 of the Trade Act of 1974, the President may provide duty-free treatment for any eligible article from any BDC, but he must consider various factors including:

(i) The effect such action will have on furthering the economic development of developing countries;
(ii) The extent to which other major developed countries are undertaking a comparable effort to assist developing countries by granting generalized preferences with respect to imports of products of such countries;
(iii) The anticipated impact of such action on US producers of like or directly competitive products;[5] and
(iv) The extent of the beneficiary developing country's competitiveness with respect to eligible articles.[6]

III. ELIGIBILITY REQUIREMENTS

A. Eligible Countries

In order to be eligible for GSP benefits, a country must have been certified as a BDC by the President of the US. Approximately 130 countries and territories currently have been designated as BDC'S. Specifically excluded from the list of BDCs are developed countries like Australia, Canada, Japan, Switzerland, the European Union Member States, Norway, New Zealand and Monaco.[7] The Trade

---

3. *See* Pub. L. No. 93-618, 88 Stat. 1978.01975 (codified as amended at 19 U.S.C. §§ 2101–2495 (1989)).
4. *See,* e.g., Section 505 of the Trade Act of 1974, as amended by Section 506 of the Trade and Tariff Act of 1984, which continued the GSP in existence until 1993; Pub. L. No. 98-573, 98 Stat. 48 (1984). *See also* Pub. L. 104-188 (extension to 1997), Pub. L. 107-210 (Retroactive extension from September 30, 2001, expired December 31, 2006), H.R. 6406 (extension until 2008).
5. *Id.* at Section 501.
6. This fourth criterion was added by Section 502 of the Trade and Tariff Act of 1984. This additional criterion has formalized a policy known as 'graduation,' whereby benefits for certain products produced in the more advanced developing countries have been denied or removed once these countries have been deemed to have become fully competitive in a particular product.
7. *See* Section 502(b) of the Trade Act of 1974. Section 503 of the Trade and Tariff Act of 1984 deleted Hungary from the list of excluded BDGS. On November 3, 1989, Hungary was officially redesignated as an eligible BDC. 54 Fed. Reg. 46.357 (1989).

Act also precludes the President from designating any country a BDC if such country is a communist country:[8]

(i) Such country is a party to an arrangement of countries and participates in any action pursuant to such arrangement, the effect of which is —
   (a) To withhold supplies of vital commodity resources from international trade or to raise the price of such commodities to an unreasonable level; and
   (b) To cause serious disruption of the world economy;[9]

(ii) Such country affords preferential treatment to the products of a developed country, other than the US, which has, or is likely to have, a significant adverse effect on US commerce;

(iii) Such country has nationalized, expropriated or otherwise seized ownership or control of property, including patents, trademarks, or copyrights,[10] owned by a US citizen or by a corporation, partnership or association which is 50 per cent or more beneficially owned by US citizens, without paying prompt, adequate and effective compensation in accordance with the governing norms of international law;

(iv) Such country fails to act in good faith in recognizing as binding, or in enforcing, arbitral awards in favor of US persons, which have been made by appointed tribunals.

(v) Such country aids or abets, by granting sanctuary from prosecution, any individual or group which has committed an act of international terrorism; and

(vi) Such country has not taken or is not taking steps to afford internationally recognized worker rights to workers in the country.

Paragraphs (iii), (iv), (v) and (vi) shall not, however, prevent the designation of any country as a BDC if the President determines that such designation will be in the national economic interest of the United States and reports such determination to Congress with his reasons therefore.

In determining whether to designate any country a BDC, the President also must take into account other factors such as: an expression by such country of its desire to be so designated; the country's level of economic development; whether that country has been extended GSP treatment by other major developed countries; and the extent to which such country has assured the US it will provide equitable and reasonable access to its markets and basic commodity resources.[11]

---

8. A communist country may, however, be designated a BDC if: the products of such country receive nondiscriminatory treatment; such country is a WTO member and a member of the International Monetary Fund; and, such country is not dominated or controlled by international communism. *See Id.* at Section 502(f)(1).
9. *See Id.*, Section 502(b)(2).
10. Such property includes patents, trademarks and copyrights. *See* Section 503(c) of the Trade and Tariff Act of 1984.
11. *Id.*, Section 502(c). Other criteria added by Section 503(c) of the Trade and Tariff Act of 1984, are: the extent to which such country has assured the U.S. that it will refrain from engaging

B. Eligible Products

The only articles that can qualify for GSP treatment are those which are imported directly from a BDC into the customs territory of the US.[12] In addition, the sum of:

(i) The cost or value of the materials produced in the BDC; and
(ii) The direct costs of processing operations performed in such BDC, must be at least 35 per cent of the appraised value of such article at the time of its entry into the customs territory of the US.[13] However, the following import-sensitive articles are expressly excluded from the list of eligible articles: textile and apparel articles which are subject to textile agreements; certain watches; import-sensitive semi-manufactured and manufactured glass products; import sensitive electronic and steel articles, and any other articles which the President determines to be import sensitive in the context of the GSP.[14]

Approximately 3,000 items currently have been designated as eligible for duty-free treatment from BDCs. However, the list of eligible countries and products changes from time to time. A current list of eligible countries follows at the end of this chapter.

IV. ADDING OR REMOVING PRODUCTS

Each year, a general review is held where parties can request the addition, removal or redesignation of an article. Also, articles that had become ineligible because

---

in unreasonable export practices; the extent to which such country is providing adequate and effective means under its laws for foreign nationals to secure, exercise and enforce exclusive rights in intellectual property; the extent to which such country has taken action to reduce trade distorting investment practices and policies, and reduce or eliminate barriers to trade in services; and whether or not such country has taken or is taking steps to afford workers in that country internationally recognized worker rights.

Consistent with this new provision in the Trade and Tariff Act of 1984, President Reagan suspended Chile's GSP status in response to alleged worker rights violations. *See* 5 Int'l Trade Rep. at 10. The GSP status of other countries has been subject to review due to similar allegations made by organized labor in the United States.

12. *Id.* at Section 503(b)(i).
13. *Id.* at Section 503(b)(2). The method of calculating this 35 per cent is set out in 19 C.F.R. § 10.177, 10.178. In *Madison Galleries, Ltd. v. United States.* 870 F.2d 627, 630 (Fed. Cir. 1989), the court liberalized the standard for GSP eligibility by striking down Customs' interpretation requiring all components of the article to be the 'growth, produce, or manufacturer' of a beneficiary developing country. Also, materials from outside the BDC can be counted toward the 35 per cent requirement if 'substantially transformed' within the BDC.
14. *Id.* at Section 503(c)(1). Subsequently added to this list are footwear, handbags, luggage, flat goods, work gloves, and leather apparel which were not eligible articles on April 1, 1984. *See* Section 5-4(b) of the Trade and Tariff Act of 1984. On November 4, 1989, the President determined that certain types of watches not currently produced in the U.S. would be eligible for GSP. *See* 54 Fed. Reg. 46348 (1989).

they exceeded certain limits, referred to as the competitive need limits, can be the subject of a request for 'competitive need waivers.' Generally, products are removed from the GSP program if imports of that product from anyone country exceed 50 per cent of the appraised value of all US imports of that product during the preceding calendar year. Certain advanced developing countries may be selected to receive a reduced competitive need limit of only 25 per cent of total US imports.[15]

In 2006, the GSP was amended to give the President the authority to end waivers after five years on products that constitute 150 per cent of the dollar value competitive need limit or 75 per cent of US imports of the product.[16] There was a strong sentiment in the Congress to limit benefits for more advanced developing countries.

Products can also be removed from the GSP if the amount of total US imports of that article exceeded a certain dollar value. This dollar value is adjusted each year, but currently is approximately USD 120 million. Finally, under what is known as the *de minimis* rule, a product that exceeds the quantitative competitive need limits may still be eligible if the dollar value is very small. This dollar value *de minimis* amount is also adjusted annually and was approximately USD 13 million in 2006. Each year an executive order is issued which announces the changes in the products eligible for GSP, as well as the current competitive need limit amounts and *de minimus* levels in effect. This notice is published in the *Federal Register* of each year.[17] Changes take effect on July 1st of each year.[18]

The procedures to add or remove a product from GSP, or to seek a waiver of the competitive need limitations, are set out in the regulations of the US Trade Representative. 15 C.F.R. Section 2007.1, *et seq.* These regulations set out the requirements for petitions and the information that must be contained in them.

In recent years the US Trade Representative has been particularly strict in not accepting petitions that do not comply with the regulations. For example, the regulations require historical data on sales, exports, production, capacity, capacity utilization, costs, profits and employment for three years prior to the date of filing of the petition.[19] Many petitions, particularly those that are not prepared by experienced lawyers, are rejected because of incomplete data or failure to follow the requirements set out in the regulations.

---

15. *See* 15 C.F.R. § 2007.8(2) for the applicable criteria for a reduction in the competitive need limitation.
16. H.R. 6406 § 8001.
17. Exporters and importers and their representatives are advised to carefully monitor exports, particularly in the last quarter of the year to determine if they are close to the competitive need limits.
18. This month period allows an exporter to expedite or delay shipments depending on whether they will be losing or gaining GSP benefits. In a special review for countries in the Andean Region the effective date was August 1, 1990.
19. 15 C.F.R. § 2007.1(b) and (c).

A. Petition Filing Requirements

Petitions to add or remove products, or seeking competitive need waivers, must be filed before June 1st of each year. Petitions for redesignation of products that lost eligibility because they exceeded competitive need limits, but are now eligible because they have fallen below the limits, are filed in a special review held in February of each year. This review is announced in the *Federal Register* and often parties have as little as two weeks to submit petitions.[20]

B. Acceptance of Petitions for Review

Petitions that are filed in the general review are reviewed for adequacy and decisions are made whether to accept the petitions for further consideration within six to eight weeks.[21] However, in recent years the decision date actually has been later. For example, in 1989, the announcement of products accepted for review was made on August 10th. This resulted in a shortened period in which to prepare pre-hearing briefs. Those products accepted for review are given further consideration by the GSP Subcommittee, an interagency panel consisting of representatives of various government agencies including the USTR, the United States International Trade Commission, the Treasury, State and Commerce Departments, the Departments of Labor and Agriculture and sometimes representatives from the Defense Department and the Justice Department. The GSP Subcommittee reports to a higher level interagency Trade Policy Staff Committee. Pre-hearing briefs, generally prepared by legal counsel, are usually filed a month before the hearings which are often held in late September or early October. Post-hearing and rebuttal briefs are then filed and deliberations of the Committee take place. Parties may arrange meetings with Committee members to discuss their submissions. The United States International Trade Commission (USITC) generally also is asked to submit comments on each product.[22] These comments are made to the US Trade Representative, although a public version usually also is released.

---

20. 15 C.F.R. § 2007.3.
21. The USTR generally has denied redesignation to products from the advanced developing countries. However, in October 1989 the USTR requested the ITC to conduct a Section 332 investigation on the probable economic effect of redesignating certain products including those of the advanced developing countries. The USTR has since indicated that it may reevaluate its policies regarding redesignation in the near future, and did in fact redesignate many products from advanced developing countries such as Mexico in its decisions announced in May 1990. More recently, however, most redesignation requests for countries like Brazil have been denied.
22. *See* 15 C.F.R. § 2007.2(c). In recent years, the USITC has held their own parallel hearings and briefing schedule within a week or two of the USTR hearings. Some consider this to be burdensome or duplicative, although the issues considered by the ITC are not identical to those before the USTR. The ITC concentrates on the economic impact of granting or removing GSP treatment on U.S. industries producing a like or competitive product, and on consumers, while the USTR focuses on policy issues and the competitiveness of the beneficiary developing country in regard to the product involved.

Usually, in May or June of each year, the decisions are announced, and they take effect on July 1st.[23]

C. ACCEPTANCE OF PRODUCTS

GSP decisions generally have been held to be non-appealable in the courts since they are discretionary decisions of the President made through his trade representative upon the recommendations of the inter-agency panel. However, if procedural rights are ignored, court appeals may be entertained.

In recent years, GSP decision have become increasingly linked to policy issues such as BDC practices relating to foreign investment and protection of intellectual property, and workers' rights. The GSP program expired on July 1, 1995. Legislation to renew the program retroactively was pending in the US Congress at the time of preparation of this second addition. It is likely, however, that further extensions of the program will occur although with increased limitations. For example, in 1988, Taiwan, Korea, Singapore and Hong Kong were all removed from the GSP program.[24]

The following countries, territories and associations of countries eligible for treatment as one country (pursuant to section 502(a)(3) of the Trade Act of 1974 (19 U.S.C. 2462(a)(3)) are designated beneficiary developing countries for the purposes of the Generalized System of Preferences, provided for in Title V of the Trade Act of 1974, as amended (19 U.S.C. 2461 *et seq.*):

Independent Countries

Albania
Angola
Antigua and Barbuda
Argentina
Almenia
Bahrain
Bangladesh
Barbados
Belarus
Belize
Benin
Bhutan
Bolivia
Gambia
Ghana
Grenada
Guatemala
Guinea
Guinea Bissau
Guyana
Haiti
Honduras
Hungary
India
Indonesia
Jamaica
Peru
Philippines
Poland
Thomania, Russia
Rwanda
St. Kitts and Nevis
Saint Lucia
Saint Vincent and the Grenadines
Sao Tome and Principe
Senegal
Seychelles
Sierra Leone

23. A description of the GSP designation process can be found in Glick, *The Generalized System of Preferences, Yesterday, Today, and Tomorrow*, 30 Fed. B. News and J. 284 (1983).
24. Any new GSP program is likely to attempt to further limit and contract benefits to the more advanced developing countries. A further discussion of changes in the GSP program appears in Glick, *The Generalized Systems of Preferences Revisited*, 32 Fed. B. News and J. 284 (1985).

Bosnia & Herzegovina
Botswana
Brazil
Bulgaria
Burkina Faso
Burundi
Cameroon
Cape Verde
Central African Republic
Chad
Chile
Colombia
Comoros
Congo
Costa Rica
Cote d'Ivoire
Croatia
Cyprus
Czech Republic
Djibouti
Dominica
Dominion Republic
Ecuador
Egypt
El Salvador
Equatorial Guinea
Fiji
Jordan
Kazakhstan
Kenya
Kiribati
Kyrgyzstan
Lebanon
Lesotho
Lithuania
Macedonia (former Yugoslav Republic of)
Madagascar
Malawi
Malaysia
Mali
Malta
Mauritius
Moldova
Morocco
Mozambique
Namibia
Nepal
Niger
Oman
Pakistan
Panama
Papua New Guinea
Paraguay
Solomon Islands
Somalia
South Africa
Sri Lanka
Suriname
Swaziland
Tanzania
Thailand
Togo
Tonga
Trinidad and Tobago
Tunisia
Turkey
Tuvalu
Uganda
Ukraine
Uruguay
Uzbekistan
Vanuatu
Venezuela
Western Samoa
Yemen Arab Republic (Sanaa)
Zaire
Zambia
Zimbabwe

Chapter 20

Section 337 of the Tariff Act of 1930 Unfair Trade Practices and Methods of Competition in the Importation of Products into the United States

I. INTRODUCTION

Section 337 of the Tariff Act of 1930,[1] deals with unfair trade practices relating to patents, copyrights and trademarks and, unlike the other statutes discussed, provides for an evidentiary hearing before an administrative law judge. Thus, issues relating to discovery and evidence that do not arise in other types of cases are of significance in Section 337 cases.

The US International Trade Commission (hereinafter the 'Commission' or 'ITC') administers Section 337 of the Tariff Act of 1930, which was designed by Congress to provide US industries with a vehicle to prevent unfair competition from imported goods that violate US patents, trademarks, copyrights or antitrust laws. Although the Commission conducts the investigation, its final determination is subject to presidential review based on policy considerations, and review by the Appeals for the Federal Circuit (CAFC) on legal issues. Section 337 of the Tariff Act of 1930 was intended by Congress to be a remedy 'in addition to' other actions available in the federal and state courts. It is a remedy that has been frequently utilized to aid US industries faced with

---

1. 19 U.S.C. § 1337 (1995). *See* Appendix A for complete text. For a general introductory discussion of Section 337, *see* L.A. Glick, 'Section 337 of the Tariff Act of 1930: A Trade Relief Measure for All Seasons,' 29 *Fed. Bar News* & J. 31 (January 1982).

imported goods that infringe patents, trademarks and copyrights or violate antitrust laws.

Section 337 originally was enacted as part of the Tariff Act of 1930. Section 337 was amended by the Trade Act of 1974.[2] Since that time, there has been a tremendous increase in the number of cases brought under this section, and the Commission has expanded and developed its procedures for handling these cases. Section 337 also was amended by the Trade Act of 1979[3] and most recently by the Omnibus Trade and Competitiveness Act of 1988.

In the Omnibus Trade and Competitiveness Act of 1988, Congress specifically found that 'the existing protection under Section 337 of the Tariff Act of 1930 against unfair trade practices is cumbersome and costly and has not provided United States owners of intellectual property rights with adequate protection against foreign companies violating such rights,'[4] significant changes have been made in the law. Some of the provisions of the old law that were refined or changed may still be discussed for historical purposes.

In 1988 a formal complaint was filed with the disputes panel of the General Agreement on Tariffs and Trade (GATT) challenging the legality of Section 337 on grounds that it subjects foreign firms to different standards of adjudication for intellectual property disputes than the standards for domestic firms. The European Economic Community (EEC) filed the complaint in 1985, charging that Section 337 violated the nondiscrimination provision of Article III of the GATT relating to national treatment, since domestic companies accused of patent, copyright or trademark infringement are not subjected to the provisions of Section 337 and have the advantage of defending these claims in the court system which has stricter evidence standards and which allows for the filing of counterclaims. The GATT Panel found against the United States. On February 1, 1990, the Office of the United States Trade Representative requested written comments on a proposal to remove jurisdiction over patent-based Section 337 cases from the ITC and transfer this jurisdiction to a new specialized court, or, to create a new division in the Court of International Trade to hear these cases.

In 1995, Section 337 was substantially modified to fully conform with the provisions of Uruguay Round of GATT agreements. We will begin with a short description of the revised statute, followed by a discussion of the procedures for conducting an investigation, and a discussion of some of the more significant cases handled by the ITC.

---

2. *See* 19 U.S.C. § 2101 *et seq.* Because of the significant changes in the law in 1974, all cases discussed herein are post-1974.
3. Pub. Law No. 96-39; 19 U.S.C. § 2501 *et seq.*
4. 19 U.S.C. 1341(a)(2) (1995), including amendments in the Omnibus Trade and Competitiveness Act of 1988, Pub. Law No. 103-465 (1995).

II. DESCRIPTION OF THE STATUTE AND REGULATIONS

Section 337, as amended in 1995, prohibits the following:

(A) Unfair methods of competition and unfair acts in the importation of articles (other than articles provided for in subparagraphs (B), (C), and (D)) into the United States, or in the sale of such articles by the owner, importer, or consignee, the threat or effect of which is
  (i) To destroy or substantially injure an industry in the United States;
  (ii) To prevent the establishment of such an industry; or
  (iii) To restrain or monopolize trade and commerce in the United States.

(B) The importation into the United States, the sale for importation, or the sale within the United States after importation by the owner, importer, or consignee, of articles that –
  (i) Infringe a valid and enforceable United States patent or a valid and enforceable United States copyright registered under Title 17, United States Code; or
  (ii) Are made, produced, processed, or mined under, or by means of, a process covered by the claims of a valid and enforceable United States patent.

(C) The importation into the United States, the sale for importation, or the sale within the United States after importation by the owner, importer, or consignee, of articles that – infringe a valid and enforceable United States trademark registered under the Trademark Act of 1946.

(D) The importation into the United States, the sale for importation, or the sale within the United States after importation by the owner, importer, or consignee, of a semiconductor chip product in a manner that constitutes infringement of a mask work registered under Chapter 9 of Title 17, United States Code.

Subparagraphs (B), (C), and (D) of Paragraph (1) apply only if an industry in the United States, relating to the articles protected by the patent, copyright, trademark, or mask work concerned, exists or is in the process of being established.[5]

The Commission can impose various remedies, when it finds a violation of the statute. The most common remedy is an 'exclusion order' which is an exclusion of articles from entry into the United States. This is an effective remedy and one reason for the popularity of the statute among US producers. This remedy does not apply to importations prior to the investigation or during the course of the investigation, but only to goods imported after the date the order becomes final.[6] Usually, these exclusion orders are broad in nature, known as 'general' exclusion orders, applying to all goods which infringe or violate the property rights adjudicated,

---

5. 19 U.S.C. § 1337(a), including amendments in the Omnibus Trade and Competitiveness Act of 1988, Pub. Law No. 100-418. 102 Stat. 1941.
6. 19 U.S.C. § 1337(d).

whether or not the affected parties appeared at the trial. However, since exclusion orders were found generally to violate GATT provisions, the ITC can only issue exclusion orders where they are shown necessary to prevent circumvention of specific orders or where a pattern of violation exists and it is difficult to identify the persons responsible.[7] In deciding whether to issue a general exclusion order, the Commission balances the complainant's interest in obtaining protection from all potential foreign infringements of the complainant's rights against the need to avoid disruption of legitimate trade.

A provisional remedy during the pendency of the investigation is exclusion of articles from entry temporarily during an investigation. This is called a Temporary Exclusion Order (TEO) and is similar to a Temporary Restraining Order (TRO) in Federal Courts.[8]

The Commission has adopted special rules pertaining to TEOs.

Interim rules, that became effective November 21, 1988, govern the posting and possible forfeiture of the temporary relief bonds posted by complainants seeking TEOs. *See* 53 *Fed. Reg.* 49, 118; 19 C.F.R. part 210. TEOs have been granted in a number of recent cases and can provide a quick and effective remedy for domestic producers while imposing a serious burden on foreign respondents. For a TEO to be issued, the complaining party must post a bond with the proceeds going to the respondent (and not the Treasury) if there is a final negative determination; conversely, if there is a final affirmative determination, the proceeds from the bond will go to the complainant. In the case of a final affirmative determination (but before Presidential action), the importer must post bond to enter the goods into the United States with the proceeds of such bond going to the complainant if the President does not disapprove of the ITC decision. However, this remedy has been granted infrequently since it requires a high standard of proof.

A third remedy is a cease and desist order.[9] This remedy is designed to attack the specific unfair acts found in an investigation without the necessity of excluding goods from the United States. Cease and desist orders are directed at a United States importer and require specific action. For example, if a patent infringement was found, and exports had ceased during the course of the investigation, an importer with a significant inventory of the infringing products in the US could be ordered to discontinue sales of the product. Unlike an exclusion order, which is *in rem* in nature

7. As a result of the recent amendments to Customs Regulations, 19 C.F.R. 12.39(b), ITC has the authority to issue seizure and forfeiture orders against articles and like articles for which exclusion orders have been issued under certain conditions and the Secretary of Treasury has the authority to enforce those orders. Section 12.39(b) provides the procedures for the enforcement on exclusion orders. Once the three statutory conditions are met, ITC is allowed to issue a seizure and forfeiture order. The ITC then notifies the Secretary of the Treasury of the issuance of the order, and Customs will notify all ports of entry of the order and identify the article, importers or consignees all subject to the order. Seizures issued by ITC apply only to articles and like articles which have been denied entry by reason of an exclusion order, and for which the importer has been notified in writing.
8. 19 U.S.C. § 1337(c).
9. *Certain Woodworking Machines*, 337-TA-174, 8 I.T.R.D. (B.N.A.) 1251 (1985).

(affects the goods), a cease and desist order is *in personam* in nature and requires personal jurisdiction over the named party. Fines and penalties can be levied for violations of these orders.

A provision in the Trade Agreements Act of 1979[10] amended Section 337 to provide the Commission with the authority to impose a civil penalty for non-compliance with a cease-and-desist order. This provision was later amended by the Omnibus Trade and Competitiveness Act of 1988. The amount of a fine was increased to the greater of USD 100,000 for each day imports occur, or twice the domestic value of the imported goods.

A list of outstanding Exclusion Orders as of the date of completion of this chapter is set out below:

Outstanding Section 337 Exclusion Orders

Investigation No.	*Investigation Title*	*US Patent Number(s)*	*Date Patent(s) Expires*
337-TA-055	Certain Novelty Glasses	Non-patent	–
337-TA-069	Certain Airtight Cast-Iron Stoves	Non-patent	–
337-TA-087	Certain Coin-Operated Audio Visual Games and Components Thereof	Non-patent	–
337-TA-105	Certain Coin-Operated Audio Visual Games and Components Thereof	Non-patent	–
337-TA-112	Certain Cube Puzzles	Non-patent	–
337-TA-114	Certain Miniature Plug-In Blade Fuses	Non-patent	–
337-TA-118	Certain Sneakers with Fabric Uppers and Rubber Soles	Non-patent	–
337-TA-137	Certain Heavy Duty Staple Gun Tackers	Non-patent	–
337-TA-152	Certain Plastic Food Storage Containers	Non-patent	–
337-TA-167	Certain Single Handle Faucets	Non-patent	–
337-TA-174	Certain Woodworking Machines	Non-patent	–
337-TA-195	Certain Cloisonné Jewelry	Non-patent	–
337-TA-197	Certain Compound Action Metal Cutting Snips and Components Thereof	Non-patent	–

10. *See also Certain Aramid Fiber,* 337-TA-194, 8 I.T.R.D. (B.N.A.) 1967 (1986).

Outstanding Section 337 Exclusion Orders (continued)

Investigation No.	*Investigation Title*	*US Patent Number(s)*	*Date Patent(s) Expires*
337-TA-229	Certain Nut Jewelry and Parts Thereof	Non-patent	–
337-TA-231	Certain Soft Sculpture Dolls, Popularly Known as 'Cabbage Patch Kids,' Related Literature and Packaging Therefore	Non-patent	–
337-TA266	Certain Re-closable Bags and Tubing	Non-patent	–
337-TA-279	Certain Plastic Light Duty Screw Anchors	Non-patent	–
337-TA-285	Certain Chemiluminescent Compositions and Components Thereof and Methods of Using, and Products Incorporating the Same	Non-patent	–
337-TA-287	Certain Strip Lights	Non-patent	–
337-TA-295	Certain Novelty Teleidoscopes	Non-patent	–
337-TA-319	Certain Automotive Fuel Caps and Radiator Caps and Related Packaging and Promotional Materials	Non-patent	–
337-TA-321	Certain Soft Drinks and Their Containers	Non-patent	–
337-TA-333	Certain Woodworking Accessories	4,805,505	–
337-TA-360	Certain Devices for Connecting Computers via Telephone Lines	5,003,579	Feb. 13, 2007
337-TA-365	Certain Audible Alarm Devices for Divers	4,950,107 5,106,236	–
337-TA-374	Certain Electrical Connectors and Products Containing Same	5,383,792	Jan. 22, 2008
337-TA-376	Certain Variable Speed Wind Turbines and Components Thereof	5,083,039	–
337-TA-378	Certain Asian-Style Kamaboko Fish Cakes	Non-patent	–
337-TA-380	Certain Agricultural Tractors Under 50 Power Take-Off Horsepower	Non-patent	–

Outstanding Section 337 Exclusion Orders (continued)

Investigation No.	*Investigation Title*	*US Patent Number(s)*	*Date Patent(s) Expires*
337-TA-383	Certain Hardware Logic Emulation Systems and Components Thereof	5,329,470	Apr. 28, 2009
		5,109,353	Apr. 28, 2009
		5,036,473	Oct. 5, 2008
		5,448,496	Oct. 5, 2008
		5,452,231	Oct. 5, 2008

III. COMMISSION STANDARDS IN SECTION 337 CASES

Unlike a US District Court which only considers the infringement issue, if the Commission finds infringement of a patent, trademark or copyright, it also must consider several additional elements before it imposes a remedy. The statute requires the Commission to consider various public interest factors in determining whether a remedy should be imposed in a particular case, and in determining 'which remedy is appropriate.' These factors include the affects of the remedy on the public health and welfare; competitive conditions in the United States; the production of competitive articles in the US, and possible effects on US consumers.[11] The Commission solicits comments from various Government agencies, including the Department of Justice, Federal Trade Commission, and the Department of Health and Human Services, in making its determination. In a few cases, the Commission has held that the public interest factors outweigh the proprietary rights of the complainant and refused to exclude the imported products on this basis. It is also important to note that no Section 337 investigation may be initiated where the complainant has already sought injunctive relief in the district court with respect to a particular party and claim. Conversely, no injunctive relief will be available in district courts against a party where the complainant has sought relief against such party based on the same underlying claim in an action pursued under Section 337.

In civil cases before a district court involving parties that are also parties to a Section 337 proceeding before the ITC, at the request of the respondent, the district court will stay the proceedings for any claim involving the same issues until the ITC case is finished. The ITC record shall be transmitted to the district court and will be admissible in the civil action.

If the Commission determines that goods are to be excluded from entry, or if a cease and desist order is to be imposed, it must determine the amount of a bond under which the goods will be allowed entry during the 60-day period in which the Commission's determination is considered by the President. Exclusion orders are generally preferred to cease and desist orders in trademark cases. *In re Certain*

11. 19 U.S.C. § 1337(d), (e) and (f).

Single Handle Faucets, 7 I.T.R.D. (BNA) 1470, 1471 (1984). In order to obtain a general exclusion order, the ITC requires that there be 'both

(i) a widespread pattern of unauthorized use of the protected article, and
(ii) business conditions from which it can be inferred that manufacturers other than the named respondents may attempt to enter the US market with infringing articles (cites omitted)' *Id.* at 1471.

Once the Commission determines that a violation exists and a remedy should be imposed, it must send the record of the investigation to the President of the United States. The President may refuse to implement the Commission's remedy for policy reasons, but cannot substitute another remedy.[12]

IV. PROCEDURES FOR INVESTIGATIONS UNDER § 337

A. BACKGROUND

An important provision of Section 337, different from other trade laws, requires that investigations be carried out by the Commission under the terms of the Administrative Procedure Act.[13] Each party has a right to fully investigate the facts of the case. This is done by various discovery mechanisms such as interrogatories,[14] oral depositions[15] and requests for documents.[16] The facts gathered by the parties are presented at hearings before an Administrative Law Judge.[17] Hearings provide an opportunity for parties to cross-examine witnesses as in a normal district court proceeding. However, the rules of evidence are more liberal than in the courts. For example, hearsay evidence can be admitted. To be admissible, evidence must be shown to be relevant, material and reliable.[18]

One aspect of ITC investigations that makes them particularly attractive to domestic companies and burdensome to counsel for accused importers is the rule that an investigation must be completed within one year. The ITC must conclude its investigation at the earliest practical time and must set a target date for final determination. In cases involving temporary exclusion orders, all discovery and

---

12. 19 U.S.C. § 1337(j)(2) (1995).
13. *See.* e.g., *Headboxes and Papermaking Machine Forming Sections for the Continuous Production of Paper and Components Thereof,* 337-TA-82, 2 I.T.R.D. (BNA) 5481 (1981) (disapproved by the President because the remedy was too broad).
14. 19 C.F.R. § 210.32 (1995).
15. 19 C.F.R. § 210.32 (1995).
16. 19 C.F.R. § 210.31 (1995).
17. 19 C.F.R. § 210.42 (1995).
18. 19 C.F.R. § 210.37(b) (1995).

the hearing must be completed within three (3) months from the date the notice of institution of the investigation is published.[19]

B. Institution of the Investigation

Section 337 investigations may be instituted either based upon a complaint filed with the Commission,[20] or by the Commission on its own motion.[21] Most past investigations have been instituted by persons filing complaints with the Commission, although recently the staff has recommended a few investigations on their own. Historically, most Section 337 cases have involved allegations of patent infringement. Counterclaims may be raised in Section 337 cases. Such counterclaims will immediately be removed to district court and shall be presumed to have been raised on the date of the original petition in the ITC action for the purposes of tolling any relevant statutes of limitation and providing actual notice of infringement.

There have also been some significant cases involving other types of unfair trade practices. The Commission has entertained cases based on misappropriation of trade secrets,[22] unauthorized use of trademarks,[23] passing off of goods,[24] improper designations of origin,[25] violation of copyrights and even false advertising.[26] In addition, there have been various antitrust-type investigations based on allegations of pricing at levels which were lower than the foreign manufacturer's cost of production, and attempted monopolization or monopolization of United States industries.[27] These have been less frequent in recent years.

When a complaint is brought to the Commission, it is directed to a staff legal office, the Office of Unfair Imports (O.U.I.), which conducts a preliminary investigation of the complaint to determine whether it meets certain procedural rules of the Commission. The staff may attempt to contact the named respondents in order to obtain additional information and to determine the factual basis for certain allegations stated in the complaint. During the thirty (30) days after the filing of a complaint, it is reviewed by the staff and recommendations are made to the Commission as to whether it meets the rules and presents a cause of action which should be considered by the Commission as a basis for an investigation.

---

19. 19 C.F.R. § 210.41(e)(2).
20. 19 C.F.R. § 210.8(a) (1994).
21. 19 C.F.R. § 210.8(b) (1994).
22. *See* e.g., *Certain Apparatus for the Continuous Production of Copper Rod,* 337-TA-52, 2 I.T.R.D. (BNA) 5006 (1979).
23. *Certain Airtight Cast iron Stoves,* 337-TA-69, 3 I.T.R.D. (BNA) 1158 (1980).
24. *Id.*
25. *Certain Surface Grinding Machines and the Literature for Promotion Thereof,* 337-TA-9S.
26. *Certain Coin Operated Audio-Visual Games and Components Thereof,* (viz. Rally-X and PacMan), 337-TA-I0S, 4 I.T.R.D. (BNA) 1403 (1982),
27. *See,* e.g., *Certain Electronic Audio and Related Equipment,* 337-TA-7, 1 I.T.R.D. (BNA) 5211 (1976).

PRACTICE COMMENT: O.U.I., unlike the office of the General Counsel which is legal advisor to the Commission, is an independent Party to § 337 proceedings charged with representing the public interest. As such, it is proper, and generally advisable, for prospective complainants' counsel to discuss a draft of their complaint with O.U.I. staff prior to filing. Similarly, once a complaint is filed, but prior to initiation of an investigation, counsel for prospective respondents may wish to meet with the O.U.I. staff to discuss deficiencies and weaknesses in the complaint with the hope that the O.U.I. will recommend against initiation. This has occurred on a number of occasions.

In the past, the Commission generally has taken the position that Section 337 only requires that a complaint meet the requirements of its rules in order for an investigation to be instituted. However, there have been indications recently, perhaps due to the Commission's increased caseload, that the Commission may adopt a different interpretation of the statute. Under this interpretation, complaints which meet the rules may not be instituted if there is a reason for the Commission to believe that they lack merit.[28]

Although it is likely, at least in patent-based investigations, that the Commission will generally continue instituting complaints as long as they meet the basic procedural requirements of the Commission's rules; some decisions have raised questions concerning this. For example, in Docket 1056, Fruit Preserves in Containers Having Lids with Gingham Cloth-Designs, decided on June 20, 1984, the Commission voted 3-2 not to institute an investigation despite the pro forma sufficiency of the petition, due to insufficient evidence of injury. It is important for complainants, therefore, to draft sufficiently detailed allegations in the complaint and, where possible, to support the allegations with documentary and physical evidence to ensure that the Commission has a sufficient basis to institute an investigation.

In cases where the Commission does not believe sufficient information exists to warrant institution of a Section 337 investigation, it may order a preliminary investigation under Section 603 of the Trade Act of 1974.[29]

If the Commission determines that a Section 337 investigation should be instituted, a notice is published in the *Federal Register* and copies of the complaint are sent to those named as respondents. At this point, the Commission assigns the investigation to an Administrative Law Judge, who will control the conduct of the investigation until he or she reports an initial finding of violation to the Commission.

The date of the publication of a Notice of Investigation in the *Federal Register* begins the one-year time limit for the Commission to complete its investigation. Respondents named in the investigation have twenty (20) days in which to answer the complaint[30] or thirty (30) days if they are overseas.

---

28. For example, the Commission postponed institution in the case of *Certain Portable Kerosene Hearers,* Docket 921, until more information could be received from the complainant.
29. 19 U.S.C. § 2482 (1995).
30. 19 C.F.R. § 210.13(a) (1995).

V. SETTLEMENT AND PRE-TRIAL TERMINATION

Many of the investigations instituted never go to a hearing and are settled or terminated before a final decision by the Commission. Parties can initiate a variety of procedures during the course of the investigation in order to terminate it. For example, the parties to patent infringement actions often reach terms for the settlement of a case based on license of the patent.[31] It also is possible that the respondents named in an investigation may discover that their sales in the US market are not sufficient to justify the expense of fully defending an action. In such an event, the respondents can agree not to import the product into the United States for the life of the patent and accept a consent order agreement.[32]

Cases can also be disposed of in the pre-trial stage by motions to terminate based on settlements or by motions for summary determination when there are no material issues of fact in dispute. On October 11, 1988, the Commission issued for public comment proposed rules concerning enforcement procedures that affect consent orders and consent order agreements.

VI. SUBSTANTIVE ISSUES

It is necessary for the complainant to prove that there has been an unfair act, that there is a domestic industry, and also, in cases involving common law trademarks and other forms of common law unfair competition, that there has been injury to this domestic industry.

Under prior law, in contrast to patent infringement actions in district court, Section 337 was not intended to protect US industries from unfair acts unless these acts caused injury to the domestic industry. Under the current law, this injury test applies only to non-statutory actions for common law trademark, passing off or unfair competition violations.

A. INJURY

Historically, the questions of injury and the existence of a domestic industry have been extremely important in determining the outcome of cases. However, as noted above, Section 1342(a) of the Omnibus Trade and Competitiveness Act of 1988[33] amended Section 337 of the Tariff Act of 1930 and eliminated the need to demonstrate injury to, or the prevention of the establishment of, an industry in the US in cases involving intellectual property protected by valid and enforceable US patents; copyrights; registered 'mask works' (computer chips); or, in cases involving the importation and sale of a product allegedly made, produced or mined under,

---

31. 19 C.F.R. § 210.21(b) (1995).
32. 19 C.F.R. § 210.21(c) (1995).
33. Pub. L. 100-418; 102 Stat. 1212.

or by means of, a process covered by the claims of a valid and enforceable US patent. Thus, without the injury test, even small amounts of imports from developing countries that do not injure US producers, but use US patents, trademarks, copyrights, or mask works, could be excluded. The need to establish injury is still required in cases involving non-registered, common law trademarks, or other common law remedies such as passing off, copying or trade dress.

In regard to injury, the Commission generally has looked at the following criteria: 1) lost sales or royalties; 2) lost profits; 3) decline in production; 4) decline in employment; 5) underselling and price suppression; 6) volume and ratio of imports; and 7) the capacity of foreign manufacturers and exporters. Many of these factors were set out in the Commission's decisions in *Certain Rotary Scraping Tools,* 337 TA-62, 2 I.T.R.D. (B.N.A.) 5233 (1980), and *Certain Roller Units,* 337-TA-44, 1 I.T.R.D. (BNA) 5503 (1979). Not all of these elements need be present to constitute injury. There is no mechanical test for demonstrating the necessary quantum of injury. A violation can be found when a mere threat of injury exists and often, mere proof of foreign capacity and lower prices, coupled with contracts to sell the products in the United States, may establish a tendency to injure sufficient to constitute a violation.

B. Section 337 as an Antitrust Remedy

Section 337 has not been used frequently as an antitrust-type remedy. However, the legislative history and the broad language of the statute contemplate this possibility. The statute successfully has been used to combat predatory pricing schemes cognizable under the antidumping law, although the Justice Department objected to the use of Section 337 for this purpose.[34] Because this area overlapped with the antidumping law of 1921, the statute was amended as part of the 1979 Trade Agreements Act to require that the Commission refer complaints based solely on violations of the antidumping and countervailing duty laws to the Commerce Department. However, the Commission can still maintain actions that involve claims under the antitrust laws if they are combined with other claims cognizable under Section 337 (*i.e.*, patent or trademark infringement).

VII. CONCLUSION

Section 337 has proven to be an extremely effective remedy for US industries seeking protection of intellectual property rights. The majority of cases disposed of to date have been terminated as a result of settlement agreements or consent orders, or alternatively, terminated without a decision on the merits. Commission decisions themselves do not have any *res judicata* effect on actions involving the

34. *See Certain Welded Stainless Steel Pipe & 0 Tube,* 337-TA-29, 1 I.T.R.D. (BNA) 5245 (1978).

same patents in a district court. However, if the Court of Appeals for the Federal Circuit (CAFC) affirms a finding of invalidity in an ITC case, it could prevent enforcement of the patent in the district courts since the CAFC is also the court of appeal for all patent decisions from district courts.

Exporters and importers should therefore be aware of the potential for actions against their products under Section 337 and review their use of patents, trademarks and copyrights to determine if there is a potential of infringing rights of a US company.

Chapter 21
Legislation and Policy Issues

I. INTRODUCTION

This chapter will discuss legislation and policy issues regarding the US Customs and Border Protection Services and various trade laws. Some of a historical nature from earlier editions of this book and some discuss more recent developments. The historical discussion will focus on changes in the customs laws in the Omnibus Trade and Competitiveness Act of 1988,[1] regulations implementing the US–Canada Free Trade Agreement which is now part of The North American Free Trade Agreement, certain hearings before subcommittees of the Committee on Ways and Means of the US House of Representatives and miscellaneous regulations which were being reviewed by the US Customs. The more recent developments will include a discussion of the many Free Trade Agreements, some in effect and others still under negotiation or awaiting Congressional approval. Among the agreements discussed are: The Central American Free Trade Agreement (CAFTA), the US–Columbia Free Trade Agreement, the US–Chile Free Trade Agreement, the US–Jordan Free Trade Agreement, the US–Israel Free Trade Agreement, the US–Morocco Free Trade Agreement, the US–Bahrain Free Trade Agreement, the US–Panama Free Trade Agreement, the US–Peru Free Trade Agreement, the US–Singapore Free Trade Agreement, and the proposed Free Trade Agreement of the Americas (FTAA).

---

1. Pub. L. No. 100-418, 102 Stat. 1312, effective January 1, 1989.

II. DISCUSSION

A. THE OMNIBUS TRADE AND COMPETITIVENESS ACT OF 1988

Title I, Subtitle H, Part I of the Omnibus Trade and Competitiveness Act of 1988 (Act) amended various provisions of the customs laws.

1. Restrictions Against Imported Pornography

Section 1901 of the Act amends Section 305 of the Tariff Act of 1930 which prohibits the importation of immoral material.[2] It allows a customs officer, upon seizure of immoral material, to inform the US Attorney of the district either at 'the office at which such seizure took place; or the district to which the goods were destined.

2. Duty Free Stores

Section 555(b) of the Tariff Act of 1930 is amended to authorize Customs to designate duty free stores as a separate class of bonded warehouse.[3] Section 1908 also provides certain statutory control over the operations of duty free stores. Duty free shops are to be located within 25 miles of the port of entry from which the customer will leave the US;

The section contains other specific provisions, for example:

(1) Duty free shops must establish procedures designed to provide reasonable assurance that the merchandise sold in the stores will leave the customs territory of the United States;[4]
(2) Duty free shops located in airports will be subject to control by the Customs Service;[5] and
(3) Duty free shops must post a notice stating that the duty free merchandise has not been subject to any tax in the United States, will be so subject

---

2. 19 U.S.C. § 1305(a). Immoral material which is prohibited from entering the U.S. includes

> any book, pamphlet, paper, writing, advertisement, circular, print, picture, or drawing containing any matter advocating or urging treason or insurrection against the United States, or forcible resistance to any law of the United States, or containing any threat to take the life of or inflict bodily harm upon any person in the United States, or any obscene book pamphlet, paper, writing, advertisement, circular, print, picture, drawing, or other representation, figure, or image on or of paper or other material, or any case, instrument, or other article which is obscene or immoral, or any drug or medicine or any article whatever. for causing unlawful abortion, or any lottery ticket, or any printed paper that may be used as a lottery ticket, or any advertisement of any lottery.

3. Section 1908, Pub. 1. No. 100-418, 102 Stat. 1315.
4. *See* Section 1908(b)(3)(A), (F).
5. *See* Section 1908(b)(3)(B). Prerule *Customs* Regulations regarding duty free stores have been published. *See* 53 Fed. Reg. 42, 335 (1988).

if it returns to the customs territory of the United States, is subject to the customs laws of the country to which it is taken, and must mark the merchandise to identify that it was sold at a duty free store.[6]

3. Caribbean Basin Initiative

Section 1909 of the Act sets forth certain Congressional findings as to the economic and political importance of the Caribbean Basin Initiative (CBI) and states that it is the intent of Congress to strengthen 'the trade elements of the Caribbean Basin Initiative . . . in a manner consistent with the promotion of economic and political stability in the Caribbean and Central America.'

Section 1909 also amends Section 212(e) of the CBI to allow the President to withdraw or suspend benefits under the CBI to specific articles as well as withdraw beneficiary status from a country. Notice of the President's proposed action under this section must be published in the *Federal Register,* and the US Trade Representative will accept comments and hold a hearing on the matter.

4. Other Amendments

There are several other miscellaneous amendments to the Customs laws contained in the Act. Section 507 of the Tariff Act of 1930[7] is amended to allow for any 'detectable moisture and impurities present in, or upon, the imported crude oil or petroleum products.' Section 503(c)(1)(B) of the Trade Act of 1974[8] is amended to except watches which the President has determined will not materially injure the domestic industry, from the general exclusion of watches from eligibility under the Generalized System of Preferences.[9] Section 1904 of the Act amended Section 623(c) of the Tariff Act of 1930[10] to authorize Customs to publish standards for cancellation of customs bonds. Other changes were made in Section 1905 as well; the Pontiac/Oakland, Michigan Airport is added to the list of airports which will have customs services available for a user fee. Section 1910 of the Act amended the 'grandfather clauses' in Section 423 of the Tax Reform Act of 1986 (regarding producers of ethyl alcohol): to include two Caribbean-owned facilities; to extend the benefits until December 31, 1989; to limit the total imports which may receive the preferential treatment; and to order the ITC and the General Accounting Office to study the production of ethanol in the Caribbean and the potential impact on the domestic industry. Finally, Section 1911 of the Act requires the US Trade Representative to gather recommendations for improving enforcement of the restrictions on imports from Cuba.

---

6. Section 1908(b)(3)(C), (D).
7. 19 U.S.C. § 1507.
8. 19 U.S.C. § 2463(c)(1)(b).
9. Section 1903.
10. 19 U.S.C. § 1623(c).

B. US–Canada Free Trade Agreement and the North American Free Trade Agreement (NAFTA)

The US and Canada entered into an agreement (CFTA) which was designed to

> eliminate barriers to trade in goods and services between the two parties, facilitate conditions of fair competition within the free-trade areas, liberalize significantly conditions for investments within the free-trade area, establish effective procedures for the joint administration of the CFTA and the resolution of disputes, and lay the foundation for further bilateral and multilateral cooperation to expand and enhance the benefits of the CFTA.'[11]

The agreement provides preferential tariff treatment to goods which originate in the US or Canada, phasing out the *ad valorem* user fees described in 19 C.F.R. § 24.23 and the flat rate of duty for goods accompanying any person, described in 19 C.F.R. § 148.102, over the next five years.

US Customs is authorized to implement the portions of the agreement which deal with the rules of origin and other trade issues. In order to carry out this role the Customs Service has published interim regulations.[12]

1. Eligibility

Under the interim regulations, any goods which are classifiable under a heading of the Harmonized Tariff Schedule of the United States (HTS) which has a 'CA' in the 'Special' column may be eligible for preferential treatment under the CFTA if the goods are 'originating goods' and are shipped directly to the US from Canada.[13]

'Originating goods' are goods which are 'wholly obtained or produced in the Territory of Canada or the United States, or both' or have undergone a process in one of the two nations which results in a change in its classification under the HTS.[14] Specific rules of origin may be found in General Note 3(c)(vii) of the HTS. Under certain circumstances, assembling goods in either country, even without a change in tariff classification, may also be sufficient to qualify the goods as 'originating goods.'[15] If the changes in tariff classification are due solely to simple packaging, diluting, or combining operations, then they are not 'originating goods' for purposes of the CFTA.[16]

Some of the rules of origin established for the CFTA require that there be a value content determination with regard to the product.[17] In those cases, Section 10.305 provides certain relevant definitions. For example, the direct costs of

11. 53 Fed. Reg. 51762.
12. All references to the regulations in the following discussion will be by the section number, but they are published at 53 *Fed. Reg.* 51, 762–77.
13. 19 C.F.R. § 10.302.
14. 19 C.F.R. § 10.303.
15. 19 C.F.R. § 10.303(c).
16. 19 C.F.R. § 10.304.
17. *See,* e.g., HTS General Note 3(c)(vii)(F), (H), and (Q).

processing or assembling are 'the costs directly incurred in, or that can be reasonably allocated to, the production of goods.'[18] These costs may include:

(1) all labor costs;
(2) inspection and testing costs;
(3) energy, fuel, dies, molds, tooling, depreciation and maintenance of the equipment;
(4) development, design, and engineering costs;
(5) rent, mortgage, depreciation, property insurance, maintenance, taxes and costs of utilities for real property used to produce the goods; and
(6) royalty or licensing payments for the right to the goods.

Costs which are not included in the direct costs include:

(1) general business expenses;
(2) import/export brokerage costs;
(3) costs of communication;
(4) costs of packing for export;
(5) royalty payments related to an agreement to distribute or sell the goods;
(6) costs on real property used by administrative personnel; and
(7) profit.

The 'value of originating materials' is the total of the price paid for all the materials used in manufacturing the product and certain other related costs, if they are not included in the price of the materials.[19] The 'value of the goods when exported to the United States' is the total of the direct costs and the value of the originating materials.[20]

To be eligible for preferential treatment under the CFTA, the goods must not only be 'originating goods,' but must also be 'directly shipped to the United States from Canada.'[21] Goods are shipped directly if they have been shipped from Canada to the US without passing through a third country.[22] If the goods do pass through a third country, they will be deemed to have been shipped directly if they did not enter the commerce of the third country, did not undergo any processing other than was necessary for transportation in the third country and all relevant documents show the US as the final destination.[23]

There are two special regulations dealing with determining whether automobiles are originating goods. The manufacturer of the automobile may elect to calculate the value-content requirement for the vehicles based on averages over the manufacturer's 12-month financial year.[24] The manufacturer's election to average becomes binding upon the entry of the first vehicles to the US.

---

18. 19 C.F.R § 10.305(a).
19. 19 C.F.R. § 10.305(b).
20. 19 C.F.R. § 10.305(c).
21. 19 C.F.R. § 10.302.
22. 19 C.F.R. § 10.306(a).
23. 19 C.F.R. § 10.306(b).
24. 19 C.F.R. § 10.310(a).

2. Procedures

In order to claim a preference under the CFTA, the entry summary must include the code 'CA' before the HTS subheading under which the goods are to enter the US.[25] At the time the preference is claimed there must be an Exporter's Certificate of Origin signed by the person causing the exportation from Canada.[26] All information on the Certificate is subject to verification by Customs.[27] The Certificate of Origin should be made on Customs Form 353 or in an approved computer format.[28] The Certificate is not required for formal entries under 19 C.F.R. § 143.21, or if the district director elects to waive the requirement.

Unlike the other claims for preferences, manufacturers electing to average need not submit an Exporter's Certificate of Origin to claim a preference under the CFTA. The declaration of election is sufficient.[29] The declaration is to be submitted to the US Customs Service, Regulatory Audit Division, Detroit, Michigan, on Customs Form 355.[30] Manufacturers electing to average must also submit quarterly vehicle cost reports on Customs Form 356 and an annual vehicle cost report must be submitted, within 90 days of the end of the manufacturer's fiscal year, on Customs Form 357.[31] The necessary reports may be submitted in alternative formats provided they contain the information required in Customs Forms 355-7. The US–Canadian Free Trade Agreement while still in force has largely been superseded by the North American Free Trade Agreement (NAFTA). NAFTA is discussed only briefly in Chapter 4, I, E and Chapter 7, II, E since it is the subject of a separate book by the author entitled, Understanding the North American Free Trade Agreement, 2nd Edition, also published by Kluwer Law International. The reader is referred to that book for an extensive discussion of all aspects of NAFTA.

C. Committee Hearings

The Subcommittee on Oversight of the House Committee on Ways and Means undertook an investigation of the Customs Service in 1988. In a hearing on September 27, 1988, the Honorable J. J. Pickle, Chairman of the Subcommittee, stated that the investigation had raised some serious problems with regard to how the Customs Service operates. He stated,

I have concluded that the Customs Service operates, by and large, with a free hand – much as a 'Lone Ranger.' . . . [I]t seems that Customs has grown somewhat insensitive to the concerns of the trade community . . . We must . . . carefully

25. 19 C.F.R. § 10.307(a).
26. 19 C.F.R. § 10.307(c)–(e).
27. 19 C.F.R. § 10.309.
28. 19 C.F.R. § 10.307.
29. 19 C.F.R. § 10.310(c).
30. 19 C.F.R. § 10.311(a).
31. 19 C.F.R. § 10.311(b), (c).

consider whether the legitimate concerns of the domestic trade community are being properly addressed by Customs.'[32]

During the hearing, the Subcommittee questioned the then Commissioner of the Customs Service, Mr. William Von Raab, extensively regarding particular examples of abuse, inconsistency and insensitivity by the Customs Service to the trade community. Mr. Von Raab responded to the questions and entered a statement into the record. This statement indicated that the Customs Service considered that it had a very broad mandate with regard to commercial and enforcement operations and that, to a certain degree, these missions were inconsistent with one another.[33] In his view, Customs is charged with both the strict enforcement of all the customs laws and with facilitating the flow of cargo into and out of the US. 'Today . . . the Customs Service has begun to shift its focus to dealing with the enormous burdens and complexities of facilitating the movement of cargo . . . while at the same time strengthening the trade law enforcement mission.'[34]

Mr. Von Raab indicated that the Customs Service has been developing several programs in pursuit of these goals. Many of the programs are designed to increase the efficiency with which the necessary paperwork is conducted. Customs is implementing a paperless electronic entry system which has reduced quota processing times dramatically; it is attempting to eliminate paper backups for entries and entry summaries; and it is encouraging the use of electronic funds transfer.[35] The Service is also developing an automated system for handling all commercial processing.

Mr. Von Raab also reaffirmed the Customs Service's commitment to enforcing the various trade agreements to which the US is a party. The Customs Service will continue to 'pursue all Customs disciplines in fighting fraud . . . Increased prosecution and penalties resulting from these investigat[ions] will play a major role in ensuring that the integrity of trade agreements are maintained.'[36] Finally, in response to the multitude of complaints regarding inconsistent tariff classification by the Customs Service, Mr. Von Raab said that Customs is restructuring the tariff classification procedures somewhat. Customs is hiring more personnel who will be responsible almost exclusively for classifying goods. These personnel will undergo rigorous training in their duties and in the proper manner in which to respond to the trading community.

---

32. The Honorable J.J. Pickle, Opening Statement, Subcommittee on Oversight Hearing, September 27, 1988.
33. William Von Raab, Statement before the Subcommittee on Oversight House Committee on Ways and Means, September 27, 1988.
34. *Id.*
35. *Id.* at 4–7.
36. *Id.* at 13.

D. Central American–Dominican Republic–United States Free Trade Agreement (CAFTA-DR)

The Central America-Dominican Republic-United States Free Trade Agreement was signed on August 5, 2004, creating the second-largest US export market in Latin America, behind only Mexico, and the tenth largest US export market in the world. <www.export.gov /fta/CAFTA> (last visited April 6, 2007). Originally, the agreement encompassed only the United States and the Central American countries of Costa Rica, El Salvador, Guatemala, Honduras, and Nicaragua, and was called CAFTA. *Id.* However, with the addition of the Dominican Republic in 2004, the agreement was renamed CAFTA-DR. *See* <www.ustr.gov/Trade_Agreements/ Bilateral/CAFTA/ Section_Index.html>(follow link to CAFTA Background).

The US Congress approved the CAFTA-DR in July 2005 and the President signed it into law on August 2, 2005. *See* Press Release, USTR, *Statement of USTR Rob Portman on Signing of US-Central American-Dominican Republic Free Trade Agreement* (August 2, 2005) *available at* <www.ustr.gov/Trade_Agreements/ Bilateral/CAFTA/Section_Index.html>. The Agreement has been approved by the legislatures in the Dominican Republic, El Salvador, Guatemala, Honduras and Nicaragua. Approval is pending in Costa Rica. *See* <www.Export.gov>, *supra.*

CAFTA-DR replaces and enhances the US preferential market access extended unilaterally under the Caribbean Basin Economic Recovery Act (CBERA), the Caribbean Basin Trade Partnership Act (CBTPA), and the Generalized System of Preferences (GSP). However, unlike these other programs, CAFTA-DR is a bilateral program where the country must agree to reciprocal tariff and non-tariff measures to open these markets. See US Congressional Research Service, The Dominican Republic–Central America–United States Free Trade Agreement (RL31870; August 1, 2006), by J. F. Hornbeck, at 1. The Agreement covers trade in goods, services, government procurement, intellectual property, and investment, and addresses labor and environment issues. *Id.* The CAFTA-DR also specifies rules for transitional safeguards, tariff rate quotas, and trade capacity building. *Id.* It does not address antidumping and countervailing duties. *Id.*

Although all parties of the CAFTA-DR have the same set of obligations, each country defines its own market access schedule. *Id.* at 18. Each product is placed in one of eight tariff elimination 'staging categories,' defining the time period over which customs duties will be eliminated. *Id.* For the CAFTA-DR countries, all non-textile and non-agricultural goods enter the US duty free immediately. *Id.* Most commercial and farm goods attain duty-free status immediately, as well. *Id.* Tariffs for remaining items are being phased out incrementally over five to twenty years, duty-free treatment for the most sensitive agricultural products being delayed the longest. *Id.*

The CAFTA-DR removes all duties on textile and apparel imports that qualify under the agreement's rules of origin, retroactive to January 1, 2004, and allows for safeguard measures during the duty phase-out period. *Id.* Central American and Dominican apparel has long been entering the US duty free as long as it is assembled from US yarn and fabric under the 'yarn forward' rule. *Id.* at 19. Duty-free access under CAFTA-DR differs from earlier agreements in that it applies to textiles and garments assembled from components made in either the CAFTA-DR countries or the US, rather than just the US. *Id.* One exception is so-called enhanced 'cumulation rule,' which allows duty-free treatment for a limited quantity of woven apparel assembled from components made in Canada and Mexico. *Id.* There are also exceptions for certain goods containing limited Tariff phase-out schedules on agricultural products are the greatest, with up to 20 years for some products (e.g., rice and dairy). *Id.* at 20. Other than sugar imported by the US, fresh potatoes and onions imported by Costa Rica, and white corn imported by the other Central American countries – which will continue to be subject to quotas increasing by approximately 2 per cent each year – all agricultural trade will ultimately become duty-free. *Id.* The parties may not impose safeguard duties pursuant to the WTO Agreement on Agriculture on originating goods.<www.ustr.gov/Trade_Agreements/Bilateral/CAFTA/Briefing_Book/Section_Index.html>.

CAFTA-DR has made substantial commitments to liberalization in cross-border services trade, telecommunications, and financial services. *Id.* These commitments improve upon WTO commitments in terms of sectors covered and elimination of restrictions, and they provide for the elimination of barriers in most service sectors and regulatory transparency. CRS Report, *supra*, at 24.

CAFTA-DR includes core obligations for national treatment, most-favored nation treatment, and additional market access obligations to promote foreign direct investment in the CAFTA-DR countries. *Id.* at 23. The Agreement clarifies rules on expropriation and compensation, investor-state dispute settlement, and the expeditious free flow of investment-related payments and transfers. *Id.* It includes provisions on cross-border trade in financial services, new financial services, regulatory transparency, and objective and impartial administration of domestic regulation as well as commitments relating to branching, asset management and use of foreign-based portfolio. *See* USTR Short Summary, *supra.*

In government procurement contracts, the Agreement grants companies non-discriminatory rights to bid on contracts from a broad range of Central American ministries, agencies, and departments, with minor exceptions. CRS Report, *supra*, at 25. It also includes provisions that require the use of transparent and fair procurement procedures, including clear advance notices of purchases and effective review. *Id.*

The intellectual property rights provisions in the CAFTA-DR provide that all businesses receive equal treatment and that the CAFTA-DR countries ratify or accede to various international IP agreements. *Id.* The Agreement defines labor standards for all member countries. *Id.* at 28. It establishes a dispute settlement mechanism for arbitrating formal complaints against noncompliance, and it also includes a permanent Committee on Trade Capacity Building to coordinate assistance to the Central American. *Id.* at 28–32.

E. US–Columbia Free Trade Agreement

The United States and Colombia signed the US–Colombia Trade Promotion Agreement on November 22, 2006. Press Release, USTR, United States and

Colombia Sign Trade Promotion Agreement (November 22, 2006), *available at* <www.ustr.gov/TradeAgreements/Bilateral/Colombia_FTA/Section_Index.html>. Both countries must still enact implementing legislation before the Agreement can enter into force. <www.export.gov/fta/Colombia> (last visited April 6, 2007).

This comprehensive trade agreement covers trade in goods, services, government procurement, intellectual property, and investment. It also addresses labor and environment issues. *See* USTR Fact Sheet, Trade Facts: Free Trade With Colombia – Summary of the Agreement (February 27, 2006), *available at* <www.ustr.gov/Trade_Agreements/Bilateral/Colombia_FTA/Section Index.html>. It was preceded by the Andean Trade Preference and Drug Enforcement Act (ATPDEA), which was enacted by President George W. Bush on August 6, 2002. <www.whitehouse.gov/news/releases/2002/10/20021031-9.html.> ATPDEA was set to expire on December 31, 2006 but was extended for six months until June 30, 2007. US Federal News, *Reps. Seek Extension Of Trade Preferences For Andean Nations* (March 29, 2007). Congress is currently considering a second two-year extension until the free trade agreement can be implemented, but it is unclear whether it will pass. *Id.*

Upon implementation, the Agreement would eliminate duties on most US exports of consumer and industrial products to Colombia. *See* US–Colombia TPA Final Texts *available at* <www.ustr.gov/Trade Agreements/Bilateral/Colombia FTA/Final_Text/Section_Index.html>. Additional US exports would receive duty-free treatment within five or ten years of implementation. USTR Fact Sheet, *supra*, at 1. Colombia will join the WTO Information Technology Agreement (ITA), which would remove Colombia's trade barriers to information technology products. *Id.*

In agriculture, the Agreement grants immediate duty-free treatment to certain farm products from both countries, while some US tariffs on Colombian products such as sugar would remain in place. US Congressional Research Service, US–Colombia Trade Promotion Agreement (RS22419; September 21, 2006), by M. Angeles Villarreal, at 4. The US and Colombia made separate side commitments regarding sanitary and phytosanitary barriers that would be attached to the Agreement. *Id.*

In textiles and apparel, products that meet the Agreement's rules of origin requirements receive immediate duty-free treatment. *Id.* The customs procedures provisions include requirements for transparency and efficiency, procedural certainty and fairness, information sharing, and special procedures for the release of express delivery shipments. *Id.* These customs cooperation commitments allow for verification of claims of origin or preferential treatment and denial of preferential treatment or entry if the claims cannot be verified. USTR Fact Sheet, *supra*. The rules of origin requirements are generally based on the 'yarn forward' standard to encourage production and economic integration between the US and Columbia. *Id.* at 2. A safeguard provision provides for temporary tariff relief if imports prove to be damaging to domestic producers. *Id.* A *de minimis* provision allows limited amounts of specified third-country content to go into US and Colombian apparel, providing flexibility to producers in both countries. *Id.*

In government procurement contracts, the Agreement grants US companies a nondiscriminatory right to bid on contracts from a broad range of Colombian government ministries, agencies, public enterprises, and regional governments. CRS Report, *supra*, at 5. The Agreement also requires fair and transparent procurement procedures, such as advance notice of purchases and timely and effective bid review procedures. *Id.*

In services, Colombia would grant market access to US firms in most service sectors. *Id.* Colombia would dismantle services and investment barriers to the telecommunications, financial services, construction, professional services, and energy sectors, including requirements that US firms hire nationals rather than Americans to provide professional services. *Id.*

The Agreement's investment provisions intend to protect all forms of US investment in Colombia, including enterprises, debt, concessions and similar contracts, and intellectual property. USTR Fact Sheet, *supra*, at 3. It grants US investors the right to be treated equally to Colombian investors in establishing, acquiring and operating investments in Colombia. *Id.* The Agreement provides US investors in Colombia substantive and procedural protections that foreign investors have under the US legal system, including due process protections and the right to receive fair market value for property in the event of an expropriation. CRS Report, *supra*, at 5. Disputes are subject to a transparent, binding international arbitration mechanism. *Id.* Investor-state arbitration is available for breach of investment claims by investors. *Id.*

In all categories of intellectual property rights, US companies will be treated no less favorably than Colombian companies, and the agreement makes a number of important improvements to IP protections, including penalties on piracy and counterfeiting. USTR Fact Sheet, *supra*, at 3.

The core obligations of the Agreement, including labor and environmental provisions, are subject to dispute settlement provisions. *Id.* at 7. The Agreement includes an enforcement mechanism providing for monetary penalties to enforce commercial, labor, and environmental obligations of the agreement. CRS Report, *supra*, at 5.

The labor and environmental obligations of the Agreement require both parties to effectively enforce their own domestic labor and environmental laws. *Id.* The labor provisions include procedural guarantees ensuring that workers and employers have fair, equitable, and transparent access to labor tribunals. *Id.*

The Agreement also creates a Trade Capacity Building Committee, which will help Colombia build its capacity to implement its obligations. Likely assistance programs include those for small and medium-sized enterprises and rural farmers and for improvements in transportation infrastructure and telecommunications. USTR Fact Sheet, *supra*, at 7.

F. US–Australia Free Trade Agreement

The United States–Australia Free Trade Agreement (USAFTA) is a preferential agreement between the two countries that is similar to NAFTA. President Bush signed the Agreement into law on August 3, 2004 and the USAFTA came into force on January 1, 2005.[37]

The USAFTA was the first FTA between the US and a developed country since 1998, when the US signed an agreement with Canada. The agreement contains 23 chapters covering numerous topics such as agriculture, textiles, customs administration, sanitary and phytosanitary measures, technical barriers to trade, telecommunications, intellectual property rights, financial services, investment, government procurement, e-commerce, labor, environment, and rules of origin.[38]

Immediate benefits were realized once the agreement took effect. More than ninety-nine per cent of US manufactured goods exports to Australia immediately became duty free. The same was true for US agricultural exports to Australia, which total more than USD 400 million.[39] It is anticipated that American industries will see immediate benefits in manufacturing sectors such as autos, chemicals, construction and electrical equipment. Agricultural products will also benefit from the FTA including processed foods, soybeans, and alcoholic beverages.[40] According to former US Trade Representative Robert Zoellick, 'by opening trade in goods and services; eliminating barriers in the agricultural sector, investment, and government procurement; and increasing protection for intellectual property; the agreement will strengthen US–Australian economic ties and has the potential to increase trade between our countries by billions of dollars.'[41]

The agreement grants significant access to government procurement in both countries. For instance, US suppliers are granted rights to bid on contracts to supply Australian government entities, and Australia gains non-discriminatory access to the procurement of most US federal agencies. The agreement requires that procurements be conducted in a fair, transparent manner, and confirms that bribery for government contracts is a criminal offense. These measures, among many others help to promote equal access to government contracts.[42]

The FTA also sets out measures for sanitary and phytosanitary issues. In conjunction with existing WTO mandates, the agreement establishes two committees to ensure that the WTO provisions are followed.

The US–Australia FTA establishes rules for determining the origin of the goods being traded to establish eligibility under the agreement. The USAFTA defines originating goods as those that 1) are wholly obtained or produced entirely in the country, 2) are produced in the country wholly from originating materials,

---

37. *See* Press Release, U.S. Department of State, *President Bush Signs U.S.-Australia Free Trade Agreement, August 3, 2004,* Australia-United States Free Trade Agreement, *available at* <www/fta.gov.au/default.aspx?FolderID=246&ArticleID=193>. (last visited March 28, 2007).
38. *See* Office of the United States Trade Representative, *Summary of the U.S.-Australia Free Trade Agreement,* February 8, 2004.
39. *See* Press Release, Office of the United States Trade Representative, *Landmark U.S.-Australia Free Trade Agreement Goes Into Effect Today*, January 1, 2005.
40. *See* USTR Summary, 1–2.
41. *See* USTR Press Release, January 1, 2005.
42. *See* USTR Summary, 5.

or 3) are produced in the country partly from non-originating materials that have undergone a qualifying change in tariff classification.[43]

G. US–CHILE FTA SUMMARY

The US–Chile Free Trade Agreement (USFTA) entered into force on January 1, 2004. At the time of implementation, Chile was only the fifth country to have completed an FTA with the US.[44]

1. Tariff Elimination

Immediately upon implementation, 90 per cent of US exports to Chile and 95 per cent of Chilean exports to the US became tariff-free.[45] For the remaining items, the US and Chile negotiated a twelve-year schedule to phase-out tariffs based upon the relative sensitivity of the subject product.[46] Several key sectors that gained immediate duty-free access included agricultural equipment, construction equipment, autos and auto parts, computers, medical equipment, and textiles that met the agreement's rules of origin.[47] Over 75 per cent of US agricultural goods will be duty free within the first four years, although some products will continue to be subject to duties for the full twelve-year phase-out period.[48] Tariffs on wine were equalized at the lower US levels before being eliminated.[49]

The agreement obligated the US to immediately eliminate tariffs on any non-agricultural Chilean goods designated as articles eligible for duty-free treatment under GSP.[50] Also eliminated were duties on goods imported into either country, or re-entering the other party after undergoing repair or alteration.[51]

---

43. *U.S.-Australia* Free *Trade Agreement*, Art. 5.1, May 18, 2004, *available at* <www.ustr.gov/Trade_Agreements/Bilateral/Australia_FTA/Final_Text/Section_Index.html> (final text).
44. J.F. Hornbeck, U.S. Congressional Research Service RL31144, *The U.S.-Chile Free Trade Agreement: Economic and Trade Policy Issues*, at 15 (Updated September 10, 2003).
45. USTR Fact Sheet, *The U.S. Chile Free Trade Agreement: An Early Record of Success* (June 4, 2004), *available at* <www.ustr.gov/Document_Library/Fact_Sheets/2004/The_USChile_Free_Trade_Agreement_An_Early_Record_of_Success.html>.
46. *United States – Chile Free Trade Agreement*, Art. 3.3, annex 3.3, June 6, 2003, *available at* <www.ustr.gov/Trade_Agreements/Bilateral/Chile_FTA/FinalTexts/Section_Index.html> (final text) [hereinafter *USCFTA*].
47. USTR Fact Sheet, *Free Trade With Chile: Summary of the U.S.-Chile Free Trade Agreement* (December 11, 2002), *available at* <www.ustr.gov/Document_Library/Fact_Sheets/2002/Free_Trade_with_Chile_Summary_of_the_US-Chile_Free_Trade_Agreement.html> [hereinafter *USTR Summary*].
48. *Id.*
49. *Id.*
50. *USCFTA, supra* note 3, Art. 3.3, Para. 3.
51. *See id* at 3.9.

2. Non-tariff Barriers

Chile sought to address US antidumping statutes in the text of the FTA, but the US offered only to make the trade remedies process more transparent.[52] The agreement explicitly preserves the antidumping and countervailing duty measures available to the parties under existing agreements.[53]

The US Non-tariff Barrier focused on Chile's price band system for domestic agricultural prices, and sanitary and phytosanitary regulations that acted to restrict US agricultural and meat imports.[54] The non-tariff barriers section prohibits import or export price requirements, except as employed in antidumping and countervailing duty measures.[55]

The USCFTA established a four-year schedule for eliminating Chile's tax on luxury goods, while simultaneously annually increasing, by USD 2,500, the threshold for application of the tax.[56]

3. Trade Remedies

The trade remedies chapter allows either country to employ certain 'safeguard measures' to counteract serious harm to an industry that results from drastically increased imports under the agreement's reduced duties.[57] Subject to various procedural requirements and time limits, the safeguard measures involve either suspension of further tariff reductions, or increasing the duty rate to the most-favored-nation rate.[58] The parties may only employ safeguard measures once on any good, for a maximum of three years, and only during the transition period before duties are completely eliminated.[59]

4. Dispute Settlement

The USCFTA establishes a multi-step system for settlement of disputes arising under the agreement.[60] Either party may invoke the dispute settlement provisions to resolve questions of interpretation or application of the agreement, when a party believes that the other party has failed to fulfill its obligations under the agreement, or when a party feels that an otherwise allowable measure of the other party is causing 'nullification or impairment' of certain goals of the agreement.[61]

---

52. Hornbeck, *supra* at 12.
53. *USCFTA*, *supra* note 3, Art. 8.8.
54. Hornbeck, *supra* at 12.
55. *USCFTA*, *supra* note 3, Art. 3.11(2)(a).
56. *See id.* Art. 3.14, annex 3.14.
57. *See id.* Art. 8.1.
58. *Id.*
59. *See id.* Art. 8.2, Paras 1,3.
60. *See id.* Articles 22.4–22.6.
61. *See id.* Art. 22.2.

Dispute settlement proceedings begin with a choice of forum by the complaining party if the dispute arises under more than one trade agreement.[62] The first step in the dispute settlement process under USCFTA is a request for consultations with the other party.[63] If the dispute has not been resolved within sixty days (fifteen for disputes involving perishable goods), the either party may request a meeting of the Free Trade Commission that administers the agreement, and the commission may make recommendations.[64] If within thirty days of the commission convening the parties still have not resolved the dispute, either party may request the formation of an arbitral panel (consisting of individuals from a roster of panelists named by the parties) except that parties may not request arbitration of disputes over proposed measures.[65] Failure to implement the final report of an arbitration panel or with the terms of a settlement made pursuant to its determinations, subjects a party to suspension of benefits under USCFTA.[66] However, in the case of failure to implement an arbitration panel final report regarding a dispute arising under the articles governing enforcement of labor laws (Article 18.2, Para. 1(a)) or enforcement of environmental laws (Article 19.2, Para. 1(a)), the complaining party's only recourse is a request to the arbitral panel to impose an annual monetary fine.[67]

5. Government Procurement

The parties must accord treatment to the other each other's goods, services, and suppliers to government entities that is no less favorable than the most favorable treatment they accord to their own goods, services or suppliers.[68] At the time of implementation, the adjustable monetary value thresholds for application of this chapter to central government entities were USD 56,190 for goods and services, and USD 6,481,000 for construction services.[69] In Chile, the government entities covered by the agreement include most Chilean government agencies, thirteen regional governments, eleven ports and airports, and several hundred municipalities.[70]

With limited exceptions, the government entities covered by the government procurement provisions, must publish notice of each intended procurement, including tender submission deadlines; all criteria the entity will consider in awarding the contract; and an address where suppliers can obtain documents relating to the procurement.[71] Central government entities must publish notice of

---

62. *See id.* Art. 22.3.
63. *See id.* Art. 22.4.
64. *See id.* Art. 22.5.
65. *See id.* Art. 22.6, Paras. 1, 3.
66. *See id.* Art. 22.15, Para. 2.
67. *See id.* Art. 22.16.
68. *See id.* Art. 9.2, Para. 1.
69. *See id.* annex 9.1, Secs. A, G. The goods and services threshold was higher for municipalities and other covered entities.
70. *USTR Summary*, *supra* note 4.
71. *USCFTA*, *supra* note 3, Articles 9.4, 9.6.

intended procurement in a 'single-point-of-entry' electronic format.[72] In general, the procuring entity must publish notice of the intended procurement thirty days before the deadline for submission of tenders.[73]

The agreement requires legislative measures by the parties to make it a crime for procurement officials to solicit or accept bribes, or for any person to offer bribes to any procurement official, foreign or domestic.[74] The parties must each designate an impartial judicial authority to hear supplier challenges to domestic procurement decisions.[75]

6. Services

The chapter governing trade in services does not apply to financial services (which are covered in a separate chapter), or air transportation services.[76] The parties may not restrict market access for services by imposing limitations on the number of service suppliers, or the total value of services, and may not require that a service be supplied through a particular type of legal entity or joint venture.[77]

The requirements for national treatment (Article 11.2), most-favored-nation treatment (Article 11.3), and market access (Article 11.4), and the prohibition of local presence requirements (Article 11.5) do not apply to existing non-conforming practices of the parties.[78] In an annex, Chile agreed not to impose any new restrictions on express delivery services, or to direct revenues from its postal services monopoly to benefit express delivery services.[79]

The requirement that parties afford service providers most-favored-nation treatment does not extend to require the parties to recognize the education, certifications, or licenses of the other party, even if they recognize education, certifications, or licenses of a non-party.[80] Annex 11.9 includes provisions regarding specific professions. The parties must allow nationals of the other party to practice or advise on the law of any country in which that person is authorized to practice law.[81] The agreement also establishes a three-year schedule for implementation of a temporary licensing system for engineers that requires government cooperation with the relevant professional association in each country.[82]

72. *See id.* Art. 9.17, Para. 2.
73. *See id.* Art. 9.5.
74. *See id.* Art. 9.12.
75. *See id.* Art. 9.13.
76. *See id.* Art. 11.1, Para. 4.
77. *See id.* Art. 11.4.
78. *See id.* Art. 11.6.
79. *See id.* annex 11.6, Para. 4.
80. *See id.* Art. 11.9, Para. 2.
81. *See id.* annex 11.9, sec. B, Para. 1.
82. *Id.* Sec. C.

7. Financial Services

The agreement's financial services market access requirements are similar to those for services in general.[83] The countries may not limit the number of financial institutions of the other party allowed to supply services, the total value of allowed financial service transactions, or the types of legal entities authorized to supply financial services.[84] Each country is also obligated to allow financial institutions of the other country to provide any new financial services that would be allowed under existing domestic law.[85] Additionally, the agreement prohibits either country from requiring that senior management of financial institutions be of a particular nationality, or that boards of directors be composed of more than a minority of nationals of that country.[86]

8. Agriculture

The agreement prohibits export subsidies for agricultural products exported to the other party, except where required by the exporting party to compete with a third country's exports to the importing party.[87] In addition to the general safeguard measures set out in Article 8.1, the agreement contains specific safeguard measures that may be employed when agricultural goods originating from a party are exported to the other party at a unit price that is 90 per cent or less of a 'trigger price' established by the parties.[88] However, the agricultural safeguard measures are available only during the twelve-year implementation period, and only for goods that have not yet achieved duty-free status under the agreement.[89]

9. Intellectual Property

The US–Chile FTA reaffirmed the two countries' obligations under the Trade Related Intellectual Property Rights (TRIPS) Agreement, and added another layer of protection for US industries that was intended to increase revenues for a number of US industries dependent on strong patent and trademark enforcement. [90] The FTA includes a chapter on electronic commerce, that prohibits duties on digital products, and guarantees rights equal to those accorded to home-country and third-country digital products.[91]

---

83. *See id.* Art. 12.4.
84. *Id.*
85. *See id.* Art. 12.6.
86. *See id.* Art. 12.7.
87. *See id.* Art. 3.16, Paras 2–3.
88. *See id.* Art. 3.18, Paras 2–3.
89. *Id.* at Para. 6.
90. Hornbeck, *supra* at 13.
91. *USCFTA*, *supra* note 3, Art. 15.3–15.4. Digital products are defined at article 15.6 as, 'computer programs, text, video, images, sound recordings, and other products that are digitally

The chapter establishing rules on national treatment and market access for goods included a provision on 'distinctive products.'[92] This article requires Chile to prohibit sales of products labeled as 'Kentucky Bourbon' or 'Tennessee Whiskey,' unless those products conform to US regulations governing their manufacture.[93] Similarly, the US may not allow sales of products labeled as certain Chilean alcoholic beverages, unless they conform to the appropriate Chilean regulations.[94]

10. Investment

The FTA added to protections already enjoyed by US investors in Chile under the WTO agreement on Trade Related Investment Measures (TRIMS) and the WTO General Agreement on Trade in Services (GATS).[95]

11. Labor

Chile had said that it was against any language allowing for trade sanctions in cases of noncompliance with labor provisions.[96] The agreement requires the parties to enforce their own labor laws, but recognizes that the parties will exercise discretion in investigating and prosecuting labor violations, and allows that '*bona fide* decision[s] regarding the allocation of resources' comply with the agreement's requirements.[97]

H. US–Israel FTA Summary

The United States–Israel Free Trade Area Agreement (the 'Agreement'), the United States' first free trade agreement, entered into force August 19, 1985. The agreement currently includes US imports from Qualified Industrial Zones (QIZs) formed by Israeli agreements with both Jordan and Egypt.[98] The major provisions of the Agreement are set out below.

1. Tariff Reduction and Elimination

The Agreement established four classes of goods: one class became duty-free upon implementation of the Agreement; one received incrementally reduced tariffs

---

encoded and transmitted electronically, regardless of whether a Party treats such products as a good or a service under its domestic law.'

92. *See id.* Art. 3.15.
93. *See id.* Art. 3.15, Para. 1.
94. *Id.* at Para. 2.
95. Hornbeck, *supra* at 13.
96. *Id.* at 14.
97. *USCFTA*, *supra* note 3, Art. 18.2, Para. 1.
98. Carol Migdalovitz, U.S. Congressional Research Service IB82008, *Israel: Background and Relations With the United States*, at 8 (May 18, 2006).

before becoming duty-free at the end of four years; one class received incrementally reduced tariff rates before becoming duty-free at the end of ten years; and the last class was subject to general duty rates for the first five years, a duty rate determined by consultation of the parties for the second five years, and became duty-free at the end of ten years.[99] The different classes of goods were organized by their numbers in the respective US and Israeli tariff schedules then in use.[100]

Although the Agreement eliminated tariffs on agricultural products, Article 6 of the Agreement allowed the parties to maintain non-tariff measures, such as quotas and fees, to restrict agricultural imports in accordance with agricultural policies.[101] The US and Israel subsequently agreed to refrain from any measures authorized by Article 6 from January 1, 2004 through December 31, 2008.[102]

2. Trade-in Services

Article 16 of the Agreement committed the parties to cooperate to minimize restrictions on trade in services between the two countries, and to make a declaration with specific provisions to govern their cooperative efforts.[103] The Declaration on Trade in Services acknowledged the rights and obligations created by other bilateral and multilateral agreements and established general principles to guide the parties' policies affecting trade in services.[104] The declaration establishes 'national treatment' as the governing principle of trade in services between the parties and commits the parties to consult with their respective political subdivisions and regulatory agencies to ensure consistency with the principles of the declaration.[105] The declaration states that the parties will notify each other of laws and regulations that discriminate against a service exported from the other party, and that they will provide service suppliers of the other party with 'reasonable access' to domestic proceedings relating to the regulation of trade in services.[106]

3. Government Procurement

The US and Israel each agreed to waive 'Buy National' restrictions on government agency purchases with a contract value of USD 50,000 or more.[107] The agreement applied to government agencies of each country that would have been subject to the GATT/WTO 1981 Agreement on Government Procurement when the FTA

---

99. *Agreement on the Establishment of a Free Trade Area*, U.S.-Isr., annexes 1–2, April 22, 1985, 24 I.L.M. 657, 667–69, (1985) [hereinafter *FTAA*].
100. *Id.*
101. *See id.* Art. 6, 24 I.L.M. at 659.
102. *United States-Israel Agricultural Agreement*, July 27, 2004, *available at* <www.ustr.gov/assets/Trade_Agreements/Bilateral/Israel/asset_upload_file899_7902.pdf>.
103. *FTAA*, *supra* note 1, Art. 16, 24 I.L.M. at 663.
104. *Declaration on Trade in Services*, U.S.-Isr., April 22, 1985, 24 I.L.M. 679 (1985).
105. *Id.*
106. *Id.*
107. *FTAA*, *supra* note 1, Art.15, Paras 2–3, 24 I.L.M. at 662–63.

entered into force, even if those agencies did not meet the threshold requirement of the Agreement on Government Procurement.[108] Israel additionally committed the Ministry of Defense to waive 'Buy National' restrictions, 'subject to exceptions comparable in character and extent' to the exceptions included in the United States' entity list in the Agreement on Government Procurement.[109] The parties exempted their respective defense agencies from the one-year implementation deadline for the article on government procurement, and Israel pledged to relax offset requirements on purchases by government agencies other than the Ministry of Defense.[110]

4. Dispute Settlement

The agreement allows the parties to invoke the dispute settlement mechanism ('Joint Committee') to resolve disputes over the interpretation of the agreement, when one party asserts that the other party has failed to uphold its obligations under the agreement, or when one party asserts that measures taken by the other party 'severely distort the balance of trade benefits' or 'substantially undermine fundamental objectives' of the agreement.[111]

The agreement requires consultations before a matter may be referred to the Joint Committee, and if the dispute has not been resolved within sixty days of referral to the Joint Committee, either party may refer the dispute to a 'conciliation panel.'[112] The panel is comprised of one member appointed by each country, and a chairman selected by the two appointed members.[113] If the panel fails to bring about a mutually agreeable resolution within three months of the first member's selection, then the panel must present a report to the parties with findings of fact and determinations as to the validity of the claim, as well as a proposal for settlement of the problem.[114]

After the conciliation panel has presented its report, the complaining party is authorized by the agreement to take 'any appropriate measure.'[115] The parties may invoke other applicable international dispute settlement mechanisms, but once a party has invoked either the conciliation panel or another applicable mechanism, that mechanism has exclusive jurisdiction over the dispute.[116]

---

108. *Id.*
109. *See id.* Art. 15, Para. 3, 24 I.L.M. at 663.
110. *See id.* Art. 15, Para. 6, 24 I.L.M. at 663. The implementation deadline was actually the later of one year from entry into force of the FTA, or one year from Israel's completion of a list of exempt government entities under Article 15, Paragraph 3.
111. *See id.* Art. 19, Para. 1(a), 24 I.L.M. at 664–65.
112. *See id.* Art. 19, Para. 1(b)–(d), 24 I.L.M. at 665.
113. *See id.* Art. 19, Para. 1(d), 24 I.L.M. at 665.
114. *See id.* Art. 19, Para. 1(e), 24 I.L.M. at 665.
115. *See id.* Art. 19, Para. 2, 24 I.L.M. at 665.
116. *See id.* Art. 19, Para. 1(f), 24 I.L.M. at 665.

5. Labor and Environment

The FTAA does not include provisions that relate to labor or environmental standards in either country.

I. US–Jordan Free Trade Agreement

The United States–Jordan Free Trade Agreement (USJFTA) was signed on October 24, 2000. It was ratified by both houses of Congress and signed into law by President Bush on September 28, 2001. The treaty took effect on December 17, 2001. The US–Jordan Free Trade Agreement was America's third free trade agreement and the first with an Arab country.[117] The agreement proposed to eliminate all tariff and non-tariff barriers to bilateral trade within ten years from its inception for nearly all agricultural goods and industrial products. This reduction in tariff barriers will take place as duties on goods are phased-out, leading to duty-free trade between the countries.[118]

According to the CRS Report for Congress, 'in addition to covering traditional reductions in barriers to trade in goods and services, the FTA also deals with other issues that became part of the US trade agenda during the Clinton Administration such as intellectual property rights, e-commerce, and labor and environmental standards.'[119] As the first trade agreement to include provisions addressing e-commerce, both countries agreed to avoid imposing duties and barriers on things such as electronic transmissions, digitized products, and electronic services.[120] Additionally, the FTA includes current standards for copyright protections and contains trade-related environmental and labor provisions that allow each country to set its own labor and environmental standards.

Article 9 of the agreement speaks directly to government procurement, and states that the countries will enter into negotiations regarding this topic. Additionally, Annex 2.2 sets the standard for the FTA's Rules of Origin. A qualifying product of origin is an 'article [that] is wholly the growth, product, or manufacture of a Party or is a new or different article of commerce that has been grown, produced, or manufactured in a party.'[121]

The Jordan FTA also promotes cooperative dispute resolution. Both the US and Jordan agreed to resolve disagreements through consultations rather than through formal dispute settlement procedures. However, for any dispute that cannot be solved through cooperation, the FTA creates a multi-step, transparent dispute settlement process for the countries to follow.

---

117. *See* White House Press Release, *Overview of U.S.-Jordan Free Trade* Agreement, September 28, 2001.
118. *See* Congressional Research Service, (CRS) Report RL30652, *U.S.-Jordan Free Trade Agreement*, May 1, 2001 at 12.
119. CRS Report, 1.
120. *See* White House Press Release, *supra* note 1.
121. *See* U.S.-Jordan Free Trade Agreement, *Rules of Origin*, Annex 2.2.

J. US–Oman FTA

The US–Oman Free Trade Agreement was signed on January 19, 2006. The US Congress passed the necessary implementing legislation on September 19, 2006, and the President signed that implementing legislation into law on September 26, 2006.[122] The agreement will enter into force with an exchange of notes between the President and the Government of Oman.[123]

1. Tariff Provisions

The agreement creates five classes of goods for the purposes of reducing or eliminating tariffs: goods that will continue to receive duty free treatment; goods that will become duty free on the date the agreement enters into force; goods that will receive five equal annual tariff reductions before becoming duty free in year five; goods that will receive ten equal annual tariff reductions before becoming duty free in year ten; and goods that will be subject to general duty rates for the first nine years of the agreement before becoming duty free in year ten.[124]

The FTA includes a separate chapter on textiles and apparel. In addition to the safeguard provisions of the agreement, the parties may employ emergency tariff increases (to most-favored-nation levels) if imports of textiles or apparel benefiting from the agreement increase drastically enough to cause or threaten serious injury to a domestic industry producing a competing textile or apparel article.[125] The party taking emergency action must provide a compensatory concession liberalizing the trade of textiles and apparel in another area.[126] Additionally, the textiles and apparel chapter creates specific obligations regarding Oman's country of origin labeling and enforcement, including a provision requiring Oman to conduct on-site inspections of enterprises claiming to produce originating textiles and apparel for export to the US.[127]

2. Trade-in Services

The chapter governing trade in services does not apply to financial services, air transportation services, government procurement, or subsidies or grants provided by a party, including government-sponsored loans.[128] The parties may not restrict

---

122. Mary Jane Bolle, U.S. Congressional Research Service RL33328, *U.S.-Oman Free Trade Agreement*, at 14 (updated October 10, 2006).
123. *United States-Oman Free Trade Agreement Implementation Act*, Pub. L. No. 109-283, § 101(b), 120 Stat. 1191, 1192 (2006).
124. *United States-Oman Free Trade Agreement*, annex 2-B, January19, 2006, *available at* <www.ustr.gov/Trade_Agreements/Bilateral/Oman_FTA/Final_Text/Section_Index.html> (final text) [hereinafter *USOFTA*].
125. *See id.* Art. 3.1, Para. 1.
126. *Id.* at Para. 6.
127. *See id.* Art. 3.3, Para. 3.
128. *See id.* Art. 11.1, Para. 4.

market access for services by imposing limitations on the number of service suppliers, or the total value of services, and may not require that a service be supplied through a particular type of legal entity or joint venture.[129]

The requirements for national treatment (Article 11.2), most-favored-nation treatment (Article 11.3), and market access (Article 11.4), and the prohibition of local presence requirements (Article 11.5) do not apply to existing non-conforming practices of the parties.[130] In an article on specific commitments, the parties expressed their intention not to impose any new restrictions on market access for express delivery services, or to direct revenues from postal services monopolies to benefit express delivery services.[131] The parties also agreed to ensure that monopoly postal service suppliers do not use their monopoly position to compete to provide express delivery services in a manner inconsistent with the parties' obligations under the FTA.[132]

The requirement that parties afford service providers most-favored-nation treatment does not extend to require the parties to recognize the education, certifications, or licenses of the other party, even if they recognize education, certifications, or licenses of a non-party.[133] Annex 11.9 (Professional Services) does not include provisions regarding any specific professional service suppliers, but the annex does establish a basic process for the relevant authorities of each party to determine mutually acceptable standards for licensing and certification of professional service suppliers in general.[134]

3. Government Procurement

The parties must accord treatment to the other each other's goods, services, and suppliers that is no less favorable than the most favorable treatment they accord to their own goods, services or suppliers.[135] At the time of implementation, the adjustable monetary value thresholds for application of this chapter to central government entities will be USD 193,000 for goods and services, and USD 8,422,165 for construction services.[136] Notable exceptions to the government procurement provisions include Oman's Ministry of Awqaf and Religious Affairs' procurement of construction services for religious buildings, and procurement activities of the United States' Federal Aviation Administration.[137]

---

129. *See id.* Art. 11.4.
130. *See id.* Art. 11.6.
131. *See id.* Art. 11.12, Paras 2, 4.
132. *See id.* Art. 11.12, Para. 3.
133. *See id.* Art. 11.9, Para. 2.
134. *See id.* annex 11.9, Paras 1–3.
135. *See id.* Art. 9.2, Para. 1.
136. *See id.* annex 9.1, Secs. A, B, G. Oman central level government procurement will be subject to a non-adjustable USD 260,000 (United States Dollar) goods and services threshold for the first two years. The thresholds will be higher for municipalities and other covered entities.
137. *Id.* at Sec. A.

With limited exceptions, the government entities covered by the government procurement provisions must publish notice of each intended procurement, including tender submission deadlines, all criteria the entity will consider in awarding the contract, and an address where suppliers can obtain documents relating to the procurement.[138] In general, the procuring entity must publish notice of the intended procurement forty days before the deadline for submission of tenders.[139]

The agreement obligates the parties to put procedures in place to temporarily or permanently disqualify suppliers who have engaged in illegal acts in the procurement process, including fraud.[140] The parties must each designate an impartial judicial authority to hear supplier challenges to domestic procurement decisions.[141]

4. Dispute Settlement

The agreement establishes a multi-step system for settlement of disputes arising under the agreement.[142] Either party may invoke the dispute settlement provisions to resolve questions of interpretation or application of the agreement, when a party believes that the other party has failed to fulfill its obligations under the agreement, or when a party feels that an otherwise allowable measure of the other party is causing 'nullification or impairment' of certain goals of the agreement.[143]

Dispute settlement proceedings begin with a choice of forum by the complaining party if the dispute arises under more than one trade agreement.[144] The chosen forum will then have exclusive jurisdiction over the dispute.[145] The first step in the US–Oman FTA's dispute settlement process is a request for consultations with the other party.[146] If the dispute has not been resolved within sixty days (twenty for disputes involving perishable goods), then either party may refer the dispute to the Joint Committee that administers the agreement and the committee.[147] If within sixty days (thirty where perishable goods are involved) of referral to the committee, the committee has not resolved the dispute, the complaining party may request the formation of a dispute resolution panel, except that parties may not refer disputes over proposed measures to a panel.[148]

Parties will each appoint one member of the dispute settlement panel, and in the event they cannot agree on a chairperson, one party will be chosen by lot to select a chairperson who is not a national of that party.[149] Failure to implement the

138. *See id.* Articles 9.4, 9.6.
139. *See id.* Art. 9.5.
140. *See id.* Art. 9.10.
141. *See id.* Art. 9.11.
142. *See id.* Articles 20.3–20.7.
143. *See id.* Art. 20.2.
144. *See id.* Art. 20.4.
145. *Id.* at Para. 3.
146. *See id.* Art. 20.5.
147. *See id.* Art. 20.6.
148. *See id.* Art. 20.7, Paras 1–2.
149. *Id.* at Para. 3(c).

final report of an arbitration panel, or to comply with the terms of a compensation agreement made pursuant to its determinations, ultimately subjects a party to suspension of an equivalent amount of benefits under the agreement.[150] However, in the case of failure to implement an arbitration panel final report regarding a dispute arising under the articles governing enforcement of labor laws (Article 16.2, Para. 1(a)) or enforcement of environmental laws (Article 17.2, Para. 1(a)), the complaining party's only recourse is a request to the dispute settlement panel to impose an annual monetary fine.[151] These monetary fines, assessed for failure to enforce domestic labor or environmental laws, are capped at fifteen million dollars annually.[152]

K. US–Peru TPA Summary

The United States and Peru signed the US–Peru Trade Promotion Agreement ('USPTPA') on April 12, 2006. The Peruvian Congress approved the USPTPA in June of 2006.[153] Implementing legislation was passed on December 4, 2007 by the US Congress and became Public Law 110–138 on December 14, 2007.[154]

1. Tariff Provisions

Eighty per cent of US exports of consumer and industrial products will become duty-free upon entry into force of the USPTPA, including exports of agricultural and construction equipment, auto parts, information technology equipment, forest products, and medical and scientific equipment.[155]

The agreement creates five main classes of goods for the purposes of reducing or eliminating tariffs: goods that will continue to receive duty free treatment; goods that will become duty free on the date the agreement enters into force; goods that will receive five equal annual tariff reductions before becoming duty free in year five; goods that will receive ten equal annual tariff reductions before becoming duty free in year ten; and goods that will be subject to general duty rates for the first nine years of the agreement before becoming duty free in year ten.[156] The annexes to the countries' respective tariff schedules create additional

150. *See id.* Art. 20.11.
151. *See id.* Art. 20.12.
152. *Id.* at Para. 2.
153. M. Angeles Villarreal, U.S. Congressional Research Service RS22391, *U.S.-Peru Trade Promotion Agreement*, at 1 (updated January 24, 2007).
154. *See* 19 U.S.C. § 3803(c)(1).
155. USTR Fact Sheet, *Summary of the U.S.-Peru Trade Promotion Agreement* (December 2005), *available at* <www.ustr.gov/assets/Document_Library/Fact_Sheets/2005/asset_upload_file490_8547.pdf> [hereinafter *USTR Summary*].
156. *United States–Peru Trade Promotion Agreement*, annex 2.3, January 19, 2006, *available at* <www.ustr.gov/Trade_Agreements/Bilateral/Peru_FTA/Final_Text/Section_Index.html> (final text) [hereinafter *USPTPA*].

categories of goods subject to staged tariff reductions; the last categories of goods to become duty-free will occur in year seventeen of the agreement.[157]

The USPTPA includes a separate chapter on textiles and apparel. In addition to the general safeguard provisions of the agreement, during the transition period the parties may employ textile or apparel safeguard measures (that increase tariffs to most-favored-nation levels) if imports of textiles or apparel benefiting from the agreement increase drastically enough to cause or threaten serious injury to a domestic industry producing a competing good.[158] Textile or apparel safeguard measures may only be applied after an investigation by the relevant authority of the party, and the party applying the safeguard must provide a compensatory concession liberalizing the trade of textiles and apparel in another area.[159] Additionally, the textiles and apparel chapter creates specific procedures for bilateral cooperation to verify country of origin labeling and compliance with general regulations, including a provision requiring an exporting party to arrange joint on-site inspections of enterprises at the request of the importing party.[160]

2. Trade-in Services

The chapter governing trade in services does not apply to financial services (which are covered in a separate chapter), air transportation services, government procurement, or subsidies or grants provided by a party, including government-sponsored loans.[161] The parties may not restrict market access for services by imposing limitations on the number of service suppliers, or the total value of services, and may not require that a service be supplied through a particular type of legal entity or joint venture.[162]

As a result of a 'grandfather clause,' the requirements for national treatment (Article 11.2), most-favored-nation treatment (Article 11.3), and market access (Article 11.4), and the prohibition of local presence requirements (Article 11.5) do not apply to existing non-conforming practices of the parties.[163]

The requirement that parties afford service providers most-favored-nation treatment does require a party to recognize the education, certifications, or licenses of the other party, even if the party recognizes the education, certifications, or licenses of a non-party.[164] Annex 11-B (Professional Services) establishes a basic voluntary process for the relevant authorities of each party to determine mutually acceptable standards for licensing and certification of professional service suppliers.[165] The Professional Services Annex also provides for reciprocal temporary

157. *See id.* annex 2.3 – Peru Notes, annex 2.3 – U.S. Notes.
158. *See id.* Art. 3.1, Para. 1.
159. *Id.* Paras. 4, 7.
160. *See id.* Art. 3.2, Paras 3–5.
161. *See id.* Art. 11.1, Para. 4.
162. *See id.* Art. 11.4.
163. *See id.* Art. 11.6.
164. *See id.* Art. 11.9, Para. 2.
165. *See id.* annex 11-B, Paras 1–3.

licensing of engineers under a program to be discussed in the Working Group on Professional Services that the parties must form.[166]

In an annex specifically addressing express delivery services, the parties agreed to maintain current levels of market openness and to ensure that postal services monopolies do not compete in a manner inconsistent with the parties' obligations regarding national treatment or most-favored-nation treatment.[167]

3. Financial Services

The separate chapter governing trade in financial services interacts to a limited extent with provisions of the chapters on investment (Chapter 10) and general trade in services (Chapter 11).[168] Financial services refer generally to insurance and insurance-related services, and banking and banking-related services.[169] The obligations created in the financial services chapter do not apply to measures relating to public retirement plans or social security systems, except where the parties allow private financial institutions to compete with public entities, or other financial institutions, to provide these services.[170]

The agreement's financial services market access requirements are similar to those for services in general.[171] The signatory countries may not limit the number of financial institutions of the other party allowed to supply services, the total value of allowed financial service transactions, or the types of legal entities authorized to supply financial services.[172] Each country is also obligated to allow financial institutions of the other country to provide any new financial services that would be allowed under existing domestic law.[173] Additionally, the agreement prohibits either country from requiring that senior management of financial institutions be of a particular nationality, or that boards of directors be composed of more than a minority of nationals of that country.[174]

Specifically, the parties agree to allow outside financial institutions to provide investment advice and portfolio management services to 'collective investment schemes' (e.g., mutual funds) registered in their territories.[175] Insurance and related services generally may be supplied on a cross-border basis, both from the territory of one party into the territory of another, and by nationals of one party in the territory of another.[176] The parties separately confirmed that a country may require

---

166. *Id.* Para. 12.
167. *See id.* annex 11-D.
168. *See id.* Art. 12.1, Para. 2.
169. *See id.* Art. 12.20.
170. *Id.* Para. 3.
171. *See id.* Art. 12.4.
172. *Id.*
173. *See id.* Art. 12.6.
174. *See id.* Art. 12.8.
175. *See id.* annex 12.15.
176. *See id.* annex 12.5.1.

insurance company branches to bring capital into the territory of that country and convert it into local currency in order to comply with solvency measures.[177]

4. Government Procurement

The parties must accord treatment in the procurement of government services to each other's goods, services, and suppliers that is no less favorable than the most favorable treatment they accord to their own goods, services or suppliers.[178] At the time of implementation, the adjustable monetary value thresholds for application of this chapter to central government entities will be USD 193,000 for goods and services, and USD 7,407,000 for construction services.[179]

With limited exceptions, the government entities covered by the government procurement provisions must publish notice of each intended procurement, including tender submission deadlines, a description of the procurement, the time frame for delivery, and an address where suppliers can obtain documents relating to the procurement.[180] Upon request, the procuring entity must also provide suppliers with tender documentation to allow suppliers to submit responsive tenders, including all criteria the entity will consider in awarding the contract.[181]

In general, the procuring entity must publish notice of the intended procurement forty days before the deadline for submission of tenders.[182] Procuring entities can shorten the submission period for tenders by publishing the required notice in an electronic medium and simultaneously making the tender documentation available in an electronic medium.[183]

The agreement obligates the parties to put procedures in place to temporarily or permanently disqualify suppliers who have engaged in illegal acts in the procurement process, including fraud.[184] The parties must each designate an impartial judicial authority to hear supplier challenges to domestic procurement decisions.[185]

177. *Understanding Regarding Financial Services and Services Measures*, U.S.-Peru, April 12, 2006, *available at* <www.ustr.gov/assets/Trade_Agreements/Bilateral/Peru_TPA/Final_Texts/asset_upload file4_9519.pdf>.
178. *USPTPA*, *supra* note 4, Art. 9.2, Para. 1.
179. *See id.* annex 9.1, Secs. A, B, G. The thresholds will be higher for municipalities and other covered entities.
180. *See id.* Art. 9.4. The exceptions are contained in Article 9.8 and include procurement after no tenders were submitted in response to a notice of intended procurement, and procurement of goods or services from an original supplier where another supplier could not adequately supply interchangeable goods.
181. *See id.* Art. 9.6.
182. *See id.* Art. 9.5.
183. *Id.* Para. 3.
184. *See id.* Art. 9.10.
185. *See id.* Art. 9.11.

5. Dispute Settlement

The agreement establishes a multi-step system for settlement of disputes arising under the agreement.[186] Either party may invoke the dispute settlement provisions to resolve questions of interpretation or application of the agreement, when a party believes that the other party has failed to fulfill its obligations under the agreement, or when a party feels that an otherwise allowable measure of the other party is causing 'nullification or impairment' of certain goals of the agreement.[187]

Dispute settlement proceedings begin with a choice of forum by the complaining party if the dispute arises under more than one trade agreement.[188] The chosen forum will then have exclusive jurisdiction over the dispute.[189]

The first step in the dispute settlement process under the USPTPA is a request for consultations with the other party.[190] If the dispute has not been resolved within sixty days (fifteen for disputes involving perishable goods), then either party may request a meeting of the Free Trade Commission that administers the agreement, and the commission may make recommendations.[191] The commission must meet within ten days of the request, but may use available technological means of communication as an alternative to meeting in person.[192]

If within thirty days of the commission convening the parties still have not resolved the dispute, either party may request the formation of an arbitral panel (consisting of individuals from a roster of qualified panelists named by the parties) except that parties may not request arbitration of disputes over proposed measures.[193]

Failure to implement the final report of an arbitration panel, or to comply with the terms of a settlement made pursuant to its determinations, subjects a party to suspension of benefits under the USPTPA.[194] The party complained against can attempt to agree on alternative compensation with the complaining party.[195] If the parties cannot agree on compensation for the offending measure, or if the party complained against fails to uphold its obligations under the compensation agreement, the complaining party can then suspend trade benefits equivalent to the harm it has suffered.[196] However, in the case of failure to implement an arbitration panel final report regarding a dispute arising under the articles governing enforcement of labor laws (Article 17.2, Para. 1(a)) or enforcement of environmental laws (Article 18.2, Para. 1(a)), the complaining party's first recourse is a request to the arbitral panel

186. *See id.* Articles 21.4–21.6.
187. *See id.* Art. 21.2.
188. *See id.* Art. 21.3, Para. 1.
189. *Id.* Para. 2.
190. *See id.* Art. 21.4.
191. *See id.* Art. 21.5, Para. 4.
192. *Id.* Paras 4, 6.
193. *See id.* Art. 21.6, Paras 1, 6.
194. *See id.* Art. 21.16.
195. *Id.* Para. 1.
196. *Id.* Para. 2.

to impose an annual monetary fine to be paid into a fund.[197] If the party found to be in violation does not pay the fine assessed by the panel, the complaining party may then resort to a proportional suspension of tariff benefits.[198]

The dispute settlement chapter also includes a provision regarding disputes between private parties in the free trade area. The agreement requires the US and Peru to provide procedures to ensure that private parties observe agreements to arbitrate and that arbitral awards are enforced.[199] Compliance with obligations under either the United Nations Convention on the Recognition and Enforcement of Foreign Arbitral Awards or the Inter-American Convention on International Commercial Arbitration satisfies the requirements of the PTPA.[200]

6. Labor and Environment Provisions

Similar to certain other trade agreements negotiated by the US under the President's trade promotion authority, the USPTPA includes provisions regarding labor and the environment in the text of the agreement, as opposed to in a separate instrument like a side letter.[201] The agreement requires the parties to enforce their own labor laws, but recognizes that the parties will exercise discretion in investigating and prosecuting labor violations, and provides that '*bona fide* decision[s] regarding the allocation of resources' comply with the agreement's requirements.[202] The agreement employs the same wording for the countries' obligation to enforce their environmental laws.[203]

L. US–Panama TPA Summary

The US and Panama announced on December 19, 2006 that they had concluded negotiations on a free trade agreement subject to further negotiations on labor provisions.[204] The countries must enter into the proposed US–Panama Trade Promotion Agreement (USPTPA) by July 1, 2007 for it to receive expedited consideration under the President's trade promotion authority.[205] The following is a summary of the draft text of the agreement.

---

197. *See id.* Art. 21.17.
198. *Id.* Para. 5.
199. *See id.* Art. 21.22, Para. 2.
200. *Id.* Para. 3.
201. *See USTR Summary*, *supra* note 3; *PTPA*, *supra* note 4, Chapters 17, 18.
202. *USPTPA*, *supra* note 4, Art. 17.2, Para. 1.
203. *See id.* Art. 18.2, Para. 1.
204. Press Release, USTR, *U.S. and Panama Complete Trade Promotion Agreement Negotiations* (December 19, 2006), *available at* <www.ustr.gov/Document_Library/Press_Releases/2006/December/US_Panama_CompleteTrade Promotion_Agreement_Negotiations.html> [hereinafter *USTR Press Release*].
205. *See* 19 U.S.C. § 3803(c)(1).

1. Tariff Provisions

The USPTPA establishes nine main categories for the purposes of eliminating tariffs on goods originating in the signatory states ('originating goods'). Tariffs on originating goods will either be eliminated on the date the agreement enters into force, or will be incrementally reduced before being eliminated in years five, ten, fifteen, or seventeen.[206] Eighty-eight per cent of consumer and industrial goods would become duty-free immediately, and one hundred per cent of those goods would become duty-free within ten years.[207] Several of the agreement's tariff categories maintain general duty rates for a number of years before incremental reductions begin.[208] The tariff schedules the two countries attach to the agreement may contain exceptions to these general categories.[209]

The proposed text of the USPTPA chapter on tariff elimination includes sections covering agricultural goods, and textiles and apparel. The agreement allows the signatory countries to take 'agricultural safeguard measures' in the form of limited increases of duties on agricultural imports where quantities of specified imports exceed certain trigger levels.[210] For the most part the trigger levels are expressed as percentages of tariff rate quotas (e.g., Panama's trigger for pork is 130 per cent of the quota for US pork), and the agricultural safeguard measures only apply during the transition period before an agricultural good becomes entirely duty free.[211] In the agriculture section the US also provides special treatment relating to sugar, which would allow compensation to be paid to Panama's sugar exporters in lieu of according duty-free treatment to sugar.[212]

The textiles and apparel section creates enforceable obligations for the signatory countries to cooperate in monitoring and regulating trade in textiles. For example, an importing country can withhold preferential tariff treatment of related goods when an exporting country refuses to organize a joint on-site inspection visit to verify a manufacturer's country of origin claims.[213]

2. Government Procurement

The parties must accord treatment to each other's goods, services, and suppliers to government entities that is no less favorable than the most favorable treatment

---

206. *See* USTR, *Proposed U.S.-Panama Trade Promotion Agreement Texts*, annex 3.3, Para. 1, <www.ustr.gov/Trade_Agreements/Bilateral/Panama_FTA/Draft_Text/Section_Index.html> (last visited June 15, 2007) [hereinafter *Proposed USPTPA*].
207. USTR Fact Sheet, *Free Trade With Panama: Summary of the Agreement* (January2007), *available at* <www.ustr.gov/assets/Document_Library/Fact_Sheets/2007/assetupload_file975_10234.pdf > [hereinafter *USTR Summary*].
208. *Proposed USPTPA*, *supra* note 3, annex 3.3, Para. 1.
209. *Id.*
210. *See id.* Art. 3.17.
211. *See id.* annex 3.17; Art. 3.17 Para. 5.
212. *See id.* Art. 3.18.
213. *See id.* Chap. 3, Sec. G.

they accord to their own goods, services or suppliers.[214] At the time of implementation, the adjustable monetary value thresholds for application of this chapter to central government entities will be USD 193,000 for goods and services, and USD 7,407,000 for construction services.[215]

The agreement is expected to create opportunities for US firms to participate in procurements relating to the multi-billion dollar expansion of the Panama Canal, scheduled to begin in 2008.[216] A special section of the government procurement annex governs procurements by the Panama Canal Authority, and sets the adjustable thresholds at USD 593,000 for goods and services, and USD 12,000,000 for construction services.[217] The agreement would also allow a limited amount of procurement to be set aside for Panamanian firms, and a ten per cent price preference for Panamanian small businesses.[218]

With limited exceptions, the government entities covered by the government procurement provisions must publish notice of each intended procurement, including tender submission deadlines, date of delivery of goods or services, and an address where suppliers can obtain documents relating to the procurement.[219] In general, the procuring entity must publish notice of the intended procurement at least forty days before the deadline for submission of tenders, with an exception for urgently needed procurement and for government entities that procure goods and services for re-sale.[220] Entities must electronically publish, or provide upon request, documentation to allow for the submission of responsive tenders, including all criteria that will be used in awarding a contract.[221]

Some exceptions apply. For example, a covered entity need not request tenders via an open submission process for procurement of prototypes, additional construction services included in the objectives of an earlier tender, or in some cases additional goods or services from an original supplier.[222] The parties must each adopt procedures to temporarily or permanently disqualify suppliers who engage in illegal procurement activities, and each country must designate an independent administrative or judicial authority to hear supplier challenges to domestic procurement decisions.[223]

---

214. *See id.* Art. 9.2, Para. 1.
215. *See id.* annex 9.1, Sec. A. The goods and services threshold will be higher for municipalities and other covered entities.
216. *USTR Summary*, *supra* note 4.
217. *Proposed USPTPA*, *supra* note 3, annex 9.1, Sec. D. The construction services threshold applicable to Panama Canal Authority procurements will decrease after 12 years.
218. *Id.*
219. *See id.* Art. 9.4.
220. *See id.* Art. 9.5.
221. *See id.* Art. 9.6.
222. *See id.* Art. 9.9.
223. *See id.* Articles 9.13, 9.15.

3. Trade-in Services

The USPTPA follows a model for trade agreements that includes separate chapters for financial services, investment, telecommunications, electronic commerce, and cross-border trade in services in general. The parties may not restrict market access for services by imposing limitations on the number of service suppliers, or the total value of services supplied, and may not require that a service be supplied through a particular type of legal entity or joint venture.[224] Panama had previously pursued policies that created barriers to trade in services, including restricting provision of certain professional services to Panamanian nationals.[225]

There is a 'grandfather clause' that provides that the requirements for national treatment (Article 11.2), most-favored-nation treatment (Article 11.3), and market access (Article 11.4), and the prohibition of local presence requirements (Article 11.5) do not apply to existing non-conforming practices of the parties.[226] Panama obligated itself not to impose any new restrictions on market access for express delivery services, and both countries pledged not to direct revenues from postal services monopolies to benefit express delivery services.[227] The parties also agreed to ensure that monopoly postal service suppliers do not use their monopoly position to compete to provide express delivery services in a manner inconsistent with the parties' obligations under the FTA.[228]

The requirement that parties afford service providers most-favored-nation treatment does not require the parties to recognize the education, certifications, or licenses of the other party, even if they recognize education, certifications, or licenses of a non-party.[229] Annex 11.9 (Professional Services) does not include provisions regarding any specific professional service suppliers, but the annex does establish a basic process for the relevant authorities of each party to determine mutually acceptable standards for licensing and certification of professional service suppliers in general.[230]

4. Dispute Settlement

The USPTPA establishes a multi-step system for settlement of disputes arising under the agreement.[231] Either party may invoke the dispute settlement provisions to resolve questions of interpretation or application of the agreement, when a party believes that the other party has failed to fulfill its obligations under the agreement,

224. *See id.* Art. 11.4.
225. *USTR Summary*, *supra* note 4.
226. *Proposed USPTPA*, *supra* note 3, Art. 11.6.
227. *See id.* Art. 11.13.
228. *Id.*
229. *See id.* Art. 11.9, Para. 2.
230. *See id.* annex 11.9, Paras 1–3.
231. *See id.* Articles 20.4–20.6.

or when a party feels that an otherwise allowable measure of the other party is causing 'nullification or impairment' of certain goals of the agreement.[232]

Dispute settlement proceedings begin with a choice of forum by the complaining party if the dispute arises under more than one trade agreement.[233] A request for a panel (which would be the last step in the USPTPA) under any applicable agreement creates exclusive jurisdiction over the dispute in that panel.[234]

The first step in the dispute settlement process under USPTPA is a request for consultations with the other party.[235] If the dispute has not been resolved within sixty days (fifteen for disputes involving perishable goods), then either party may request a meeting of the bilateral Free Trade Commission that administers the agreement, and the commission may make recommendations.[236] If within thirty days of the commission convening the parties still have not resolved the dispute, either party may request the formation of an arbitral panel (consisting of individuals from a roster of panelists named by the parties) except that parties may not request arbitration of disputes over proposed measures.[237]

Failure to implement the final report of an arbitration panel, or to comply with the terms of a settlement made pursuant to its determinations, subjects a party to suspension of benefits under USPTPA.[238] However, in the case of failure to implement an arbitration panel final report regarding a dispute arising under the articles governing enforcement of labor laws (Article 16.2, Paragraph 1(a)) or enforcement of environmental laws (Article 17.2, Paragraph 1(a)), the complaining party's only recourse is a request to the arbitral panel to impose an annual monetary fine, except that the complaining party may suspend tariff benefits to enforce payment of the fine.[239]

5. Labor and Environment Provisions

Like some other trade agreements negotiated by the US under the President's trade promotion authority, the USPTPA includes provisions regarding labor and the environment in the text of the agreement, as opposed to in a separate instrument like a side letter.[240] The agreement requires the parties to enforce their own labor laws, but recognizes that the parties will exercise discretion in investigating and prosecuting labor violations, and allows that '*bona fide* decision[s] regarding the allocation of resources' comply with the agreement's requirements.[241] The

232. *See id.* Art. 20.2.
233. *See id.* Art. 20.3.
234. *Id.*
235. *See id.* Art. 20.4.
236. *See id.* Art. 20.5.
237. *See id.* Art. 20.6, Paras 1, 4.
238. *See id.* Art. 20.15, Para. 2.
239. *See id.* Art. 20.16.
240. *See USTR Summary*, *supra* note 4; *Proposed USPTPA*, *supra* note 3, Chapters 16, 17.
241. *Proposed USPTPA*, *supra* note 4, Art. 16.2, Para. 1.

agreement employs the same wording for the countries' obligations to enforce their environmental laws.[242]

M. US–Korea Free Trade Agreement

Negotiations for a free trade agreement between the United States and Korea began in February, 2006 and continued through eight negotiating rounds in June, 2006. On April 1, 2007, these talks culminated in the formation of the United States–Korea Free Trade Agreement, or KORUS FTA.[243] Also on April 1, President Bush sent a formal notification to Congress informing them of his intention to enter into a free trade agreement with Korea.[244] The agreement is awaiting congressional approval prior to implementation. There is no determined date that the agreement will come into force.

KORUS is one of the more significant trade agreements the United States has entered into in over a decade. Korea is the world's tenth largest economy and a major trading partner of the US, with bilateral trade in 2006 over USD 70 billion. The United States–Korea FTA will 'provide US farmers, ranchers, manufacturers, and service providers exciting new market opportunities in a growing, dynamic country.'[245]

The agreement covers numerous economic sectors and will hopefully be greatly beneficial for both countries. It is anticipated that KORUS will be especially beneficial for American farmers, as it eliminates or phases out Korean tariffs on a wide range of agricultural products. Once implemented, more than USD 1 billion worth of US agricultural exports to Korea will become duty-free at once, and remaining tariffs will be phased out over a ten year period. Manufacturers of industrial goods and consumer products will also benefit from the new FTA, as nearly 95 per cent of bilateral trade in consumer and industrial products will become duty-free within three years of the agreement's implementation. Additionally, most remaining tariffs will be eliminated over a ten year time period.[246]

In addition to these products, KORUS should protect US investors in Korea and expand market access and investment opportunities in many service sectors such as telecommunications and e-commerce.[247] Finally, the agreement requires both member countries to enforce their own labor and environmental laws.

According to the USTR, the FTA will 'strengthen the more than fifty-year-old alliance between the United States and Korea,' and 'help cement important

242. *See id.* Art. 17.2, Para. 1.
243. *See* Office of the United States Trade Representative, Press Release, *United States and Korea Conclude Historic Trade Agreement*, April 2, 2007.
244. *See* White House Press Release, April 1, 2007.
245. *See* USTR Press Release, 1.
246. *Id.*
247. *Id.* at 2.

political and economic reforms that Korea has undertaken in the past decade and help promote strong economic relations with the region.' [248]

N. US–Singapore FTA

The US–Singapore Free Trade Agreement (USSFTA) was signed on May 6, 2003, and entered into force on January 1, 2004.[249] At the time of signing, Singapore was the United States' twelfth largest trading partner, with bilateral trade of goods and services approaching forty billion dollars.[250]

1. Tariff Provisions

At entry into force of the USSFTA Singapore eliminated tariffs on all US goods not already entering Singapore duty free.[251] For the US, however, the agreement resulted in various categories of goods for the purposes of reducing and eliminating tariffs in stages over ten years: goods that would continue to receive duty-free treatment or become duty-free upon entry into force of the agreement; goods that would be subject to equal annual tariff reductions before becoming duty free in years four, eight, and ten; and certain goods that would continue to be subject to tariffs before becoming duty-free in year ten.[252] Additionally, the agreement permitted the US to maintain tariff rate quotas (TRQs) on duty-free imports of various agricultural products, such as beef, cheese, and cotton which would be phased out over ten years.[253]

To increase the flexibility of the agreement's rules of origin for various high-tech and medical goods, the US and Singapore created an 'Integrated Sourcing Initiative.' The initiative requires the parties to grant preferential tariff treatment to imports of each other's subject high-tech and medical goods regardless of the origin of the inputs used in the good's manufacture.[254] The agreement includes an annex listing the various categories of the goods that qualify for preferential tariff treatment if the finished product is imported into one signatory country from the other.[255] Although the agreement calls for the parties to meet to consider expanding the list of goods subject to the Integrated Sourcing Initiative's definition of

---

248. *Id.*
249. Proclamation No. 7747, 68 Fed. Reg. 75,793 (December 31, 2003).
250. USTR Fact Sheet, *Quick Facts: U.S.-Singapore Free Trade Agreement* (May 6, 2003), *available at* <www.ustr.gov/Document_Library/Fact_Sheets/2003/Quick_Facts_US-Singapore_Free_Trade_Agreement.html>.
251. *U.S.-Singapore Free Trade Agreement*, annex 2C, May 6, 2003, *available at* <www.ustr.gov/Trade_Agreements/Bilateral/Singapore_FTA/Final_Texts/Section_Index.html> [hereinafter *USSFTA*].
252. *See id.* annex 2B, Para. 4.
253. *See id.* annex 1 to annex 2B.
254. *See id.* Art. 3.2, Para. 1.
255. *See id.* annex 3B.

'originating' goods,[256] in the implementing legislation, the US Congress did not grant authority to the President to modify the list by proclamation.[257]

2. Trade-in Services

In general, the USSFTA establishes that the parties may not restrict market access for services by imposing limitations on the number of service suppliers, or the total value of services, and may not require that a service be supplied through a particular type of legal entity or joint venture.[258] Separate chapters of the agreement govern financial services (Chapter 10), telecommunications (Chapter 9), electronic commerce (Chapter 14), and investments (Chapter 15).

A 'grandfather clause' in the agreement allows that the requirements for national treatment (Article 8.3), most-favored-nation treatment (Article 8.4), and market access (Article 8.5), and the prohibition of local presence requirements (Article 8.6) would not apply to existing non-conforming practices of the parties.[259] Two annexes (8A and 8B) to the trade in services chapter list the parties' existing non-conforming trade-in-services measures. For example, despite its national treatment and most-favored-nation treatment obligations, the US Overseas Private Investment Corporation (OPIC) will not offer insurance and loan guarantees to certain aliens or foreign-controlled domestic enterprises.[260]

Singapore's annex lists numerous non-conforming measures limiting provision of certain professional services such as accounting, architecture, and land surveying.[261] Also, in a chapter containing various general provisions, both countries reserve the right to adopt measures that they subjectively believe to be necessary to protect their 'essential security interests.'[262]

In general, the requirement that parties accord service providers national and most-favored-nation treatment does not require a party to recognize the education, certifications, or licenses of the other party, even if the party recognizes the education, certifications, or licenses of a non-party.[263] Annex 8C (Professional Services) establishes a voluntary process for the authorities of each party to determine mutually acceptable standards for licensing and certification of professional service suppliers.[264] The Professional Services Annex also provides for reciprocal temporary licensing of mutually agreed upon professional services suppliers.[265]

---

256. *See id.* Art. 3.2, Para. 2.
257. *U.S.-Singapore Free Trade Agreement Implementation Act*, Pub. L. No. 108–78, § 202(o)(2)(A)(i), 117 Stat. 948, 961 (2003).
258. *USSFTA*, *supra* note 3, Art. 8.5.
259. *See id.* Art. 8.7.
260. *See id.* annex 8A, Schedule of the US at 5.
261. *See id.* annex 8A, Schedule of Singapore at 9–11.
262. *See id.* Art. 21.2. The agreement provides that a country can take measures 'that it considers necessary' to its essential security or international peace and security.
263. *See id.* Art. 8.9, Para. 2.
264. *See id.* annex 8C, Paras 1–3.
265. *Id.* Para. 4.

3. Financial Services

A separate chapter of the USSFTA governs the treatment accorded to financial institutions of the parties and the bilateral trade in financial services. The USSFTA's financial services market access requirements are similar to those for services in general.[266] The signatory countries may not limit the number of financial institutions of the other party allowed to supply services, the total value of allowed financial service transactions, or the types of legal entities authorized to supply financial services.[267] Each country is also obligated to allow financial institutions of the other country to provide any new financial services that would be allowed under existing domestic law.[268] Additionally, the agreement prohibits either country from requiring that senior management of financial institutions be of a particular nationality, or that boards of directors be composed of more than a simple majority of nationals of that country.[269]

As with trade-in services in general, the financial services chapter includes a 'grandfather clause' that allows the parties to maintain existing measures that do not conform with certain financial services obligations incurred under the USSFTA.[270] For example, notwithstanding the US obligation to treat Singapore financial institutions equally favorable to its own financial institutions, the US reserves the right to grant advantages (e.g., exemptions from taxes and regulations) to government-sponsored entities like the Federal Home Loan Mortgage Corporation.[271] Singapore limits to six the number of foreign banks that can receive 'Qualifying Full Bank' (QFB) privileges, but agreed to phase this measure out with regard to US banks, allowing US banks to establish numerous customer service locations, offer ATM network services, and provide point-of-sale debit services.[272]

If financial services disputes arise under the agreement, the parties have the option to agree that each member of the dispute settlement panel must have expertise or experience in financial services law or practice.[273] In dispute settlement proceedings, financial services benefits may only be suspended as the result of a panel finding of an inconsistent measure when that measure affects the financial services sector.[274]

---

266. *See id.* Art. 10.4.
267. *Id.*
268. *See id.* Art. 10.6.
269. *See id.* Art. 10.8.
270. *See id.* Art. 10.9.
271. *See id.* annex 10B, Non-Conforming Measures of the U.S. at 4.
272. *See id.* annex 10B, Non-Conforming Measures of Singapore at 3.
273. *See id.* Art. 10.18, Paras 1–3.
274. *Id.*, Para. 4.

4. Government Procurement

The US and Singapore confirmed their respective rights and obligations under the WTO Agreement on Government Procurement.[275] In fact, nearly the entire GPA is incorporated into the USSFTA and forms the bulk of the agreement's government procurement rules.[276] At the time of implementation, the adjustable monetary value thresholds for application of this chapter to US central government entities were USD 56,190 for goods and services, and USD 6,481,000 for construction services.[277] The thresholds for application of the USSFTA's government procurement provisions to Singapore's central government agencies was S$102,710 for purchases of goods and services, and S$11,376,000 for construction services.[278]

5. Dispute Settlement

The USSFTA established a multi-level system for settlement of disputes arising under the agreement.[279] Either party may invoke the dispute settlement provisions to resolve questions of interpretation or application of the agreement, when a party believes that the other party has failed to fulfill its obligations under the agreement, or when a party feels that an otherwise allowable measure of the other party is causing 'nullification or impairment' of certain goals of the agreement.[280]

The first step in the USSFTA's dispute settlement process is a request for consultations with the other party.[281] If consultations have not resolved the dispute within sixty days, then either party may refer the dispute to the Joint Committee that administers the agreement.[282] If within sixty days of referral to the committee, the committee has not resolved the dispute, the complaining party may request the formation of a dispute settlement panel.[283]

Parties will each appoint one member of the dispute settlement panel, and in the event they cannot agree on a chairperson, a chairperson will be chosen by lot from a contingent list of five potential panelists appointed by the each party.[284] Failure to implement the final report of an arbitration panel, or to comply with the terms of a compensation agreement made pursuant to its determinations, ultimately

---

275. *See id.* Art. 13.1, Para. 1.
276. *See id.* Art. 13.3.
277. *See id.* annex 13A. The thresholds will be higher for covered entities other than those at the central level of government.
278. *Id.*
279. *See id.* Articles 20.3–20.4.
280. *See id.* Art. 20.4, Para. 1.
281. *See id.* Art. 20.3.
282. *See id.* Art. 20.4, Para. 1. Unlike some later US FTAs, the USSFTA does not contain a provision for a mandatory expedited dispute resolution procedure in cases involving perishable goods.
283. *See id.* Art. 20.4, Para. 4.
284. *Id.*

subjects a party to suspension of an equivalent amount of benefits under the agreement.[285]

However, in the case of failure to implement an arbitration panel final report regarding a dispute arising under the articles governing enforcement of labor laws (Article 17.2, Paragraph 1(a)) or enforcement of environmental laws (Article 18.2, Paragraph 1(a)), the complaining party's only recourse is a request to the dispute settlement panel to impose an annual monetary fine.[286] Monetary fines assessed for failure to enforce domestic labor or environmental laws are paid into a fund for labor and environmental initiatives and are limited to fifteen million US dollars annually.[287]

The USSFTA allows for a choice of forum by the complaining party if the dispute arises under more than one trade agreement.[288] Only a request for the formation of a dispute settlement panel (*i.e.,* not a request for consultations or a referral to Joint Committee) acts as a choice of forum request and the chosen forum will then have exclusive jurisdiction over the dispute.[289]

6. Labor and Environment Provisions

The labor and environmental chapters of the USSFTA both employ similar language to establish the two countries' obligations in these areas. The primary obligation under each chapter is that the countries enforce their respective labor and environmental laws as far as they relate to the bilateral trade.[290] Although there is no blanket prohibition against weakening labor and environmental laws, the agreement does 'recognize that it is inappropriate' for a party to weaken those laws in order to stimulate trade.[291]

Enforcement of a country's own laws is the only provision in the labor and environment chapters that is enforceable by the USSFTA's dispute settlement process.[292] All other disputes arising from provisions of the environmental and labor chapters must first be submitted for consultation, and beyond that may only be referred to the relevant administrative subcommittee, which may attempt structure a resolution, but may not make findings or determinations.[293]

285. *See id.* Art. 20.6.
286. *See id.* Art. 20.7, Para. 1.
287. *Id.* Paras 2, 4.
288. *See id.* Art. 20.4, Para. 3.
289. *Id.*
290. *See id.* Articles 17.2, Para. 1(a), 18.2, Para. 1(a).
291. *See id.* Articles 17.2, Para. 2, 18.2, Para. 2.
292. *See id.* Articles 17.6, Para. 5, 18.7, Para. 5.
293. *See id.* Articles 17.6, Paras 1–3, 18.7, Paras 1–3.

O. US–Bahrain FTA

The United States and Bahrain signed the US–Bahrain Free Trade Agreement (USBFTA) in September of 2004. The USBFTA enjoyed broad support among trade groups representing various sectors of the US economy, including the National Association of Manufacturers and PhRMA, among others.[294] Congress passed implementing legislation that was signed into law in January 2006.[295] The USBFTA subsequently entered into force on August 1, 2006.[296]

1. Tariff Provisions

The USBFTA established three main categories of goods for the purposes of reducing and eliminating tariffs: those goods that would continue to receive duty-free treatment; those that became duty-free upon entry into force of the agreement; and those that will be subject to ten annual staged tariff reductions before becoming duty-free in year ten of the agreement.[297] Each country included additional categories, and the US included quotas that will restrict duty-free imports of certain agricultural products (beef, liquid dairy, cheese, butter) in the first ten years of the agreement.[298]

Trade in originating textile and apparel articles became duty-free upon entry into force of the agreement.[299] The separate textiles and apparel chapter sets out specific procedures for bilateral cooperation to verify country of origin labeling and compliance with general regulations, including a provision requiring an exporting party to permit joint on-site inspections of enterprises at the request of the importing party.[300] The USBFTA created a ten-year grace period to allow for duty-free treatment of numerous textile and apparel articles that do not conform to the agreement's rules of origin because they are produced or assembled from more than *de minimis* amounts of non-originating fiber, yarn, or fabric.[301]

---

294. Martin A. Weiss, U.S. Congressional Research Service RS21846, *Proposed U.S.-Bahrain Free Trade Agreement*, at 2 (Updated April 4, 2005).
295. *See U.S.-Bahrain Free Trade Agreement Implementation Act*, Pub. L. No. 109–169, 119 Stat. 3581 (2006).
296. Proclamation No. 8039, 71 Fed. Reg. 43, 635 (August 1, 2006).
297. *U.S.-Bahrain Free Trade Agreement*, annex 2-B, Para. 1, September 14, 2004, *available at* <www.ustr.gov/Trade_Agreements/Bilateral/Bahrain_FTA/final_texts/SectionIndex.html> [hereinafter *USBFTA*].
298. *See id.* Chapter 2, annex 1 to U.S. General Notes.
299. USTR Fact Sheet, *Bahrain Free Trade Agreement* (May 27, 2004), *available at* <www.ustr.gov/Trade_Agreements/Bilateral/Bahrain_FTA/Briefing_Book/Bahrain_Free_Trade_Agreement_Fact_Sheet.html>.
300. *USBFTA*, *supra* note 4, Art. 3.3, Paras 3–5.
301. *See id.* Art. 3.2, Para. 8.

2. Trade-in Services

In general, the USBFTA establishes that the parties may not restrict market access for services by imposing limitations on the number of service suppliers, or the total value of services, and may not require that a service be supplied through a particular type of legal entity or joint venture.[302] Separate chapters of the agreement govern financial services (Chapter 11), telecommunications (Chapter 12), and electronic commerce (Chapter 13).

A 'grandfather clause' in the agreement allows that the requirements for national treatment (Article 10.2), most-favored-nation treatment (Article 10.3), and market access (Article 10.4), and the prohibition of local presence requirements (Article 10.5) do not apply to existing non-conforming practices of the parties.[303] Two annexes to the USBFTA list existing non-conforming trade-in-services measures of the parties. For example, despite its 'national treatment' obligations, the US will continue to treat the release of certain controlled technologies to foreign nationals in the United States as an export, and to require that the foreign national receive a license from the Department of Commerce Bureau of Industry and Security.[304] Bahrain's annex enumerates certain measures that violate the agreement's prohibition on local presence requirements in service sectors such as accounting, advertising, and consultancy, but also establishes timelines to phase out non-conforming local presence requirements in some sectors.[305]

The requirement that parties afford service providers most-favored-nation treatment does not require a party to recognize the education, certifications, or licenses of the other party, even if the party recognizes the education, certifications, or licenses of a non-party.[306] Annex 10-B (Professional Services) establishes a basic voluntary process for the relevant authorities of each party to determine mutually acceptable standards for licensing and certification of professional service suppliers.[307] The Professional Services Annex also provides for temporary reciprocal licensing of mutually agreed upon professional services suppliers.[308]

3. Financial Services

A separate chapter of the USBFTA governs the treatment accorded to financial institutions of the parties and the bilateral trade in financial services. The agreement's financial services market access requirements are similar to those provided for services in general.[309] The signatory countries may not limit the number of financial institutions of the other party that are allowed to supply services, the

302. *See id.* Art. 10.4.
303. *See id.* Art. 10.6.
304. *See id.* annex I, Schedule of the U.S. at 2.
305. *See id.* annex I, Schedule of Bahrain at 1–2.
306. *See id.* Art. 10.9, Para. 2.
307. *See id.* annex 10-B, Paras 1–3.
308. *Id.*, Para. 4.
309. *See id.* Art. 11.4.

total value of allowed financial service transactions, or the types of legal entities authorized to supply financial services.[310] Each country is also obligated to permit financial institutions of the other country to provide any new financial services that would be allowed under its existing domestic law.[311] Additionally, the agreement prohibits either country from requiring that senior management of financial institutions be of a particular nationality, or that boards of directors be composed of more than a minority of nationals of that country.[312]

As with trade in services in general, the financial services chapter includes a 'grandfather clause' provision that allows the parties to maintain existing measures that do not conform with certain financial services obligations incurred under the USBFTA.[313] For example, notwithstanding their obligations to treat financial institutions of the other country as well as their own financial institutions, both countries reserve the right to grant advantages (e.g., exemptions from taxes and regulations) to government-sponsored entities like the Federal home Loan Mortgage Corporation in the US, and the Bahrain Housing Bank in Bahrain.[314] In dispute settlement proceedings, financial services benefits may only be suspended as the result of a panel finding of an inconsistent measure when that measure affects the financial services sector.[315]

4. Government Procurement

The parties must accord treatment in the procurement of government services to each other's goods, services, and suppliers that is no less favorable than the most favorable treatment they accord to their own goods, services or suppliers.[316] At the time of implementation, the adjustable monetary value thresholds for application of this chapter to US central government entities were USD 175,000 for goods and services, and USD 7,611,532 for construction services.[317] For the first two years the agreement is in force, the thresholds for application of the USBFTA's government procurement provisions to Bahrain's central government agencies will be USD 200,000 for purchases of goods and services, and USD 8,000,000 for construction services; the adjustable thresholds will then harmonize with those in place for US entities.[318]

With limited exceptions, the government entities covered by the government procurement provisions must publish notice of each intended procurement, including

---

310. *Id.*
311. *See id.* Art. 11.6.
312. *See id.* Art. 12.8.
313. *See id.* Art. 11.9.
314. *See id.* annex III, Non-Conforming Measures of the U.S. at 15, Non-Conforming Measures of Bahrain at 2.
315. *See id.* Art. 11.20, Para. 4.
316. *See id.* Art. 9.2, Para. 1.
317. *See id.* annex 9-A-1, Para. 1. The thresholds will be higher covered entities other than those at the central level of government.
318. *Id.* Para. 2.

tender submission deadlines, a description of the procurement, the time frame for delivery and an address where suppliers can obtain documents relating to the procurement.[319] The exceptions to the open tender process include procurement after no tenders were submitted in response to a notice of intended procurement, and procurement of goods or services from an original supplier where another supplier could not adequately supply interchangeable goods.[320]

In general, the procuring entity must publish notice of the intended procurement forty days before the deadline for submission of tenders.[321] Procuring entities can shorten the submission period for tenders by up to five days by publishing the required notice in an electronic medium.[322] Upon request, the procuring entity must also provide suppliers with tender documentation to allow suppliers to submit responsive tenders, including all criteria the entity will consider in awarding the contract.[323]

The USBFTA obligates the parties to put procedures in place to temporarily or permanently disqualify suppliers who have engaged in illegal acts in the procurement process, including fraud.[324] The parties must each designate an impartial judicial authority to hear supplier challenges to domestic procurement decisions.[325]

5. Dispute Settlement

The USBFTA established a multi-step system for settlement of disputes arising under the agreement.[326] Either party may invoke the dispute settlement provisions of the USBFTA to resolve any questions of interpretation or application of the agreement, when a party believes that the other party has failed to fulfill its obligations under the USBFTA, or when a party feels that an otherwise allowable measure of the other party is causing 'nullification or impairment' of certain goals of the agreement.[327]

The first step in the USBFTA's dispute settlement process is a request for consultations with the other party.[328] If consultations have not resolved the dispute within 60 days (20 for disputes involving perishable goods), then either party may refer the dispute to the Joint Committee that administers the agreement and the committee.[329] If within 60 days (30 where perishable goods are involved) of referral to the committee, the committee has not resolved the dispute, the complaining

319. *See id.* Art. 9.4.
320. *See id.* Art. 9.8.
321. *See id.* Art. 9.5.
322. *Id.* Para. 3.
323. *See id.* Art. 9.6.
324. *See id.* Art. 9.10.
325. *See id.* Art. 9.11.
326. *See id.* Articles 19.4–19.7.
327. *See id.* Art. 19.2.
328. *See id.* Art. 19.5.
329. *See id.* Art. 19.6.

party may request the formation of a dispute resolution panel, except that parties may not refer disputes over proposed measures to a panel.[330]

Parties will each appoint one member of the dispute settlement panel, and in the event they cannot agree on a chairperson, one party will be chosen by lot to select a chairperson who is not a national of that party.[331] Failure to implement the final report of an arbitration panel, or to comply with the terms of a compensation agreement made pursuant to its determinations, ultimately subjects a party to suspension of an equivalent amount of benefits under the USBFTA.[332]

However, in the case of failure to implement an arbitration panel final report regarding a dispute arising under the articles governing enforcement of labor laws (Article 15.2, Paragraph 1(a)) or enforcement of environmental laws (Article 16.2, Paragraph 1(a)), the complaining party's only recourse is a request to the dispute settlement panel to impose an annual monetary fine.[333] These monetary fines assessed for failure to enforce domestic labor or environmental laws are paid into a fund for labor and environmental initiatives and are limited to fifteen million US dollars annually.[334]

The USBFTA allows for a choice of forum by the complaining party if the dispute arises under more than one trade agreement.[335] Only a request for the formation of a dispute settlement panel (*i.e.,* not a request for consultations or a referral to Joint Committee) acts as a choice of forum and the chosen forum will then have exclusive jurisdiction over the dispute.[336]

6. Labor and Environment Provisions

The labor and environment chapters both employ similar language which establishes the countries' obligations in these areas. The primary obligation is that the countries enforce their own labor and environmental laws insofar as they relate to the bilateral trade.[337] Although there is no blanket prohibition against weakening labor and environmental laws, the agreement does 'recognize that it is inappropriate' for a party to weaken those laws in order to stimulate trade.[338]

Enforcement of each country's laws is the only provision in the labor and environment chapters that is enforceable by the USBFTA's dispute settlement process.[339] All other disputes arising from provisions of the environmental and labor chapters must first be submitted for consultation, and beyond that may only

330. *See id.* Art. 19.7.
331. *Id.* Para. 3.
332. *See id.* Art. 19.11.
333. *See id.* Art. 19.12
334. *Id.* Para. 2.
335. *See id.* Art. 19.4, Para. 1.
336. *See id.* Art. 19.4, Paras 3–4.
337. *See id.* Articles 15.2, Para. 1(a), 16.2, Para. 1(a).
338. *See id.* Articles 15.2, Para. 2, 16.2, Para. 2.
339. *See id.* Articles 15.6, Para. 5, 16.8, Para. 5.

be referred to the relevant administrative subcommittee, which may attempt a resolution, but may not make binding findings or determinations.[340]

P. US–Morocco FTA

The US and Morocco signed the United States–Morocco Free Trade Agreement (USMFTA) on June 15, 2004. The US Congress passed the required implementing legislation and the USMFTA entered into force on January 1, 2006.[341]

1. Tariff Provisions

Before implementation of the USMFTA, the average tariff rate on US products entering Morocco was twenty per cent, compared to the average four per cent tariff levied on Moroccan products imported into the US.[342] In addition to providing for continued duty-free treatment and immediate elimination of tariffs on certain goods, the USMFTA established various categories of goods for the purposes of reducing and eliminating tariffs in stages.[343] Eight separate categories of goods are subject to equal annual tariff reductions before tariffs on those goods are eliminated in years two through fifteen of the agreement.[344] Two other categories of goods are subject to initially small percentage tariff reductions before larger reductions take effect, and tariffs on those goods will then be eliminated in years ten and eighteen of the agreement.[345]

Both the US and Morocco included additional categories of goods in their tariff schedules under the agreement, with Morocco phasing out some tariffs as late as year twenty-five and maintaining a most-favored-nation duty rate on one category of goods.[346] In a side letter, the parties confirmed that Morocco will continue to impose a quarter per cent tax on all imports.[347]

The USMFTA provides that each country may maintain tariff-rate quotas (TRQs) to restrict the volume of duty-free agricultural imports.[348] In general, the

---

340. *See id.* Articles 15.6, Paras 1–3, 16.8, Paras 1–3.
341. *See U.S.-Morocco Free Trade Agreement Implementation Act*, Pub. L. No. 108-302, 118 Stat. 1103 (2004); Proclamation No. 7971, 70 Fed. Reg. 76, 651 (December 27, 2005).
342. USTR Fact Sheet, *Free Trade With Morocco* (January 17, 2003), *available at* <www.ustr.gov/Document_Library/Fact_Sheets/2003/Free_Trade_with_Morocco_Helping_to_Solidify_Economic_Reforms.html>.
343. *U.S.-Morocco Free Trade Agreement*, annex IV, Para. 1, June 15, 2004, <www.ustr.gov/Trade_Agreements/Bilateral/Morocco_FTA/FInal_Text/Section_Index.html> [hereinafter *USMFTA*].
344. *Id.*
345. *Id.*
346. *See id.* annex IV, Tariff Schedule of Morocco, General Notes, Para. 3.
347. *Side Letter on Parafiscal Tax*, U.S.-Morocco, June 15, 2004, *available at* <www.ustr.gov/assets/Trade_Agreements/Bilateral/Morocco_FTA/FInal_Text/assetupload_file946_3822.pdf>.
348. *See id.* Art. 3.2.

quantity of allowable duty-free imports increases each year before the quotas are lifted during the second decade of the agreement.[349] The US has instituted fifteen-year TRQs on Moroccan exports of beef, sugar, and cotton, among other agricultural products.[350] In addition to other agriculture quotas, Morocco has put in place a ten-year TRQ on US exports of common wheat that is tied to Moroccan domestic production, increasing in proportion to any production shortfall in a given year.[351]

Reduction and elimination of tariffs on textiles and apparel are governed by complex provisions in a separate chapter of the USMFTA.[352] The rules of origin for textiles and apparel are relaxed for the first ten years of the agreement to allow for duty-free treatment of numerous articles that do not conform to the rules of origin because they are produced or assembled from more than *de minimis* amounts of non-originating fiber, yarn, or fabric.[353] Additionally, the USMFTA provides for duty-free treatment for a limited volume of articles whose sole non-originating content is cotton fiber from one or more least-developed countries of sub-Saharan Africa.[354]

2. Trade-in Services

In general, the USMFTA establishes that the parties may not restrict market access for services by imposing limitations on the number of service suppliers, or the total value of services, and may not require that a service be supplied through a particular type of legal entity or joint venture.[355] Separate chapters of the agreement govern investment, (Chapter 10), financial services (Chapter 12), telecommunications (Chapter 13), and electronic commerce (Chapter 14).

A 'grandfather clause' in the agreement allows that the requirements for national treatment (Article 11.2), most-favored-nation treatment (Article 11.3), and market access (Article 11.4), and the prohibition of local presence requirements (Article 11.5) do not apply to existing non-conforming practices of the parties, which are listed in Annex I of the USMFTA.[356] Additionally, the above requirements do not limit a country's ability to implement measures respecting the particular sectors, sub-sectors or activities included by the parties in their respective schedules to Annex II of the agreement.[357] For example, despite its 'national treatment' obligations, the US will continue to allow only air carriers that are

---

349. *See id.* annex IV, Tariff Schedule of Morocco, General Notes, annex 1; Tariff Schedule of the U.S., General Notes, annex 1.
350. *See id.* annex IV, Tariff Schedule of the U.S., General Notes, annex 1, Paras 2, 8, 11.
351. *See id.* annex IV, Tariff Schedule of Morocco, General Notes, annex 1, Para. 10.
352. *See id.* Chapter. 4.
353. *See id.* Art. 4.3.
354. *Id.* Para. 15.
355. *See id.* Art. 11.4.
356. *See id.* Art. 11.6.
357. *Id.* Para. 2.

'citizens' of the US to provide domestic air service.[358] A non-conforming Moroccan practice is its exclusion of foreign nationals from the profession of licensed tour and mountain guides.[359]

The requirement that parties accord service providers most-favored-nation treatment does not require a party to recognize the education, certifications, or licenses of the other party, even if the party recognizes the education, certifications, or licenses of a non-party.[360] Annex 11-B (Professional Services) establishes a basic voluntary process for the relevant authorities of each party to determine mutually acceptable standards for licensing and certification of professional service suppliers.[361] The Professional Services Annex also provides for reciprocal temporary licensing of mutually agreed upon professional services suppliers.[362]

3. Financial Services

A separate chapter of the USMFTA governs the treatment accorded to financial institutions of the parties and the bilateral trade in financial services. The agreement's financial services market access requirements are similar to those for services in general.[363] The signatory countries may not limit the number of financial institutions of the other party allowed to supply services, the total value of allowed financial service transactions, or the types of legal entities authorized to supply financial services.[364] Each country is also obligated to allow financial institutions of the other country to provide any new financial services that would be allowed under existing domestic law.[365] Additionally, the agreement prohibits either country from requiring that senior management of financial institutions be of a particular nationality, or that boards of directors be composed of more than a minority of nationals of that country.[366]

As with trade in services in general, the financial services chapter includes a 'grandfather clause' provision that allows the parties to maintain existing measures that do not conform to certain financial services obligations incurred under the USMFTA.[367] For example, notwithstanding the requirement to provide open market access to financial institutions of the other country, Morocco requires that stock brokerage firms be incorporated in Morocco.[368] The US requires that all directors of a national bank be US citizens, despite the agreement's provision that citizenship requirements may not be imposed on more than a minority of a financial

358. *See id.* annex I, Schedule of the U.S. at 7.
359. *See id.* annex I, Schedule of Morocco at 1.
360. *See id.* Art. 11.9, Para. 2.
361. *See id.* annex 11-B, Paras 1–3.
362. *Id.* Para. 4.
363. *See id.* Art. 12.4.
364. *Id.*
365. *See id.* Art. 12.6.
366. *See id.* Art. 12.8.
367. *See id.* Art. 12.9.
368. *See id.* annex III, Non-Conforming Measures of Morocco at 11.

institution's directors.[369] In dispute settlement proceedings, financial services benefits may only be suspended as the result of a panel finding of an inconsistent measure when that measure affects the financial services sector.[370]

4. Government Procurement

The parties must accord treatment in the procurement of government services to each other's goods, services, and suppliers that is no less favorable than the most favorable treatment they accord to their own goods, services or suppliers.[371] At the time of implementation, the adjustable monetary value thresholds for application of this chapter to US central government entities were USD 175,000 for goods and services, and USD 6,725,000 for construction services.[372] The US reserved the right to set aside certain contracts for, or grant price preferences to small and minority-owned businesses.[373]

With limited exceptions, the government entities covered by the government procurement provisions must publish notice of each intended procurement, including tender submission deadlines, a description of the procurement, the time frame for delivery, and an address where suppliers can obtain documents relating to the procurement.[374] The exceptions to the open tender process include procurement after no tenders were submitted in response to a notice of intended procurement, and procurement of goods or services from an original supplier where another supplier could not adequately supply interchangeable goods.[375]

In general, the procuring entity must publish notice of the intended procurement at least forty days before the deadline for submission of tenders.[376] Upon request, the procuring entity must also provide suppliers with tender documentation to allow suppliers to submit responsive tenders, including all criteria the entity will consider in awarding the contract.[377]

The USMFTA obligates the parties to put procedures in place to temporarily or permanently disqualify suppliers who have engaged in illegal acts in the procurement process, including fraud.[378] The parties must each designate an impartial judicial authority to hear supplier challenges to domestic procurement decisions.[379]

---

369. *See id.* annex III, Non-Conforming Measures of the U.S. at 6.
370. *See id.* Art. 12.17, Para. 4.
371. *See id.* Art. 9.2, Para. 1.
372. *See id.* annex 9-A-1. The thresholds are higher for entities other than those at the central level of government.
373. *See id.* annex 9-F, Schedule of the U.S., Para. 1.
374. *See id.* Art. 9.4.
375. *See id.* Art. 9.9.
376. *See id.* Art. 9.5.
377. *See id.* Art. 9.6.
378. *See id.* Art. 9.11.
379. *See id.* Art. 9.12.

5. Dispute Settlement

The USMFTA established a multi-step system for settlement of disputes arising under the agreement.[380] Either party may invoke the dispute settlement provisions to resolve questions of interpretation or application of the agreement, when a party believes that the other party has failed to fulfill its obligations under the agreement, or when a party feels that an otherwise allowable measure of the other party is causing 'nullification or impairment' of certain goals of the agreement.[381]

The first step in the USMFTA's dispute settlement process is a request for consultations with the other party.[382] If consultations have not resolved the dispute within sixty days (twenty for disputes involving perishable goods), then either party may refer the dispute to the Joint Committee that administers the agreement and the committee.[383] If within sixty days (thirty where perishable goods are involved) of referral to the committee, the committee has not resolved the dispute, the complaining party may refer the matter to a dispute resolution panel, except that parties may not refer disputes over proposed measures to a panel.[384] Parties may each appoint one member of the dispute settlement panel, and in the event they disagree on a chairperson, the chairperson of the panel will be chosen by lot from the parties' reserve lists of eligible panelists.[385]

Failure to implement the final report of an arbitration panel, or to comply with the terms of a compensation agreement made pursuant to its determinations, ultimately subjects a party to suspension of an equivalent amount of benefits under the agreement.[386] However, in the case of failure to implement an arbitration panel final report regarding a dispute arising under the articles governing enforcement of labor laws (Article 16.2, Para. 1(a)) or enforcement of environmental laws (Article 17.2, Para. 1(a)), the complaining party's only recourse is a request to the dispute settlement panel to impose an annual monetary fine.[387] Monetary fines assessed for failure to enforce domestic labor or environmental laws are paid into a fund for labor and environmental initiatives and are capped at fifteen million dollars annually.[388]

The USMFTA allows for a choice of forum by the complaining party if the dispute arises under more than one trade agreement.[389] Only a request for the formation of a dispute settlement panel (*i.e.*, not a request for consultations or a

380. *See id.* Articles 20.4–20.7.
381. *See id.* Art. 20.2.
382. *See id.* Art. 20.5.
383. *See id.* Art. 20.6.
384. *See id.* Art. 20.7.
385. *Id.* Para. 3.
386. *See id.* Art. 20.11.
387. *See id.* Art. 20.12
388. *Id.* Para. 4.
389. *See id.* Art. 20.4, Para. 1.

referral to Joint Committee) acts as a choice of forum and the chosen forum will then have exclusive jurisdiction over the dispute.[390]

6. Labor and Environment Provisions

The labor and environment chapters of the USMFTA both employ similar language to set out each country's obligations as to labor and environment measures. The primary obligation is that the countries enforce their own labor and environmental laws insofar as they relate to the bilateral trade.[391] One week before the USMFTA was signed, a Moroccan labor law went into effect that raised the age for employment from twelve to fifteen, reduced the work week to forty-four hours and provided for overtime pay, called for periodic review of the minimum wage, and guaranteed rights of association and collective bargaining.[392] Although there is no blanket prohibition against weakening labor and environmental laws, the agreement does 'recognize that it is inappropriate' for a party to weaken those laws in order to stimulate trade.[393]

Enforcement by each country of its own laws is the only provision in the labor and environment chapters that is enforceable through the USMFTA's dispute settlement process.[394] All other disputes arising from provisions of the environmental and labor chapters must first be submitted for consultation, and beyond that may only be referred to the relevant administrative subcommittee, which may attempt to structure a resolution, but may not make findings or determinations.[395]

Q. Proposed Free Trade Agreement of the Americas (FTAA)

In 1994, 34 western hemisphere nations met at summit in Miami and discussed implementing a free trade area throughout the Americas. The goal of the Free Trade Area of the Americas, or FTAA, is the progressive elimination of trade and investment barriers within the western hemisphere. *See* World Agriculture and Trade, *Free Trade Area of the Americas: What are the Benefits for US Agriculture*, April, 2000. This proposed agreement was viewed by some as an extension of the North American Free Trade Agreement. At the initial meeting in 1994, the member countries set a completion deadline of January 1, 2005. Since 1994, there have been many summits and many trade ministerial meetings. Unfortunately, the negotiation process for the FTAA has been repeatedly stalled, and the deadline has expired. *See* Congressional Research Service, Report RS20864, *A Free Trade*

---

390. *See id.* Art. 20.4, Paras 3–4.
391. *See id.* Articles 16.2, Para. 1(a), 17.2, Para. 1(a).
392. Raymond J. Ahearn, U.S. Congressional Research Service RS21464, Morocco-U.S. Free Trade Agreement at 6 (updated May 26, 2005).
393. *See id.* Articles 16.2, Para. 2, 17.2, Para. 2.
394. *See id.* Articles 16.6, Para. 5, 17.7, Para. 5.
395. *See id.* Articles 16.6, Paras 1–3, 17.7, Paras 1–3.

Area of the Americas: Major Policy Issues and Status of Negotiations, January 3, 2005.

The central purpose of the FTAA is to promote economic growth and prosperity through the reduction of barriers to trade and investment in the Western Hemisphere. The FTAA has six main objectives: to promote prosperity through increased integration and free trade, to establish a Free Trade Area in which barriers to trade in goods, services and investment are progressively eliminated, to maximize market openness, to facilitate the integration of smaller economies into the FTAA, to strive to make trade liberalization and environmental policies mutually supportive, and secure the observance and protection of workers' rights. *See* Terry L. McCoy, Center for Latin American Studies, *The Free Trade Area of the Americas: Opportunities and Challenges for Florida*, 3.

When the FTAA was proposed, one of the key concepts was that all 34 countries would have to agree together. However, this premise has proved extremely challenging, as US priorities differ significantly from those of key Latin American countries. *See* CRS Report, 3. Brazil and Argentina have emerged as the leaders of Latin American resistance to the FTAA. Throughout the negotiation process, the US has pushed for a single comprehensive agreement to reduce trade barriers for goods, while increasing intellectual property protection. Brazil however, favors a measured, multi-track approach that calls for a series of bilateral agreements to reduce tariffs on specific goods, and a hemispheric pact on rules of origin and dispute resolution procedures. *See* CRS Report, 3.

Two of the main points of disagreement during the FTAA negotiations were intellectual property rights and agricultural subsidies. The US favors strong IP rights, as numerous US producers have been hurt by intellectual property violations in Latin America. Additionally, the US believes that no Latin American country has laws equal to the US for protecting these rights. The Latin American countries, again led by Argentina and Brazil, strongly favor a reduction in US agricultural subsidies. They want to open the US market to exports from their countries. This is significant because agriculture is traditionally a much protected sector in the US. However, for Latin American countries, agriculture is a large portion of their economic output, and they would greatly benefit from a reduction in US subsidies. *See* CRS Report, 3.

For now, the FTAA negotiations have stalled. At the end of 2005, leaders from Argentina, Brazil, Paraguay, Uruguay, and Venezuela made it clear that they would not consider a new round of negotiations until the United States changes its trade and economic policies. *See Dissent Stalls Goals of Trade Talks: Bush Leaves Summit Without Agreement*, Chicago Tribune, November 6, 2005. There was no information available as to when talks will resume. Notably, a round of negotiations for Cancun failed to produce any results. The US, however, has not given up its objective of a FTAA. Many of the issues of contention are the same as those being fought out by the US and certain more advanced developing countries such as Brazil and India in the Dotha Round of World Trade Organization negotiations.

R. Update: FTAs Pending Further Negotiation at Time of Publication

1. United Arab Emirates

President Bush notified Congress of his intention to begin negotiating a trade agreement with the United Arab Emirates (UAE) in November of 2004.[396] At the time of publication, talks have not resulted in an agreement, reportedly because the UAE is unwilling to initiate labor reforms for the limited benefits of an FTA to the UAE economy.[397] Also possibly impeding negotiations were security-related concerns aroused by a Dubai firm's stake in the management of US ports.[398]

The Bush administration hoped to add a UAE trade agreement to several already negotiated in the region (Jordan, Morocco, and Bahrain) to further open the area to trade and investment.[399] The ultimate goal in the region is a Middle-East Free Trade Area (MEFTA), which is seen as achieving the dual goals of trade liberalization and regional security through economic development.[400]

2. Malaysia

President Bush notified Congress of his intent to negotiate a free trade agreement with Malaysia on March 8, 2006.[401] The effort to form an agreement with Malaysia is part of a larger initiative to strengthen trade ties with individual Association of Southeast Asian Nations (ASEAN) Member States.[402] Negotiations commenced on October 30, 2006, but could be delayed by differing positions on liberalization of trade in services.[403] The US seeks the adoption of a negative list approach that would require the countries to allow cross-border supply of all services except those specifically exempted, while Malaysia seeks an agreement that specifically identifies service sectors to be included in the agreement.[404]

---

396. Press Release, USTR, *U.S. Begins FTA Negotiations With UAE and Oman* (March 8, 2005), *available at* <www.ustr.gov/Document_Library/Press_Releases/2005/March/United_States_to_Begin_Free_Trade_Negotiations_This_Week_with_the_United_Arab_Emirates_Oman.html>.
397. Kenneth Katzman, U.S. Congressional Research Service RS21852, *The UAE: Issues For U.S. Policy*, at 6 (updated May 1, 2007).
398. Ian F. Fergusson, U.S. Congressional Research Service RL33463, *Trade Negotiations During the 110th Congress*, at 13 (updated January 3, 2007).
399. *See* Press Release, USTR, *supra* note 1.
400. *Id.*
401. Press Release, USTR, *United States, Malaysia Announce Intention to Negotiate Free Trade Agreement* (March 8, 2006), *available at* <www.ustr.gov/Document_Library/Press Releases/2006/March/United_States,_Malaysia_Announce_Intention_to_Negotiate Free Trade Agreement.html>.
402. *Id.*
403. Fergusson, *supra* note 3, at 12.
404. *Id.*

3. Thailand

The Bush administration announced in October 2003 that it would begin free trade agreement negotiations with Thailand.[405] US agricultural interests were particularly interested in an agreement with Thailand to lower duties and other barriers in the 16th largest market for US agricultural exports.[406] Negotiations began in June of 2004, but were interrupted by political events in Thailand in 2006.[407] Negotiations may have faced other obstacles. For example, in January 2006, negotiations in Thailand drew demonstrations against proposed intellectual property rights (IPR) provisions.[408]

4. South African Customs Union

The US and the South African Customs Union (SACU) began Free Trade Agreement (FTA) negotiations in 2003 to expand the trade relationship already doubled by the African Growth and Opportunity Act (AGOA).[409] SACU includes South Africa, Botswana, Lesotho, Namibia, and Swaziland. FTA negotiations were set aside in 2006, in favor of more limited talks focused on developing a 'joint-work program' to address trade and investment issues, with the possibility of trade and investment-related agreements in the short-term, and a more extensive FTA in the long-term.[410] Possible reasons for the breakdown in FTA negotiations include a failure to agree on the scope of the negotiations and diminished incentive for SACU to participate after the extension of AGOA tariff preferences through 2015.[411]

5. Antiterrorism Programs

In addition to the Bioterrorism Act discussed in Chapter 18, there are two other customs programs that evolved since September 11, 2001 to combat terrorism and promote the safety of inbound cargo. These are voluntary programs and do not have many references in the customs laws or regulations so they are not discussed in other sections. However, because of their importance to exporters and importers

---

405. Press Release, USTR, *USTR Notifies Congress of Intent to Initiate FTA Negotiations With Thailand* (February 14, 2004), *available at* <www.ustr.gov/Document_Library/Press_Releases/2004/February/USTR_Notifies_Congress_of_Intent_to_Initiate_FTA_Negotiations with Thail.html>.
406. *Id.*
407. Fergusson, *supra* note 3, at 12.
408. *Id.*
409. Press Release, USTR, *U.S.-SACU Agree to Pursue Concrete Steps to Deepen Trade and Investment Relations* (April 18, 2006), *available at* <www.ustr.gov/Document_Library/Press_Releases/2006/April/US-SACUAgree_to_Pursue_Concrete_Steps_to_Deepen_Trade_Investment_Relations.html>.
410. *Id.*
411. Danielle Langton, U.S. Congressional Research Service RS21387, *U.S.-SACU Free Trade Agreement Negotiations* (updated January 3, 2007).

they are being briefly discussed here and materials about them appear in the Appendices.

A. Customs Trade Partnership Against Terrorism (CTPAT) - this program is a voluntary partnership between customs and the trade community. Companies agree to provide a security profile to customs and meet certain security standards and in return, they can be certified as CTPAT companies that are placed in a lower risk group and which receive less inspections and less intensive inspections (e.g. X-rays versus offloading of trailers). This certification is akin to an ISO standard for quality and many original equipment manufacturers, such as in the automotive industry, are requiring their vendors to have this CTPAT certification. At this time the following types of entities can apply for CTPAT:

    U.S. importers; foreign manufacturers/exporters in Mexico and Canada, U.S truck and rail carriers, customs brokers and air freight forwarders, and shipping lines. The author has helped many companies obtain CTPAT certifications first starting with a security audit of their facilities and a report on deficiencies below CTPAT minimum standards. These standards involve physical plant security, supply chain security, information security and personnel security. Two documents that appear in Appendix B (7,8) provide more details on these requirements.

B. Free and Secure Trade (FAST) - this is also a voluntary program and only CTPAT certified companies are eligible. Membership in FAST enables companies to use special FAST lanes at the U.S. border with Mexico and Canada saving time and money. To apply for FAST, the exporter, importer and carriers must all be CTPAT certified. More information on FAST appears in Appendix B.9.

Appendix A

Frequently Used Customs Forms

TABLE OF CONTENTS

19. Certificate of Registration (#4455)
20. General Declaration (outward/inward) Agriculture, Customs, Immigration, and Public Health (#7507)
21. United States–Canada Transit Manifest (#7512B)
22. Drawback Notice (#7514)
23. Entry and Manifest of Merchandise Free of Duty, Carrier's Certificate and Release (#7523)
24. Inward Cargo Manifest for Vessel under Five Tons, Ferry, Train, Car, Vehicle, etc. (#7533)
25. Entry Declaration (#7501)

OMB No. 1651-0029

CENSUS USE ONLY

U.S. DEPARTMENT OF HOMELAND SECURITY
Bureau of Customs and Border Protection

APPLICATION FOR FOREIGN-TRADE ZONE ADMISSION AND/OR STATUS DESIGNATION

19 CFR 146.22, 146.32, 146.35-146.37, 146.39-146.41, 146.44, 146.53, 146.66

1. ZONE NO. AND LOCATION *(Address)*

2. PORT CODE

3. IMPORTING VESSEL (& FLAG)/OTHER CARRIER | 4. EXPORT DATE | 5. IMPORT DATE | 6. ZONE ADMISSION NO.

7. U.S. PORT OF UNLADING | 8. FOREIGN PORT OF LADING | 9. BILL OF LADING/AWB NO. | 10. INWARD M'FEST NO.

11. INBOND CARRIER | 12. I.T. NO. AND DATE | 13. I.T. FROM *(Port)*

14. STATISTICAL INFORMATION FURNISHED DIRECTLY TO BUREAU OF CENSUS BY APPLICANT? ☐ YES ☐ NO

15. NO. OF PACKAGES AND COUNTRY OF ORIGIN CODE	16. DESCRIPTION OF MERCHANDISE	17. HTSUS NO.	18. QUANTITY (HTSUS)	19. GROSS WEIGHT	20. SEPARATE VALUE & AGGR CHGS.
		21. HARBOR MAINTENANCE FEE (19 CFR 24.24) ➡			

22. I hereby apply for admission of the above merchandise into the Foreign-Trade Zone. I declare to the best of my knowledge and belief that the above merchandise is not prohibited entry into the Foreign-Trade Zone within the meaning of section 3 of the Foreign-Trade Zones Act of 1934, as amended, and section 146.31, Customs Regulations.

23. I hereby apply for the status designation indicated:

☐ NONPRIVILEGED FOREIGN (19 CFR 146.42) ☐ PRIVILEGED FOREIGN (19 CFR 146.41) ☐ ZONE RESTRICTED (19 CFR 146.44) ☐ DOMESTIC (19 CFR 146.43)

24. APPLICANT FIRM NAME | 25. BY *(Signature)* | 26. TITLE | 27. DATE

F.T.Z. AGREES TO RECEIVE MERCHANDISE INTO THE ZONE ➡ | 28. FOR THE F.T.Z. OPERATOR *(Signature)* | 29. TITLE | 30. DATE

PERMIT — **Permission is hereby granted to transfer the above merchandise into the Zone.** | 31. PORT DIRECTOR OF CBP: BY *(Signature)* | 32. TITLE | 33. DATE

PERMIT — The above merchandise has been granted the requested status. | 34. PORT DIRECTOR OF CBP: BY *(Signature)* | 35. TITLE | 36. DATE

PERMIT TO TRANSFER

37. The goods described herein are authorized to be transferred: ☐ without exception ☐ except as noted below

38. CBP OFFICER AT STATION *(Signature)* | 39. TITLE | 40. STATION | 41. DATE

42. RECEIVED FOR TRANSFER TO ZONE *(Driver's Signature)* | 43. CARTMAN | 44. CHL NO. | 45. DATE

FTZ OPERATOR'S REPORT OF MERCHANDISE RECEIVED AT ZONE

46. To the Port Director of CBP: The above merchandise was received at the Zone on the date shown except as noted below:

47. FOR THE FTZ OPERATOR *(Signature)* | 48. TITLE | 49. DATE

(See back of form for Paperwork Reduction Act Notice.) *Previous Editions are Obsolete* **CBP Form 214 (02/96)**

OMB No. 1651-0029

CENSUS USE ONLY

U.S. DEPARTMENT OF HOMELAND SECURITY
Bureau of Customs and Border Protection

APPLICATION FOR FOREIGN-TRADE ZONE ADMISSION AND/OR STATUS DESIGNATION

19 CFR 146.32, 146.40

1. ZONE NO. AND LOCATION *(Address)*

2. PORT CODE

3. IMPORTING VESSEL (& FLAG)/OTHER CARRIER	4. EXPORT DATE	5. IMPORT DATE	6. ZONE ADMISSION NO.

7. U.S. PORT OF UNLADING	8. FOREIGN PORT OF LADING	9. BILL OF LADING/AWB NO.	10. INWARD M'FEST NO.

11. INBOND CARRIER	12. I.T. NO. AND DATE	13. I.T. FROM *(Port)*

14. STATISTICAL INFORMATION FURNISHED DIRECTLY TO BUREAU OF CENSUS BY APPLICANT? ☐ YES ☐ NO

15. NO. OF PACKAGES AND COUNTRY OF ORIGIN CODE	16. DESCRIPTION OF MERCHANDISE	17. HTSUS NO.	18. QUANTITY (HTSUS)	19. GROSS WEIGHT	20. SEPARATE VALUE & AGGR CHGS.
		21. HARBOR MAINTENANCE FEE (19 CFR 24.24) ➡			

22. I hereby apply for admission of the above merchandise into the Foreign-Trade Zone. I declare to the best of my knowledge and belief that the above merchandise is not prohibited entry into the Foreign-Trade Zone within the meaning of section 3 of the Foreign-Trade Zones Act of 1934, as amended, and section 146.31, Customs Regulations.

23. I hereby apply for the status designation indicated:

☐ NONPRIVILEGED FOREIGN (19 CFR 146.42) ☐ PRIVILEGED FOREIGN (19 CFR 146.41) ☐ ZONE RESTRICTED (19 CFR 146.44) ☐ DOMESTIC (19 CFR 146.43)

24. APPLICANT FIRM NAME	25. BY *(Signature)*	26. TITLE	27. DATE
F.T.Z. AGREES TO RECEIVE MERCHANDISE INTO THE ZONE ➡	28. FOR THE F.T.Z. OPERATOR *(Signature)*	29. TITLE	30. DATE
PERMIT — **Permission is hereby granted to transfer the above merchandise into the Zone.**	31. PORT DIRECTOR OF CBP: BY *(Signature)*	32. TITLE	33. DATE
PERMIT — The above merchandise has been granted the requested status.	34. PORT DIRECTOR OF CBP: BY *(Signature)*	35. TITLE	36. DATE

PERMIT TO TRANSFER

37. The goods described herein are authorized to be transferred: ☐ without exception ☐ except as noted below

38. CBP OFFICER AT STATION *(Signature)*	39. TITLE	40. STATION	41. DATE
42. RECEIVED FOR TRANSFER TO ZONE *(Driver's Signature)*	43. CARTMAN	44. CHL NO.	45. DATE

FTZ OPERATOR'S REPORT OF MERCHANDISE RECEIVED AT ZONE

46. To the Port Director of CBP: The above merchandise was received at the Zone on the date shown except as noted below:

47. FOR THE FTZ OPERATOR *(Signature)*	48. TITLE	49. DATE

(See back of form for Paperwork Reduction Act Notice.) STATISTICAL COPY **CBP Form 214A (08/00)**

OMB No. 1651-0029

U.S. DEPARTMENT OF HOMELAND SECURITY
Bureau of Customs and Border Protection

APPLICATION FOR FOREIGN-TRADE ZONE ADMISSION AND/OR STATUS DESIGNATION

CONTINUATION SHEET

19 CFR 146.22, 146.32, 146.35-146.37, 146.39-146.41, 146.44, 146.53, 146.66

1. ZONE NO. AND LOCATION (Address)

2. PORT CODE

6. ZONE ADMISSION NO.

15. NO. OF PACKAGES AND COUNTRY OF ORIGIN CODE	16. DESCRIPTION OF MERCHANDISE	17. HTSUS NO.	18. QUANTITY (HTSUS)	19. GROSS WEIGHT	20. SEPARATE VALUE & AGGR CHGS.

(See back of form for Paperwork Reduction Act Notice.)

CBP Form 214B (08/00)

OMB No. 1651-0029

U.S. DEPARTMENT OF HOMELAND SECURITY
Bureau of Customs and Border Protection

APPLICATION FOR FOREIGN-TRADE ZONE ADMISSION AND/OR STATUS DESIGNATION

CONTINUATION SHEET

19 CFR 146.32, 146.40

1. ZONE NO. AND LOCATION *(Address)*

2. PORT CODE

6. ZONE ADMISSION NO.

15. NO. OF PACKAGES AND COUNTRY OF ORIGIN CODE	16. DESCRIPTION OF MERCHANDISE	17. HTSUS NO.	18. QUANTITY (HTSUS)	19. GROSS WEIGHT	20. SEPARATE VALUE & AGGR CHGS.

(See back of form for Paperwork Reduction Act Notice.) STATISTICAL COPY **CBP Form 214C (08/00)**

Approved through OMB No. 1651-0029

U.S. DEPARTMENT OF HOMELAND SECURITY
Bureau of Customs and Border Protection

APPLICATION FOR FOREIGN-TRADE ZONE ACTIVITY PERMIT

19 CFR 146.52, 146.66

1. ZONE NO. AND LOCATION *(Address)*

2. ZONE ADMISSION NO.

3. APPLICATION DATE

4. TYPE OF ACTIVITY FOR WHICH PERMIT REQUESTED

☐ Manipulate ☐ Manufacture ☐ Exhibit ☐ Destroy ☐ Temporary Removal

5. FULL DESCRIPTION OF THE ACTIVITY *(Include designation of the exact place in zone where the operation is to be performed and, in the case of a proposed manipulation or manufacture, a statement as to whether merchandise with one zone status is to be packed, commingled, or combined with merchandise having different zone status. If additional space required, attach separate sheet. If first application for manufacturing of this kind, state whether Foreign-Trade Zones board has occurred in proposed operation.)*

6. ZONE LOT NO. OR UNIQUE IDENTIFIER	7. MARKS AND NUMBERS	8. DESCRIPTION OF MERCHANDISE	9. QUANTITY	10. WEIGHTS, MEASURES	11. ZONE STATUS

If any merchandise is to be manipulated in any way or manufactured, I agree to maintain the records provided for in sections 146.21(a), 146.23, and 146.52(d) of the Customs Regulations and to make them available to CBP officers for inspection.

12. APPLICANT FIRM NAME	13. BY *(Signature)*	14. TITLE
APPROVED BY FOREIGN-TRADE ZONE OPERATOR ➡	15. BY *(Signature)*	16. TITLE

PERMIT

The application made above is hereby approved and permission is granted to manipulate, manufacture, exhibit, destroy, or temporarily removed, as requested, on condition that the applicable regulations are complied with and the records required to be maintained will be available for inspection.

17. PORT DIRECTOR OF CBP: By *(Signature)*	18. TITLE	19. DATE

FTZ OPERATOR'S

20. TO THE PORT DIRECTOR OF CBP:
I certify that the goods described herein have been disposed of as directed except as noted below.

21. FOR THE FTZ OPERATOR: *(Signature)*	22. TITLE	23. DATE

CBP Form 216 (01/01)

DEPARTMENT OF THE TREASURY
UNITED STATES CUSTOMS SERVICE

Approved through 03/31/96
OMB No. 1515-0087

DECLARATION OF UNACCOMPANIED ARTICLES

19 CFR 145.12, 145.43, 148.110, 148.113-148.116

The arriving traveler or head of a family must complete a **SEPARATE** Customs Form 255 for **EACH** unaccompanied package or container sent from American Samoa, Guam, or the U.S. Virgin Islands. **PLEASE PRINT** the information in blocks 1 - 8 and **SIGN block 9.**

1. FAMILY NAME	GIVEN NAME	MIDDLE INITIAL	2. NUMBER OF FAMILY MEMBERS INCLUDED IN FAMILY DECLARATION	
3. PERMANENT ADDRESS			4. DATE OF ARRIVAL	5. VESSEL, OR AIRLINE & FLIGHT NO.
			6. PORT OF ARRIVAL	

7. DESCRIPTION OF ARTICLE(S) IN PACKAGE	8. PRICE	10. CUSTOMS USE ONLY (After arrival of traveler)

9. I declare that the above articles were acquired in American Samoa, Guam or the U.S. Virgin Islands by me or those members of my family included in my declaration. I further declare that the above information is valid and correct to the best of my knowledge and belief. I will pay any customs duties and internal revenue taxes which are found to be due upon arrival of the articles.

SIGNATURE

X

11. CUSTOMS OFFICER SIGNATURE DATE

WARNING
FALSE CLAIMS ARE PUNISHABLE BY LAW

IMPORTANT

IMPORTER: To receive your entitled exemptions and appropriate rates of duty, you must SEND THE YELLOW COPY OF CUSTOMS FORM 255 TO THE VENDOR IMMEDIATELY AFTER CUSTOMS VALIDATION (Blocks 10 and 11).

VENDOR: 1. Enclose this form in an envelope marked "U.S. Customs Form 255 enclosed" and securely attach it to the outside of the package or container.

2. Mark the package or container "UNACCOMPANIED TOURIST SHIPMENT."

CUSTOMS USE ONLY (After arrival of article)

12. ARRIVAL DATE	13. MAIL OR INFORMAL ENTRY NO.
14. RELEASE DATE	15. CUSTOMS OFFICER
16. DISCREPANCIES BETWEEN CF 255 AND SHIPMENT	

Paperwork Reduction Act Notice: The Paperwork Reduction Act of 1980 says we must tell you why we are collecting this information, how we will use it, and whether you have to give it to us. We ask for this information to carry out the Customs Service Laws of the United States. This form is used by travelers to the U.S. Virgin Islands, Guam, or American Samoa to allow personal duty exemptions and/or a flat 5% rate of duty to be granted to tourist purchases that are mailed to the U.S. from these insular possessions. Your response is required to obtain or retain a benefit.

Statement Required by 5 CFR 1320.21: The estimated average burden associated with this collection of information is 5 minutes per respondent or recordkeeper depending on individual circumstances. Comments concerning the accuracy of this burden estimate and suggestions for reducing this burden should be directed to U.S. Customs Service, Paperwork Management Branch, Washington DC 20229, and to the Office of Management and Budget, Paperwork Reduction Project (1515-0087), Washington DC 20503.

Customs Form 255 (081591)

U.S. DEPARTMENT OF HOMELAND SECURITY
Bureau of Customs and Border Protection

OMB No. 1651-0098
Exp. 02/28/2009
See back of form for Paperwork Reduction Act Notice.

NORTH AMERICAN FREE TRADE AGREEMENT
CERTIFICATE OF ORIGIN

Please print or type

19 CFR 181.11, 181.22

1. EXPORTER NAME AND ADDRESS TAX IDENTIFICATION NUMBER:	2. BLANKET PERIOD FROM TO
3. PRODUCER NAME AND ADDRESS TAX IDENTIFICATION NUMBER:	4. IMPORTER NAME AND ADDRESS TAX IDENTIFICATION NUMBER:

5. DESCRIPTION OF GOOD(S)	6. HS TARIFF CLASSIFICATION NUMBER	7. PREFERENCE CRITERION	8. PRODUCER	9. NET COST	10. COUNTRY OF ORIGIN

I CERTIFY THAT:

- THE INFORMATION ON THIS DOCUMENT IS TRUE AND ACCURATE AND I ASSUME THE RESPONSIBILITY FOR PROVING SUCH REPRESENTATIONS. I UNDERSTAND THAT I AM LIABLE FOR ANY FALSE STATEMENTS OR MATERIAL OMISSIONS MADE ON OR IN CONNECTION WITH THIS DOCUMENT;
- I AGREE TO MAINTAIN AND PRESENT UPON REQUEST, DOCUMENTATION NECESSARY TO SUPPORT THIS CERTIFICATE, AND TO INFORM, IN WRITING, ALL PERSONS TO WHOM THE CERTIFICATE WAS GIVEN OF ANY CHANGES THAT COULD AFFECT THE ACCURACY OR VALIDITY OF THIS CERTIFICATE;
- THE GOODS ORIGINATED IN THE TERRITORY OF ONE OR MORE OF THE PARTIES, AND COMPLY WITH THE ORIGIN REQUIREMENTS SPECIFIED FOR THOSE GOODS IN THE NORTH AMERICAN FREE TRADE AGREEMENT AND UNLESS SPECIFICALLY EXEMPTED IN ARTICLE 411 OR ANNEX 401, THERE HAS BEEN NO FURTHER PRODUCTION OR ANY OTHER OPERATION OUTSIDE THE TERRITORIES OF THE PARTIES; AND
- THIS CERTIFICATE CONSISTS OF ☐ PAGES, INCLUDING ALL ATTACHMENTS.

11.	11a. AUTHORIZED SIGNATURE		11b. COMPANY	
	11c. NAME *(Print or Type)*		11d. TITLE	
	11e. DATE *(MM/DD/YYYY)*	11f. TELEPHONE NUMBER ▶	*(Voice)*	*(Facsimile)*

CBP Form 434 (04/97)

PAPERWORK REDUCTION ACT NOTICE: This information is needed to carry out the terms of the North American Free Trade Agreement (NAFTA). NAFTA requires that, upon request, an importer must provide CBP with proof of the exporters written certification of the origin of the goods. The certification is essential to substantiate compliance with the rules of origin under the Agreement. You are required to give us this information to obtain a benefit.

The estimated average burden associated with this collection of information is 15 minutes per respondent or recordkeeper depending on individual circumstances. Comments concerning the accuracy of this burden estimate and suggestions for reducing this burden should be directed to Bureau of Customs and Border Protection, Information Services Branch, Washington, DC 20229, and to the Office of Management and Budget, Paperwork Reduction Project (1651-0098), Washington DC 20503.

NORTH AMERICAN FREE TRADE AGREEMENT CERTIFICATE OF ORIGIN INSTRUCTIONS

For purposes of obtaining preferential tariff treatment, this document must be completed legibly and in full by the exporter and be in the possession of the importer at the time the declaration is made. This document may also be completed voluntarily by the producer for use by the exporter. Please print or type:

FIELD 1: State the full legal name, address (including country) and legal tax identification number of the exporter. Legal taxation number is: in Canada, employer number or importer/exporter number assigned by Revenue Canada; in Mexico, federal taxpayer's registry number (RFC); and in the United States, employer's identification number or Social Security Number.

FIELD 2: Complete field if the Certificate covers multiple shipments of identical goods as described in Field # 5 that are imported into a NAFTA country for a specified period of up to one year (the blanket period). "FROM" is the date upon which Certificate becomes applicable to the good covered by the blanket Certificate (it may be prior to the date of signing this Certificate). "TO" is the date upon which the blanket period expires. The importation of a good for which preferential treatment is claimed based on this Certificate must occur between these dates.

FIELD 3: State the full legal name, address (including country) and legal tax identification number, as defined in Field #1, of the producer. If more than one producer's good is included on the Certificate, attach a list of additional producers, including the legal name, address (including country) and legal tax identification number, cross-referenced to the good described in Field #5. If you wish this information to be confidential, it is acceptable to state "Available to CBP upon request". If the producer and the exporter are the same, complete field with "SAME". If the producer is unknown, it is acceptable to state "UNKNOWN".

FIELD 4: State the full legal name, address (including country) and legal tax identification number, as defined in Field #1, of the importer. If the importer is not known, state "UNKNOWN"; if multiple importers, state "VARIOUS".

FIELD 5: Provide a full description of each good. The description should be sufficient to relate it to the invoice description and to the Harmonized System (H.S.) description of the good. If the Certificate covers a single shipment of a good, include the invoice number as shown on the commercial invoice. If not known, indicate another unique reference number, such as the shipping order number.

FIELD 6: For each good described in Field #5, identify the H.S. tariff classification to six digits. If the good is subject to a specific rule of origin in Annex 401 that requires eight digits, identify to eight digits, using the H.S. tariff classification of the country into whose territory the good is imported.

FIELD 7: For each good described in Field #5, state which criterion (A through F) is applicable. The rules of origin are contained in Chapter Four and Annex 401. Additional rules are described in Annex 703.2 (certain agricultural goods), Annex 300-B, Appendix 6 (certain textile goods) and Annex 308.1 (certain automatic data processing goods and their parts). **NOTE: In order to be entitled to preferential tariff treatment, each good must meet at least one of the criteria below.**

Preference Criteria

A The good is "wholly obtained or produced entirely" in the territory of one or more of the NAFTA countries as referenced in Article 415. **Note: The purchase of a good in the territory does not necessarily render it "wholly obtained or produced".** If the good is an agricultural good, see also criterion F and Annex 703.2. *(Reference: Article 401(a) and 415)*

B The good is produced entirely in the territory of one or more of the NAFTA countries and satisfies the specific rule of origin, set out in Annex 401, that applies to its tariff classification. The rule may include a tariff classification change, regional value-content requirement, or a combination thereof. The good must also satisfy all other applicable requirements of Chapter Four. If the good is an agricultural good, see also criterion F and Annex 703.2. *(Reference: Article 401(b))*

C The good is produced entirely in the territory of one or more of the NAFTA countries exclusively from originating materials. Under this criterion, one or more of the materials may not fall within the definition of "wholly produced or obtained", as set out in article 415. All materials used in the production of the good must qualify as "originating" by meeting the rules of Article 401(a) through (d). If the good is an agricultural good, see also criterion F and Annex 703.2. *Reference: Article 401(c).*

D Goods are produced in the territory of one or more of the NAFTA countries but do not meet the applicable rule of origin, set out in Annex 401, because certain non-originating materials do not undergo the required change in tariff classification. The goods do nonetheless meet the regional value-content requirement specified in Article 401(d). This criterion is limited to the following two circumstances:

1. The good was imported into the territory of a NAFTA country in an unassembled or disassembled form but was classified as an assembled good, pursuant to H.S. General Rule of Interpretation 2(a), or
2. The good incorporated one or more non-originating materials, provided for as parts under the H.S., which could not undergo a change in tariff classification because the heading provided for both the good and its parts and was not further subdivided into subheadings, or the subheading provided for both the good and its parts and was not further subdivided.

NOTE: This criterion does not apply to Chapters 61 through 63 of H.S. *(Reference: Article 401(d))*

E Certain automatic data processing goods and their parts, specified in Annex 308.1, that do not originate in the territory are considered originating upon importation into the territory of a NAFTA country from the territory of another NAFTA country when the most-favored-nation tariff rate of the good conforms to the rate established in Annex 308.1 and is common to all NAFTA countries. *(Reference: Annex 308.1)*

F The good is an originating agricultural good under preference criterion A, B, or C above and is not subject to a quantitative restriction in the importing NAFTA country because it is a "qualifying good" as defined in Annex 703.2, Section A or B (please specify). A good listed in Appendix 703.2B.7 is also exempt from quantitative restrictions and is eligible for NAFTA preferential tariff treatment if it meets the definition of "qualifying good" in Section A of Annex 703.2. **NOTE 1: This criterion does not apply to goods that wholly originate in Canada or the United States and are imported into either country. NOTE 2: A tariff rate quota is not a quantitative restriction.**

FIELD 8: For each good described in Field #5, state "YES" if you are the producer of the good. If you are not the producer of the good, state "NO" followed by (1), (2), or (3), depending on whether this certificate was based upon: (1) your knowledge of whether the good qualifies as an originating good; (2) your reliance on the producer's written representation (other than a Certificate of Origin) that the good qualifies as an originating good; or (3) a completed and signed Certificate for the good, voluntarily provided to the exporter by the producer.

FIELD 9: For each good described in field #5, where the good is subject to a regional value content (RVC) requirement, indicate "NC" if the RVC is calculated according to the net cost method; otherwise, indicate "NO". If the RVC is calculated over a period of time, further identify the beginning and ending dates (MM/DD/YYYY) of that period. *(Reference: Article 402.1, 402.5).*

FIELD 10: Identify the name of the country ("MX" or "US" for agricultural and textile goods exported to Canada; "US" or "CA" for all goods exported to Mexico; or "CA" or "MX" for all goods exported to the United States) to which the preferential rate of CBP duty applies, as set out in Annex 302.2, in accordance with the Marking Rules or in each party's schedule of tariff elimination.

For all other originating goods exported to Canada, indicate appropriately "MX" or "US" if the goods originate in that NAFTA country, within the meaning of the NAFTA Rules of Origin Regulations, and any subsequent processing in the other NAFTA country does not increase the transaction value of the goods by more than seven percent; otherwise indicate "JNT" for joint production. *(Reference: Annex 302.2)*

FIELD 11: This field must be completed, signed, and dated by the exporter. When the Certificate is completed by the producer for use by the exporter, it must be completed, signed, and dated by the producer. The date must be the date the Certificate was completed and signed.

CBP Form 434 (04/97)(Back)

U.S. DEPARTMENT OF HOMELAND SECURITY
Bureau of Customs and Border Protection

NORTH AMERICAN FREE TRADE AGREEMENT
CERTIFICATE OF ORIGIN CONTINUATION SHEET

OMB No. 1651-0098.
Expires 02/28/2009.
See CBP Form 434 for Paper- work Reduction Act Notice.

19 CFR 181.11, 181.22

5. DESCRIPTION OF GOOD(S)	6. HS TARIFF CLASSIFICATION NUMBER	7. PREFERENCE CRITERION	8. PRODUCER	9. NET COST	10. COUNTRY OF ORIGIN

CBP Form 434A (12/93)

U.S. DEPARTMENT OF HOMELAND SECURITY
Bureau of Customs and Border Protection

OMB No. 1651-0098.
Exp. 02/28/2009
See back of form for Paperwork Reduction Act Notice.

NAFTA VERIFICATION OF ORIGIN QUESTIONNAIRE

19 CFR 181.72

This questionnaire is sent to you pursuant to 19 CFR 181.72, The questionnaire will be used in

determining if the ....

described on the NAFTA Certificate of Origin (CO) dated .... and signed by ....

originates under the NAFTA. If necessary, additional information may be requested at a later date.

☐ **EXPORTER** If this box is checked, you are being sent this questionnaire as the exporter of the imported good. If you relied upon a Certificate of Origin or written representation from the Producer to prepare your Certificate of Origin, provide a copy of what it was that you relied upon, and then go directly to Section V and complete it. If you relied upon your knowledge of the good, complete the questionnaire.	☐ **PRODUCER OF GOOD** If this box is checked, you are being sent this questionnaire as the producer of the imported good. The good was exported by .... Complete the questionnaire.
☐ **EXPORTER/PRODUCER** If this box is checked, you are being sent this questionnaire as the exporter and also the producer of the imported good. Complete the questionnaire.	☐ **PRODUCER OF MATERIAL** If this box is checked, you are being sent this questionnaire because .... identified you as the producer of the material(s) used in the production of the good described above. Complete the questionnaire.

You have until .... to return the completed and signed questionnaire to the requesting CBP office. You may fax your response. If a reply cannot be made by this date, please contact the CBP office by mail, telephone, or fax. If additional space is needed for your response, attach additional pages as needed. When the verification is completed, the exporter/producer will receive a written determination of the findings. The producer of a verified material will also be notified of the results of the verification of the material. The confidential business information collected on the questionnaire may only be disclosed to those authorities responsible for the administration and enforcement of determinations of origin, and of customs and revenue matters.

The questionnaire must be signed and dated by an individual who can certify as to the accuracy of the information provided in the questionnaire. Failure to complete and return this questionnaire may result in the denial of preferential treatment under the NAFTA.

SECTION I ▶ PRODUCTION PROCESS

Provide a ***brief*** description of the production process for the good/material being verified.

SECTION II ▶ NON-ORIGINATING/UNKNOWN MATERIALS OR COMPONENTS

Provide the following information for each *non-originating* material or component and for each material or component whose origin is unknown, used to produce the good being verified. If none were used, state "NONE".

Description of the material or component	HS#

HS# — Provide the six digit Harmonized System number or if the rule of origin of the good requires eight digits, supply eight.

CBP Form 446 (04/97)

SECTION III ▶ ORIGINATING MATERIALS OR COMPONENTS

Provide the following information for each *originating* material or component used to produce the good being verified. If none were used, state "NONE".

Description of the material or component	Basis of Originating Status	Name and Address of the Supplier or, **if known**, Name & Address of the Manufacturer

Description of the Material or Component:
If the material or component is self-produced (**Self-Produced material** or component is a material or component that is produced by the producer of a good and used in the production of that good) and designated as an intermediate material (**Intermediate material** is a self-produced material or component, designated by the producer, that meets the rules of origin and that is incorporated into the final good), place the letter 'D' before the name of the material or component in the table. If the material or component is self-produced but designated as an intermediate material, then each material used in the production of this self-produced material or component must be identified separately.

Basis of Originating Status:
Describe type of information (i.e. certificate of origin, affidavit, etc.) which was relied upon to determine the originating status of the material or component.

SECTION IV ▶ ADDITIONAL QUESTIONS

1. Has a classification ruling been issued with respect to any of the materials or components produced? If yes, provide a copy of the ruling. ☐ Yes ☐ No
2. Was the de minimis provision used to determine whether the good being verified was originating? ☐ Yes ☐ No
3. Is the good being verified an originating fungible good? If yes, check below which inventory management method you used: ☐ Yes ☐ No
   ☐ LIFO ☐ FIFO ☐ Average ☐ Specific Identification
4. Did any of the originating materials used in the production of the good qualify as an originating fungible material? ☐ Yes ☐ No
   If yes, attach a list of the materials that qualify as originating materials under the fungible materials provisions, and check below which inventory management method you used:
   ☐ LIFO ☐ FIFO ☐ Average ☐ Specific Identification
5. Was the sale of the good/material to a related person? ☐ Yes ☐ No
6. If a Regional Value Content (RVC) was used in ascertaining whether the good being verified originates, identify the method used. ☐ Transaction Value ☐ Net Cost
7. What was the estimated qualifying percentage for RVC? ________ %
8. Was the RVC calculated using accumulation? ☐ Yes ☐ No
   If yes, provide the name and address of each supplier.

SECTION V ▶ CERTIFICATION

I certify that the information on this document is true and accurate and I assume the responsibility for proving such representations. I understand that I am liable for any false statements or relevant omissions made on or in connection with this document.

Authorized Signature	Company Name *(Print or Type)*
Name *(Print or Type)*	Title *(Print or Type)*
Telephone	Date *(MM/DD/YYYY)*

PAPERWORK REDUCTION ACT NOTICE: The requested information is needed to carry out the terms of the North American Fee Trade Agreement Implementation Act (NAFTA). NAFTA provides that the CBP administration may determine by means of a written Implementation Act questionnaire whether a good imported into its territory qualifies as an originating good. Failure to provide the requested information may result in the loss of preferential tariff treatment under the NAFTA.

The estimated average burden associated with this collection of information is 45 minutes per respondent or recordkeeper depending on individual circumstances. Comments concerning the accuracy of this burden estimate and suggestions for reducing this burden should be directed to Bureau of Customs and Border Protection, Information Services Branch, Washington DC 20229, and to the Office of Management and Budget, Paperwork Reduction Project (1651-0098), Washington, DC 20503.

CBP Form 446 (Back)(04/97)

OMB No. 1651-0016

U.S. DEPARTMENT OF HOMELAND SECURITY
Bureau of Customs and Border Protection

CERTIFICATE OF ORIGIN

(ARTICLES SHIPPED FROM INSULAR POSSESSIONS, EXCEPT PUERTO RICO, TO THE UNITED STATES 1)

19 CFR 7.3

1. PORT	
2. DATE	3. CERTIFICATE NO.
4. NAME OF PERSON COMPLETING CERTIFICATE	
5. NAME OF FIRM	

6. SHIPPERS EXPORT DEC. NO.	7. DATE FILED	8. CARRIER *(Vessel or Airline)*	9. DESTINATION *(Port of)*
10. CONSIGNED TO			11. LOCATION OF CONSIGNEE *(City and State)*

12. MARKS AND NUMBERS	13. QUANTITY	14. DESCRIPTION OF ARTICLES	FOREIGN MATERIALS 2		MATERIALS DESCRIBED IN GENERAL NOTE 3 (a)(iv)(B)(2) 3		
			15. Description	16. Value	17. Description	18. Date Imported into Insuler Possession	19. Date Incorporated into Imported Goods

20. INSULAR POSSESSION WHERE MERCHANDISE WAS PRODUCED OR MANUFACTURED	21. INSULAR POSSESSION OF WHICH MATERIALS ARE THE GROWTH, PRODUCT, OR MANUFACTURE
22. ADDRESS OF SHIPPER	I declare that I am the person named above, acting in the capacity indicated; that the description and other particulars of the merchandise specified above are correct as set forth in this certificate; that the said merchandise was produced or manufactured in the insular possession named above, and from the materials grown, produced, or manufactured in the insular possession also named above, or of the United States, or of both; that if foreign materials were used therein, their description and value are shown above.
	23. SIGNATURE OF SHIPPER

VERIFICATION OF CBP OFFICER ▶	I hereby certify that I have investigated the foregoing statements and am satisfied that they are correct to the best of my knowledge and belief.	24. DATE	25. SIGNATURE OF CBP OFFICER

SEE BACK OF FORM FOR FOOTNOTES AND PAPERWORK REDUCTION ACT NOTICE.

CBP Form 3229 (08/93)

PAPERWORK REDUCTION ACT NOTICE: This form is used by importers/exporters to claim preferential duty treatment in 19 U.S.C. 1202 General Note 3(a)(iv), HTSUS, and by the Bureau of Customs and Border Protection to determine eligibility. It is required to obtain or retain a benefit.

Statement Required by 5 CFR 1320.21: The estimated average burden associated with this collection of information is 20 minutes per respondent or recordkeeper depending on individual circumstances. Comments concerning the accuracy of this burden estimate and suggestions for reducing this burden should be directed to Customs and Border Protection, Information Services Branch, Washington DC 20229, and to the Office of Management and Budget, Paperwork Reduction Project (1651-0016), Washington DC 20503.

FOOTNOTES

1 General Note 3(a)(iv), Harmonized Tarriff Schedule of the United States (HTSUS).

2 Each "foreign material" (i.e., a material which originated in sources other than an insular possession or the United States) shall be listed on a separate line under columns 15 and 16. Columns 15 and 16 do not apply to materials which are not considered "foreign" under General Note 3(a)(iv)(B)(1), (2), HTSUS.

"VALUE" as used in this certificate, refers to the sum of (a) the actual purchase price of each foreign material used, or where a material is provided to the manufacturer without charge, or at less than fair market value, the total of all expenses incurred in the growth, production, or manufacture of the material, including general expenses, plus an amount for profit; and (b) the cost of transporting those materials to the insular possession, but excluding any duties or taxes assessed by the insular possession and any charges which may accrue after landing;

If the materials used in an article originated only in an insular possession or the United States, state "none" in column 15 and leave column 16 blank.

3 Columns 17, 18, and 19 shall be completed if the article incorporates any material described in General Note 3(a)(iv)(B)(2), HTSUS, which is not considered "foreign material" under General Note 3(a)(iv). Each such material shall be listed on a separate line. If no such materials are used, state "none" in column 17 and leave columns 18 and 19 blank.

EXCERPT FROM GENERAL NOTES, HARMONIZED TARIFF SCHEDULE OF THE UNITED STATES

General Note 3(a)(iv)

(iv) Products of Insular Possessions

(A) Except as provided in additional U.S. note 5 of chapter 91 and except as provided in additional U.S. note 2 of chapter 96, and except as provided in section 423 of the Tax Reform Act of 1986, goods imported from insular possessions of the United States which are outside the CBP territory of the United States are subject to the rates of duty set forth in column 1 of the tariff schedule, except that all such goods the growth or product of any such possession, or manufactured or produced in any such possession from materials the growth, product or manufacture of any such possession or of the CBP territory of the United States, or of both, which do not contain foreign materials to the value of more than 70 percent of their total value (or more than 50 percent of their total value with respect to goods described in section 213(b) of the Caribbean Basin Economic Recovery Act), coming to the CBP territory of the United States directly from any such possession, and all goods previously imported into the CBP territory of the United States with payment of all applicable duties and taxes imposed upon or by reason of importation which were shipped from the United States, without remission, refund, or drawback of such duties or taxes, directly to the possession from which they are being returned by direct shipment, are exempt from duty.

(B) in determining whether goods produced or manufactured in any such insular possession contain foreign materials to the value of more than 70 percent, no material shall be considered foreign which either -

(1) at the time such goods are entered, or

(2) at the time such material is imported into the insular possession.

may be imported into the CBP territory from a foreign country, and entered free of duty; except that no goods containing material to which (2) of this subparagraph applies shall be exempt from duty under subparagraph (A) unless adequate documentation is supplied to show that the material has been incorporated into such goods during the 18-month period after the date on which such material is imported into the insular possession.

U.S. DEPARTMENT OF HOMELAND SECURITY
Bureau of Customs and Border Protection

DECLARATION FOR FREE ENTRY OF UNACCOMPANIED ARTICLES

19 CFR 148.6, 148.52, 148.53, 148.77

FORM APPROVED OMB NO. 1651-0014

PAPERWORK REDUCTION ACT NOTICE: This request is in accordance with the Paperwork Reduction Act. We ask for the information in order to carry out the laws and regulations administered by the CBP. These regulations and forms apply to importers to ensure that they are complying with the law and to allow us to figure, collect, or refund the right amount of duty and tax. It is mandatory. The estimated average burden associated with this collection of information is 10 minutes per respondent depending on individual circumstances. Comments concerning the accuracy of this burden estimate and suggestions for reducing this burden should be directed to the Bureau of Customs and Border Protection, Information Services Branch, Washington, DC 20229, and to the Office of Management and Budget, Paperwork Reduction Project (1651-0014), Washington, DC 20503.

PART I -- TO BE COMPLETED BY ALL PERSONS SEEKING FREE ENTRY OF ARTICLES (Please consult with the CBP official for additional information or assistance. REMEMBER--All of your statements are subject to verification. False declarations or failure to declare articles could result in penalties.)

1. IMPORTER'S NAME (Last, first and middle)
2. IMPORTER'S DATE OF BIRTH
3. IMPORTER'S DATE OF ARRIVAL
4. IMPORTER'S U.S. ADDRESS
5. IMPORTER'S PORT OF ARRIVAL
6. NAME OF ARRIVING VESSEL CARRIER AND FLIGHT/TRAIN
7. NAME(S) OF ACCOMPANYING HOUSEHOLD MEMBERS (wife, husband, minor children, etc.)

8. THE ARTICLES FOR WHICH FREE ENTRY IS CLAIMED BELONG TO ME AND/OR MY FAMILY AND WERE IMPORTED ➡
A. DATE
B. NAME OF VESSEL/CARRIER
C. FROM (Country)
D. B/L OR AWB OR I.T. NO.
E. NUMBER AND KINDS OF CONTAINERS
F. MARKS AND NUMBERS

PART II -- TO BE COMPLETED BY ALL PERSONS EXCEPT U.S. PERSONNEL AND EVACUEES

9. RESIDENCY ('X" appropriate box)
I declare that my place of residence abroad ☐ is ☐ was ➡
A. NAME OF COUNTRY
B. LENGTH OF TIME Yr. Mo.

C. RESIDENCY STATUS UPON MY/OUR ARRIVAL ("X" One)
☐ (1) Returning resident of the U.S.
(2) Nonresident: ☐ a. Emigrating to the U.S. ☐ b. Visiting the U.S.

10. STATEMENT(S) OF ELIGIBILITY FOR FREE ENTRY OF ARTICLES
I the undersigned further declare that ("X" all applicable items and submit packing list):

A. Applicable to RESIDENT AND NONRESIDENT

☐ (1) All household effects acquired abroad for which free entry is sought were used abroad for at least one year by me or my family in a household of which I or my family was a resident member during such period of use, and are not intended for any other person or for sale. (9804.00.05, HTSUSA)

☐ (2) All instruments, Implements, or tools of trade, occupation or employment, and all professional books for which free entry is sought were taken abroad by me or for my account or I am an emigrant who owned and used them abroad. (9804.00.10, 9804.00.15, HTSUSA)

B. Applicable to RESIDENT ONLY

☐ All personal effects for which free entry is sought were taken abroad by me or for my account. (9804.00.45, HTSUSA)

C. Applicable to NONRESIDENT ONLY

☐ (1) All articles of apparel, personal adornment, toiletries and similar personal effects for which free entry is sought were actually owned by me and in the possession of myself, or those members of my family who accompanied me, at the time of departure to the United States and that they are appropriate and are intended for our personal use and not for any other person nor for sale. (9804.00.20 HTSUSA)

☐ (2) Any vehicles, trailers, bicycles or other means of conveyance being imported are for the transport of me and my family and such incidental carriage of articles as are appropriate to my personal use of the conveyance. (9804.00.35, HTSUSA)

PART III -- TO BE COMPLETED BY U.S. PERSONNEL AND EVACUEES ONLY

I, the undersigned, the owner, importer, or agent of the importer of the personal and household effects for which free entry is claimed, hereby certify that they were in direct personal possession of the importer, or of a member of the importer's family residing with the importer, while abroad, and that they were imported into the United States because of the termination of assignment to extended duty (as defined in section 148.74(d) of the Customs Regulations) at a post or station outside the United States and the CBP Territory of the United States, or because of Government orders or instructions evacuating the importer to the United States; and that they are not imported for sale or for the account of any other person and that they do not include any alcoholic beverages or cigars. Free entry for these effects is claimed under Subheading No. 9805.00.50, Harmonized Tariff Schedule of the United States.

1. DATE OF IMPORTER'S LAST DEPARTURE FROM THE U.S.
2. A COPY OF THE IMPORTER'S TRAVEL ORDERS IS ATTACHED AND THE ORDERS WERE ISSUED ON:

PART IV -- TO BE COMPLETED BY ALL PERSONS SEEKING FREE ENTRY OF ARTICLES (Certain articles may be subject to duty and/or other requirements and must be specifically declared herein. Please check all applicable items and list them separately in item D on the reverse.)

A. For U.S. Personnel, Evacuees, Residents and Non-Residents

☐ (1) Articles for the account of other persons.
☐ (2) Articles for sale or commercial use.
☐ (3) Firearms and/or ammunition.
☐ (4) Alcoholic articles of all types or tobacco products.
☐ (5) Fruits, plants, seeds, meats, or birds.
☐ (6) Fish, wildlife, animal products thereof.

B. For Residents and Non-Residents ONLY

☐ (7) Foreign household effects acquired abroad and used less than one year.
☐ (8) Foreign household effects acquired abroad and used more than one year.

C. For Resident ONLY

☐ (9) Personal effects acquired abroad.
☐ (10) Foreign made articles acquired in the United States and taken abroad on this trip or acquired abroad on another trip that was previously declared to CBP.
☐ (11) Articles taken abroad for which alterations or repairs were performed abroad.

CBP Form 3299 (10/95)

D. LIST OF ARTICLES

(1) ITEM NUMBER CHECKED IN PART IV, A., B., C.	(2) DESCRIPTION OF MERCHANDISE	(3) VALUE OR COST OF REPAIRS	(4) FOREIGN MERCHANDISE TAKEN ABROAD THIS TRIP: *State where in the U.S. the foreign merchandise was acquired or when and where it was previously declared to CBP.*

PART V -- CARRIER'S CERTIFICATE AND RELEASE ORDER

The undersigned carrier, to whom of upon whose order the articles described in PART I, 8., must be released, hereby certifies that the person named in Part I, 1., is the owner or consignee of such articles within the purview of section 484(h), Tariff Act of 1930.

In accordance with the provisions of section 484(h), Tariff Act of 1930, authority is hereby given to release the articles to such consignee.

1. NAME OF CARRIER	2. SIGNATURE OF AGENT (Print and sign) Date

PART VI -- CERTIFICATION TO BE COMPLETED BY ALL PERSONS SEEKING FREE ENTRY

I, the undersigned, certify that this declaration is correct and complete.

1. "X" One
☐ A. Authorized Agent* (From facts obtained from the importer) ☐ B. Importer

2. SIGNATURE	3. DATE

**An Authorized Agent is defined as a person who has actual knowledge of the facts and who is specifically empowered under a power of attorney to execute this declaration (see 19 CFR 141.19, 141.32, 141.33).*

PART VII -- CBP USE ONLY (Inspected and Released)	1. SIGNATURE OF CBP OFFICIAL	2. DATE

CBP Form 3299 (10/95)(Back)

U.S. DEPARTMENT OF HOMELAND SECURITY
Bureau of Customs and Border Protection

Form Approved
OMB No. 1651-0011

DECLARATION FOR FREE ENTRY OF RETURNED AMERICAN PRODUCTS

19 CFR 7.8, 10.1, 10.5, 10.66, 10.67, 12.41, 123.4, 143.23, 145.35

1. PORT	2. DATE	3. ENTRY NO. & DATE
4. NAME OF MANUFACTURER		5. CITY AND STATE OF MANUFACTURE
6. REASON FOR RETURN		7. U.S. DRAWBACK PREVIOUSLY ☐ CLAIMED ☐ UNCLAIMED 8. PREVIOUSLY IMPORTED UNDER HTSUS 864.05? ☐ YES ☐ NO

9. MARKS, NUMBERS, AND DESCRIPTION OF ARTICLES RETURNED	10. VALUE*

* If the value of the article is $10,000 or more and the articles are not clearly marked with the name and address of U.S. manufacturer, please attach copies of any documentation or other evidence that you have that will support or substantiate your claim for duty free status as American Goods Returned.

11. I declare that the information given above is true and correct to the best of my knowledge and belief; that the articles described above are the growth, production, and manufacture of the United States and are returned without having been advanced in value or improved in condition by any process of manufacture or other means; that no drawback bounty, or allowance have been paid or admitted thereon, or on any part thereof; and that if any notice(s) of exportation of articles with benefit of drawback ☐ was ☐ were filed upon exportation of the merchandise from the United States, such notice(s) ☐ has ☐ have been abandoned.

12. NAME OF DECLARANT	13. TITLE OF DECLARANT
14. NAME OF CORPORATION OR PARTNERSHIP (If any)	15. SIGNATURE (See note)
16. SIGNATURE OF AUTHORIZING CBP OFFICER	

NOTE: If the owner or ultimate consignee is a corporation, this form must be signed by the president, vice president, secretary, or treasurer of the corporation, or by any employee or agent of the corporation who holds a power of attorney and a certificate by the corporation that such employee or agent has or will have knowledge of the pertinent facts.

PAPERWORK REDUCTION ACT NOTICE: This information is needed to ensure that importers/exporters are complying with customs laws, to allow us to compute and collect the right amount of money, to enforce other agency requirements, and to collect accurate statistical information on imports. Your response is mandatory. The estimated average burden associated with this collection is 6 minutes per respondent or recordkeeper depending on individual circumstances. Comments concerning the accuracy of this burden estimate and suggestions for reducing this burden should be directed to Bureau of Customs and Border Protection, Information Services Branch, Washington DC 20229, and to the Office of Management and Budget, Paperwork Reduction Project (1651-0011), Washington DC 20503.

Previous Editions are Obsolete **CBP Form 3311 (06/96)**

U.S. DEPARTMENT OF HOMELAND SECURITY
Bureau of Customs and Border Protection

OMB No. 1651-0093
Exp. 02/28/2009

DECLARATION OF OWNER
FOR MERCHANDISE OBTAINED (OTHERWISE THAN) IN PURSUANCE OF A PURCHASE OR AGREEMENT TO PURCHASE

19 CFR 24.11(a)(1), 141.20

This declaration must be presented at the port of entry within 90 days after the date of entry in order to comply with Section 485(d), of the Tariff Act of 1930. **LINE OUT EACH PHRASE SHOWN IN ITALICS NOT APPLICABLE TO THIS DECLARATION.**

1. NAME OF OWNER		2. ADDRESS OF OWNER (STREET, CITY, STATE, ZIP CODE)		3. SUPERSEDING BOND SURETY CODE
4. PORT OF ENTRY	5. PORT CODE	6. IMPORTER NUMBER OF AUTHORIZED AGENT (SHOW HYPHENS)		7. VESSEL/CARRIER ARRIVED FROM
8. IMPORTER NUMBER OF OWNER (SHOW HYPHENS)		9. ENTRY NUMBER	10. DATE OF ENTRY	11. DATE OF ARRIVAL

I, the undersigned, representing the above named owner in the capacity indicated herein, declare that they are the actual owners for CBP purposes of the merchandise covered by the entry identified in Blocks 9 and 10 above, and that they will pay all additional and increased duties thereon pursuant to Section 485(d), of the Tariff Act of 1930, and that such entry exhibits a full and complete account of all the merchandise imported by them in the vessel identified in the entry and obtained by them (otherwise than) in pursuance of a purchase, or an agreement to purchase, except as listed in columns 20-26 below.

I also declare to the best of my knowledge and belief that all statements appearing in the entry and in the invoice or invoices and other documents presented therewith and in accordance with which the entry was made, are true and correct in every respect; that the entry and invoices set forth the true prices, values, quantities, and all information as required by the law and the regulations made in pursuance thereof; that the invoices and other documents are in the same state as when received; that I have not received and do not know of any other invoice, paper, letter, document, or information showing a different currency, price, value, quantity, or description of the said merchandise; and that if any time hereafter I discover any information showing a different state of facts, I will immediately make the same known to the Port Director of CBP at the port of entry.

I further declare, if the merchandise was entered by means of a seller's or shipper's invoice, that no CBP invoice for any of the merchandise covered by the said seller's or shipper's invoice can be produced due to causes beyond my control, and that if entered by means of a statement of the value or the price paid in the form of an invoice it is because neither seller's, shipper's, nor CBP invoice can be produced at this time.

12. EXCEPTIONS (IF ANY)	13. NOMINAL CONSIGNEE OR AUTHORIZED AGENT FILED BY:

14. I REQUEST THAT:
- ☐ BILLS, REFUNDS, AND NOTICES OF LIQUIDATION
- ☐ BILLS ONLY
- ☐ CHECKS FOR REFUNDS ONLY
- ☐ NOTICES OF LIQUIDATION ONLY

BE ADDRESSED TO ME IN CARE OF THE AUTHORIZED AGENT WHOSE IMPORTER NUMBER IS SHOWN ABOVE.

15. SIGNATURE OF PRINCIPAL MEMBER OF FIRM **X**	16. DATE	17. ADDRESS OF PRINCIPAL MEMBER OF FIRM (STREET, CITY, STATE, ZIP CODE)
18. TITLE		

19. EXECUTE THIS PORTION ONLY IF OWNER DOES NOT HAVE AN IMPORT NUMBER (I.E., HAS NOT FILED CBP FORM **5106**)

IRS EMPLOYER NUMBER OF FIRM OWNER SUFFIX	NAME
OR IF NO EMPLOYER NUMBER: SSN OF INDIVIDUAL OWNER	ADDRESS (STREET, CITY, STATE, ZIP CODE)
OR IF NEITHER OF THE ABOVE NUMBERS: CUSTOMS SERIAL NUMBER	**NOTE:** IF OWNER HAS NO IRS OR SOCIAL SECURITY NUMBER OR A CBP SERIAL NUMBER HAS NOT BEEN PREVIOUSLY ASSIGNED, FILE AN ADDITIONAL COPY OF THIS FORM. THE COPY WILL BE RETURNED TO OWNER WITH A CBP SERIAL NUMBER ASSIGNED. SUCH NUMBER SHALL BE USED BY OWNER IN ALL FUTURE CBP TRANSACTIONS REQUIRING THE IMPORTER NUMBER.

20. NUMBER OF PACKAGES	21. SELLER OR SHIPPER	22. PLACE AND DATE OF INVOICE	23. AMOUNT PAID OR TO BE PAID IN FOREIGN CURRENCY	24. RATE OF EXCHANGE	25. ENTERED VALUE (FOREIGN CURRENCY)	26. ENTERED VALUE (U.S. DOLLARS)

CBP Form 3347 (12/02)

U.S. DEPARTMENT OF HOMELAND SECURITY
Bureau of Customs and Border Protection

OMB No. 1651-0093
Exp. 02/28/2009

DECLARATION OF CONSIGNEE WHEN ENTRY IS MADE BY AN AGENT

19 CFR 141.19(B)(2)

If this declaration is made by an agent who does not present with the entry the declaration of the consignee, or who does not have proper authority to execute such declaration for this principal, bond must be given to produce such declaration in accordance with Section 485(c), Tariff Act of 1930.

THIS DECLARATION MUST BE PRESENTED TO THE PORT DIRECTOR OF CBP AT THE PORT OF ENTRY WITHIN SIX MONTHS AFTER THE DATE OF THE BOND GIVEN THEREFORE, UNLESS AN EXTENSION OF TIME IS GRANTED BY THE PORT DIRECTOR.

1. NAME OF CONSIGNEE	2. ADDRESS (STREET, CITY, STATE, ZIP CODE)

3. VESSEL/CARRIER ARRIVED FROM	4. NAME OF VESSEL/CARRIER	5. ENTRY NUMBER	6. DATE

7. NUMBER OF PACKAGES	8. SELLER OR SHIPPER	9. PLACE AND DATE OF INVOICE	10. AMOUNT PAID OR TO BE PAID IN FOREIGN CURRENCY	11. RATE OF EXCHANGE	12. ENTERED VALUE (FOREIGN CURRENCY)	13. ENTERED VALUE (U.S. DOLLARS)

COMPLETE SECTION I, OR SECTION II, OR SECTION III (CHECK ONE) AND SECTION IV.

☐ SECTION I — DECLARATION OF NOMINAL CONSIGNEE

14. NAME OF OWNER	15. ADDRESS (STREET, CITY, STATE, ZIP CODE)

I, the undersigned, herewith declare that the consignee in whose name the entry covering the merchandise described herein was made, is not the actual owner of the said merchandise, but that such entry exhibits a full and complete account of all the merchandise imported in the vessel indicated therein by the above name person who is the actual owner for CBP purposes of the said merchandise except as listed below.

☐ SECTION II — DECLARATION OF CONSIGNEE FOR MERCHANDISE OBTAINED IN PURSUANCE OF A PURCHASE OR AGREEMENT TO PURCHASE

I, the undersigned, representing the above name consignee, herewith declare that they are the consignees for CBP purposes of the merchandise described herein, that the entry covering the said merchandise exhibits a full and complete account of all the merchandise imported by them in the vessel indicated in the said entry and that the said merchandise was obtained by them in pursuance of a purchase or an agreement to purchase, except as listed below.

☐ SECTION III — DECLARATION OF CONSIGNEE FOR MERCHANDISE OBTAINED OTHERWISE THAN IN PURSUANCE OF A PURCHASE OR AGREEMENT TO PURCHASE

I, the undersigned, representing the above name consignee, herewith declare that they are the consignees for CBP purposes of the merchandise described herein, that the entry covering the said merchandise exhibits a full and complete account of all the merchandise imported by them in the vessel indicated in the said entry and that the said merchandise was obtained by them in pursuance of a purchase or an agreement to purchase, except as listed below.

16. EXCEPTIONS (IF ANY)

☐ SECTION IV — GENERAL DECLARATION

I also declare, to the best of my knowledge and belief, that all statements appearing in the entry and in the invoice or invoices and other documents presented herewith and in accordance with which the entry is made, are true and correct in every respect; that the entry and invoices set forth the true prices, values, quantities, and all information as required by the law and the regulations made in pursuance thereof, that the invoices and other documents are in the same state as when received; that I have not received and do not know of any other invoices, paper, letter, document, or information showing a different currency, price, value, quantity, or description of the said merchandise, and that if at any time hereafter I discover any information showing a different state of facts, I will immediately make the same known to the port director of CBP at the port of entry.

17. SIGNATURE	18. ADDRESS	19. DATE

20. TITLE (CHECK ONE)

☐ PRINCIPAL ☐ MEMBER OF THE FIRM ☐ PRINCIPAL OFFICER OF THE CORPORATION: TITLE ____________ ☐ AUTHORIZED AGENT

CBP Form 3347A (12/02)

U.S. DEPARTMENT OF HOMELAND SECURITY
Bureau of Customs and Border Protection

Form Approved
OMB No. 1651-0024
Exp. 11/30/2008

ENTRY/IMMEDIATE DELIVERY

19 CFR 142.3, 142.16, 142.22, 142.24

1. ARRIVAL DATE	2. ELECTED ENTRY DATE	3. ENTRY TYPE CODE/NAME	4. ENTRY NUMBER
5. PORT	6. SINGLE TRANS. BOND	7. BROKER/IMPORTER FILE NUMBER	
	8. CONSIGNEE NUMBER		9. IMPORTER NUMBER
10. ULTIMATE CONSIGNEE NAME		11. IMPORTER OF RECORD NAME	
12. CARRIER CODE	13. VOYAGE/FLIGHT/TRIP	14. LOCATION OF GOODS-CODE(S)/NAME(S)	
15. VESSEL CODE/NAME			
16. U.S. PORT OF UNLADING	17. MANIFEST NUMBER	18. G. O. NUMBER	19. TOTAL VALUE
20. DESCRIPTION OF MERCHANDISE			

21. IT/BL/ AWB CODE	22. IT/BL/AWB NO.	23. MANIFEST QUANTITY	24. H.S. NUMBER	25. COUNTRY OF ORIGIN	26. MANUFACTURER NO.

27. CERTIFICATION

I hereby make application for entry/immediate delivery. I certify that the above information is accurate, the bond is sufficient, valid, and current, and that all requirements of 19 CFR Part 142 have been met.

SIGNATURE OF APPLICANT

X

PHONE NO. DATE

29. BROKER OR OTHER GOVT. AGENCY USE

28. CBP USE ONLY

☐ OTHER AGENCY ACTION REQUIRED, NAMELY:

☐ CBP EXAMINATION REQUIRED.

☐ ENTRY REJECTED, BECAUSE:

DELIVERY AUTHORIZED: SIGNATURE DATE

PAPERWORK REDUCTION ACT NOTICE: This information is to determine the admissibility of imports into the United States and to provide the necessary information for the examination of the cargo and to establish the liability for payment of duties and taxes. Your response is necessary. The estimated average burden associated with this collection of information is 15 minutes per respondent depending on individual circumstances. Comments concerning the accuracy of this burden estimate and suggestions for reducing this burden should be directed to Bureau of Customs and Border Protection, Information Services Branch, Washington, DC 20229, and to the Office of Management and Budget, Paperwork Reduction Project (1651-0024), Washington, DC 20503.

CBP Form 3461 (01/89)

Form Approved OMB No. 1651-0012. Expires 07/31/2009.

U.S. DEPARTMENT OF HOMELAND SECURITY
Bureau of Customs and Border Protection

LIEN NOTICE

19 U.S.C. 66, 1564; 19 CFR 141.112

1. PORT	2. CBP ASSIGNED NO.
3. DATE OF NOTICE	4. DATE OF ARRIVAL

5. NAME OF CONSIGNEE/IMPORTER	6. NAME OF CARRIER	7. B/L NO. OR CBP 7512 NO.

8. LOCATION OF GOODS

9. MARKS AND NUMBERS	10. NO. OF PACKAGES	11. REMARKS

12. AMOUNTS CLAIMED ▶	A. Freight	B. Charges	C. Contributions to General Average	D. TOTAL

13. STATEMENT OF AGENT

I, the Undersigned, agent of the above named carrier, certify that the carrier has a lien on the above listed merchandise in accordance with Sections 564 and 613 of the Tariff Act of 1930. I further certify that the information set forth in this notice is true to the best of my knowledge and belief, and that the sum claimed is due and unpaid and was a subsisting lien upon the goods described at the time they passed into Bureau of Customs and Border Protection (CBP) custody. I understand that sale of this merchandise by the Government for any reason does not entitle claimants to advance notice in the absence of a written request identifying the goods with this notice. I also, agree, upon the discharge or satisfaction of this lien, to promptly notify the CBP office at the above-named port by filing a written release or receipt showing payment of the claim in full.

SIGNATURE OF AGENT Date

14. NAME AND ADDRESS OF LIENHOLDER

15. SIGNATURE AND TITLE OF LEINHOLDER Date

16. STATEMENT OF CLAIMANT
The amounts claimed as due and unpaid have been satisfied.

SIGNATURE OF CLAIMANT Date

DISPOSITION *(CBP Use Only)*

17. NAME OF CBP OFFICER	18. SIGNATURE OF CBP OFFICER	19. DATE

CBP Form 3485 (08/90)

Form Approved OMB No. 1651-0004

U.S. DEPARTMENT OF HOMELAND SECURITY
Bureau of Customs and Border Protection

APPLICATION FOR EXPORTATION OF ARTICLES UNDER SPECIAL BOND

19 CFR 10.38

TO CBP PORT DIRECTOR

1. TO: CBP Port Director *(Address)*	2. FROM: *(Name and Address of Importer or Agent)*

ATTACH COPY OF EXPORT INVOICE DESCRIBING ARTICLES TO BE EXPORTED

3. Name of Exporting Carrier	4. Date of Departure	5. Country of Origin	6. No. of Export Packages
7. Port of Entry	8. Entry Number	Date	9. Date Bonded Period Expires
10. Date Articles Available for CBP Examination	11. Signature of Importer or Agent		12. Date

(FOR CBP USE ONLY)

NOTICE TO IMPORTER TO DELIVER ARTICLES TO BE EXAMINED AND IDENTIFIED FOR EXPORTATION

13. Place of CBP Examination	Date
14. Date	15. CBP PORT DIRECTOR BY:

REPORT OF EXAMINATION

☐ 16. The articles covered by this application have been examined and agree with the invoice in content and No. of export pkgs. and are approved for export.

17. No. of Export Packages	18. Date of Delivery for Exportation	19. Marks and Numbers on Export Packages

☐ 20. The articles covered by this application do not agree with the invoice in content or in number of packages as follows

21. SIGNATURE OF EXAMINING CBP OFFICER	22. DATE

REPORT OF EXPORTATION

23. Home of Exporting Conveyance *(Vessel, Railroad, Airline and Flight Number)*

24. Date of Departure	PAPERWORK REDUCTION ACT NOTICE: The Paperwork Reduction Act says we must tell you why we are collecting this information, and whether you have to give it to us. We need this information to ensure that importers and exporters are complying with the Customs laws of the United States and allow us to figure and collect the right amount of revenue. Your response is mandatory. The estimated average burden associated with this collection of information is 8 minutes per respondent or recordkeeper depending on individual circumstances. Comments concerning the accuracy of this burden estimate and suggestions for reducing this burden should be directed to Bureau of Customs and Border Protection, Information Services Group, Washington, DC 20229, and to the Office of Management and Budget, Paperwork Reduction Project (1651-0004), Washington, DC 20503.
25. Manifest No.	
26. SIGNATURE OF CBP OFFICER	

(CBP officer must return one copy of this form to port of origin upon exportation.)

(Previous Editions are Obsolete)

CBP Form 3495 (08/99)

U.S. DEPARTMENT OF HOMELAND SECURITY
Bureau of Customs and Border Protection

Form Approved
OMB No. 1651-0006
Expires 07/31/2009
See back of form for Paperwork Reduction Act Notice.

APPLICATION AND APPROVAL TO MANIPULATE, EXAMINE, SAMPLE OR TRANSFER GOODS

19 CFR 19.8, 19.11, 158.43

1. GOODS CONSIGNED TO *(Name)*	2. GOODS EXPORTED FROM	3. PORT AND DATE OF APPLICATION
4. LOCATION OF GOODS	5. CARRIER OR SHIP *(Name)*	6. BILL OF LADING OR CBP 7512 NO.
7. IS AREA BONDED? ☐ YES ☐ NO	8. ENTRY INFORMATION ☐ Warehouse ☐ Consumption	Number: .... Date:

PERMISSION IS REQUESTED TO: (Describe the complete operation to be performed under CBP supervision on the goods listed below):

		FOR CBP USE ONLY
9. MARKS AND NUMBERS	10. DESCRIPTION	11. MANIPULATED VALUE

12. SIGNATURE OF APPLICANT

APPROVED

13. DATE	14. SIGNATURE AND TITLE OF APPROVING CBP OFFICER

Customs and Border Protection Officers Report on Reverse

CBP Form 3499 (10/95)

CUSTOMS AND BORDER PROTECTION OFFICER'S REPORT

Date:

MANIPULATION COMPLETED AS REQUESTED: When goods are repacked the CBP (warehouse) officer will report hereon the marks and numbers of packages repacked and the marks and numbers of packages and the weights or guage of same after repacking.

(CBP Officer and Title)

PAPERWORK REDUCTION ACT NOTICE: The Paperwork Reduction says we must tell you why we are collecting this information, how we will use it, and whether you have to give it to us. We ask for the information in order to carry out the Bureau of Customs and Border Protection laws of the United States. This form is used by importers as an application to examine, sample, repack or transfer merchandise under CBP supervision; as a request for manipulation of merchandise in a bonded warehouse; and as an application for abandonment or destruction of merchandise in bond. It is required to obtain or retain a benefit. The estimated average burden associated with this collection of information is 6 minutes per respondent depending on individual circumstances. Comments concerning the accuracy of this burden estimate and suggestions for reducing this burden should be directed to Bureau of Customs and Border Protection, Information Services Branch, Washington, DC 20229, and to the Office of Management and Budget, Paperwork Reduction Project (1651-0006), Washington, DC 20503.

CBP Form 3499 (10/95)(Back)

Form Approved. OMB No. 1651-0010

U.S. DEPARTMENT OF HOMELAND SECURITY
Bureau of Customs and Border Protection

CERTIFICATE OF REGISTRATION

19 CFR 10.8, 10.9, 10.68, 148.1, 148.8, 148.32, 148.37

(NOTE: Number of copies to be submitted varies with type of transaction. Inquire at Port Director's office as to number of copies required.)

NO.

VIA *(Carrier)*	B/L or INSURED NO.	DATE

NAME, ADDRESS, AND ZIP CODE TO WHICH CERTIFIED FORM IS TO BE MAILED *(If Applicable)*

ARTICLES EXPORTED FOR:

- ☐ ALTERATION*
- ☐ REPAIR*
- ☐ USE ABROAD
- ☐ REPLACEMENT
- ☐ PROCESSING*
- ☐ OTHER, *(specify)*

*** NOTE:** *The cost or value of alterations, repairs, or processing abroad is subject to CBP duty.*

LIST ARTICLES EXPORTED

Number Packages	Kind of Packages	Description

SIGNATURE OF OWNER OR AGENT *(Print or Type and Sign)*	DATE

The Above-Described Articles Were:

EXAMINED		LADEN under my supervision	
DATE	PORT	DATE	PORT
SIGNATURE OF CBP OFFICER		SIGNATURE OF CBP OFFICER	

CERTIFICATE ON RETURN

Duty-free entry is claimed for the described articles as having been exported without benefit of drawback and are returned unchanged except as noted: (use reverse if needed)

SIGNATURE OF IMPORTER *(Print or Type and Sign)*	DATE

NOTE: Certifying officers shall draw lines through all unused spaces with ink or indelible pencil.

Paperwork Reduction Act Notice: This request is in accordance with the Paperwork Reduction Act. The information to be provided is submitted by importers/exporters. Completion of this form is mandatory and to your benefit. The estimated average burden associated with this collection of information is 3 minutes per respondent depending on individual circumstances. Comments concerning the accuracy of this burden estimates and suggestions for reducing this burden should be directed to Bureau of Customs and Border Protection, Information Services Branch, Washington, DC 20229, and to the Office of Management and Budget, Paperwork Reduction Project (1651-0010), Washington, DC 20503.

CBP Form 4455 (06/00)

U.S. DEPARTMENT OF HOMELAND SECURITY
Bureau of Customs and Border Protection

Form Approved
O.M.B. No. 1651-0002
See back of form for Paperwork Reduction Act Notice.

GENERAL DECLARATION
(Outward/Inward)
AGRICULTURE, CUSTOMS, IMMIGRATION, AND PUBLIC HEALTH

19 CFR 122.43,122.52,122.54,122.73,122.144

Owner or Operator ....

Marks of Nationality and Registration .... **Flight No.** .... **Date** ....

Departure from .... (Place) **Arrival at** .... (Place)

FLIGHT ROUTING
("Place" Column always to list origin, every en-route stop and destination)

PLACE	TOTAL NUMBER OF CREW	NUMBER OF PASSENGERS ON THIS STAGE 1)
		Departure Place:
		Embarking ....
		Through on same flight ....
		Arrival Place:
		Disembarking ....
		Through on same flight ....
		NUMBER OF SED's AND AWB's
		SED's ______ AWB's ______

Declaration of Health

Persons on board known to be suffering from illness other than airsickness or the effects of accidents, as well as those cases of illness disembarked during the flight:

Any other condition on board which may lead to the spread of disease:

Details of each disinsecting or sanitary treatment (place, date, time, method) during the flight. If no disinsecting has been carried out during the flight give details of most recent disinsecting:

Signed, if required ....
Crew Member Concerned

For official use only

I declare that all statements and particulars contained in this General Declaration, and in any supplementary forms required to be presented with this General Declaration are complete, exact and true to the best of my knowledge and that all through passengers will continue/have continued on the flight.

SIGNATURE Authorized Agent or Pilot-in-Command

1) Not to be completed when passenger manifests are presented.

CBP Form 7507 (12/96)

GENERAL DECLARATION

Notes and Specifications

NOTE 1. An arrival-departure card (CBP Form I-94) for each passenger on board shall be presented to the immigration officer at the port of first arrival.

NOTE 2. List surname, given name and middle initial of each crew member in the column headed "Total Number of Crew."

NOTE 3. Air cargo manifests shall be attached hereto.

NOTE 4. If copies of air waybills/consignment notes are attached, their numbers shall be entered on separate cargo manifest CBP Form 7509 to be attached hereto. If copies of air waybills/consignment notes are not attached to this form, a separate cargo manifest CBP Form 7509 completed to show the full information required shall be furnished.

NOTE 5. If the airline or operator consolidates a shipment with other shipments, or encloses the goods in other wrappers or containers, either separately or with other goods, the changes in packing and/or marks and numbers must be clearly stated in the air way-bill/consignment note.

NOTE 6. Declaration of Health (U.S. Public Health Service requirements):
First two items-- To be completed **immediately upon landing** or **immediately before landing,** by pilot-in-command or appropriate crew member designated by him. Make entries in clear handwriting. Person making entries is to initial the first item unless he signs the general declaration.

Third item-- If entry is duplicated, it is to be (a) initialed by person signing the general declaration or (b) signed by his authorized agent having knowledge of measures applied.

NOTE 7. This General Declaration and/or attached manifests or air waybills should not bear erasures or corrections except those approved by the proper public authorities concerned nor contain interlineations or several listings on the same line. As many extra sheets may be added as necessary.

The information requested by the official General Declaration may be furnished on ICAO Annex 9, Appendix 1, provided the form approximates (but does not exceed) 8 1/2" x 14", and is printed on white paper of appropriate quality.

This form may be printed by private parties provided it conforms to official form in size, wording, arrangement, and quality and color of paper.

PAPERWORK REDUCTION ACT NOTICE: This request is in accordance with the Paperwork Reduction Act. We ask for the information in order to carry out the laws and regulations administered by the Bureau of Customs and Border Protection. These regulations and forms apply to the agent or pilot-in-command to make entry of the aircraft as required by statute, to bring the aircraft under United States control, deliver passengers and their baggage to their destination, and cargo to the appropriated consignee/owner for payment of duties and taxes. It is mandatory. The estimated average burden associated with this collection of information is 5 minutes per respondent depending on individual circumstances. Comments concerning the accuracy of this burden estimate and suggestions for reducing this burden should be directed to Bureau of Customs and Border Protection, Information Services Branch, Washington, DC 20229, and to the Office of Management and Budget, Paperwork Reduction Project (1651-0002), Washington, DC 20503.

CBP Form 7507 (12/96)(Back)

See back of form for Paperwork Reduction Act Notice.

UNITED STATES - CANADA TRANSIT MANIFEST

Form Approved; OMB No. 1515-0005

TRANSIT MANIFEST NO.

DEPARTMENT OF THE TREASURY **DEPARTMENT OF NATIONAL REVENUE**

☐ **CARRIER IN TRANSIT THROUGH CANADA** ☐ **CARRIER IN TRANSIT THROUGH UNITED STATES**

STATE PROVINCE LICENSE PLATE NO.

TRACTOR: TRAILER: OTHER:

PORT OF DEPARTURE	PORT OF RE-ENTRY[1]
CANADA PERMIT NO.	CANADA CUSTOMS BOND NO.
NAME AND ADDRESS OF IMPORTING CARRIER *(Print or Type)*	NAME OF OPERATOR OR AGENT OF CARRIER *(Print or Type)*

PORT AND DATE OF ARRIVAL	CUSTOMS SEAL NOS.	PORT AND DATE OF EXIT	**Seals Intact:** ☐ YES ☐ NO *(If "No", report on reverse)*
			Other Irregularity: ☐ YES ☐ NO *(If "Yes", report on reverse)*
	INITIALS OF CUSTOMS OFFICER		INITIALS OF CUSTOMS OFFICER

WAYBILL NUMBERS	NUMBER OF PACKAGES	VALUE[2]	WAYBILL NUMBERS	NUMBER OF PACKAGES	VALUE[2]

I certify that I have received from customs at the port of arrival all goods described in the waybills listed in this manifest, which will be transported under bond and delivered to customs at the ports of exit and re-entry; that this manifest and related waybills contain a true account of all the goods on board the vehicle; that any discrepancy, error, or omission in this account, or any irregularity in the transit movement of this shipment will be immediately reported to customs.

SIGNATURE OF OPERATOR OR AGENT OF CARRIER

[1]To be entered by customs officer at port of re-entry.

[2]Value to be shown only for goods transiting the United States; if estimated, so state.

CUSTOMS FORM 7512B (062591) **CANADA 8½**

Prepare in *Quadruplicate;* White - *Arrival copy,* Blue - *Exit copy,* Green - *Re-entry copy,* Pink - *Carrier copy.*

DEPARTMENT OF HOMELAND SECURITY
U.S. Customs and Border Protection

OMB No. 1651-0075

DRAWBACK NOTICE

(Lading/Foreign Trade Zone Transfer)
19 CFR 191.92, 191.93, 191.163

1. FUNCTION OF DOCUMENT
☐ Lading of Supplies/Equipment
☐ Transfer to a Foreign Trade Zone

2. Port Number	3. Port	4. Notice Number

5. Articles to be Laden/Transferred by (Name)	6. Location (Port and Place or City and State)
7. Destination or Zone Number	8. Vessel, Aircraft, or Zone Lot No.

9. Marks and Numbers	10. Number and Kind of Packages, Contents and Quantity

11. Forward Executed Certificate to (Name and Address)

12. Port Where Drawback Entry to be Filed

13. Name of Manufacturer or Producer

14. No. of Crew*	15. No. of Pass*	16. Duration of Voyage*

The above-described articles are to be ☐ laden as stated above ☐ transferred to a foreign-trade zone for the sole purpose of exportation, destruction (except distilled spirits, wines, and fermented malt liquors), or storage and are not to be returned to customs territory of the United States for domestic consumption.

To the best of my knowledge and belief said articles are unused and are entitled on lading or transfer to drawback of the duties paid on the imported materials used in their manufacture, or of the internal revenue tax paid on the domestic materials used.

*Items 14 and 15 not required in cases where supplies consist of lubricating and fuel oils for operation of vessel. Items 14, 15, and 16 not required if drawback on a single lading is less than $25.

17. Exporter, Transferor or Agent Signature, Title Date

CUSTOMS CERTIFICATION
(Do not use when Blanket Certificate of Lading is completed on reverse hereof)

18. Vessel/Aircraft Registry or Foreign Trade Zone Number

19. Destination or Zone Lot Number

20. Date Vessel or Aircraft was cleared (or departed under permit) or Date Articles Received.

21. ☐ **FOREIGN TRADE ZONE TRANSFER:** I certify that I have inspected the packages bearing the marks and numbers as described in this notice of transfer and find them to be as stated and that they were assigned the zone lot number in Block 19.

☐ **LADING:** The vessel (or vehicle or aircraft) specified herein was cleared (or departed under permit).

Signature Title Date

22. DECLARATION OF MASTER OR OTHER OFFICER
I declare that the information given above is true and correct to the best of my knowledge and belief; that I have knowledge of the facts set forth herein; that the articles described in this notice of lading were received in the quantities stated, from the person, and on the date, indicated above; that said articles were laden on the vessel (or aircraft) named above for use on said vessel (or aircraft) as supplies (or equipment), except as noted below; and that at the time of lading of the articles, the said vessel (or aircraft) was engaged in the business or trade checked below: (It is not necessary for a foreign vessel to show its class of trade.)

☐ Fisheries	☐ Whaling	☐ Trade between Atlantic and Pacific Ports of the U.S.	☐ Trade between the U.S. and any of its possessions	☐ Foreign Trade	☐ Trade between Hawaii or Alaska and any other port of the U.S.

RECEIPT OF FOREIGN TRADE ZONE OPERATOR, OR MASTER OR OTHER OFFICER

23. Name of Foreign Trade Zone Operator or Airline	24. Articles Received From	25. Date Received or Laden

26. Name and title of Individual Receiving Articles	27. Signature

28. Exceptions

CBP Form 7514 (07/05)

BLANKET CERTIFICATE OF LADING FOR FUEL LADEN AIRCRAFT

Aircraft	Airline	Country of Registry	Month and Year

The aircraft hereunder are registered in that country unless otherwise indicated in the column "A/C No."

FOR AIRLINE USE							FOR CBP USE ONLY	
Flight No.	A/C No.	Foreign Destination	Trade	Type of Fuel Laden	Quantity	Date of Lading	Date of Clearance	Remarks

CBP Port Director	By	Title

ENDORSEMENT

Name

I hereby authorize the above-mentioned person to make entry and receive the drawback on the within-described articles.

Name of Transferor

Signature	Title

Paperwork Reduction Act Notice We require this information to enforce the Customs laws of the United States. This form is used to record and verify receipt and use of supplies in operating vessels or aircraft and to transfer articles manufactured or produced in the United States into a foreign trade zone. Your response is mandatory.

The estimated average burden associated with this collection of information is 15 minutes per respondent or record-keeper depending on individual circumstances. Comments concerning the accuracy of this burden estimate and suggestions for reducing the burden should be directed to U.S. Customs and Border Protection, Information Services Branch, Washington, DC 20229.

CBP Form 7514 (BACK)(07/05)

U.S. DEPARTMENT OF HOMELAND SECURITY
Bureau of Customs and Border Protection

OMB No. 1651-0013

ENTRY AND MANIFEST OF MERCHANDISE FREE OF DUTY, CARRIER'S CERTIFICATE AND RELEASE

19 U.S.C. 1433, 1484, 1498; 19 CFR 123.4, 143.23

1. NO.

The undersigned, as the importer of merchandise described below, which arrived at the port or station identified, hereby claims free entry therefore under the provisions of the applicable law indicated.

2. PORT CODE

3. DATE

4. VESSEL OR OTHER CONVEYANCE

5. ARRIVAL DATE

6. COUNTRY OF EXPORTATION

7. MARKS AND NUMBERS	8. DESCRIPTION AND QUANTITY OF MERCHANDISE	9. VALUE	10. HTSUS HEADING NO. OR P.L. NO.

11. IMPORTER OF RECORD *(Name and Address)*

12. AGENT'S SIGNATURE

13. INSPECTED AND PASSED FREE OF DUTY BY:

14. OWNER, PURCHASER, OR CONSIGNEE *(If different from Importer of Record)*

15. SIGNATURE *(Inspector)*

16. DATE

CARRIER'S CERTIFICATE AND RELEASE ORDER

The undersigned carrier, to whom or upon whose order the articles described above must be released, hereby certifies that the person or firm named above as the importer is the owner purchaser, or consignee of such articles within the purview of section 484(h), Tariff Act of 1930. In accordance with the provisions of section 484(j), Tariff Act of 1930, authority is hereby given to release the articles to such consignee.

17. CARRIER

18. AGENT'S SIGNATURE

PAPERWORK REDUCTION ACT NOTICE: The Paperwork Reduction Act says we must tell you why we are collecting this information, how we will use it and whether you have to give it to us. We ask for the information to carry out the customs laws of the United States. This form is used by carriers and importers as a manifest for the entry of merchandise free of duty under certain conditions and by CBP to authorize the entry of such merchandise. It is also used by the carrier to show that the articles being imported are to be released to the importer or consignee. It is mandatory. The estimated average burden associated with this collection of information is 5 minutes per respondent or recordkeeper depending on individual circumstances. Comments concerning the accuracy of this burden estimate and suggestions for reducing this burden should be directed to Bureau of Customs and Border Protection, Information Services Branch, Washington, DC 20229, and to the Office of Management and Budget, Paperwork Reduction Project (1651-0013), Washington DC 20503.

CBP Form 7523 (05/96)

DEPARTMENT OF THE TREASURY
UNITED STATES CUSTOMS SERVICE

OMB No. 1515-0049

INWARD CARGO MANIFEST FOR VESSEL UNDER FIVE TONS, FERRY, TRAIN, CAR, VEHICLE, ETC.

(INSTRUCTIONS ON REVERSE)

19 CFR 123.4, 123.7, 123.61

Customs Manifest/In Bond Number

Page No.

1. Name or Number and Description of Importing Conveyance	2. Name of Master or Person in Charge	
3. Name and Address of Owner	4. Foreign Port of Lading	5. U.S. Port of Destination
6. Port of Arrival	7. Date of Arrival	

Column No. 1	Column No. 2	Column No. 3	Column No. 4	Column No. 5
Bill of Lading or Marks & Numbers or Address of Consignee on Packages	Car Number and Initials	Number and Gross Weight (in kilos or pounds) of Packages and Description of Goods	Name of Consignee	For Use By Customs Only

CARRIER'S CERTIFICATE

To the District Director of Customs, Port of Arrival:

The undersigned carrier, to whom or upon whose order the articles described above must be released, hereby certifies that .... of .... is the owner or consignee of such articles within the purview of section 484(h), Tariff Act of 1930.

I certifiy that this manifest is correct and true to the best of my knowledge.

Date .... Master or Person in charge ....
(Signature)

This form for sale by District Directors of Customs

Customs Form 7533 (080295)

Form Approved OMB No. 1651-0022

DEPARTMENT OF HOMELAND SECURITY
U.S. Customs and Border Protection

ENTRY SUMMARY

1. Filer Code/Entry No.		2. Entry Type	3. Summary Date
4. Surety No.	5. Bond Type	6. Port Code	7. Entry Date

8. Importing Carrier	9. Mode of Transport	10. Country of Origin	11. Import Date
12. B/L or AWB No.	13. Manufacturer ID	14. Exporting Country	15. Export Date

16. I.T. No.	17. I.T. Date	18. Missing Docs	19. Foreign Port of Lading	20. U.S. Port of Unlading

21. Location of Goods/G.O. No.	22. Consignee No.	23. Importer No.	24. Reference No.

25. Ultimate Consignee Name and Address	26. Importer of Record Name and Address
City State Zip	City State Zip

27. Line No.	28. Description of Merchandise 29. A. HTSUS No. B. ADA/CVD No.	30. A. Grossweight B. Manifest Qty.	31. Net Quantity in HTSUS Units	32. A. Entered Value B. CHGS C. Relationship	33. A. HTSUS Rate B. ADA/CVD Rate C. IRC Rate D. Visa No.	34. Duty and I.R. Tax Dollars Cents

Other Fee Summary for Block 39	35. Total Entered Value $	**CBP USE ONLY**		TOTALS
		A. LIQ CODE	B. Ascertained Duty	37. Duty
	Total Other Fees $	REASON CODE	C. Ascertained Tax	38. Tax
36. DECLARATION OF IMPORTER OF RECORD (OWNER OR PURCHASER) OR AUTHORIZED AGENT			D. Ascertained Other	39. Other
			E. Ascertained Total	40. Total

I declare that I am the ☐ Importer of record and that the actual owner, purchaser, or consignee for CBP purposes is as shown above, **OR** ☐ owner or purchaser or agent thereof. I further declare that the merchandise ☐ was obtained pursuant to a purchase or agreement to purchase and that the prices set forth in the invoices are true, **OR** ☐ was not obtained pursuant to a purchase or agreement to purchase and the statements in the invoices as to value or price are true to the best of my knowledge and belief. I also declare that the statements in the documents herein filed fully disclose to the best of my knowledge and belief the true prices, values, quantities, rebates, drawbacks, fees, commissions, and royalties and are true and correct, and that all goods or services provided to the seller of the merchandise either free or at reduced cost are fully disclosed.
I will immediately furnish to the appropriate CBP officer any information showing a different statement of facts.

41. DECLARANT NAME	TITLE	SIGNATURE	DATE

42. Broker/Filer Information (Name, address, phone number)	43. Broker/Importer File No.

CBP Form 7501 (04/05)

DEPARTMENT OF HOMELAND SECURITY
U.S. Customs and Border Protection

ENTRY SUMMARY CONTINUATION SHEET

OMB No. 1651-0022

1. Filer Code/Entry No.

27.	28. Description of Merchandise			32.	33.	34.	
Line No.	29. A. HTSUS No. B. ADA/CVD No.	30. A. Grossweight B. Manifest Qty.	31. Net Quantity in HTSUS Units	A. Entered Value B. CHGS C. Relationship	A. HTSUS Rate B. ADA/CVD Rate C. IRC Rate D. Visa No.	Duty and I.R. Tax Dollars	Cents

CBP Form 7501 (04/05)

DEPARTMENT OF HOMELAND SECURITY
U.S. Customs and Border Protection

ENTRY SUMMARY CONTINUATION SHEET

OMB No. 1651-0022

1. Filer Code/Entry No.

27.	28. Description of Merchandise			32.	33.	34.	
	29.	30.	31.		A. HTSUS Rate	Duty and I.R. Tax	
Line No.	A. HTSUS No. B. ADA/CVD No.	A. Grossweight B. Manifest Qty.	Net Quantity in HTSUS Units	A. Entered Value B. CHGS C. Relationship	B. ADA/CVD Rate C. IRC Rate D. Visa No.	Dollars	Cents

CBP Form 7501 (04/05)

DEPARTMENT OF HOMELAND SECURITY
U.S. Customs and Border Protection

ENTRY SUMMARY CONTINUATION SHEET

OMB No. 1651-0022

1. Filer Code/Entry No.

27.	28. Description of Merchandise			32.	33.	34.
Line No.	29. A. HTSUS No. B. ADA/CVD No.	30. A. Grossweight B. Manifest Qty.	31. Net Quantity in HTSUS Units	A. Entered Value B. CHGS C. Relationship	A. HTSUS Rate B. ADA/CVD Rate C. IRC Rate D. Visa No.	Duty and I.R. Tax: Dollars / Cents

CBP Form 7501 (04/05)

DEPARTMENT OF HOMELAND SECURITY
U.S. Customs and Border Protection

ENTRY SUMMARY CONTINUATION SHEET

OMB No. 1651-0022

1. Filer Code/Entry No.

27.	28. Description of Merchandise			32.	33.	34.
Line No.	29. A. HTSUS No. B. ADA/CVD No.	30. A. Grossweight B. Manifest Qty.	31. Net Quantity in HTSUS Units	A. Entered Value B. CHGS C. Relationship	A. HTSUS Rate B. ADA/CVD Rate C. IRC Rate D. Visa No.	Duty and I.R. Tax: Dollars Cents

CBP Form 7501 (04/05)

Appendix B

Related Official Source Materials

TABLE OF CONTENTS

1. Compliance Policy Guide

Guidance for FDA and CBP Staff

Issued December 2003
Revised June 2004, August 2004, November 2004, March 2005.

TABLE OF CONTENTS

Sec. 110.310: Prior Notice of Imported Food Under the Public Health Security and Bioterrorism Preparedness and Response Act of 2002

This Compliance Policy Guide (CPG) is being revised The draft revisions are found in Section C, items 7 and 8; The revised text is indicated as [NEW]. This guidance document represents the Food and Drug Administration's (FDA) and Customs and Border Protection's (CBP) current thinking on this topic. It does not create or confer any rights for or on any person and does not operate to bind FDA, CBP, or the public. An alternative approach may be used if such approach satisfies the requirements of the applicable statute and regulations.

I. INTRODUCTION

The purpose of this document is to provide guidance on FDA's and CBP's strategy for enforcing and otherwise achieving compliance with the requirements of the interim final rule for submitting prior notice for food imported or offered for import into the United States (68 Fed. Reg. 58974 (Oct. 10, 2003) (codified at 21 CFR 1.276–1.285)).

FDA's guidance documents, including this Compliance Policy Guide (CPG), do not establish legally enforceable responsibilities. Instead, guidance documents describe the agency's current thinking on a topic and should be viewed only as recommendations, unless specific regulatory or statutory requirements are cited. The use of the word *should* in agency guidance documents means that something is suggested or recommended, but not required.

II. BACKGROUND

The Public Health Security and Bioterrorism Preparedness and Response Act of 2002 (Bioterrorism Act), section 307, added section 801(m) to the Federal Food, Drug, and Cosmetic Act (the Act) to require that FDA receive prior notice for food imported or offered for import into the United States. Section 801(m) also provides that if an article of food arrives at the port of arrival with inadequate prior notice (e.g., no prior notice, inaccurate prior notice, or untimely prior notice), the food is subject to refusal of admission under section 801(m)(1) of the Act and may not be delivered to the importer, owner, or consignee. If an article of food is refused under section 801(m)(1) of the Act, unless CBP concurrence is obtained for export and the article is immediately exported from the port of arrival under CBP supervision, it must be held within the port of entry for the article unless directed by CBP or FDA.

The Bioterrorism Act, section 305, also amended Chapter IV of the Act by adding section 415 to require domestic and foreign facilities that manufacture, process, pack, or hold food for consumption in the United States to register with FDA, and amended Chapter VIII of the Act by adding section 801(1) to require any food for human and animal consumption from an unregistered foreign facility that is imported or offered for import to be held at the port of entry until the foreign facility has been registered.

On October 10, 2003, FDA and CBP issued interim final regulations establishing the requirements for registration and requiring that FDA receive prior notice of the importation of food beginning on December 12, 2003 (68 FR 58994 and 68 FR 58974). For the purposes of prior notice, 'food' has the meaning given in section 201 (f) of the Act, and is defined as (1) articles of food or drink for man or other animals, (2) chewing gum, and (3) articles used as components of any such article, except that it does not include food contact substances or pesticides. The requirements for prior notice do not apply to:

1. Food for an individual's personal use when it is carried by or otherwise accompanies the individual when arriving in the United States;

2. Food that was made by an individual in his/her personal residence and sent by that individual as a personal gift (i.e., for non-business reasons) to an individual in the United States;
3. Food that is imported then exported without leaving the port of arrival until export;
4. Meat food products that at the time of importation are subject to the exclusive jurisdiction of the U.S. Department of Agriculture (USDA) under the Federal Meat Inspection Act (21 U.S.C. 601 et seq.);
5. Poultry products that at the time of importation are subject to the exclusive jurisdiction of USDA under the Poultry Products Inspection Act (21 U.S.C. 451 et seq.);
6. Egg products that at the time of importation are subject to the exclusive jurisdiction of USDA under the Egg Products Inspection Act (21 U.S.C. 1031 et seq.).
7. Prior notice also is not required under FDA requirements for food brought into the United States in a diplomatic pouch, The Vienna Convention on Diplomatic Relations (1961) provides: 'The diplomatic bag shall not be opened or detained.' Art. 27(3): Any baggage or cargo marked 'diplomatic bag' or 'diplomatic pouch' is immune from search, including by electronic devices, and thus its contents are not subject to FDA's prior notice requirements.

Information required to be submitted in a prior notice includes, with certain exceptions, the registration numbers assigned to the foreign manufacturer's and shipper's facilities that are associated with the article of food. FDA's monitoring of compliance by foreign facilities with the requirement to register under section 415 of the Act will be accomplished primarily through the prior notice review process. If an article of food is from a foreign manufacturer that is not registered as required and is imported or offered for import, then the food is subject to refusal under section 801(m)(1) of the Act for failure to provide adequate prior notice. Likewise, the failure to provide the correct registration number of the relevant foreign manufacturer, if registration is required, renders the identity of that facility incomplete for purposes of prior notice. In addition, if an article of food is imported or offered for import from any foreign facility that is not registered as required, then the food is subject to being held under section 801(l) of the Act.

In the preamble to the interim final rule, FDA stated that it planned to provide guidance to its staff regarding the agency's enforcement policies. Accordingly, this CPG describes general policies regarding the enforcement of the prior notice requirements, including the requirement to provide a required registration number.

The requirements for submitting prior notice to FDA were effective beginning December 12, 2003. During the first eight months following this effective date, FDA and CBP focused their resources on education to achieve compliance with the prior notice requirements. The agencies will continue this education and outreach, including the following:

1. FDA and CBP will distribute information flyers at the ports.
2. FDA and CBP plan to:
   a. Gather data to track compliance with the prior notice requirements and to determine how best to use their resources to educate industry and the public in order to achieve full compliance.
   b. Provide industry and the public with summary information about the level of compliance with the prior notice requirements, including data on the types of errors in submitted prior notices.
   c. Provide the summary information on FDA's website at *www.fda.gov*.
   d. Utilize the data and summary information to assist the industry and the public in improving the submission of prior notice.

FDA may consider the failure to provide adequate prior notice as a factor in determining whether and where to examine an article of food. However, if FDA decides not to refuse an article of food under 21 CFR 1.283 or 1.285, this decision has no bearing on whether the article of food is admissible or will be granted admission under other provisions of the Act or other U.S. laws. Thus, for food that is imported or offered for import, FDA will continue its normal review, investigative, and enforcement activities for food safety and security concerns to determine whether the food is subject to refusal under section 801 (a) of the Act. In addition, if FDA decides not to refuse an article of food under 21 CFR 1.283 or 1.285, this decision does not affect FDA's ability to initiate other types of actions – such as seizures, injunctions, prosecutions, or 'debarments under sections 302, 303, 304, and 306 of the Act – that may be necessary. Likewise, it does not affect CBP's ability to initiate other types of actions that may be necessary.

III. REGULATORY ACTION GUIDANCE

FDA's Prior Notice Review Center, in conjunction with CBP headquarters, should use the information below to make decisions about whether to refuse a shipment of food pursuant to 21 CFR 1.283 or 1.285 or take other actions for violations under sections 801(m) and 415 of the Act.

The following definitions and descriptions apply to this Compliance Policy Guide (CPG).

A. Types of Violations

1. *Inadequate Prior Notice*
   a. *No Prior Notice* – The article of food arrives at the port of arrival and no prior notice has been submitted and confirmed by FDA for review.

b. *Inaccurate Prior Notice* – Prior notice has been submitted and confirmed by FDA for review, but upon review of the notice or examination of the article of food, the prior notice is determined to be inaccurate,
c. *Untimely Prior Notice* – Prior notice has been submitted and confirmed by FDA for review, but the full time that applies under 21 CFR 1.279 for prior notice has not elapsed when the article arrives, unless FDA has already reviewed the prior notice, determined its response to the prior notice, and advised CBP of that response.

2. *Unregistered Facility* – The article of food is imported or offered for import from a foreign facility that is not registered as required.
3. *No PN Confirmation*
   a. When a copy of the Prior Notice (PN) Confirmation is required for food carried by or otherwise accompanying an individual, but cannot be provided by the individual.
   b. When the PN Confirmation Number is not affixed to an article of food that arrives by international mail.
   c. When the PN Confirmation Number for an article of food for which prior notice was submitted through PNSI is not provided to CBP or FDA upon arrival.

B. Actions in Response to Violations

1. *Education/Communication* – To the extent possible:
   a. Distribute information flyers at the ports to carriers and others associated with the shipment of food.
   b. Provide, to the extent practicable, notice of the violation and of the prior notice and registration requirements to the person(s) who transmits and/or files the prior notice.
   c. When an article of food that is carried by or otherwise accompanying an individual is not for personal use and has inadequate prior notice or the individual cannot provide FDA or CBP with a copy of the prior notice (PN) confirmation, provide the individual with an information sheet on prior notice.
   d. When an article of food arrives by international mail with inadequate prior notice or the PN confirmation number is not affixed, provide an information sheet on prior notice and forward the package to the addressee.
   e. When an article of food is imported or offered for import for non commercial purposes with a non-commercial shipper as set out below under Section C.4, provide an information sheet on prior notice to the importer, owner, consignee, or shipper.
2. *Assessment of CBP Civil Monetary Penalties* – CBP, in consultation with FDA, may assess civil monetary penalties for violation of 19 U.S.C.

1595a(b) against any party who aids or abets the importation of any merchandise contrary to law.

3. *Refusal* – FDA, in consultation with CBP, may refuse admission of an article of food under section 801(m)(1) of the Act or place it under hold under section 801(l) of the Act for violations under sections 801(m) and 415 of the Act. If an article of food is refused or placed under hold under these provisions, unless CBP concurrence is obtained for export and the article is immediately exported from the port of arrival under CBP supervision, it must be held within the port of entry for the article unless directed by CBP or FDA (21 CFR 1.283(a) and 1.285(a),(b)). For food that is carried by or otherwise accompanying an individual, and is refused, and if, before leaving the port, the individual does not arrange to have the food held at the port or exported, the article of food shall be destroyed (21 CFR 1.283(b) and 1.285(h)). For food that arrives by international mail and is refused, if there is a return address, the parcel will be returned to sender stamped 'No Prior Notice – FDA Refused.' If there is no return address, or if FDA determines that the article of food in the parcel appears to present a hazard, FDA may dispose of or destroy the parcel (21 CFR 1.283(e) and 1.285(k)).
4. The phrase '*the action FDA and CBP staff typically should consider taking*' used in this CPG means that FDA and CBP staff, exercising enforcement discretion pursuant to their agency's policies and procedures, may take these actions or may take different or additional actions if they believe particular circumstances warrant them.

C. Policy

This policy provides guidance to FDA and CBP staff when they encounter the prior notice situations described within this section.

The policy contains several references to Tables 1 and 2, which are set out below.

1. *Shipments of food, other than food covered by another section of this CPG*

   In general, for any prior notice violation, the action FDA and CBP staff typically should consider taking is refusal and/or assessment of CBP Civil Monetary Penalties.

   a. *Manufacturer.* Table 1 lists the prior notice requirements for providing information about the identity of the manufacturer for an article of food that is no longer in its natural state. If there is a prior notice violation because this information is not provided, FDA and CBP should typically consider not taking any regulatory action under the circumstances described in the first column of Table 2 if the information in the second column of that table is provided.

Table 1. Requirements for the Identity of the Manufacturer (see 21 CFR 1.281)

In the Following Circumstances	*Provide the Following Information*
1. Any article of food, when the facility that manufactured the food *is required* to be registered.	Name, Registration Number, City, and Country of the facility that manufactured the food.
2. Any article of food, when the facility that manufactured the food is not required to be registered.	Name, Street Address, City, and Country of the facility that manufactured the food, as well as a reason code identifying this situation and the reason the facility is not required to be registered.
3. An article of food that is for transshipment, storage and export, or further manipulation and export.	Name, Street Address (or Registration Number in lieu of Street Address), City, and Country of the facility that manufactured the food.
4. An article of food that is sent by an individual as a personal gift (i.e., for nonbusiness reasons) to an individual in the United States. Note: Under this circumstance, you should also refer to Section C.3 of this CPG.	Name, Registration Number (or Street Address if the facility is not required to be registered), City, and Country of the facility that manufactured the food or Name and Address of the firm that appears on the label under 21 CFR 101.5.

Table 2. Enforcement Discretion Policy for the Identity of the Manufacturer

If, After a Good Faith Effort, the Person Submitting Prior Notice Does not Know…	*Then the Person Submitting Prior Notice Should Provide ...*
1. The Registration Number of the facility that manufactured the food (and the facility *is required* to be registered).	Name, Street Address, City, and Country of the facility that manufactured the food, and a reason code identifying this situation.*

Table 2. (continued)

If, After a Good Faith Effort, the Person Submitting Prior Notice Does not Know…	*Then the Person Submitting Prior Notice Should Provide ...*
2. Either the Registration Number or the name and full address of the facility that manufactured the food.	Name, Street Address, City, and Country of the headquarters of the facility that manufactured the food, and a reason code identifying this situation.*
3. The information in items 1 and 2 of this table.	Name, Street Address, City, and Country of the invoicing firm, and a reason code identifying this situation.*

* Notes for Table 2:

- If the facility that manufactured the food is a foreign facility that is required to be registered and either its registration number is not provided or the name and address of a different facility (i.e., the manufacturing facility's headquarters or the invoicing firm) is provided, then it will be more difficult and/or may take more time for FDA and CBP to verify the identity of the manufacturing facility and its registration status and to determine whether the article of food is subject to being held under section 801(l) of the Act. As a result, if an article of food is imported or offered for import with the alternative information provided in Table 2 in lieu of the identity of the facility that manufactured the food, and if FDA has concerns that the food may pose a serious health threat, then the food may be delayed at the port of arrival until the verification is completed.
- As with other types of prior notice violations, FDA may consider the failure to provide required information about the facility that manufactured the food as a factor in determining whether and where to examine the article of food.
- We intend to reject prior notice submissions unless the prior notice includes a valid registration number or an appropriate reason code selected from among those provided in *the Prior Notice System Interface (PNSI)* and *the Automated Broker Interface of the Automated Commercial System (ABI/ACS) (see Appendix 1)*. Rejected submissions are not confirmed for FDA review.

b. *Express Courier.* If prior notice is inadequate because it does not include the required anticipated arrival information and/or planned shipment information, FDA and CBP should typically consider not taking any regulatory action if:
   1) The article of food is imported or offered for import via an express courier;
   2) The person submitting prior notice is not the express courier;
   3) The prior notice is submitted via the Prior Notice System Interface (PNSI); and
   4) The prior notice includes the shipment's tracking number in lieu of the required anticipated arrival information and/or planned shipment information.

c. *Time Frame.* FDA and CBP should typically consider not taking any regulatory action if there is a prior notice violation because the prior notice was submitted more than 5 calendar days before the anticipated date of arrival, provided that: (1) the prior notice was submitted less than 10 calendar days before the anticipated date of arrival; and (2) the prior notice was submitted through the Prior Notice System Interface (PNSI). In addition, under the same conditions, FDA should typically provide the Prior Notice Confirmation Number when prior notice has been confirmed for review even if prior notice was submitted more than 5 calendar days before the anticipated date of arrival. Because of the way the Automated Broker Interface of the Automated Commercial System (ABI/ACS) is programmed, when prior notice is submitted through ABI/ACS, the Prior Notice Confirmation Number cannot be provided more than 5 calendar days before the anticipated date of arrival.

Please note that if any of the prior notice information, except the anticipated arrival information, the estimated quantity, or the planned shipment information, changes after FDA has confirmed the prior notice submission for review, the prior notice must be resubmitted (21 CFR 1.282(a)). The resubmission must be confirmed by FDA for review no less than 2, 4, or 8 hours before arriving at the port of arrival, with the minimum time depending on the mode of transportation (21 CFR 1.279(a)). If prior notice is resubmitted, the previous prior notice should be cancelled (21 CFR 1.282(b)).

2. *Food carried by or ótherwise accompanying an individual that is not for personal use*

In general, the action FDA and CBP staff typically should consider taking is education/communication for minor or inadvertent prior notice violations and refusal for all other prior notice violations.

Manufacturer. Table 1 lists the prior notice requirements for providing information about the identity of the manufacturer for an article of food that is no longer in its natural state. If there is a prior notice violation due to the fact that this information is not provided, FDA and CBP should typically consider not taking any regulatory action under the circumstances described in the fast column of Table 2 if the information in the second column of that table is provided.

3. *Food imported or offered for import for non-commercial purposes with a non commercial shipper, irrespective of the type of carrier*

FDA and CBP should typically consider not taking any regulatory action when an article of food is imported or offered for import for non-commercial purposes with a non-commercial shipper. Generally, staff should consider a non-commercial purpose to be when the food is purchased or otherwise acquired by an individual for non-business purposes and the shipper is an individual (e.g., the individual delivers the food to a post office or common carrier for delivery to self, family member, or friend for non-business purposes, i.e., not for sale, resale, barter, business use, or commercial use.)

Examples of foods imported or offered for import that may be covered by this non-commercial category are:

- food in household goods, including military, civilian, governmental agency, and diplomatic transfers;
- food purchased by a traveler and mailed or shipped to the traveler's U.S. address by the traveler, not the commercial establishment; and
- gifts purchased at a commercial establishment and shipped by the purchaser, not the commercial establishment.

Note that the shipper and the carrier are different entities, and the carrier is likely to be a commercial entity even when the shipper is an individual. Thus, the food for non-commercial purposes may arrive by international mail or any other mode of transportation, but must be shipped by one individual to another individual (self, family member, or friend) to be considered for non-commercial purposes. For example, when an individual ships his or her own household goods, even when the goods are delivered to a mover or carrier for international movement, the individual is the shipper, e.g., the owner or exporter of the article of food who consigns and ships the article from a foreign country or the person who sends an article of food by international mail to the United States (see § 1.276(b)(12) of the prior notice interim final rule). In another example, when an individual purchases food at Store A and sends that food to an individual by mail, the individual is the shipper and the carrier is the mail service. If the individual uses an express courier, the result is the same: the individual is the shipper and the express courier is the carrier. However, if Store A ships the food, Store A is the shipper. Since Store A is not an individual, this last example is not covered by the policy described above because the food was not imported or offered for import with a non-commercial shipper. (While a 'person' sometimes can be an individual, partnership, corporation, or association, see 21 U.S.C. 321 (e), by 'individual' we mean a sole human being, not a partnership, corporation, or association.)

4. *Food arriving by international mail that is **not** food imported or offered for import for non-commercial purposes with a non-commercial shipper*
   In general, the action FDA and CBP staff typically should consider taking is education/communication for minor or inadvertent prior notice violations and refusal for all other prior notice violations.

   Manufacturer. Table 1 lists the prior notice requirements for providing information about the identity of the manufacturer for an article of food that is no longer in its natural state, If there is a prior notice violation because this information is not provided, FDA and CBP should typically consider not taking any regulatory action under the circumstances described in the first column of Table 2 if the information in the second column of that table is provided.

5. *Gift Pack purchased or otherwise acquired by an individual and imported or offered for import for non-business purposes*
FDA and CBP staff should typically consider not taking regulatory action if there is a prior notice violation because a single prior notice is submitted for a gift pack and the identity of the facility that packed the gift pack is submitted in lieu of the identity of the manufacturer, provided that the ,gift pack is purchased or otherwise acquired by an individual and imported or offered for import for non-business purposes. The person submitting the prior notice should provide the appropriate reason code, selected from among those provided in the Prior Notice System Interface (PNSI) and the Automated Broker Interface of the Automated Commercial System (ABI/ACS) (see Appendix 1).
Food is considered to be for non-business purposes when it is not for sale, resale, barter, business use, or commercial use. The policy described in this section applies irrespective of where the individual who purchased or otherwise acquired the gift pack lives and irrespective of the type of carrier. While the policy also applies irrespective of whether it involves a commercial or non-commercial shipper, please note that the guidance contained in section C.3 of this CPG applies to gift packs, and other foods, that are imported or offered for import for noncommercial purposes with a non-commercial shipper. More information about non-commercial purposes, the difference between shippers and carriers, and the difference between commercial and non-commercial shippers is contained in section C.3 of this CPG.
For the purpose of this CPG, gift packs are considered to be food that is described with FDA Product Code 37Y–01 (human food) or FDA Product Code 72B–99 (animal food). Examples of gift packs that may be covered are:
   - A gift basket containing fresh fruit and/or vegetables.
   - A gift box containing crackers and cheeses and canned condensed soups.
   - A gift basket of crackers, cheeses and fresh fruit.
   - A wicker basket with champagne, port, scotch whisky, smoked salmon, cheese, tea, coffee, chutney, pistachio nuts, biscuits, marmalade, honey, butter biscuits, crackers, cake, mustard; olive oil, and olives.
   - Tote bag with infant clothing, bib, booties, and coffee and candy for the parents; or a toy dispenser with hard candy and powdered candy.
   - A gift bag with multiple pet food items such as rawhide chews and dog biscuits, with or without non-food items.
6. *Food imported or offered for import for quality assurance, research or analysis purposes only, not for human or animal consumption or resale*
If the article of food is imported or offered for import for quality assurance, research or analysis purposes only, not for human or animal consumption and not for resale, then FDA and CBP should follow the enforcement

policies described in section C.1 of this CPG. Please note that with respect to item 1 of Table 2, there is a specific reason code for samples of food that are imported or offered for import for quality assurance, research or analysis purposes (see Appendix 1). This reason code should be used when it is applicable.

For the purpose of this CPG, samples of food are considered to be imported or offered for import for quality assurance, research or analysis purposes when they are imported in small quantities (i.e., quantities consistent with the quality assurance, research, or analysis purposes) and the entire sample is used up by the analysis or is destroyed after analysis or a reasonable retention period after analysis. The analysis may include sensory analysis or evaluations such as those organoleptic analyses for testing the quality of tea or for testing for histamines. Evidence that an article of food is imported for quality assurance, research, or analysis purposes only might include, among other evidence, that the food and shipment documents are marked accordingly. The policy in this section does not apply to samples intended for test marketing, such as tasting at trade shows or product promotional tasting events.

Information about when samples are 'food' for the purposes of prior notice is provided in the 2nd Edition of Guidance for Industry, Prior Notice of Imported Food, Questions and Answers, May 2004. This guidance states that, in general, prior notice is required for samples of food, including animal feed, for research and development and test marketing (Q&A, Section C., Question 1.3). However, if the samples are items that are in such early stages of research and development that they cannot yet be considered food for the purposes of prior notice, then they would not be subject to prior notice requirements (Q&A, Section C., Question 1.3). In addition, if the sample is in a form that is not an article of food, such as a slurry of lettuce for pesticide analysis or a sterile sample container filled with juice for heavy metal analysis, then prior notice would not apply (Q&A, Section C., Question 17.2).

7. *Imported Food Arriving From and Exiting To the Same Country* [NEW]
Food that is shipped by land through the United States is subject to the prior notice requirements, 21 CFR 1.277(a), even if it is shipped a short distance and travels from and to the same country. This section describes the specific policy regarding the enforcement of the prior notice requirements in this situation.

The IFR requires that prior notice be submitted electronically through either the Automated Broker Interface of the Automated Commercial System (ABI/ACS) or the Prior Notice System Interface (PNSI). You must submit prior notice through ABI/ACS or PNSI and FDA will consider prior notice inadequate if prior notice is submitted in any other form. However, under the below listed specific circumstances, if the prior notice is submitted by fax instead of through ABI/ACS or PNSI, FDA and CBP may consider not taking regulatory action.

If there is a prior notice violation because the prior notice is submitted by fax instead of through ABI/ACS or PNSI and/or it does not contain the required information about the manufacturer or grower; the carrier's Standard Carrier Abbreviation Code (SCAC), International Air Transportation Association (IATA) code, or name and country of the carrier; the planned shipment information; and/or the FDA product code, FDA and CBP staff should typically consider not taking regulatory action if:

- The food being imported or offered for import is for shipment by land through the United States, and will not be manufactured, processed, packaged, unloaded or transferred from conveyance to conveyance, or modified in any other way while in transit.
- The food is exported to the same country from which it was imported (i.e. Canada-United States-Canada or Mexico-United States-Mexico).
- The importing conveyance is physically sealed before it enters the United States and the integrity of the aforementioned seal is maintained during the time the shipment is in-transit through the United States. FDA and CBP should randomly examine the shipments to ensure that the food imported from the country is the same food that is exported back to that country.
- The food being imported or offered for import represents a relatively regular/routine shipment by land that arrives at and exits from specific border crossings, such that FDA and/or CBP are sufficiently familiar with the typical shipment.
- The number of the regular/routine shipments by land between the two border points is relatively low, e.g. an average of less than one shipment per day.
- The transportation route through the United States is relatively short, e.g. less than 100 miles.
- Due to the geography, the only practical transportation route available for the shipment is through the United States.
- The prior notice is received by FDA at least 36 hours before the food arrives at the port of arrival to provide sufficient time for FDA to receive, review, and respond to the alternative form of prior notice submission.

If a copy of invoice for the food is submitted in lieu of the prior notice submission, it should be legible and in English and the fax cover sheet should provide the remaining information, including the submitter, the anticipated port of arrival, and the anticipated time of arrival.

Please note that if any of the prior notice information, except the anticipated arrival information, the estimated quantity, or the planned shipment information, changes after FDA has confirmed the prior notice submission for review, the prior notice must be resubmitted (21 CFR 1.282(a)). However, the enforcement policy described above, including the amount of time FDA believes it will need to conduct its prior notice review, applies to re-submissions as well as original submissions.

A submitter who is considering submitting an alternative form of prior notice for routine shipments of food that are shipped short distances by land in-transit through the United States should contact the FDA Prior Notice Center at 703-621-7809 before the first alternative submission.

8. *Planned Shipment Information – Harmonized Tariff Schedule code* [NEW]
   FDA and CBP should typically consider not taking regulatory action when there is a prior notice violation because the prior notice submission does not include the 6-digit HTS code for the article of food.

   However, prior notice submitters are reminded that the HTS Code is required by CBP independent of prior notice. *See* 19 CFR 143 Subpart D – Electronic Entry Filing, which sets forth the requirements for electronic filing, and specifically 19 CFR 143.32(f), which references the Customs and Trade Automated Interface Requirements (CATAIR) as the defining document for what data has to be submitted. Therefore, filers should keep in mind that ABI/ACS will not accept a submission that lacks the HTS code.

IV. APPENDIX 1: REASON CODES FOR REGISTRATION NUMBER OF MANUFACTURER NOT PROVIDED

A. Facility is out of business
B. Facility is private residence (21 CFR 1.227(b)(2))
C. Facility is a restaurant (21 CFR 1.226(d); 1.227(b)(10))
D. Facility is retail food establishment (21 CFR 1.226(c); 1.227(b) (11))
E. Facility is non-processing fishing vessel (21 CFR 1.226(f))
F. Facility is non-bottled drinking water collection and distribution establishment (21 CFR 1.227(b)(2))
G. Individual gift – label name/address in lieu of registration number (21 CFR 1.281(a)(6), (b)(5), and (c)(6))
H. Grower – satisfies farm exemption (21 CFR 1.226(b); 1.227(b)(3))
I. Samples – quality assurance, research or analysis purposes only
J. U.S. manufacturing facility that is not required to register
K. Unable to determine the registration number of the manufacturer.
L. Unable to determine identity of manufacturer – providing identity of manufacturer's headquarters
M. Unable to determine identity of manufacturer or headquarters – providing invoicing firm's identity
O. Gift pack for non-business purposes – providing single prior notice and identity of packer.

2. Compliance Policy Guide

Guidance for FDA and CBP Staff

Issued December 2003
Revised June 2004, August 2004, November 2004, March 2005 and November 2005

TABLE OF CONTENTS

Sec. 110.310: Prior Notice of Imported Food Under the Public Health Security and Bioterrorism Preparedness and Response Act of 2002

This Compliance Policy Guide (CPG) is being revised to finalize the previous draft sections, found in section III. C, items 7 and 8; the revised text is indicated as [NEW]. This guidance document represents the Food and Drug Administration's (FDA) and Customs and Border Protection's (CBP) current thinking on this topic. It does not create or confer any rights for or on any person and does not operate to bind FDA, CBP, or the public. An alternative approach may be used if such approach satisfies the requirements of the applicable statute and regulations.

I. INTRODUCTION

The purpose of this document is to provide guidance on FDA's and CBP's strategy for enforcing and otherwise achieving compliance with the requirements of the interim final rule for submitting prior notice for food imported or offered for import into the United States (68 Fed. Reg. 58974 (Oct.10, 2003) (codified at 21 CFR 1.276–1.285)).

FDA's guidance documents, including this Compliance Policy Guide (CPG), do not establish legally enforceable responsibilities. Instead, guidance documents describe the agency's current thinking on a topic and should be viewed only as recommendations, unless specific regulatory or statutory requirements are cited. The use of the word should in agency guidance documents means that something is suggested or recommended, but not required.

II. BACKGROUND

The Public Health Security and Bioterrorism Preparedness and Response Act of 2002 (Bioterrorism Act), section 307, added section 801(m) to the Federal Food, Drug, and Cosmetic Act (the Act) to require that FDA receive prior notice for food imported or offered for import into the United States. Section 801(m) also provides that if an article of food arrives at the port of arrival with inadequate prior notice (e.g., no prior notice, inaccurate prior notice, or untimely prior notice), the food is subject to refusal of admission under section 801(m)(1) of the Act and may not be delivered to the importer, owner, or consignee. If an article of food is refused under section 801(m)(1) of the Act, unless CBP concurrence is obtained for export and the article is immediately exported from the port of arrival under CBP supervision, it must be held within the port of entry for the article unless otherwise directed by CBP or FDA.

The Bioterrorism Act, section 305, also amended Chapter IV of the Act by adding section 415 to require domestic and foreign facilities that manufacture, process, pack, or hold food for consumption in the United States to register with FDA, and amended Chapter VIII of the Act by adding section 801(l) to require any food for human and animal consumption from an unregistered foreign facility that is imported or offered for import to be held at the port of entry until the foreign facility has been registered.

On October 10, 2003, FDA and CBP issued interim final regulations establishing the requirements for registration and requiring that FDA receive prior notice of the importation of food beginning on December 12, 2003 (68 FR 58994 and 68 FR 58974). For the purposes of prior notice, 'food' has the meaning given in section 201(f) of the Act, and is defined as (1) articles of food or drink for man or other animals, (2) chewing gum, and (3) articles used as components of any such article, except that it does not include food contact substances or pesticides. The requirements for prior notice do not apply to:

1. Food for an individual's personal use when it is carried by or otherwise accompanies the individual when arriving in the United States;

2. Food that was made by an individual in his/her personal residence and sent by that individual as a personal gift (i.e., for non-business reasons) to an individual in the United States;
3. Food that is imported then exported without leaving the port of arrival until export;
4. Meat food products that at the time of importation are subject to the exclusive jurisdiction of the U.S. Department of Agriculture (USDA) under the Federal Meat Inspection Act (21 U.S.C. 601 et seq.);
5. Poultry products that at the time of importation are subject to the exclusive jurisdiction of USDA under the Poultry Products Inspection Act (21 U.S.C. 451 et seq.);
6. Egg products that at the time of importation are subject to the exclusive jurisdiction of USDA under the Egg Products Inspection Act (21 U.S.C. 1031 et seq.).
7. Prior notice also is not required under FDA requirements for food brought into the United States in a diplomatic pouch. The Vienna Convention on Diplomatic Relations (1961) provides: 'The diplomatic bag shall not be opened or detained.' Art. 27(3): Any baggage or cargo marked 'diplomatic bag' or 'diplomatic pouch' is immune from search, including by electronic devices, and thus its contents are not subject to FDA's prior notice requirements.

Information required to be submitted in a prior notice includes, with certain exceptions, the registration numbers assigned to the foreign manufacturer's and shipper's facilities that are associated with the article of food. FDA's monitoring of compliance by foreign facilities with the requirement to register under section 415 of the Act will be accomplished primarily through the prior notice review process. If an article of food is from a foreign manufacturer that is not registered as required and is imported or offered for import, then the food is subject to refusal under section 801(m)(1) of the Act for failure to provide adequate prior notice. Likewise, the failure to provide the correct registration number of the relevant foreign manufacturer, if registration is required, renders the identity of that facility incomplete for purposes of prior notice. In addition, if an article of food is imported or offered for import from any foreign facility that is not registered as required, then the food is subject to being held under section 801(l) of the Act.

In the preamble to the interim final rule, FDA stated that it planned to provide guidance to its staff regarding the agency's enforcement policies. Accordingly, this CPG describes general policies regarding the enforcement of the prior notice requirements, including the requirement to provide a required registration number.

The requirements for submitting prior notice to FDA were effective beginning December 12, 2003. During the first eight months following this effective date, FDA and CBP focused their resources on education to achieve compliance with the prior notice requirements. The agencies will continue this education and outreach, including the following:

1. FDA and CBP will distribute information flyers at the ports.
2. FDA and CBP plan to:
   a. Gather data to track compliance with the prior notice requirements and to determine how best to use their resources to educate industry and the public in order to achieve full compliance.
   b. Provide industry and the public with summary information about the level of compliance with the prior notice requirements, including data on the types of errors in submitted prior notices.
   c. Provide the summary information on FDA's website at *www.fda.gov*.
   d. Utilize the data and summary information to assist the industry and the public in improving the submission of prior notice.

FDA may consider the failure to provide adequate prior notice as a factor in determining whether and where to examine an article of food. However, if FDA decides not to refuse an article of food under 21 CFR 1.283 or 1.285, this decision has no bearing on whether the article of food is admissible or will be granted admission under other provisions of the Act or other U.S. laws. Thus, for food that is imported or offered for import, FDA will continue its normal review, investigative, and enforcement activities for food safety and security concerns to determine whether the food is subject to refusal under section 801(a) of the Act. In addition, if FDA decides not to refuse an article of food under 21 CFR 1.283 or 1.285, this decision does not affect FDA's ability to initiate other types of actions – such as seizures, injunctions, prosecutions, or debarments under sections 302, 303, 304, and 306 of the Act – that may be necessary. Likewise, it does not affect CBP's ability to initiate other types of actions that may be necessary.

III. REGULATORY ACTION GUIDANCE

FDA's Prior Notice Review Center, in conjunction with CBP headquarters, should use the information below to make decisions about whether to refuse a shipment of food pursuant to 21 CFR 1.283 or 1.285 or take other actions for violations under sections 801(m) and 415 of the Act.

The following definitions and descriptions apply to this Compliance Policy Guide (CPG).

A. Types of Violations

1. Inadequate Prior Notice
   a. No Prior Notice – The article of food arrives at the port of arrival and no prior notice has been submitted and confirmed by FDA for review.

b. Inaccurate Prior Notice – Prior notice has been submitted and confirmed by FDA for review, but upon review of the notice or examination of the article of food, the prior notice is determined to be inaccurate.
c. Untimely Prior Notice – Prior notice has been submitted and confirmed by FDA for review, but the full time that applies under 21 CFR 1.279 for prior notice has not elapsed when the article arrives, unless FDA has already reviewed the prior notice, determined its response to the prior notice, and advised CBP of that response.

2. Unregistered Facility – The article of food is imported or offered for import from a foreign facility that is not registered as required.
3. No PN Confirmation
   a. When a copy of the Prior Notice (PN) Confirmation is required for food carried by or otherwise accompanying an individual, but cannot be provided by the individual.
   b. When the PN Confirmation Number is not affixed to an article of food that arrives by international mail.
   c. When the PN Confirmation Number for an article of food for which prior notice was submitted through PNSI is not provided to CBP or FDA upon arrival.

B. Actions in Response to Violations

1. Education/Communication – To the extent possible:
   a. Distribute information flyers at the ports to carriers and others associated with the shipment of food.
   b. Provide, to the extent practicable, notice of the violation and of the prior notice and registration requirements to the person(s) who transmits and/or files the prior notice.
   c. When an article of food that is carried by or otherwise accompanying an individual is not for personal use and has inadequate prior notice or the individual cannot provide FDA or CBP with a copy of the prior notice (PN) confirmation, provide the individual with an information sheet on prior notice.
   d. When an article of food arrives by international mail with inadequate prior notice or the PN confirmation number is not affixed, provide an information sheet on prior notice and forward the package to the addressee.
   e. When an article of food is imported or offered for import for non-commercial purposes with a non-commercial shipper as set out below under Section C.4, provide an information sheet on prior notice to the importer, owner, consignee, or shipper.
2. Assessment of CBP Civil Monetary Penalties – CBP, in consultation with FDA, may assess civil monetary penalties for violation of 19 U.S.C.

1595a(b) against any party who aids or abets the importation of any merchandise contrary to law.

3. Refusal – FDA, in consultation with CBP, may refuse admission of an article of food under section 801 (m)(1) of the Act or place it under hold under section 801(l) of the Act for violations under sections 801 (m) and 415 of the Act. If an article of food is refused or placed under hold under these provisions, unless CBP concurrence is obtained for export and the article is immediately exported from the port of arrival under CBP supervision, it must be held within the port of entry for the article unless directed by CBP or FDA (21 CFR 1.283(a) and 1.285(a),(b)). For food that is carried by or otherwise accompanying an individual, and is refused, and if, before leaving the port, the individual does not arrange to have the food held at the port or exported, the article of food shall be destroyed (21 CFR 1.283(b) and 1.285(h)). For food that arrives by international mail and is refused, if there is a return address, the parcel will be returned to sender stamped 'No Prior Notice – FDA Refused.' If there is no return address, or if FDA determines that the article of food in the parcel appears to present a hazard, FDA may dispose of or destroy the parcel (21 CFR 1.283(e) and 1.285(k)).
4. The phrase 'the action FDA and CBP staff typically should consider taking' used in this CPG means that FDA and CBP staff, exercising enforcement discretion pursuant to their agency's policies and procedures, may take these actions or may take different or additional actions if they believe particular circumstances warrant them.

C. Policy

This policy provides guidance to FDA and CBP staff when they encounter the prior notice situations described within this section.

The policy contains several references to Tables 1 and 2, which are set out below.

1. *Shipments of food, other than food covered by another section of this CPG*

   In general, for any prior notice violation, the action FDA and CBP staff typically should consider taking is refusal and/or assessment of CBP Civil Monetary Penalties.

   a. *Manufacturer.* Table 1 lists the prior notice requirements for providing information about the identity of the manufacturer for an article of food that is no longer in its natural state. If there is a prior notice violation because this information is not provided, FDA and CBP should typically consider not taking any regulatory action under the circumstances described in the first column of Table 2 if the information in the second column of that table is provided.

Table 1. Requirements for the Identity of the Manufacturer (see 21 CFR 1.281)

In the Following Circumstances	*Provide the Following Information*
1. Any article of food, when the facility that manufactured the food *is required* to be registered.	Name, Registration Number, City, and Country of the facility that manufactured the food.
2. Any article of food, when the facility that manufactured the food is not required to be registered.	Name, Street Address, City, and Country of the facility that manufactured the food, as well as a reason code identifying this situation and the reason the facility is not required to be registered.
3. An article of food that is for transshipment, storage and export, or further manipulation and export.	Name, Street Address (or Registration Number in lieu of Street Address), City, and Country of the facility that manufactured the food.
4. An article of food that is sent by an individual as a personal gift (i.e., for nonbusiness reasons) to an individual in the United States. Note: Under this circumstance, you should also refer to Section C.3 of this CPG.	Name, Registration Number (or Street Address if the facility is not required to be registered), City, and Country of the facility that manufactured the food or Name and Address of the firm that appears on the label under 21 CFR 101.5.

Table 2. Enforcement Discretion Policy for the Identity of the Manufacturer

If, After a Good Faith Effort, the Person Submitting Prior Notice Does not Know…	*Then the Person Submitting Prior Notice Should Provide…*
1. The Registration Number of the facility that manufactured the food (and the facility *is required* to be registered).	Name, Street Address, City, and Country of the facility that manufactured the food, and a reason code identifying this situation.*

Table 2. (continued)

If, After a Good Faith Effort, the Person Submitting Prior Notice Does not Know…	*Then the Person Submitting Prior Notice Should Provide…*
2. Either the Registration Number or the name and full address of the facility that manufactured the food.	Name, Street Address, City, and Country of the headquarters of the facility that manufactured the food, and a reason code identifying this situation.*
3. The information in items 1 and 2 of this table.	Name, Street Address, City, and Country of the invoicing firm, and a reason code identifying this situation.*

* Notes for Table 2:

- If the facility that manufactured the food is a foreign facility that is required to be registered and either its registration number is not provided or the name and address of a different facility (i.e., the manufacturing facility's headquarters or the invoicing firm) is provided, then it will be more difficult and/or may take more time for FDA and CBP to verify the identity of the manufacturing facility and its registration status and to determine whether the article of food is subject to being held under section 801(l) of the Act. As a result, if an article of food is imported or offered for import with the alternative information provided in Table 2 in lieu of the identity of the facility that manufactured the food, and if FDA has concerns that the food may pose a serious health threat, then the food may be delayed at the port of arrival until the verification is completed.
- As with other types of prior notice violations, FDA may consider the failure to provide required information about the facility that manufactured the food as a factor in determining whether and where to examine the article of food.
- We intend to reject prior notice submissions unless the prior notice includes a valid registration number or an appropriate reason code selected from among those provided in *the Prior Notice System Interface (PNSI)* and *the Automated Broker Interface of the Automated Commercial System (ABI/ACS) (see Appendix 1).* Rejected submissions are not confirmed for FDA review.

b. *Express Courier.* If prior notice is inadequate because it does not include the required anticipated arrival information and/or planned shipment information, FDA and CBP should typically consider not taking any regulatory action if:
   1) The article of food is imported or offered for import via an express courier;
   2) The person submitting prior notice is not the express courier;
   3) The prior notice is submitted via the Prior Notice System Interface (PNSI); and
   4) The prior notice includes the shipment's tracking number in lieu of the required anticipated arrival information and/or planned shipment information.

c. *Time Frame.* FDA and CBP should typically consider not taking any regulatory action if there is a prior notice violation because the prior notice was submitted more than 5 calendar days before the anticipated date of arrival, provided that: (1) the prior notice was submitted less than 10 calendar days before the anticipated date of arrival; and (2) the prior notice was submitted through the Prior Notice System Interface (PNSI). In addition, under the same conditions, FDA should typically provide the Prior Notice Confirmation Number when prior notice has been confirmed for review even if prior notice was submitted more than 5 calendar days before the anticipated date of arrival. Because of the way the Automated Broker Interface of the Automated Commercial System (ABI/ACS) is programmed, when prior notice is submitted through ABI/ACS, the Prior Notice Confirmation Number cannot be provided more than 5 calendar days before the anticipated date of arrival.

Please note that if any of the prior notice information, except the anticipated arrival information, the estimated quantity, or the planned shipment information, changes after FDA has confirmed the prior notice submission for review, the prior notice must be resubmitted (21 CFR 1.282(a)). The resubmission must be confirmed by FDA for review no less than 2, 4, or 8 hours before arriving at the port of arrival, with the minimum time depending on the mode of transportation (21 CFR 1.279(a)). If prior notice is resubmitted, the previous prior notice should be cancelled (21 CFR 1.282(b)).

2. *Food carried by or otherwise accompanying an individual that is not for personal use*
In general, the action FDA and CBP staff typically should consider taking is education/communication for minor or inadvertent prior notice violations and refusal for all other prior notice violations.

Manufacturer. Table 1 lists the prior notice requirements for providing information about the identity of the manufacturer for an article of food that is no longer in its natural state. If there is a prior notice violation due to the fact that this information is not provided, FDA and CBP should typically consider not taking any regulatory action under the circumstances described in the first column of Table 2 if the information in the second column of that table is provided.
3. *Food imported or offered for import for non-commercial purposes with a non-commercial shipper, irrespective of the type of carrier*
FDA and CBP should typically consider not taking any regulatory action when an article of food is imported or offered for import for non-commercial purposes with a non-commercial shipper. Generally, staff should consider a non-commercial purpose to be when the food is purchased or otherwise acquired by an individual for non-business purposes and the shipper is an individual (e.g., the individual delivers the food to a post

office or common carrier for delivery to self, family member, or friend for non-business purposes, i.e., not for sale, resale, barter, business use, or commercial use.)

Examples of foods imported or offered for import that may be covered by this non-commercial category are:

- food in household goods, including military, civilian, governmental agency, and diplomatic transfers;
- food purchased by a traveler and mailed or shipped to the traveler's U.S. address by the traveler, not the commercial establishment; and
- gifts purchased at a commercial establishment and shipped by the purchaser, not the commercial establishment.

Note that the shipper and the carrier are different entities, and the carrier is likely to be a commercial entity even when the shipper is an individual. Thus, the food for non-commercial purposes may arrive by international mail or any other mode of transportation, but must be shipped by one individual to another individual (self, family member, or friend) to be considered for non-commercial purposes. For example, when an individual ships his or her own household goods, even when the goods are delivered to a mover or carrier for international movement, the individual is the shipper, e.g., the owner or exporter of the article of food who consigns and ships the article from a foreign country or the person who sends an article of food by international mail to the United States (see § 1.276(b)(12) of the prior notice interim final rule). In another example, when an individual purchases food at Store A and sends that food to an individual by mail, the individual is the shipper and the carrier is the mail service. If the individual uses an express courier, the result is the same: the individual is the shipper and the express courier is the carrier. However, if Store A ships the food, Store A is the shipper. Since Store A is not an individual, this last example is not covered by the policy described above because the food was not imported or offered for import with a non-commercial shipper. (While a 'person' sometimes can be an individual, partnership, corporation, or association, see 21 U.S.C. 321(e), by 'individual' we mean a sole human being, not a partnership, corporation, or association.)

4. *Food arriving by international mail that is **not** food imported or offered for import for non-commercial purposes with a non-commercial shipper*
In general, the action FDA and CBP staff typically should consider taking is education/communication for minor or inadvertent prior notice violations and refusal for all other prior notice violations.

Manufacturer. Table 1 lists the prior notice requirements for providing information about the identity of the manufacturer for an article of food that is no longer in its natural state. If there is a prior notice violation because this information is not provided, FDA and CBP should typically consider not taking any regulatory action under the circumstances described in the first column of Table 2 if the information in the second column of that table is provided.

5. *Gift Pack purchased or otherwise acquired by an individual and imported or offered for import for non-business purposes*
   FDA and CBP staff should typically consider not taking regulatory action if there is a prior notice violation because a single prior notice is submitted for a gift pack and the identity of the facility that packed the gift pack is submitted in lieu of the identity of the manufacturer, provided that the gift pack is purchased or otherwise acquired by an individual and imported or offered for import for non-business purposes. The person submitting the prior notice should provide the appropriate reason code, selected from among those provided in the Prior Notice System Interface (PNSI) and the Automated Broker Interface of the Automated Commercial System (ABI/ACS) (see Appendix 1).

   Food is considered to be for non-business purposes when it is not for sale, resale, barter, business use, or commercial use. The policy described in this section applies irrespective of where the individual who purchased or otherwise acquired the gift pack lives and irrespective of the type of carrier. While the policy also applies irrespective of whether it involves a commercial or non-commercial shipper, please note that the guidance contained in section C.3 of this CPG applies to gift packs, and other foods, that are imported or offered for import for non-commercial purposes with a non-commercial shipper. More information about non-commercial purposes, the difference between shippers and carriers, and the difference between commercial and non-commercial shippers is contained in section C.3 of this CPG.

   For the purpose of this CPG, gift packs are considered to be food that is described with FDA Product Code 37Y–01 (human food) or FDA Product Code 72E–99 (animal food). Examples of gift packs that may be covered are:
   - A gift basket containing fresh fruit and/or vegetables.
   - A gift box containing crackers and cheeses and canned condensed soups.
   - A gift basket of crackers, cheeses and fresh fruit.
   - A wicker basket with champagne, port, scotch whisky, smoked salmon, cheese, tea, coffee, chutney, pistachio nuts, biscuits, marmalade, honey, butter biscuits, crackers, cake, mustard, olive oil, and olives.
   - Tote bag with infant clothing, bib, booties, and coffee and candy for the parents; or a toy dispenser with hard candy and powdered candy.
   - A gift bag with multiple pet food items such as rawhide chews and dog biscuits, with or without non-food items.
6. *Food imported or offered for import for quality assurance, research or analysis purposes only, not for human or animal consumption or resale*
   If the article of food is imported or offered for import for quality assurance, research or analysis purposes only, not for human or animal consumption and not for resale, then FDA and CBP should follow the

enforcement policies described in section C.1. of this CPG. Please note that with respect to item 1 of Table 2, there is a specific reason code for samples of food that are imported or offered for import for quality assurance, research or analysis purposes (see Appendix 1). This reason code should be used when it is applicable.

For the purpose of this CPG, samples of food are considered to be imported or offered for import for quality assurance, research or analysis purposes when they are imported in small quantities (i.e., quantities consistent with the quality assurance, research, or analysis purposes) and the entire sample is used up by the analysis or is destroyed after analysis or a reasonable retention period after analysis. The analysis may include sensory analysis or evaluations such as those organoleptic analyses for testing the quality of tea or for testing for histamines. Evidence that an article of food is imported for quality assurance, research, or analysis purposes only might include, among other evidence, that the food and shipment documents are marked accordingly. The policy in this section does not apply to samples intended for test marketing, such as tasting at trade shows or product promotional tasting events.

Information about when samples are 'food' for the purposes of prior notice is provided in the 2nd Edition of Guidance for Industry, Prior Notice of Imported Food, Questions and Answers, May 2004. This guidance states that, in general, prior notice is required for samples of food, including animal feed, for research and development and test marketing (Q&A, Section C., Question 1.3). However, if the samples are items that are in such early stages of research and development that they cannot yet be considered food for the purposes of prior notice, then they would not be subject to prior notice requirements (Q&A, Section C., Question 1.3). In addition, if the sample is in a form that is not an article of food, such as a slurry of lettuce for pesticide analysis or a sterile sample container filled with juice for heavy metal analysis, then prior notice would not apply (Q&A, Section C., Question 17.2).

7. *Imported Food Arriving From and Exiting To the Same Country* [NEW] Food that is shipped by land through the United States is subject to the prior notice requirements, 21 CFR 1.277(a), even if it is shipped a short distance and travels from and to the same country. This section describes the specific policy regarding the enforcement of the prior notice requirements in this situation.

   FDA and CBP staff should typically consider not taking regulatory action if there is no prior notice and each of the following conditions is met:

   – The food is exported to the same country from which it was imported (i.e. Canada-United States-Canada or Mexico-United States-Mexico).
   – Due to the geography, the only practical transportation route available for the shipment is through the United States.

- The importing conveyance is physically sealed before it enters the United States and the integrity of the aforementioned seal is maintained during the time the shipment is in-transit through the United States. FDA and CBP should randomly examine the shipments to ensure that the food imported from the country is the same food that is exported back to that country.
- The food being imported or offered for import is for shipment by land through the United States, and will not be manufactured, processed, packaged, unloaded or transferred from conveyance to conveyance, or modified in any other way while in transit.
- The food being imported or offered for import represents a relatively regular/routine shipment by land that arrives at and exits from specific border crossings, such that FDA and/or CBP are sufficiently familiar with the typical shipment.
- The number of the regular/routine shipments by land between the two border points is relatively low, e.g., an average of one or less shipments per day.
- The transportation route through the United States is relatively short, e.g., less than 100 miles.
- Before the import or series of imports, the FDA Prior Notice Center is contacted regarding the above. The public can contact the Prior Notice Center at 866-521-2297.

8. *Planned Shipment Information – Harmonized Tariff Schedule code*

   FDA and CBP should typically consider not taking regulatory action when there is a prior notice violation because the prior notice submission does not include the 6-digit HTS code for the article of food.

   However, prior notice submitters are reminded that the HTS Code is required by CBP independent of prior notice. See 19 CFR 143 Subpart D – Electronic Entry Filing, which sets forth the requirements for electronic filing, and specifically 19 CFR 143.32(f), which references the Customs and Trade Automated Interface Requirements (CATAIR) as the defining document for what data has to be submitted. Therefore, filers should keep in mind that ABI/ACS will not accept a submission that lacks the HTS code.

IV. APPENDIX 1: REASON CODES FOR REGISTRATION NUMBER OF MANUFACTURER NOT PROVIDED

A. Facility is out of business
B. Facility is private residence (21 CFR 1.227(b)(2))
C. Facility is a restaurant (21 CFR 1.226(d); 1.227(b)(10))
D. Facility is retail food establishment (21 CFR 1.226(c); 1.227(b)(11))
E. Facility is non-processing fishing vessel (21 CFR 1.226(f))

F. Facility is non-bottled drinking water collection and distribution establishment (21 CFR 1.227(b)(2))
G. Individual gift – label name/address in lieu of registration number (21 CFR 1.281(a)(6), (b)(5), and (c)(6))
H. Grower – satisfies farm exemption (21 CFR 1.226(b); 1.227(b)(3))
I. Samples – quality assurance, research or analysis purposes only
J. U.S. manufacturing facility that is not required to register
K. Unable to determine the registration number of the manufacturer
L. Unable to determine identity of manufacturer – providing identity of manufacturer's headquarters
M. Unable to determine identity of manufacturer or headquarters – providing invoicing firm's identity
N. Gift pack for non-business purposes – providing single prior notice and identity of packer

3. Part 318 – Food Safety and Inspection Service, USDA – Entry into Official Establishments; Reinspection and Preparation of Products

Subpart A–General

Sec.

318.1	Products and other articles entering official establishments.
318.2	Reinspection, retention, and disposal of meat and poultry products at official establishments.
318.3	Designation of places of receipt of products and other articles for reinspection.
318.4	Preparation of products to be officially supervised; responsibilities of official establishments; plant operated quality control.
318.5	Requirements concerning procedures.
318.6	Requirements concerning ingredients and other articles used in preparation of products.
318.8	Preservatives and other substances permitted in product for export only; handling; such product not to be used for domestic food purposes.
318.9	Samples of products, water, dyes, chemicals, etc., to be taken for examination.
318.10	Prescribed treatment of pork and products containing pork to destroy trichinae.
318.11	[Reserved]

318.12 Manufacture of dog food or similar uninspected article at official establishments.
318.13 Mixtures containing product but not amendable to the Act.
318.14 Adulteration of product by polluted water; procedure for handling.
318.15 Tagging chemicals, preservatives, cereals, spices, etc., 'U.S. retained.'
318.16 Pesticide chemicals and other residues in products.
318.17 Requirements for the production of cooked beef, roast beef, and cooked corned beef products.
318.18 Handling of certain material for mechanical processing.
318.19 Compliance procedure for cured pork products.
318.20 Use of animal drugs.
318.21 Accreditation of chemistry laboratories.
318.22 Determination of added water in cooked sausages.
318.23 Heat-processing and stabilization requirements for uncured meat patties.
318.24 Product prepared using advanced meat/bone separation machinery; process control.

Subparts B–F [Reserved]

Subpart G–Canning and Canned Products

318.300 Definitions.
318.301 Containers and closures.
318.302 Thermal processing.
318.303 Critical factors and the application of the process schedule.
318.304 Operations in the thermal processing area.
318.305 Equipment and procedures for heat processing systems.
318.306 Processing and production records.
318.307 Record review and maintenance.
318.308 Deviations in processing.
318.309 Finished product inspection.
318.310 Personnel and training.
318.311 Recall procedure.

AUTHORITY: 7 U.S.C. 138f, 450, 1901–1906; 21 U.S.C. 601–695; 7 CFR 2.18, 2.53.

SUBPART A – GENERAL

SOURCE: 35 FR 15586, Oct. 3, 1970, unless otherwise noted.

§ 318.1 Products and other Articles Entering Official Establishments

(a) Except as otherwise provided in paragraphs (g) and (h) of this section or § 318.12, no product shall be brought into an official establishment unless it has been prepared only in an official establishment and previously inspected and passed by a Program employee, and is identified by an official inspection legend as so inspected and passed. Notwithstanding the foregoing provisions of this subparagraph, product imported in accordance with part 327 of this subchapter and not prepared in the United States outside an official establishment, may enter any official establishment subject in other respects to the same restrictions as apply to domestic product. Products received in an official establishment during the Program employees absence shall be identified and maintained in a manner acceptable to such employee. Product entering any official establishment shall not be used or prepared thereat until it has been reinspected in accordance with § 318.2. Any product originally prepared at any official establishment may not be returned into any part of such establishment, except the receiving area approved under § 318.3, until it has been reinspected by the inspector.
(b) No slaughtered poultry or poultry product shall be brought into an official establishment unless it has been (1) previously inspected and passed and is identified as such in accordance with the requirements of the Poultry Products Inspection Act (21 U.S.C. 451 et seq.) and the regulations thereunder, and has not been prepared other than in an establishment inspected under said Act, or (2) has been inspected and passed and is identified as such in accordance with the requirements of a State law.

(c) Every article for use as an ingredient in the preparation of meat food products, when entering any official establishment and at all times while it is in such establishment, shall bear a label showing the name of the article, the amount or percentage therein of any substances restricted by this part or part 317 of this subchapter, and a list of ingredients in the article if composed of two or more ingredients: *Provided,* That in the case of articles received in tank car lots, only one such label shall be used to identify each lot. In addition, the label must show the name and address of the shipper.

(d) To ensure the safe use of preparations used in hog scalding water or in the denuding of tripe, the label or labeling on containers of such preparations shall bear adequate directions to ensure use in compliance with any limitations prescribed in 21 CFR Chapter I, Subchapter A or Subchapter B, or 9 CFR Chapter III, Subchapter A or Subchapter E.

(e) Dyes, chemicals, or other substances the use of which is restricted to certain products may be brought into or kept in an official establishment only if such products are prepared thereat. No prohibited dye, chemical, preservative, or other substance shall be brought into or kept in an official establishment.

(f) [Reserved]

(g) Glands and organs, such as cotyledons, ovaries, prostate glands, tonsils, spinal cords, and detached lymphatic, pineal, pituitary, parathyroid, suprarenal, pancreatic and thyroid glands, used in preparing pharmaceutical, organotherapeutic, or technical products and which are not used as human food (whether or not prepared at official establishments) may be brought into and stored in edible product departments of inspected establishments if packaged in suitable containers so that the presence of such glands and organ will in no way interfere with the maintenance of sanitary conditions or constitute an interference with inspection. Glands or organs which are regarded as human food products, such as livers, testicles, and thymus glands, may be brought into official establishments for pharmaceutical, organotherapeutic or technical purposes, only if U.S. inspected and passed and so identified. Lungs and lung lobes derived from livestock slaughtered in any establishment may not be brought into any official establishment except as provided in §318.12(a).

(h)(1) Carcasses of game animals, and carcasses derived from the slaughter by any person of livestock of his own raising in accordance with the exemption provisions of paragraph 23(a) of the Act, and parts of such carcasses, may be brought into an official establishment for preparation, packaging, and storing in accordance with the provisions of § 303.1(a)(2) of this subchapter.

(2) Meat, meat byproducts, and meat food products bearing official marks showing that they were inspected and passed under State inspection in any State not designated in § 331.2 of this subchapter may be received by official establishments for storage and distribution solely in intrastate commerce. The presence of such State inspected products must not create any unsanitary condition or otherwise result in adulteration of any products at the official establishment or interfere with the conduct of inspection under this subchapter. In addition, such State inspected products must be stored separately and apart from the federally inspected products in the official establishment.

(i) The operator of the official establishment shall furnish such information as is necessary to determine the origin of any product or other article entering the official establishment. Such information shall include, but is not limited to, the name and address of the seller or supplier, transportation company, agent, or broker involved in the sale or delivery of the product or article in question.

(j) Any product or any poultry or poultry product or other article that is brought into an official establishment contrary to any provision of this section may be required by the Administrator to be removed immediately from such establishment by the operator thereof, and failure to comply with such requirement shall be deemed a violation of this regulation. If any slaughtered poultry or poultry products or other articles are received at an official establishment and are suspected of being adulterated or misbranded under the Poultry Products Inspection Act or the Federal Food, Drug, and Cosmetic Act, or applicable State laws, the appropriate governmental authorities will be notified.

[35 FR 15586, Oct. 3, 1970, as amended at 36 FR 11639, June 17, 1971; 38 FR 5152, Feb. 26, 1973; 48 FR 6091, Feb. 10, 1983; 49 FR 32055, Aug. 10, 1984; 64 FR 72174, Dec. 23, 1999]

§ 318.2 REINSPECTION, RETENTION, AND DISPOSAL OF MEAT AND POULTRY PRODUCTS AT OFFICIAL ESTABLISHMENTS

(a) All products and all slaughtered poultry and poultry products brought into any official establishment shall be identified by the operator of the official establishment at the time of receipt at the official establishment and shall be subject to reinspection by a Program employee at the official establishment in such manner and at such times as may be deemed necessary to assure compliance with the regulations in this subchapter.

(b) All products, whether fresh, cured, or otherwise prepared, even though previously inspected and passed, shall be reinspected by Program employees as often as they may deem necessary in order to ascertain that they are not adulterated or misbranded at the time they enter or leave official establishments and that the requirements of the regulations in this subchapter are complied with.

(c) Reinspection may be accomplished through use of statistically sound sampling plans that assure a high level of confidence. The circuit supervisor shall designate the type of plan and the program employee shall select the specific plan to be used in accordance with instructions issued by the Administrator.[1]

(d) A U.S. retained tag shall be placed by a Program employee at the time of reinspection at any official establishment on all products which are suspected on such reinspection of being adulterated or misbranded, and such products shall be held for further inspection. Such tags shall be removed only by authorized Program employees. When further inspection is made, if the product is found to be adulterated, all official inspection legends or other official marks for which the product is found to be ineligible under the regulations in this subchapter, shall be removed or defaced and the product will be subject to condemnation and disposal in accordance with part 314 of this subchapter, except that a determination regarding adulteration may be deferred if a product has become soiled or unclean by falling on the floor or in any other accidental way or if the product is affected with any other condition which the inspector deems capable of correction, in which case the product shall be cleaned (including trimming if necessary) or otherwise handled in a manner approved by the inspector to assure that it will not be adulterated or misbranded and shall then be presented for reinspection and disposal in accordance with this section. If upon final inspection, the product is found to be neither adulterated nor misbranded, the inspector shall remove the U.S. retained tag. If a product is found upon reinspection to be misbranded, it shall be held under a U.S. retained tag, or a U.S. detention tag as provided in part 329 of this subchapter, pending correction of the misbranding or issuance of an order under section 7 of the Act to withhold from use the labeling or container of the product, or the institution of a judicial seizure action under section 403 of Act or other appropriate action. The inspector shall make a complete record of each transaction under this paragraph and shall report his action to the area supervisor.

---

1 Further information concerning sampling plans which have been adopted for specific products may be obtained from the Circuit Supervisors of Program circuits. These sampling plans are developed for individual products by the Washington staff and will be distributed for field use as they are developed. The type of plan applicable depends on factors such as whether the product is in containers, stage of preparation, and procedures followed by the establishment operator. The specific plan applicable depends on the kind of product involved, such as liver, oxtails, etc.

§ 318.3 Designation of Places of Receiptof Products and Other Articles for Reinspection

Every official establishment shall designate, with the approval of the circuit supervisor, a dock or place at which products and other articles subject to reinspection under § 318.2 shall be received, and such products and articles shall be received only at such dock or place.

[35 FR 15586, Oct. 3, 1970; 36 FR 11903, June 23, 1971]

§ 318.4 Preparation of Products to be Officially Supervised; Responsibilities of Official Establishments; Plant Operated Quality Control

(a) All processes used in curing, pickling, rendering, canning, or otherwise preparing any product in official establishments shall be supervised by Program employees unless such preparation is conducted as a custom operation exempted from inspection under § 303.1(a)(2) of this subchapter in any official establishment or consists of operations that are exempted from inspection under § 303.1(d) of this subchapter and are conducted in a retail store in an establishment subject to inspection only because the State or Territory in which the establishment is located is designated under paragraph 301(c) of the Act. No fixtures or appliances, such as tables, trucks, trays, tanks, vats, machines, implements, cans, or containers of any kind, shall be used unless they are of such materials and construction as will not contaminate or otherwise adulterate the product and are clean and sanitary. All steps in the preparation of edible products shall be conducted carefully and with strict cleanliness in rooms or compartments separate from those used for inedible products.

(b) It shall be the responsibility of the operator of every official establishment to comply with the Act and the regulations in this subchapter. In order to carry out this responsibility effectively, the operator of the establishment shall institute appropriate measures to assure the maintenance of the establishment and the preparation, marking, labeling, packaging and other handling of its products strictly in accordance with the sanitary and other requirements of this subchapter. The effectiveness of such measures will be subject to review by the Department.

(c) *Applying for Total Plant Quality Control.* Any owner or operator of an official establishment preparing meat food product who has a total plant quality control system or plan for controlling such product, after antemortem and postmortem inspection, through all stages of preparation, may request the Administrator to evaluate it to determine whether or not that system is adequate to result in product being in compliance with the requirements of the Act and therefore qualify as a

U.S. Department of Agriculture (USDA) Total Plant Quality Control Establishment. Such a request shall, as a minimum, include:

(1) A letter to the Administrator from the establishment owner of operator stating the company's basis and purpose for seeking an approved quality control system and willingness to adhere to the requirements of the system as approved by the Department; that all the establishment's data, analyses, and information generated by its quality control system will be maintained to enable the Department to monitor compliance and available to Department personnel; that plant quality control personnel will have authority to halt production or shipping of product in cases where the submitted quality control system requires it; and that the owner or operator (or his/her designee) will be available for consultation at any time Department personnel consider it necessary.

(2) In the case of an establishment having one or more fulltime persons whose primary duties are related to the quality control system, an organizational chart showing that such people ultimately report to an establishment official whose quality control responsibilities are independent of or not predominantly production responsibilities. In the case of an establishment which does not have fulltime quality control personnel, information indicating the nature of the duties and responsibilities of the person who will be responsible for the quality control system.

(3) A list identifying those parts and sections of the Federal meat inspection regulations which are applicable to the operations of the establishment applying for approval of a quality control system. This list shall also identify which part of the quality control system will serve to maintain compliance with the applicable regulations.

(4) Detailed information concerning the manner in which the system will function. Such information should include, but not necessarily be limited to, questions of raw material control, the critical check or control points, the nature and frequency of tests to be made, the nature of charts and other records that will be used, the length of time such charts and records will be maintained in the custody of the official establishment, the nature of deficiencies the quality control system is designed to identify and control, the parameters or limits which will be used, and the points at which corrective action will occur and the nature of such corrective action – ranging from least to most severe: *Provided,* That, subsequent to approval of the total plant quality control system by the Administrator, the official establishment may produce a new product for test marketing provided labeling for the product has been approved by the Administrator, the inspector in charge has determined that the procedures for preparing the product will assure that all Federal requirements are met, and the production for test marketing does not exceed 6 months. Such new product shall not be produced at that establishment after the 6-month period unless approval of the quality control system for that product has been received from the Administrator.

(d) [Reserved]

(e) *Evaluation and Approval of Total Plant Quality Control.* (1) The Administrator shall evaluate the material presented in accordance with the provisions of paragraph (c) of this section. If it is determined by the Administrator, on the basis of the evaluation, that the total quality control system will result in finished products controlled in this manner being in full compliance with the requirements of the Act and regulations thereunder, the total quality control system will be approved and plans will be made for implementation under departmental supervision.

(2) In any situation where the system is found by the Administrator to be unacceptable, formal notification shall be given to the applicant of the basis for the denial. The applicant will be afforded an opportunity to modify the system in accordance with the notification. The applicant shall also be afforded an opportunity to submit a written statement in response to this notification of denial and a right to request a hearing with respect to the merits or validity of the denial. If the applicant requests a hearing and the Administrator, after review of the answer, determines the initial determination to be correct, he shall file with the Hearing Clerk of the Department the notification, answer and the request for hearing, which shall constitute the complaint and answer in the proceeding, which shall thereafter be conducted in accordance with Rules of Practice which shall be adopted for this proceeding.

(3) The establishment owner or operator shall be responsible for the effective operation of the approved total plant quality control system to assure compliance with the requirements of the Act and regulations thereunder. The Secretary shall continue to provide the Federal inspection necessary to carry out his responsibilities under the Act.

(f) *Labeling Logo.* Owners and operators of official establishments having a total plant quality control system approved under the provisions of paragraph (c) of this section, may only use, as a part of any labeling, the following logo. Any

labeling bearing the logo and any wording of explanation with respect to this logo shall be approved as required by parts 316 and 317 of this subchapter.

(g) *Termination of Total Plant Quality Control.* (1) The approval of a total plant quality control system may be terminated at any time by the owner or operator of the official establishment upon written notice to the Administrator.

(2) The approval of a total plant quality control system may be terminated upon the establishment's receipt of a written notice from the Administrator under the following conditions:

(i) If adulterated or misbranded meat food product is found by the Administrator to have been prepared for or distributed in commerce by the subject establishment. In such case, opportunity will be provided to the establishment owner or operator to present views to the Administrator within 30 days of the date of terminating the approval. In those instances where there is conflict of facts, a hearing, under applicable Rules of Practice, will be provided to the establishment owner or operator to resolve the conflict. The Administrator's termination of approval shall remain in effect pending the final determination of the proceeding.

(ii) If the establishment fails to comply with the quality control system or program to which it has agreed after being notified by letter from the Administrator or his designee. Prior to such termination, opportunity will be provided to the establishment owner or operator to present views to the Administrator within 30 days of the date of the letter. In those instances where there is a conflict of facts, a hearing, under applicable Rules of Practice, will be provided to the establishment owner or operator to resolve the conflict. The Administrator's termination of quality control approval shall remain in effect pending the final determination of the proceeding.

(3) If approval of the total establishment quality control system has been terminated in accordance with the provisions of this section, an application and request for approval of the same or a modified total establishment quality control system will not be evaluated by the Administrator for at least 6 months from the termination date.

(h)(1) *Operating Schedule Under Total Plant Quality Control.* An official establishment with an approved total plant quality control system may request approval for an operating schedule of up to 12 consecutive hours per shift. Permission will be granted provided that:

(i) The official establishment has satisfactorily operated under a total plant quality control system for at least 1 year.

(ii) All products prepared and packaged, or processed after the end of 8 hours of inspection shall only be a continuation of the processing monitored by the inspector and being conducted during the last hour of inspection.

(iii) All immediate containers of products prepared and packaged shall bear code marks that are unique to any period of production beyond the 8 hours of inspection. The form of such code marks will remain constant from day to day, and a facsimile of the code marks and their meaning shall be provided to the inspector.

(2) *Application.* Applications shall be submitted to the Regional Director and shall specify how the conditions in § 318.4(h)(1) have been or will be met.

(3) *Monitoring by Inspectors.* In order to verify that an establishment is preparing and shipping product in accordance with the approved total plant quality control system and the Act and regulations after the 8 hours of inspection, the official establishment may be provided overtime inspection services at the discretion of the circuit supervisor and charged for such services.

(Reporting requirements were approved by the Office of Management and Budget under control number 0583–0015)

[35 FR 15586, Oct. 3, 1970, as amended at 36 FR 12003, June 24, 1971; 45 FR 54322, Aug. 15, 1980; 51 FR 32304, Sept. 11, 1986; 62 FR 45024, Aug. 25, 1997; 62 FR 54759, Oct. 22, 1997; 65 FR 34389, May 30, 2000]

§ 318.5 Requirements Concerning Procedures

(a)(1) Care shall be taken to assure that product is not adulterated when placed in freezers. If there is doubt as to the soundness of any frozen product, the inspector will require the defrosting and reinspection of a sufficient quantity thereof to determine its actual condition.

(2) Frozen product may be defrosted in water or pickle in a manner and with the use of facilities which are acceptable to the inspector. Before such product is defrosted, a careful examination shall be made to determine its condition. If necessary, this examination shall include defrosting of representative samples by means other than in water or pickle.

(b) Product, such as pork tenderloins, brains, sweetbreads, stew, or chop suey, shall not be packed in hermetically sealed metal or glass containers, unless subsequently heat processed or otherwise treated to preserve the product in a manner approved by the Administrator in specific cases.

(c) Care shall be taken to remove bones and parts of bones from product which is intended for chopping.

(d) Heads for use in the preparation of meat food products shall be split and the bodies of the teeth, the turbinated and ethmoid bones, ear tubes, and horn butts removed, and the heads then thoroughly cleaned.

(e) Kidneys for use in the preparation of meat food products shall first be freely sectioned and then thoroughly soaked and washed. All detached kidneys, including beef kidneys with detached kidney fat, shall be inspected before being used in or shipped from the official establishment.

(f) Cattle paunches and hog stomachs for use in the preparation of meat food products shall be thoroughly cleaned on all surfaces and parts immediately after being emptied of their contents, which shall follow promptly their removal from the carcasses.

(g) Clotted blood shall be removed from hog hearts before they are shipped from the official establishment or used in the preparation of meat food products.

(h) Beef rounds, beef bungs, beef middles, beef bladders, calf rounds, hog bungs, hog middles, and hog stomachs which are to be used as containers of any meat food product shall be presented for inspection, turned with the fat surface exposed.

(i) Portions of casings which show infection with Oesophagostomum or other noduleproducing parasite, and weasands infected with the larvae of Hypoderma lineatum, shall be rejected, except that when the infestation is slight and the nodules and larvae are removed, the casing or weasand may be passed.

[35 FR 15586, Oct. 3, 1970; 36 FR 11903, June 23, 1971]

§ 318.6 Requirements Concerning Ingredients and Other Articles used in Preparation of Products

(a) All ingredients and other articles used in the preparation of any product shall be clean, sound, healthful, wholesome, and otherwise such as will not result in the product being adulterated. Official establishments shall furnish inspectors accurate information on all procedures involved in product preparation including product composition and any changes in such procedures essential for inspectional control of the product.

(b)(1) The only animal casings that may be used as containers of product are those from sheep, swine, or goats. Casings from cattle may be used as containers of products. However, if casings from cattle are derived from the small intestine, the small intestine must comply with the requirements in 9 CFR 310.22(a)(3). Establishments that use casings derived from the small intestine of cattle as containers for products must demonstrate, through documentation, that the small intestine from which the casing was derived complies with the requirements in 9 CFR 310.22(a)(3).

(2) Casings for products shall be carefully inspected by Program employees. Only those casings which have been carefully washed and thoroughly flushed with clean water immediately before stuffing and are suitable for containers, are clean, and are passed on such inspection shall be used, except that preflushed animal casings packed in salt or salt and glycerine solution or other approved medium may be used without additional flushing provided they are found to be clean and otherwise acceptable and are thoroughly rinsed before use.

(3) Hog and sheep casings intended for use as containers of product may be treated by soaking in or applying thereto sound, fresh pineapple juice or papain or bromelin or pancreatic extract to permit the enzymes contained in these substances to act on the casings to make them less resistant. The casings shall be handled in a clean and sanitary manner throughout and the treatment shall be followed by washing and flushing the casings with water sufficiently to effectively remove the substance used and terminate the enzymatic action.

(4) On account of the invariable presence of bone splinters, detached spinal cords shall not be used in the preparation of edible product other than for rendering

where they constitute a suitable raw material. Detached spinal cords from cattle 30 months of age and older shall not be used as raw materials for edible rendering.

(5) Testicles if handled as an edible product may be shipped from the official establishment as such, but they shall not be used as an ingredient of a meat food product.

(6) Tonsils shall be removed and shall not be used as ingredients of meat food products.

(7) Blood from livestock prepared in accordance with § 310.20 of this subchapter may be used as an ingredient of a meat food product for which a standard is prescribed in part 319 of this subchapter, if permitted by such standard, and may be used in any meat food product for which no such standard is prescribed in part 319 of this subchapter if it is a common and usual ingredient of such product.

(8) Intestines shall not be used as ingredients in any meat food product for which a standard is prescribed in part 319 of this subchapter and shall not be used in other products unless the products are labeled in accordance with § 317.8(b)(3) of this subchapter. When small intestine from cattle is used in a meat food product or for edible rendering, it must comply with the requirements in 9 CFR 310.22(a)(3).

(9) Poultry products and egg products (other than shell eggs) which are intended for use as ingredients of meat food products shall be considered acceptable for such use only when identified as having been inspected and passed for wholesomeness by the Department under the regulations in 7 CFR part 59 or 9 CFR part 362 or 381 and when found to be sound and otherwise acceptable when presented for use. Poultry products and egg products (other than shell eggs) which have not been so inspected and passed for wholesomeness shall not be used in the preparation of such meat food products.

(10) Dry milk products which are intended for use as ingredients of meat food products shall be considered acceptable for such use only when produced in a plant approved by the Department under the regulations in 7 CFR part 58, and when found to be sound and otherwise acceptable when presented for use. Dry milk products prepared in a plant not so approved shall not be used in the preparation of such meat food products.

(11) [Reserved]

(12) Ingredients for use in any product may not bear or contain any pesticide chemical or other residues in excess of level permitted in § 318.16.

(13) Use of 'Mechanically Separated (Kind of Poultry),' as defined in § 381.173 of this chapter, in the preparation of meat food products shall accord with § 381.174 and all other applicable provisions of this subchapter.

[35 FR 15586, Oct. 3, 1970, as amended at 38 FR 14368, June 1, 1973; 38 FR 29214, Oct. 23, 1973; 39 FR 1973, Jan. 16, 1974; 41 FR 23702, June 11, 1976; 49 FR 19623, May 9, 1984; 50 FR 6, Jan. 2, 1985; 60 FR 55982, Nov. 3, 1995; 69 FR 1874, Jan. 12, 2004; 70 FR 53050, Sept. 7, 2005]

§ 318.8 Preservatives and Other Substances Permitted in Product for Export only; Handling; such Product Not to be Used for Domestic Food Purposes

(a) Preservatives and other substances not permitted in domestic product under the regulations in this subchapter may be used in the preparation and packing of product intended for export provided the product (1) accords to the specifications or directions of the foreign purchaser; (2) is not in conflict with the laws of the country to which it is intended for export; and

(3) is labeled on the outside container to show that it is intended for export, and is otherwise labeled as required by this subchapter for such export product.

(b) The preparation and packing of export product as provided for in paragraph (a) of this section shall be done in a manner acceptable to the inspector in charge so that the identity of the export product is maintained conclusively and the preparation of domestic product is adequately protected. The preservatives and other substances not permitted in domestic product shall be stored in a room or compartment separate from areas used to store other supplies and shall be held under Program lock. Use of the preservatives or other substances shall be under the direct supervision of a Program employee.

(c) The packing of all articles under paragraph (a) of this section shall be conducted under the direct supervision of a Program employee.

(d) No article prepared or packed for export under paragraph (a) of this section shall be sold or offered for sale for domestic use or consumption, but unless exported shall be destroyed for food purposes under the direct supervision of a Program employee.

(e) The contents of the container of any article prepared or packed for export under paragraph (a) of this section shall not be removed, in whole or in part, from such container prior to exportation, except under the supervision of a Program employee. If such contents are removed prior to exportation, then the article shall be either repacked, in accordance with the provisions of paragraphs (b) and (c) of this section, or destroyed for food purposes under the direct supervision of a Program employee.

(f) Permission must be obtained from the Administrator before meats packed in borax are shipped from one official establishment to another or to an unofficial establishment for storage, except such meat prepared for the account of Federal agencies.

(g) At all times, the identity of meat to which borax has been added shall be effectively maintained. In no case shall such meat, nor any trimmings or fat derived from such meat, whether unwashed or washed, or otherwise treated, be diverted to domestic use.

(h) Salt used for bulking meat previously packed in borax may not again be used in an edible products department other than in connection with the packing of meat in borax. Only metal equipment should be used for handling such meat. Particularly effective cleansing will be required if wooden equipment such as trucks, washing vats, etc., is used. Boxes from which boraxed meat has been removed may be used for repacking meat in borax, but their use as containers for other meat will be dependent upon the effective removal of all traces of borax.

(i) The following instructions pertain to export cured pork packed in borax for the account of Federal agencies. The meat may be packed in borax in a room in which there is boraxfree meat, provided proper care is taken to see that the boraxfree meat is not affected by the borax. Under the same condition, meat packed in borax may be received, unpacked, defrosted, soaked, washed, smoked, and repacked in a room where there is other meat. However, meat originally packed in borax shall at all times be subject to the restrictions of meat so packed, even though repacked without borax. After packing or repacking, borax packed meat may be stored in a room with meat not packed in borax, provided a reasonable degree of separation is maintained between the two classes of product.

[35 FR 15586, Oct. 3, 1970; 36 FR 11903, June 23, 1971, as amended at 38 FR 29214, Oct. 23, 1973]

§ 318.9 Samples of Products, Water, Dyes, Chemicals, etc., to be taken for Examination

Samples of products, water, dyes, chemicals, preservatives, spices, or other articles in any official establishment shall be taken, without cost to the Program, for examination, as often as may be deemed necessary for the efficient conduct of the inspection.

§ 318.10 Prescribed Treatment of Pork and Products Containing Pork to Destroy Trichinae

(a)(1) All forms of fresh pork, including fresh unsmoked sausage containing pork muscle tissue, and pork such as bacon and jowls, other than those covered by paragraph (b) of this section, are classed as products that are customarily well cooked in the home or elsewhere before being served to the consumer. Therefore, the treatment of such products for the destruction of trichinae is not required.

(2) Pork from carcasses or carcass parts that have been found free of trichinae as described under paragraph (e) or (f) of this section is not required to be treated for the destruction of trichinae.

(b) Products named in this paragraph, and products of the character hereof, containing pork muscle tissue (not including pork hearts, pork stomachs, and pork livers), or the pork muscle tissue which forms an ingredient of such products, shall be effectively heated, refrigerated, or cured to destroy any possible live trichinae, as prescribed in this section at the official establishment where such products are prepared: Bologna, frankfurter, vienna, and other cooked sausage; smoked sausage; knoblauch sausage; mortadella; all forms of summer or dried sausage, including mettwurst; flavored pork sausages such as those containing wine or similar flavoring materials; cured pork sausage; sausage containing cured and/or smoked pork; cooked loaves; roasted, baked, boiled, or cooked hams, pork shoulders, or pork shoulder picnics; Italianstyle hams; Westphaliastyle hams; smoked boneless pork shoulder butts; cured meat rolls; capocollo (capicola, capacola); coppa; fresh or cured boneless pork shoulder butts, hams, loins, shoulders, shoulder picnics, and similar pork cuts, in casings or other containers in which ready-to-eat delicatessen articles are customarily enclosed (excepting Scotch-style hams); breaded pork products; cured boneless pork loins; boneless back bacon; bacon used for wrapping around patties, steaks and similar products; and smoked pork cuts such as hams, shoulders, loins, and pork shoulder picnics (excepting smoked hams, and smoked pork shoulder picnics which are specially prepared for distribution in tropical climates or smoked hams delivered to the Armed Services); ground meat mixtures containing pork and beef, veal, lamb, mutton, or goat meat and other product consisting of mixtures of pork and other ingredients, which the Administrator determines at the time the labeling for the product is submitted for approval in accordance with part 317 of the regulations in this subchapter or upon subsequent reevaluation of the product, would be prepared in such a manner that the product might be eaten rare or without thorough cooking because of the appearance of the finished product or otherwise. Cured boneless pork loins shall be subjected to prescribed treatment for destruction of trichinae prior to being shipped from the establishment where cured.

(c) The treatment shall consist of heating, refrigerating, or curing, as follows:

(1) *Heating.* (i) All parts of the pork muscle tissue shall be heated according to one of the time and temperature combinations in the following table:

Minimum internal temperature		
Degrees fahrenheit	*Degrees centigrade*	*Minimum time*
120	49.0	21 hours.
122	50.0	9.5 hours.
124	51.1	4.5 hours.
126	52.2	2 hours.
128	53.4	1 hour.
130	54.5	30 minutes.
132	55.6	15 minutes.
134	56.7	6 minutes.
136	57.8	3 minutes.
138	58.9	2 minutes.
140	60.0	1 minute.
142	61.1	1 minute.
144	62.2	Instant.

(ii) Time and temperature shall be monitored by a calibrated recording instrument that meets the requirements of paragraph (d) of this section, except for paragraph (c)(1)(iv).

(iii) The time to raise product temperature from 60 °F to 120 °F shall not exceed 2 hours unless the product is cured or fermented.

(iv) Time, in combination with temperatures of 138 °F to 143 °F, need not be monitored if the product's minimum thickness exceeds 2 inches (5.1 cm) and refrigeration of the product does not begin within 5 minutes of attaining 138 °F (58.9 °C).

(v) The establishment shall use procedures which insure the proper heating of all parts of the product. It is important that each piece of sausage, each ham, and other product treated by heating in water be kept entirely submerged throughout the heating period; and that the largest pieces in a lot, the innermost links of bunched sausage or other massed articles, and pieces placed in the coolest part of a heating cabinet or compartment or vat be included in the temperature tests.

(2) *Refrigerating.* At any stage of preparation and after preparatory chilling to a temperature of not above 40 °F or preparatory freezing, all parts of the muscle tissue of pork or product containing such tissue shall be subjected continuously to a temperature not higher than one of those specified in table 1, the duration of such refrigeration at the specified temperature being dependent on the thickness of the meat or inside dimensions of the container.

(i) Group 1 comprises product in separate pieces not exceeding 6 inches in thickness, or arranged on separate racks with the layers not exceeding 6 inches in depth, or stored in crates or boxes not exceeding 6 inches in depth, or stored as solidly frozen blocks not exceeding 6 inches in thickness.

(ii) Group 2 comprises product in pieces, layers, or within containers, the thickness of which exceeds 6 inches but not 27 inches, and product in containers including tierces, barrels, kegs, and cartons having a thickness not exceeding 27 inches.

(iii) The product undergoing such refrigeration or the containers thereof shall be so spaced while in the freezer as will insure a free circulation of air between the pieces of meat, layers, blocks, boxes, barrels, and tierces in order that the temperature of the meat throughout will be promptly reduced to not higher than 5 °F., –10 °F., or –20 °F., as the case may be.

(iv) In lieu of the Methods prescribed in Table 1, the treatment may consist of commercial freeze drying or controlled freezing, at the center of the meat pieces, in accordance with the times and temperatures specified in Table 2.

Table 1. Required Period of Freezing at Temperature Indicated

Temperature °F.	*Group 1 (Days)*	*Group 2 (Days)*
5	20	30
–10	10	20
–20	6	12

Table 2. Alternate Periods of Freezing at Temperatures Indicated

Minimum internal temperature		
Degrees Fahrenheit	*Degrees centigrade*	*Minimum Time*
0	–17.8	106 hours.
–5	–20.6	82 hours.
–10	–23.3	63 hours.
–15	–26.1	48 hours.
–20	–28.9	35 hours.
–25	–31.7	22 hours.
–30	–34.5	8 hours.
–35	–37.2	1/2 hour.

(v) During the period of refrigeration the product shall be kept separate from other products and in the custody of the Program in rooms or compartments equipped and made secure with an official Program lock or seal. The rooms or compartments containing product undergoing freezing shall be equipped with accurate thermometers placed at or above the highest level at which the product undergoing treatment is stored and away from refrigerating coils. After completion of the prescribed freezing of pork to be used in the preparation of product covered by paragraph (b) of this section the pork shall be kept under close supervision of an inspector until it is prepared in finished form as one of the products enumerated in paragraph (b) of this section or until it is transferred under Program control to another official establishment for preparation in such finished form.

(vi) Pork which has been refrigerated as specified in this subparagraph may be transferred in sealed railroad cars, sealed motortrucks, sealed trailers, or sealed closed containers to another official establishment at the same or another location, for use in the preparation of product covered by paragraph

(b) of this section. Such vehicles and containers shall be sealed and transported between official establishments in accordance with § 325.7 of this subchapter.

(3) *Curing* – (i) *Sausage.* The sausage may be stuffed in animal casings, hydrocellulose casings, or cloth bags. During any stage of treating the sausage for the destruction of live trichinae, except as provided in Method 5, these coverings shall not be coated with paraffin or like substance, nor shall any sausage be washed during any prescribed period of drying. In the preparation of sausage, one of the following methods may be used:

Method No. 1. The meat shall be ground or chopped into pieces not exceeding threefourths of an inch in diameter. A drycuring mixture containing not less than 3 ⅓ pounds of salt to each hundredweight of the unstuffed sausage shall be thoroughly mixed with the ground or chopped meat. After being stuffed, sausage having a diameter not exceeding 3½ inches, measured at the time of stuffing, shall be held in a drying room not less than 20 days at a temperature not lower than 45 °F., except that in sausage of the variety known as pepperoni, if in casings not exceeding 1⅜ inches in diameter measured at the time of stuffing, the period of drying may be reduced to 15 days. In no case, however, shall the sausage be released from the drying room in less than 25 days from the time the curing materials are added, except that sausage of the variety known as pepperoni, if in casings not exceeding the size specified, may be released at the expiration of 20 days from the time the curing materials are added. Sausage in casings exceeding 3½ inches, but not exceeding 4 inches, in diameter at the time of stuffing, shall be held in a drying room not less than 35 days at a temperature not lower than 45 °F., and in no case shall the sausage be released from the drying room in less than 40 days from the time the curing materials are added to the meat.

Method No. 2. The meat shall be ground or chopped into pieces not exceeding three-fourths of an inch in diameter. A drycuring mixture containing not less than 3⅓ pounds of salt to each hundredweight of the unstuffed sausage shall be thoroughly mixed with the ground or chopped meat. After being stuffed, sausage having a diameter not exceeding 3½ inches, measured at the time of stuffing, shall be smoked not less than 40 hours at a temperature not lower than 80 °F., and finally held in a drying room not less than 10 days at a temperature not lower than 45 °F. In no case, however, shall the sausage be released from the drying room in less than 18 days from the time the curing materials are added to the meat. Sausage exceeding 3½ inches, but not exceeding 4 inches, in diameter at the time of stuffing, shall be held in a drying room, following smoking as above indicated, not less than 25 days at a temperature not lower than 45 °F., but in no case shall the sausage be released from the drying room in less than 33 days from the time the curing materials are added to the meat.

Method No. 3. The meat shall be ground or chopped into pieces not exceeding three-fourths of an inch in diameter. A drycuring mixture containing not less than 3⅓ pounds of salt to each hundredweight of the unstuffed sausage shall be thoroughly mixed with the ground or chopped meat. After admixture with the salt and other curing materials and before stuffing, the ground or chopped meat shall be held at a temperature not lower than 34 °F for not less than 36 hours. After being stuffed, the sausage shall be held at a temperature not lower than 34 °F. for an additional period of time sufficient to make a total of not less than 144 hours from the time the curing materials are added to the meat, or the sausage shall be held for the time specified in a picklecuring medium of not less than 50° strength (salometer reading) at a temperature not lower than 44 °F Finally, sausage having a diameter not exceeding 3½ inches, measured at the time of stuffing, shall be smoked for not less than 12 hours. The temperature of the smokehouse during this period at no time shall be lower than 90 °F.; and for 4 consecutive hours of this period the smokehouse shall be maintained at a temperature not lower than 128 °F. Sausage exceeding 3½ inches, but not exceeding 4 inches, in diameter at the time of stuffing shall be smoked, following the prescribed curing, for not less than 15 hours. The temperature of the smokehouse during the 15-hour period shall at no time be lower than 90 °F, and for 7 consecutive hours of this period the smokehouse shall be maintained at a temperature not lower than 128 °F. In regulating the temperature of the smokehouse for the treatment of sausage under this Method, the temperature of 128 °F shall be attained gradually during a period of not less than 4 hours.

Method No. 4. The meat shall be ground or chopped into pieces not exceeding one-fourth of an inch in diameter. A drycuring mixture containing not less than 2½ pounds of salt to each hundredweight of the unstuffed sausage shall be thoroughly mixed with the ground or chopped meat. After admixture with the salt and other curing materials and before stuffing, the ground or chopped sausage shall be held as a compact mass, not more than 6 inches in depth, at a temperature not lower than 36 °F for not less than 10 days. At the termination of the holding period, the sausage shall be stuffed in casings or cloth bags not exceeding 3⅓ inches in diameter, measured at the time of stuffing. After being stuffed, the sausage shall be held in a drying room at a temperature not lower than 45 °F for the remainder of a 35-day period, measured from the time the curing materials are added to the meat. At any time after stuffing, if the establishment operator deems it desirable, the product may be heated in a water bath for a period not to exceed 3 hours at a temperature not lower than 85 °F, or subjected to smoking at a temperature not lower than 80 °F, or the product may be both heated and smoked as specified. The time consumed in heating and smoking, however, shall be in addition to the 35-day holding period specified.

Method No. 5. The meat shall be ground or chopped into pieces not exceeding three-fourths of an inch in diameter. A drycuring mixture containing not less than 3⅓ pounds of salt to each hundredweight of the unstuffed sausage shall be thoroughly mixed with the ground or chopped meat. After being stuffed, the sausage shall be held for not less than 65 days at a temperature not lower than 45 °F. The coverings for sausage prepared according to this Method may be coated at any stage of the preparation before or during the holding period with paraffin or other substance approved by the Administrator.

Method No. 6. (A) *Basic requirements.* The meat shall be ground or chopped into pieces not exceeding three-fourths of an inch in diameter. A drycuring mixture containing not less than 3.33 pounds of salt to each hundred-weight of the unstuffed sausage, excluding the weight of dry ingredients, shall be thoroughly mixed with the ground or chopped meat. After the curing mixture has been added, the sausage shall be held for two time periods, a holding period and a drying period. The holding period will be for a minimum of 48 hours at a room temperature not lower than 35 °F. This holding period requirement may be fulfilled totally or in part before the drying period and then the remainder, if any, after the drying period or as an extension of the drying period. During the drying period, the sausage shall be held in a drying room at a temperature not lower than 50 (10.0 °F. (10.0 °C) for a period of time determined by Tables 3A, 3B, and 4. The length

Table 3A. Sausage Drying Room Times by Method No. 6

Diameter of casing at time of stuffing[1]	*Days in drying room*[2]
Up to:	
1 inches	14
1½ inches	15
2 inches	16
2½ inches	18
3 inches	20
3½ inches	23
4 inches	25
4½ inches	30
5 inches	35
5½ inches	43
6 inches	50

1. The drying room times for flattened or oval sausages shall use a diameter derived by measuring the circumference and dividing by 3.14 (pi).
2. Drying room time may be modified as set forth in Tables 3B and 4.

Table 3B. Percentage Reduction in Drying Room Time (Table 3A) Permitted by Holding Times and Temperatures Prior to Drying [1]

Minimum Time	*Minimum Temperature*[2]									
	70 °F	*75 °F*	*80 °F*	*85 °F*	*90 °F*	*95 °F*	*100 °F*	*105 °F*	*110 °F*	*120 °F*
	21.1°C	*23.9°C*	*26.7°C*	*29.5°C*	*32.2°C*	*35.0°C*	*37.9°C*	*40.6°C*	*43.3°C*	*48.9°C*
24 hours	4	5	8	10	15	23	37	57	90	100[3]
48 hours	9	12	18	25	35	49	88	100[3]	100[3]	100
72 hours	14	19	28	39	55	74	100[3]	100	100	100
96 hours	19	26	38	53	75	98	100	100	100	100
120 hours	24	33	48	67	95	100[3]	100	100	100	100

1. In computing the days to be deducted, the number with any fraction shall be rounded to the next lower whole number and shall be deducted from the required total drying time. Example: Sausage stuffed in 3" diameter casing requires 20 days in the drying room (from Drying Room Times, Table 3A). If allowed to ferment, after addition of curing materials, at 80 °F. for 48 hours, the 20 day drying time may be reduced 18% (from Table 3B). Eighteen percent of 20 day equals 3.6 days. Twenty days minus 3 days equals 17 days. The total drying time required in the drying room, therefore, will be 17 days.
2. Either room temperature or internal product temperature shall be used for sausages that will be subsequently dried to a moisture-protein ratio of 2.3:1 or less. Internal product temperature shall be used for all other sausages.
3. Trichinae will be destroyed during fermentation or smoking at the temperature and length of time indicated. Therefore, no drying room period is required for products so treated.

Table 4. Reduced Salt Content – Drying
[Required percentage increase in drying room time (Table 3A) for added salt of less than 3.33 pounds per hundredweight of sausage]

Minimum pounds of salt added to sausage[1]	*Increase in drying room time*[2]
3.3	1
3.2	4
3.1	7
3.0	10
2.9	13
2.8	16
2.7	19
2.6	22
2.5	25
2.4	28
2.3	31
2.2	34
2.1	37
2.0	40

1. Calculate the salt content for column 1 as follows: Multiply the pounds of salt in the sausage formulation by 100. Then divide this number by the total weight of sausage formulation minus the weight of dry ingredients and round down to the next lowest 0.1%. Percents may be substituted for pounds.
   Example: 120 lbs. pork, 3.56 lbs. salt, 2 lbs. spices, 0.5 lbs. wine, 1 lb. water and starter culture, 0.8 lbs. sugar, .012 lbs. sodium nitrite total weight is 127.872 lbs.

   $$(3.56 \times 100)/(127.872 - 3.56 - 2 - .8 - .012) = 356/121.5 = 2.93$$

   Therefore, the sausage drying time must be increased by 13 percent.
2. In computing the days to be added to the required total drying time, fractions shall be rounded to the next higher whole number and added to the required total drying time.
   Example: Sausage stuffed in 3½ inch diameter casing requires 23 days in the drying room (from Drying Room Times). If the quantity of salt added per hundredweight of sausage is 2 pounds instead of 3.33 pounds, the drying room time must be increased by 40 percent (from Reduced Salt Content-Drying Room Times), or 9.2 days. The 9.2 is rounded up to 10 days and is added to the 23 days to equal 33 days. The total drying time required in the drying room, therefore, will be 33 days.

of the drying period, established in (c)(3)(i)(A), may be modified as provided in paragraphs (c)(3)(i)(B) and (c)(3)(i)(C) of this section.

(B) *Reduction in Drying Room Time.* During the holding period, the sausage may be smoked or fermented. If the temperature is increased to 70 °F. (21.1 °C) or higher, while the sausage is being held after adding curing materials but before the drying period, the subsequent drying room times prescribed for this *Method* may be reduced according to the schedule in Table 3B. No interpolation of values is permissible.

(C) *Reduced Salt Content – Drying Room Times.* Salt content of less than 3.33 pounds for each hundredweight of sausage formulation, excluding dry ingredients, (such as salts, sugars, and spices), may be permitted provided the drying time is increased according to the schedule contained in Table 4.

TRICHINA TREATMENT OF SAUSAGE BY METHOD NO. 6;

Method No. 7, Dry Sausages. (A) *General Requirements.* The establishment shall use meat particles reduced in size to no more than ¼ inch in diameter. The establishment shall add a curing mixture containing no less than 2.7 pounds of salt per hundred pounds of meat and mix it uniformly throughout the product. The establishment shall hold, heat, and dry the product according to paragraph (B) or (C) below.

(B) *Holding, Heating, and Drying Treatment, Large Sausages.* Except as permitted in (C) below, the establishment shall subject sausages in casings not exceeding 105 mm in diameter, at the time of stuffing, to all of the following minimum chamber temperatures and time periods.

Treatment Schedule for Sausages 105 Millimeters (4⅛ Inches) or Less in Diameter

Minimum chamber temperature		*Minimum time (hours)*
(°F)	(°C)	
50	10	12
90	32.2	1
100	37.8	1
110	43.3	1
120	48.9	1
125	51.7	7

Following the preceding treatment, the establishment shall dry the sausages at a temperature not lower than 50 °F (10 °C) for not less than 7 days.

Treatment Schedule for Sausages 55 Millimeters (2⅛ Inches) or Less in Diameter

Minimum chamber temperature		*Minimum time (hours)*
(°F)	(°C)	
50	10	12
100	37.8	1
125	51.7	6

(C) *Heating and Drying Treatment, Small Sausages.* Alternatively, the establishment may subject sausages in casings not exceeding 55 mm in diameter, at the time of stuffing, to all of the following minimum chamber temperatures and time periods.

Following the preceding heat treatment, the establishment shall dry the sausages at a temperature not lower than 50 °F (10 °C) for not less than 4 days.

(ii) *Capocollo (capicola, capacola).* Boneless pork butts for capocollo shall be cured in a drycuring mixture containing not less than 4½ pounds of salt per hundredweight of meat for a period of not less than 25 days at a temperature not lower than 36 °F. If the curing materials are applied to the butts by the process known as churning, a small quantity of pickle may be added. During the curing period the butts may be overhauled according to any of the usual processes of overhauling, including the addition of pickle or dry salt if desired. The butts shall not be subjected during or after curing to any treatment designed to remove salt from the meat, except that superficial washing may be allowed. After being stuffed, the product shall be smoked for a period of not less than 30 hours at a temperature not lower than 80 °F., and shall finally be held in a drying room not less than 20 days at a temperature not lower than 45 °F.

(iii) *Coppa.* Boneless pork butts for coppa shall be cured in a drycuring mixture containing not less than 4½ pounds of salt per hundredweight of meat for a period of not less than 18 days at a temperature not lower than 36 °F. If the curing mixture is applied to the butts by the process known as churning, a small quantity of pickle may be added. During the curing period the butts may be overhauled according to any of the usual processes of overhauling, including the addition of pickle or dry salt if desired. The butts shall not be subjected during or after curing to any treatment designed to remove salt from the meat, except that superficial washing may be allowed. After 251 being stuffed, the product shall be held in a drying room not less than 35 days at a temperature not lower than 45 °F.

(iv) *Hams and pork shoulder picnics.* In the curing of hams and pork shoulder picnics, one of the Methods below shall be used. For calculating days per pound, the establishment shall use the weight of the heaviest ham or picnic in the lot.

Method No. 1. The hams and pork shoulder picnics shall be cured by a drysalt curing process not less than 40 days at a temperature no lower than 36 °F. The products shall be laid down in salt, not less than 4 pounds to each hundredweight of product, the salt being applied in a thorough manner to the lean meat of each item. When placed in cure, the products may be pumped with pickle if desired. At least once during the curing process, the products shall be overhauled (turned over for the application of additional cure) and additional salt applied, if necessary, so that the lean meat of each item is thoroughly covered. After removal from cure, the products may be soaked in water at a temperature not higher than 70 °F for not more than 15 hours, during which time the water may be changed once, but they shall not be subjected to any other treatment designed to remove salt from the meat except that superficial washing may be allowed. The products shall finally be dried or smoked at a time and temperature not less than a combination prescribed in Table 5 of Method No. 3.

Method No. 2. [Reserved]

Method No. 3. (A) *Curing.* (Other than bag curing): Establishments shall cure hams and shoulders by using a cure mixture containing not less than 70 percent salt by weight to cover all exposed muscle tissue and to pack the hock region. Total curing time consists of a mandatory cure contact time and an optional equalization time.

(B) *Cure Contact Time.* This is the cure contact period, during which the establishment shall keep exposed muscle tissue coated with the cure mixture at least 28 days but for no less than 1.5 days per pound of ham or shoulder. Overhaul is optional so long as the exposed muscle tissue remains coated with curing mixture.

(C) *Equalization.* The establishment may provide an equalization period after the minimum cure contact period in (B) above to permit the absorbed salt to permeate the product's inner tissues. Equalization is the time after the excess cure has been removed from the product at the end of the cure contact period until the product is placed in the drying room and the drying period begins. The total curing time (equalization plus cure contact) shall be at least 40 days and in no case less than 2 days per pound of an uncured ham or shoulder.

(D) *Removing Excess Cure.* After the required cure contact period, the establishment may remove excess cure mixture from the product's surface mechanically or by rinsing up to 1 minute with water, but not by soaking.

(E) *Bag Curing.* Bag curing is a traditional ham curing technique in which the manufacturer wraps the ham and all of the cure mixture together in kraft paper then hangs them individually. The paper keeps the extra cure mixture in close contact with the product making reapplication of salt unnecessary, and it protects the product from mites and insects. Establishments may employ the bag curing Method as an alternative to (A) through (D) above. An establishment which elects to use the bag curing Method shall apply a cure mixture containing at least 6 pounds of salt per 100 pounds of uncured product. The establishment shall rub the curing mixture into the exposed muscle tissue, pack the hock region with the curing mixture, and use uncoated wrapping paper to wrap the product together with any remaining curing mixture. The bag cured product shall remain wrapped throughout the curing period and may or may not remain wrapped during the drying period. In any case, the curing period shall be at least 40 days but not less than 2 days per pound of an uncured ham or shoulder. After curing, the cured product shall be exposed to a drying time and temperature prescribed in Table 5.

(F) *Curing Temperature.* During the curing period the establishment shall use one of the following procedures:

(1) The establishment shall control the room temperature at not less than 35 °F (1.7 °C) nor greater than 45 °F (7.2 °C) for the first 1.5 days per pound of an uncured ham or shoulder, and not less than 35 °F (1.7 °C) nor greater than 60 °F (15.6 °C) for the remainder of the curing period.

(2) The establishment shall monitor and record daily product temperature. The room temperature need not be controlled but days on which the product temperature drops below 35 °F (1.7 °C) shall not be counted as curing time. If the product temperature exceeds 45 °F (7.2 °C) within the first period of 1.5 days per pound of an uncured ham or shoulder or if it exceeds 60 °F (15.6 °C) for the remainder of the curing period, the establishment shall cool the product back to the 45 °F (7.2 °C) maximum during the first period or 55 °F (12.8 °C) maximum during the remainder of the period.

(3) The establishment shall begin curing product only between the dates of December 1 and February 13. The room temperature need not be controlled, but the establishment shall monitor and record daily room temperatures, and days in which the room temperature drops below 35 °F (1.7 °C) shall not be counted as curing time.

(G) *Drying.* After the curing period, establishments shall use one of three procedures for drying:

(1) The establishment shall subject the product to a controlled room temperature for a minimum time and minimum temperature combination prescribed in Table 5 or for a set of such combinations in which the total of the fractional periods (in column 4 of Table 5) exceeds 1.5.

(2) Establishments using uncontrolled room temperatures shall monitor and record the internal product temperature. The drying period shall be complete when, from the days which can be counted as curing time, one of the time/temperature combinations of Table 5 is satisfied or when the total of the fractional values for the combinations exceeds 1.5.

(3) Establishments using uncontrolled room temperatures shall dry the product for a minimum of 160 days including the entire months of June, July, and August. This procedure is obviously dependent on local climatic conditions and no problem exists with respect to current producers who use this procedure. Future applicants shall demonstrate that their local monthly average temperatures and the local monthly minimum temperatures are equal to or warmer than the normal average temperatures and normal minimum temperatures compiled by the National Oceanic and Atmospheric Administration for Boone, North Carolina, station 31–0977, 1951 through 1980.

*Table 5. Minimum Drying Days at a Minimum Temperature**

Minimum Drying Temperature		*Minimum days at drying temperature*	*Fractional period for one day of drying*
Degrees fahrenheit	*Degrees centigrade*		
130	54.4	1.5	.67
125	51.7	2	.50
120	48.9	3	.33
115	46.1	4	.25
110	43.3	5	.20
105	40.6	6	.17
100	37.8	7	.14
95	35.0	9	.11
90	32.2	11	.091
85	29.4	18	.056
80	26.7	25	.040
75	23.9	35	.029

* Interpolation of these times or temperatures is not acceptable; establishments wishing to use temperatures or times not in this Table shall first validate their efficacy as provided by 318.10(c)(4) of this section.

Monthly Temperatures (°F) for Boone Nc, 1951–1980

Jan.	Feb.	Mar.	Apr.	May	June	July	Aug.	Sep.
Normal average temperatures								
32.2	34.1	41.3	51.2	59.1	65.1	68.3	67.5	61.6
Normal minimum temperatures								
28.8	24.2	30.8	39.6	48.1	54.7	58.5	57.6	51.6

Drying Times and Temperatures for Trichina Inactivation in Hams and Shoulders

Method No. 4. (A) Cure: Establishments shall cure hams and shoulders by using a cure mixture containing not less than 71.5 percent salt by weight to cover all exposed muscle tissue and to pack the hock region. Establishments may substitute potassium chloride (KCl) for up to half of the required salt on an equal weight basis.

(B) *Curing.* Establishments shall apply the cure at a rate not less than 5.72 pounds of salt and KCl per hundred pounds of fresh meat. The cure shall be applied in either three or four approximately equal amounts (two or three overhauls) at separate times during the first 14 days of curing.

(C) *Cure Contact Time.* Establishments shall keep the product in contact with the cure mixture for no less than 2 days per pound of an uncured ham or shoulder but for at least 30 days. Establishments shall maintain the curing temperature at no less than 35 °F (1.7 °C) during the cure contact time.

(D) *Equalization.* After the cure contact period, establishments shall provide an added equalization period of no less than 1 day per pound of an uncured ham or shoulder but at least 14 days. Equalization is the time after the excess cure has been removed from the product, the end of the cure contact period, and before the drying period begins. Establishments may substitute additional cure contact days for an equal number of equalization days.

(E) *Removing Excess Cure.* After the required cure contact period, the establishment may remove excess cure mixture from the product's surface mechanically or by rinsing up to 1 minute with water, but not by soaking.

(F) *Drying.* After the curing period, establishments shall use one of the controlled temperature methods for drying listed in Method No. 3 of this subparagraph.

Method No. 5 (A) *Curing.* The establishment shall cure the ham to a minimum brine concentration of 6 percent by the end of the drying period. Brine concentration is calculated as 100 times the salt concentration divided by the sum of the salt and water concentrations.

$$\text{Percent brine} = 100 \times [\text{salt}] / ([\text{salt}] + [\text{water}])$$

The Agency will accept the brine concentration in the biceps femoris as a reasonable estimate of the minimum brine concentration in the ham.

(B) *Drying and Total Process Times.* The establishment shall dry the cured ham at a minimum temperature of 55 °F (13 °C) for at least 150 days. The total time of drying plus curing shall be at least 206 days.

(C) *Ensuring an Acceptable Internal Brine Concentration.* (1) To establish compliance, the establishment shall take product samples from the first 12 lots of production as follows: From each lot,

(i) One sample shall be taken from each of 5 or more hams;

(ii) Each sample shall be taken from the biceps femoris. As an alternative to the use of the biceps femoris, the Agency shall consider other method(s) of sampling the drycured hams to determine the minimum internal brine concentration, as long as the establishment proposes it and submits data and other information to establish its sufficiency to the Director of the Processed Products Inspection Division;

(iii) Each sample shall weigh no less than 100 grams;

(iv) The samples shall be combined as one composite sample and sealed in a water vapor proof container;

(v) The composite sample shall be submitted to a laboratory accredited under the provisions of § 318.21 to be analyzed for salt and water content using methods from the 'Official Methods of Analysis of the Association of Official Analytical Chemists (AOAC),' 15th Edition, 1990, Section 983.18 (page 931) and Section 971.19 (page 933) which are incorporated by reference. This incorporation by reference was approved by the Director of the Federal Register in accordance with 5 U.S.C. 552(a) and 1 CFR part 51. Copies may be obtained from the Association of Official Analytical Chemists, suite 400–BW, 2200 Wilson Boulevard, Arlington, VA 22201–3301. Copies may be inspected at the Office of the FSIS Hearing Clerk, room 3171, South Agriculture Building, Food Safety and Inspection Service, U.S. Department of Agriculture, Washington, DC 20250 or at the National Archives and Records Administration (NARA). For information on the availability of this material at NARA, call 202–741–6030, or go to: *http://www.archives.gov/federal_register/code\of_federal_regulations/ibr_locations.html.* If the time between sampling and submittal of the composite sample to the accredited laboratory will exceed 8 hours, then the establishment shall freeze the composite sample immediately after the samples are combined;

(vi) Once the laboratory results for the composite sample are received, the manufacturer shall calculate the internal brine concentration by multiplying the salt concentration by 100 and then dividing that figure by the sum of the salt and water concentrations;

(vii) Compliance is established when the samples from the first 12 lots of production have a minimum internal brine concentration of 6 percent. Lots being tested to establish compliance shall be held until the internal brine concentration has been determined and found to be at least 6 percent. If the minimum internal brine concentration is less than 6 percent, the lot being tested shall be held until the establishment brings the lot into compliance by further processing.

(2) To maintain compliance, the establishment shall take samples, have the samples analyzed, and perform the brine calculations as set forth above from one lot every 13 weeks. Lots being tested to maintain compliance shall not be held. If the minimum internal brine concentration is less than 6 percent in a lot being tested to maintain compliance, the establishment shall develop and propose steps acceptable to FSIS to ensure that the process is corrected.

(3) Accredited laboratory results and the brine calculations shall be placed on file at the establishment and available to Program employees for review.

Method No. 6 (A) *Curing*. The establishment shall cure the ham to a minimum brine concentration of 6 percent by the end of the drying period. Brine concentration is calculated as 100 times the salt concentration divided by the sum of the salt and water concentrations.

$$\text{Percent brine} = 100 \times [\text{salt}] / ([\text{salt}] + [\text{water}])$$

The Agency will accept the brine concentration in the biceps femoris as a reasonable estimate of the minimum brine concentration.

(B) *Drying and Total Process Times.* The establishment shall dry the cured ham at a minimum temperature of 110 °F (43 °C) for at least 4 days. The total time of drying plus curing shall be at least 34 days.

(c) *Ensuring an Acceptable Internal Brine Concentration.* (1) To establish compliance the establishment shall take product samples from the first 12 lots of production as follows: From each lot,

(i) One sample shall be taken from each of 5 or more hams;

(ii) Each sample shall be taken from the biceps femoris. As an alternative to the use of the biceps femoris, the Agency will consider other methods of sampling the drycured hams to determine internal brine concentration, as long as the establishment proposes it and submits data and other information to establish its sufficiency to the Director of the Processed Products Inspection Division;

(iii) Each sample shall weigh no less than 100 grams;

(iv) The samples shall be combined as one composite sample and sealed in a water vapor proof container;

(v) The composite sample shall be submitted to a laboratory accredited under the provisions of § 318.21 to be analyzed for salt and water content using methods from the 'Official Methods of Analysis of the Association of Official Analytical Chemists (AOAC),' 15th Edition, 1990, section 983.18 (page 931) and section 971.19 (page 933) which are incorporated by reference. This incorporation by reference was approved by the Director of the Federal Register in accordance with 5 U.S.C. 552(a) and 1 CFR part 51. Copies may be obtained from the Association of Official Analytical Chemists, suite 400–BW, 2200 Wilson Boulevard, Arlington, VA 22201–3301. Copies may be inspected at the Office of the FSIS Hearing Clerk, room 3171, South Agriculture Building, Food Safety and Inspection Service, U.S. Department of Agriculture, Washington, DC 20250 or at the National Archives and Records Administration (NARA). For information on the availability of this material at NARA, call 202–741–6030, or go to: *http://www.archives.gov/federal_register/code_of_federal_regulations/ibr_locations.html.* If the time between sampling and submittal of the composite sample to the accredited laboratory will exceed 8 hours, then the establishment shall freeze the composite sample immediately after the samples are combined;

(vi) Compliance is established when the samples from the first 12 lots of production have a minimum internal brine concentration of 6 percent. Lots being tested to establish compliance shall be held until the internal brine concentration has been determined and found to be at least 6 percent. If the minimum internal brine concentration is less than 6 percent, the lot being tested shall be held until the establishment brings the lot into compliance by further processing.

(2) To maintain compliance, the establishment shall take samples, have the samples analyzed, and perform the brine calculations as set forth above from one lot every 13 weeks. Lots being tested to maintain compliance shall not be held. If the minimum internal brine concentration is less than 6 percent in a lot being tested to maintain compliance, the establishment shall develop and propose steps acceptable to FSIS to ensure that the process is corrected.

(3) Accredited laboratory results and the brine calculations shall be placed on file in the establishment and available to Program employees for review.

(v) *Boneless pork loins and loin ends.* In lieu of heating or refrigerating to destroy possible live trichinae in boneless loins, the loins may be cured for a period of not less than 25 days at a temperature not lower than 36 °F. by the use of one of the following methods:

Method No. 1. Application of a drysalt curing mixture containing not less than 5 pounds of salt to each hundredweight of meats.

Method No. 2. Application of a pickle solution of not less than 80° strength (salometer) on the basis of not less than 60 pounds of pickle to each hundredweight of meat.

Method No. 3. Application of a pickle solution added to the drysalt cure prescribed as Method No. 1 in this subdivision (v) provided the pickle solution is not less than 80° strength (salometer).

After removal from cure, the loins may be soaked in water for not more than 1 hour at a temperature not higher than 70 °F. or washed under a spray but shall not be subjected, during or after the curing process, to any other treatment designed to remove salt.

Following curing, the loins shall be smoked for not less than 12 hours. The minimum temperature of the smokehouse during this period at no time shall be lower than 100 °F., and for 4 consecutive hours of this period the smokehouse shall be maintained at a temperature not lower than 125 °F.

Finally, the product shall be held in a drying room for a period of not less than 12 days at a temperature not lower than 45 °F.

(4) The Administrator shall consider additional processing methods upon petition by manufacturers, and shall approve any such Method upon his/her determination that it can be properly monitored by an inspector and that the safety of such methods is adequately documented by data which has been developed by following an experimental protocol previously reviewed and accepted by the Department.

(d) General instructions: When necessary to comply with the requirements of this section, the smokehouses, drying rooms, and other compartments used in the treatment of pork to destroy possible live trichinae shall be suitably equipped, by the operator of the official establishment, with accurate automatic recording thermometers. Circuit supervisors are authorized to approve for use in sausage smokehouses, drying rooms, and other compartments, such automatic recording thermometers as are found to give satisfactory service and to disapprove and require discontinuance of use, for purposes of the regulations in this subchapter, any thermometers (including any automatic recording thermometers) of the establishment that are found to be inaccurate or unreliable.

(e) The requirements for using the pooled sample digestion technique to analyze pork for the presence of trichina cysts are:

(1) The establishment shall submit for the approval of the Regional Director its proposed procedure for identifying and pooling carcasses, collecting and

pooling samples, testing samples (including the name and address of the laboratory), communicating test results, retesting individual carcasses, and maintaining positive identification and clear separation of pork found to be trichinafree from untested pork or trichinapositive pork.

(2) The establishment shall use the services of a laboratory approved by the Administrator for all required testing. Such approval shall be based on adequacy of facilities, reagents, and equipment, and on demonstration of continuing competency and reliability in performing the pooled sample digestion technique for trichinae.

(3) The establishment shall sample no less than 5 grams of diaphragm muscle or tongue tissue from each carcass or no less than 10 grams of other muscle tissue. Samples may be pooled but a pool shall not consist of more than 100 grams of sample. Sampling and sample preparation are subject to inspection supervision.

(4) Pork or products made from tested pork shall not be released as trichina free from the official establishment without treatment until the inspector in charge receives a laboratory report that the tested pork is free of trichina cysts.

(f) *Approval of other tests for trichinosis in pork.* The Administrator shall consider any additional analytical method for trichinosis upon petition by a manufacturer, and may approve that method upon the determination that it will detect at least 98 percent of swine bearing cysts present at a tissue density equal to or less than one cyst per gram of muscle from the diaphragm pillars at a 95 percent confidence level. Any such petitions shall be supported by any data and other information that the Administrator finds necessary. Notice of any approval shall be given in the Federal Register, and the approved method will be incorporated into this section.

[35 FR 15586, Oct. 3, 1970, as amended at 38 FR 31517; Nov. 15, 1973; 39 FR 40580, Nov. 19, 1974; 50 FR 5229, Feb. 7, 1985; 50 FR 48075, Nov. 21, 1985; 52 FR 12517, Apr. 17, 1987; 57 FR 27874, June 22, 1992; 57 FR 33633, July 30, 1992; 57 FR 56440, Nov. 30, 1992]

§ 318.11 [Reserved]

§ 318.12 Manufacture of Dog Food or Similar Uninspected Article at Official Establishments

(a) When dog food, or similar uninspected article is manufactured in an edible product department, there shall be sufficient space allotted and adequate equipment provided so that the manufacture of the uninspected article in no way interferes with the handling or preparation of edible products. Where necessary to avoid adulteration of edible products, separate equipment shall be provided for the uninspected article. To assure the maintenance of sanitary conditions in the edible product departments, the operations incident to the manufacture of the uninspected article will be subject to the same sanitary requirements that apply to all operations in edible product departments. The manufacture of the uninspected article shall be limited to those hours during which the establishment operates under inspectional supervision; and there shall be no handling, other than receiving at the official establishment, of any of the product ingredient of the uninspected article, other than during the regular hours of inspection. The materials used in the manufacture of the uninspected article shall not be used so as to interfere with the inspection of edible product or the maintenance of sanitary conditions in the department or render any edible product adulterated. The meat, meat byproducts, and meat food product ingredients of the uninspected article may be admitted into any edible products department of an official establishment only if they are U.S. Inspected and Passed. Products within § 314.11 of this subchapter or parts of carcasses of kinds not permitted under the regulations in this subchapter to be prepared for human food (e.g., lungs or intestines), which are produced at any official establishment, may be brought into the inedible products department of any official establishment for use in uninspected articles under this section. The uninspected article may be stored in, and distributed from, edible product departments: *Provided,* That adequate facilities are furnished, there is no interference with the maintenance of sanitary conditions, and such article is properly identified.

(b) When dog food or similar uninspected article is manufactured in a part of an official establishment other than an edible product department, the area in which the article is manufactured shall be separated from edible product departments in the manner required for separation between edible product departments and inedible product departments. Sufficient space must be allotted and adequate equipment provided so that the manufacture of the uninspected article does not interfere with the proper functioning of the other operations at the establishment. Except as provided in § 314.11 of this subchapter, nothing in this paragraph shall be construed as permitting any deviation from the requirement that dead animals, condemned products, and similar materials of whatever origin, must be placed in the inedible product rendering equipment, and without undue delay. The manufacture of the uninspected article must be such as not to interfere with the maintenance of general sanitary conditions on the premises, and it shall be subject to inspectional supervision similar to that exercised over other inedible product departments. There shall be no movement of any product from an inedible product department to any edible product department. Trucks, barrels, and other equipment shall be cleaned before being returned to edible product departments from inedible product departments. Unoffensive material prepared outside edible product departments may be stored in, and distributed from, edible product departments only if packaged in clean, properly identified, sealed containers.

(c) Animal food shall be distinguished from articles of human food, so as to avoid distribution of such animal food as human food. To accomplish this, such animal food shall be labeled or otherwise identified in accordance with § 325.11(d) of this subchapter.

[35 FR 15586, Oct. 3, 1970, as amended at 36 FR 11639, June 17, 1971; 53 FR 24679, June 30, 1988]

§ 318.13 Mixtures Containing Product but not Amendable to the Act

Mixtures containing product but not classed as a meat food product under the Act shall not bear the inspection legend or any abbreviation or representation thereof unless manufactured under the food inspection service provided for in part 350 of subchapter B of this chapter. When such mixtures are manufactured in any part of an official establishment, the sanitation of that part of the establishment shall be supervised by Program employees, and the manufacture of such mixtures shall not cause any deviation from the requirement of § 318.1.

[35 FR 15586, Oct. 3, 1970, as amended at 38 FR 29215, Oct. 23, 1973]

§ 318.14 Adulteration of Product by Polluted Water; Procedure for Handling

(a) In the event there is polluted water (including but not limited to flood water) in an official establishment, all products and ingredients for use in the preparation of such products that have been rendered adulterated by the water shall be condemned.

(b) After the polluted water has receded from an official establishment, all walls, ceilings, posts, and floors of the rooms and compartments involved, including the equipment therein, shall, under the supervision of an inspector, be cleaned thoroughly by the official establishment personnel. An adequate supply of hot water under pressure is essential to make such cleaning effective. After cleaning, a solution of sodium hypochlorite containing approximately one-half of 1 percent available chlorine (5,000 p/m) or other equivalent disinfectant approved by the Administrator[1] shall be applied to the surface of the rooms and equipment and rinsed with potable water before use.

(c) Hermetically sealed containers of product which have been contaminated by polluted water shall be examined promptly by the official establishment under supervision of an inspector and rehandled as follows:

(1) Separate and condemn all product in damaged or extensively rusted containers.

(2) Remove paper labels and wash the remaining containers in warm soapy water, using a brush where necessary to remove rust or other foreign material. Disinfect these containers by either of the following methods:

(i) Immerse in a solution of sodium hypochlorite containing not less than 100 p/m of available chlorine or other equivalent disinfectant approved by the Administrator,[1] rinse in potable water, and dry thoroughly; or

(ii) Immerse in 212 °F water, bring temperature of the water back to 212 °F and maintain the temperature at 212 °F for 5 minutes, then remove containers from water and cool them to 95 °F and dry thoroughly.

---

1. A list of approved disinfectants is available upon request to Scientific Services, Meat and Poultry Inspection Program, Food Safety and Inspection Service, U.S. Department of Agriculture, Washington, DC 20250.

(3) After handling as described in paragraph (c)(2) of this section, the containers may be relacquered, if necessary, and then relabeled with approved labels applicable to the product therein.

(4) The identity of the canned product shall be maintained throughout all stages of the rehandling operations to insure correct labeling of the containers.

[35 FR 15586, Oct. 3, 1970, as amended at 38 FR 34455, Dec. 14, 1973]

§ 318.15 Tagging Chemicals, Preservatives, Cereals, Spices, Etc., 'U.S. Retained'

When any chemical, preservative, cereal, spice, or other substance is intended for use in an official establishment, it shall be examined by a Program employee and if found to be unfit or otherwise unacceptable for the use intended, or if final decision regarding acceptance is deferred pending laboratory or other examination, the employee shall attach a 'U.S. retained' tag to the substance or container thereof. The substance so tagged shall be kept separate from other substances as the circuit supervisor may require and shall not be used until the tag is removed, and such removal shall be made only by a Program employee after a finding that the substance can be accepted, or, in the case of an unacceptable substance, when it is removed from the establishment.

§ 318.16 Pesticide Chemicals and Other Residues in Products

(a) *Nonmeat ingredients.* Residues of pesticide chemicals, food additives and color additives or other substances in or on ingredients (other than meat, meat byproducts, and meat food products) used in the formulation of products shall not exceed the levels permitted under the Federal Food, Drug, and Cosmetic Act, and such nonmeat ingredients must otherwise be in compliance with the requirements under that Act.

(b) *Products, and meat, meat byproduct, or other meat food product ingredients.* Products, and products used as ingredients of products, shall not bear or contain any pesticide chemical, food additives, or color additive residue in excess of the level permitted under the Federal Food, Drug, and Cosmetic Act and the regulations in this subchapter, or any other substance that is prohibited by such regulations or that otherwise makes the products adulterated.

(c) *Standards and procedures.* Instructions specifying the standards and procedures for determining when ingredients of finished products are in compliance with this section shall be issued to the inspectors by the Administrator. Copies of such instructions will be made available to interested persons upon request made to the Administrator.

§ 318.17 Requirements for the Production of Cooked Beef, Roast Beef, and Cooked Corned Beef Products

(a) Cooked beef, roast beef, and cooked corned beef products must be produced using processes ensuring that the products meet the following performance standards:

(1) *Lethality.* A 6.5-$\log_{10}$ reduction of *Salmonella* or an alternative lethality that achieves an equivalent probability that no viable *Salmonella* organisms remain in the finished product, as well as the reduction of other pathogens and their toxins or toxic metabolites necessary to prevent adulteration, must be demonstrated to be achieved throughout the product. The lethality process must include a cooking step. Controlled intermediate step(s) applied to raw product may form part of the basis for the equivalency.

(2) *Stabilization.* There can be no multiplication of toxigenic microorganisms such as *Clostridium botulinum,* and no more than 1-$\log_{10}$ multiplication of *Clostridium perfringens* within the product.

(b) For each product produced using a process other than one conducted in accordance with the Hazard Analysis and Critical Control Point (HACCP) system requirements in part 417 of this chapter, an establishment must develop and have on file and available to FSIS, a process schedule, as defined in § 301.2 of this chapter. Each process schedule must be approved in writing by a process authority for safety and efficacy in meeting the performance standards established for the product in question. A process authority must have access to the establishment in order to evaluate and approve the safety and efficacy of each process schedule.

(c) Under the auspices of a processing authority, an establishment must validate new or altered process schedules by scientifically supportable means, such as information gleaned from the literature or by challenge studies conducted outside the plant.

[64 FR 744, Jan. 6, 1999]

§ 318.18 Handling of Certain Material for Mechanical Processing

Material to be processed into 'Mechanically Separated (Species)' shall be so processed within 1 hour from the time it is cut or separated from carcasses or parts of carcasses, except that such product may be held for no more than 72 hours at 40 °F. (4 °C.) or less, or held indefinitely at 0 °F. (–18 °C.) or less. 'Mechanically Separated (Species)' shall, directly after being processed, be used as an ingredient in a meat food product except that it may be held prior to such use for no more than 72 hours at 40 °F. (4 °C.) or less or indefinitely at 0 °F (–18 °C.) or less.

[43 FR 26423, June 20, 1978, as amended at 47 FR 28256, June 29, 1982]

§ 318.19 Compliance Procedure for Cured Pork Products

(a) *Definitions.* For the purposes of this section:

(1) A *product* is that cured pork article which is contained within one *Group* as defined in paragraph (a)(2) of this section and which purports to meet the criteria for a single product designated under the heading 'Product Name and Qualifying Statements' in the chart in § 319.104 or the chart in § 319.105.

(2) A *Product Group* or a *Group* means one of the following:

Group I, consisting of cured pork products which have been cooked while imperviously encased. Any product which fits into the Group will be placed in this Group regardless of any other considerations.

Group II, consisting of cured pork products which have been water cooked. Any product which does not fit into Group I but does fit into Group II will be placed into Group II regardless of any other considerations.

Group III, consisting of boneless smokehouse heated cured pork products. Any boneless product that does not fit into Group I or Group II shall be placed in Group III.

Group IV, consisting of bonein or semiboneless smokehouse heated cured pork products. Any product that is not completely boneless or still contains all the bone which is traditional for bonein product, and does not fit into Group I, Group II, or Group III shall be placed in this Group.

(3) A *lot* is that product from one production shift.

(4) A *production rate* is frequency of production, expressed in days per week.

(5) *Protein fat free percentage, protein fat free content, PFF percentage, PFF content or PFF* of a product means the meat protein (indigenous to the raw, unprocessed pork cut) content expressed as a percent of the nonfat portion of the finished product.

(b) *Normal Compliance Procedures.* The Department shall collect samples of cure pork products and analyze them for their PFF content. Analyses shall be conducted in accordance with the 'Official methods of Analysis of the Association of Official Analytical Chemists §§ 950.46, and 928.08 (Chapter 39).[1] The 'Official Methods of Analysis of the Association of Official Analytical Chemists,' 15th edition, 1990, is incorporated by reference with the approval of the Director of the Federal Register in accordance with 5 U.S.C. 552(a) and 1 CFR part 51. Each analytical result shall be recorded and evaluated to determine whether future sampling of product Groups within an official establishment shall be periodic or daily under the provisions of paragraph (b)(1) of this section, and if the affected lot and

1. A copy of the "Official methods of Analysis of the Association of Official Analytical Chemists," 15th edition, 1990, is on file with the Director, Office of the Federal Register, and may be purchased from the Association of Official Analytical Chemists, Inc., 2200 Wilson Boulevard, Suite 400, Arlington, Virginia 22201.

subsequent production of like product shall be U.S. retained, or administratively detained, as appropriate, as provided in paragraph (b)(2) of this section.[2]

(1) *Criteria to determine sampling frequency of Product Groups.* For each official plant preparing cured pork products, Product Groups shall be sampled periodically or daily. Analytical results shall be evaluated and the sampling frequency determined as follows:

(i) Determine the difference between the individual PFF analysis and the applicable minimum PFF percentage requirement of § 319.104 or § 319.105. The resulting figure shall be negative when the individual sample result is less than the applicable minimum PFF percentage requirement and shall be positive when the individual sample result is greater than the applicable minimum PFF percentage requirement.

(ii) Divide the resulting number by the standard deviation assigned to the Product Group represented by the sample to find the Standardized Difference. The standard deviation assigned to Groups I and II is 0.75 and to Groups III and IV is 0.91.

(iii) Add 0.25 to the Standardized Difference to find the Adjusted Standardized Difference.

(iv) Use the lesser of 1.90 and the Adjusted Standardized Difference as the Sample Value.

(v) Cumulatively total Sample Values to determine the Group Value. The first Sample Value in a Group shall be the Group Value, and each succeeding Group Value shall be determined by adding the most recent Sample Value to the existing Group Value; provided, however, that in no event shall the Group Value exceed 1.00. When calculation of a Group Value results in a figure greater than 1.00, the Group Value shall be 1.00 and all previous Sample Values shall be ignored in determining future Group Values.

(vi) The frequency of sampling of a Group shall be periodic when the Group Value is greater than –1.40 (e.g., –1.39, –1.14, 0, 0.50, etc.) and shall be daily

---

2. Rules for Rounding:

1. Laboratory results for percent meat protein and fat will be reported to the second decimal place (hundredths).

2. PFF and Sample Values for charting purposes will be calculated from the reported laboratory results to the second decimal place. Rounding of calculations to reach two decimal places will be done by the following rule:

All values of five-thousandths (0.005) or more will be rounded up to the next highest hundredth. All values of less than five-thousandths (0.005) will be dropped.

3. For compliance with the Absolute Minimum PFF requirements, the PFF will be rounded to the first decimal place (tenths). Rounding of calculations to reach one decimal place will be done by the following rule:

All PFF values of five-hundredths (0.05) or more will be rounded up to the next highest tenth.
All PFF values of less than five-hundredths (0.05) will be dropped.

4. For product disposition (pass-fail of a minimum PFF standard for retained product) the average PFF calculation will be rounded to the first decimal place. Individual PFF Values will be calculated to the nearest hundredth as in (2) above. The average, however, will be rounded to the nearest tenth as in (3) above.

when the Group Value is –1.40 or less (e.g., –1.40, –1.45, –1.50, etc.); provided, however, that once daily sampling has been initiated, it shall continue until the Group Value is 0.00 or greater, and each of the last seven Sample Values is –1.65 or greater (e.g., –1.63, –1.50, etc.), and there is no other product within the affected Group being U.S. retained as produced, under provisions of paragraph (b)(2) or (c).

(2) *Criteria for U.S. retention or administrative detention of cured pork products for further analysis.* Cured prok products shall be U.S. retained, or administratively detained, as appropriate, when prescribed by paragraphs (b)(2) (i) or (ii) of this section as follows:

(i) *Absolute Minimum PFF Requirement.* In the event that an analysis of an individual sample indicates a PFF content below the applicable minimum requirement of § 319.104 or § 319.105 by 2.3 or more percentage points for a Group I or II product, or 2.7 or more percentage points for a Group III or IV product, the lot from which the sample was collected shall be U.S. retained if in an official establishment and shall be subject to administrative detention if not in an official establishment unless returned to an official establishment and there U.S. retained. Any subsequently produced lots of like product and any lots of like product for which production dates cannot be established shall be U.S. retained or subject to administrative detention. Such administratively detained product shall be handled in accordance with part 329 of this subchapter, or shall be returned to an official establishment and subjected to the provisions of paragraph (c)(1) (i) or (ii) of this section, or shall be relabeled in compliance with the applicable standard, under the supervision of a program employee, at the expense of the product owner. Disposition of such U.S. retained product shall be in accordance with paragraph (c) of this section.

(ii) *Product Value requirement.* The Department shall maintain, for each product prepared in an official establishment, a Product Value. Except as provided in paragraph (c)(2) of this section, calculation of the Product Value and its use to determine if a product shall be U.S. retained shall be as follows:

(A) Determine the difference between the individual PFF analysis and applicable minimum PFF percentage requirement of § 319.104 and § 319.105. The resulting figure shall be negative when the individual sample result is less than the applicable minimum PFF percentage requirement and shall be positive when the individual sample result is greater than the applicable minimum PFF percentage requirement.

(B) Divide the difference determined in paragraph (b)(2)(ii)(A) of this section by the standard deviation assigned to the product's Group in paragraph (b)(1)(ii) of this section to find the standardized difference.

(C) Use the lesser of 1.65 and the standardized difference as the Sample Value.

(D) Cumulatively total Sample Values to determine the Product Value. The first Sample Value of a product shall be the Product Value, and each succeeding Product Value shall be determined by adding the most recent Sample Value to the existing Product Value; provided, however, that in no event shall the Product Value exceed 1.15. When calculation of a Product Value results in a figure greater than 1.15, the Product Value shall be 1.15, and all previous Sample Values shall be ignored in determining future Product Values.

(E) Provided daily group sampling is in effect pursuant to the provisions of paragraph (b)(1) of this section, and provided further the Product Value is –1.65 or less (e.g., –1.66), the affected lot (if within the official establishment) and all subsequent lots of like product prepared by and still within the official establishment shall be U.S. retained and further evaluated under paragraph (c) of this section. Except for release of individual lot pursuant to paragraph (c)(1), subsequently produced lots of like product shall continue to be U.S. retained until discontinued pursuant to paragraph (c)(2) of this section.

(c) *Compliance procedure during product retention.* When a product lot is U.S. retained under the provisions of paragraph (b)(2) of this section, the Department shall collect three randomly selected samples from each such lot and analyze them individually for PFF content. The PFF content of the three samples shall be evaluated to determine disposition of the lot as provided in paragraph (c)(1) of this section and the action to be taken on subsequently produced lots of like product as provided in paragraph (c)(2) of this section.[3]

(1) A product lot which is U.S. retained under the provisions of paragraph (b)(2) of this section may be released for entry into commerce provided one of the following conditions is met:

(i) The average PFF content of the three samples randomly selected from the lot is equal to or greater than the applicable minimum PFF percentage required by § 319.104 or § 319.105. Further processing to remove moisture for the purpose of meeting this provision is permissible. In lieu of further analysis to determine the effects of such processing, each 0.37 percent weight reduction due to moisture loss resulting from the processing may be considered the equivalent of a 0.1 percent PFF gain.

(ii) The lot of the product is relabeled to conform to the provisions of § 319.104 or § 319.105, under the supervision of a program employee.

(iii) The lot is one that has been prepared subsequent to preparation of the lot which, under the provisions of paragraph (c)(2) of this section, resulted in discontinuance of U.S. retention of new lots of like product. Such lot may be released for entry into commerce prior to receipt of analytical results for which sampling has been conducted. Upon receipt of such results, they shall be subjected to the provisions of paragraphs (b)(2)(i) and (c)(2) of this section.

(2) The PFF content of three randomly selected samples from each U.S. retained lot shall be used to maintain the Product Value described in paragraph

---

3. If the processor does not wish to have the product evaluated in this manner, alternate sampling plans may be used provided such plans have been formulated by the processor and approved by the Administrator prior to evaluation by the three-sample criteria, and provided the analyses specified in such plans are performed at the expense of the processor.

(c)(2)(ii). The manner and effect of such maintenance shall be as follows: (i) Find the average PFF content of the three samples.

(ii) Determine the difference between that average and the applicable minimum PFF percentage requirement of § 319.104 or § 319.105. The resulting figure shall be negative when the average of the sample results is less than the applicable minimum PFF percentage requirement and shall be positive when the average of the sample results is greater than the applicable minimum PFF requirements.

(iii) Divide the resulting figure by the standard deviation assigned to the product's Group in paragraph (b)(1)(ii) of this section, to find the standardized difference.

(iv) Use the lesser of 1.30 and the standardized difference as the Sample Value.

(v) Add the first Sample Value thus calculated to the latest Product Value calculated under the provisions of paragraph (c)(2)(ii) of this section to find the new Product Value. To find each succeeding Product Value, add the most recent Sample Value to the existing Product Value; provided, however, that in no event shall the Product Value exceed 1.15. When the addition of a Sample Value to an existing Product Value results in a figure greater than 1.15, the Product Value shall be 1.15 and all previous Sample Values shall be ignored in determining future Product Values.

(vi) New lots of like product shall continue to be retained pending disposition in accordance with paragraph (c)(1) of this section until, after 5 days of production, the Product Value is 0.00 or greater, and the PFF content of no individual sample from a U.S. retained lot is less than the Absolute Minimum PFF requirement specified in paragraph (b)(2)(i) of this section. Should an individual sample fail to meet its Absolute Minimum PFF requirement, the 5-day count shall begin anew.

(vii) When U.S. retention of new lots is discontinued under the above provisions, maintenance of the Product Value shall revert to the provisions of paragraph (b)(2)(ii) of this section.

(3) For purposes of this section, the plant owner or operator shall have the option of temporarily removing a product from its Product Group, provided product lots are being U.S. retained, as produced, and provided further that the average production rate of the product, over the 8-week period preceding the week in which the first U.S. retained lot was prepared, is not greater than 20 percent of the production rate of its Group. When a product is thus removed from its Group, analytical results of product samples shall not cause daily sampling of the Group. When pursuant to paragraph (c)(2)(vi) of this section, new lots of the product are no longer being U.S. retained, the product shall again be considered with its Group.

(d) *Adulterated and misbranded products.* Products not meeting specified PFF requirements, determined according to procedures set forth in this section, may be deemed adulterated under section 1(m)(8) of the Act (21 U.S.C. 601(m)(8)) and misbranded under section 1(n) of the Act (21 U.S.C. 601(n)).

(e) *Quality control.* Cured pork products bearing on their labeling the statement 'X% of Weight is Added Ingredients' shall be prepared only under a quality control system or program in accordance with § 318.4 of this subchapter. With respect to any other cured pork product, official establishments may institute quality control procedures under § 318.4 of this subchapter. Cured pork products produced in such establishments may be exempt from the requirements of this section, provided in plant quality control procedures are shown to attain the same or higher degree of compliance as the procedures set forth in this section; provided, however, that all cured pork products produced shall be subject to the applicable Absolute Minimum PFF content requirement, regardless of any quality control procedures in effect.

[49 FR 14877, Apr. 13, 1984; 49 FR 33434, Aug. 23, 1984, as amended at 59 FR 33642, June 30, 1994; 60 FR 10304, Feb. 24, 1995; 62 FR 45025, Aug. 25, 1997].

§ 318.20 Use of Animal Drugs

Animal drug residues are permitted in meat and meat food products if such residues are from drugs which have been approved by the Food and Drug Administration and any such drug residues are within tolerance levels approved by the Food and Drug Administration, unless otherwise determined by the Administrator and listed herein.

[50 FR 32165, Aug. 9, 1985].

§ 318.21 Accreditation of Chemistry Laboratories

(a) *Definitions – Accredited laboratory* – A non-Federal analytical laboratory that has met the requirements for accreditation specified in this section and hence, at an establishment's discretion, may be used in lieu of an FSIS laboratory for analyzing official regulatory samples. Payment for the analysis of official samples is to be made by the establishment using the accredited laboratory.

Accreditation – Determination by FSIS that a laboratory is qualified to analyze official samples of product subject to regulations in this subchapter and part 381 of this chapter for the presence and amount of all four food chemistry analytes (protein, moisture, fat, and salt); or a determination by FSIS that a laboratory is qualified to analyze official samples of product subject to regulations in this subchapter and part 381 of this chapter for the presence and amount of one of several classes of chemical residue, in accordance with the requirements of the Accredited Laboratory Program. Accreditations are granted separately for the food chemistry analysis of official samples and for the analysis of such samples for any one of the several classes of chemical residue. A laboratory may hold more than one accreditation.

AOAC Methods – Methods of chemical analysis, Chapter 39, Association of Official Analytical Chemists (AOAC), published in the 'Official Methods of Analysis of the Association of Official Analytical Chemists,' 15th edition, 1990.[1] The 'Official Methods of Analysis of the Association of Official Analytical Chemists,' 15th edition, 1990, is incorporated by reference with the approval of the Director of the Federal Register in accordance with 5 U.S.C. 552(a) and 1 CFR part 51.

Chemical residue misidentification – see 'correct chemical residue identification' definition.

Coefficient of variation (CV) – The standard deviation of a distribution of analytical values multiplied by 100, and divided by the mean of those values.

Comparison Mean – The average, for a sample, of all accredited and FSIS laboratories' average results, each of which has a large deviation measure of zero, except when only two laboratories perform the analysis, as in the case of split sample analysis by both an accredited laboratory and an FSIS laboratory. In the latter case, the comparison mean is the average of the two laboratories' results. For food chemistry, a result for a laboratory is the obtained analytical value; for chemical residues, a result is the logarithmic transformation of the obtained analytical value.

Correct chemical residue identification – Correct identification by a laboratory of a chemical residue whose concentration, in a sample, is equal to or greater than the minimum reporting level for that residue, as determined by the median of all positive analytical values obtained by laboratories analyzing the sample. Failure of a laboratory to report the presence such a chemical residue is considered a misidentification. In addition, reporting the presence of a residue at a level equal to or above the minimum reporting level that is not reported by 90 percent or more of all other laboratories analyzing the sample, is considered a misidentification.

CUSUM – A class of statistical procedures for assessing whether or not a process is 'in control'. Each CUSUM value is constructed by accumulating incremental values obtained from observed results of the process, and then determined to either exceed or fall within acceptable limits for that process. The initial CUSUM values for each laboratory whose application for accreditation is accepted are set at zero. The four CUSUM procedures are:

(1) Positive systemic laboratory difference CUSUM (CUSUM-P) – monitors how consistently an accredited laboratory gets numerically greater results than the comparison mean;

(2) Negative systematic laboratory difference CUSUM (CUSUM-N) – monitors how consistently an accredited laboratory gets numerically smaller results than the comparison mean;

---

1. A copy of the 'Official methods of Analysis of the Association of Official Analytical Chemists,' 15th edition, 1990, is on file with the Director, Office of the Federal Register, and may be purchased from the Association of Official Analytical Chemists, Inc., 2200 Wilson Boulevard, Suite 400, Arlington, Virginia 22201.

(3) Variability CUSUM (CUSUM-V) – monitors the average 'total discrepancy' (i.e., the combination of the random fluctuations and systematic differences) between an accredited laboratory's results and the comparison mean;

(4) Individual large discrepancy CUSUM (CUSUM-D) – monitors the magnitude and frequency of large differences between the results of an accredited laboratory and the comparison mean.

Individual large deviation – An analytical result from a non-Federal laboratory that differs from the sample comparison mean by more than would be expected assuming normal laboratory variability.

Initial accreditation check sample – A sample prepared and sent by an FSIS laboratory to a non-Federal laboratory to ascertain if the non-Federal laboratory's analytical capability meets the standards for granting accreditation.

Interlaboratory accreditation maintenance check sample – A sample prepared and sent by FSIS to a non-Federal laboratory to assist in determining if acceptable levels of analytical capability are being maintained by the accredited laboratory.

Large deviation measure – A measure that quantifies an unacceptably large difference between a non-Federal laboratory's analytical result and the sample comparison mean.

Minimum proficiency level – The minimum concentration of a residue at which an analytical result will be used to assess a laboratory's quantification capability. This concentration is an estimate of the smallest concentration for which the average coefficient of variation (CV) for reproducibility (i.e., combined within and between laboratory variability) does not exceed 20 percent. (See Table 2.)

Minimum reporting level – The number such that if any obtained analytical value equals or exceeds this number, then the residue is reported together with the obtained analytical value.

Official Sample – A sample selected by a Program employee in accordance with FSIS procedures for regulatory use.

Probation – The period commencing with official notification to an accredited laboratory that its check or split sample results no longer satisfy the performance requirements specified in this rule, and ending with official notification that accreditation is either fully restored, suspended, or revoked.

QA (quality assurance) recovery – The ratio of a laboratory's unadjusted analytical value of a check sample residue to the residue level fortified by the FSIS laboratory that prepared the sample, multiplied by 100. (See Table 2.)

QC (quality control) recovery – The ratio of a laboratory's unadjusted analytical value of a quality control standard to the fortification level of the standard, multiplied by 100. (See Table 2.)

Refusal of Accreditation – An action taken when a laboratory which is applying for accreditation is denied the accreditation.

Responsibly connected – Any individual who or entity which is a partner, officer, director, manager, or owner of 10 per centum or more of the voting stock of the applicant or recipient of accreditation or an employee in a managerial or executive capacity or any employee who conducts or supervises the chemical analysis of FSIS official samples.

Revocation of Accreditation – An action taken against a laboratory which removes its right to analyze official samples.

Split sample – An official sample divided into duplicate portions, one portion to be analyzed by an accredited laboratory (for official regulatory purposes) and the other portion by an FSIS laboratory (for comparison purposes).

Standardizing Constant – The number which is the result of a mathematical adjustment to the 'standardized value.' Specifically, the number equals the square root of the expected variance of the difference between the accredited or applying laboratory's result and the comparison mean on a sample, taking into consideration the standardizing value, the correlation and number of repeated results by a laboratory on a sample, and the number of laboratories that analyzed the sample.

Standardized Difference – The quotient of the difference between a laboratory's result on a sample and the comparison mean of the sample divided by the standardizing constant.

Standardizing Value – A number representing the performance standard deviation of an individual result (see Tables 1 and 2 and footnotes to the Tables for determining exact procedures for calculation).

Suspension of Accreditation – Action taken against a laboratory which temporarily removes its right to analyze official samples. Suspension of accreditation ends when accreditation is either fully restored or revoked.

Systematic laboratory difference – A comparison of one laboratory's results with the comparison means on samples that shows, on average, a consistent

Table 1. Standardizing Values for Food Chemistry

[By Product Class and Analyte]

Product/Class	*Moisture*	*Protein*[1]	*Fat*[2]	*Salt*[3]
Cured Pork/ Canned Ham	0.50	0.060	0.26 (0.30)	0.127
Ground Beef	0.71	0.060	(0.35)	0.127
Other	0.57	0.060	0.20 (0.30)	0.127

1. To obtain the standardizing value for a sample the appropriate entry in this column is multiplied by $X^{0.65}$ where X is the comparison mean of the sample.
2. To obtain the standardizing value for a sample, the appropriate entry in this column is multiplied by $X^{0.25}$, where X is the comparison mean of the sample. The appropriate entry is equal to the value in parentheses when X is equal to or greater than 12.5 percent, otherwise it is equal to 0.26.
3. To obtain the standardizing value for a sample, when the comparison mean of the sample, X, is less than 1.0 percent, the standardizing value equals 0.127, otherwise the appropriate entry is multiplied by $X^{0.25}$. When X is equal to or greater than 4.0 percent for dry salami and pepperoni products, the standardizing value equals 0.22.

Table 2. Minimum Proficiency Levels, Percent Expected Recoveries (QC and QA), and Standardizing Values for Chemical Residues

Class of Residues	*Minimum Proficiency Level*	*Percent Expected Recovery (QC and QA)*	*Standardizing Value*[3]
Chlorinated Hydrocarbons:[1]			
Aldrin	0.10 ppm	80–110	0.20
Benzene Hexachloride	0.10 ppm	80–110	0.20
Chlordane	0.30 ppm	80–110	0.20
Dieldrin	0.10 ppm	80–110	0.20
DDT	0.15 ppm	80–110	0.20
DDE	0.10 ppm	80–110	0.20
TDE	0.15 ppm	80–110	0.20
Endrin	0.10 ppm	80–110	0.20
Heptachlor	0.10 ppm	80–110	0.20
Heptachlor Epoxide	0.10 ppm	80–110	0.20
Lindane	0.10 ppm	80–110	0.20
Methoxychlor	0.50 ppm	80–110	0.20
Toxaphene	1.00 ppm	80–110	0.20
Hexachlorobenzene	0.10 ppm	80–110	0.20
Mirex	0.10 ppm	80–110	0.20
Nonachlor	0.15 ppm	80–110	0.20
Polychlorinated Biphenyls:	0.50 ppm	80–110	0.20
Arsenic [2]	0.20 ppm	90–105	0.25
Sulfonamides [2]	0.08 ppm	70–120	0.25
Volatile Nitrosamine [2]	5 ppm	70–110	0.25

1. Laboratory statistics are computed over all results (excluding PCB results), and for specific chemical residues.
2. Laboratory statistics are only computed for specific chemical residues.
3. The standardizing value of all initial accreditation and probationary check samples computations is 0.15.

relationship. A laboratory that is reporting, on average, numerically greater results than the comparison mean has a positive systematic laboratory difference and, conversely, numerically smaller results indicate a negative systematic laboratory difference.

Variability – Random fluctuations in a laboratory's processes that cause its analytical results to deviate from a true value.

Variance – The expected average of the squared differences of sample results from an expected sample mean.

(b) *Laboratories accredited for analysis of protein, moisture, fat, and salt content of meat and meat products* – (1) *Applying for accreditation.* Application for accreditation shall be made on designated forms provided by FSIS, or otherwise in writing, by the owner or manager of a non-Federal analytical laboratory and sent to the Accredited Laboratory Program, Food Safety and Inspection Service, U.S. Department of Agriculture, Washington, DC 20250-3700, and shall specify the kinds of accreditation that are wanted by the owner or manager of the laboratory. A laboratory whose accreditation has been refused or revoked may reapply for accreditation after 60 days from the effective date of that action, and must provide written documentation specifying what corrections were made.

(i) At the time that an Application for Accreditation is filed with the Accredited Laboratory Program, FSIS, and annually thereafter upon receipt of the bill issued by FSIS on the anniversary date of each accreditation, the management of a laboratory shall reimburse the program at the rate specified in 9 CFR 391.5 for the cost of each accreditation that is sought for the laboratory or that the laboratory holds.

(ii) Simultaneously with the initial application for accreditation, the management of a laboratory shall forward a check, bank draft, or money order in the amount specified in 9 CFR 391.5 made payable to the U.S. Department of Agriculture along with the completed application for the accreditation(s) sought by the laboratory. Accreditation will not be granted or continued, without further procedure, for failure to pay the accreditation fee(s). The fee(s) paid shall be nonrefundable and shall be credited to the account from which the expenses of the laboratory accreditation program are paid.

(iii) Annually on the anniversary date of each accreditation, FSIS will issue a bill in the amount specified in 9 CFR 391.5.

(iv) Bills are payable upon receipt by check, bank draft, or money order, made payable to the U.S. Department of Agriculture, and become delinquent 30 days from the date of the bill. Accreditation will be terminated without further procedure for having a delinquent account. The fee(s) paid shall be nonrefundable and shall be credited to the account from which the expenses of 266 the Accredited Laboratory Program are paid.

(v) The accreditation of a laboratory that was accredited by FSIS on or before December 13, 1993 and was not on probation and whose accreditation on that date was not in suspension or revocation shall be continued, provided that such laboratory reapply for accreditation in accordance with the provisions of this paragraph (b)(1) by January 12, 1994 (30 days after the effective date of this section), and that the reapplication be accepted by the Agency. The CUSUM values for such laboratory will be reset at zero upon acceptance of its reapplication. The accreditation of a laboratory that is on probation shall be continued, provided that the laboratory reapply for accreditation by February 11, 1994 (60 days after the effective date of this section), that the reapplication be accepted by the Agency, and that the laboratory satisfy the terms of the probation.

(2) *Criteria for obtaining accreditation.* Non-Federal analytical laboratories may be accredited for the analyses of moisture, protein, fat, and salt content of meat and meat food products. Accreditation will be given only if the applying laboratory successfully satisfies the requirements presented below, for all four analytes. This accreditation authorizes official FSIS acceptance of the analytical test results provided by these laboratories on official samples. To obtain FSIS accreditation for moisture, protein, fat, and salt analyses, a non-Federal analytical laboratory must:

(i) Be supervised by a person holding, as a minimum, a bachelor's degree in either chemistry, food science, food technology, or a related field and having 1 year's experience in food chemistry, or equivalent qualifications, as determined by the Administrator.

(ii) Demonstrate acceptable levels of systematic laboratory difference, variability, and individual large deviations in the analyses of moisture, protein, fat, and salt content using AOC methods. An applying laboratory will successfully demonstrate these capabilities if its moisture, protein, fat, and salt results from a 36 check sample accreditation study each satisfy the criteria presented below.[2] If the laboratory's analysis of an analyte (or analytes) from the first set of 36 check samples does not meet the criteria for obtaining accreditation, a second set of 36 check samples will be provided within 30 days following the date of receipt by FSIS of a request from the applying laboratory. The second set of samples shall be analyzed for only the analyte(s) for which unacceptable initial results had been obtained by the laboratory. If the results of the second set of samples do not meet the accreditation criteria, the laboratory may reapply after a 60-day waiting period, commencing from the date of refusal of accreditation by FSIS. At that time, a new application, all fees, and all documentation of corrective action required for accreditation must be submitted.

(A) *Systematic laboratory difference:* The absolute value of the average standardized difference must not exceed 0.73 minus the product of 0.17 and the standard deviation of the standardized differences.

(B) *Variability:* The estimated standard deviation of the standardized differences must not exceed 1.15.

(C) *Individual large deviations:* One hundred times the average of the large deviation measures of the individual samples must be less than 5.0.[3]

---

2. All statistical computations are rounded to the nearest tenth, except where otherwise noted.
3. A result will have a large deviation measure equal to zero when the absolute value of the result's standardized difference, (d), is less than 2.5, and otherwise a measure equal to $1-(2.5/d)^4$.

(iii) Allow inspection of the laboratory by FSIS officials prior to the determination of granting accredited status.

(iv) Pay the accreditation fee by the date required.

(3) *Criteria for maintaining accreditation.* To maintain accreditation for moisture, protein, fat, and salt analyses, a non-Federal analytical laboratory must:

(i) Report analytical results of the moisture, protein, fat, and salt content of official samples, weekly, on designated forms to the FSIS Eastern Laboratory, College Station Road, P.O. Box 6085, Athens, GA 30604, or to the address designated by the Assistant Administrator, Office of Public Health and Science.

(ii) Maintain laboratory quality control records for the most recent 3 years that samples have been analyzed under this Program.

(iii) Maintain complete records of the receipt, analysis, and disposition of official samples for the most recent 3 years that samples have been analyzed under this Program.

(iv) Maintain a standards book, which is a permanently bound book with sequentially numbered pages, containing all readings and calculations for standardization of solutions, determination of recoveries, and calibration of instruments. All entries are to be dated and signed by the analyst immediately upon completion of the entry and by his/her supervisor within 2 working days. The standards book is to be retained for a period of 3 years after the last entry is made.

(v) Analyze interlaboratory accreditation maintenance check samples and return the results to FSIS within 3 weeks of sample receipt. This must be done whenever requested by FSIS and at no cost to FSIS.

(vi) Inform the Accredited Laboratory Program, Food Safety and Inspection Service, U.S. Department of Agriculture, Washington, DC 20250-3700, by certified or registered mail, within 30 days, when there is any change in the laboratory's ownership, officers, directors, supervisory personnel, or other responsibly connected individual or entity.

(vii) Permit any duly authorized representative of the Secretary to perform both announced and unannounced onsite laboratory reviews of facilities and records during normal business hours, and to copy any records pertaining to the laboratory's participation in the Accredited Laboratory Program.

(viii) Use official AOAC Methods[4] on official and check samples. The 'Official Methods of Analysis of the Association of Official Analytical Chemists,' 15th edition, 1990, is incorporated by reference with the approval of the Director of the Federal Register in accordance with 5 U.S.C. 552(a) and 1 CFR part 51.

(ix) Demonstrate that acceptable limits of systematic laboratory difference, variability, and individual large deviations are being maintained in the analyses of

---

4. A copy of the 'Official Methods of Analysis of the Association of Analytical Chemists,' 15th edition, 1990, is on file with the Director, Office of the Federal Register, and may be purchased from the Association of Official Analytical Chemists, Inc., 2200 Wilson Boulevard, Suite 400, Arlington, Virginia 22201.

moisture, protein, fat, and salt content. An accredited laboratory will successfully demonstrate the maintenance of these capabilities if its moisture, protein, fat, and salt results from interlaboratory accreditation maintenance check samples and/or split samples satisfy the criteria presented below.[5]

(A) *Systematic laboratory difference:*

(*1*) *Positive systematic laboratory difference:* The standardized difference between the accredited laboratory's result and that of the FSIS laboratory for each split or interlaboratory accreditation maintenance check sample is used to determine a CUSUM value, designated as CUSUM-P. This value is computed and evaluated as follows:

(*i*) Determine the CUSUM increment for the sample. The CUSUM increment is set equal to:

2.0, if the standardized difference is greater than 1.6,

–2.0, if the standardized difference is less than –1.6,

or

the standardized difference minus 0.4, if the standardized difference lies between –1.6 and 2.4, inclusive.

(*ii*) Compute the new CUSUM-P value. The new CUSUM-P value is obtained by adding algebraically, the CUSUM increment to the last previously computed CUSUM-P value. If this computation yields a value smaller than 0, the new COSUM-P value is set equal to 0. [COSUM-P values are initialized at zero; that is, the COSUM-P value associated with the first sample is set equal to the CUSUM increment for that sample.]

(*iii*) Evaluate the new COSUM-P value. The new COSUM-P value must not exceed 5.2.

(*2*) *Negative systematic laboratory difference:* The standardized difference between the accredited laboratory's result and that of the FSIS laboratory for each split or interlaboratory accreditation maintenance check sample is used to determine a CUSUM value, designated as COSUM-N. This value is computed and evaluated as follows:

(*i*) Determine the CUSUM increment for the sample. The CUSUM increment is set equal to:

2.0, if the standardized difference is greater than 1.6,

–2.0, if the standardized difference is less than –2.4,

or

the standardized difference plus 0.4, if the standardized difference lies between –2.4 and 1.6, inclusive.

---

5. All statistical computations are rounded to the nearest tenth, except where otherwise noted.

(*ii*) Compute the new COSUM-N value. The new COSUM-N value is obtained by subtracting, algebraically, the CUSUM increment to the last previously computed COSUM-N value. If this computation yields a value smaller than 0, the new COSUM-N value is set equal to 0. [COSUM-N values are initialized at zero; that is, the COSUM-N value associated with the first sample is set equal to the CUSUM increment for that sample.]

(*iii*) Evaluate the new COSUM-N value. The new COSUM-N value must not exceed 5.2.

(B) *Variability:* The absolute value of the standardized difference between the accredited laboratory's result and that of the FSIS laboratory for each split sample or interlaboratory accreditation maintenance check sample is used to determine a CUSUM value, designated as COSUM-V. This value is computed and evaluated as follows:

(*1*) Determine the CUSUM increment for the sample. The CUSUM increment is set equal to the larger of –0.4 and the absolute value of the standardized difference minus 0.9. If this computation yields a value larger than 1.6, the increment is set equal to 1.6.

(*2*) Compute the new COSUM-V value. The new COSUM-V value is obtained by adding, algebraically, the CUSUM increment to the last previously computed COSUM-V value. If this computation yields a value less than 0, the new COSUM-V value is set equal to 0. [COSUM-V values are initialized at zero; that is, the COSUM-V value associated with the first sample is set equal to the CUSUM increment for that sample.]

(3) Evaluate the new COSUM-V value. The new COSUM-V value must not exceed 4.3.

(C) *Large deviations:* The large deviation measure of the accredited laboratory's result for each split sample or interlaboratory accreditation maintenance check sample is used to determine a CUSUM value, designated as COSUM-D.[6] This value is computed and evaluated as follows:

(*1*) Determine the CUSUM increment for the sample. The CUSUM increment is set equal to the value of the large deviation measure minus 0.025.

(*2*) Compute the new COSUM-D value. The new COSUM-D value is obtained by adding, algebraically, the CUSUM increment to the last previously computed COSUM-D value. If this computation yields a value less that 0, the new COSUM-D value is set equal to 0. [COSUM-D values are initialized at zero; that is, the COSUM-D value associated with the first sample is set equal to the CUSUM increment for that sample.]

(*3*) Evaluate the new COSUM-D value. The new COSUM-D value must not exceed 1.0.

(x) Meet the following requirements if placed on probation pursuant to paragraph (e) of this section:

(A) Send all official samples that have not been analyzed as of the date of written notification of probation to a specified FSIS laboratory by certified mail or

---

6. *See* footnote 3.

private carrier or, as an alternative, to an accredited laboratory approved for food chemistry. Mailing expenses will be paid by FSIS.

(B) Analyze a set of check samples similar to those used for initial accreditation, and submit the analytical results to FSIS within 3 weeks of receipt of the samples.

(C) Satisfy criteria for check samples specified in paragraphs (b)(2)(ii) (A), (B), and (C) of this section.

(xi) Expeditiously report analytical results of official samples to the FSIS Eastern Laboratory, College Station Road, P.O. Box 6085, Athens, GA 30604, or to the address designated by the Assistant Administrator, Office of Public Health and Science. The Federal inspector at any establishment may assign the analysis of official samples to an FSIS laboratory if, in the inspector's judgment, there are delays in receiving test results on official samples from an accredited laboratory.

(xii) Pay the required accreditation fee when it is due.

(c) *Laboratories accredited for analysis of a class of chemical residues in meat and meat food products* – (1) *Applying for accreditation.* Application for accreditation shall be made on designated forms provided by FSIS, or otherwise in writing, by the owner or manager of the non-Federal analytical laboratory and sent to the Accredited Laboratory Program, Food Safety and Inspection Service, U.S. Department of Agriculture, Washington, DC 20250-3700, and shall specify the kinds of accreditation that are wanted by the owner or manager of the laboratory. A laboratory whose accreditation has been refused or revoked may reapply for accreditation after 60 days from the effective date of that action, and must provide written documentation specifying what corrections were made.

(i) At the time that an Application for Accreditation is filed with the Accredited Laboratory Program, FSIS, and annually thereafter upon receipt of the bill issued by FSIS on the anniversary date of each accreditation, the management of a laboratory shall reimburse the program at the rate specified in 9 CFR 391.5 for the cost of each accreditation that is sought for the laboratory or that the laboratory holds.

(ii) Simultaneously with the initial application for accreditation, the management of a laboratory shall forward a check, bank draft, or money order in the amount specified in 9 CFR 391.5 made payable to the U.S. Department of Agriculture along with the completed application for the accreditation(s) sought for the laboratory. Accreditation will not be granted or continued, without further procedure, for failure to pay the accreditation fee(s). The fee(s) paid shall be nonrefundable and shall be credited to the account from which the expenses of the laboratory accreditation program are paid.

(iii) Annually on the anniversary date of each accreditation, FSIS will issue a bill in the amount specified in 9 CFR 391.5.

(iv) Bills are payable upon receipt by check, bank draft, or money order, made payable to the U.S. Department of Agriculture, and become delinquent 30 days from the date of the bill. Accreditation will be terminated without further procedure for having a delinquent account. The fee(s) paid shall be nonrefundable and shall be credited to the account from which the expenses of the Accredited Laboratory Program are paid.

(v) The accreditation of a laboratory that was accredited by FSIS on or before December 13, 1993 and was not on probation and whose accreditation on that date was not in suspension or revocation shall be continued, provided that such laboratory reapply for accreditation in accordance with the provisions of this paragraph (c)(1), by January 12, 1994 (30 days of the effective date of this section), and that the reapplication be accepted by the Agency. The CUSUM values for such laboratory will be reset at zero upon acceptance of its reapplication. The accreditation of a laboratory that is on probation shall be continued, provided that such laboratory reapply for accreditation by February 11, 1994 (60 days of the effective date of this section), that the reapplication be accepted by the Agency, and that the laboratory satisfy the terms of the probation.

(2) *Criteria for obtaining accreditation.* Non-Federal analytical laboratories may be accredited for the analysis of a class of chemical residues in meat and meat food products. Accreditation will be given only if the applying laboratory successfully satisfies the requirements presented below. This accreditation authorizes official FSIS acceptance of the analytical test results provided by these laboratories on official samples. To obtain FSIS accreditation for the analysis of a class of chemical residues, a non-Federal analytical laboratory must:

(i) Be supervised by a person holding, as a minimum, a bachelor's degree in either chemistry, food science, food technology, or a related field. Further, either the supervisor or the analyst assigned to analyze the sample must have 3 years' experience determining analytes at or below part per million levels, or equivalent qualifications, as determined by the Administrator.

(ii) Demonstrate acceptable limits of systematic laboratory difference, variability, individual large deviations, recoveries, and proper identification in the analysis of the class of chemical residues for which application was made, using FSIS approved procedures. An applying laboratory will successfully demonstrate these capabilities if its analytical results for each specific chemical residue provided in a check sample accreditation study containing a minimum of 14 samples satisfy the criteria presented in this paragraph (c)(2)(ii).[7] In addition, if the laboratory is requesting accreditation for the analysis of chlorinated hydrocarbons, all analytical results for the residue class must collectively satisfy the criteria. [Conformance to criteria (c)(2)(ii) (A), (B), (C), (D), (E), and (F) will only be determined when six or more analytical results with associated comparison means at or above the logarithm of the minimum proficiency level are available.] If the results of the first set of check samples do not meet these criteria for obtaining accreditation, a second set of at least 14 samples will be provided within 30 days following the date of receipt by FSIS of a request from the applying laboratory. If the results of the second set of samples do not meet accreditation criteria, the laboratory may reapply after a 60-day waiting period, commencing from the date

7. All statistical computations are rounded to the nearest tenth, except where otherwise noted.

of refusal of accreditation by FSIS. At that time, a new application, all fees, and all documentation of corrective action required for accreditation must be submitted.

(A) *Systematic laboratory difference:* The absolute value of the average standardized difference must not exceed 1.67 (2.00 if there are less than 12 analytical results) minus the product of 0.29 and the standard deviation of the standardized differences.

(B) *Variability:* The standard deviation of the standardized differences must not exceed a computed limit. This limit is a function of the number of analytical results used in the computation of the standard deviation, and of the amount of variability associated with the results from the participating FSIS laboratories.

(C) *Individual large deviations:* One hundred times the average of the large deviation measures of the individual analytical results must be less than 5.0.[8]

(D) *QA recovery:* The average of the QA recoveries of the individual analytical results must lie within the range given in Table 2 under the column entitled 'Percent Expected Recovery.'

(E) *QC recovery:* All QC recoveries must lie within the range given in Table 2 under 'Percent Expected Recovery.' Supporting documentation must be made available to FSIS upon request.

(F) *Correct identification:* There must be correct identification of all chemical residues in all samples.

(iii) Allow inspection of the laboratory by FSIS officials prior to the determination of granting accredited status.

(iv) Pay the accreditation fee by the date required.

(3) *Criteria for maintaining accreditation.* To maintain accreditation for analysis of a class of chemical residues, a nonFederal analytical laboratory must:

(i) [Reserved]

(ii) Maintain laboratory quality control records for the most recent 3 years that samples have been analyzed under this Program.

(iii) Maintain complete records of the receipt, analysis, and disposition of official samples for the most recent 3 years that samples have been analyzed under the Program.

(iv) Maintain a standards book, which is a permanently bound book with sequentially numbered pages, containing all readings and calculations for standardization of solutions, determination of recoveries, and calibration of instruments. All entries are to be dated and signed by the analyst immediately upon completion of the entry and by his/her supervisor within 2 working days. The standards book is to be retained for a period of 3 years after the last entry is made.

(v) Analyze interlaboratory accreditation maintenance check samples and return the results to FSIS within 3 weeks of sample receipt. This must be done whenever requested by FSIS and at no cost to FSIS.

---

8. A result will have a large deviation measure equal to zero when the absolute value of the result's standardized difference, (d), is less than 2.5 and otherwise a measure equal $1-(2.5/d)^4$.

(vi) Inform the Accredited Laboratory Program, Food Safety and Inspection Service, U.S. Department of Agriculture, Washington, DC 20250-3700, by certified or registered mail, within 30 days of any change in the laboratory's ownership, officers, directors, supervisory personnel, or any other responsibly connected individual or entity.

(vii) Permit any duly authorized representative of the Secretary to perform both announced and unannounced onsite laboratory reviews of facilities and records during normal business hours, and to copy any records pertaining to the laboratory's participation in the Accredited Laboratory Program.

(viii) Use analytical procedures designated and approved by FSIS.

(ix) Demonstrate that acceptable limits of systematic laboratory difference, variability, and individual large deviations are being maintained in the analysis of samples, in the chemical residue class for which accreditation was granted. A laboratory will successfully demonstrate the maintenance of these capabilities if its analytical results for each specific chemical residue found in interlaboratory accreditation maintenance check samples and/or split samples satisfy the criteria presented in this paragraph (c)(3)(ix).[9,10] In addition, if the laboratory is accredited for the analysis of chlorinated hydrocarbons, all analytical results for the residue class must collectively satisfy the criteria.

(A) *Systematic laboratory difference:*

(*1*) *Positive systematic laboratory difference:* The standardized difference between the accredited laboratory's result and that of the FSIS laboratory for each split and/or interlaboratory accreditation maintenance check sample is used to determine a CUSUM value, designated as COSUM-P.[11] This value is computed and evaluated as follows:

(*i*) Determine the CUSUM increment for the sample. The CUSUM increment is set equal to:

2.0, if the standardized difference is greater than 2.5,

–2.0, if the standardized difference is less than –1.5,

or

the standardized difference minus 0.5, if the standardized difference lies between –1.5 and 2.5, inclusive.

---

9. All statistical computations are rounded to the nearest tenth, except where otherwise noted.
10. An analytical result will only be used in the statistical evaluation of the laboratory if the associated comparison mean is equal to or greater than the logarithm of the minimum proficiency level for the residue.
11. When determining compliance with this criterion for all chlorinated hydrocarbon results in a sample collectively, the following statistical procedure must be followed to account for the correlation of analytical results within a sample: the average of the standardized differences of the analytical results within the sample, divided by a constant, is used in place of a single standardized difference to determine the COSUM-P (or COSUM-N) value for the sample. The constant is a function of the number of analytical results used to compute the average standardized difference.

(*ii*) Compute the new COSUM-P value. The new COSUM-P value is obtained by adding, algebraically, the CUSUM increment to the last previously computed COSUM-P value. If this computation yields a value smaller than 0, the new COSUM-P value is set equal to 0. [COSUM-P values are initialized at zero; that is, the COSUM-P value associated with the first sample is set equal to the CUSUM increment for that sample.]

(*iii*) Evaluate the new COSUM-P value. The new COSUM-P value must not exceed 4.8.

(2) *Negative systematic laboratory difference:* The standardized difference between the accredited laboratory's result and that of the FSIS laboratory for each split and/or interlaboratory accreditation maintenance check sample is used to determine a CUSUM value, designated as COSUM-N.[12] This value is computed and evaluated as follows:

(i) Determine the CUSUM increment for the sample. The CUSUM increment is set equal to:

2.0, if the standardized difference is greater than 1.5,

–2.0, if the standardized difference is less than –2.5,

or

the standardized difference plus 0.5, if the standardized difference lies between –2.5 and 1.5, inclusive.

(*ii*) Compute the new COSUM-N value. The new COSUM-N value is obtained by subtracting, algebraically, the CUSUM increment to the last previously computed COSUM-N value. If this computation yields a value smaller than 0, the new COSUM-N value is set equal to 0. [COSUM-N values are initialized at zero; that is, the COSUM-N value associated with the first sample is set equal to the CUSUM increment for that sample.]

(*iii*) Evaluate the new COSUM-N value. The new COSUM-N value must not exceed 4.8.

(B) *Variability:* The absolute value of the standardized difference between the accredited laboratory's result and that of the FSIS laboratory for each split and/or interlaboratory accreditation maintenance check sample is used to determine a CUSUM value, designated as COSUM-V.[13] This value is computed and evaluated as follows:

---

12. *See* footnote 11.
13. When determining compliance with this criterion for all chlorinated hydrocarbon results in a sample collectively, the following statistical procedure must be followed to account for the correlation of analytical results within a sample: the square root of the sum of the within sample variance and the average standardized difference of the sample, divided by a constant, is used in place of the absolute value of the standardized difference to determine the COSUM-V value for the sample. The constant is a function of the number of analytical results used to compute the average standardized difference.

(*1*) Determine the CUSUM increment for the sample. The CUSUM increment is set equal to the larger of –0.4 and the absolute value of the standardized difference minus 0.9. If this computation yields a value larger than 1.6, the increment is set equal to 1.6.

(*2*) Compute the new COSUM-V value. The new COSUM-V value is obtained by adding, algebraically, the CUSUM increment to the last previously computed COSUM-V value. If this computation yields a value less than 0, the new COSUM-V value is set equal to 0. [COSUM-V values are initialized at zero; that is, the COSUM-V value associated with the first sample is set equal to the CUSUM increment for that sample.]

(*3*) Evaluate the new COSUM-V value. The new COSUM-V value must not exceed 4.3.

(C) *Large Deviations:* The large deviation measure of the accredited laboratory's result for each split and/or interlaboratory accreditation maintenance check sample is used to determine a CUSUM value, designated as COSUM-D.[14] This value is computed and evaluated as follows:

(*1*) Determine the CUSUM increment for the sample. The CUSUM increment is set equal to the large deviation measure minus 0.025.

(*2*) Compute the new COSUM-D value. The new COSUM-D is obtained by adding, algebraically, the CUSUM increment to the last previously computed COSUM-D value. If this computation yields a value less than 0, the new COSUM-D value is set equal to 0. [COSUM-D values are initialized at zero; that is, the COSUM-D value associated with the first sample is set equal to the CUSUM increment for that sample.]

(*3*) Evaluate the new COSUM-D value. The new COSUM-D value must not exceed 1.0.

(x) Meet the following requirements if placed on probation pursuant to paragraph (e) of this section:

(A) Send all official samples that have not been analyzed as of the date of written notification of probation to a specified FSIS laboratory by certified mail or private carrier or, as an alternative, to an accredited laboratory accredited for this specific chemical residue. Mailing expense will be paid by FSIS.

(B) Analyze a set of check samples similar to those used for initial accreditation, and submit analytical results to FSIS within 3 weeks of receipt of the samples.

(C) Satisfy criteria for check samples as specified in paragraphs (c)(2)(ii) (A), (B), (C), (D), (E), and (F) of this section.

(xi) Expeditiously report analytical results of official samples to the Eastern Laboratory, College Station Road, P.O. Box 6085, Athens, GA 30604, or to the address designated by the Assistant Administrator, Office of Public Health and Science. The Federal inspector at any establishment may assign the analysis of

---

14. A result will have a large deviation measure equal to zero when the absolute value of the result's standardized difference, (d), is less than 2.5, and otherwise a measure equal to $1-(2.5/d)^4$.

official samples to an FSIS laboratory if, in the judgment of the inspector, there are delays in receiving test results on official samples from an accredited laboratory.

(xii) Every QC recovery associated with reporting of official samples must be within the appropriate range given in Table 2 under 'Percent Expected Recovery.' Supporting documentation must be made available to FSIS upon request.

(xiii) Demonstrate that acceptable levels of systematic laboratory difference, variability, individual large deviations, recoveries, and proper identification are being maintained in the analysis of interlaboratory accreditation maintenance check samples, in the chemical residue class for which accreditation was granted. A laboratory will successfully demonstrate the maintenance of these capabilities if its analytical results for each specific chemical residue found in interlaboratory accreditation maintenance check samples satisfy the criteria presented below. In addition, if the laboratory is accredited for the analysis of chlorinated hydrocarbons, all analytical results for the residue class must collectively satisfy the criteria.

(A) *Systematic laboratory difference* – (*1*) *Positive systematic laboratory difference:* The standardized difference between the accredited laboratory's result and the comparison mean for each interlaboratory accreditation maintenance check sample is used to determine a CUSUM value, designated as COSUM-P.[15] This value is computed and evaluated as follows:

(i) Determine the CUSUM increment for the sample. The CUSUM increment is set equal to:

2.0, if the standardized difference is greater than 2.5,

–2.0, if the standardized difference is less than –1.5,

or

the standardized difference minus 0.5, if the standardized difference lies between –1.5 and 2.5, inclusive.

(*ii*) Compute the new COSUM-P value. The new COSUM-P value is obtained by adding, algebraically, the CUSUM increment to the last previously computed COSUM-P value. If this computation yields a value smaller than 0, the new COSUM-P value is set equal to 0. [COSUM-P values are initialized at zero; that is, the COSUM-P value associated with the first sample is set equal to the CUSUM increment for that sample.]

(*iii*) Evaluate the new COSUM-P value. The new COSUM-P value must not exceed 4.8.

(*2*) *Negative systematic laboratory difference:* The standardized difference between the accredited laboratory's result and the comparison mean for each interlaboratory accreditation maintenance check sample is used to determine a CUSUM value, designated as COSUM-N.[16] This value is computed and evaluated as follows:

(*i*) Determine the CUSUM increment for the sample. The CUSUM increment is set equal to:

15. *See* footnote 11.

16. *See* footnote 11.

2.0, if the standardized difference is greater than 1.5,

–2.0, if the standardized difference is less than –2.5,

or

the standardized difference plus 0.5, if the standardized difference lies between –2.5 and 1.5, inclusive.

(*ii*) Compute the new COSUM-N value. The new COSUM-N value is obtained by subtracting, algebraically, the CUSUM increment to the last previously computed COSUM-N value. If this computation yields a value smaller than 0, the new COSUM-N value is set equal to 0. [COSUM-N values are initialized at zero; that is, the COSUM-N value associated with the first sample is set equal to the CUSUM increment for that sample.]

(*iii*) Evaluate the new COSUM-N value. The new COSUM-N value must not exceed 4.8.

(B) *Variability:* The absolute value of the standardized difference between the accredited laboratory's result and the comparison mean for each interlaboratory accreditation maintenance check sample is used to determine a CUSUM value, designated as COSUM-V.[17] This value is computed and evaluated as follows:

(*1*) Determine the CUSUM increment for the sample. The CUSUM increment is set equal to the larger of –0.4 or the absolute value of the standardized difference minus 0.9. If this computation yields a value larger than 1.6, the increment is set equal to 1.6.

(*2*) Compute the new COSUM-V value. The new COSUM-V value is obtained by adding, algebraically, the CUSUM increment to the last previously computed COSUM-V value. If this computation yields a value less than 0, the new COSUM-V value is set equal to 0. [COSUM-V values are initialized at zero; that is, the COSUM-V value associated with the first sample is set equal to the CUSUM increment for that sample.]

(*3*) Evaluate the new COSUM-V value. The new COSUM-V value must not exceed 4.3.

(C) *Large deviations:* The large deviation measure of the accredited laboratory's result for each interlaboratory accreditation maintenance check sample is used to determine a CUSUM value, designated as COSUM-D.[18] This value is computed and evaluated as follows:

(*1*) Determine the CUSUM increment for the sample. The CUSUM increment is set equal to the value of the large deviation measure minus 0.025.

(*2*) Compute the new COSUM-D value. The new COSUM-D is obtained by adding, algebraically, the CUSUM increment to the last previously computed COSUM-D value. If this computation yields a value less than 0, the new COSUM-D value is set equal to 0. [COSUM-D values are initialized at zero; that is, the

---

17. *See* footnote 13.

18. A result will have a large deviation measure equal to zero when the absolute value of the result's standardized difference, (d), is less than 2.5, and otherwise a measure equal to $1-(2.5/d)^4$.

COSUM-D value associated with the first sample is set equal to the CUSUM increment for that sample.]

(*3*) Evaluate the new COSUM-D value. The new COSUM-D value must not exceed 1.0.

(D) Each QC Recovery is within the range given in Table 2 under 'Percent Expected Recovery'. Supporting documentation must be made available to FSIS upon request.

(E) Not more than 1 residue misidentification in any 2 consecutive check samples.

(F) Not more than 2 residue misidentifications in any 8 consecutive check samples.

(xiv) Pay the accreditation fee when it is due.

(d) *Refusal of accreditation.* Upon a determination by the Administrator, a laboratory shall be refused accreditation for the following reasons:

(1) A laboratory shall be refused accreditation for moisture, protein, fat, and salt analysis for failure to meet the requirements of paragraph (b)(1) or (b)(2) of this section.

(2) A laboratory shall be refused accreditation for chemical residue analysis for failure to meet the requirements of paragraph (c)(1) or (c)(2) of this section.

(3) A laboratory shall be refused subsequent accreditation for failure to return to an FSIS laboratory, by certified mail or private carrier, all official samples which have not been analyzed as of the notification of a loss of accreditation.

(4) A laboratory shall be refused accreditation if the applicant or any individual or entity responsibly connected with the applicant has been convicted of or is under indictment or if charges on an information have been brought against the applicant or responsibly connected individual or entity in any Federal or State court concerning the following violations of law:

(i) Any felony.

(ii) Any misdemeanor based upon acquiring, handling, or distributing of unwholesome, misbranded, or deceptively packaged food or upon fraud in connection with transactions in food.

(iii) Any misdemeanor based upon a false statement to any governmental agency.

(iv) Any misdemeanor based upon the offering, giving or receiving of a bribe or unlawful gratuity.

(e) *Probation of accreditation.* Upon a determination by the Administrator, a laboratory shall be placed on probation for the following reasons:

(1) If the laboratory fails to complete more than one interlaboratory accreditation maintenance check sample analysis within 12 consecutive months as required by paragraphs (b)(3)(v) and (c)(3)(v) of this section.

(2) If the laboratory fails to meet any of the criteria set forth in paragraphs (b)(3)(v) and (b)(3)(ix) and (c)(3)(v) and (c)(3)(ix) of this section.

(f) *Suspension of accreditation.* The accreditation of a laboratory shall be suspended if the laboratory or any individual or entity responsibly connected with the laboratory is indicted or if charges on an information have been brought against the laboratory or responsibly connected individual or entity in any Federal or State court concerning any of the following violations of law:

(1) Any felony.

(2) Any misdemeanor based upon acquiring, handling or distributing of unwholesome, misbranded, or deceptively packaged food or upon fraud in connection with transactions in food.

(3) Any misdemeanor based upon a false statement to any governmental agency.

(4) Any misdemeanor based upon the offering, giving or receiving of a bribe or unlawful gratuity.

(g) *Revocation of accreditation.* The accreditation of a laboratory shall be revoked for the following reasons:

(1) An accredited laboratory which is accredited to perform analysis under paragraph (b) of this section shall have its accreditation revoked for failure to meet any of the requirements of paragraph (b)(3) of this section except for the following circumstances. If the accredited laboratory fails to meet the criteria for reporting the analytical results on interlaboratory accreditation maintenance check samples as set forth in paragraph (b)(3)(v) of this section or if, at any time, the CUSUM results from the analysis of such interlaboratory accreditation maintenance check samples and/or split samples have not satisfied the criteria specified in paragraph (b)(3)(ix) of this section and there have been, during the previous 12 months, no other occasions on which such CUSUM results have not satisfied such criteria, the laboratory shall be placed on probation; but if there have been such other occasions during those 12 months, the laboratory's accreditation will be revoked.

(2) An accredited laboratory which is accredited to perform analysis for a class of chemical residues under paragraph (c) of this section shall have the accreditation to perform this analysis revoked if it fails to meet any of the requirements in paragraph (c)(3) of this section except for the following circumstances. If the accredited laboratory fails to meet any of the criteria set forth in paragraphs (c)(3)(v), (c)(3)(ix), and (c)(3)(xiii) of this section and it has not so failed during the 12 months preceding its failure to meet the criteria, it shall be placed on probation, but if it has so failed at any time during those 12 months, its accreditation will be revoked.

(3) An accredited laboratory shall have its accreditation revoked if the Administrator determines that the laboratory or any responsibly connected individual or any agent or employee has:

(i) Altered any official sample or analytical finding, or,

(ii) Substituted any analytical result from any other laboratory for its own.

(4) An accredited laboratory shall have its accreditation revoked if the laboratory or any individual or entity responsibly connected with the laboratory is convicted in a Federal or State court of any of the following violations of law:

(i) Any felony.

(ii) Any misdemeanor based upon acquiring, handling, or distributing of unwholesome, misbranded, or deceptively packaged food or upon fraud in connection with transactions in food.

(iii) Any misdemeanor based upon a false statement to any governmental agency.

(iv) Any misdemeanor based upon the offering, giving or receiving of a bribe or unlawful gratuity.

(h) *Notification and hearings.* Accreditation of any laboratory shall be refused, suspended, or revoked under the conditions previously described herein. The owner or operator of the laboratory shall be sent written notice of the refusal, suspension, or revocation of accreditation by the Administrator. In such cases, the laboratory owner or operator will be provided an opportunity to present, within 30 days of the date of the notification, a statement challenging the merits or validity of such action and to request an oral hearing with respect to the denial, suspension, or revocation decision. An oral hearing shall be granted if there is any dispute of material fact joined in such responsive statement. The proceeding shall thereafter be conducted in accordance with the applicable rules of practice which shall be adopted for the proceeding. Any such refusal, suspension, or revocation shall be effective upon the receipt by the laboratory of the notification and shall continue in effect until final determination of the matter by the Administrator.

(Reporting and recordkeeping requirements approved by the Office of Management and Budget under control number 0583–0015)

[52 FR 2185, Jan. 20, 1987, as amended at 58 FR 65260, 65262–65264, Dec. 13, 1993; 59 FR 33642, June 30, 1994; 59 FR 66448, Dec. 27, 1994; 60 FR 10305, Feb. 24, 1995; 69 FR 254, Jan. 5, 2004]

§ 318.22 Determination of Added Water in Cooked Sausages

(a) For purposes of this section, the following definitions apply.

(1) *Cooked sausage.* Cooked sausage is any product described in § 319.140 and §§ 319.180–319.182 of this chapter.

(2) *Group 1 Protein-Contributing Ingredients.* Ingredients of livestock or poultry origin from muscle tissue which is skeletal or which is found in the edible organs, with or without the accompanying and overlying fat, and the portions of bone, skin, sinew, nerve, and blood vessels which normally accompany the muscle tissue and which are not separated from it in the process of dressing; meat byproducts; mechanically separated (species); and poultry products; except those ingredients processed by hydrolysis, extraction, concentrating or drying.

(3) *Group 2 Protein-Contributing Ingredients.* Ingredients from Gorup 1 protein-contributing ingredients processed by hydrolysis, extraction, concentrating, or drying, or any other ingredient which contributes protein.

(b) The amount of added water in cooked sausage is calculated by:

(1) Determining by laboratory analysis the total percentage of water contained in the cooked sausage; and

(2) Determining by laboratory analysis the total percentage of protein contained in the cooked sausage; and

(3) Calculating the percentage of protein in the cooked sausage contributed by the Group 2 protein-contributing ingredients; and

(4) Subtracting one pecent from the total percentage of protein calculated in (b)(3); and

(5) Subtracting the remaining percentage of protein calculated in (b)(3) from the total protein content determined in (b)(2); and

(6) Calculating the percentage of indigenous water in the cooked sausage by multiplying the percentage of protein determined in (b)(5) by 4, (This amount is the percentage of water attributable to Group 1 protein-contributing ingredients and one percent of Group 2 protein-contributing ingredients in a cooked sausage.); and

(7) Subtracting the percentage of water calculated in (b)(6) from the total percentage of water determined in (b)(1). (This amount is the percentage of added water in a cooked sausage.)[1]

[55 FR 7299, Mar. 1, 1990]

§ 318.23 Heat-Processing and Stabilization Requirements for Uncured Meat Patties

(a) *Definitions.* For purposes of this section, the following definitions shall apply:

(1) *Patty.* A shaped and formed, comminuted, flattened cake of meat food product.

Permitted Heat-Processing Temperature/Time Combinations for Fully-Cooked Patties

Minimum internal temperature at the center of each patty (Degrees)		*Minimum holding time after required internal temperature is reached (Time)*	
Fahrenheit	*Or centigrade*	*Minutes*	*Or seconds*
151	66.1	.68	41
152	66.7	.54	32
153	67.2	.43	26
154	67.8	.34	20
155	68.3	.27	16
156	68.9	.22	13
157 (and up)	69.4 (and up)	.17	10

1. The equation for the narrative description of the calculation for added water is as follows: AW=TW-(TP-(P-1.0))4, Where AW=Added Water, TW-Total Water Determined by Laboratory Analysis, TP=Total Protein Determined by Laboratory Analysis, P=Protein Contributed by Group 2 Protein Contributing Ingredients, 1.0=Percent Allowance for Group 2 Protein-Contributing Ingredients, 4=Moisture-Protein Ratio for Cooked Sausage.

(2) *Comminuted.* A processing term describing the reduction in size of pieces of meat, including chopping, flaking, grinding, or mincing, but not including chunking or sectioning.

(3) *Partially-cooked patties.* Meat patties that have been heat processed for less time or using lower internal temperatures than are prescribed by paragraph (b)(1) of this section.

(4) *Charmarked patties.* Meat patties that have been marked by a heat source and that have been heat processed for less time or using lower internal temperatures than are prescribed by paragraph (b)(1) of this section.

(b) *Heat-processing procedures for fully-cooked patties.* (1) Official establishments which manufacture fully-cooked patties shall use one of the following heat-processing procedures:

(2) The official establishment shall measure the holding time and temperature of at least one fully-cooked patty from each production line each hour of production to assure control of the heat process. The temperature measuring device shall be accurate within 1 degree F.

(3) Requirements for handling heating deviations. (i) If for any reason a heating deviation has occurred, the official establishment shall investigate and identify the cause; take steps to assure that the deviation will not recur; and place on file in the official establishment, available to any duly authorized FSIS program employee, a report of the investigation, the cause of the deviation, and the steps taken to prevent recurrence.

(ii) In addition, in the case of a heating deviation, the official establishment may reprocess the affected product, using one of the *Method*s in paragraph (b)(1) in this section; use the affected product as an ingredient in another product processed to one of the temperature and time combinations in paragraph (b)(1) in this section, provided this does not violate the final product's standard of composition, upset the order of predominance of ingredients, or perceptibly affect the normal product characteristics; or relabel the affected product as a partially-cooked patty product, if it meets the stabilization requirements in paragraph (c) of this section.

(c) *Stabilization.* (1) Fully cooked, partially cooked, and char-marked meat patties must be produced using processes ensuring no multiplication of toxigenic microorganisms such as *Clostridium botulinum,* and no more than a 1 $\log_{10}$ multiplication of *Clostridium perfringens,* within the product.

(2) For each meat patty product produced using a stabilization process other than one conducted in accordance with the Hazard Analysis and Critical Control Point (HACCP) system requirements in part 417 of this chapter, an establishment must develop and have on file, available to FSIS, a process schedule, as defined in § 301.2 of this chapter. Each process schedule must be approved in writing by a process authority for safety and efficacy in meeting the performance standards established for the product in question. A process authority must have access to an establishment in order to evaluate and approve the safety and efficacy of each process schedule.

(3) Under the auspices of a processing authority, an establishment must validate new or altered process schedules by scientifically supportable means,

such as information gleaned from the literature or by challenge studies conducted outside the plant.

(4) Partially cooked patties must bear the labeling statement 'Partially cooked: For Safety Cook Until Well Done (Internal Meat Temperature 160 degrees F.).' The labeling statement must be adjacent to the product name, and prominently placed with such conspicuousness (as compared with other words, statements, designs or devices in the labeling) as to render it likely to be read and understood by the ordinary individual under customary conditions of purchase and use.

(5) Charmarked patties must bear the labeling statement 'Uncooked, Charmarked: For Safety, Cook Until Well Done (Internal Meat Temperature 160 degrees F.).' The labeling statement shall be adjacent to the product name, at least onehalf the size of the largest letter in the product name, and prominently placed with such conspicuousness (as compared with other words, statements, designs or devices in the labeling) as to render it likely to be read and understood by the ordinary individual under customary conditions of purchase and use.

[64 FR 744, Jan. 6, 1999]

§ 318.24 Product Prepared Using Advanced Meat/Bone Separation Machinery; Process Control

(a) *General.* Meat, as defined in § 301.2 of this subchapter, may be derived by mechanically separating skeletal muscle tissue from the bones of livestock, other than skulls or vertebral column bones of cattle 30 months of age and older as provided in § 310.22 of this subchapter, using advances in mechanical meat/bone separation machinery (*i.e.,* AMR systems) that, in accordance with this section, recover meat –

(1) Without significant incorporation of bone solids or bone marrow as measured by the presence of calcium and iron in excess of the requirements in this section, and

(2) Without the presence of any brain, trigeminal ganglia, spinal cord, or dorsal root ganglia (DRG).

(b) *Process control.* As a prerequisite to labeling or using product as meat derived by the mechanical separation of skeletal muscle tissue from live-stock bones, the operator of an establishment must develop, implement, and maintain procedures that ensure that the establishment's production process is in control.

(1) The production process is not in control if the skulls entering the AMR system contain any brain or trigeminal ganglia tissue, if the vertebral column bones entering the AMR system contain any spinal cord, if the recovered product fails otherwise under any provision of paragraph (c)(1), if the product is not properly labeled under the provisions of paragraph (c)(2), or if the spent bone materials are not properly handled under the provisions of paragraph (c)(3) of this section.

(2) The establishment must document its production process controls in writing. The program must be designed to ensure the ongoing effectiveness of the process controls. If the establishment processes cattle, the program must be in its

HACCP plan, its Sanitation SOP, or other prerequisite program. The program shall describe the ongoing verification activities that will be performed, including the observation of the bones entering the AMR system for brain, trigeminal ganglia, and spinal cord; the testing of the product exiting the AMR system for bone solids, bone marrow, spinal cord, and DRG as prescribed in paragraph (c)(1) of this section; the use of the product and spent bone materials exiting the AMR system; and the frequency with which these activities will be performed.

(3) The establishment shall maintain records on a daily basis sufficient to document the implementation and verification of its production process.

(4) The establishment shall make available to inspection program personnel the documentation described in paragraphs (b)(2) and (b)(3) of this section and any other data generated using these procedures.

(c) *Noncomplying product.* (1) Notwithstanding any other provision of this section, product that is recovered using advanced meat/bone separation machinery is not meat under any one or more of the following circumstances:

(i) *Bone solids.* The product's calcium content, measured by individual samples and rounded to the nearest 10th, is more than 130.0 mg per 100 g.

(ii) *Bone marrow.* The product's added iron content, measured by duplicate analyses on individual samples and rounded to the nearest 10th, is more than 3.5 mg per 100 g.[1]

(iii) *Brain or trigeminal ganglia.* Skulls that enter the AMR system have tissues of brain or trigeminal ganglia.

(iv) *Spinal cord.* Vertebral column bones that enter the AMR system have tissues of spinal cord, or the product that exits the AMR system contains spinal cord.

---

1. The excessive iron (ExcFe) measurement for an analyzed sample is equal to the obtained iron (Fe) result expressed in mg/100 g measured and rounded to the nearest 100th or more for that sample, minus the product of three factors: (1) The iron to protein ratio (IPR) factor associated with corresponding hand-deboned product; (2) the obtained protein (P) result (%) for that sample; and (3) a constant factor of 1.10. In formula, this can be written as: $ExcFe = mFe - IPR \times Protein \times 1.10$, where ExcFe represents the excess iron, expressed in units of mg/100 g; mFe represents the measured level of iron (Fe, mg/ 100 g), IPR is the iron to protein ratio for the appropriate hand-deboned product, and 'Protein' is the measured level of protein rounded to the nearest 100th and expressed as a percentage of the total weight of the sample. In lieu of data demonstrating otherwise, the values of IPR to be used in the above formula are as follows: For beef products the value of IPR is equal to 0.104, except for any combination of bones that include any beef neckbone product, for which the value of 0.138 is to be used; for pork product, the IPR value is 0.052. Other IPR values can be used provided that the operator of an establishment has verified and documented the ratio of iron content to protein content in the skeletal muscle tissue attached to bones prior to their entering the AMR system, based on analyses of hand-deboned samples, and the documented value is to be substituted for the IPR value (as applicable) in the above formula with respect to product that the establishment mechanically separates from those bones.

(v) *DRG.* The product that exits the AMR system contains DRG.

(2) If product that may not be labeled or used as 'meat' under this section meets the requirements of § 319.5 of this subchapter, it may bear the name 'Mechanically Separated (Species)' except as follows:

(i) If skulls or vertebral column bones of cattle younger than 30 months of age that enter the AMR system have tissues of brain, trigeminal ganglia, or spinal cord, the product that exits the AMR system shall not be used as an ingredient of a meat food product.

(ii) If product that exits the AMR system contains spinal cord or DRG from bones of cattle younger than 30 months of age, it shall not be used as an ingredient of a meat food product.

(iii) If product derived from any bones of cattle of any age does not comply with (c)(1)(i) or (ii), it may bear a common or usual name that is not false or misleading, except that the product may not bear the name 'Mechanically Separated (Beef).'

(3) Spent skulls or vertebral column bone materials from cattle younger than 30 months of age that exit the AMR system shall not be used as an ingredient of a meat food product.

[69 FR 1884, Jan. 12, 2004]

SUBPARTS B–F [RESERVED]

SUBPART G – CANNING AND CANNED PRODUCTS

SOURCE: 51 FR 45619, Dec. 19, 1986, unless otherwise noted.

§ 318.300 DEFINITIONS

(a) *Abnormal container.* A container with any sign of swelling or product leakage or any evidence that the contents of the unopened container may be spoiled.

(b) *Acidified low acid product.* A canned product which has been formulated or treated so that every component of the finished product has a pH of 4.6 or lower within 24 hours after the completion of the thermal process unless data are available from the establishment's processing authority demonstrating that a longer time period is safe.

(c) *Bleeders.* Small orifices on a retort through which steam, other gasses, and condensate are emitted from the retort throughout the entire thermal process.

(d) *Canned product.* A meat food product with a water activity above 0.85 which receives a thermal process either before or after being packed in a hermetically sealed container. Unless otherwise specified, the term 'product' as used in this subpart G shall mean 'canned product.'

(e) *Closure technician.* The individual(s) identified by the establishment as being trained to perform specific container integrity examinations as required by this subpart and designated by the establishment to perform such examinations.

(f) *Code lot.* All production of a particular product in a specific size container marked with a specific container code.

(g) *Comeup time.* The elapsed time, including venting time (if applicable), between the introduction of the heating medium into a closed retort and the start of process timing.

(h) *Critical factor.* Any characteristic, condition or aspect of a product, container, or procedure that affects the adequacy of the process schedule. Critical factors are established by processing authorities.

(i) *Headspace.* That portion of a container not occupied by the product.

(1) *Gross headspace.* The vertical distance between the level of the product (generally the liquid surface) in an upright rigid container and the top edge of the container (i.e., the flange of an unsealed can, the top of the double seam on a sealed can, or the top edge of an unsealed jar).

(2) *Net headspace.* The vertical distance between the level of the product (generally the liquid surface) in an upright rigid container and the inside surface of the lid.

(j) *Hermetically sealed containers.* Airtight containers which are designed and intended to protect the contents against the entry of microorganisms during and after thermal processing.

(1) *Rigid container.* A container, the shape or contour of which, when filled and sealed, is neither affected by the enclosed product nor deformed by external mechanical pressure of up to 10 pounds per square inch gauge (0.7 kg/ cm^2) (i.e., normal firm finger pressure).

(2) *Semirigid container.* A container, the shape or contour of which, when filled and sealed, is not significantly affected by the enclosed product under normal atmospheric temperature and pressure, but can be deformed by external mechanical pressure of less than 10 pounds per square inch gauge (0.7 kg/ cm^2) (i.e., normal firm finger pressure).

(3) *Flexible container.* A container, the shape or contour of which, when filled and sealed, is significantly affected by the enclosed product.

(k) *Incubation tests.* Tests in which the thermally processed product is kept at a specific temperature for a specified period of time in order to determine if outgrowth of microorganisms occurs.

(l) *Initial temperature.* The temperature, determined at the initiation of a thermal process cycle, of the contents of the coldest container to be processed.

(m) *Low acid product.* A canned product in which any component has a pH value above 4.6.

(n) *Process schedule.* The thermal process and any specified critical factors for a given canned product required to achieve shelf stability.

(o) *Process temperature.* The minimum temperature(s) of the heating medium to be maintained as specified in the process schedule.

(p) *Process time.* The intended time(s) a container is to be exposed to the heating medium while the heating medium is at or above the process temperature(s).

(q) *Processing authority.* The person(s) or organization(s) having expert knowledge of thermal processing requirements for foods in hermetically sealed containers, having access to facilities for making such determinations, and designated by the establishment to perform certain functions as indicated in this subpart.

(r) P*rogram employee.* Any inspector or other individual employed by the Department or any cooperating agency who is authorized by the Secretary to do any work or perform any duty in connection with the Program (see §301.2(f)).

(s) *Retort.* A pressure vessel designed for thermal processing of product packed in hermetically sealed containers.

(t) *Seals.* Those parts of a semirigid container and lid or of a flexible container that are fused together in order to hermetically close the container.

(u) *Shelf stability.* The condition achieved by application of heat, sufficient, alone or in combination with other ingredients and/or treatments, to render the product free of microorganisms capable of growing in the product at nonrefrigerated conditions (over 50 °F or 10 °C) at which the product is intended to be held during distribution and storage. Shelf stability and shelf stable are synonymous with commercial sterility and commercially sterile, respectively.

(v) *Thermal process.* The heat treatment necessary to achieve shelf stability as determined by the establishment's processing authority. It is quantified in terms of:

(1) Time(s) and temperature(s); or

(2) Minimum product temperature.

(w) *Venting.* The removal of air from a retort before the start of process timing.

(x) *Water activity.* The ratio of the water vapor pressure of the product to the vapor pressure of pure water at the same temperature.

§ 318.301 Containers and Closures

(a) *Examination and cleaning of empty containers.* (1) Empty containers, closures, and flexible pouch roll stock shall be evaluated by the establishment to ensure that they are clean and free of structural defects and damage that may affect product or container integrity. Such an examination should be based upon a statistical sampling plan.

(2) All empty containers, closures, and flexible pouch roll stock shall be stored, handled, and conveyed in such a manner that will prevent soiling and damage that could affect the hermetic condition of the sealed container.

(3) Just before filling, rigid containers shall be cleaned to prevent incorporation of foreign matter into the finished product. Closures, semirigid containers, preformed flexible pouches, and flexible pouch roll stock contained in original wrappings do not need to be cleaned before use.

(b) *Closure examinations for rigid containers (cans) – (1) Visual examinations.* A closure technician shall visually examine the double seams formed by each closing machine head. When seam defects (e.g., cutovers, sharpness, knocked down flanges, false seams, droops) are observed, necessary corrective actions, such as adjusting or repairing the closing machine, shall be taken. In addition to the double seams, the entire container shall be examined for product leakage or obvious defects. A visual examination shall be performed on at least one container from each closing machine head, and the observations, along with any corrective actions, shall be recorded. Visual examinations shall be conducted with sufficient frequency to ensure proper closure and should be conducted at least every 30 minutes of continuous closing machine operation. Additional visual examinations shall be made by the closure technician at the beginning of production, immediately following every jam in the closing machine and after closing machine adjustment (including adjustment for changes in container size).

(2) *Teardown examinations.* Teardown examinations of double seams formed by each closing machine head shall be performed by a closure technician at a frequency sufficient to ensure proper closure. These examinations should be made at intervals of not more than 4 hours of continuous closing machine operation. At least one container from each closing head shall be examined on the packer's end during each regular examination period. Examination results along with any necessary corrective actions, such as adjusting or repairing the closing machine, shall be promptly recorded by the closure technician. The establishment shall have container specification guidelines for double seam integrity on file and available for review by Program employees. A teardown examination of the can maker's end shall be performed on at least one container selected from each closing machine during each examination period except when teardown examinations are made on incoming empty containers or when, in the case of self-manufactured containers, the containers are made in the vicinity of the establishment and the container plant records are made available to Program employees. Additional teardown examinations on the packer's end should be made at the beginning of production, immediately following every jam in a closing machine and after closing machine adjustment (including adjustment for a change in container size). The following procedures shall be used in teardown examinations of double seams:

(i) One of the following two methods shall be employed for dimensional measurements of the double seam.

(*a*) *Micrometer measurement.* For cylindrical containers, measure the following dimensions (Figure 1) at three points approximately 120 degrees apart on the double seam excluding and at least onehalf inch from the side seam juncture:

(*1*) Double seam length – W;

(*2*) Double seam thickness – S;

(*3*) Body hook length – BH; and

(*4*) Cover hook length – CH.

Maximum and minimum values for each dimensional measurement shall be recorded by the closure technician.

(*b*) *Seamscope or seam projector.* Required measurements of the seam include thickness, body hook, and overlap. Seam thickness shall be obtained by micrometer. For cylindrical containers, at least two locations, excluding the side seam juncture, shall be used to obtain the required measurements.

(ii) *Seam tightness.* Regardless of the dimensional measurement method used to measure seam dimensions, at a minimum, the seam(s) examined shall be stripped to assess the degree of wrinkling.

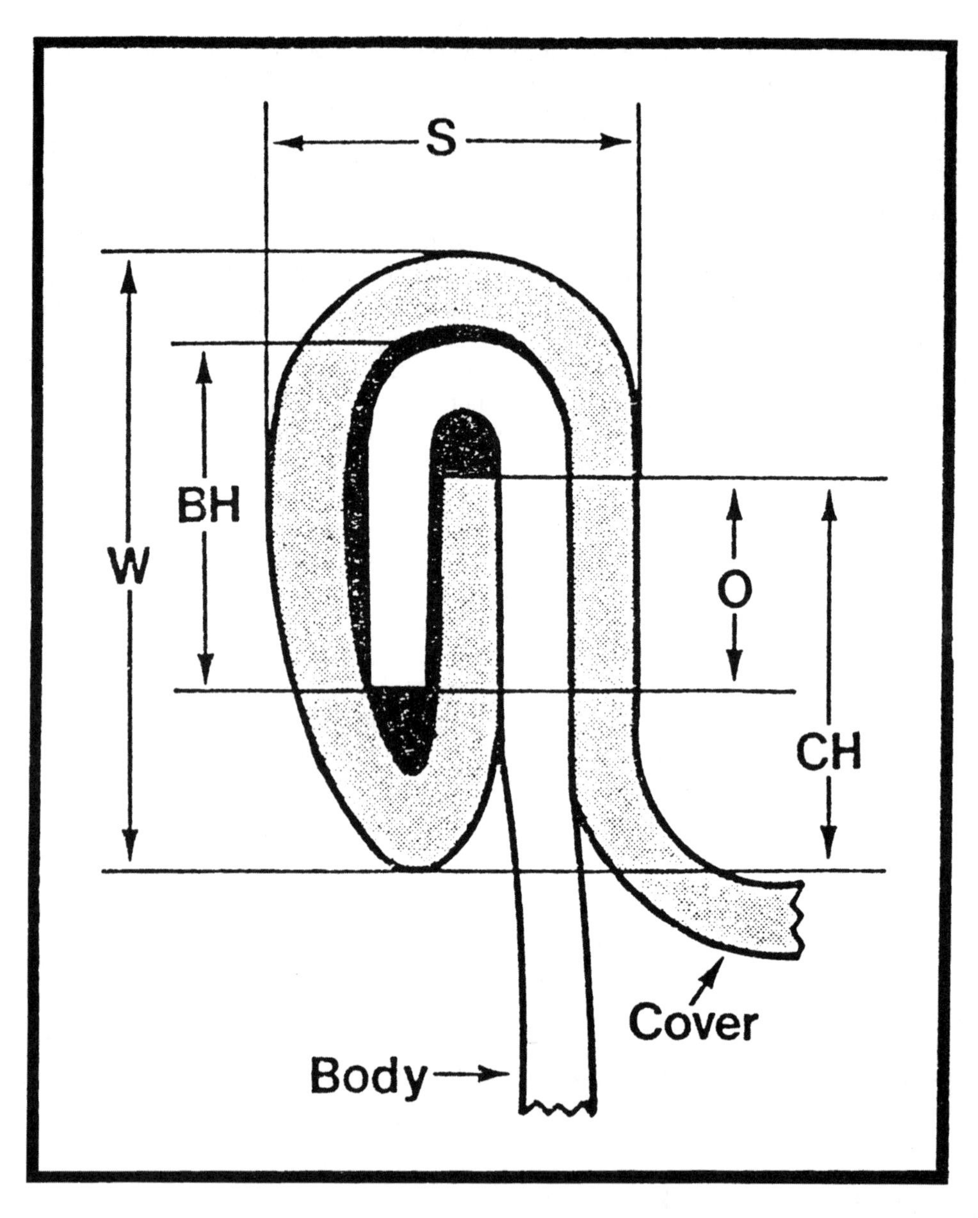

(iii) *Side seam juncture rating.* Regardless of the dimensional measurement method used to measure seam dimensions, the cover hook shall be stripped to examine the cover hook droop at the juncture for containers having side seams.

(iv) *Examination of noncylindrical containers.* Examination of noncylindrical containers (e.g., square, rectangular, 'D'-shaped, and irregularly-shaped) shall be conducted as described in paragraphs (b)(2) (i), (ii), and (iii) of this section except that the required dimensional measurements shall be made on the double seam at the points listed in the establishment's container specification guidelines.

(c) *Closure examinations for glass containers* – (1) *Visual examinations.* A closure technician shall visually assess the adequacy of the closures formed by each closing machine. When closure defects, such as loose or cocked caps, fractured or cracked containers and low vacuum jars, are observed, necessary corrective actions, such as adjusting or repairing the closing machine shall be taken and recorded. In addition to the closures, the entire container shall be examined for defects. Visual examinations shall be made with sufficient frequency to ensure proper closure and should be conducted at least every 30 minutes of continuous closing machine operation. Additional visual examinations shall be made by the closure technician and the observations recorded at the beginning of production, immediately following every jam in the closing machine, and after closing machine adjustment (including adjustment for a change in container size).

(2) *Closure examinations and tests.* Depending upon the container and closure, tests shall be performed by a closure technician at a frequency sufficient to ensure proper closure. These examinations should be made either before or after thermal processing and at intervals of not more than 4 hours of continuous closing machine operation. At least one container from each closing machine shall be examined during each regular examination period. Examination results along with any necessary corrective actions, such as adjusting or repairing the closing machine, shall be promptly recorded by the closure technician. The establishment shall have specification guidelines for closure integrity on file and available for review by Program employees. Additional closure examinations should be made at the beginning of production, immediately following every jam in the closing machine, and after closing machine adjustment (including adjustment for a change in container size).

(d) *Closure examinations for semirigid and flexible containers* – (1) *Heat seals* – (i) *Visual examinations.* A closure technician shall visually examine the seals formed by each sealing machine. When sealing defects are observed, necessary corrective actions, such as adjusting or repairing the sealing machine, shall be taken and recorded. In addition to examining the heat seals, the entire container shall be examined for product leakage or obvious defects. Visual examinations shall be performed before and after the thermal processing operation and with sufficient frequency to ensure proper closure. These examinations should be conducted at least in accordance with a statistical sampling plan. All defects noted and corrective actions taken shall be promptly recorded.

(ii) *Physical tests.* Tests determined by the establishment as necessary to assess container integrity shall be conducted by the closure technician at a frequency sufficient to ensure proper closure. These tests shall be performed after the thermal processing operation and should be made at least every 2 hours of continuous production. The establishment's acceptance guidelines for each test procedure shall be on file and available for review by Program employees. Test results along with any necessary corrective actions, such as adjusting or repairing the sealing machine, shall be recorded.

(2) Double seams on semirigid or flexible containers shall be examined and the results recorded as provided in paragraph (b) of this section. Any additional

measurements specified by the container manufacturer shall also be made and recorded.

(e) *Container coding.* Each container shall be marked with a permanent, legible, identifying code mark. The mark shall, at a minimum, identify in code the product (unless the product name lithographed or printed elsewhere on the container) and the day and year the product was packed.

(f) *Handling of containers after closure.*

(1) Containers and closures shall be protected from damage which may cause defects that are likely to affect the hermetic condition of the containers. The accumulation of stationary containers on moving conveyors should be minimized to avoid damage to the containers.

(2) The maximum time lapse between closing and initiation of thermal processing shall be 2 hours. However, the Administrator may specify a shorter period of time when considered necessary to ensure product safety and stability. A longer period of time between closing and the initiation of thermal processing may be permitted by the Administrator.

(Approved by the Office of Management and Budget under control number 0583-0015)

§ 318.302 Thermal Processing

(a) *Process schedules.* Prior to the processing of canned product for distribution in commerce, an establishment shall have a process schedule (as defined in § 318.300(n) of this subpart) for each canned meat product to be packed by the establishment.

(b) *Source of process schedules.* (1) Process schedules used by an establishment shall be developed or determined by a processing authority.

(2) Any change in product formulation, ingredients, or treatments that are not already incorporated in a process schedule and that may adversely affect either the product heat penetration profile or sterilization value requirements shall be evaluated by the establishment's processing authority. If it is determined that any such change adversely affects the adequacy of the process schedule, the processing authority shall amend the process schedule accordingly.

(3) Complete records concerning all aspects of the development or determination of a process schedule, including any associated incubation tests, shall be made available by the establishment to the Program employee upon request.

(c) *Submittal of process information.* (1) Prior to the processing of canned product for distribution in commerce, the establishment shall provide the inspector at the establishment with a list of the process schedules (including alternate schedules) along with any additional applicable information, such as the retort comeup operating procedures and critical factors.

(2) Letters or other written communications from a processing authority recommending all process schedules shall be maintained on file by the establishment. Upon request by Program employees, the establishment shall make available such letters or written communications (or copies thereof). If critical factors are identi-

fied in the process schedule, the establishment shall provide the inspector with a copy of the procedures for measuring, controlling, and recording these factors, along with the frequency of such measurements, to ensure that the critical factors remain within the limits used to establish the process schedule. Once submitted, the process schedules and associated critical factors and the procedures for measuring (including the frequency), controlling, and recording of critical factors shall not be changed without the prior written submittal of the revised procedures (including supporting documentation) to the inspector at the establishment.

(Approved by the Office of Management and Budget under control number 0583-0015)

§ 318.303 Critical Factors and the Application of the Process Schedule

Critical factors specified in the process schedule shall be measured, controlled and recorded by the establishment to ensure that these factors remain within the limits used to establish the process schedule. Examples of factors that are often critical to process schedule adequacy may include:

(a) *General.*
- (1) Maximum fillin weight or drained weight;
- (2) Arrangement of pieces in the container;
- (3) Container orientation during thermal processing;
- (4) Product formulation;
- (5) Particle size;
- (6) Maximum thickness for flexible, and to some extent semirigid containers during thermal processing;
- (7) Maximum pH;
- (8) Percent salt;
- (9) Ingoing (or formulated) nitrite level (ppm);
- (10) Maximum water activity; and
- (11) Product consistency or viscosity.

(b) *Continuous rotary and batch agitating retorts.*
- (1) Minimum headspace; and
- (2) Retort reel speed.

(c) *Hydrostatic retorts.*
- (1) Chain or conveyor speed.

(d) *Steam/air retorts.*
- (1) Steam/air ratio; and
- (2) Heating medium flow rate.

§ 318.304 Operations in the Thermal Processing Area

(a) *Posting of processes.* Process schedules (or operating process schedules) for daily production, including minimum initial temperatures and operating procedures for thermal processing equipment, shall be posted in a conspicuous place near the thermal processing equipment. Alternatively, such information shall be available to the thermal processing system operator and the inspector.

(b) *Process indicators and retort traffic control.* A system for product traffic control shall be established to prevent product from bypassing the thermal processing operation. Each basket, crate or similar vehicle containing unprocessed product, or at least one visible container in each vehicle, shall be plainly and conspicuously marked with a heat sensitive indicator that will visually indicate whether such unit has been thermally processed. Exposed heat sensitive indicators attached to container vehicles shall be removed before such vehicles are refilled with unprocessed product. Container loading systems for crateless retorts shall be designed to prevent unprocessed product from bypassing the thermal processing operation.

(c) *Initial temperature.* The initial temperature of the contents of the coldest container to be processed shall be determined and recorded by the establishment at the time the processing cycle begins to assure that the temperature of the contents of every container to be processed is not lower than the minimum initial temperature specified in the process schedule. Thermal processing systems which subject the filled and sealed containers to water at any time before process timing begins shall be operated to assure that such water will not lower the temperature of the product below the minimum initial temperature specified in the process schedule.

(d) *Timing devices.* Devices used to time applicable thermal processing operation functions or events, such as process schedule time, comeup time and retort venting, shall be accurate to assure that all such functions or events are achieved. Pocket watches and wrist watches are not considered acceptable timing devices. Analog and digital clocks are considered acceptable. If such clocks do not display seconds, all required timed functions or events shall have at least a 1-minute safety factor over the specified thermal processing operation times. Temperature/time recording devices shall correspond within 15 minutes to the time of the day recorded on written records required by § 318.306.

(e) *Measurement of pH.* Unless other methods are approved by the Administrator, potentiometric Methods using electronic instruments (pH meters) shall be used for making pH determinations when a maximum pH value is specified as a critical factor in a process schedule.

(Approved by Office of Management and Budget under control number 0583-0015)

§ 318.305 Equipment and Procedures for Heat Processing Systems

(a) *Instruments and controls common to different thermal processing systems* – (1) *Indicating temperature devices.* Each retort shall be equipped with at least one indicating temperature device that measures the actual temperature within the retort.

The indicating temperature device, not the temperature/time recording device, shall be used as the reference instrument for indicating the process temperature.

(i) *Mercury-in-glass thermometers.* A mercury-in-glass thermometer shall have divisions that are readable to 1F °(or 0.5C°) and whose scale contains not more than 17F°/inch (or 4.0C°/cm) of graduated scale. Each mercury-in-glass thermometer shall be tested for accuracy against a known accurate standard upon installation and at least once a year to ensure its accuracy. Records that specify the date, standard used, test method, and the person or testing authority performing the test shall be maintained on file by the establishment and made available to Program employees. A mercury-in-glass thermometer that has a divided mercury column or that cannot be adjusted to the standard shall be repaired and tested for accuracy before further use, or replaced.

(ii) *Other devices.* Temperatureindicating devices, such as resistance temperature detectors, used in lieu of mercury-in-glass thermometers, shall meet known, accurate standards for such devices when tested for accuracy. The records of such testing shall be available to FSIS program employees.

(2) *Temperature/time recording devices.* Each thermal processing system shall be equipped with at least one temperature/time recording device to provide a permanent record of temperatures within the thermal processing system. This recording device may be combined with the steam controller and may be a recording/controlling instrument. When compared to the known accurate indicating temperature device, the recording accuracy shall be equal to or better than 1F °(or 0.5C°) at the process temperature. The temperature recording chart should be adjusted to agree with, but shall never be higher than, the known accurate indicating temperature device. A means of preventing unauthorized changes in the adjustment shall be provided. For example, a lock or a notice from management posted at or near the recording device warning that only authorized persons are permitted to make adjustments, are satisfactory means for preventing unauthorized changes. Airoperated temperature controllers shall have adequate filter systems to ensure a supply of clean, dry air. The recorder timing mechanism shall be accurate.

(i) *Charttype devices.* Devices using charts shall be used only with the correct chart. Each chart shall have a working scale of not more than 55F°/ inch (or 12C°/ cm) within a range of 20F °(or 11C°) of the process temperature. Chart graduations shall not exceed 2F degrees (or 1C degree) within a range of 10F degrees (or 5C degrees) of the process temperature. Multipoint plotting chart-type devices shall print temperature readings at intervals that will assure that the parameters of the process time and process temperature have been met. The frequency of recording should not exceed 1-minute intervals.

(ii) *Other devices.* Temperature/time recording devices or procedures used in lieu of chart-type devices must meet known accurate standards for such devices or procedures when tested for accuracy. Such a device must be accurate enough for ensuring that process time and temperature parameters have been met.

(3) *Steam controllers.* Each retort shall be equipped with an automatic steam controller to maintain the retort temperature. This may be a recording/controlling instrument when combined with a temperature/time recording device.

(4) *Air valves.* All air lines connected to retorts designed for pressure processing in steam shall be equipped with a globe valve or other equivalent-type valve or piping arrangement that will prevent leakage of air into the retort during the process cycle.

(5) *Water valves.* All retort water lines that are intended to be closed during a process cycle shall be equipped with a globe valve or other equivalent-type valve or piping arrangement that will prevent leakage of water into the retort during the process cycle.

(b) *Pressure processing in steam* – (1) *Batch still retorts.* (i) The basic requirements and recommendations for indicating temperature devices and temperature/time recording devices are described in paragraphs (a) (1) and (2) of this section. Additionally, bulb sheaths or probes of indicating temperature devices and probes of temperature/time recording devices shall be installed either within the retort shell or in external wells attached to the retort. External wells shall be connected to the retort through at least a 3/4 inch (1.9 cm) diameter opening and equipped with a $^1/_{16}$ inch (1.6 mm) or larger bleeder opening so located as to provide a constant flow of steam past the length of the bulb or probe. The bleeder for external wells shall emit steam continuously during the entire thermal processing period.

(ii) Steam controllers are required as described under paragraph (a)(3) of this section.

(iii) *Steam inlet.* The steam inlet to each retort shall be large enough to provide steam for proper operation of the retort, and shall enter at a point to facilitate air removal during venting.

(iv) *Crate supports.* Vertical still retorts with bottom steam entry shall employ bottom retort crate supports. Baffle plates shall not be used in the bottom of retorts.

(v) *Steam spreader.* Perforated steam spreaders, if used, shall be maintained to ensure they are not blocked or otherwise inoperative. Horizontal still retorts shall be equipped with perforated steam spreaders that extend the full length of the retort unless the adequacy of another arrangement is documented by heat distribution data or other documentation from a processing authority. Such information shall be maintained on file by the establishment and made available to Program employees for review.

(vi) *Bleeders and condensate removal.* Bleeders, except those for external wells of temperature devices, shall have $^1/_8$ inch (or 3 mm) or larger openings and shall be wide open during the entire process, including the comeup time. For horizontal still retorts, bleeders shall be located within approximately 1 foot (or 30 cm) of the outermost locations of containers at each end along the top of the retort. Additional bleeders shall be located not more than 8 feet (2.4 m) apart along the top. Bleeders may be installed at positions other than those specified above, as long as the establishment has heat distribution data or other documentation from the manufacturer or from a processing authority demonstrating that the bleeders accomplish removal of air and circulate the steam within the retort. This information shall be maintained on file by the establishment and made available to Program employees for review. All bleeders shall be arranged in a way that enables the retort operator to observe that they are functioning properly. Vertical retorts shall have at least one bleeder opening located in the portion of the retort opposite the steam inlet. All bleeders shall be arranged so that the retort operator can observe that they are functioning properly. In retorts having a steam inlet above the level of the lowest container, a bleeder shall be installed in the bottom of the retort to remove condensate. The condensate bleeder shall be so arranged that the retort operator can observe that it is functioning properly. The condensate bleeder shall be checked with sufficient frequency to ensure adequate removal of condensate. Visual checks should be performed at intervals of not more than 15 minutes and the results recorded. Intermittent condensate removal systems shall be equipped with an automatic alarm system that will serve as a continuous monitor of condensate bleeder functioning. The automatic alarm system shall be tested at the beginning of each shift for proper functioning and the results recorded. If the alarm system is not functioning properly, it must be repaired before the retort is used.

(vii) *Stacking equipment – (a) Equipment for holding or stacking containers in retorts.* Crates, trays, gondolas, carts, and other vehicles for holding or stacking product containers in the retort shall be so constructed to ensure steam circulation during the venting, comeup, and process times. The bottom of each vehicle shall have perforations at least 1 inch (2.5 cm) in diameter on 2 inch (or 5 cm) centers or the equivalent unless the adequacy of another arrangement is documented by heat distribution data or other documentation from a processing authority and such information is maintained on file by the establishment and made available to Program employees for review.

(*b*) *Divider plates.* Whenever one or more divider plates are used between any two layers of containers or placed on the bottom of a retort vehicle, the establishment shall have on file documentation that the venting procedure allows the air to be removed from the retort before timing of the thermal process is started. Such documentation shall be in the form of heat distribution data or documentation from a processing authority. This information shall be made available to Program employees for review.

(viii) *Bleeder and vent mufflers.* If mufflers are used on bleeders or vent systems, the establishment shall have on file documentation that the mufflers do not impede the removal of air from the retort. Such documentation shall consist of either heat distribution data or documentation from the muffler manufacturer or from a processing authority. This information shall be made available to Program employees for review.

(ix) *Vents – (a)* Vents shall be located in that portion of the retort opposite the steam inlet and shall be designed, installed, and operated in such a way that air is removed from the retort before timing of the thermal process is started. Vents shall be controlled by a gate, plug cock, or other fullflow valve which shall be fully opened to permit rapid removal of air from retorts during the venting period.

(*b*) Vents shall not be connected to a closed drain system without an atmospheric break in the line. Where a retort manifold connects several pipes from a single retort, the manifold shall be controlled by a gate, plug cock, or other fullflow valve and the manifold shall be of a size such that the cross-sectional area of the manifold is larger than the total cross-sectional area of all connecting vents. The discharge shall not be connected to a closed drain without an atmospheric break in the line. A manifold header connecting vents or manifolds from several still retorts shall lead to the atmosphere. The manifold header shall not be controlled by a valve and shall be of a size such that the cross-sectional area is at least equal to the total cross-sectional area of all connecting retort manifold pipes from the maximum number of retorts to be vented simultaneously.

(*c*) Some typical installations and operating procedures are described below. Other retort installations, vent piping arrangements, operating procedures or auxiliary equipment such as divider plates may be used provided there is documentation that the air is removed from the retort before the process is started. Such documentation shall be in the form of heat distribution data or other documentation from the equipment manufacturer or processing authority. This information shall be maintained on file by the establishment and made available to Program employees for review.

(*d*) For crateless retort installations, the establishment shall have heat distribution data or other documentation from the equipment manufacturer or from a processing authority that demonstrates that the venting procedure used accomplishes the removal of air and condensate. This information shall be maintained on file by the establishment and made available to Program employees for review.

(*e*) Examples of typical installations and operating procedures that comply with the requirements of this section are as follows:

(*1*) Venting horizontal retorts.

(*i*) Venting through multiple 1 inch (2.5 cm) vents discharging directly to the atmosphere.

(*ii*) Venting through multiple 1 inch (2.5 cm) vents discharging through a manifold to the atmosphere.

Specifications (Figure 1): One, 1 inch (2.5 cm) vent for every 5 feet (1.5 m) of retort length, equipped with a gate, plug cock, or other full-flow valve and discharging to atmosphere. The end vents shall not be more than 2½ feet (or 75 cm) from ends of retort. *Venting method* (*Figure 1*): Vent valves shall be wide open for at least 5 minutes and to at least 225 °F (or 107 °C), or at least 7 minutes and to at least 220 °F (or 104.5 °C)

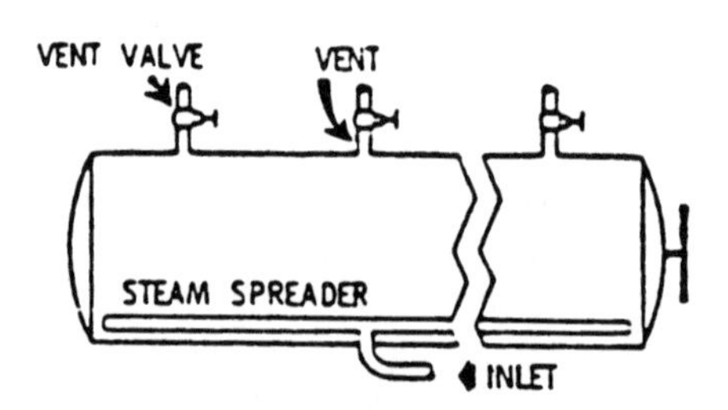

Figure 1.

Specifications (Figure 2): One, 1-inch (2.5 cm) vent for every 5 feet (1.5 m) of retort length; vents not over 2½ inches 6.4 cm), and for retorts 15 feet (4.6 m) and over in length, 3 inches (7.6 cm).

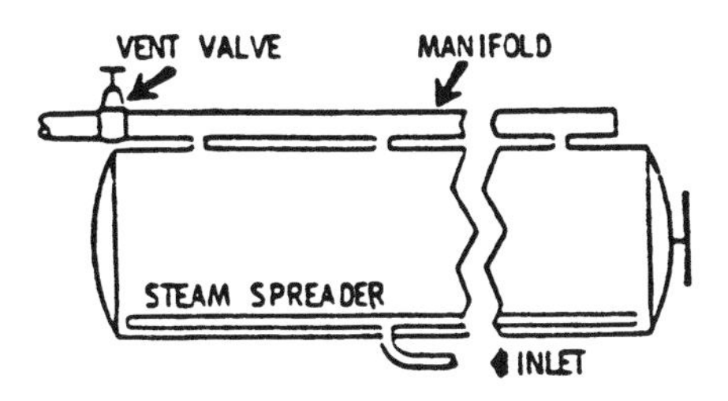

Figure 2.

Venting method (*Figure 2*): The manifold vent gate, plug cock, or other full-flow valve shall be wide open for at least 6 minutes and to at least 225 °F (or 107 °C) or for at least 8 minutes and to at least 220 °F (or 104.5 °C).

(*iii*) Venting through water spreaders.

Specifications (Figure 3): Size of vent and vent valve. For retorts less than 15 feet (4.6 m) in length, 2 inches (or 5 cm); for retorts 15 feet (4.6 m) and over in length, 2½ inches (6.4 cm).

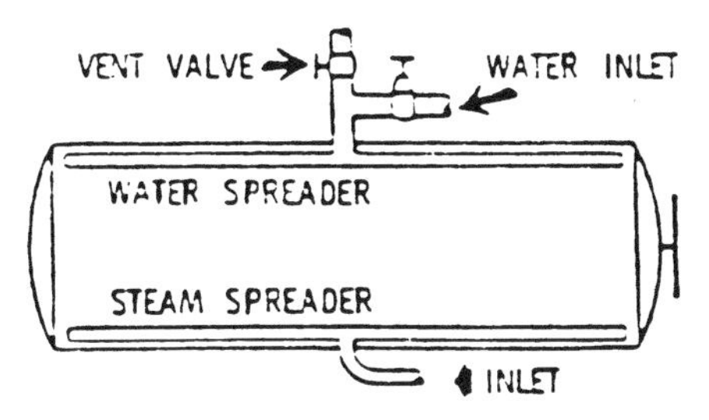

Figure 3.

Size of water spreader (Figure 3): For retorts less than 15 feet (4.6 m) in length, 1½ inches (3.8 cm); for retorts 15 feet (4.6 m) and over in length, 2 inches (or 5 cm). The number of holes shall be such that their total cross-sectional area is equal to the cross-sectional area of the vent pipe inlet.

Venting method (Figure 3): The gate, plug cock, or other full-flow valve on the water spreader vent shall be wide open for at least 5 minutes and to at least 225 °F (or 107 °C), or for at least 7 minutes and to at least 220 °F (or 104.5 °C).

(*iv*) Venting through a single 2½ inch (6.4 cm) top vent for retorts not exceeding 15 feet (4.6 m) in length.

Specifications (Figure 4): A 2½ inch (6.4 cm) vent equipped with a 2½ inch (6.4 cm) gate, plug cock, or other full-flow valve and located within 2 feet (61 cm) of the center of the retort.

Venting method (Figure 4): The vent valve shall be wide open for at least 4 minutes and to at least 220 °F (or 104.5 °C).

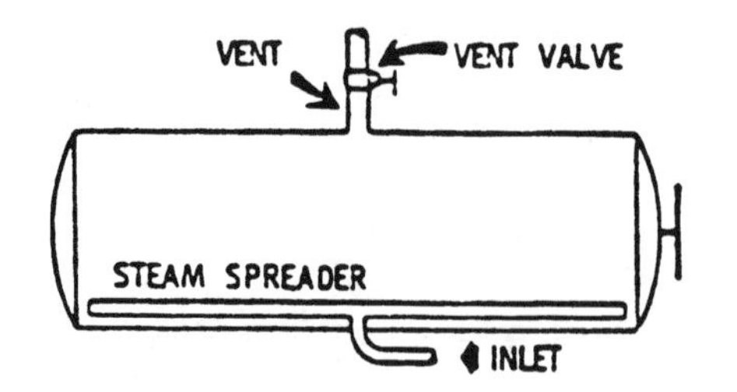

Figure 4.

(*2*) Venting vertical retorts.

(*i*) Venting through a 1½ inch (3.8 cm) overflow.

Specifications (Figure 5): A 1½ inch (3.8 cm) overflow pipe equipped with a 1½ inch (3.8 cm) gate, plug cock, or other full-flow valve and with not more than 6 feet (1.8 m) of 1½ inch (3.8 cm) pipe beyond the valve before a break to the atmosphere or to a manifold header.

Venting method (Figure 5): The vent valve shall be wide open for at least 4 minutes and to at least 218 °F (or 103.5 °C), or for at least 5 minutes and to at least 215 °F (or 101.5 °C).

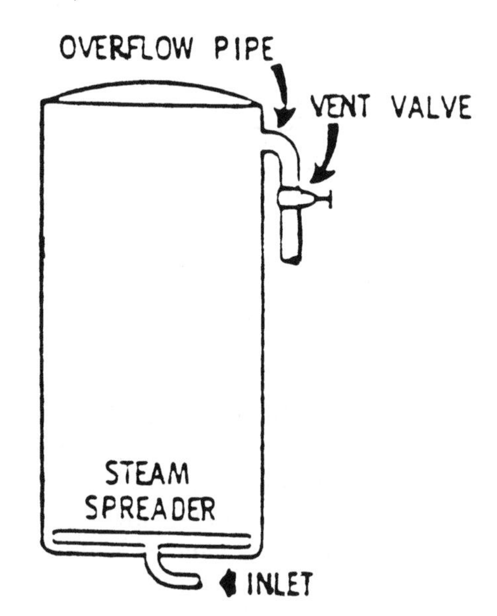

Figure 5.

(*ii*) Venting through a single 1 inch (2.5 cm) side or top vent.

Specifications (Figure 6 or 7): A 1 inch (2.5 cm) vent in lid or top side, equipped with a gate, plug cock, or other full-flow valve and discharging directly into the atmosphere or to a manifold header.

Venting method (Figure 6 or 7): The vent valve shall be wide open for at least 5 minutes and to at least 230 °F (110 °C), or for at least 7 minutes and to at least 220 °F (or 104.5 °C).

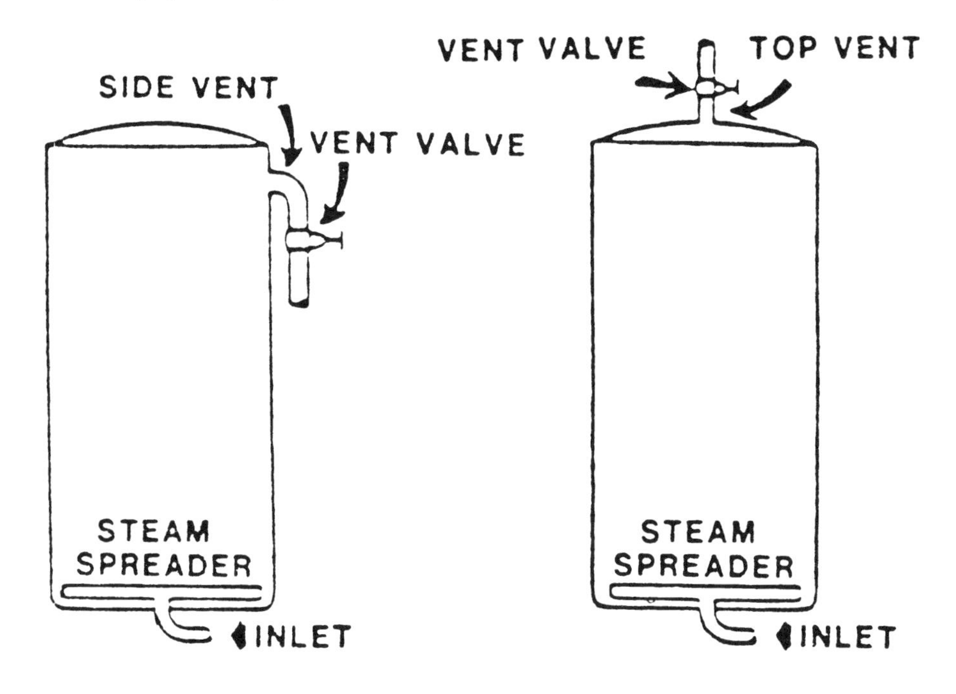

(2) *Batch agitating retorts.* (i) The basic requirements for indicating temperature devices and temperature/time recording devices are described in paragraphs (a)(1) and (2) of this section. Additionally, bulb sheaths or probes of indicating temperature devices and probes of temperature/time recording devices shall be installed either within the retort shell or in external wells attached to the retort. External wells shall be connected to the retort through at least a ¾ inch (1.9 cm) diameter opening and equipped with a $\frac{1}{16}$ (1.6 mm) or larger bleeder opening so located as to provide a constant flow of steam past the length of the bulbs or probes. The bleeder for external wells shall emit steam continuously during the entire thermal processing period.

(ii) Steam controllers are required as described in paragraph (a)(3) of this section.

(iii) *Steam inlet.* The steam inlet to each retort shall be large enough to provide steam for proper operation of the retort and shall enter at a point(s) to facilitate air removal during venting.

(iv) *Bleeders.* Bleeders, except those for external wells of temperature devices, shall be ⅛ inch (or 3 mm) or larger and shall be wide open during the entire process including the comeup time. Bleeders shall be located within approximately 1 foot (or 30 cm) of the outermost location of containers, at each end along the top of the retort. Additional bleeders shall be located not more than 8 feet (2.4 m) apart along the top. Bleeders may be installed at positions other than those specified above, as long as the establishment has heat distribution data or other documentation from the manufacturer or from a processing authority that the bleeders accomplish removal of air and circulate the steam within the retort. This information shall be maintained on file by the establishment and made available to Program employees for review. All bleeders shall be arranged in a way that enables the retort operator to observe that they are functioning properly.

(v) *Venting and condensate removal.* The air in the retort shall be removed before processing is started. Heat distribution data or other documentation from the manufacturer or from the processing authority who developed the venting procedure shall be kept on file by the establishment and made available to Program employees for review. At the time the steam is turned on, the drain shall be opened to remove steam condensate from the retort. A bleeder shall be installed in the bottom of the retort to remove condensate during retort operation. The condensate bleeder shall be so arranged that the retort operator can observe that it is functioning properly. The condensate bleeder shall be checked with sufficient frequency to ensure adequate removal of condensate. Visual checks should be performed at intervals of not more than 15 minutes and the results recorded. Intermittent condensate removal systems shall be equipped with an automatic alarm system that will serve as a continuous monitor of condensate bleeder functioning. The automatic alarm system shall be tested at the beginning of each shift for proper functioning and the results recorded. If the alarm system is not functioning properly, it must be repaired before the retort is used.

(vi) *Retort or reel speed timing.* The retort or reel speed shall be checked before process timing begins and, if needed, adjusted as specified in the process schedule. In addition, the rotational speed shall be determined and recorded at least once during process timing of each retort load processed. Alternatively, a recording tachometer can be used to provide a continuous record of the speed. The accuracy of the recording tachometer shall be determined and recorded at least once per shift by checking the retort or reel speed using an accurate stopwatch. A means of preventing unauthorized speed changes on retorts shall be provided. For example, a lock or a notice from management posted at or near the speed adjustment device warning that only authorized persons are permitted to make adjustments are satisfactory means of preventing unauthorized changes.

(vii) *Bleeder and vent mufflers.* If mufflers are used on bleeders or vent systems, the establishment shall have documentation that the mufflers do not impede the removal of air from the retort. Such documentation shall consist of either heat distribution data or documentation from the muffler manufacturer or from a processing authority. This information shall be maintained on file by the establishment and made available to Program employees for review.

(3) *Continuous rotary retorts.* (i) The basic requirements for indicating temperature devices and temperature/time recording devices are described in paragraphs (a)(1) and (2) of this section. Additionally, bulb sheaths or probes of indicating temperature devices and probes of temperature/time recording devices shall be installed either within the retort shell or in external wells attached to the retort. External wells shall be connected to the retort through at least a ¾ inch (1.9 cm) diameter opening and equipped with a $\frac{1}{16}$ inch (1.6 mm) or larger bleeder opening so located as to provide a constant flow of steam past the length of the

bulbs or probes. The bleeder for external wells shall emit steam continuously during the entire thermal processing period.

(ii) Steam controllers are required as described in paragraph (a)(3) of this section.

(iii) *Steam inlet.* The steam inlet to each retort shall be large enough to provide steam for proper operation of the retort, and shall enter at a point(s) to facilitate air removal during venting.

(iv) *Bleeders.* Bleeders, except those for external wells of temperature devices, shall be ⅛ inch (3.2 mm) or larger and shall be wide open during the entire process, including the comeup time. Bleeders shall be located within approximately 1 foot (or 30 cm) of the outermost location of containers at each end along the top of the retort. Additional bleeders shall be located not more than 8 feet (2.4 m) apart along the top of the retort. Bleeders may be installed at positions other than those specified above, as long as the establishment has heat distribution data or other documentation from the manufacturer or a processing authority that the bleeders accomplish removal of air and circulate the steam within the retort. This information shall be maintained on file by the establishment and made available to Program employees for review. All bleeders shall be arranged so that the retort operator can observe that they are functioning properly.

(v) *Venting and condensate removal.* The air in the retort shall be removed before processing is started. Heat distribution data or other documentation from the manufacturer or from the processing authority who developed the venting procedure shall be kept on file by the establishment and made available to Program employees for review. At the time the steam is turned on, the drain shall be opened to remove steam condensate from the retort. A bleeder shall be installed in the bottom of the shell to remove condensate during the retort operation. The condensate bleeder shall be so arranged that the retort operator can observe that it is functioning properly. The condensate bleeder shall be checked with sufficient frequency to ensure adequate removal of condensate. Visual checks should be performed at intervals of not more than 15 minutes and the results recorded. Intermittent condensate removal systems shall be equipped with an automatic alarm system that will serve as a continuous monitor of condensate bleeder functioning. The automatic alarm system shall be tested at the beginning of each shift for proper functioning and the results recorded. If the alarm system is not functioning properly, it must be repaired before the retort is used.

(vi) *Retort speed timing.* The rotational speed of the retort shall be specified in the process schedule. The speed shall be adjusted as specified, and recorded by the establishment when the retort is started, and checked and recorded at intervals not to exceed 4 hours to ensure that the correct retort speed is maintained. Alternatively, a recording tachometer may be used to provide a continuous record of the speed. If a recording tachometer is used, the speed shall be manually checked against an accurate stopwatch at least once per shift and the results recorded. A means of preventing unauthorized speed changes on retorts shall be provided. For example, a lock or a notice from management posted at or near the speed adjustment device warning that only authorized persons are permitted to make adjustments are satisfactory means of preventing unauthorized changes.

(vii) *Bleeders and vent mufflers.* If mufflers are used on bleeders or vent systems, the establishment shall have documentation that the mufflers do not impede the removal of air from the retort. Such documentation shall consist of either heat distribution data or other documentation from the muffler manufacturer or from a processing authority. This information shall be maintained on file by the establishment and made available to Program employees for review.

(4) *Hydrostatic retorts.* (i) The basic requirements for indicating temperature devices and temperature/time recording devices are described in paragraphs (a)(1) and (2) of this section. Additionally, indicating temperature devices shall be located in the steam dome near the steam/water interface. Where the process schedule specifies maintenance of particular water temperatures in the hydrostatic water legs, at least one indicating temperature device shall be located in each hydrostatic water leg so that it can accurately measure water temperature and be easily read. The temperature/time recorder probe shall be installed either within the steam dome or in a well attached to the dome. Each probe shall have a 1/16 inch (1.6 mm) or larger bleeder opening which emits steam continuously during the processing period. Additional temperature/time recorder probes shall be installed in the hydrostatic water legs if the process schedule specifies maintenance of particular temperatures in these water legs.

(ii) Steam controllers are required as described in paragraph (a)(3) of this section.

(iii) *Steam inlet.* The steam inlets shall be large enough to provide steam for proper operation of the retort.

(iv) *Bleeders.* Bleeder openings 1/4 inch (or 6 mm) or larger shall be located in the steam chamber(s) opposite the point of steam entry. Bleeders shall be wide open and shall emit steam continuously during the entire process, including the comeup time. All bleeders shall be arranged in such a way that the operator can observe that they are functioning properly.

(v) *Venting.* Before the start of processing operations, the retort steam chamber(s) shall be vented to ensure removal of air. Heat distribution data or other documentation from the manufacturer or from a processing authority demonstrating that the air is removed from the retort prior to processing shall be kept on file at the establishment and made available to Program employees for review.

(vi) *Conveyor speed.* The conveyor speed shall be calculated to obtain the required process time and recorded by the establishment when the retort is started. The speed shall be checked and recorded at intervals not to exceed 4 hours to ensure that the correct conveyor speed is maintained. A recording device may be used to provide a continuous record of the conveyor speed. When a recording device is used, the speed shall be manually checked against an accurate stopwatch at least once per shift by the establishment. A means of preventing unauthorized speed changes of the conveyor shall be provided. For example, a lock or a notice from management posted at or near the speed adjustment device warning that only authorized persons are permitted to make adjustments are satisfactory means of preventing unauthorized changes.

(vii) *Bleeders and vent mufflers.* If mufflers are used on bleeders or vent systems, the establishment shall have documentation that the muffler do not impede the removal of air from the retort. Such documentation shall consist of either heat distribution data or other documentation from the muffler manufacturer or from a processing authority. This information shall be maintained on file by the establishment and made available to Program employees for review.

(c) *Pressure processing in water* – (1) *Batch still retorts.* (i) The basic requirements for indicating temperature devices and temperature/time recording devices are described in paragraphs (a)(1) and (2) of this section. Additionally, bulbs or probes of indicating temperature devices shall be located in such a position that they are beneath the surface of the water throughout the process. On horizontal retorts, the indicating temperature device bulb or probe shall be inserted directly into the retort shell. In both vertical and horizontal retorts, the indicating temperature device bulb or probe shall extend directly into the water a minimum of 2 inches (or 5 cm) without a separable well or sleeve. In vertical retorts equipped with a recorder/controller, the controller probe shall be located at the bottom of the retort below the lowest crate rest in such a position that the steam does not strike it directly. In horizontal retorts so equipped, the controller probe shall be located between the water surface and the horizontal plane passing through the center of the retort so that there is no opportunity for direct steam impingement on the controller probe. Air-operated temperature controllers shall have filter systems to ensure a supply of clean, dry air.

(ii) *Pressure recording device.* Each retort shall be equipped with a pressure recording device which may be combined with a pressure controller.

(iii) *Steam controllers* are required as described in paragraph (a)(3) of this section.

(iv) *Heat distribution.* Heat distribution data or other documentation from the equipment manufacturer or a processing authority demonstrating uniform heat distribution within the retort shall be kept on file at the establishment and made available to Program employees for review.

(v) *Crate supports.* A bottom crate support shall be used in vertical retorts. Baffle plates shall not be used in the bottom of the retort.

(vi) *Stacking equipment.* For filled flexible containers and, where applicable, semirigid containers, stacking equipment shall be designed to ensure that the thickness of the filled containers does not exceed that specified in the process schedule and that the containers do not become displaced and overlap or rest on one another during the thermal process.

(vii) *Drain valve.* A nonclogging, water-tight drain valve shall be used. Screens shall be installed over all drain openings.

(viii) *Water level.* There shall be a means of determining the water level in the retort during operation (i.e., by using a gauge, electronic sensor, or sight glass indicator). For retorts requiring complete immersion of containers, water shall cover the top layer of containers during the entire comeup time and thermal processing periods and should cover the top layer of containers during cooling. For retorts using cascading water or water sprays, the water level shall be maintained within the range specified by the retort manufacturer or processing authority during the entire comeup, thermal processing, and cooling periods. A means to ensure that water circulation continues as specified throughout the comeup, thermal processing, and cooling periods shall be provided. The retort operator shall check and record the water level at intervals to ensure it meets the specified processing parameters.

(ix) *Air supply and controls.* In both horizontal and vertical still retorts, a means shall be provided for introducing compressed air or steam at the pressure required to maintain container integrity. Compressed air and steam entry shall be controlled by an automatic pressure control unit. A nonreturn valve shall be provided in the air supply line to prevent water from entering the system. Overriding air or steam pressure shall be maintained continuously during the comeup, thermal processing, and cooling periods. If air is used to promote circulation, it shall be introduced into the steam line at a point between the retort and the steam control valve at the bottom of the retort. The adequacy of the air circulation for maintaining uniform heat distribution within the retort shall be documented by heat distribution data or other documentation from a processing authority, and such data shall be maintained on file by the establishment and made available to Program employees for review.

(x) *Water recirculation.* When a water recirculation system is used for heat distribution, the water shall be drawn from the bottom of the retort through a suction manifold and discharged through a spreader that extends the length or circumference of the top of the retort. The holes in the water spreader shall be uniformly distributed. The suction outlets shall be protected with screens to keep debris from entering the recirculation system. The pump shall be equipped with a pilot light or a similar device to warn the operator when it is not running, and with a bleeder to remove air when starting operations. Alternatively, a flowmeter alarm system can be used to ensure proper water circulation. The adequacy of water circulation for maintaining uniform heat distribution within the retort shall be documented by heat distribution or other documentation from a processing authority and such data shall be maintained on file by the establishment and made available to Program employees for review. Alternative methods for recirculation of water in the retort may be used, provided there is documentation in the form of heat distribution data or other documentation from a processing authority maintained on file by the establishment and made available to Program employees for review.

(xi) *Cooling water entry.* In retorts for processing product packed in glass jars, the incoming cooling water should not directly strike the jars, in order to minimize glass breakage by thermal shock.

(2) *Batch agitating retorts.* (i) The basic requirements and recommendations for indicating temperature devices and temperature/time recording devices are described in paragraphs (a)(1) and (2) of this section. Additionally, the indicating temperature device bulb or probe shall extend directly into the water without a separable well or sleeve. The recorder/controller probe shall be located between

the water surface and the horizontal plane passing through the center of the retort so that there is no opportunity for steam to directly strike the controller bulb or probe.

(ii) *Pressure recording device.* Each retort shall be equipped with a pressure recording device which may be combined with a pressure controller.

(iii) Steam controllers are required as described in paragraph (a)(3) of this section.

(iv) *Heat distribution.* Heat distribution data or other documentation from the equipment manufacturer or a processing authority shall be kept on file by the establishment and made available to Program employees for review.

(v) *Stacking equipment.* All devices used for holding product containers (e.g., crates, trays, divider plates) shall be so constructed to allow the water to circulate around the containers during the comeup and thermal process periods.

(vi) *Drain valve.* A nonclogging, water-tight drain valve shall be used. Screens shall be installed over all drain openings.

(vii) *Water level.* There shall be a means of determining the water level in the retort during operation (i.e., by using a gauge, electronic sensor, or sight glass indicator). Water shall completely cover all containers during the entire comeup, thermal processing, and cooling periods. A means to ensure that water circulation continues as specified throughout the comeup, thermal processing, and cooling periods shall be provided. The retort operator shall check and record the adequacy of the water level with sufficient frequency to ensure it meets the specified processing parameters.

(viii) *Air supply and controls.* Retorts shall be provided with a means for introducing compressed air or steam at the pressure required to maintain container integrity. Compressed air and steam entry shall be controlled by an automatic pressure control unit. A nonreturn valve shall be provided in the air supply line to prevent water from entering the system. Overriding air or steam pressure shall be maintained continuously during the comeup, thermal processing, and cooling periods. If air is used to promote circulation, it shall be introduced into the steam line at a point between the retort and the steam control valve at the bottom of the retort. The adequacy of the air circulation for maintaining uniform heat distribution within the retort shall be documented by heat distribution data or other documentation from a processing authority, and such data shall be maintained on file by the establishment and made available to Program employees for review.

(ix) *Retort or reel speed timing.* The retort or reel speed timing shall be checked before process timing begins and, if needed, adjusted as specified in the process schedule. In addition, the rotational speed shall be determined and recorded at least once during process timing of each retort load processed. Alternatively, a recording tachometer can be used to provide a continuous record of the speed. The accuracy of the recording tachometer shall be determined and recorded at least once per shift by the establishment by checking the retort or reel speed using an accurate stopwatch. A means of preventing unauthorized speed changes on retorts shall be provided. For example, a lock or a notice from management posted at or near the speed adjustment device warning that only authorized persons are permitted to make adjustments are satisfactory means of preventing unauthorized changes.

(x) *Water recirculation.* If a water recirculation system is used for heat distribution, it shall be installed in such a manner that water will be drawn from the bottom of the retort through a suction manifold and discharged through a spreader which extends the length of the top of the retort. The holes in the water spreader shall be uniformly distributed. The suction outlets shall be protected with screens to keep debris from entering the recirculation system. The pump shall be equipped with a pilot light or a similar device to warn the operator when it is not running and with a bleeder to remove air when starting operations. Alternatively, a flowmeter alarm system can be used to ensure proper water circulation. The adequacy of water circulation for maintaining uniform heat distribution within the retort shall be documented by heat distribution data or other documentation from a processing authority, and such data shall be maintained on file by the establishment and made available to Program employees for review. Alternative methods for recirculation of water in the retort may be used provided there is documentation in the form of heat distribution data or other documentation from a processing authority maintained on file by the establishment and made available to Program employees for review.

(xi) *Cooling water entry.* In retorts for processing product packed in glass jars, the incoming cooling water should not directly strike the jars, in order to minimize glass breakage by thermal shock.

(d) *Pressure processing with steam/air mixtures in batch retorts.* (1) The basic requirements for indicating temperature devices and temperature/time recording devices are described in paragraphs (a)(1) and (2) of this section. Additionally, bulb sheaths or probes for indicating temperature devices and temperature/time recording devices or controller probes shall be inserted directly into the retort shell in such a position that steam does not strike them directly.

(2) Steam controllers are required as described in paragraph (a)(3) of this section.

(3) *Recording pressure controller.* A recording pressure controller shall be used to control the air inlet and the steam/air mixture outlet.

(4) *Circulation of steam/air mixtures.* A means shall be provided for the circulation of the steam/air mixture to prevent formation of low-temperature pockets. The efficiency of the circulation system shall be documented by heat distribution data or other documentation from a processing authority, and such data shall be maintained on file by the establishment and made available to Program employees for review. The circulation system shall be checked to ensure its proper functioning and shall be equipped with a pilot light or a similar device to warn the operator when it is not functioning. Because of the variety of existing designs, reference shall be made to the equipment manufacturer for details of installation, operation, and control.

(e) *Atmospheric cookers* – (1) *Temperature/time recording device.* Each atmospheric cooker (e.g., hot water bath) shall be equipped with at least one temperature/time recording device in accordance with the basic requirements described in paragraph (a)(2) of this section.

(2) *Heat distribution.* Each atmospheric cooker shall be equipped and operated to ensure uniform heat distribution throughout the processing system during the thermal process. Heat distribution data or other documentation from the manufacturer or a processing authority demonstrating uniform heat distribution within the cooker shall be kept on file by the establishment and made available to Program employees for review.

(f) *Other systems.* All other systems not specifically delineated in this section and used for the thermal processing of canned product shall be adequate to produce shelfstable products consistently and uniformly.

(g) *Equipment maintenance.* (1) Upon installation, all instrumentation and controls shall be checked by the establishment for proper functioning and accuracy and, thereafter, at any time their functioning or accuracy is suspect.

(2) At least once a year each thermal processing system shall be examined by an individual not directly involved in daily operations to ensure the proper functioning of the system as well as all auxiliary equipment and instrumentation. In addition, each thermal processing system should be examined before the resumption of operation following an extended shutdown.

(3) Air and water valves that are intended to be closed during thermal processing shall be checked by the establishment for leaks. Defective valves shall be repaired or replaced as needed.

(4) Vent and bleeder mufflers shall be checked and maintained or replaced by the establishment to prevent any reduction in vent or bleeder efficiency.

(5) When water spreaders are used for venting, a maintenance schedule shall be developed and implemented to assure that the holes are maintained at their original size.

(6) Records shall be kept on all maintenance items that could affect the adequacy of the thermal process. Records shall include the date and type of maintenance performed and the person conducting the maintenance.

(h) *Container cooling and cooling water.* (1) Potable water shall be used for cooling except as provided for in paragraphs (h)(2) and (3) of this section.

(2) Cooling canal water shall be chlorinated or treated with a chemical approved by the Administrator as having a bactericidal effect equivalent to chlorination. There shall be a measurable residual of the sanitizer in the water at the discharge point of the canal. Cooling canals shall be cleaned and replenished with potable water to prevent the buildup of organic matter and other materials.

(3) Container cooling waters that are recycled or reused shall be handled in systems that are so designed, operated, and maintained so there is no buildup of microorganisms, organic matter, and other materials in the systems and in the waters. System equipment, such as pipelines, holding tanks and cooling towers, shall be constructed and installed so that they can be cleaned and inspected. In addition, the establishment shall maintain, and make available to Program employees for review, information on at least the following:

(i) System design and construction;

(ii) System operation including the rates of renewal with fresh, potable water and the means for treating the water so that there is a measurable residual of an acceptable sanitizer, per paragraph (h)(2) of this section, in the water at the point where the water exits the container cooling vessel;

(iii) System maintenance including procedures for the periodic cleaning and sanitizing of the entire system; and

(iv) Water quality standards, such as microbiological, chemical and physical, monitoring procedures including the frequency and site(s) of sampling, and the corrective actions taken when water quality standards are not met.

(i) *Post-process handling of containers* Containers shall be handled in a manner that will prevent damage to the hermetic seal area. All worn and frayed belting, can retarders, cushions, and the like shall be replaced with nonporous materials. To minimize container abrasions, particularly in the seal area, containers should not remain stationary on moving conveyors. All post-process container handling equipment should be kept clean so there is no buildup of microorganisms on surfaces in contact with the containers.

(Approved by the Office of Management and Budget under control number 0583-0015)

[51 FR 45619, Dec. 19, 1986, as amended at 65 FR 34389, May 30, 2000]

§ 318.306 Processing and Production Records

At least the following processing and production information shall be recorded by the establishment: date of production; product name and style; container code; container size and type; and the process schedule, including the minimum initial temperature. Measurements made to satisfy the requirements of § 318.303 regarding the control of critical factors shall be recorded. In addition, where applicable, the following information and data shall also be recorded:

(a) *Processing in steam* – (1) *Batch still retorts.* For each retort batch, record the retort number or other designation, the approximate number of containers or the number of retort crates per retort load, product initial temperature, time steam on, the time and temperature vent closed, the start of process timing, time steam off, and the actual processing time. The indicating temperature device and the temperature recorder shall be read at the same time at least once during process timing and the observed temperatures recorded.

(2) *Batch agitating retorts.* In addition to recording the information required for batch, still steam retorts in paragraph (a)(1) of this section, record the functioning of the condensate bleeder(s) and the retort or reel speed.

(3) *Continuous rotary retorts.* Record the retort system number, the approximate total number of containers retorted, product initial temperature, time steam on, the time and temperature vent closed, time process temperature reached, the time the first can enters and the time the last can exits the retort. The retort or reel speed shall be determined and recorded at intervals not to exceed 4 hours. Readings of the indicating temperature device(s) and temperature recorder(s) shall

be made and recorded at the time the first container enters the retort and thereafter with sufficient frequency to ensure compliance with the process schedule. These observations should be made and recorded at intervals not exceeding 30 minutes of continuous retort operation. Functioning of the condensate bleeder(s) shall be observed and recorded at the time the first container enters the retort and thereafter as specified in § 318.305(b)(3)(v).

(4) *Hydrostatic retorts.* Record the retort system number, the approximate total number of containers retorted, product initial temperature, time steam on, the time and temperature vent(s) closed, time process temperature reached, time first containers enter the retort, time last containers exit the retort, and, if specified in the process schedule, measurements of temperatures in the hydrostatic water legs. Readings of the temperature indicating device, which is located in the steam/water interface, and the temperature recording device shall be observed and the temperatures recorded at the time the first containers enter the steam dome. Thereafter, these instruments shall be read and the temperatures recorded with sufficient frequency to ensure compliance with the temperature specified in the process schedule and should be made at least every hour of continuous retort operation. Container conveyor speed, and for agitating hydrostatic retorts, the rotative chain speed, shall be determined and recorded at intervals of sufficient frequency to ensure compliance with the process schedule and should be performed at least every 4 hours.

(b) *Processing in water* – (1) *Batch still retorts.* For each retort batch, record the retort number or other designation, the approximate number of containers or number of retort crates per retort load, product initial temperature, time steam on, the start of process timing, water level, water recirculation rate (if critical), overriding pressure maintained, time steam off, and actual processing time. The indicating temperature device and the temperature recorder shall be read at the same time at least once during process timing and the observed temperatures recorded.

(2) *Batch agitating retorts.* In addition to recording the information required in paragraph (b)(1) of this section, record the retort or reel speed.

(c) *Processing in steam/air mixtures.* For each retort batch, record the retort number or other designation, the approximate number of containers or number of retort crates per retort load, product initial temperature, time steam on, venting procedure, if applicable, the start of process timing, maintenance of circulation of the steam/air mixture, air flow rate or forced recirculation flow rate (if critical), overriding pressure maintained, time steam off, and actual processing time. The indicating temperature device and the temperature recorder shall be read at the same time at least once during process timing and the observed temperatures recorded.

(d) *Atmospheric cookers* – (1) *Batch-type systems.* For each cooker batch, record the cooker number or other designation and the approximate number of containers. In addition, record all critical factors of the process schedule such as cooker temperature, initial temperature, the time the thermal process cycle begins and ends, hold time, and the final internal product temperature.

(2) *Continuous-type systems.* Record the cooker number or other designation, the time the first containers enter and the last containers exit a cooker, and the

approximate total number of containers processed. In addition, record all critical factors of the process schedule such as the initial temperature, cooker speed, and final internal product temperature.

(Approved by the Office of Management and Budget under control number 0583-0015)

§ 318.307 Record Review and Maintenance

(a) *Process records.* Charts from temperature/time recording devices shall be identified by production date, container code, processing vessel number or other designation, and other data as necessary to enable correlation with the records required in § 318.306. Each entry on a record shall be made at the time the specific event occurs, and the recording individual shall sign or initial each record form. No later than 1 working day after the actual process, the establishment shall review all processing and production records to ensure completeness and to determine if all product received the process schedule. All records, including the temperature/time recorder charts and critical factor control records, shall be signed or initialed and dated by the person conducting the review. All processing and production records required in this subpart shall be made available to Program employees for review.

(b) *Automated process monitoring and recordkeeping.* Automated process monitoring and recordkeeping systems shall be designed and operated in a manner that will ensure compliance with the applicable requirements of §318.306.

(c) *Container closure records.* Written records of all container closure examinations shall specify the container code, the date and time of container closure examination, the measurement(s) obtained, and any corrective actions taken. Records shall be signed or initialed by the container closure technician and shall be reviewed and signed by the establishment within 1 working day after the actual production to ensure that the records are complete and that the closing operations have been properly controlled. All container closure examination records required in this subpart shall be made available to Program employees for review.

(d) *Distribution of product.* Records shall be maintained by the establishment identifying initial distribution of the finished product to facilitate, if necessary, the segregation of specific production lots that may have been contaminated or are otherwise unsound for their intended use.

(e) *Retention of records.* Copies of all processing and production records required in § 318.306 shall be retained for no less than 1 year at the establishment, and for an additional 2 years at the establishment or other location from which the records can be made available to Program employees within 3 working days.

(Approved by the Office of Management and Budget under control number 0583-0015)

[51 FR 45619, Dec. 19, 1986, as amended at 65 FR 34389, May 30, 2000]

§ 318.308 Deviations in Processing

(a) Whenever the actual process is less than the process schedule or when any critical factor does not comply with the requirements for that factor as specified in the process schedule, it shall be considered a deviation in processing.

(b) Deviations in processing (or process deviations) must be handled according to:

(1)(i) A HACCP plan for canned product that addresses hazards associated with microbial contamination, or,

(ii) Alternative documented procedures that will ensure that only safe and stable product is shipped in commerce; or

(iii) Paragraph (d) of this section.

(c) [Reserved]

(d) Procedures for handling process deviations where the HACCP plan for thermally processed/commercially sterile product does not address food safety hazards associated with microbial contamination, where there is no approved total quality control system, or where the establishment has no alternative documented procedures for handling process deviations.

(1) *Deviations identified in-process.* If a deviation is noted at any time before the completion of the intended process schedule, the establishment shall:

(i) Immediately reprocess the product using the full process schedule; or

(ii) Use an appropriate alternate process schedule provided such a process schedule has been established in accordance with § 318.302 (a) and (b) and is filed with the inspector in accordance with § 318.302(c); or

(iii) Hold the product involved and have the deviation evaluated by a processing authority to assess the safety and stability of the product. Upon completion of the evaluation, the establishment shall provide the inspector the following:

(*a*) A complete description of the deviation along with all necessary supporting documentation;

(*b*) A copy of the evaluation report; and

(*c*) A description of any product disposition actions, either taken or proposed.

(iv) Product handled in accordance with paragraph (d)(1)(iii) of this section shall not be shipped from the establishment until the Program has reviewed all of the information submitted and approved the product disposition actions.

(v) If an alternate process schedule is used that is not on file with the inspector or if an alternate process schedule is immediately calculated and used, the product shall be set aside for further evaluation in accordance with paragraphs (d)(1)(iii) and (iv) of this section.

(vi) When a deviation occurs in a continuous rotary retort, the product shall be handled in accordance with paragraphs (d)(1)(iii) and (iv) of this section or in accordance with the following procedures:

(*a*) Emergency stops.

(*1*) When retort jams or breakdowns occur during the processing operations, all containers shall be given an emergency still process (developed per § 318.302(b)) before the retort is cooled or the retort shall be cooled promptly and all containers removed and either reprocessed, repacked and reprocessed, or destroyed. Regardless of the procedure used, containers in the retort in-take valve and in transfer valves between retort shells at the time of a jam or breakdown shall be removed and either reprocessed, repacked and reprocessed and or destroyed. Product to be destroyed shall be handled as 'U.S. Inspected and Condemned', as defined in § 301.2(ttt) of this subchapter, and disposed of in accordance with part 314 of this subchapter.

(*2*) The time the retort reel stopped and the time the retort is used for an emergency still retort process shall be noted on the temperature/time recording device and entered on the other production records required in § 318.306.

(*b*) Temperature drops. When the retort temperature drops below the temperature specified in the process schedule, the reel shall be stopped and the following actions shall be taken:

(*1*) For temperature drops of less than 10 °F (or 5.5 °C) either, (*i*) all containers in the retort shall be given an emergency still process (developed per § 318.302(b)) before the reel is restarted; (*ii*) container entry to the retort shall be prevented and an emergency agitating process (developed per § 318.302(b)) shall be used before container entry to the retort is restarted; or (*iii*) container entry to the retort shall be prevented and the reel restarted to empty the retort. The discharged containers shall be reprocessed, repacked and reprocessed, or destroyed. Product to be destroyed shall be handled as 'U.S. Inspected and Condemned', as defined in § 318.2(ee) of this subchapter, and disposed of in accordance with part 314 of this subchapter.

(*2*) For temperature drops of 10 °F (or 5.5 °C) or more, all containers in the retort shall be given an emergency still process (developed per § 318.302(b)). The time the reel was stopped and the time the retort was used for a still retort process shall be marked on the temperature/time recording device by the establishment and entered on the other production records required in § 318.306. Alternatively, container entry to the retort shall be prevented and the reel restarted to empty the retort. The discharged containers shall be either reprocessed, repacked and reprocessed, or destroyed. Product to be destroyed shall be handled as 'U.S. Inspected and Condemned', as defined in § 301.2(ee) of this subchapter, and disposed of in accordance with part 314 of this subchapter.

(2) *Deviations identified through record review.* Whenever a deviation is noted during review of the processing and production records required by § 318.307(a) and (b), the establishment shall hold the product involved and the deviation shall be handled in accordance with paragraphs (d)(1) (iii) and (iv) of this section.

(e) Process deviation file. The establishment shall maintain full records regarding the handling of each deviation. Such records shall include, at a minimum, the appropriate processing and production records, a full description of the corrective actions taken, the evaluation procedures and results, and the disposition of the affected product. Such records shall be maintained in a separate file or in a log that contains the appropriate information. The file or log shall be retained in accordance with § 318.307(e) and shall be made available to Program employees upon request.

(Approved by the Office of Management and Budget under control number 0583-0015)

[51 FR 45619, Dec. 19, 1986, as amended at 53 FR 49848, Dec. 12, 1988; 62 FR 45025, Aug. 25, 1997; 65 FR 34389, May 30, 2000; 65 FR 53532, Sept. 5, 2000]

§ 318.309 Finished Product Inspection

(a) Finished product inspections must be handled according to:

(1) A HACCP plan for canned product that addresses hazards associated with microbiological contamination;

(2) An FSIS-approved total quality control system;

(3) Alternative documented procedures that will ensure that only safe and stable product is shipped in commerce; or

(4) Paragraph (d) of this section.

(b)–(c) [Reserved]

(d) Procedures for handling finished product inspections where the HACCP plan for thermally processed/commercially sterile product does not address food safety hazards associated with microbial contamination, where there is no approved total quality control system, or where the establishment has no alternative documented procedures for handling process deviations.

(1) *Incubation of shelf stable canned product* – (i) *Incubator.* The establishment shall provide incubation facilities which include an accurate temperature/time recording device, an indicating temperature device, a means for the circulation of the air inside the incubator to prevent temperature variations, and a means to prevent unauthorized entry into the facility. The Program is responsible for the security of the incubator.

(ii) *Incubation temperature.* The incubation temperature shall be maintained at 95±5 °F (35±2.8 °C). If the incubation temperature falls below 90 °F (or 32 °C) or exceeds 100 °F (or 38 °C) but does not reach 103 °F (or 39.5 °C), the incubation temperature shall be adjusted within the required range and the incubation time extended for the time the sample containers were held at the deviant temperature. If the incubation temperature is at or above 103 °F (or 39.5 °C) for more than 2 hours, the incubation test(s) shall be terminated, the temperature lowered to within the required range, and new sample containers incubated for the required time.

(iii) *Product requiring incubation.* Shelf stable product requiring incubation includes:

(*a*) Low acid products as defined in § 318.300(m); and

(*b*) Acidified low acid products as defined in § 318.300(b).

(iv) *Incubation samples.* (*a*) From each load of product processed in a batchtype thermal processing system (still or agitation), the establishment shall select at least one container for incubation.

(*b*) For continuous rotary retorts, hydrostatic retorts, or other continuous-type thermal processing systems, the establishment shall select at least one container per 1,000 for incubation.

(*c*) Only normal-appearing containers shall be selected for incubation.

(v) *Incubation time.* Canned product requiring incubation shall be incubated for not less than 10 days (240 hours) under the conditions specified in paragraph (d)(1)(ii) of this section.

(vi) *Incubation checks and record maintenance.* Designated establishment employees shall visually check all containers under incubation each working day and the inspector shall be notified when abnormal containers are detected. All abnormal containers should be allowed to cool before a final decision on their condition is made. For each incubation test the establishment shall record at least the product name, container size, container code, number of containers incubated, in and out dates, and incubation results. The establishment shall retain such records, along with copies of the temperature/ time recording charts, in accordance with § 318.307(e).

(vii) *Abnormal containers.* The finding of abnormal containers (as defined in § 318.300(a)) among incubation samples is cause to officially retain at least the code lot involved.

(viii) *Shipping.* No product shall be shipped from the establishment before the end of the required incubation period except as provided in this paragraph or paragraph (b) or (c) of this section. An establishment wishing to ship product prior to the completion of the required incubation period shall submit a written proposal to the area supervisor. Such a proposal shall include provisions that will assure that shipped product will not reach the retail level of distribution before sample incubation is completed and that product can be returned promptly to the establishment should such action be deemed necessary by the incubation test results. Upon receipt of written approval from the area supervisor, product may be routinely shipped provided the establishment continues to comply with all requirements of this subpart.

(2) *Container condition* – (i) *Normal containers.* Only normal-appearing containers shall be shipped from an establishment as determined by an appropriate sampling plan or other means acceptable to Program employees.

(ii) *Abnormal containers.* When abnormal containers are detected by any means other than incubation, the establishment shall inform the inspector, and the affected code lot(s) shall not be shipped until the Program has determined that the product is safe and stable. Such a determination will take into account the cause and level of abnormals in the affected lot(s) as well as any product disposition actions either taken or proposed by the establishment.

(Approved by the Office of Management and Budget under control number 0583-0015)

[51 FR 45619, Dec. 19, 1986, as amended at 57 FR 37872, Aug. 21, 1992; 57 FR 55443, Nov. 25, 1992; 62 FR 45025, Aug. 25, 1997; 65 FR 34389, May 30, 2000; 65 FR 53532, Sept. 5, 2000]

§ 318.310 PERSONNEL AND TRAINING.

All operators of thermal processing systems specified in § 318.305 and container closure technicians shall be under the direct supervision of a person who has successfully completed a school of instruction that is generally recognized as adequate for properly training supervisors of canning operations.

[51 FR 45619, Dec. 19, 1986]

§ 318.311 RECALL PROCEDURE.

Establishments shall prepare and maintain a current procedure for the recall of all canned product covered by this subpart. Upon request, the recall procedure shall be made available to Program employees for review.

(Approved by the Office of Management and Budget under control number 0583-0015)

4. US Customs and Border Protection

Notice: Mandatory Electronic Manifest (e-Manifest)

Dear Sir or Madam:

As mandated by Section 343(a) of the Trade Act of 2002, CBP is implementing mandatory electronic manifest (e-Manifest) for all truck carriers and other parties transmitting advance electronic cargo information to U.S. Customs and Border Protection (CBP).

As required by Section 123.92(e) of CBP regulations (19 CFR 123.92(e)), CBP must provide notice to affected carriers 90 days in advance that the approved data interchange is in place and fully operational at a port, and that carriers must commence the presentation of the required cargo information through the approved system. Notice is to be provided by way of publication in the Federal Register that the electronic data interchange (EDI) system is in place and fully operational.

The Federal Register Notice announcing required advance electronic presentation of cargo information for truck carriers was published on October 27, 2006 [71 FR 62922]. In this notice, truck carriers were notified that on January 25, 2007, they would be required to use the Automated Commercial Environment (ACE) e-Manifest system to present advance electronic cargo information regarding shipments arriving at selected ports of entry.

Those ports initially impacted include all ports in the states of Washington and Arizona, as well as the following ports in the state of North Dakota: Pembina, Neche, Walhalla, Maida, Hannah, Sarles, and Hansboro. For complete details regarding this notice and all of the CBP issued Federal Register Notices regarding e-Manifest: Trucks, please visit the CBP website at: *http://www.cbp.gov/xp/cgov/toolbox/about/modernization/ace/frnnotices.xml.*

CBP will issue additional Federal Register Notices announcing final implementation dates for subsequent ports 90 days prior to such implementation.

The Pre-Arrival Processing System (PAPS), QP/WP (an Automated Broker Interface (ABI) in-bond processing system that allows ABI filers to create and process in-bond shipments), Free and Secure Trade (FAST), and Border Release Advanced Screening and Selectivity (BRASS) will continue to be used as cargo release and in-bond authorizing mechanisms. While use of those systems will no longer satisfy advance electronic cargo information requirements, carriers should continue to work with the appropriate parties, (i.e. brokers, importers) regarding the use of these systems. Use of these systems is still required to obtain the release of shipments.

If you have any questions concerning the submission of required advance electronic information, please contact *ACENow@dhs.gov*.

Sincerely,

Louis Samenfink
Executive Director, Cargo Systems Program Office
Office of Information Technology
U.S. Customs and Border Protection

MANDATORY e-MANIFEST POLICY

Q: Where is the electronic manifest (e-Manifest) capability currently available?

A: The e-Manifest capability for trucks is available at all land border ports featuring the Automated Commercial Environment (ACE), the commercial trade processing and communications system being developed by U.S. Customs and Border Protection (CBP) to facilitate legitimate trade while strengthening border security. ACE is currently deployed at all land ports along the southern border, as well as most land ports along the northern border, with the exception of those in Maine, Idaho, Montana, New Hampshire, Alaska, and certain ports in North Dakota and Minnesota.

Q: When and how will e-Manifests become mandatory?

A: Use of e-Manifests is currently voluntary, however, CBP announced in Federal Register Notice (FRN) 71 FR 62922, dated October 27, 2006, that it will begin implementation of a mandatory e-Manifest policy at the specified ports named in the Federal Register 90 days after publication of this notice in the Federal Register, on January 25, 2007.

Q: Which ports will be the first to require e-Manifests?

A: All ports in the states of Washington and Arizona. Also, the following ports in the state of North Dakota: Pembina, Neche, Walhalla, Maida, Hannah, Sarles, and Hansboro.

Q: What is the mandatory e-Manifest policy rollout schedule for the remaining land border ports?

A: The dates for implementation of the mandatory e-Manifest policy at additional ports will be announced later. The port groupings and order of implementation listed in the FRN are subject to change. Schedules detailing when each port will implement the policy will be announced via subsequent Federal Register Notices (FRNs), as well as on the CBP Modernization Web site, 90 days before each implementation.

Q: How will the mandatory e-Manifest policy be enforced?

A: As implementation of the policy begins at the first group of ports on January 25, 2007, CBP intends to exercise enforcement discretion in the form of informed compliance notices given to carriers who arrive without submitting or attempting an e-Manifest. This discretionary period will last for a limited period of time (approximately 60 days) and will be followed by enforcement action against carriers who fail to participate. Enforcement action will take the form of a denial of permit to proceed into the U.S. or monetary penalties of up to $5,000 for violation of the Trade Act of 2002. CBP intends, for a short period of time during this first enforcement phase, to continue to exercise limited enforcement discretion for those carriers who are attempting to file e-Manifests. December 2006 At some point CBP will begin to fully enforce the mandatory e-Manifest regulations for all parties, subject to the requirements, who fail to file an e-Manifest.

Q: Will carriers be able to continue using other entry/release systems to submit entries and obtain cargo releases?

A: Yes. The Pre-Arrival Processing System (PAPS) and other entry/release processes will continue to be in use at all ACE and non-ACE ports throughout and after the transition to ACE and implementation of the mandatory e-Manifest policy. ACE supports existing entry/release processes, including PAPS, the Border Release Advanced Selectivity System (BRASS), In-bond processing, and Section 321 processing, as well as the Free and Secure Trade (FAST) program. ACE integrates existing entry and release processes and adds some new automated methods to obtain release of cargo and request the in-bond movement of cargo. All existing entry and release methods will continue to be used for the purpose of entry submission and obtaining release of cargo. Once mandatory filing of e-Manifests has been implemented, PAPS and electronic in-bond (QP/WP) messages will continue to be used for the purpose of obtaining the release or authorized movement of cargo, but these entry methods will not be considered sufficient notification to CBP of the anticipated arrival of cargo.

Q: Will carriers be able to continue using other entry/release systems to comply with the Trade Act of 2002 advance cargo rule?

A: Not at border crossings that have implemented the mandatory e-Manifest policies. All commercial cargo, with certain exceptions, is subject to advance cargo information requirements pursuant to 19 CFR 123.92(b) and will require the filing of advance cargo information in the form of either an e-Manifest or a FAST/NCAP electronic declaration prior to the arrival of a conveyance at an applicable U.S. land border crossing. The advance cargo rule was enacted to help combat terrorism and otherwise unsafe or illegal transports by requiring the submission of cargo information electronically, in advance of the arrival of the conveyance (See 69 *FR* 51007, published August 17, 2004). Temporary exceptions enumerated in the above referenced Federal Register Notice include merchandise which is informally entered on Customs Form (CF) 368 or CF 368 A (cash collection or receipt); merchandise unconditionally or conditionally free, not exceeding $2000 in value, eligible for entry on CF 7523; domestic cargo transiting Canada or Mexico; and products of the United States being returned, for which entry is prescribed on CF 3311 (US goods returned). However it should be noted that with the exception of CF 368 (A) the above manifest shipment release types can be reported as shipments on an e-Manifest as well as Section 321 (certain goods valued under $200); goods astray; and merchandise which is released under exceptions listed in General Headnote 1. The appropriate Customs Forms and supporting documentation will be required in addition to the electronic manifest. Merchandise entered under a CF

3299 (household effects, tools of trade) are NOT listed under 123.92(b) as being exempted from advance cargo information requirements and will required an e-Manifest to be filed. Although a truck hauling Instruments of International Traffic (ITT) is required to present a manifest they are not required to file an e-Manifest however the filing of an e-Manifest is acceptable and recommended.

During the transition period at ports where ACE is not available or e-Manifest use is not yet mandatory, current processes will continue to be used to comply with the rule until the mandatory policy is implemented, including FAST National Customs Automation Program (NCAP) electronic messages.

The advance cargo rule mandated pre-filing of an entry at least one hour prior to the arrival of the truck. Through use of PAPS the carrier was able to temporarily use the pre-filed entry to comply with the advance cargo rule. At the time of the advance cargo rule implementation, there was no e-Manifest capability. Use of PAPS implied a barcode would be used to enable a CBP officer to pull up the entry by scanning, rather than typing an entry number. The barcode is not needed by CBP if an e-Manifest has been filed. The shipment control number (SCN) reported in the shipment record of a manifest will be recorded in the prefiled entry so that the entry and manifest shipment records will be automatically associated upon arrival of the truck.

For more details on Trade Act of 2002 advance electronic information, visit the CBP Web site, *http://www.cbp.gov/xp/cgov/import/communications_to_trade/advance_info/*.

Q. How does use of e-Manifests impact PAPS?

A. CBP will continue to use PAPS as a mechanism for the submission of entry data in conjunction with a carrier's ACE e-Manifest. It is recommended PAPS continue to be used in all cases where it is currently being used for filing entries, even when filing an e-Manifest. Use of PAPS means the entry is filed via the Automated Broker Interface (ABI) prior to the arrival of the truck. ACE e-Manifest eliminates the need for a carrier to present a PAPS barcode to the CBP officer. The earlier an entry is filed, the better for everyone. Advance submissions give both the carrier and the broker time to confirm that the entry data filed by the broker (through PAPS) matches the manifest data filed by the carrier (through an e-Manifest). The e-Manifest data will need to be associated with the corresponding entry data.

The e-Manifest provides for automated submission of trip, conveyance, crew, equipment, and shipment data. Some release processes that do not use PAPS as the release process today have been automated in e-Manifest: Trucks such as Section 321, Goods Astray, General Headnote 1, In-bond requests and the declaration of Instruments of International Traffic. In the e-Manifest environment, the PAPS entry is the responsibility of the broker/importer of record, as far as CBP enforcement is concerned, and the carrier is solely responsible for the manifest. So, if the entry is not on file, the broker could be liable for broker compliance penalties if this happens on a frequent basis. Lack of an e-Manifest will ultimately result in a denial to proceed, which means the truck could be turned around at the border, unable to cross until compliance with the policy is achieved.

Q. Does the phasing in of the mandatory e-Manifest policy mean carriers will have to use two systems until ACE deployment is complete if they are crossing at ACE and non-ACE ports?

A. It depends on the situation. There are three types of scenarios possible during the transition period:

1. **At a port that has mandated the use of e-Manifests:** a carrier must transmit, at least one hour prior to the arrival of the truck (30 minutes if FAST qualified), an e-Manifest to comply with the advance cargo rule. In addition, arrangements must be made, as before, for the release of the cargo being carried. These releases can be obtained by previously used methods such as a pre filed entry through PAPS. In-bond requests can be made via the e-Manifest. Carrier declarations supported by special provisions of the regulations, such as Section 321, General Head note 1 or Goods Astray rules, can be declared by the carrier via e-Manifest. e-Manifests will be required for cargo that is released via paper processes, such as Customs Form (CF)-3299 Unaccompanied Articles, CF-3311 Free US Goods Returned or CF-7523 Free of Duty. These paper processes can be identified in the e-Manifest declaration as the designated release type. These CBP forms and appropriate supporting documentation will be required to be available upon request.
2. **At a port that has deployed ACE but has not mandated the filing of e-Manifests:** it will be the carrier's option to comply with the advance cargo rule by either filing an e-Manifest or following the previously prescribed methods, namely PAPS or QP/WP. Previously documented exceptions will continue to exist, such as cargo moving in-transit from point to point in the United States, and certain informal entries.
3. **At ports where ACE is not yet deployed:** carriers will continue to use the same systems and paper manifests they are using now until the transition to ACE is made.

Q: With use of e-Manifests currently a relatively low percentage of the number of manifests filed, is CBP going to be able to handle suddenly requiring 100 percent of manifests to be filed electronically at ACE ports?

A: The system is designed to handle high volumes of electronic manifests and the transition has begun. The question will be whether carriers are ready. We have been seeing numbers of e-Manifests filed increase dramatically in the past few months, from 1,000 e-Manifests submitted in April 2006 to more than 12,000 filed in September, to more than 22,000 submitted in November 2006, and the trend is continuing as the feature becomes available at more ports. To date, more than 80,000 e-Manifests have been filed since the first e-Manifest was submitted in 2005.

The number of ACE carrier accounts more than doubled in that same time period, and now stands at more than 4,000 as of December 2006. The more carries use e-Manifests, the easier it will be for everyone, and the sooner the better. As with any change in procedures, there may be a learning curve for some carriers, who may experience transitional issues. We are hoping to see even greater growth in e-Manifest filings in the next few weeks prior to the mandatory policy being implemented. Carriers are encouraged to establish ACE truck carrier accounts, or contact a customs broker, service provider, or other authorized filer as soon as possible to discuss how to submit e-Manifests. Lists of brokers and software providers can be found on the CBP Web site, www.cbp.gov/modernization, under *Broker and Importer Information on ACE*, and *Truck Carrier Information on* ACE. Truck carriers should be making plans now to avoid being stuck in the last minute influx of carriers rushing to comply.

e-MANIFEST DESCRIPTION

Q: What is an e-Manifest?

A: With the current system, carriers must present a paper manifest to CBP before a shipment can enter the United States. An e-Manifest is the submission of trip, conveyance, equipment, crew, passenger, and shipment details electronically. Filing manifests electronically can be accomplished either by Electronic Data Interchange (EDI) or via the Internet by using the ACE Secure Data Portal.

Q: How does an e-Manifest work?

A: As a truck approaches the primary booth, ACE is used to retrieve e-Manifest details for the CBP officer to review. If the truck is equipped with a CBP-approved electronic transponder, ACE will automatically retrieve e-Manifest details along with matching pre-filed entries or in-bond requests.

Q: Does a carrier need to have a transponder to participate in ACE e-Manifest?

A: No, transponder technology is not required for participation in ACE. If a truck does not have a transponder, the officer uses the vehicle license plate or trip number to retrieve the e-Manifest.

Q: How do e-Manifests save time?

A: Time spent at the borders is reduced when carriers are able to submit electronic manifests to CBP for review before the truck's arrival. This process frequently eliminates the need for an officer to spend time processing paper manifests and barcodes. As release times are lessened, truckers will have additional time to haul more shipments to make more money.

Several carrier companies have reported a significant time and cost savings by no longer having to have someone fax paper shipping documents – that process has been eliminated. Carriers report driver paperwork has been cut dramatically. Some companies have experienced administrative start-up and training costs, and have added monitoring procedures to verify the status of manifest filings, but report those procedures have not added a significant amount of effort, and the time-savings of e-Manifest are a net benefit. With clear, positive benefits, carriers currently using e-Manifests report they would not go back to the old system. Carriers using e-Manifests also report an approximately fifty-percent decrease in the number of times a driver has to get out of the truck at the border to process cargo. Prior to ACE deployment, most drivers were required to stop and enter the processing center.

Q: Has the use of e-Manifests resulted in a decrease in processing times?

A: Yes. Although the effect of ACE on truck processing time at land border ports continues to vary by port, trucks were processed, on average, 22 percent faster than the pre-ACE baseline during October and November 2006 at key ACE ports. The ACE ports reviewed to develop the average were: Detroit Ambassador Bridge, and Port Huron, Michigan; Laredo and El Paso, Texas; Otay Mesa, California; Nogales, Arizona; and Pembina, North Dakota. As additional ports and more drivers use e-Manifests, the processing times are expected to decrease more as lines become shorter for everyone, even those who have not yet begun to use e-Manifests. The mandatory policy is expected to increase time savings yet again when all carriers are required to use e-Manifests.

Q: How do electronic manifests help ensure border security?

A: Access to advance shipment data enables CBP officers to prescreen trucks and shipments, freeing up time to inspect suspicious cargo without delaying the border crossings of legitimate carriers. Automating the process also allows information to be integrated electronically with CBP systems to provide better cargo screening. It is a win-win for everyone to ensure the border crossing process is smooth, safe, and as efficient as possible – that goods flow freely in and out of our nation for the benefit of all. Moving goods to market faster will have positive impacts on U.S., Mexican, and Canadian economies, benefiting consumers and business alike.

Q: What information is required for an e-Manifest?

A: An e-Manifest provides the same information as the current paper manifest, including: crew identification (driver/passenger); description of conveyance (vehicle/truck/cab); description of equipment as applicable (trailer/container/chassis); and shipment details (cargo). More specific detail on information required is listed in the ACE Truck Manifest Notice published on March 21, 2005 (70 FRN 13514). The cargo information required enables high-risk shipments to be identified for purposes of ensuring cargo safety and security and preventing smuggling pursuant to the laws enforced and administered by CBP.

FILING AN e-MANIFEST

Q: How can an e-Manifest be filed?

A: An e-Manifest can be submitted through one or both of the following channels: the Web-based ACE Secure Data Portal, or via a CBP-approved Electronic Data Interchange (EDI).

Q: When must an e-Manifest be received by CBP?

A: Generally, an e-Manifest must be received at least one hour prior to the carrier reaching the first port of arrival in the United States. For truck carriers arriving with shipments qualified for clearance under the FAST (Free and Secure Trade) program, an e-Manifest is required when following FAST/PAPS procedures or a FAST/NCAP electronic message must be received at least 30 minutes prior to the carrier reaching the first port of arrival in the United States.

Q: What is the ACE Secure Data Portal?

A: The ACE Secure Data Portal is essentially a customized, secure Web site for authorized users that connects CBP, the trade community, and participating government agencies with a single, centralized on-line access point for communications and information.

Q: What features and abilities are provided by the portal?

A: With the portal:

- Carriers have the ability to input data, track the CBP status of a truck and its cargo, and develop a variety of reports.
- Data regarding trucks, trailers, drivers, shippers, and consignees can be stored and reused, saving time for truck carriers entering recurring trip data and resulting in fewer opportunities for mistakes.
- A broker download feature, also available via EDI, enables carriers to quickly transmit shipment details to a customs broker or other entry filer, helping carriers and filers reconcile manifest and entry data, minimizing errors and reducing delays.
- ACE makes it easier for CBP officers to release cargo, which can save time for truckers.
- There is no charge to use the portal, but users must provide their own high-speed Internet access (dial-up service does not have the capacity for portal navigation), and a compatible web browser must be used. To use the portal, a carrier must establish an ACE account. Currently, more than 2,600 carriers have established ACE accounts. Through the portal, e-Manifests can be filed with CBP at no charge.

Q: What are the options for companies choosing to use EDI for filing e-Manifests?

A: EDI filing options:

- Some companies may opt to develop their own EDI software, which will need to be tested for compatibility with CBP systems.
- Companies may also purchase or lease software from EDI software providers.
- A list of EDI software providers can be found on the CBP Modernization Web site, at *http://www.cbp.gov/modernization.* Scroll down the middle and click on 'Truck Carrier Information on ACE'. Once in the car-

rier information section, look to the right of the page and click on **ACE Electronic Truck Manifest Software Developers**. The list is continually growing, with more and more companies becoming eligible to transmit e-Manifests via EDI. Please note that inclusion on this list does not constitute endorsement by CBP.

- Another option is to use a third party to transmit the e-Manifest via EDI. Third parties usually charge a fee to help carriers file manifests with CBP. Some customs brokers have the ability to file e-Manifests. Lists of customs brokers can be found on the CBP Web site www.cbp.gov/modernization, under '*Broker and Importer Information on ACE*,' and 'Truck Carrier Information on ACE.' Click on the '*Ports of Entry*' link: *http://www.cbp.gov/xp/cgov/toolbox/ports/*. For a list of brokers operating at each port, click on the appropriate state, followed by specific port links, then click on '*Brokers: View List*'
- Carriers may also use a combination of EDI and the ACE Secure Data Portal to file e-Manifests with CBP.
- An ACE account is not needed to file an e-Manifest via EDI.

Q: What are the costs for filing e-Manifests?

A: CBP does not charge a fee for filing an e-Manifest via the ACE Secure Data Portal, although users must provide their own high speed Internet access. No special software is required to use the portal, only a compatible Internet Web browser. If a third party is used to file e-Manifests on behalf of a carrier, the fee would be determined by the third party. If a company chooses to file e-Manifests directly with CBP via EDI, software will either need to be developed, purchased, or leased. The software must be tested for CBP system compatibility. There may be administrative set-up and training costs, although e-Manifests eventually should reduce administrative costs.

FUTURE PREPARATION FOR e-MANIFEST

Q: How can a truck carrier prepare for the mandatory e-manifest policy?

A: Truck carriers should establish ACE truck carrier accounts as soon as possible, or contact a customs broker, service provider, or other authorized filer to discuss how to submit e-Manifests.

Remember, ACE and e-Manifests will soon be a business necessity for everyone. Don't let your truck get caught in the last minute traffic jam of carriers rushing to comply with the new e-Manifest requirements. Beat the rush and start using the e-Manifest process now, before the mandatory policy takes effect, to ensure a smooth transition as CBP moves toward implementing the mandatory policy.

SPECIFIC ADDITIONAL GUIDELINES FOR CARRIERS FILING e-MANIFESTS

Q: What additional information/documentation do I need for border crossings using e-Manifests? Do I still need paper?

A: Yes, the driver should have in his possession a paper manifest with PAPS barcodes if the shipments are being released via the PAPS process. This manifest should not be given to the CBP primary booth officer unless requested. This manifest is maintained as a back up in case there are problems with the e-Manifest submission, system outages, or other irregularities that may require further inspection.

After successfully transmitting an e-Manifest, carriers or their agents should prepare and provide the driver with a CBP Form 7533 (Inward Cargo Manifest) or a plain paper printout. These documents should be annotated with the following minimum information in at least 22 point type:

- **'ACE Electronic Manifest'** should be printed on the document.
- **'Trip number: Standard Carrier Alpha Code (SCAC), plus up to 16 alpha/numeric characters (A/N)':** This should be clearly labeled as 'trip number' and must be in text. [Note: this is not the shipment control number or PAPS number).
- **Driver's Name**
- **Truck (Tractor) License Plate** (Must be the one that is listed in the e-Manifest transmission to CBP)

A code '3 of 9' barcode label may be provided in addition to the text for these elements. In addition, the following data elements may be added in smaller letters (12 point type maximum):

- Shipment Control Number (SCN): (PAPS or other shipment ID SCAC, plus up to 12 alpha numeric characters)
- Shipment Description for each SCN

Carriers should not place PAPS barcode labels on any forms to be handed to CBP officers in primary booths.

If invoices and PAPS bar-coded manifests are provided to the driver they should remain in the driver's control and not be given to CBP except upon request. CBP officers should only use these documents for CBP system downtime or validation/examination of shipments.

Free and Secure Trade (FAST) manifest cover sheets will continue to be used for FAST shipments.

5. Required Advance Electronic Presentation of Cargo Information for Truck Carriers, ACE Truck Manifest (Federal Register, Vol. 72, No. 12, 19 CFR Part 123)

AGENCY: Customs and Border Protection, Department of Homeland Security.
ACTION: Notice.

SUMMARY: Pursuant to section 343(a) of the Trade Act of 2002 and implementing regulations, truck carriers and other eligible parties are required to transmit advance electronic truck cargo information to the Bureau of Customs and Border Protection (CBP) through a CBP-approved electronic data interchange. In a previous notice, CBP designated the Automated Commercial Environment (ACE) Truck Manifest System as the approved interchange and announced that the requirement that advance electronic cargo information be transmitted through ACE would be phased in by groups of ports of entry. The previous notice identified the first group of ports where use of the ACE Truck Manifest System is mandated. This notice announces the second group of land border ports that will require truck carriers to file electronic manifests through the ACE Truck Manifest System.

DATES: Trucks entering the United States through land border ports of entry in the states of California, Texas, and New Mexico will be required to transmit the advance information through the ACE Truck Manifest system effective April 19, 2007.

SUPPLEMENTARY INFORMATION

BACKGROUND

Section 343(a) of the Trade Act of 2002, as amended (the Act; 19 U.S.C. 2071 note), required that CBP promulgate regulations providing for the mandatory transmission of electronic cargo information by way of a CBP-approved electronic data interchange (EDI) system before the cargo is brought into or departs the United States by any mode of commercial transportation (sea, air, rail or truck). The cargo information required is that which is reasonably necessary to enable high-risk shipments to be identified for purposes of ensuring cargo safety and security and preventing smuggling pursuant to the laws enforced and administered by CBP.

On December 5, 2003, CBP published in the **Federal Register** (68 FR 68140) a final rule to effectuate the provisions of the Act. In particular, a new § 123.92 (19 CFR 123.92) was added to the regulations to implement the inbound truck cargo provisions. Section 123.92 describes the general requirement that, in the case of any inbound truck required to report its arrival under § 123.1(b), if the truck will have commercial cargo aboard, CBP must electronically receive certain information regarding that cargo through a CBP-approved EDI system no later than 1 hour prior to the carrier's reaching the first port of arrival in the United States. For truck carriers arriving with shipments qualified for clearance under the FAST (Free and Secure Trade) program, § 123.92 provides that CBP must electronically receive such cargo information through the CBP-approved EDI system no later than 30 minutes prior to the carrier's reaching the first port of arrival in the United States.

ACE TRUCK MANIFEST TEST

On September 13, 2004, CBP published a notice in the **Federal Register** (69 FR 55167) announcing a test allowing participating Truck Carrier Accounts to transmit electronic manifest data for inbound cargo through ACE, with any such transmissions automatically complying with advance cargo information requirements as provided in section 343(a) of the Trade Act of 2002. Truck Carrier Accounts participating in the test were given the ability to electronically transmit the truck manifest data and obtain release of their cargo, crew, conveyances, and equipment via the ACE Portal or electronic data interchange messaging.

A series of notices announced additional deployments of the test, with deployment sites being phased in as clusters. Clusters were announced in the following notices published in the **Federal Register:** 70 FR 30964 (May 31, 2005); 70 FR 43892 (July 29, 2005); 70 FR 60096 (October 14, 2005); 71 FR 3875 (January 24, 2006); 71 FR 23941 (April 25, 2006); 71 FR 42103 (July 25, 2006); and 71 FR 77404 (December 26, 2006).

CBP continues to test ACE at various ports. CBP will continue, as necessary, to announce in subsequent notices in the **Federal Register** the deployment of the ACE truck manifest system test at additional ports.

DESIGNATION OF ACE TRUCK MANIFEST SYSTEM AS THE APPROVED DATA INTERCHANGE SYSTEM

In a notice published October 27, 2006, (71 FR 62922), CBP designated the Automated Commercial Environment (ACE) Truck Manifest System as the approved EDI for the transmission of required data and announced that the requirement that advance electronic cargo information be transmitted through ACE would be phased in by groups of ports of entry.

ACE will be phased in as the required transmission system at some ports even while it is still being tested at other ports. However, the use of ACE to transmit advance electronic truck cargo information will not be required in any port in which CBP has not first conducted the test.

The October 27, 2006, document identified all land border ports in the states of Washington and Arizona and the ports of Pembina, Neche, Walhalla, Maida, Hannah, Sarles, and Hansboro in North Dakota as the first group of ports where use of the ACE Truck Manifest System is mandated.

ACE MANDATED AT PORTS OF ENTRY IN CALIFORNIA, TEXAS AND NEW MEXICO

Applicable regulations (19 CFR 123.92(e)) require CBP, 90 days prior to mandating advance electronic information at a port of entry, to publish notice in the **Federal Register** informing affected carriers that the EDI system is in place and fully operational. Accordingly, CBP is announcing in this document that, effective 90 days from the date of publication of this notice, truck carriers entering the United States at any land border port of entry in the states of California, Texas, and New Mexico will be required to present advance electronic cargo information regarding truck cargo through the ACE Truck Manifest System.

Although other systems that have been deemed acceptable by CBP for transmitting advance truck manifest data will continue to operate and may still be used in the normal course of business for purposes other than transmitting advance truck manifest data, use of systems other than ACE will no longer satisfy advance electronic cargo information requirements at a port of entry in California, Texas and New Mexico as of April 19, 2007.

COMPLIANCE SEQUENCE

CBP will be publishing subsequent notices in the **Federal Register** as it phases in the requirement that truck carriers utilize the ACE system to present advance electronic truck cargo information at other ports. ACE will be phased in as the mandatory EDI system at the ports identified below in the sequential order in which they are listed. The sequential order provided below is somewhat different from that announced in the October 27, 2006, notice. Although further changes to this order are not currently anticipated, CBP will state in future notices if changes do occur. In any event, as mandatory ACE is phased in at these remaining ports, CBP will always provide 90 days' notice through publication in the **Federal Register** prior to requiring the use of ACE for the transmission of advance electronic truck cargo information at a particular group of ports.

The remaining ports at which the mandatory use of ACE will be phased in, listed in sequential order, are as follows:

1. All ports of entry in the state of New York and Michigan.
2. All ports of entry in the states of Vermont, New Hampshire, and Maine.
3. All ports of entry in the states of Idaho and Montana.
4. The remaining ports of entry in the state of North Dakota and the land border port of Minnesota.
5. All ports of entry in the state of Alaska.

Dated: January 16, 2007.

Deborah J. Spero,
Acting Commissioner, Customs and Border Protection.

[FR Doc. E7–762 Filed 1–18–07; 8:45 am]
BILLING CODE 9111–14–P

6. U.S. Customs and Border Protection

Fact Sheet: Automated Commercial Environment (ACE)

The Automated Commercial Environment (ACE) is the commercial trade processing system being developed by U.S. Customs and Border Protection (CBP) to facilitate legitimate trade while strengthening border security.

INTEGRATED ON-LINE ACCESS

The ACE Secure Data Portal, essentially a customized Web page, connects CBP, the trade community, and participating government agencies by providing a single, centralized, online access point for communications and information related to cargo shipments.

PERIODIC PAYMENTS

With the ACE account-based system, monthly payment and statement capabilities are available. Duties and fees no longer have to be paid on a transaction-per-transaction basis, and companies can more easily track their activities through customized account views and reports that better meet their business needs. ACE periodic payment users have the ability to wait until the 15th working day of the next month to pay for shipments released during the previous calendar month. This provides a potentially significant cash flow benefit. To date, more than 9 billion dollars in duties and fees have been paid through the ACE monthly statement process since the first payment was made in July 2004. A total of $752 million in payments were collected via December 21, 2006 monthly statements, representing approximately 33 percent of adjusted total statement collections.

ACE ACCOUNT FACTS

There are currently nearly 4,500 ACE portal accounts, including more than 700 importer accounts, nearly 500 broker accounts, and more than 3,200 carrier accounts. Non-portal ACE accounts are also available, which enable importers to use authorized brokers with ACE portal accounts to make payments without the importer creating a separate ACE portal account.

ELECTRONIC MANIFESTS (e-MANIFESTS)

All carriers are required to submit manifests detailing shipment, carrier, and other information to enter the United States. e-Manifests are simply electronically filed manifests.

The e-Manifest feature is available at all ACE land border ports. To date, nearly 100,000 truck e-Manifests have been filed through an Electronic Data Interchange (EDI) or the ACE Secure Data Portal. Nearly 400 companies have met CBP compatibility tests to file e-Manifests through EDI.

EDI testing is not needed to file e-Manifests through the portal. Parties may submit e-Manifests with CBP directly at no charge, or authorized brokers, service providers, or other third parties designated by the carrier may also be used to help with fi lings, usually for a fee. In 2007, CBP will begin to make the filing of e-Manifests mandatory, in a phased approach. In the coming months, check our Web site and the Federal Register for notices that will detail which ports will become mandatory, on what dates. Notice will be provided at a minimum of 90 days before a mandatory policy is implemented.

ACE LOCATIONS

Total number of ACE ports: 65

States where ACE is deployed: Arizona, California, Michigan, Minnesota, New Mexico, New York, North Dakota, Texas, Vermont, and Washington.

CBP is working diligently to fi nish deployment at all 99 land-border ports. Eventually ACE will reach all ports when, in the coming years, capabilities are deployed for air, rail, and sea cargo processing.

7. C-TPAT Foreign Manufacturer Security Criteria

These minimum security criteria are fundamentally designed to be the building blocks for foreign manufacturers to institute effective security practices designed to optimize supply chain performance to mitigate the risk of loss, theft, and contraband smuggling that could potentially introduce terrorists and implements of terrorism into the global supply chain. The determination and scope of criminal elements targeting world commerce through internal conspiracies requires companies, and in particular, foreign manufacturers to elevate their security practices.

At a minimum, on a yearly basis, or as circumstances dictate such as during periods of heightened alert, security breach or incident, foreign manufacturers must conduct a comprehensive assessment of their international supply chains based upon the following C-TPAT security criteria. Where a foreign manufacturer out-sources or contracts elements of their supply chain, such as another foreign facility, warehouse, or other elements, the foreign manufacturer must work with these business partners to ensure that pertinent security measures are in place and are adhered to throughout their supply chain. The supply chain for C-TPAT purposes is defined from point of origin (manufacturer/supplier/vendor) through to point of distribution – and recognizes the diverse business models C-TPAT members employ.

C-TPAT recognizes the complexity of international supply chains and security practices, and endorses the application and implementation of security measures based upon risk.[1] Therefore, the program allows for flexibility and the customization of security plans based on the member's business model.

---

1. Foreign manufacturers shall have a documented and verifiable process for determining risk throughout their supply chains based on their business model (i.e., volume, country of origin, routing, C-TPAT membership, potential terrorist threat via open source information, having inadequate security, past security incidents, etc.).

Appropriate security measures, as listed throughout this document, must be implemented and maintained throughout the Foreign manufacturer's supply chains – based on risk.[2]

BUSINESS PARTNER REQUIREMENT

Foreign manufacturers must have written and verifiable processes for the selection of business partners including, carriers, other manufacturers, product suppliers and vendors (parts and raw material suppliers, etc).

SECURITY PROCEDURES

For those business partners eligible for C-TPAT certification (carriers, importers, ports, terminals, brokers, consolidators, etc.) the foreign manufacturer must have documentation (e.g., C-TPAT certificate, SVI number, etc.) indicating whether these business partners are or are not C-TPAT certified.

For those business partners not eligible for C-TPAT certification, the foreign manufacturer must require that their business partners to demonstrate that they are meeting C-TPAT security criteria via written/electronic confirmation (e.g., contractual obligations; via a letter from a senior business partner officer attesting to compliance; a written statement from the business partner demonstrating their compliance with C-TPAT security criteria or an equivalent World Customs Organization (WCO) accredited security program administered by a foreign customs authority; or, by providing a completed foreign manufacturer security questionnaire). Based upon a documented risk assessment process, non-C-TPAT eligible business partners must be subject to verification of compliance with C-TPAT security criteria by the foreign manufacturer.

POINT OF ORIGIN

Foreign manufacturers must ensure that business partners develop security processes and procedures consistent with the C-TPAT security criteria to enhance the integrity of the shipment at point of origin, assembly or manufacturing. Periodic reviews of business partners' processes and facilities should be conducted based on risk, and should maintain the security standards required by the foreign manufacturer.

---

2. Foreign manufacturer shall have a documented and verifiable process for determining risk throughout their supply chains based on their business model (i.e., volume, country of origin, routing, potential terrorist threat via open source information, etc.).

PARTICIPATION/CERTIFICATION IN A FOREIGN CUSTOMS ADMINISTRATION SUPPLY CHAIN SECURITY PROGRAM

Current or prospective business partners who have obtained a certification in a supply chain security program being administered by foreign Customs Administration should be required to indicate their status of participation to the foreign manufacturer.

SECURITY PROCEDURES

On U.S. bound shipments, foreign manufacturers should monitor that C-TPAT carriers that subcontract transportation services to other carriers use other C-TPAT approved carriers, or non-C-TPAT carriers that are meeting the C-TPAT security criteria as outlined in the business partner requirements.

As the foreign manufacturer is responsible for loading trailers and containers, they should work with the carrier to provide reassurance that there are effective security procedures and controls implemented at the point-of-stuffing.

Container and Trailer Security

Container and trailer integrity must be maintained to protect against the introduction of unauthorized material and/or persons. At the point-of-stuffing, procedures must be in place to properly seal and maintain the integrity of the shipping containers and trailers. A high security seal must be affixed to all loaded containers and trailers bound for the U.S. All seals must meet or exceed the current PAS ISO 17712 standard for high security seals. In those geographic areas where risk assessments warrant checking containers or trailers for human concealment or smuggling, such procedures should be designed to address this risk at the manufacturing facility or point-of-stuffing.

CONTAINER INSPECTION

Procedures must be in place to verify the physical integrity of the container structure prior to stuffing, to include the reliability of the locking mechanisms of the doors. A seven-point inspection process is recommended for all containers:

- Front wall
- Left side
- Right side
- Floor
- Ceiling/Roof
- Inside/outside doors
- Outside/Undercarriage

TRAILER INSPECTION

Procedures must be in place to verify the physical integrity of the trailer structure prior to stuffing, to include the reliability of the locking mechanisms of the doors. The following five-point inspection process is recommended for all trailers:

- Fifth wheel area – check natural compartment/skid plate
- Exterior – front/sides
- Rear – bumper/doors
- Front wall
- Left side

CONTAINER AND TRAILER SEALS

The sealing of trailers and containers, to include continuous seal integrity, are crucial elements of a secure supply chain, and remains a critical part of a foreign manufacturers' commitment to CTPAT. The foreign manufacturer must affix a high security seal to all loaded trailers and containers bound for the U.S. All seals must meet or exceed the current PAS ISO 17712 standards for high security seals.

Written procedures must stipulate how seals are to be controlled and affixed to loaded containers and trailers, to include procedures for recognizing and reporting compromised seals and/or containers/trailers to US Customs and Border Protection or the appropriate foreign authority. Only designated employees should distribute seals for integrity purposes.

CONTAINER AND TRAILER STORAGE

Containers and trailers under foreign manufacturer control or located in a facility of the foreign manufacturer must be stored in a secure area to prevent unauthorized access and/or manipulation. Procedures must be in place for reporting and neutralizing unauthorized entry into containers/trailers or container/trailer storage areas.

Physical Access Controls

Access controls prevent unauthorized entry to facilities, maintain control of employees and visitors, and protect company assets. Access controls must include the positive identification of all employees, visitors, and vendors at all points of entry.

EMPLOYEES

An employee identification system must be in place for positive identification and access control purposes. Employees should only be given access to those secure areas needed for the performance of their duties. Company management or security personnel must adequately control the issuance and removal of employee, visitor and vendor identification badges. Procedures for the issuance, removal and changing of access devices (e.g. keys, key cards, etc.) must be documented.

VISITORS

Visitors must present photo identification for documentation purposes upon arrival. All visitors should be escorted and should visibly display temporary identification.

DELIVERIES (INCLUDING MAIL)

Proper vendor ID and/or photo identification must be presented for documentation purposes upon arrival by all vendors. Arriving packages and mail should be periodically screened before being disseminated.

CHALLENGING AND REMOVING UNAUTHORIZED PERSONS

Procedures must be in place to identify, challenge and address unauthorized/ unidentified persons.

Personnel Security

Processes must be in place to screen prospective employees and to periodically check current employees.

PRE-EMPLOYMENT VERIFICATION

Application information, such as employment history and references must be verified prior to employment.

BACKGROUND CHECKS/INVESTIGATIONS

Consistent with foreign regulations, background checks and investigations should be conducted for prospective employees. Once employed, periodic checks and reinvestigations should be performed based on cause, and/or the sensitivity of the employee's position.

PERSONNEL TERMINATION PROCEDURES

Companies must have procedures in place to remove identification, facility, and system access for terminated employees.

Procedural Security

Security measures must be in place to ensure the integrity and security of processes relevant to the transportation, handling, and storage of cargo in the supply chain.

DOCUMENTATION PROCESSING

Procedures must be in place to ensure that all information used in the clearing of merchandise/ cargo, is legible, complete, accurate, and protected against the exchange, loss or introduction of erroneous information. Documentation control must include safeguarding computer access and information.

MANIFESTING PROCEDURES

To help ensure the integrity of cargo, procedures must be in place to ensure that information received from business partners is reported accurately and timely.

SHIPPING AND RECEIVING

Departing cargo being shipped should be reconciled against information on the cargo manifest. The cargo should be accurately described, and the weights, labels, marks and piece count indicated and verified. Departing cargo should be verified against purchase or delivery orders. Drivers delivering or receiving cargo must be positively identified before cargo is received or released. Procedures should also be established to track the timely movement of incoming and outgoing goods.

CARGO DISCREPANCIES

All shortages, overages, and other significant discrepancies or anomalies must be resolved and/ or investigated appropriately. Customs and/or other appropriate law enforcement agencies must be notified if anomalies, illegal or suspicious activities are detected – as appropriate.

Physical Security

Cargo handling and storage facilities in international locations must have physical barriers and deterrents that guard against unauthorized access. Foreign manufacturer should incorporate the following C-TPAT physical security criteria throughout their supply chains as applicable.

FENCING

Perimeter fencing should enclose the areas around cargo handling and storage facilities. Interior fencing within a cargo handling structure should be used to segregate domestic, international, high value, and hazardous cargo. All fencing must be regularly inspected for integrity and damage.

GATES AND GATE HOUSES

Gates through which vehicles and/or personnel enter or exit must be manned and/or monitored. The number of gates should be kept to the minimum necessary for proper access and safety.

PARKING

Private passenger vehicles should be prohibited from parking in or adjacent to cargo handling and storage areas.

BUILDING STRUCTURE

Buildings must be constructed of materials that resist unlawful entry. The integrity of structures must be maintained by periodic inspection and repair.

LOCKING DEVICES AND KEY CONTROLS

All external and internal windows, gates and fences must be secured with locking devices. Management or security personnel must control the issuance of all locks and keys.

LIGHTING

Adequate lighting must be provided inside and outside the facility including the following areas: entrances and exits, cargo handling and storage areas, fence lines and parking areas.

ALARMS SYSTEMS AND VIDEO SURVEILLANCE CAMERAS

Alarm systems and video surveillance cameras should be utilized to monitor premises and prevent unauthorized access to cargo handling and storage areas.

Information Technology Security

PASSWORD PROTECTION

Automated systems must use individually assigned accounts that require a periodic change of password. IT security policies, procedures and standards must be in place and provided to employees in the form of training.

ACCOUNTABILITY

A system must be in place to identify the abuse of IT including improper access, tampering or the altering of business data. All system violators must be subject to appropriate disciplinary actions for abuse.

Security Training and Threat Awareness

A threat awareness program should be established and maintained by security personnel to recognize and foster awareness of the threat posed by terrorists and contraband smugglers at each point in the supply chain. Employees must be made aware of the procedures the company has in place to address a situation and how to report it. Additional training should be provided to employees in the shipping and receiving areas, as well as those receiving and opening mail.

Additionally, specific training should be offered to assist employees in maintaining cargo integrity, recognizing internal conspiracies, and protecting access controls. These programs should offer incentives for active employee participation.

8. Implementation Plan – Minimum Security Criteria for Foreign Manufacturers

Customs-Trade Partnership Against Terrorism (C-TPAT) Implementation Plan – Minimum Security Criteria for Foreign Manufacturers

August 22, 2006

U.S. Customs and Border Protection (CBP) has developed minimum-security criteria for Foreign Manufacturers already enrolled in the C-TPAT program, or for those wishing to join the voluntary, incentive-based supply chain security program. These new minimum-security criteria help solidify membership expectations, and more clearly define and establish the baseline level of security measures, which must be employed by member Foreign Manufacturers. The foreign manufacturer minimum-security criteria is effective as of August 29, 2006.

For New Foreign Manufacturers Wishing To Join C-TPAT: Foreign Manufacturers wishing to join the C-TPAT program on or after August 29, 2006, will need to meet or exceed the security criteria before they will be 'certified' and eligible for benefits. Applications for new membership will only be accepted electronically, via the C-TPAT web-based online application for Foreign Manufacturers, (C-TPAT for Foreign Manufacturers) with the submission of a completed, comprehensive security-profile that is required at time of application.

For Existing C-TPAT Member Foreign Manufacturers: For Foreign Manufacturers who are already members of the C-TPAT program, a 90-day implementation approach will be followed which provides existing members with sufficient time to address the security measures outlined in the criteria.

Existing member Foreign Manufacturers will have 90 calendar days from the August 29, 2006 effective date to address all of the following security areas:

- *Container and Trailer Security* (seals, container/trailer security, etc.)
- *Physical Access Controls* (employees, visitors, etc.)
- *Physical Security* (fencing, lighting, parking, etc.)
- *Personnel Security* (background checks, employee hiring, etc.)
- *Procedural Security* (documentation, manifesting procedures, etc.)
- *Security Training and Threat Awareness*
- *Information Technology Security* (passwords and accountability)
- *Business Partner Requirements.*

Certifications: Existing C-TPAT member Foreign Manufacturers will not be required to provide a written certification that the security criteria have been met, nor will previously submitted and accepted security profiles need to be resubmitted. It will be understood that Foreign Manufacturers must meet or exceed these baseline security criteria by the end of the implementation timeframe. CBP will continue to use validations to gauge whether or not Foreign Manufacturers have adopted these security criteria. Those Foreign Manufacturers found to be deficient, may have their benefits suspended, or removed from the program entirely.

Foreign Manufacturers in Canada and Mexico failing to meet security criteria as evidenced through a validation, or because of a resulting seizure due to compromised supply chain security, will be have their Free and Secure Trade (FAST) program benefits immediately suspended until notification from the C-TPAT office.

To assist in the implementation of these security criteria the trade is encouraged to submit questions to the C-TPAT Industry Partnership email address at *Industry.Partnership@dhs.gov*.

In closing, as a voluntary, incentive based supply chain security program, the new C-TPAT security criteria for Foreign Manufacturers are risk based, flexible, and designed to help CBP achieve its twin goals of security and facilitation. CBP will continue to work with members who demonstrate a commitment towards strengthening their entire supply chain and benefits will be provided accordingly.

9. U.S. Customs and Border Protection – FAST Program

OVERVIEW

The FAST program is a bilateral initiative between the United States and Mexico designed to ensure security and safety while enhancing the economic prosperity of both countries. In developing this program, Mexico and the United States have agreed to coordinate to the maximum extent possible, their commercial processes for clearance of commercial shipments at the border. This will promote free and secure trade by using common risk-management principles, supply chain security, industry partnership, and advanced technology to improve the efficiency of screening and clearing commercial traffic at our shared border.

OBJECTIVES

FAST is an ambitious program both in terms of its scope and its implementation dates. For the United States and Mexico, the initiative's objectives promise to revolutionize the processing of transborder trade:

1. The program aims to increase the integrity of supply chain security by offering expedited clearance to carriers and importers enrolled in Customs Trade Partnership Against Terrorism (C-TPAT).
2. It's designed to streamline and to integrate registration processes for drivers, carriers, and importers; minimizing paperwork and ensuring only low risk participants are enrolled as members.
3. The initiative seeks to expedite the clearance of transborder shipments of compliant partners by reducing Customs information requirements, dedicating lanes at major crossings to FAST participants, using common technology, and physically examining cargo transported by these low-risk clients with minimal frequency.

4. The program is a catalyst for both Customs administrations to participate in the enhanced technologies by using transponders, which would make it easier to clear low risk shipments, and would mitigate the cost of program participation for FAST partners.

BENEFITS

FAST approved U.S./Mexico highway carriers will benefit from:

1. Dedicated lanes (where available) for greater speed and efficiency in the clearance of FAST transborder shipments.
2. Reduced number of examinations for continued compliance with Customs FAST requirements.
3. A strong and ongoing partnership with the Mexican and Customs (C-TPAT) administrations.
4. Enhanced supply chain security and safety while protecting the economic prosperity of both countries.
5. The knowledge that they are carrying shipments for a C-TPAT approved importer.
6. A head start for the upcoming modifications to FAST that will expand eligible electronic cargo release methods. The FAST processing of Pre-Arrival Processing System (PAPS) is currently in use and will commence at locations along the U.S./Mexico border this year.

INAUGURATION

The initial phase of FAST for the United States and Mexico bound commercial shipments began on September 27, 2003 at the Port of El Paso, Texas. Additional dedicated FAST lane processing is available at the following locations:

FAST Southern Border Operations

	U.S. Border	*Mexico Border*
Currently Available		
	Laredo, Texas	Nuevo Laredo, Tamaulipas
	Hidalgo, Texas	Reynosa, Tamaulipas
	El Paso, Texas	Ciudad Juarez, Chihuahua
	Otay Mesa, California	Tijuana, Baja California
	Brownsville, Texas	Matamoros, Tamaulipas
	Calexico, California	Mexacali, Baja

FAST Southern Border Operations (continued)

	U.S. Border	*Mexico Border*
Operational By Summer 2005		
	Tecate, California	Tecate, Baja California
	San Luis, Arizona	San Luis, Sonora
	Douglas, Arizona	Agua Prieta, Sonora
	Nogales, Arizona	Nogales
	Santa Teresa, New Mexico	San Jeronimo, Chihuahua
	Del Rio, Texas	Villa Acuna, Coahila
	Eagle Pass, Texas	Pierdas Negras, Coahuila
	Rio Grande City, Texas	Cd. Camargo, Tamulipas

QUALIFICATIONS

FAST is a harmonized clearance process for shipments of known compliant importer. Thus, any truck using FAST lane processing must be a C-TPAT approved carrier, carrying qualifying goods from a C-TPAT approved manufacturer, importer, and the driver must possess a valid FAST-Commercial Driver Card. FAST processing is based upon advanced electronic transmission of information. The following are the key components:

- **Manufacturer Registration:** Mexican manufacturers who are C-TPAT certified will be allowed to participate in the FAST program along the U.S./Mexico Border. Mexican related party manufacturers that are whole or majority owned subsidiaries of current C-TPAT importers that are controlled by the C-TPAT importer and are included in the importer's C-TPAT security profile will be eligible for FAST processing upon completion of the C-TPAT Importer Related Party Manufacturer Information by the C-TPAT importer. Mexican related party manufacturers who are NOT included in the C-TPAT importer's security profile must go through the entire application process for C-TPAT certification. Once certified, these parties will be eligible for FAST processing. Please note that per FAST requirements, Mexican manufacturers must ensure that high security mechanical seals are used on all loaded containers or trailers destined for the United States, and where appropriate, must follow ISO/PSA standard 17712. Refer to U.S./ Mexico Border C-TPAT/FAST Seal Requirements for more information.

- **Importer Registration:** Importers will complete a FAST Application to Customs and Border Protection in the United States. Importers authorized to use the FAST program for clearance into the United States will have a demonstrated history of complying with all relevant legislative and regulatory requirements, and will have made a commitment to security enhancing business practices as required by C-TPAT. Please note that per FAST requirements, importers participating in FAST have responsibilities to ensure that high security mechanical seals are used on all loaded containers or trailers destined for the United States, and where appropriate, must follow ISO/PSA standard 17712. Refer to U. S./Mexico Border C-TPAT/ FAST Seal Requirements for more information.
- **Carrier Registration:** Carriers will complete the FAST U.S./Mexico Border Highway Carrier Application Process requirements that include corporate information, a security profile, and a written U.S./Mexico Border Highway Carrier Agreement. In order to qualify for FAST Highway Carrier membership into the United States and Mexico, a carrier application must be submitted to the FAST Processing Center. An independent risk assessment will be performed and once the assessment is complete, an approval for FAST participation will be authorized. For the United States, a FAST approved carrier will have met all aspects of C-TPAT through the FAST registration process. Carriers must ensure that all of their employed drivers are in possession of a valid FAST Commercial Driver Identification Card or other identification issued **only** by CBP. Please note that per FAST requirements, carriers participating in FAST have responsibilities to ensure that high security mechanical seals are used on all loaded containers or trailers destined for the U. S., and where appropriate, must follow ISO/PSA standard 17712. Refer to U.S./Mexico Border C-TPAT/FAST Seal Requirements for more information.
- **Commercial Driver Application:** Drivers must complete a single FAST U.S./Mexico Border Commercial Driver Application for the United States and Mexico. CBP will assess the application for risk. Applicants identified as low risk will report to an enrollment center where they will be interviewed, have their original identification and citizenship documents reviewed, fingerprinted and have a digital photo taken. Low-risk applicants will then be issued a FAST – Commercial Driver Identification Card.
  - **FAST Driver Enrollment Centers:** FAST commercial driver enrollment centers are operational at the ports of:
    Otay Mesa, California
    Calexico, California
    Nogales, Arizona
    El Paso, Texas
    Laredo, Texas
    Pharr, Texas
    Brownsville, Texas

- To date, 5,597 FAST cards have been issued to drivers at the SW border.

CARGO RELEASE METHODS

Two present cargo release methods exist for FAST processing. The first method is FAST, which is the modified version of the National Customs Automated Prototype (NCAP) and the Pre-Arrival Processing System (PAPS). More detailed information on these two release methods may be obtained from Federal Register Notice Volume 68, Number 186, published on September 25, 2003, titled the Modification to the Free and Secure Trade Prototype. The initial implementation of the FAST prototype began in December 16, 2002 in Detroit, Michigan. Both cargo release methods are the only accepted electronic transactions available for FAST processing.

- **FAST:** Modified NCAP/Prototype is the first complete paperless cargo release mechanism put into place Customs and Border Protection. This paperless processing is achieved through electronic data transmissions and transponder technology. FAST is highly automated and allows for the expedited release of highly compliant cargo from major importers, reducing congestion at our land borders.
- **The Pre-Arrival Processing System (PAPS):** PAPS is a Customs Automated Commercial System (ACS) border cargo release mechanism that utilizes barcode technology to expedite the release of commercial shipments while processing each shipment through Border Cargo Selectivity (BCS) and the Automated Targeting System (ATS).

ADDITIONAL INFORMATION

For additional information, reference the www.CBP.gov web address or contact a local CBP FAST representative at any of the FAST sites indicated. Designated FAST team members are available to answer questions at designated FAST ports.

10. Monetary Guidelines for Setting Bond Amounts for Importation Subject to Enhanced Bonding Requirements (Federal Register, Vol. 71, No. 205, USCBP-2006-0019)

SUMMARY: This Notice serves to provide additional information on the process used to determine bond amounts for importations involving elevated collection risks and to seek public comment on that process. The process published in this Notice is in effect. Public comments will assist CBP in identifying factors that may further improve the process to ensure the bond amounts protect the revenue and facilitate trade. After consideration of the comments, a revised version of the Monetary Guidelines for Setting Bond Amounts Customs Directive 99-3510-004 July 23, 1991 (1991 Monetary Guidelines) will be published.

DATES: Comments must be received on or before December 26, 2006.

ADDRESSES: Commenters must submit comments, identified by *docket number*, by *one* of the following methods:

- Federal eRulemaking Portal: *http:// www.regulations.gov.* Follow the instructions for submitting comments via docket number USCBP-2006-0119.
- Mail: Trade and Commercial Regulations Branch, Office of Regulations and Rulings in the Office of International Trade, Bureau of Customs and Border Protection, 1300 Pennsylvania Avenue, NW. (Mint Annex), Washington, DC 20229.

Instructions: All submissions received must include the agency name and docket number for this Notice. All comments received will be posted without change to *http:// www.regulations.gov*, including any personal information provided. For detailed instructions on submitting comments, see the 'Public Participation' heading of the SUPPLEMENTARY INFORMATION section of this document.

Docket: For access to the docket to read background documents or comments received, go to *http:// www.regulations.gov.* Submitted comments may also be inspected during regular business days between the hours of 9 a.m. and 4:30 p.m. at the Office of Regulations and Rulings in the Office of International Trade, Bureau of Customs and Border Protection, 799 9th Street, NW., 5th Floor, Washington, DC. Arrangements to inspect submitted comments should be made in advance by calling Joseph Clark at (202) 572– 8768.

SUPPLEMENTARY INFORMATION

PUBLIC PARTICIPATION

Interested persons are invited to submit written data, views, or arguments on all aspects of this Notice. CBP also invites comments that relate to the economic, environmental, or federalism effects that might result from this Notice. Comments that will provide the most assistance to CBP in developing these procedures will reference a specific portion of this Notice, explain the reason for any recommended change, and include data, information, or authority that support such recommended change.

BACKGROUND

A key CBP mission is to collect all import duties determined to be due to the United States. Under customs statutes and regulations release of merchandise prior to the determination of all duties that may be owed is ordinarily permitted, provided the importer posts a bond or other security to insure payment of duties and compliance with other applicable laws and regulations. Estimated duties are collected at entry, a bond is posted, and final duties await liquidation at a later point in time.

In the case of antidumping (AD) or countervailing duties (CVD) determined by the Department of Commerce (DOC) (which administers the AD/CVD laws in conjunction with the U.S. International Trade Commission), the administrative and judicial process for determining the appropriate rate of duty for AD/CVD merchandise may significantly delay the liquidation of an entry of AD/CVD merchandise. At liquidation, CBP follows DOC instructions regarding the applicable AD/CVD rate. CBP must collect the duties owed of whatever nature. However, importers have increasingly failed to pay additional AD/CVD duties determined to be due at liquidation. Recent defaults for AD/CVD supplemental bills are substantially higher than defaults that were the previous norm and are unprecedented. This troubling trend caused an internal policy review of revenue protection strategies at CBP.

During the review, CBP reconsidered its general continuous bond formula which provides that the minimum continuous bond may be in an amount equal to the greater of $50,000 or ten percent of the amount of the previous year's duties, taxes and fees. In response to the growing collection problem, CBP announced an enhanced customs bonding requirement for those continuous bonds that secure the promise to pay all duties finally determined to be due on certain merchandise subject to AD/CVD. *Amendment to Bond Directive 99-3510-004 For Certain Merchandise Subject to Antidumping Countervailing Duty Cases* (July 9, 2004) (July 2004 Amendment to the Bond Guidelines); see also *Clarification to the July 9, 2004 Amended Monetary Guidelines for Setting Bond Amounts* (August 10, 2005) (August 2005 Clarification). Application of the enhanced bonding requirement thus far has been limited in scope – having been applied to merchandise subject to the first antidumping orders involving aquaculture merchandise imposed after issuance of the July 2004 Amendment to the Bond Guidelines. Aquaculture is the industry sector with the highest share of total defaults in recent years.

CBP commenced its policy of reviewing the sufficiency of continuous bonds related to imports of AD/CVD merchandise with the release of its July 2004 Amendment to the Bond Guidelines. That document and the August 2005 Clarification were posted on CBP's Web site.

The bond guidelines are designed to ensure the amount of the continuous bond reflects a reasonable amount necessary to secure against non-payment of any additional revenue ultimately legally owed and not paid in cash deposits at entry. As noted earlier,

U.S. laws and regulations afford importers the opportunity to post such bonds in order to facilitate prompt release of the goods at the border without creating an undue burden on importers or international trade and commerce.

CBP includes guidelines on determining sufficient bond amounts in its regulations at 19 CFR 113.13. The regulations direct CBP to review bonds periodically and to notify the principal in writing if CBP determines the bond amount is insufficient to adequately protect the revenue and ensure compliance with U.S. laws and regulations. The principal has 30 days from date of notification to remedy the deficiency. During those 30 days, principals have frequently requested CBP to adjust its bond determination.

This Notice seeks public comment on the procedures for setting bond amounts on merchandise subject to increased default risk and, therefore, designated as Special Category Merchandise that may be subject to enhanced bonding requirements. An explanation of Special Category Merchandise appears later in this document under 'Procedures for Setting Bond Amount.' History of compliance with customs laws and regulations, ability to pay, existence of assets available as recourse for nonpayment, past payment history, similarity to previous circumstances giving rise to uncollected revenue problems, and other relevant factors will be considered in determining whether to reduce the bond amount otherwise required under the enhanced bond formula. Importers will be offered the opportunity to submit information on their financial condition related to the risk of non-collection for that importer and CBP will determine bond amounts based on that information, the importer's compliance history and other relevant information available to CBP. In the absence of a submission by the importer, CBP would calculate the bond amount using the formulas set forth below.

This document will be incorporated into the 1991 Monetary Guidelines and represents the comprehensive and exclusive statement of the policy and processes expressed in the July 2004 Amendment to the Bond Guidelines, the Bond Formulas posted on CBP's Web site, and the August 2005 Clarification. After consideration of any comments received, an incorporated policy will be published.

PROCEDURE FOR SETTING BOND AMOUNT

In order to provide a consistent bond formula and to ensure the bond amounts protect the revenue and facilitate trade, CBP issued bond guidelines. Under the August 2005 Clarification, CBP indicated that it would designate Special Categories of Merchandise and designate Covered Cases within those Special Categories. CBP will continue to evaluate on an industry wide basis those types of merchandise where additional bond requirements may be needed. However, because importers are only affected when merchandise is subject to different bond requirements, CBP will only designate Special Categories, that is, merchandise for which an enhanced bond amount may be required.

Designation of Special Categories

- Special Categories may be designated when additional bond requirements in the form of greater continuous entry bonds or other security may be required.
- At least 60 days before new bonding requirements take effect, CBP will provide public notice of designation of a Special Category in the Customs Bulletin and on the CBP's Web site (*http://www.cbp.gov*). The notice will solicit comment from affected parties and will provide a description of the reasons for the Special Category. Affected parties will have 30 days from the date the designation notice is published to submit comments.
- When conditions no longer exist that warrant the Special Category designation, the designation will be removed and the public will be notified through the Customs Bulletin and the CBP Web site.

Criteria for Special Categories

In considering which merchandise should be designated Special Category merchandise subject to enhanced bond requirements, the following criteria shall be considered:

1. Previous collection problems concerning the industry involved;
2. The similarity to previous imports or industries experiencing uncollected revenue problems;
3. Payment history;

4. Indications that liquidated duty rates may exceed existing security;
5. Any other factors that are deemed relevant.

All Special Categories will be monitored on a regular basis to determine whether a material change in factors has occurred so that the amount of the required bond for the Special Categories should be adjusted up or down or that the conditions that warranted the designations no longer exist.

Continuous Bond Formulas for Special Category Merchandise

CBP will review the sufficiency of bonds covering Special Category merchandise. Importers of Special Category merchandise may be required to obtain larger continuous bonds. In such circumstances, importers will be offered the opportunity to submit information on their financial condition related to the risk of non-collection for that importer, and CBP will determine bond amounts based on that information, the importer's compliance history, and other relevant information available to CBP. In the absence of a submission by the importer, CBP may calculate the bond amount using the formulas determined on the basis of the risk of non-collection posed by the Special Category merchandise. These formulas may be adjusted in accordance with the revenue risks identified for future importations of designated Special Category merchandise.

For Special Category merchandise which is merchandise subject to AD/CVD, the formulas determined on the basis of the risk of non-collection will be based upon the importer's previous 12 months cumulative import value of merchandise subject to the AD/CVD Order and the rate that the DOC establishes in its Order or, if the bond amount is established after an administrative review, it will be calculated using the rate determined by DOC in the most recent administrative review. The amount of additional coverage will be calculated using the following formula:

- AD/CVD rate established in DOC Order (or the rate established in the most recently completed administrative review) × previous 12 months' cumulative import value of subject merchandise.

For example, if an importer has imported $1 million of the subject AD/ CVD merchandise during the previous 12 months and the DOC rate is 40%, the importer's continuous bond amount will be increased by $400,000.

For new importers with no prior history of imports who import Special Category merchandise subject to AD/ CVD, the continuous bond will be calculated in accordance with the following formula:

- DOC deposit rate in effect on date of entry × the importer's estimated annual value of imported goods subject to the case.

Periodic reviews will be conducted to monitor the sufficiency of the continuous bonds for Special Category merchandise. CBP may adjust the rates in the formulas set forth above to calculate different bond amounts as circumstances warrant. CBP is committed to protecting its ability to collect the amount of money determined to be due at liquidation and to requiring continuous bonds in an amount reasonably necessary to cover its additional financial risk.

Absent exceptional circumstances, the above formulas will determine the bond amounts where a submission has not been made by the principal. Nothing in this policy affects the CBP's authority to require additional security if CBP believes that acceptance of a transaction secured by a continuous bond would place the revenue in jeopardy or otherwise hamper the enforcement of customs laws or regulations.

Notice Timing and Adjustment Factors for Individual Importers

In implementing the bond requirements for imports of Special Category merchandise, CBP shall:

(1) Provide the principal subject to the revised bond requirements with notice of the new bond requirements not less than 30 days before the revised requirements will take effect. Such notice will include a description of the rationale for the new requirements and offer the principal the opportunity to submit information on its financial condition related to the risk of non-collection of that principal, which CBP will use along with other information, such as the importer's compliance history, to determine bond amounts. The notice will inform the principal that in the absence of a submission by the principal, CBP may calculate the bond amount using the formulas determined on the basis of the risk of non-collection for the Special Category merchandise. The notice will provide examples of additional information that might be submitted in support of the former calculation, how the bond amount would be calculated if the formula were applied, and a description of the procedures for responding to the notice.

(2) Provide the principal 30 days from the date of the mailing of the notice to respond, including by providing evidence of factors that could support a bond amount other than that resulting from the formula. Such responses may be filed individually or by groups of principals who share common characteristics. Principals who import from the same foreign manufacturer/ exporter share common characteristics. Depending upon available resources and workload, CBP shall endeavor to issue decisions to those who respond within 45 days of receipt of a complete, legible response and, in any event, shall issue decisions within a reasonable time. The new bond requirement will not take effect with respect to a principal until 14 days after the date of CBP's reply to the principal's response. The reply to the principal will include the rationale for the determination. In the absence

of a submission by the principal, CBP may calculate the bond amount using the formulas determined on the risk of non-collection posed by the Special Category merchandise as provided in the notice. The bond requirement will take effect with respect to that principal 30 days after the date of the mailing of the notice.

(3) Consistent with 19 CFR 113.13(b), consider the following factors when determining a bond amount, other than the amount resulting from the formula, for a principal who has responded in accordance with (2) above:

(a) The prior record of the principal regarding timely payment of duties, taxes and charges with respect to the transactions involving such payments;
(b) The prior record of the principal in complying with CBP demands for redelivery, the obligation to hold unexamined merchandise intact, and other requirements relating to enforcement and administration of CBP and other laws and regulations;
(c) The value and nature of the merchandise involved in the transaction(s) to be secured;
(d) The degree and type of supervision that CBP will exercise over the transaction(s);
(e) The prior record of the principal in honoring bond commitments, including the payment of liquidated damages and AD/CVD;
(f) Any additional information contained in any application for a bond, or contained in any request for adjustment of the bond amount, including information that provides proof of ability to pay such as independently audited financial statements, tax returns submitted by the principal, availability of assets, including securities in the United States and elsewhere, credit rating, and length of time in business; and
(g) Any other relevant information.

(4) If CBP determines that the principal has a record of compliance with customs laws and regulations and that the principal has demonstrated an ability to pay, CBP may decide not to require an increased bond amount even though the principal imports Special Category merchandise.

A request for reconsideration may be made by submitting a new bond application and CBP Form 301 at any time after six months from the date of the notice of new bond amount set forth in paragraph (1) above, if no response to CBP's notice was received under paragraph (2). If the principal filed a response under paragraph (2) requesting a bond amount other than that resulting from the formula, the principal may request further reconsideration at any time after six months from the date of the decision issued under paragraph (2). A request for reconsideration of the bond amount based on a material error by CBP that affects the bond amount may be made at any time.

At any time after CBP determines a bond amount for a principal below that provided by the formula, if the principal fails to remain compliant with customs laws and regulations, CBP will recalculate the principal's bond amount in accordance with the formulas outlined in this notice.

Affected Parties

This Notice affects only continuous bonds for imports of Special Category merchandise. This Notice does not affect laws and regulations regarding cash deposits or other security with respect to merchandise subject to AD/CVD proceedings. CBP notes those initial deposits and bonds sometimes are not sufficient to cover the final assessed duty liabilities. Defaults on such additional duty liability have increased.

Congress has provided CBP authority to require security in order to ensure the payment of all duties determined to be due to the United States, including any revenue collection gaps between estimated duty deposits and final assessed duties that the importer fails to satisfy. Please note that this Notice does not limit CBP's authority to require additional security under 19 CFR 113.13(d) and the requirements of the 1991 Monetary Guidelines remain in effect consistent with this Notice.

Dated: October 20, 2006.

Deborah J. Spero
Acting Commissioner, Customs and Border Protection.

[FR Doc. E6–17885 Filed 10–23–06; 8:45 am]
BILLING CODE 9111–14–P

11. 'J – List' Exceptions

Articles of a class or kind listed below are excepted from the requirements of country of origin marking in accordance with the provisions of section 304(a)(3)(J), Tariff Act of 1930, as amended (19 U.S.C. 1304(a)(3)(J)). However, in the case of any article described in this list which is imported in a container, the outermost container in which the article ordinarily reaches the ultimate purchaser is required to be marked to indicate the origin of its contents in accordance with the requirements of subpart C of this part. All articles are listed in Treasury Decisions 49690, 49835, and 49896. A reference different from the foregoing indicates an amendment.

Articles	References
Art, works of.	
Articles classified under sub-headings 9810.00.15, 9810.00.25, 9810.00.40 and 9810.00.45, Harmonized Tariff Schedule of the United States.	T.D. 66–153.
Articles entered in good faith as antiques and rejected as unauthentic.	
Bagging, waste.	
Bags, jute.	
Bands, steel.	
Beads, unstrung.	
Bearings, ball, 5/8-inch or less in diameter.	
Blanks, metal, to be plated.	
Bodies, harvest hat.	
Bolts, nuts, and washers.	
Briarwood in blocks.	
Briquettes, coal or coke.	
Buckles, 1 inch or less in greatest dimension	
Burlap.	
Buttons.	
Cards, playing.	
Cellophane and celluloid in sheets, bands, or strips.	
Chemicals, drugs, medicinal, and similar substances, when imported in capsules, pills, tablets, lozenges, or troches.	
Cigars and cigarettes.	
Covers, Straw bottle	
Dies, diamond wire, unmounted.	

Articles	References
Dowels, wooden.	
Effects, theatrical.	
Eggs.	
Feathers.	
Firewood.	
Flooring, not further manufactured than planed, tongued and grooved.	T.D.s 49750; 50366(6).
Flowers, artificial, except bunches.	
Flowers, cut.	
Glass, out to shape and size for use in clocks, hand, pocket, and purse mirrors, and other glass of similar shapes and sizes, not including lenses or watch crystals.	
Glides, furniture, except glides with prongs.	
Hairnets.	
Hides, raw.	
Hooks, fish (except snelled fish hooks).	T.D. 50205(3).
Hoops (wood), barrel.	
Laths.	
Leather, except finished.	
Livestock.	
Lumber, sawed	T.D.s 49750; 50366(6).
Metal bars, except concrete reinforcement bars; billets, blocks, blooms; ingots; pigs; plates; sheets, except galvanized sheets; shafting; slabs; and metal in similar forms.	
Mica not further manufactured than cut or stamped to dimensions, shape or form.	
Monuments.	
Nails, spikes, and staples.	
Natural products, such as vegetables, fruits, nuts, berries, and live or dead animals, fish and birds; all the foregoing which are in their natural state or not advanced in any manner further than is necessary for their safe transportation.	
Nets, bottle, wire.	
Paper, newsprint.	
Paper, stencil.	
Paper, stock.	
Parchment and vellum.	
Parts for machines imported from same country as parts.	

Articles	References
Pickets (wood).	
Pins, tuning. Plants, shrubs and other nursery stock.	
Plugs, tie.	
Poles, bamboo.	
Posts (wood), fence.	
Pulpwood.	
Rags (Including wiping rags)	
Rails, joint, bars, and tie plates covered by subheadings 7302.10.10 through 7303.90.00, Harmonized Tariff Schedule of the United States.	
Ribbon.	
Rivets.	
Rope, including wire rope; cordage; cords; twines, threads, and yams.	
Scrap and waste.	
Screws. Shims, track.	
Shingles (wood), bundles of (except bundles of red-cedar shingles).	T.D. 49750.
Skins, fur, dressed or dyed.	
Skins, raw fur.	
Sponges.	
Springs, watch.	
Stamps, postage and revenue, and other articles covered in subheadings 9704.00.00 and 4807.00.00, Harmonized Tariff Schedule of the United States.	T.D. 66-153.
Staves (wood), barrel.	
Steel, hoop.	
Sugar, maple.	
Ties (wood), railroad.	
Tides, not over 1 inch in greatest dimension.	
Timbers, sawed.	
Tips, penholder.	
Trees, Christmas.	
Weights, analytical and precision in sets.	T.D.s 49750; 51802.
Wicking, candle.	
Wire, except barbed.	

[T.D. 72–262, 35 FR 20318, Sept. 29, 1972, as amended by T.D. 85–123, 50 FR 29954, July 23, 1985; T.D. 89–1, 53 FR 51256, Dec. 21, 1988; T.D. 95–79, 60 FR, 49752. Sept. 27, 1995]

Index

D

Q

R